Instructor's Manual and Test Bank for Sigelman's

Life-Span Human Development

Third Edition

Elizabeth Rider
Elizabethtown College

Jennifer Kofkin

Brooks/Cole Publishing Company

I(T)P® An International Thomson Publishing Company

Pacific Grove • Albany • Belmont • Bonn • Boston • Cincinnati • Detroit
Johannesburg • London • Madrid • Melbourne • Mexico City • New York
Paris • Singapore • Tokyo • Toronto • Washington

Senior Assistant Editor: *Faith B. Stoddard*
Editorial Assistant: *Stephanie M. Andersen*
Production Coordinator: *Dorothy Bell*

Cover Design: *Roy R. Neuhaus/Terri Wright*
Cover Art: *Hamish MacEwan/SuperStock*
Printing and Binding: *Globus Printing*

For more information, contact:

BROOKS/COLE PUBLISHING COMPANY
511 Forest Lodge Road
Pacific Grove, CA 93950
USA

International Thomson Publishing Europe
Berkshire House 168-173
High Holborn
London WC1V 7AA
England

Thomas Nelson Australia
102 Dodds Street
South Melbourne, 3205
Victoria, Australia

Nelson Canada
1120 Birchmount Road
Scarborough, Ontario
Canada M1K 5G4

International Thomson Editores
Seneca 53
Col. Polanco
11560 México, D. F., México

International Thomson Publishing GmbH
Königswinterer Strasse 418
53227 Bonn
Germany

International Thomson Publishing Asia
60 Albert Street
#15-01 Albert Complex
Singapore 189969

International Thomson Publishing Japan
Hirakawacho Kyowa Building, 3F
2-2-1 Hirakawacho
Chiyoda-ku, Tokyo 102
Japan

Printed in the United States of America

5 4 3 2

ISBN 0-534-35960-4

CONTENTS

INTRODUCTION

This Instructor's Manual has been designed specifically for use with Carol Sigelman's text *Life-Span Human Development*, *3rd edition*. The introduction to this manual contains sections on course objectives, student note-taking, writing in psychology, as well as suggestions for course projects. The introduction is followed by chapter-by-chapter supplements to the text, and a test bank.

The chapter-by-chapter supplements include the following:

<u>Learning Objectives</u>. The learning objectives in this Instructor's Manual also appear in the student Study Guide. They can be used to help focus lecture content, or as discussion or essay questions.

<u>Chapter Outline</u>. The detailed outline of each chapter may be used to help prepare lecture notes, or may be used as is as a quick reference in the classroom.

<u>Suggestions for Class Discussions or Projects</u>. Several ideas are presented that can be a basis for class discussions or student projects. In most cases, special materials and excessive preparation are not required.

<u>Suggested Films and Videos</u>. This section lists a number of relevant films and videos, and includes their source, type (VHS or 16 mm film), length, and a brief description. The films and videos are varied and can be used to supplement lecture topics and exemplify concepts discussed in class or in the text.

<u>Suggested Readings</u>. The suggested readings can be used by the instructor to strengthen background on a lecture topic, or may be assigned as additional readings for students.

<u>Transparency Masters</u>. The transparency masters can be copied onto transparency sheets for use in class. Many of the transparencies organize and summarize points from the chapter, and can help structure lectures or discussion of the material. In some chapters, a transparency may correspond to one of the Suggestions for Class Discussion.

A <u>Test Bank</u> follows the chapter-by-chapter materials described above. The test bank includes well over 100 questions for each chapter of the text, prepared by Dr. Elizabeth Rider at Elizabethtown College in Pennsylvania. There are multiple choice, true-false, and essay questions covering a wide range of topics and difficulty levels. Within each category, the questions are arranged in the order that the material is presented in the text and are keyed to the text with page numbers. The multiple choice questions are divided into two types: those that assess largely factual (F) understanding of material and those that assess more conceptual (C) understanding of material. The answers to factual questions are spelled out very clearly in the text, while the answers to conceptual questions require students to use their factual knowledge in some way. They may need to compare/contrast material, apply it to new situations, analyze it, or integrate several pieces to arrive at a new understanding.

Some questions in the test bank are also located in the Brooks/Cole Study Center on the world wide web (http://www.brookscole.com/psychology). These are designated with "www" in the left margin. Other questions appear in the student Study Guide that accompanies the text and are designated with "SG" in the left margin. These are clustered together at the end of the multiple choice and essay sections so that instructors can readily see what students who use the Study Guide have available to them. The Study Guide provides a sample answer for one of the essay questions.

Every instructor is faced with the difficult task of evaluating students. Specification of course objectives can facilitate the evaluation process. Assignments designed to assess specific objectives will provide the material necessary for an informed evaluation. In addition, the provision of course objectives to students at the beginning of the course allows them to be clear about expectations. It might also be helpful to the instructor and the students to have a mid-term review of these objectives (perhaps including a student self-assessment of progress).

There are many ways to think about course objectives. A number of years ago, Benjamin Bloom introduced a useful taxonomy for classifying *cognitive* objectives. The six levels of this taxonomy are summarized below, along with an example of the type of question that would assess each particular level. These are also included in the Study Guide for students in order to help them understand the different levels of "knowing" material.

1. Knowledge--The ability to identify, recall, or recognize information
       EX: Define "accommodation"

2. Comprehension--The ability to demonstrate, explain, and rephrase information.
       EX: Explain the concept of accommodation in your own words.

3. Application--The ability to apply or generalize; to *use* the principles.
       EX: Indicate how accommodation relates to the process of equilibration.

4. Analysis--The ability to break a principle into component parts and understand how the parts relate; to analyze or deduce knowledge.
       EX: Discuss how Piaget's notion of nurture differs from Freud's.

5. Synthesis--The ability to put old knowledge together in new ways; to formulate or modify knowledge.
       EX: In what way(s) would Piaget's description of the preoperational stage need to be modified in order to better "fit" recent research in this area?

6. Evaluation--The ability to make judgments *based on knowledge*; to argue or to assess knowledge.
       EX: Assess the usefulness of Piaget's concept of equilibration and justify your response.

Bloom's taxonomy is hierarchical, yet overlapping. For example, analysis of a concept requires more sophisticated understanding than knowledge of that concept, but it is not isolated from earlier levels of understanding. Two frequently-used formats for assessing cognitive objectives are multiple choice and essay questions. We often think that multiple choice questions only assess lower levels of knowledge, but carefully constructed multiple choice questions can assess higher levels of knowledge than poorly constructed essay questions. For more information about test construction, see V.L. Clegg & W.E Cashin (1986) "Improving multiple-choice tests," *Idea Paper No. 16.* and W.E. Cashin (1987) "Improving essay tests," *Idea Paper No. 17*, both from the Center for Faculty Development, Kansas State University; and N.E. Gronlund (1985) *Measurement and evaluation in teaching*, 5th ed. (NY: Macmillan).

Bloom's taxonomy is, of course, only one way of thinking about course objectives. Not all course objectives are strictly cognitive, and tests are not the only method of evaluation. A list of course objective might also include, for example: research skills; experience as a practitioner in the field; critical thinking skills; writing skills; increase in self-awareness; and ability to work as a team player. Some of these objectives might not be best assessed by a test, while the course projects in this Manual might prove useful. As an instructor, you will want to confirm that your evaluation methods fit your course goals. After considering your course objectives, tailor assessment materials so that it is possible to assess the student on the outcomes that you deem important.

STUDENT NOTE-TAKING AND CLASS PERFORMANCE

When many of us think of our college experiences, we often remember sitting in a class taking notes while the professor stood at the front of the room lecturing on the material. Although this does not characterize all modern classrooms, lecturing is incorporated in many college courses. Even when lecturing is not used, students still need to keep a record of what took place in class. Unfortunately, students are often poor note-takers. Research on note-taking shows that students typically record fewer than 50% of the main points from a class. If tested on information omitted from their notes, students respond correctly about one-third of the time, but respond correctly three-quarters of the time if the material was included in their notes.

Note-taking during class has two functions that are related to academic achievement. First, note-taking increases attention, which increases encoding of material into long-term memory. The second function is to facilitate the review of class material, which is positively correlated with performance.

Listed below are some suggestions and points to consider in order to facilitate more effective note-taking by students. The points are also intended to make you think about techniques that you use in the classroom and perhaps discover ways to stimulate more active learning and better record keeping by students in your class.

1. Make students aware of the relationship between note-taking and academic performance. Note that the act of recording notes as well as the act of reviewing notes is important. The importance of reviewing increases as the interval of time between note-taking and test-taking increases.

2. In recording notes, more seems to be better than less. More notes and more ideas contained in the notes are related to higher achievement levels. However, this does not mean that students should try to take verbatim notes. Some research suggests that the relevant factor is not quantity of notes, but terseness of notes (having many ideas in few words).

3. Following one of the first classes, provide students with a model of complete and organized notes from that class. Allow them to compare their notes to this model and encourage them to modify their note-taking strategies on the basis of this comparison. Or, if time and class size permit, collect student's class notes for one class and provide individual feedback. This not only benefits students, but the instructor also gets useful information about the kinds of information that students record during a class.

4. Emphasize important ideas-- repeat them, show them on an overhead, or write them on the board. Research has found that students record about 88% of the material written on the board but only 52% of the important ideas that were not written on the board.

5. Lecture rate has an inverse effect on note-taking such that the faster the rate, the fewer notes. Provide enough pauses during the lecture for students to keep up with the lecture in their note-taking.

6. Consider providing an outline of the lectures. Outlines provide an organizational structure for note-taking and allow students to see where you are in a lecture and where you are going. Research indicates, however, that handing out complete notes can actually lead to decreased performance. Headings only, or the "bare skeleton" of notes, seem to be most effective because they provide students with some organization but also require students to be actively involved in taking their own notes.

7. Students record notes differently depending on whether they are anticipating an essay test or a multiple choice test. Thus, it may be important that students know how they will be evaluated before they record notes on that material.

8. Research also indicates that students take fewer notes in the second half of class. In fact, attention peaks after just 15-18 minutes of a class. If you have 75-minute classes, that leaves an entire hour of class after students' attention spans have peaked! This might suggest that instructors need to change their style for the second half of the class, give students a brief break, or use an activity that will "freshen up" the students.

9. Students can benefit from rewriting their notes, and as they do, reorganizing them and integrating them with material from other sources, such as their textbook.

10. Finally, there are a number of excellent videos that are available for psychology classes. When a video is turned on, students often take this as a sign that they can put down their pens and mentally relax for the duration of the video. Sometimes this is an appropriate response, but if you wish to encourage more active listening, you might try giving students a set of notes for one of the first video clips shown in the semester. This allows students to see what your expectations are for the amount of detail that they should be watching for in videos. Outlines may also be useful for videos because the audio accompanying the video often moves faster than students can reasonably take good notes. Having a framework in front of them while they watch may enable students to get more out of the video.

WRITING IN PSYCHOLOGY

Improvement of writing skills may be an implicit or explicit goal in many college courses. Fortunately, most school have resources that instructors can draw on to help students with their writing. There are, however, specific issue that may arise in undergraduate science courses, especially psychology courses. Perhaps most important is the issue of voice. It might be useful to draw distinctions early in the term between scientific papers, which tend to be written in the third person and rely upon empirical evidence generated using the scientific method, versus more personal papers that may have an intimate voice and rely on anecdotal evidence and autobiographical information to support important points.

Students should be aware of these different types of writing, and the types of evidence on which each style depends. A discussion about scientific evidence might also include a discussion of the uses and misuses of the internet, where information is not submitted to scientific review before dissemination to the public. Some students, particularly those interested in pursuing graduate studies, might appreciate the opportunity to practice writing in a more scientific style. Writing groups might be organized to help students understand these distinctions in voice (as well as help each other with the other challenges of writing). Students working in groups of about three exchange papers, and write short critiques designed to strengthen their classmates' papers. These critiques might include responses to the following basic questions:
- What was interesting?
- What were you confused about?
- What would you like to know more about?

In addition, students might also help each other assess the appropriateness of their supporting evidence, or their ability to use APA style. Each student then rewrites the paper based on peer input before handing it in for the instructor's review. Instructor's might wish to asses both the students papers, and their critiques of their peers' papers.

Guidelines for writing in APA style may be found on the internet. Two places to look are:
http://www.apa.org/students/
http://www.psych-web.com/resource/apacrib.htm

Below are several suggestions for semester-long projects. Some of them require advance preparation, but offer the promise of enriching the course as a whole. In addition to these ideas, shorter projects specific to the material presented in each chapter follow the chapter outlines in this Instructor's Manual.

1. Community service: A community service component will require some advance work in setting up placements, as well as the monitoring of placements throughout the course. There is, however, no substitution for the kind of hands-on, real-world learning that occurs in the field. Service learning can be a win-win situation in which the students' education is enhanced, and human service agencies are better able to meet the needs of the people they serve. Below are a few resources to assist in establishing service learning opportunities:

Web sites:
The National Service Learning Cooperative Clearinghouse:
　　http://www.nicsl.coled.umn.edu
American Association of Community Colleges-- Service Learning Clearinghouse
　　http://www.aacc.nche.edu/spcproj/service/service.htm
American Association for Higher Education-- Series on Service Learning
　　http://www.aahe.org/service/srv-lrn.htm

Articles:
McCluskey-Fawcett, K, & Green, P. (1992). Using community service to teach
　　developmental psychology. *Teaching of Psychology, 19*, 150-152.
Compares groups of students who either chose to write three papers as part of the course, or chose to work as volunteers in community service settings for families and children. No statistically significant difference in course satisfaction were found between the groups, but the authors describe some of the benefits they observed from the community service work.

Sugar, J.; & Livosky, M. (1988). Enriching child psychology courses with a
　　preschool journal option. *Teaching of Psychology, 15*, 93-95.
Students spend two hours each week as volunteers at a preschool. Their weekly journal entries reflect the course focus for that particular week. This is described as an optional course assignment--Students who have the motivation to do this can earn bonus percentage points.

2. Interviews and Behavioral Observations: Another means of getting students into the field would be to have them conduct observations or interviews (relating to the chapter under study) at daycare centers, preschools, nursing homes, or other agencies. Again, some advance work will be necessary to establish collaborative relationships with community agencies and organize the visits.

An alternative to visiting community agencies as a group would be to have students use the social networks that exist in the classroom to identify people of different age groups who might be observed or interviewed. A written report describing the data collected and interpreting/ evaluating them in light of developmental psychology themes might be due at the end of the observation period. Alternatively, students might discuss their findings in classroom groups.

Students will need some background information on doing behavioral observations and conducting interviews before they start, and ethics should be discussed as well. Below are a few articles that provide additional ideas on the use of observations and interviews:

McManus, J. L. (1986). "Live" case study/journal record in adolescent psychology.
　　Teaching of Psychology, 13, 70-74.

Students meet with an adolescent approximately once a week and keep a journal record of their observations and interviews with this individual.

Schwanenflugel, P. J. (1987). An interview method for teaching adolescent psychology. *Teaching of Psychology, 14*, 167-168.
Describes a project in which students interview individuals to learn about adolescent development. Students begin by using several instructor-provided questions as guidelines. Following the interview, they prepare a written report interpreting the interview in light of topics/ideas covered in class.

Walton, M. D. (1988). Interviewing across the lifespan: A project for an adult development course. *Teaching of Psychology, 15*, 198-200.
Describes a project in which students interview five individuals from different phases of life and then write a paper using these data to illustrate developmental theory and research discussed in the course. Two purposes of the project are to apply theory and research to understand "real" people, and to develop interviewing skills useful in a variety of contexts.

3. <u>Current Events Portfolio</u>: This assignment involves keeping a notebook or file of current events relevant to developmental psychology from newspapers and magazines. For each current event, students provide a brief description or explanation of how it is related to the psychological concepts covered in class or in the textbook. Portfolios can be assessed based on relevancy of the event, the accuracy of student's comments, breadth of coverage, and creativity. The best portfolios are often those that have shown multiple interpretations of current events based on more than one theory or research concept. For more information, see Rider (1992; Understanding and applying psychology through use of news clippings, *Teaching of Psychology, 19*, 161-163).

4. <u>Thought Papers/ Important Points Paper</u>: For each chapter, or periodically during the semester, have students discuss what they view as the most important point from the textbook, and their rationale for selecting these points. If you are going to use student analyses as a basis for class discussion, it helps to have students commit to their ideas in writing before the class discussion (otherwise, there may be a quick consensus about what the important points are). Better yet, have students write short papers that are copied and exchanged with other class members before the discussion. Depending on the size of the class, papers can be distributed to everyone, or within small groups, or different groups of students might write papers and distribute them to everyone on different days. These student papers then become required reading before class. Encourage students to share not only ideas from their own papers, but from the papers of their classmates as well. If students write Thought Papers for each chapter, it provides them with a nice summary of the course material, and their relationship to it, at the end of the semester.

5. <u>Internet Discussion</u>. Have students begin or join a discussion thread on a developmental topic of interest on the internet. Choose a more scholarly forum so that discussions do not entail simply personal stories. In addition, students may be required to support or refute the points they make, or the points made by others, using references to texts. Students can keep a record of these exchanges and organize them into a final paper. In addition to the information gleaned, students might also reflect on the uses/misuses of the internet.

   A good source of information for this project is John Grohol's *The Insider's Guide to Mental Health Resources Online* (Guilford Press, 1997). Although clinically oriented, this book includes information on how to find and use internet resources, and how to formulate questions that get results. It also includes addresses for joining a variety of mailing list and newsgroup discussions. The web site associated with this author is: http://www.cmhc.com/

6. <u>Psychology Through Literature</u>: Students read a novel and use the main character(s) to describe development. The book needs to be chosen carefully so that it provides ample evidence of

development for students to discuss. An article that further explains this idea is:

> Boyatzis, C. J. (1992). Let the caged bird sing: Using literature to teach developmental psychology. *Teaching of Psychology, 19*, 221-222.
> Discusses how to use literature, in this case Maya Angelou's (1969) *I know why the caged bird sings*, to illustrate developmental psychology concepts and theories.

7. Book groups: Rather than working individually or as an entire class on understanding developmental principles through literature, book groups might be formed within the classroom. Students interested in particular topics, age groups, or authors, might work together to understand the mutually-agreed upon texts. Some class time each week might be set aside to allow the groups to meet. After completion of the reading and discussion, each group might also present the book and their understanding of it to the class. Although this exercise could be used for fiction books as described above, it would work for reading psychology or other non-fiction books (e.g., Mary Pipher's book, *Reviving Ophelia*, published by Ballantine in 1995; Carol Gilligan's *In a Different Voice*, reissued by Harvard University Press in 1993; or one of the many books written by Robert Coles or Howard Gardner).

8. Psychology Through Popular Films: Students might analyze a popular movie using developmental psychology principles. Alternatively, popular films may be shown in class and discussed as a group (with or without discussion questions prepared in advance). Showing popular films is a nice break to usual class formats, and discussion of these films may prove to be quite rich. There are a wealth of films from which one might choose. Below is a short list of possibilities, including some films from different cultures. Films should be previewed to ensure that the content is appropriate for your class.

> Antonia's Line (1995, Dutch with subtitles, 102 minutes)
> Harold and Maude (1971, 92 minutes)
> Harry and Tonto (1974, 115 minutes)
> Jules and Jim (1962, French with subtitles, 104 minutes)
> My Life as a Dog (1985, Swedish with subtitles, 101 minutes)
> Searching for Bobby Fisher (1983, 111 minutes)
> Stand By Me (1986, 87 minutes)
> Strangers in Good Company (1991, Canadian, 101 minutes)
> Sugar Cane Alley (1983, Martinique French with subtitles, 106 minutes)
> Welcome to the Dollhouse (1995, 87 minutes)

An interesting variation on this assignment would be to have students watch a popular film about a particular age group *with* someone of that age group. Have students discuss commonalities and differences between their own viewpoint and that of their viewing companion. What historical and age/developmental differences affect the differing perspective on the film.

9. Communicating Across the Generation: Assignments that encourage students to communicate across different generations can help them to put their own experiences in context, including an historical context. There are several ways to do this. One way is to watch a film with someone of a different generation (see above). Another is to have students write letters. Junn describes an project in which students write two personal letters: One to a future child on the child's 18th birthday; and one to the student's parents [Junn, E. N. (1989). "Dear Mom and Dad": Using personal letters to enhance students' understanding of developmental issues. *Teaching of Psychology, 16*, 135-139]. Students might also look at Marian Wright Edelman's 1993 book, *The Measure of Our Success : A Letter to My Children and Yours* (HarperCollins). Edelman is the Director of the Children's Defense Fund, and has a valuable perspective on child development. A variation on this theme would be to have students read actual graduation addresses, and then write one of their own.
Relevant questions to be addressed in this assignment include:

- What have you learned thus far that you would you like to share with those younger than you?
- What lessons have you carried on with you from your parents, grandparents, or more distant ancestors?

Writing across one or even two generations may seem manageable. You might encourage students to think beyond this time frame. Can they, for example, think in terms of seven generations?

10. Autobiography: Autobiographical writing allows students to make the materials covered in class more personally meaningful. Autobiographical writing might take several forms.

Students may provide a chronological description of their life and then discuss it in terms of concepts covered in the course. Students might begin by constructing the facts of their life starting at birth (or prenatally if this information is available). Good sources of information for this are parents, siblings, grandparents, family photo albums, baby books, video records, scrap books, report cards, height/weight records, and so on. Included in the description should be information about their physical growth and motor skills, cognitive-intellectual development, language development, and social-personality development. Once this has been done, students can begin analyzing the facts using concepts from the course. No fact is "correct" or "incorrect," but analysis of the facts should logically connect to research, theory, and concepts covered in the text.

Another assignment for organizing autobiographical writing is modeled after a book by Rountree in which women from different walks of life reflect on turning forty [Rountree, C. (1991). *Coming into our fullness: On women turning forty*. Freedom, CA: The Crossing Press]. Students might write about Turning 20, or Turning 30 (Turning whatever decade they are closest to). This assignment might provide an opportunity to think about issues of continuity, change, and life span development. Here are some possible questions:
- What does it mean to you to be your current age?
- What developmental issues are at work in your current life stage?
- What are some historical/societal events that have affected who you are today?
- What are the more idiosyncratic/individual factors at work in your life?
- How are you the same now as you were in past decades? How are you different?
- What are the reasons for the continuities and for the changes?
- How do you expect to be the same/ different in future decades?

11. Research analysis paper: Students are asked to read, summarize and analyze a research article that investigates some aspect of developmental psychology. Articles should come from one of the major developmental journals (e.g., *Child Development*, *Developmental Psychology*, *Journal of Experimental Child Psychology*, *Merrill-Palmer Quarterly*, *Psychology and Aging*, and others). Goals of this project include familiarizing students with reading the different components of a research article, and learning how to summarize the relevant points of research.

In the summary, students might be asked to address the following questions (and perhaps others, depending on the article and goals of the assignment):
- What were the researchers trying to do (i.e., what is their question)?
- What type of study was conducted? For example, is it longitudinal, cross- sectional, sequential? Is it experimental or correlational?
- How did researchers test their question?
- What were the important findings?
- How does this research relate to concepts from the text?
- How does it relate to an issue in "real" life?

12. Original research project: If the course includes the teaching of even *basic* statistics and research methods, or if students have already taken such courses, they might conduct their own original research study. Although surveys using correlational techniques may be the method of choice, simple experiments are also possible. In addition, non-controversial research questions and study

designs will be necessary to avoid delays in the Human Subjects Committee. Although this can be an anxiety-filled project for students who, in order to complete the project in a single semester, must be continually pushed to the next phase of research (as many of us know, formulating a question can take years in and of itself, never mind data collection and analysis). Students will need to make decisions in ambiguous situations without much experience on which to draw. They can usually be pushed forward, however, if they are assured that evaluation of this project depends on the insights gained, not the numbers of subjects tested or the significance of the results.

Completing an original research project, no matter how flawed, is usually seen as an invaluable experience that allows students to approach research in general with greater appreciation and humility. In addition, the application of research design issues, ethical issues, and statistics to one's own research project allows students to learn about these topics in a much more profound way.

Students might present their results to the class at the end of the semester in a poster-session format. It might be useful for the final write-up to include not only the research paper, but also a paper on "What I Would do Differently Next Time" that allows students to show how much they learned from their mistakes, regardless of the quality of the final study.

13. <u>Annotated Bibliography</u>: Have students create an annotated bibliography to accompany the course. They might be asked to find one, two, or three articles or books for each chapter and for each one, write a brief description or summary. This might also include an explanation of how/why they chose their articles or books. The annotations could be collected throughout the course as chapters are covered, or they could all be turned in at the end of the semester (or some combination of the two). Bibliographies might also be made available to classmates, who might be interested in pursuing additional topics.

14. <u>Advice Column</u>: An advice-column format could be used in a variety of ways. You could collect actual advice column questions and have students respond to these. Alternatively, you could write a question for each chapter, have students submit a question and answer for each chapter, or have students write questions that are then answered by other students (e.g., all students put their questions in a hat and then pick one to which they respond) . Students would be responsible for answering questions using information from the text and class. These could be turned-in throughout the semester and could provide a useful springboard for class discussion.

15. <u>Evaluation of Child Care Manual</u>: Students could be asked to evaluate one of the many popular books on child development available to parents in local bookstores. The book should be one of the general books on child development or child rearing so that more of it relates to the course in general, rather than one specific aspect of the course. Points that students could consider when evaluating the book include: the author's credentials and experience; accuracy of the description of child development; reasonableness of the suggestions; theoretical orientation of the author and how this might influence their suggestions; whether or not claims are adequately supported by research; and contradictions between the book and the material in your textbook.

16. <u>Course Portfolio</u>: This is a different type of portfolio from the one described above. For this project, a specific assignment is given each week (or for each chapter) and students turn in a two page response paper (usually due within a week). Assignments vary depending on the nature of the material being covered. Examples of assignments might be replicating (on a small-scale basis) some of the research described in the book, finding and evaluating a relevant article or current event, answering a specific discussion question related to a specific topic, relating videos to course material, or reacting to a controversial issue. Anything is possible. You might use this as a vehicle for having students respond to one or more of the discussion questions that are provided in the Study Guide. The goal is to give students regular opportunities to think and write about the topics covered in each chapter. The portfolio may also include other in-class and out-of-class work that is not turned in during the semester, but is turned in at the end of the semester when the entire portfolio is submitted for review.

Agency for Instructional Technology
Box A
Bloomington, IN 47402

Churchill Films
662 N. Robertson Blvd.
Los Angeles, CA 90069

Coronet Film and Video (COR)
108 Wilmot Road
Deerfield, IL 60015

CRM/McGraw-Hill Films
2233 Faraday Avenue
Carlsbad, CA 92008
1-800-421-0833

Davidson Films, Inc.
231 "E" Street
Davis, CA 95616
916-753-9604
Fax 916-753-3719

Filmakers Library, Inc.
124 East 40th Street
Suite 901
New York, NY 10016
        212-808-4980
Fax 212-808-4983

Films for the Humanities and Sciences
P.O. Box 2053
Princeton, NJ 08543
1-800-257-5126
Fax 609-452-1602 or 609-275-3767

Films Incorporated
1144 Willmette Avenue
Wilmette, IL 60091

Harper and Row Media
Order Fulfillment
Customer Service
2350 Virginia Avenue
Hagerstown, MD 21740

Indiana University (IND)
Audio-Visual Center
Bloomington, IN 47401

Insight Media
2162 Broadway
New York, NY 10024
212-721-6316
Fax 212-799-5309

Media Guild
118 South Acacia
Box 881
Solano Beach, CA 92075

NOVA (Crown Video)
Crown Publishers, Inc.
225 Park Avenue South
New York, NY 10003

Public Broadcasting System
(PBS)
1320 Braddock Place
Alexandria, VA 22314

Pyramid Films and Audio
P.O. Box 1048
Santa Monica, CA 90406

University of Minnesota
Film and Video
Audio-Visual Education Service
Room 55, Westbrook Hall
Minneapolis, MN 55455

UNDERSTANDING LIFE-SPAN HUMAN DEVELOPMENT

LEARNING OBJECTIVES

After students have read and studied the material in this chapter, they should be able to answer the following questions:

1. What is development? What processes underlie developmental changes across the life span?

2. How has our understanding of different periods of the life-span changed historically? What cultural and subcultural differences exist in perspectives of the life span?

3. What are the three goals of life-span developmental psychology?

4. What are the seven assumptions of the life-span perspective on human development?

5. How is the scientific method used to study development?

6. What are the pros and cons of the two common methods of data collection used by developmental researchers?

7. What are the advantages and disadvantages of the cross-sectional and longitudinal designs?

8. How does the sequential design resolve the weaknesses of the cross-sectional and longitudinal designs?

9. What are the important features of the experimental method? What sorts of information can be gathered from an experimental study?

10. What are the important features of the correlational method? What sorts of information can be gathered from this type of study?

11. What problems or issues arise in studying development?

I. **What is development?**
    Systematic continuities and changes (gains and losses) from conception to death
    A. Broad areas of concern
        1. Physical development
        2. Cognitive development
        3. Psychosocial development
    B. Processes underlying change
        1. Maturation-- biological unfolding
        2. Learning-- experiential influences

II. **How do people view the life span?**
    A. Distinguishing among developmental periods
        1. Chronological age versus capabilities
        2. Age grades-- status, roles, privileges, and responsibilities based on age group
        3. Age norms-- expectations based on age grades
            a. Social clocks-- sense of timing for life transitions
            b. "Off time" (vs. "on time") events have more negative impact
    B. Historical changes in phases of the life span
        1. Children from premodern times to the present
            a. Premodern: Miniature adults, harsh treatment, possessions
            b. Modern: Need guidance and protection
            c. Current Trend: Sophisticated and self-reliant?
        2. The invention of adolescence
            a. 19th century-- need for educated work force
            b. 20th century-- entrance to adulthood further delayed
        3. A changing adulthood
            a. Longer life expectancy
            b. Middle age as distinct period
    C. Cultural differences in phases of the life span
        1. Cross-cultural differences in age grades
        2. In United States, subcultural differences in age norms

III. **What is the science of life-span human development?**
    A. Goals of study
        1. Description of human development
            a. Normal development
            b. Variations-- individual differences
        2. Explanation of human development
        3. Optimization of human development
    B. Historical beginnings
        1. Observations of own children-- Charles Darwin's baby biographies
        2. More objective study-- G. Stanley Hall's questionnaires

    C. Today's life-span perspective on development
        1. Development is a lifelong process
        2. Development is multidirectional
        3. Development involves both gain and loss
        4. Life-long plasticity in human development
        5. Development is shaped by its historical/cultural context
        6. Development is multiply influenced
        7. Understanding development requires multiple disciplines

IV.   **How is developmental research conducted?**
A. The scientific method
   1. Theory develops from observations
   2. Hypotheses generated to test theory
B. Data collection techniques
   1. Self-report measures-- interviews, questionnaires, and tests
   2. Behavioral observation
      a. naturalistic observation-- behaviors in everyday life
      b. structured observation-- create conditions to elicit a behavior
C. Describing development
   1. Cross-sectional and longitudinal designs in brief
   2. Age, cohort, and time of measurement effects
   3. Strengths and weaknesses of the cross-sectional design
      a. Can determine cohort differences in behavior
      b. Age effects and cohort effects are confounded
      c. Relatively fast and inexpensive to conduct
      d. No information about development of individuals
   4. Strengths and weaknesses of the longitudinal design
      a. Can indicate individual age changes in behavior
      b. Can show relationships between early and later behavior
      c. Age effects and time of measurement effects are confounded
      d. Costly and time-consuming
      e. Initial questions and measures may later prove uninteresting or inadequate
      f. Loss of participants-- leads to smaller, less representative sample
      g. Participants can be affected by repeated testings
   5. Sequential designs
      a. Combines cross-sectional and longitudinal approaches
      b. Can separate age effects, time of measurement effects, and cohort effects
D. Explaining development: Experimental and correlational methods
   1. The experimental method
      a. Three features
         i. Manipulate independent variable and measure effects on dependent variable
         ii. Random assignment of individuals to conditions
         iii. Experimental control of extraneous factors
      b. Strength: Can draw conclusions about cause-effect relationships
      c. Limitations: Contrived, ethical constraints
      d. Quasi-experiment-- no random assignment to treatment groups
   2. The correlational method
      a. Most frequently used method
      b. Correlation coefficient assesses extent that individuals' scores on one variable systematically related to scores on another
      c. No conclusive cause-effect relationships
         i. Direction of causality may be reversed
         ii. Third variable may cause observed association
         iii. Need convergence of many studies for conclusions

V.   **What problems arise in studying development?**
A. Choosing samples
   1. Generalizability to populations and random sampling
B. Protecting the rights of research participants
   1. Research ethics
      a. Guidelines

      i. APA and SRCD guidelines
      ii. Human-subjects review committees
    b. Concerns
      i. informed consent
      ii. debriefing
      iii. protection from harm
      iv. confidentiality

SUGGESTIONS FOR CLASS DISCUSSIONS OR PROJECTS

1. To introduce life-span developmental psychology and to illustrate that there are different views of the life span, students might be asked (perhaps on the first day of class) how they would break up the life span and how they would describe each portion of the life span. For example, when is someone a young adult, or a toddler, or a middle-aged adult? What characteristics would they use to describe each of these age groups? (These descriptions can be somewhat depressing to instructors who find that students view them as being in an older age category than they view themselves.) This exercise often points out stereotypes or misconceptions that students have about people in different periods of the life span. Some of these might be discussed on this day; others might be referred to when the appropriate section is reached during the semester.

    This introductory exercise may be augmented by the ideas presented by Bryan [Bryan, A. J. (1988). Discussion topics for developmental psychology. *Teaching of Psychology, 15*, 42-44]. Bryan presents seven group discussion topics corresponding to seven different life phases from infancy to early adulthood. Each topic presents a "real life" situation and delineates issues that students should consider in solving the problem. Students are encouraged to apply theory and research to "real life" issues.

2. Have students break into small group to discuss the tenets of life-span developmental psychology. With which do they agree and disagree? Students might then reconvene to share their ideas with the larger group. To help launch small group discussion, some provocative statements that follow from the tenets might be distributed to each group. For example:
   • Do you believe that people over the age of 80 continue to "develop" or simply to "change" -- or do they just deteriorate?
   • Are gains and losses evenly distributed across the life-span? What are some losses experienced by children? What are some gains experienced by seniors?
   • Do you believe that plasticity remain constant across the life span? What evidence do you have for your position?
   • What historical/cultural events in your lifetime are shaping development in ways different from your parents' generation?

3. To get students thinking about meaningful periods of the life span and of their own lives, ask them to draw their lives on a sheet of paper with a line across the bottom. Then have them divide the drawing into segments that represent important eras or periods to them. This method of assessing time perspectives was reported by Whitbourne and Dennefer (*International Journal of Aging and Human Development*, 1985-1986, *22*, 147-155). Adults over 40 did not perceive any meaningful eras after age 30, whereas adults under 30 viewed almost every year as a significant marker. Individuals differed in the extent to which they emphasized their past and future lives, as well. Peggy Brick also provides suggestions on how students can construct a life line [Benjamin, L. & Lowman, K. (1981). *Activities handbook for the teaching of psychology*, Washington, D.C.: APA-- see pp. 128-130].

4. Offer students an opportunity to reflect on the notion of continuity and change in development (e.g., in small groups, written reflections, journal entries). If they have watched a child, sibling, cousin, or other person close to them grow up, have them reflect on the ways that person has

changed and the ways that she or he has remained the same. Do the students have a sense of change or continuity being more important? Might there be cultural differences in terms of whether change or constancy are viewed as predominating? Which of the identified changes relate to maturation and which to learning? Students who have not watched someone grow through the years might reflect on their own development. They might also discuss their ideas with someone who has watched them grow up (e.g., a parent, older sibling).

5.   Have students design a study to test a question such as one of those listed below. Have students identify the type of study, and the data collection technique they would use, and have them clearly define their variables.
   • Do children who witness abuse within the family demonstrate lower self-esteem and
       cognitive performance than children who do not witness such abuse ?
   • In many homes, the television is turned on as soon as family members get home and
       remains on until bedtime, even if no one is actually watching. Does allowing the TV
       to run as "background noise" have any adverse effect on children's development?
   • Are writing skills related to the amount of reading that one does and to the content of the
       reading material?
   • Are sibling relationships of same-gender siblings closer than sibling relationships of other-
       gender siblings?
   • Do men and women perceive their retirements differently and does retirement affect men and
       women differently?
   • Do men and women discipline their children differently?

6.   A major hurdle in conducting research is obtaining a representative sample. Discuss or have students brainstorm ways to obtain study participants of different ages and abilities-- perhaps specifically for the studies they designed in Exercise 5 above. This is more difficult than students usually think. Students may say they would obtain participants from the local school district, not realizing that many schools have tight restrictions on research. Other recruitment techniques include soliciting participants from an after-school program, or going through newspaper birth announcements and calling parents. Older subjects might be obtained at a bingo night or an adult daycare program. Once students have generated ways of obtaining a sample, they might discuss whether these samples would be representative of the population. For example, is there something different about older adults who play bingo versus those who do not?

7.   Another important research issue is that of informed consent. Discuss or hand-out American Psychological Association (APA) or Society for Research in Child Development (SRCD) guidelines for use of humans in research. Have students, individually or in small groups, write permission letters for different populations (e.g., parent of a preschooler, parent of an adolescent, guardian of a retarded adult, elderly person). Again, the studies devised in the exercises above might be useful as students will need to have a study in mind so they can provide the hypothetical research participant with enough information to make an informed decision. Have students exchange letters and decide: a) if they received this letter, would they give permission; and b) does the letter meet APA/SRCD guidelines?

8.   For a thoughtful discussion of the issues involved in attempting to balance the risk factors associated with research with the potential benefits of research, see Thompson (1990) in the Suggested Readings. The article focuses on special concerns of conducting research with children. Thompson describes three developmental research procedures that raise ethical questions even though they are likely to be judged acceptable by Institutional Review Boards. These vignettes could be used to get students thinking about ethical concerns involved in testing children.

9.   Have students read and discuss an early study that would not be considered ethical by today's standards. A good example is provided by Dennis (1941) in *Genetic Psychological Monographs*. Dennis studied the influence of social stimulation on child development by raising a pair of twins in

virtual isolation for their first year. Ask students how the same question could be addressed so that it meets today's ethical standards.

10.   This suggestion is appropriate for chapter one or two, depending on the emphasis you choose. Ask students to generate a list of observations concerning some question of development (e.g., Do males and females behave differently? How do preschool-age children act and speak?) Then ask students to develop a theory that ties these observations together and helps to explain them. Discuss the value of developing a theory in order to impose order on the vast number of seemingly diverse observations. Students may develop different theories that all have some value and can be used to discuss eclecticism. You might want to follow-up on this suggestion by having students generate hypotheses from the theory they developed, and design a study to test at least one of the hypotheses.

SUGGESTED FILMS AND VIDEOS

Development (CRM Films, film, 32 minutes): Presents several research methods used to assess development from infancy to adolescence.

Experiments in Human Behavior (Insight Media, VHS, 35 minutes): Uses landmark psychology experiments to illustrate the scientific method, including independent and dependent variables, and experimenter bias. Also covers field experiments, participant observation, and use of questionnaires.

Methodology (CRM Films, VHS and film): Focuses on experimental design in laboratory settings. Covers independent and dependent variables, control groups, random assignment, and other basic methodological concepts.

Whatever Happened to Childhood (Churchill Films, 45 minutes): Children and adults discuss changes in our society, including changes resulting from divorce, drug use, and sexual behavior.

SUGGESTED READINGS

Appelbaum, M. I., & McCall, R. B. (1983). Design and analysis in developmental psychology. In W. Kessen (Ed.) *Handbook of Child Psychology: Vol. I. History, theory and methods* (pp. 415-476). NY: Wiley.

Borstelmann, L. J. (1983). Children before psychology: Ideas about children from antiquity to the late 1800's. In W. Kessen (Ed.) *Handbook of Child Psychology: Vol. I. History, theory and methods* (pp. 1-40). NY: Wiley.

Cairns, R. B. (1983). The emergence of developmental psychology. In W. Kessen (Ed.) *Handbook of Child Psychology: Vol. I. History, theory and methods* (pp. 41-102). NY: Wiley.

Hetherington, E. M., & Baltes, P. B. (1988). Child psychology and life-span development. In E. M. Hetherington, R. M. Lerner, & M. Perlmutter (Eds.). *Child development in life-span perspective*. Hillsdale, NJ: Lawrence Erlbaum Associates.

Hilgard, E. R. (1987). *Psychology in America: A historical survey*. NY: Harcourt, Brace, Jovanovich.

Miller, S. A. (1987). *Developmental research methods*. NJ: Prentice-Hall.

Thompson, R. A. (1990). Vulnerability in research: A developmental perspective on research risk. *Child Development, 61*, 1-16.

Vasta, R. (1979). *Studying children*. CA: W. H. Freeman & Co.

TRANSPARENCY MASTERS

1.1   Assumptions of the life-span perspective on development

1.2 (a, b, c)   Summary of developmental designs: a) Cross-sectional, b) longitudinal, and c) sequential

1.3 (a, b)   Characteristics of experimental method (a) and correlational method (b)

Assumptions of life-span perspective on development

1. Development is a lifelong process

2. Development is multidirectional

3. Development involves both gain and loss

4. There is much plasticity in human development

5. Development is shaped by its historical/cultural context

6. Development is multiply influenced

7. Understanding development requires multiple disciplines

CROSS-SECTIONAL METHOD

Procedure: Observe people of different ages (or cohorts) at one point in time

Information gained: Describes age differences

Advantages: Demonstrates age differences in behavior

                         Hints at developmental trends

                         Takes little time to conduct

                         Inexpensive

Disadvantages: Age trends may reflect cohort effects rather than true developmental change

                         Provides no information about change over time in individuals

LONGITUDINAL METHOD

Procedure: Observe people of one age group repeatedly over time

Information gained: Describes age changes

Advantages: Actually indicates how individuals are alike and different in the way they change over time

                     Can reveal links between early behavior and later behavior

Disadvantages: Age trends may reflect time-of-measurement effects (historical effects) during the study rather than true developmental change

                     Relatively time-consuming and expensive

                     Measures may later prove inadequate

                     Participants drop out

                     Participants can be affected by repeated testing

SEQUENTIAL METHOD

Procedure: Observe different cohorts on multiple occasions (combine cross-sectional and longitudinal approaches)

Information gained: Describes age differences *and* age changes

Advantages: Helps separate the effects of age, cohort, and time of measurement

                            Indicates whether developmental changes experienced by one generation or cohort are similar to those experienced by other cohorts

Disadvantages: Often complex and time-consuming

                            Despite being the strongest method, may still leave questions about whether a developmental change is generalizable

Characteristics of the Experimental Method

Manipulation of an independent variable

Random assignment to treatment groups to ensure similarity of groups

Experimental control of extraneous variables

Can establish a cause/effect relationship between independent variable and dependent variable

May not be possible for ethical reasons

May be artificial (findings from contrived experimental settings may not generalize well to the "real world")

Characteristics of the Correlational Method

Studies people who have already had different experiences

Assignment by "nature" to groups (as a result, groups may not be similar in all respects)

Lack of control over extraneous variables

Can suggest, but not firmly establish, that one variable causes another

Can be used to study issues that cannot be studied experimentally

Can be applied to data collected in natural settings (findings may generalize better to the "real world")

2

THEORIES OF HUMAN DEVELOPMENT

After students have read and studied the material in this chapter, they should be able to answer the following questions:

1. What are the characteristics of a good theory?

2. What are the five basic issues in human development? Where does each theorist stand on each of these issues?

3. What are the distinct features of Freud's psychoanalytic theory? What are the strengths and weaknesses of the theory?

4. How does Erikson's theory compare to Freud's theory? What crisis characterizes each of Erickson's psychosocial stages?

5. What are the distinct features of Skinner's operant conditioning theory and Bandura's social-learning theory? What are the strengths and weaknesses of the learning theories?

6. What is Piaget's basic perspective on cognitive development? What are the strengths and weaknesses of Piaget's theory?

7. What are the main features of the contextual theory of development? What is Bronfenbrenner's ecological approach? What are the strengths and weaknesses of the contextual perspective?

8. What are the three major world views? Which theories are consistent with each view?

I. **The nature of theories**
   A. The importance of theories
      1. Lens for interpreting any number of facts and observations
      2. Guides the collection of new information
   B. Qualities of a good theory
      1. Parsimonious-- explains wide range of phenomena simply
      2. Internally consistent-- its different parts are not contradictory
      3. Falsifiable-- generates testable hypotheses
      4. Supported-- describes, predicts, and explains human development

II. **Basic issues in human development**
   A. Assumptions about human nature: Good, bad, or neither?
      1. Hobbes-- society must control inherent selfishness and aggression
      2. Rousseau-- society must not interfere with innate goodness
      3. Locke-- child as tabula rasa
   B. The nature/nurture issue
   C. The activity/passivity issue
   D. The continuity/discontinuity issue
      1. Gradual or abrupt change
      2. Qualitative or quantitative change
      3. Developmental stages
   E. The universality/ context-specificity issue

III. **Freud: Psychoanalytic theory**
   A. Human nature-- Humans driven by undesirable biological urges
      1. Instincts
         a. Life instincts-- life-sustaining activities
         b. Death instincts-- destructive forces
      2. Unconscious motivation
   B. Three components of personality: Id, ego, and superego
      1. Id-- basic biological urges, pleasure principle
      2. Ego-- reality principle, balances between id and superego
      3. Superego-- internalized moral standards
   C. Psychosexual development
      1. Importance of libido-- sex instinct's energy shifts body locations
      2. Conflict of id and social demands leads to ego's defense mechanisms
         a. Fixation-- Development arrested at early stage
         b. Regression-- Retreat to earlier stage
      3. Five Stages
         a. Oral stage
         b. Anal stage
         c. Phallic stage-- Oedipus and Electra complexes
         d. Latency period
         e. Genital stage
   E. Strengths and weaknesses of Freud's psychoanalytic theory
      1. Difficult to test
      2. Weak support for specific aspects of the theory
      3. Greater support for broad ideas
         a. Unconscious motivation
         b. Importance of early experience, especially parenting

Chapter 2

IV.   **Erikson: Neo-Freudian psychoanalytic theory**
    A. Neo-Freudians
         1. Erikson most important; others include Adler, Jung, Horney
         2. Erikson's differences with Freud
                a. Less emphasis on sexual and more on social influences
                b. Less emphasis on id, more on rational ego
                c.   More positive view of human nature
                d. More emphasis on developmental changes in adulthood
    B. Psychosocial Development-- through resolution of eight crises
         1. Trust versus mistrust
         2. Autonomy versus shame
         3. Initiative versus guilt
         4. Industry versus inferiority
         5. Identity versus role confusion
         6. Intimacy versus isolation
         7. Generativity versus stagnation
         8. Integrity versus despair
    C. Strengths and weaknesses
         1. Its emphases on rational, adaptive nature and social influences easier to accept
         2. Influenced thinking about adolescence and beyond
         3. Like Freud, difficult to test

IV.   **Learning theories**
    A. Watson: Behaviorism
         1. Only observed behavior should be studied
         2. Tabula rasa-- only learned associations important
    B. Skinner: Operant Conditioning
         1. Reinforcers-- consequences that increase probability of future response
         2. Punishers-- consequences that suppress future response
    C. Bandura: Social Learning
         1. Humans' cognitive abilities distinguish them from animals-- can think about
             behavior and anticipate consequences
         2. Observational learning most important mechanism for behavior change
         3. Reciprocal determinism-- mutual influence of individuals and social environments
    D. Strengths and weaknesses of learning theory
         1. Learning theories are precise and testable
         2. Principles operate across the life span
         3. Practical applications
         4. Doesn't show that learning actually causes observed developmental changes
         5. Oversimplifies development by focusing on experience and downplaying
             biological influences

V.   **Cognitive-developmental theory**
    A. Piaget's basic perspective on intellectual development
         1. Cognitive structure or scheme-- organized patterns of thought or action that aids in
             adaptation to environments
         2. Constructivism--active construction of knowledge
         3. Stage progression due to interaction of biological maturation and environment
    B. Four stages of cognitive development
         1. Sensorimotor stage
         2. Preoperational stage
         3. Concrete operations stage
         4. Formal operations stage

C. Strengths and weaknesses of Piaget's theory
    1. Acceptance of many concepts
    2. Influential in education and child rearing practices
    3. Too little emphasis on motivation and emotion
    4. Questioning of stage model

VI. **Contextual theory**
    A. Bronfenbrenner's ecological approach
        1. Relationship between individual and environment is reciprocal
        2. Developing person embedded in interacting environmental systems
            a. Microsystem-- immediate environment
            b. Mesosystem-- interrelation ships between microsystems
            c. Exosystem-- influential social setting not directly experienced
            d. Macrosystem-- larger, subcultural or cultural contexts
        3. Strengths and weaknesses
            a. Emphasizes some neglected concepts
                i. Development occurs in context
                ii. Environments are dynamic
            b. Not yet a full-blown theory--- and may never be

VII. **Theories and world views**
    A. Organismic world view
        1. Humans must be understood as wholes or systems
        2. Humans are active in own development
        3. Humans evolve through distinct stages
    B. Mechanistic world view
        1. Humans, like machines, are a collection of parts
        2. Humans are relatively passive in developmental process
        3. Change is gradual and continuously
        4. Developmental pathways depend on environment
    C. Contextual world view
        1. Focus on dynamic relationship between person and environment
        2. Humans are active in developmental process
        3. Potential exists for qualitative and quantitative change
        4. Developmental pathways depend on interplay of internal and external influences
    D. Changing world views
        1. Our understanding of human development is ever-changing
        2. Contextual theory prevalent today
        3. Less extreme positions
        4. More emphasis on "minitheories"

VIII. **Applications: Developmental theory and teenage pregnancy**

IX. **Clarifying your own theoretical perspective**

SUGGESTIONS FOR CLASS DISCUSSIONS OR PROJECTS

1.   Have students read excerpts from original writings of theorists such as Freud and Piaget. It might be useful to have students search out these texts on their own. In addition to the library, some might be found on the web. For example, Psych Web (at http://www.psych-web.com) provides excerpts from classics such as Freud's *Interpretation of Dreams*. Choose the "Books" heading.
     Students could also look up additional information about some of the theorists discussed either at the library or at web sites, such as the following:

Freud: http://plaza.interport.net/nypsan
Piaget: http://www.unige.ch/piaget/
Watson: http://uts.cc.utexas.edu/~kensicki/watson.html
Bronfenbrenner: http://www.human.cornell.edu/HD/faculty/Bronfenbrenner.html

The following questions might be considered:
• Why are there web sites-- a late 20th century invention-- available for Freud, Watson, and Piaget? Are they purely historical sites, or do the theorists continue to make a contribution to current thinking? Explain.
• What links do you see between the biographical information available about these theorists and their work?

2.   Obtain some older child rearing manuals and have students discuss the theoretical underpinnings of the manuals. In many cases, it is possible to "see" the influence of theories such as behaviorism or psychoanalytic theory. In addition, students may be fascinated to read what parents were advised in previous generations. Old child rearing manuals are often available at flea-markets, second-hand book stores, libraries, or from older parents. An early publication from the U.S. Department of Labor on child care can also be used. Early editions of Benjamin Spock (1945 or 1946) can be found in most libraries. By comparing an early edition of Spock's book to a recent one, students might assess how thinking has changed across the years.
        Young (1990-- See Suggested Readings) reviewed nearly 30 years of *Infant Care* and *Parents* magazine to determine whether psychological theories and research were indeed accurately communicated to parents. She found that some advice reflected research findings, while other advice from experts reflected beliefs consistent with the larger social-cultural context, indicating that research itself is affected by culture (A Bronfenbrennarian notion).

3.   Belsky (1980) uses Bronfenbrenner's ecological model to examine the issue of child maltreatment. Choose another social problem (e.g., substance abuse, school drop out) and examine how factors at different levels of analysis (e.g., individual level, various microsystems, the macrosystem) contribute to this problem. You might also try to propose solutions for each of the identified contributing factors to demonstrate that interventions also occur at different levels, and the solutions we attempt may depend on the level at which we conceptualize the problem.

4.   Choose a difficulty parents may have with their child (advice columns are a useful source) and discuss it from the different theoretical perspectives. For example, one mother wrote to an advice column that her 2 1/2-year-old daughter was sleeping in the parents' bed every night. This began soon after the child was born and the mother found that it was easy to breast feed in the bed while her husband worked the night shift. When his work schedule changed, they wanted the daughter to sleep in her own bed, but were unsuccessful in achieving this. Students can analyze this from several perspectives, including psychoanalytic (oral gratification, unconscious motivation), learning theory (reinforcement history of both child and mother), cognitive-developmental theory (cognitive schema for bedtime ritual, assimilation and accommodation of new behaviors into cognitive structures), and contextual theory (change in the environment causes a change in the person, which in turn affects the environment). Other problems to explore might include bed-wetting, school phobia, or even ambivalence about an impending marriage. How would each theory (or selected theories) explain these problems?

5.   The issue of adoption can be used to discuss the nature-nurture issue as well as the continuity-discontinuity issue. Some questions that adopting parents might ask are listed below. Divide students into small groups and have each group discuss these questions and formulate answers before discussing them as an entire class.
        • How will early experiences affect the later development of this child?
        • Can we provide an enriched environment that will overcome any adverse early experiences?

- What if some characteristics are genetically based and our environment has no effect?
- What traits might be "lurking" in this child's genotype?

SUGGESTED FILMS AND VIDEOS

Child Development (1992, Insight Media, VHS, 30 minutes): Introduces the field of developmental psychology by giving a brief overview of the ideas of Locke, Rousseau, Watson, Freud, Erikson, Piaget, Bowlby, and Gesell, as well as some current theorists.

B.F. Skinner on Behaviorism (Insight Media, VHS, 28 minutes): Behavior modification, positive reinforcement, and programmed instruction are discussed by Skinner. Also applies behaviorism to various social concerns.

The Discovery of Animal Behavior: A Question of Learning (Films Incorporated, film or VHS, 60 minutes). Contributions of Pavlov, Skinner, Thorndike, Watson and other learning theorists are presented.

Sigmund Freud (Insight Media, VHS, 30 minutes): Profile of Freud and his theories about the human subconscious.

SUGGESTED READINGS

Belsky, Jay (1980). Child maltreatment: An ecological model. *American Psychologist*, *35*, 320-335.

Bronfenbrenner, U. (1977). Toward an experimental ecology of human development. *American Psychologist*, *35*, 513-531.

Crain, W. (1992). *Theories of development: Concepts and applications*. NJ: Prentice-Hall.

Ginsburg, H. P., & Opper, S. (1988). *Piaget's theory of intellectual development.*. NY: Prentice-Hall.

Harris, B. (1979). Whatever happened to Little Albert? *American Psychologist*, *34*, 151-160.

Lerner, R. M. (1986). *Concepts and theories of human development*, 2nd ed. NY: Random House.

Miller, P. H. (1989). *Theories of developmental psychology*, 2nd ed. NY: W. H. Freeman and Co.

Ogbu, John U. (1981). Origins of human competence: A cultural-ecological perspective. *Child Development*, *52*, 413-429.

Piaget, J. (1960). *The child's conception of the world*. NJ: Littlefield, Adams & Co.

Skinner, B. F. (1982). Baby in a box. In J. K. Gardner (Ed.) *Readings in Developmental Psychology*, 2nd ed. MA: Little, Brown & Co. [Originally appeared in *Ladies' Home Journal* , 1946 (volume 62, pp. 30-31, 135-136, 138) and describes how Skinner's daughter was raised in an "Aircrib" using principles of learning theory.]

Watson, J. A., & Raynor, R. (1920). Conditioned emotional reactions. *Journal of Experimental Psychology*, *3*, 1-14. [The famous "Little Albert" study.]

Young, K. T. (1990). American conceptions of infant development from 1955 to 1984: What the experts are telling people. *Child Development*, *61*, 17-28.

2.1   Summary of Freud's psychoanalytic theory (Main focus of the theory and position on developmental issues)

2.2   Summary of Skinner and Bandura's learning theories (Main focus of the theory and position on developmental issues)

2.3   Summary of Piaget's cognitive-developmental theory (Main focus of the theory and position on developmental issues)

2.4   Summary of Bronfenbrenner's ecological theory (Main focus of the theory and position on developmental issues)

2.5   Organismic world view

2.6   Mechanistic world view

2.7   Contextual world view

Freud's Psychoanalytic theory

Humans have basic biological urges that need to be satisfied

Human behavior is often unconsciously motivated

Psychic energy is divided among three components of personality: id, ego, superego

Sex instinct is the most important of the life instincts. Its psychic energy--the libido--shifts focus from one part of the body to another. As this happens, the child moves through five psychosexual stages: oral, anal, phallic, latency period, and genital.

Position on developmental issues:

>   Inherently selfish and aggressive

>   Nature more than nurture
>   (inborn biological forces, but parents can influence
>   how successfully stages are resolved)

>   Passively driven through stages by biological forces

>   Discontinuity (psychosexual stages)

>   Traits from early childhood carry over to adulthood

>   Universal stages of development

Learning Theories

Skinner: Behavior is influenced by its consequences. Reinforcers are consequences that increase the probability of future responding and punishers are consequences that decrease the probability of future responding.

Bandura: Human beings are cognitive beings who actively process information that they observe in their environment.

Position on developmental issues:

Humans are inherently neither good or bad

Nurture is more influential than nature

Passively shaped by environment (Skinner)
Actively involved in own development; can influence their environment (Bandura)

Development is continuous

Early traits are likely to change if the environment changes

Development is not universal; it takes many different directions depending on one's environment

Piaget's Cognitive-Developmental Theory

Intelligent behavior helps organisms adapt to their environments.

We actively construct new understandings of the world based on experiences. These understandings are constructed through processes of assimilation and accommodation.

Position on developmental issues:

Inherent tendencies are mainly positive (e.g., curiosity)

Interactionist--both nature and nurture influence development (maturation directs the movement through same sequence of stages, but experience affects the rate of movement)

Actively involved in own development

Discontinuity (stages of cognitive growth)

Cognitive abilities change significantly (qualitative change) from one stage to another

Stages are universal

Bronfenbrenner's Ecological Approach

Development must be studied within social contexts

Four major levels of environmental contexts are: microsystem, mesosystem, exosystem, and macrosystem

Position on developmental issues:

Born with neither negative or positive tendencies

Nature and nurture are both influential

Actively involved in own development (and in shaping the environment)-- both person and environment in state of flux

Potential exists for qualitative and quantitative change

Much of development is not universal-- many different paths depending on social context, including historical and cultural context

Organismic World Model

Humans are like plants and other living organisms

They are best understood as organized wholes rather than piece by piece

They are active in their own development

Internal forces are primarily responsible for development

There are distinct and universal stages

E.g., Freud, Piaget, Erikson

<u>Mechanistic Model</u>

Humans are like machines

They are best understood as a collection of parts

They are passively influenced by outside stimulation

Development or change is gradual and continuous

Development can take a number of different paths

E.g., Watson, Skinner, Bandura

Contextual Model

Humans are like an ongoing historical event or drama

They are inseparable from the environment

They are active in development and the environment is also active

Development can be both continuous and discontinuous

Development can take a number of different paths

E.g., Bronfenbrenner

3

THE GENETICS OF LIFE-SPAN DEVELOPMENT

<u>*LEARNING OBJECTIVES*</u>

After students have read and studied the material in this chapter, they should be able to answer the following questions:

1.   What do species heredity and evolution contribute to our understanding of universal patterns of development? What are the basic principles of Darwin's theory of evolution?

2.   What are the modern approaches to evolution?

3.   What are the basic workings of individual heredity, including the contributions of genes, chromosomes, the zygote, and the processes of mitosis and meiosis?

4.   What is the difference between genotype and phenotype?

5.   How are traits passed from parents to offspring? What is an example of how a child could inherit a trait through each of the mechanisms?

6.   What are the general characteristics of the chromosomal abnormalities such as Down syndrome, Turner syndrome, and Klinefelter syndrome?

7.   What methods are used to assess the influences of heredity and environment on behavioral characteristics? Describe the logic of the method, as well as strengths weaknesses of each method.

8.   How do genes, shared environmental, and nonshared environmental factors contribute to individual differences?

9.   How do genes and environments contribute to individual differences in intellectual ability across the life span?

10.   How do genes and environments contribute to individual differences in personality and temperament across the life span?

11.   How do genes and environments contribute to differences in psychological disorders?

12.   What are three ways that genes and environments correlate to influence behavior?

13.   What tests are used to screen for genetic defects? What defects can be identified with these tests? What are the advantages and disadvantages of using techniques like these to test for prenatal problems?

I. **Species heredity, evolution, and human development**
    A. Darwin's theory of evolution
        1. There is genetic variation in a species
        2. Some genes aid in adaptation more than others do
        3. Natural selection-- Genes that aid in adaptation to the environment will be passed on more often than genes that do not
    B. Modern evolutionary perspectives on development
        1. Ethology--Study of the evolved behaviors of species in their natural environments
        2. Evolutionary psychology-- Implication of Darwin for human behavior

II. **Individual heredity**
    A. Conception and the genetic code
        1. Zygote, chromosomes, mitosis, meiosis
        2. Genetic uniqueness and relatedness
            a. Crossing over-- Exchanges in pairs of chromosomes before separating
            b. Identical twins--Share 100% of their genes
            c. Fraternal twins and siblings --Share, on average, 50% of genes
        3. Determination of sex
            a. X and Y chromosomes
            b. Karyotype-- Photograph of the arrangement of chromosomes
    B. Translation of the genetic code
        1. Regulator genes -- Genes responsible for turning gene pairs on or off
        2. Genotype-- Genetic makeup one inherits
        3. Phenotype-- Actual characteristics based on genetics and environment
    C. Mechanisms of inheritance
        1. Single gene-pair inheritance
            a. Dominant and recessive genes (Mendel)
            b. Carriers-- Not have trait but can transmit to children
            c. Incomplete dominance-- Carriers show signs of having trait
            d. Codominance-- Neither gene in pair dominant or recessive
        2. Sex-linked inheritance-- Trait influenced by gene on sex chromosomes
        3. Polygenic inheritance-- Most human characteristics determined by multiple genes
    D. Mutations-- Change in one or more genes that produces new phenotype
    E. Chromosome abnormalities-- Child receives too many or to few chromosomes
        1. Down syndrome-- Trisomy 21
        2. Turner syndrome-- Female with a single X chromosome
        3. Klinefelter syndrome-- Male with an extra X chromosome

III. **Studying genetic and environmental influences**
    A. Behavioral genetics--Study of the extent to which genetic and environmental differences correspond to differences in traits.
        1. Heritability-- Proportion of trait variability attributable to genes
    B. How information is gathered.
        1. Experimental breeding of animals, e.g., selective breeding
        2. Twin and adoption studies
        3. Estimating the contributions of genes and environment
            a. Concordance rates and correlation coefficients
            b. Estimating contributions of genes, shared environment, and nonshared environment

IV. **Accounting for individual differences**
    A. Intellectual abilities

      1. Evidence for influence of genetics, shared, and nonshared environments

      2. Influence of genes becomes greater with age until adulthood

  B. Temperament and personality

      1. Temperament-- e.g., emotional reactivity and sociability

         a. Influences of individual genetic makeup and nonshared environment

         b. Siblings have different experiences of same family (and other environments)

  C. Psychological problems

      1. Schizophrenia

      2. Inherit predispositions to develop some disorders

  D. Heritability of traits

V. **Heredity and environment: A closer look**

  A. Genes and environment are at work over the entire life span

      1. Gene's are always turning on or off

      2. Unique genes exert themselves more as become adults

  B. Gene/environment interaction-- Expression of our genotype depends on the environment we experience, and how we respond to the environment depends on our genes

  C. Genes/environment correlations

      1. Passive correlation-- Parents' genes influence the environment they provide for children

      2. Evocative correlation-- Child's genotype evokes certain reactions

      3. Active correlation-- Child's genotype influences the environment she or he seeks

  D. Genetic influences on the environment-- Gene's affect similarity of environments we experience

VI. **Applications: Genetic counseling and engineering**

  A. Tay-Sachs disease

  B. Huntington's Disease

  C. Phenylketonuria (PKU)

SUGGESTIONS FOR CLASS DISCUSSIONS OR PROJECTS

1.   Two articles in Teaching of Psychology may help demonstrate the principles of gene-environment interaction. One uses a cooking metaphor to illustrate interactions of genes and environment [Miller, D. B. (1988). The nature-nurture issue: Lessons from the Pillsbury doughboy. *Teaching of Psychology, 15*, 147-149]. The second describes a simple demonstration of genetic-environment interaction, for those who have access to albino and pigmented mice [Brown, R. T. (1989). Exercise demonstrating a genetic-environment interaction. *Teaching of Psychology, 16*, 131-132].

2.   Ask students to consider how they are similar to and different from their siblings. Have them speculate about the source of these similarities and differences (genetic factors or environmental factors). Point out that a shared family environment actually contributes more to <u>differences</u> than similarities among siblings. To make this concrete for students, have them write down, or share with another student in class, an episode within their family that was interpreted one way by them and a different way by their sibling. Or for students who don't have a sibling, ask them to think of something that has happened among a group of friends that has been interpreted differently by each person present. Then ask students to speculate on how these different interpretations might lead to different developmental outcomes. For more information, see Dunn and Plomin under Suggested Readings.

3.   Advances in the study of genetics raise a variety of ethical concerns. For example, the development of tests to identify carriers of diseases and for prenatal detection of diseases (such as cystic fibrosis) is met with mixed responses. Some applaud these tests as they could prevent many infants from being born with cystic fibrosis (either because carriers decide not to conceive a child or pregnant women elect to have an abortion if a fetus with cystic fibrosis is conceived). Others believe that the test has more drawbacks than benefits. It may imply that people with cystic fibrosis should never have been born. Other discussion questions might include:
- What is the value of genetic testing for someone who is not going to consider an abortion?
- Are partners obligated to inform each other of any genetic defects in their family?
- Should parents be told their child's sex if it means that girls are more likely to be aborted than boys?

In preparation for class discussion, students might also visit the Human Genome Research Project web site (http://www.nhgri.nih.gov) to find out some recent advances in this massive federal effort to map all the genes of 46 human chromosomes. A discussion of ethical issues is included at this website.

4.   Ask students to provide examples of some behavioral traits that they believe are primarily genetically or primarily environmentally determined. What evidence do they have for their positions? Can they identify ways in which the gene-environment correlations identified by Scarr and McCartney may affect the development of these traits? Discuss ways to test the roles of genes and environment. One topic that works well is gender role development. For example, many parents believe their sons are more aggressive and active than daughters by nature, when in fact, parents behave in ways that might be encouraging these behaviors.

5.   Have students, possibly working in small groups, solve problems involving single gene-pair and sex-linked inheritance by drawing tables like those in the text (see Figure 3.4 in the text). For example: What are the odds that Arlo Guthrie will develop Huntington's disease (caused by a dominant gene) as his father Woody did? If a man and a woman are carriers of the gene for sickle-cell disease, what are their odds of having a child with sickle-cell disease? If a girl has hemophilia (sex-linked), what can we infer about her parents? If a boy has hemophilia, what can we infer about his parents? If both parents are carriers of the gene for red hair, what are their odds of having a child without red hair?

SUGGESTED FILMS AND VIDEOS

Genetic Fix (Agency for Instructional Technology, VHS, 30 minutes). Discusses genetic research and its ethical implications.

Geometry of Life (PBS, VHS, 50 minutes). This PBS documentary covers genetic research and similarities of twins.

Heredity and Environment (CRM Films, VHS or film, 28 minutes). Shows the prenatal environment and birth, and discusses genetic factors, including the role of DNA and chromosomes. Illustrates the importance of a child's postnatal environment.

Individual Differences: Infancy to Early Childhood (CRM Films, VHS or film, 18 minutes). The topic of individual differences is explored by presenting different environmental and genetic influences that affect behavior and shows the range of characteristics that are considered "normal."

Nature and Nurture (Films for the Humanities and Sciences, VHS, 52 minutes): An adapted Phil Donahue program that looks at identical twins separated at birth to address the influences of biology and environment on development.

SUGGESTED READINGS

Bouchard, T., Lykken, D., McGue, M., Segal, N., and Tellegen, A. (1990). Sources of human psychological differences: The Minnesota study of twins reared apart. *Science*, 250, 223-228.

Dunn, J. and Plomin, R. (1990). *Separate lives: Why siblings are so different*. NY: Basic.

Feldman, D. H. (1988). *Nature's gambit: Child prodigies and the development of human potential*. NY: Basic Books, Inc.

Hetherington, E. M., Reiss, D., & Plomin, R. (Eds.). (1994). *Separate social worlds of siblings: The impact of nonshared environment on development*. NJ: Lawrence Erlbaum Associates.

Maurer, D. & Maurer, C. (1988). *The world of the newborn*. New York: Basic Books.

Plomin, R. (1990). *Nature and nurture: An introduction to human behavioral genetics*. CA: Brooks/Cole.

Plomin, R., & McClearn, G. E. (Eds.). (1993). *Nature, nurture, and psychology*. Washington, D.C.: American Psychological Association.

Rosen, C. (1987, Sept.). The eerie world of reunited twins. *Discover*, pp. 36-46.

Rowe, D. C. (1993). *The limits of family experience: Genes, experience, and behavior*. NY: Guilford Publications, Inc.

Scarr, S. (1992). Developmental theories for the 1990s: Development and individual differences. *Child Development*, 63, 1-19.

Scarr, S., & McCartney, K. (1983). How people make their own environments: A theory of genotype-environmental effects. *Child Development*, 54, 424-435.

Staff, (1987, April 13). Happiness is a reunited set of twins. *U.S. News and World Report*, pp. 63-66.

TRANSPARENCY MASTERS

3.1   Mechanisms of inheritance

3.2   Behavioral genetics research

3.3   Average correlations between the intelligence scores of different pairs of individuals

3.4   Scarr & McCartney's model of gene/environment correlations

Mechanisms of Inheritance

1. Single gene-pair inheritance

One gene in a pair dominates its matched recessive gene

--Incomplete dominance occurs when the dominant gene does not completely mask the effects of the recessive gene

--Codominance occurs when both genes in a pair express themselves; neither dominates the other

2. Sex-linked inheritance

Traits are influenced by single genes located on the sex chromosomes (usually X-linked)

3. Polygenic inheritance

Traits are influenced by multiple pairs of genes

Behavioral Genetics Research

Studies the extent to which differences among people on a given variable or trait are determined by genetic and environmental differences.

Ways of estimating genetic (or environmental) influence:

    a.   <u>concordance rates</u>-- Percentage of pairs of people in which both members display the trait if one member does

    b.   <u>correlation coefficients</u>-- the extent to which, as one family member's score on the trait increases, the other family member's score also increases.

Typical subjects of behavioral genetic research:

    a. Twin Studies

        Identical twins reared together
        Identical twins reared apart
        Fraternal twins reared together
        Fraternal twins reared apart

    b.   Adoption Studies

        Child and adoptive parents
        Child and biological parents

Average correlations between the intelligence scores of different pairs of individuals

	Reared Together	Reared Apart
Identical Twins	.86	.72
Fraternal Twins	.60	.52
Biological Siblings	.47	.24
Biological Parent and Child	.42	.22
Half-Siblings	.31	---
Adopted Siblings	.34	---
Adoptive Parent and Adopted Child	.19	---

(Adapted from "Family Studies of Intelligence: A review," by T.J. Bouchard, Jr., & M. McGue, 1981, *Science, 212*, 1055-1059; and "Separated Fraternal Twins: Resemblance for Cognitive Abilities," by N.L. Pedersen, G.E. McClearn, R. Plomin, & L. Friberg, 1985, *Behavior Genetics, 15*, 407-419).

Model of Gene/Environment Correlations
(Scarr and McCartney)

Genes and environments are correlated because people with different genes not only react differently to environments they encounter, they encounter different environments.

1. ## Passive Genotype/Environment Correlations

   Parents provide their children with genes.
   Parents also provide an environment that is influenced by their own genotype.

2. ## Evocative Genotype/Environment Correlations

   Children's genotypes evoke particular responses from the environment.

3. ## Active Genotype/Environment Correlations

   Children's genotypes influence the kinds of environments they actively seek out.

4

EARLY ENVIRONMENTAL INFLUENCES ON LIFE-SPAN DEVELOPMENT

LEARNING OBJECTIVES

After students have read and studied the material in this chapter, they should be able to answer the following questions:

1.   How does develop proceed during the prenatal period? How does prenatal behavior of the fetus relate to postnatal behavior of the infant?

2.   How do mother's age, emotional state, and nutrition affect prenatal and neonatal development?

3.   How and when do various teratogens affect the developing fetus?

4.   What is the perinatal environment like? What hazards can occur during the birth process?

5.   What is the birth experience like from the mother's and father's perspectives, and different cultural perspectives?

6.   What are three universal goals of parenting? How do societies differ in the goals they emphasize? How and why do parenting practices differ cross-culturally?

7.   To what extent are the effects of the prenatal and perinatal environments long lasting? What factors influence whether effects are lasting?

8.   How can we optimize development during the prenatal and perinatal periods?

I.   **Development in the prenatal environment**
     A. Prenatal stages
        1. Conception and the germinal period
           a. Conception-- egg and sperm unite to form zygote
           b. Germinal period
              i. Zygote divides to form blastula
              ii. 8-14 days between conception and implantation of blastula
        2. The embryonic period
           a. Implantation to end of eighth prenatal week
           b. Organogenesis-- every major organ take shape
           c. Differentiation into amnion, chorion, placenta, and umbilical cord, and
                 placental barrier
           d. Sexual differentiation, testosterone
        3. The fetal period
           a. Ninth prenatal week to birth (second and third trimester)
           b. Second trimester
              i. Sex and sensory organs, bones, muscles, body systems
              ii. Age of viability
           c. Third trimester
              i. Rapid growth
              ii. Brain development-- myelination
              iii. Infant states-- organization of behavior in waking and sleeping
                  patterns
           d. Continuity between prenatal and postnatal behavior
     B. The mother's state
        1. Age
           a. Ages 16-35 are "safest"
        2. Emotional state
           a. Prolonged, severe emotional stress may be damaging
        3. Nutritional condition
           a. Malnutrition--birth defects and predisposition to adult diseases
     C. Teratogens
        1. Generalizations about effects of teratogens
           a. Effects are worst during critical period when organs are forming
           b. Not all embryos or fetuses are affected equally
           c. Susceptibility is influenced by genetic makeup of mother and fetus, and the
                 quality of the prenatal environment
           d. The same defect can be caused by different teratogens
           e. The same teratogen can cause a variety of defects
           f. The more of a teratogen that an unborn child is exposed to, the greater the
                 damage
        2. Diseases
           a. Rubella
           b. Syphilis
           c. AIDS
        3. Drugs
           a. Thalidomide
           b. Tobacco
           c. Alcohol and fetal alcohol syndrome
           d. Cocaine

4. Environmental hazards
    a. Radiation
    b. Pollutants, e.g., lead

II.   **The perinatal environment**
    A. The birth process
        1. Three stages--contractions, delivery, afterbirth
    B. Possible hazards
        1. Anoxia--oxygen shortage and cerebral palsy
            a. Breech presentation
            b. Cesarean delivery
        2. Complicated delivery
        3. Medications
        4. Identifying high-risk newborns
            a. Apgar test
    C. The mother's experience
        1. Psychological factors- attitude, knowledge, sense of control, support
        2. Cultural factors
        3. Early bonding-- engrossment
        4. Postpartum depression
    D. The father's experience

III.   **The early postnatal environment**
    A. Culture and early socialization--
        1. Three goals
            a. Survival
            b. Economic
            c. Self-actualization
        2. Cross-cultural variation:
            a. Role of infant mortality
            b. Cultural belief systems
            c. Goodness of fit-- match between infant's behavior and culture's demands

IV.   **Risk and resilience**
    A. Mitigation of negative effects of prenatal and postnatal environments
        1. Protective factors-- Prevent problems in at-risk individuals
            a. Personal resources
            b. Supportive postnatal environment
    B. Low birth weight babies

V.   **Applications: Getting life off to a good start**
    A. Before birth
        1. Prenatal care
        2. Preparation-- Lamaze method
    B. During birth
        1. Home deliveries
        2. Alternative birth centers
    C. After birth
        1. Brazelton Neonatal Behavioral Assessment Scale
        2. Neonatal intensive care
        3. Parent training and support

1.   Before discussing the prenatal environment in class, ask students to write down or comment on any changes in their lifestyles that they would want to make during the prenatal period if they were or their partner was pregnant. Many students list changes that are made salient through the media (e.g., alcohol or drug use), but hold a number of misconceptions about other factors.

2.   Describe for students, or find a short news article for them to read, on the "empathy belly." Information about the empathy belly is available from: Birthways Childbirth Resource Center Inc., 6316 159th Place NE, Washington DC, 98070 (202-881-5242). The empathy belly was designed by childbirth educator Linda Ware to provide a better understanding of what it is like to be pregnant by having people wear a specially developed vest which has a constricting rib belt to cause shortness of breath and shallow breathing, a 6-pound bladder pouch to simulate pressure placed on the bladder by the fetus, two 1-pound water-filled forms to simulate breasts, and an 11-pound water-filled form for the womb with suspended weights to simulate fetal movements. In some classes, it may be possible for students to construct their own empathy belly and then discuss changes that cannot be simulated in this way.

3.   Many students are familiar with prematurity but are not clear on its outcome. Medical technology is keeping more and more premature babies alive although many of these children have serious complications. Discuss the medical and ethical issues involved or ask students to generate their own list of concerns. A video clip of premature babies can make this a very powerful discussion. ABC's 20/20 produced a very good program on premature babies in January 1990 that is available from MPI Home Video (15825 Rob Roy Drive, Oak Forest, IL 60452; phone 708-687-7881).

4.   One feature of the comprehensive ParentsPlace web site is the provision of chat rooms and message boards where parents experiencing a particular issue (e.g., infertility over the age of 40, high-risk pregnancies) can discuss this topic with others. Students might gain a more complete understanding of the parents' perspective on such issue by reading a message board of their choice, and reporting what they learned either in a paper, or in a class discussion. The address for message boards is: http://www.parentsplace.com/genobject.cgi/talking.html

5.   Have students read and evaluate a current popular book on parenting, child rearing, or pregnancy. There are many of these on the market and their focus ranges from general to quite specific. This project is most effective if you provide students with questions or issues to focus their reading. For example, you might ask students to verify the points in the parent or pregnancy manual by comparing them to research evidence presented in the text.

6.   Have students plan the "perfect" delivery, considering preparation beforehand, setting, birth position, people present, use of drugs, and so on. Have them justify their choices. Many students are also fascinated by Frederick Leboyer's gentle birthing techniques, described in *Birth without violence* (1975). Leboyer's methods include dim lights, quiet, gentle massage until the baby breathes, and a warm bath, all to make the transition from womb to world less traumatic. Research on the Leboyer technique suggests that infants born this way fare no better at birth or later in infancy than those who undergo standard obstetrical procedures. You might want to ask students to speculate on why there is no difference between the traditional and the Leboyer procedures.

7.   *Newsweek* (11-2-87) reported that a program known as "Prenatal University" has been developed for fostering skills prior to birth. The program begins when the mother is 5 months pregnant and includes talking to the fetus through "pregaphones" and playing musical tapes. Based on what students know about prenatal capabilities, have them discuss the impact that this is likely to have on post-birth development.

A Joyous Labor (Filmakers Library, VHS, 30 minutes): Balanced presentation of birthing options available to women today. Also covers birthing customs in different cultures.

Birth of a Brain (1983, Insight Media, VHS, 33 minutes): Examines the development of the brain from prenatal period through two years of age. Includes discussion of how genetic and environmental factors affect brain development.

Childhood: Louder than Words (WNET co-production, 1991by Ambrose Video, reissued 1995 by American Brain Tumor Association, VHS, 57 minutes): Part 2 of this 7-part series explores how parents' expectations and actions come to shape a child's character and behavior. Part 3, entitled "Love's Labours," includes observations of the development of children between the ages of 6 months and 3 years

Fetal Alcohol Syndrome and Other Drug Use During Pregnancy (Films for the Humanities and Sciences, VHS, 19 minutes): Shows an 8-year-old boy born with FAS, common characteristics of FAS, and of babies born to cocaine addicted women.

High Tech Babies (Coronet, VHS, 34 minutes): Discusses the legal and ethical issues that have developed along with recent advances in medical technology.

Infant Development (Insight Media, VHS, 45 minutes): Explores physical, cognitive and emotional development of newborns, as well as development of motor skills, language, and parent-child attachment.

The Miracle of Life (1986 NOVA program available from NOVA as well as many video stores, VHS, 60 minutes): Incredible photography inside the human body. Shows male and female internal reproductive processes, conception, prenatal development, and birth.

Newborn (Insight Media, VHS, 30 minutes): Illustrates newborn capabilities, including reflexes and responses to the Apgar test.

One For My Baby (University of Minnesota Film and Video, film, 28 minutes): Discusses fetal alcohol syndrome.

Prenatal Development (Insight Media, VHS, 30 minutes): Covers development from conception to birth (includes birth). Illustrates effects of cigarette smoking, alcohol and drug use on developing fetus. Shows how fetus responds to various stimuli.

Prenatal Diagnosis: To Be or Not To Be (1982 Filmakers Library, VHS or film, 45 minutes): Illustrates how amniocentesis, fetoscopy, and ultrasound are used to detect abnormalities prenatally. Discusses ethical considerations raised by these tests.

The Process of Birth (Films for the Humanities, VHS, 30 minutes): Takes a cross-cultural look at the birthing process.

SUGGESTED READINGS

Achenbach, T. M., Phares, V., Howell, C. T., Rauh, V. A., & Nurcombe, B. (1990). Seven-year outcome of the Vermont Intervention program for low-birthweight infants. *Child Development, 61,* 1672-1681.

Dorris, M. (1989). *The broken cord.* NY: Harper and Row. [fetal alcohol syndrome]

Goldberg, S., & DiVitto, B. A. (1983). *Born too soon: Preterm birth and early development.* CA: W. H. Freeman & Co.

Klein, N. K. (1988). Children who were very how birth weight: Cognitive abilities and classroom behavior at five years of age. *The Journal of Special Education, 22,* 41- 54.

Kopp, C., & Kaler, S. (1989). Risk in infancy. *American Psychologist, 44,* 224-230.

Niebyl, J. (Ed.) (1988). *Drug use in pregnancy*, 2nd edition. Phila: Lea and Febiger.

Rutter, M. (1985). Resilience in the face of adversity: Protective factors and resistance to psychiatric disorder. *British Journal of Psychiatry, 147,* 598-611.

Werner, E. E., & Smith, R. S. (1982). *Vulnerable but invincible: A study of resilient children.* New York: McGraw Hill.

TRANSPARENCY MASTERS

4.1   Generalizations about the effects of teratogens

4.2   Potential prenatal risk factors

4.3   Potential perinatal hazards

4.4   The Apgar test

Generalizations about the effects of teratogens

1. The effects of a teratogen on an organ system are worst during the critical period when that organ system grows most rapidly.

2. Not all embryos and fetuses are affected, or affected equally, by a teratogen.

3. Susceptibility to harm is influenced by the unborn child's genetic makeup as well as by the mother's genetic makeup and the quality of the prenatal environment she provides.

4. The same defect can be caused by different teratogens.

5. A variety of defects can result from a single teratogen.

6. The higher the "dose" of a teratogen, the more likely it is that serious damage will be done.

Potential Prenatal Risk Factors

Teratogens

    a.   <u>Diseases</u>

        Sexually transmitted: Syphilis, Gonorrhea, Acquired Immune Deficiency Syndrome (AIDS), Herpes

        Other: Chicken Pox, Mumps, Diabetes Mellitus, Rubella (German measles), Hepatitis, Influenza, Hypertension, Toxemia, Toxoplasmosis

    b.   <u>Drugs</u>

        Alcohol, Antibiotics, Aspirin, Barbiturates, Hallucinogens, Narcotics (heroin, codeine), Sex Hormones (birth control pills, DES), Stimulants (caffeine, cocaine), Tobacco, Tranquilizers, Vaccines, Vitamins

Environmental Hazards

    Radiation, Pollutants (e.g., lead)

Maternal Factors

    Age, Emotional State, Nutrition

Potential Perinatal Hazards

<u>Condition</u>   <u>Possible Outcomes</u>

<u>Anoxia</u>   Cerebral Palsy
                              Mental Retardation
                              Irritability
                              Delay in motor and cognitive development

<u>Medications</u>   Sluggish
                              Irritability
                              Difficult to feed and cuddle
                              Smile less frequently
                              Deficits in motor and cognitive development
                                    for at least a year after   birth

<u>Delivery Methods</u>

     Forceps   Cranial bleeding
                              Brain damage

     Cesarean   Respiratory difficulties
                              Longer recovery period for mother

The Apgar Test

Five characteristics are rated on a three-point scale (0, 1, 2) at one minute and five minutes after birth.

Heart Rate
    0   Absent
    1   Slow (under 100 beats per minute)
    2   Over 100 beats per minute

Respiratory effort
    0   Absent
    1   Slow or irregular
    2   Good; baby is crying

Muscle tone
    0   Flaccid; limp
    1   Weak; some flexion
    2   Strong; active motion

Color
    0   Blue or pale
    1   Body pink, extremities blue
    2   Completely pink

Reflex irritability
    0   No response
    1   Frown, grimace, or weak cry
    2   Vigorous cry

5

THE PHYSICAL SELF

LEARNING OBJECTIVES

After students have read and studied the material in this chapter, they should be able to answer the following questions:

1. How do the workings of the endocrine system contribute to growth and development across the life span?

2. How is the nervous system organized?

3. What are the key processes involved in early brain development?

4. To what are extent are cells responsive to the effects of experience?

5. What is lateralization? How does it affect behavior?

6. How does the brain change with aging?

7. What is the difference between survival and primitive reflexes? What are examples of each type of reflex? What other capabilities do newborns have?

8. How does growth proceed during infancy? What principles underlie growth?

9. What physical behaviors develop during infancy?

10. What physical changes occur during childhood?

11. What physical changes occur during adolescence? What factors contribute to sexual maturity of males and females? What psychological reactions accompany variations in growth spurt and the timing of puberty?

12. What physical changes occur during adulthood?

13. How can nutrition, exercise, and changes in lifestyle affect growth and development across the life span?

I.   **The body's systems and development**
      A. The endocrine system
          1. Pituitary gland-- triggers release of hormones from all other glands and produces growth hormone
          2. Thyroid gland-- growth and development
          3. Testes-- testosterone and other androgens
          4. Ovaries-- estrogen and progesterone
          5. Adrenal glands-- maturation of bones and muscles
      B. The nervous system-
          1. Basic units-- brain, spinal cord, and neural tissue; Neurons, synapses, and myelin
          2. Early brain development-- neural tube and "primitive" portions, then cerebral cortex
              a. Key processes
                  i. Proliferation
                  ii. Migration
                  iii. Differentiation
                  iv. Synaptogenesis
              b. Brain growth spurt (and massive losses)-- plasticity
          3. Later brain development
              a. Lateralization-- increasing dominance of one hemisphere
              b. Final phase of development at 12-20 years
          4. The aging brain
              a. Normal degeneration vs. senility
              b. Despite losses, plasticity continues

II.   **The infant**
      A. The newborn
          1. Reflexes
              a. Survival reflexes
              b. Primitive reflexes-- Babinski reflex
          2. Senses
          3. Ability to learn from experience
          4. Infant states--different levels of consciousness
      B. The body: Physical growth
          1. Cephalocaudal principle-- head to tail growth
          2. Proximodistal principle-- center outward to extremities
          3. Orthogenetic principle-- increasing differentiation
      C. Physical behavior
          1. Locomotor development
              a. Developmental norms
              b. Gross and fine motor skills
              c. Crawling, walking, manipulating objects
          2. Nature, nurture, and motor development
              a. Basic motor development in part maturational
              b. Experience and parental beliefs also affect rate
              c. Dynamic systems approach-- Nature and nurture essential and inseparable

III. **The child**
      A. Growth
          1. Steady but slower-- 2-3 inches and 6-7 pounds per year
      B. Physical behavior
          1. Refinement of motor skills

2. Improvements in eye/hand coordination
3. Faster reaction times

IV. **The adolescent**
A. Physical and sexual maturation
   1. The adolescent growth spurt
   2. Sexual maturation
      a. Females-- menarche
      b. Males--ejaculation
   3. Variations in timing
      a. Genetic and hormonal influences
      b. Secular trend-- earlier maturation in industrial societies
   4. Psychological implications
      a. Concern with body image-- sex differences in concerns
      b. Rites of passage
      c. Changes in relationships with parents
   5. Early versus late development
      a. Early maturation more advantageous for boys than for girls
      b. Late maturation more disadvantageous for boys than for girls
B. Physical behavior
   1. Strength and physical competence increases
   2. Boys outperform girls-- biological and social factors

V. **The adult**
A. Physical appearance and structure
   1. Most changes after 40
      a. Wrinkles, graying and thinning hair, changes in weight
      b. Osteoporosis
      c. Aging of the joints
   2. Functioning and health
      a. Large individual variation
      b. Decrease in reserve capacity
B. The reproductive system
   1. Hormones and adult life
      a. Fluctuating hormone levels
      b. Premenstrual syndrome (PMS) in women
   2. Menopause
      a. Physical effects-- hot flashes, vaginal dryness
      b. Psychological effects- Variable, most not greatly affected
   3. The male climacteric-- loss of reproductive capacity
C. Physical behavior
   1. Slowing down
      a. Compensation for decline
D. Disease, disuse, and abuse
   1. Effects of aging confounded with effects of disease, disuse or abuse

VI. **Applications: Optimizing healthy development**
A. Nutrition
   1. Catch-up growth
   2. Obesity
B. Exercise
C. Avoiding known health risks-- smoking, heavy drinking

1.   Ask students to report on the media's portrayal of physical characteristics across the life span. For example:
- • Students might look through magazine articles and advertisements to determine: Are older people "less attractive"? Are physical changes more of a "liability" for women than men in our culture? What are psychological correlates of being more or less attractive at different ages?
- • Students might visit a greeting card shop and look at the types of cards available for various decade-marking birthdays. What do these cards tell us about popular notions of the various decades? Students might try to write alternative greeting cards for these birthdays.

2.   In order to increases students' appreciation for why young children have difficulty with tasks that involve the coordination of several abilities, ask students do a detailed task analysis of a physical activity such as hitting a ball with a bat, walking up stairs, brushing teeth. What are the step-by-step procedures or movements needed to perform these tasks? Attempts to have computers simulate complex behaviors might provide an interesting side trip in this discussion. For a list of academic research into robotics, see: http://piglet.cs.umass.edu:4321/cgi-bin/robotics-university/. Additional artificial intelligence resources may be found at http://ai.iit.nrc.ca/misc.html

3.   Several activities might encourage students to rethink their ideas about aging. Pulos describes an exercise that confronts students with their misconceptions that major declines in physical performance occur with increasing age [Pulos, S. (1993). Illustrating life-span development in physical competence. *Teaching of Psychology, 20,* 244-245]. Students predict the performance of age groups in an athletic event and compare these to actual performance in the event.
        Palmore's 1977 "Facts on Aging" quiz (*Gerontologist, 17,* 315-320) is another useful tool for stimulating discussion of myths about older adults. It is mentioned here because many of its items concern health and physical functioning, though it could also be used later in the course, as well. It is only 25 items long, and Palmore discusses why items are right or wrong. Palmore (1980) provides further information on the scale (*Gerontologist, 20,* 669-672), and it has been revised by Miller and Dodder (1980;*Gerontologist, 20,* 673-679).
        Students might also look at the web site for the the seniors' advocacy group, AARP, at http://www.aarp.org/. They will find in the Getting Answers section, information on exercise and staying active (as well as other topics, such as caregiving, and nursing homes).

4.   A 1994 report indicated that although young adults were eating healthier foods, they had gained an average of 10 pounds (from about 161 to 171 pounds) from 1986 to 1994. The conclusion many people drew from this was that young adults are exercising less than before. Have students discuss reasons for the findings. Students might also design a study to test the conclusion that was drawn from the report. They should specify the variables that they would want to control in order to have a "clean" study, whether their study is correlational or experimental, and how they would operationalize their variables.

5.   Have students describe their perception of the "ideal" male and female in terms of physical characteristics. They should be specific-- height, weight, skin and eye color, hair style and color, presence or absence of freckles or glasses, facial characteristics, body and facial hair (e.g., moustaches and beards), etc. Collect the descriptions from the entire class and calculate descriptive statistics on each area. Then compare to reality. Published height and weight averages are available for males and females. Students can discuss how close their other ideals come to actual men and women--young and old. Do these "ideals" reflect cultural and/or age biases?

6.   As a starting point for a discussion of lateralization, ask students what their left-right preferences are for various tasks (e.g., hand they use for writing, holding utensils, and brushing

their teeth, the foot they start running with, the hand with the stronger grip, the stronger eye, etc.). If possible, also find out the preferences of a group of preschoolers for comparison to confirm that left-right preferences are more clearly defined in older children. Discuss reasons why the same person might prefer their left side for some tasks but their right side for other tasks.

7.   In connection with the material on early and late maturation in adolescence, ask students of both sexes to describe their experiences and compare what they say to information in the text. Students may not want talk about their own experiences, but they would probably be comfortable describing the experiences of siblings or friends who were early or late maturers.

SUGGESTED FILMS AND VIDEOS

Adolescent Physical Development (Insight Media, VHS, 30 minutes): Describes physical changes occurring during adolescence and the psychological consequences of many of these changes. Also covers menstruation, teenage alcoholism, and anorexia.

The Child Series (CRM Films, VHS and 16 mm): A five-part documentary series that tracks the growth patterns of seven infants between birth and 6 years. Each part is approximately 30 minutes.

The Discovery Year (Films for Humanities and Sciences, VHS, 52 minutes): Made for TV program that covers sensory and motor development during the first year. Also profiles how three sets of parents respond to the different personalities of their infant daughters.

The Growing Infant (Insight Media, VHS, 30 minutes): Covers the cephalocaudal and proximodistal principles of growth, the relationship between physical and mental growth, and illustrates various motor skills.

Left Brain, Right Brain (Filmakers Library, VHS or film, 56 minutes): Dr. Norman Geschwind discusses research on hemispheric processes and Dr. Doreen Kimura demonstrates a variety of tasks used to determine hemispheric specialization. Dr. Julian Jaynes' theory of consciousness is presented and a young retarded child's (Nadia) sophisticated drawings are presented.

Physical Development in the Middle Years (Insight Media, VHS, 30 minutes): Physical developments between ages six and twelve, including discussion of individual differences and fine motor skills such as balancing and writing.

Preschool Physical Development (Insight Media, VHS, 30 minutes): The development of bones, brain and circulatory system, and laterality from three to six years of age.

SUGGESTED READINGS

Ames, L. B. (1989). *Arnold Gesell: Themes of his work*. NY: Plenum Publishing
     Corporation.

Dawson, G., & Fischer, K. (1994). *Human behavior and the developing brain*. NY: Guilford
     Publications, Inc.

Lozoff, B. (1989). Nutrition and behavior. *American Psychologist, 44*, 231-236.

Springer, S., & Deutsch, G. (1985). *Left brain, right brain*, 2nd ed. NY: W. H. Freeman & Co.

Stattin, H., & Magnussen, D. (1990). *Pubertal maturation in female development*. NJ: Lawrence Erlbaum Associates.

TRANSPARENCY MASTERS

5.1   Outline of the endocrine system, hormones, and effects on development

5.2   Survival reflexes

5.3   Primitive reflexes

5.4   Wolff's infant states

5.5   Outcomes for early and late maturing adolescents

Endocrine System

System of glands that secrete chemicals called hormones directly into the bloodstream

Pituitary

Growth hormone: Regulates growth from birth through adolescence; triggers adolescent growth spurt

Activating hormones: Signal other endocrine glands (such as the ovaries and testes) to secrete their hormones

Thyroid

Thyroxine: Affects growth and development of the brain and helps to regulate growth of the body during childhood

Testes

Testosterone: Is responsible for development of the male reproductive system during the prenatal period; directs male sexual development during adolescence

Ovaries

Estrogen and progesterone: Responsible for regulation of menstrual cycle; estrogen directs female sexual development during adolescence

Adrenal Glands

Adrenal androgens: Play a supportive role in the development of muscle and bones

Survival Reflexes in Full-Term Newborns

Breathing reflex: Permanent reflex that provides oxygen and expels carbon dioxide

Eyeblink reflex: Permanent reflex that protects eyes from bright light or foreign objects

Pupillary reflex: Permanent reflex that protects against bright lights; helps visual system adapt to low illumination

Rooting reflex: Infant reflexively turns cheek in direction of a tactile stimulus, which facilitates orientation to breast or bottle; should gradually weaken over first 6 months of life

Sucking reflex: Infant reflexively sucks on objects placed in mouth, which allows infant to take in nutrients; will gradually be modified by experience over the first few months of life

Swallowing reflex: Allows the child to take in nutrients and protects against choking; permanent but modified by experience

Primitive Reflexes in Full-Term Newborns

Babinski reflex: Infant fans and then curls toes when bottom of foot is stroked; presence at birth and disappearance within first 8 to 12 months of life indicates normal neurological development

Grasping reflex: Infant curls fingers around objects that touch the palm of its hand; present at birth but replaced by a voluntary grasp in the first 3 to 4 months of life, which signifies normal neurological development

Moro reflex: Infant will throw arms outward, arch back, and then bring arms together in response to a loud noise or a sudden change of head position; presence at birth and disappearance within the first 6 to 7 months of life indicates normal neurological development; may evolve into a startle reflex that does not disappear

Swimming reflex: Infant will show active movements of arms and legs and will involuntarily hold breath when immersed in water; presence at birth and disappearance in first 4 to 6 months signifies normal neurological development

Stepping reflex: Infants will move their legs and feet as if to walk when held upright so that their feet touch a flat surface; presence at birth and disappearance in first 8 weeks of life signifies normal neurological development; may persist if infant has regular opportunities to practice it

Infant States Described by Wolff (1966)

Regular Sleep: Babies lie still with their eyes closed
Breathing is regular, and the skin is pale

No response to mild stimuli

Irregular sleep: Irregular breathing
Eyes may move under closed eyelids
Often grimaces, jerks, and twitches
May stir a bit in response to mild stimuli

Drowsiness: Just waking or falling asleep
Eyes intermittently open and close; eyes
    have a glazed when open
Fairly inactive
Breathing is regular but more rapid than
    in regular sleep

Alert Inactivity: Scans the environment with interest
Head, trunk, and lip movements may occur
Breathing is fast and irregular

Waking activity: Sudden bursts of vigorous activity
Eyes are open, but they are not actively
    attending to their surroundings
Breathing is irregular

Crying: May begin to whimper and then burst into
    loud, agitated cries accompanied by
    strong kicks and arm movements.

Outcomes for early and late maturing adolescents

Boys:

Early maturing boys are thought to be poised, confident in social settings, and attractive; they often win athletic honors and student elections.

Late maturing boys have been found to be anxious, attention seeking, and unsure of themselves; they score lower than other students on school achievement tests.

Girls:

Early maturing girls have been found to be less popular and more likely to report symptoms of depression, at least in early adolescence. By late adolescence, though, they have more status with peers. They are more likely to rebel against parents, and are more involved in dating, drinking, and sexual activities than later maturing girls.

Late maturing girls are thought to have some anxiety, but not much as late maturing boys; they score higher on school achievement tests.

6

PERCEPTION

<u>*LEARNING OBJECTIVES*</u>

After students have read and studied the material in this chapter, they should be able to answer the following questions:

1. What are the views of empiricists and nativists on the nature/nurture issue as it relates to sensation and perception?

2. How are perceptual abilities of infants assessed?

3. What are the infants' visual capabilities? What sorts of things do infants prefer to look at?

4. How is the visual cliff used to assess depth perception? What do we know about infants' depth perception?

5. What does is mean to say that the infant is an intuitive theorist?

6. What are the auditory capabilities of infants? What do we know about infants' abilities to perceive speech?

7. What are the taste and smell capabilities of infants? To what extent are infants sensitive to touch, temperature and pain?

8. To what extent can infants integrate their sensory experiences? What is an example of cross-modal perception?

9. What role do early experiences play in the development of perceptions? What factors contribute to normal visual perception?

10. How does culture influence one's perceptions?

11. What changes occur in attention from infancy to adulthood?

12. What perceptual capabilities are involved in learning to read?

13. What changes occur in visual capabilities and visual perception during adulthood?

14. What changes in auditory capabilities and speech perception occur during adulthood?

15. What changes occur in taste and smell, and in sensitivity to touch, temperature and pain during adulthood?

16. How can hearing impaired persons be helped with their hearing loss?

I. **Issues in perceptual development**
    A. Sensation and perception
    B. Nature versus nurture
        1. Empiricists-- infant as tabula rasa, products of nurture
        2. Nativists-- infants come into the world with knowledge, products of nature
        3. Current debates

II. **The infant**
    A. Assessing perceptual abilities
        1. Habituation technique-- learning to be bored
        2. Preferential looking
        3. Operant conditioning
    B. Vision
        1. Basic capacities
            a. Infants detect brightness, colors
            b. Limitations-- visual acuity poor, limited visual accommodation
        2. Pattern perception
            a. Discrimination of forms soon after birth
            b. Infants attracted to contour, movement, and moderate complexity
            c. Preference for whatever they can see well
            d. Beginning at 2 months, explore interiors of figures
            e. Face perception
        3. Depth perception
            a. Blink in response to moving objects
            b. Size constancy
            c. Visual cliffs by 2 months, but fear of drop-offs later
        4. Organizing a world of objects
            a. Attention to irregularities
            b. Wholeness of objects-- common motion
        5. The infant as intuitive theorist
    B. Hearing
        1. Basic capacities-- hear better than see, localize sounds, discriminate sounds
        2. Perceiving speech
            a. Initially sensitive to all speech sounds (phonemes), then lose sensitivity to
               speech sounds irrelevant to native language
            b. Recognize mother's voice soon after birth
            c. Sensitive to musical sounds and will avoid nonrhythmic sounds
    C. Taste and smell
        1. Olfaction (smell) and taste work well at birth
    D. Touch, temperature, and pain
        1. All operating in some form at birth
    E. Integrating sensory information
        1. Cross-modal perception
    F. Influences on early perceptual development
        1. All senses are working to some extent by birth, and most perceptual abilities
           emerge in the first few months
        2. Early experience and the brain
            a. Maturation not enough-- need early stimulation
        3. The infant's active role
            a. Infants seek sensory experiences they need for development
            b. Gibson's three phases of exploratory behavior-- combine
               perception and action

4. Cultural variation-- language, music, drawing

III. **The child**
  A. The development of attention
     1. Increased attention span
     2. More selective attention
     3. More systematic attention
  B. Learning to read
     1. Gibson and Levin--three phases of learning to read
     2. Learning to recognize the distinctive features of letters
     3. Phonological awareness
     4. Dyslexia-- deficient phonological awareness
     5. Teaching reading-- whole language versus phonics

IV. **The adolescent**
  A. Refinement of attention--attending to relevant and ignoring irrelevant stimuli

V. **The adult**
  A. Losses occur, usually gradual and minor, beginning in early adulthood
     1. Raised sensory thresholds
     2. Declines in perceptual abilities
  B. Vision
     1. Basic capacities
        a. Loss of near vision-- presbyopia
        b. Pathological conditions-- cataracts, glaucoma
        c. Dark adaptation
     2. Attention and visual search
        a. More difficulty processing visual information that is novel or complex
  C. Hearing
     1. Basic capacities
        a. Presbycusis-- e.g., loss of sensitivity to high frequency sounds
     2. Speech perception
        a. Problems under poor listening conditions
        b. Again, more difficulty if tasks are novel and complex
  D. Taste and smell
     1. Trouble detecting weak taste stimulation and odors
  E. Touch, temperature, and pain
     1. Detection thresholds for touch and temperature increase
     2. Differences in sensitivity to pain are small and inconsistent
  F. The adult in perspective
     1. Declines in vision and hearing most important
     2. Most often vision and hearing remain reasonably good

VI. **Applications: Aiding people with hearing impairments**
  A. Early life
     1. Importance of early identification
     2. Cochlear implants
     3. Parental involvement
  B. Later life
     1. Hearing aids, cochlear implants, and environmental changes

SUGGESTIONS FOR CLASS DISCUSSIONS OR PROJECTS

1.   Bring in selected books or toys that are appropriate for infants and children of different ages. Discuss whether they capitalize on perceptual capabilities and changing preferences, and reasons why or why not. Or alternately, ask students to develop a book or activity that is appropriate for a particular age because it capitalizes on capabilities or preferences typically present at that particular age.

A related idea is to have students working in groups design a nursery that would capitalize on infants' sensory and perceptual capabilities at different ages. Students should base their design on findings of research reported in this chapter. Each group could then share their design with the class and discuss the reasons why they included particular aspects in their design.

2.   Bring into class, or have the class collect, drawing samples from children of various ages. Examples of 3-4 year olds' drawings of a person are included on Transparency 6.4. These can also be used to show students children's early attempts at mastering this fine motor skill. The tadpole and the head-only figures are very common representations at this age. Between the ages of 2 1/2 and 4, children tend to focus on the activity of drawing itself, and starting at about age 4, they try to actually represent something in their drawing. They continue to refine their drawing and representation skills throughout childhood. Being able to represent depth in drawings typically doesn't emerge until about 9 or 10 years of age. For more information on developmental changes in drawing, see Edwards (1988); Nicholls & Kennedy (1992); Willats (1977); Winner (1986).

3.   In Betty Edward's book *Drawing on the right side of the brain.*(see Suggested Readings), she recommends a number of exercises that help us to perceive the world as an artist does. Much of what keeps us from representing the world realistically is that we draw what we know, not what we see (for example, we might draw glasses on a person in the round shape we know them to be, even if we are drawing a profile in which the glasses do not have that shape at all). It might be fun to try some of the exercises in class.

These exercises might also lead nicely into a discussion of perceptual illusions, which always make for fun classroom demonstrations. Look at some perceptual illusions. What do these illusions tell us about how the brain normally perceives? What are the function of these illusions? Do young children also see these illusions? An excellent place to look for examples of illusions, and explanations of them, is the "Seeing, Hearing, and Smelling the World" web site of the Howard Hughes Medical Institute. Go to http://www.hhmi.org/senses/ and choose "Illusions Reveal the Brain's Assumptions."

You might also try Illusionworks at http://www.illusionworks.com.
For other sites, try: http://www.icase.edu/~interran/percept_links.html

4.   An article by Hugh Downs in *Parade Magazine* (April 24 1994) asked "Should elderly people be allowed to drive?" Some people think older adults should not drive because of changes in perceptual abilities and reaction time. As a group, they are cited more than younger drivers for "failure to obey signs and signals," "failure to yield right of way," and "inattention." At the same time, 15-24 year olds are more likely (28 per 100,000 people) to die in a motor vehicle accident than 40-69 year olds (10 per 100,000), 70-79 year olds (15 per 100,000), and 80+ year olds (25 per 100,000). Discuss the implications of changes in sensory and perceptual abilities across the life span for road safety. Ask students how they might revise driving tests based on evidence presented in the chapter (e.g., the fact that older adults who have good visual acuity for stationary objects may still have difficulty perceiving objects in motion). Ideally, the discussion will end on a note of appreciation for older drivers who compensate for declines in visual perception and reaction time by driving slowly and cautiously.

5.   Sensory changes across the life span might contribute to other behavioral changes. Decreases in sensitivity to taste and smell may change cooking and eating habits. Discuss these and other potentially dangerous concerns (an accidental drug overdose). Ask students to design ways to

compensate for these sensory and perceptual changes associated with aging.

6.	Simulation exercises that can help students gain insight into the sensory changes often associated with aging are presented by Shore, 1980 (*Gerontologist, 16,* 157-165).

SUGGESTED FILMS AND VIDEOS

First Adaptations (1992, Insight Media, VHS, 30 minutes): Looks at brain development and is appropriate for this chapter because it shows recreations of classic studies with the visual cliff and on visual preference.

The Knowing Nose: Exploring the Science of Scent (Filmakers Library, VHS, 46 minutes): Discusses findings on the sense of smell in humans and animals. Traces changes in sense of smell from infancy to older adulthood.

SUGGESTED READINGS

Besner, D., & Humphreys, G. (1990). *Basic processes in reading: Visual word recognition.* NJ: Lawrence Erlbaum Associates.

Edwards, B. (1989). Drawing on memories: Your history as an Artist. In *Drawing on the right side of the brain.* Los Angeles: Jeremy P. Tarcher, Inc.

Fantz, R. L. (1958). Pattern vision in young infants. *The Psychological Record, 8,* 43-47.

Gardner, H. (1980). *Artful scribbles: The significance of children's drawings.* NY: Basic Books.

Haith, M. M. (1980). *Rules that babies look by.* NJ: Lawrence Erlbaum.

Nichols, A. L., & Kennedy, J. M. (1992). Drawing development: From similarity of features to direction. *Child Development, 63,* 227-241.

Salapatek, P., & Cohen, L. (1987). *Handbook of infant perception,* volumes 1 and 2. CA: Academic Press.

Willats, J. (1977). How children learn to draw realistic pictures. *Quarterly Journal of Experimental Psychology, 29,* 367-387.

Winner, E. (1986, Aug). Where pelicans kiss seals. *Psychology Today,* 24-26, 30-35.

TRANSPARENCY MASTERS

6.1	Theories of perceptual development

6.2	Developmental changes in pattern perception

6.3	The development of attention

6.4	Examples of 3-4 year olds' drawings of a person

Theories of Perceptual Development

How do we come to perceive a more meaningful world as we get older?

Enrichment Theory (Piaget)

Stimulation that comes in through sensory receptors is confusing.

We need to add to it, or enrich it, in order to make sense out of it.

We add to it from our stored knowledge.

The more knowledge we have, the better equipped we are to construct a meaningful understanding of the world.

Differentiation Theory (Gibson)

Stimulation that comes in through the sensory receptors is complete and does not need to be added to or enriched.

We need to detect differences (differentiate) the factors that are present all the time in the stimulation in order to understand reality.

The more experience we have, the better able we are to distinguish among distinctive features of stimuli.

Developmental Changes in Pattern Perception

< 2 days   Discriminate among visual forms

                 Prefer patterned stimuli (e.g., faces):

                         Attracted to patterns with contour

                         Attracted to patterns with movement

                         Attracted to moderately complex patterns

2 months   Visually explore the interiors of figures rather than focusing on some external boundary

2-3 months   Prefer a drawing of a normal face over one of a scrambled face

                 Formation of mental representations for familiar objects

                 Recognize parents' faces

                 Look longer at attractive than unattractive faces

1 year   Prefer to look at a scrambled face over a normal face

                 Interested in understanding stimuli that are highly discrepant from existing schemata

<u>The Development of Attention</u>

Increased Attention Span	From 18 minutes on a task at 2 1/2 to 3 1/2 years to up to an hour at 5 1/2 to 6 years
More Selective Attention	Increased ability to focus attention on critical information and ignore irrelevant information
More Systematic Attention	From age 4 to age 10, increased ability to plan and carry out systematic perceptual searches

All three of these abilities further improve during adolescence.

Examples of 3-4 year olds' drawings of a person

7

COGNITION AND LANGUAGE

After students have read and studied the material in this chapter, they should be able to answer the following questions:

1. How do organization, adaptation, and disequilibrium guide development?

2. What are examples of assimilation and accommodation?

3. What are the major achievements of the sensorimotor stage?

4. What are the characteristics and limitations of preoperational thought?

5. What are the major characteristics and limitations of concrete operational thought?

6. What are the main features of formal operational thought?

7. In what ways might adult thought be more advanced than adolescent thought?

8. What are the limitations and challenges to Piaget's theory of cognitive development?

9. What is Vygotsky's perspective on cognitive development?

10. How do Vygotsky and Piaget differ in their ideas about cognition and language?

11. What components of language must children master?

12. What is the typical developmental course of language development?

13. How do learning, nativist, and interactionist perspectives explain the acquisition of language? Which explanation is best supported by research?

14. Can cognitive functioning be improved with training? Explain.

I. **Piaget's approach to cognitive development**
   A. Introduction
      1. Genetic epistemology-- how one comes to know the world
      2. Clinical method-- flexible question-and-answer technique
   B. What is intelligence?
      1. Basic life function that facilitates adaptation to environment
      2. Schemes and cognitive structures
   C. How does intelligence develop?
      1. Organization--combining schemes into new and complex schemes
      2. Adaptation--adjusting to the demands of the environment
         a. Assimilation
         b. Accommodation (from cognitive disequilibrium)
      3. Four invariant stages resulting from interaction with environment
         a. sensorimotor stage (0-2)
         b. preoperational stage (2-7 years)
         c. concrete operations (7-11 years)
         d. formal operations (11 and later)

II. **The infant (sensorimotor stage)**
   A. Dominant cognitive structures are behavioral schemes
   B. Important achievement is development of symbolic capacity
   C. Substages of the sensorimotor stage
      1. Substage 1: Reflexive activity (birth to 1 month)
      2. Substage 2: Primary circular reactions (1 to 4 months)
      3. Substage 3: Secondary circular reactions (4 to 8 months)
      4. Substage 4: Coordination of secondary schemes (8 to 12 months)
      5. Substage 5: Tertiary circular reactions (12 to 18 months)
      6. Substage 6: Beginning of thought (18 months to 2 years)
   D. The development of object permanence
      1. The A, not B, error-- looking for object where last seen, not new place
      2. Requires mental representation

III. **The child**
   A. The preoperational stage
      1. Lack of conservation
         a. Centration
         b. Irreversibility
         c. Problems with transformational thought
      2. Egocentrism
      3. Difficulty with classification
      4. Did Piaget underestimate the preschool child?-- more recent data
   B. The concrete operations stage
      1. Conservation
         a. Decentration
         b. Reversibility of thought
         c. Transformational thought
         d. Horizontal decalage-- different skills within stage occur at different times
      2. Seriation and Transitivity
      3. Other advances in cognition
         a. Less egocentrism
         b. Class inclusion
         c. Mathematical operations

IV.   **The adolescent**
A. The formal operations stage
            1. Hypothetical and abstract thinking
            2. Problem-solving strategies-- hypothetical-deductive reasoning
            3. Progress toward mastery-- early versus late formal operations
B. Implications of formal thought
            1. Positive-- Identity, complex thought, interpersonal understanding
            2. Negative-- Confusion, rebellion, and idealism
            3. Adolescent egocentrism (Elkind)
                     a. Imaginary audience
                     b. Personal fable

V.   **The adult**
A. Limitations in adult cognitive performance-- lack of expertise in a domain of knowledge
B. Growth beyond formal operations (postformal thought)-- Relativistic thinking
C. Aging and cognitive skills
            1. Poorer performance of older cohorts due to cohort effects (e.g., differences in
                 education, cognitive style, and motivation)

VI.   **Piaget in perspective**
A. Piaget's contributions
            1. Stimulating research
            2. Emphasizing active development
            3. Basic description of cognitive-developmental sequences
B. Challenges to Piaget
            1. Underestimating young minds
            2. Failing to distinguish between competence and performance
            3. Claiming that broad stages of development exist
            4. Failing to adequately explain development
            5. Giving limited attention to social influences on cognitive development

VII.   **Vygotsky's sociocultural perspective**
A. Cognitive growth occurs in a sociocultural context and evolves out of the child's social
         interactions
B. Culture and thought-- each culture has "tools of the mind"
C. Social interaction and thought
            1. Zone of proximal development- gap between what can accomplish alone versus
                 with assistance of more skilled partner
            2. Guided participation-- scaffolding of involvement in culturally relevant activities
C. Language and thought
            1. Language is primary means of passing on culturally valued ways of thinking and
                 problem solving
                     a. Social speech, private speech, inner speech

VIII.   **Mastering language**
A. What must be mastered?
            1. Phonology--sound system of language
            2. Morphology-- rules for formation of words from sounds
            3. Syntax--rules of language
            4. Semantics--meanings of language
            5. Pragmatics--rules specifying appropriate use of language
B. The course of language development
            1. Before the first words
                     a. Cooing and babbling

b. Comprehension precedes expression
2. The first words: Holophrastic speech
    a. Holophrases-- Single words convey many things
    b. Naming, questioning, requesting and demanding
    c. Talk about objects and actions on objects
    d. Vocabulary spurt around 18 months
3. Getting the meaning
    a. Assume words refer to whole objects and class of objects
    b. Assume each word has unique meaning
    c. Infer meanings by attending to contexts
    d. Overextension and underextension
4. Telegraphic speech
    a. Two or three words in simple sentences
    b. Functional grammar-- Emphasizes semantic relationship between words
5. Mastering grammatical rules
    a. Overregularization-- Applying rules to exceptions
    b. Transformational grammar-- Rules of syntax for sentence forms
6. Later language development
    a. Improve pronunciation, sentence complexity, vocabulary, ability to manipulate language
7. Language in adulthood
    a. Knowledge of phonology and grammar usually retained
    b. Knowledge of semantics may expand

C. How language develops: Three theories
1. The learning perspective
    a. Observation, imitation, and reinforcement
    b. Hard to account for syntactical rules
2. The nativist perspective
    a. Language acquisition device (LAD)
    b. Not explain how language develops and role of environment
3. The interactionist perspective
    a. Integration of native capacities with language environment
    b. Motherese
4. A critical period for language?

IX.   **Applications: Improving cognitive functioning**

SUGGESTIONS FOR CLASS DISCUSSIONS OR PROJECTS

1.   Having reviewed some of the physical, perceptual, and cognitive changes children undergo, students might examine how these capabilities underlie the development of effective toys. Neysmith-Roy suggests a Make a Toy class project [Neysmith-Roy, J. M. (1994). Constructing toys to integrate knowledge about child development. *Teaching of Psychology, 21*, 101-103]. This project helps students understand infants' and young children's cognitive, perceptual-motor, and social capabilities. Assessment criteria for the project are described.

    Alternatively, a variety of toys might be brought to class and students can identify the age groups for which the toys are appropriate. They might also discuss how children of different ages might utilize the toys.

    Students might also visit toy stores on their own and analyze some of the currently available toys, perhaps choosing a toy they might buy for children of different ages, and justifying why that toy would be appropriate.

2.   Have students work in pairs or small groups on Piagetian tasks. Holbrook describes a demonstration of a standard conservation of liquid task, as well as a "conservation-like" problem for adults. Student responses on this task are analyzed using Piagetian concepts of centration, irreversibility, and perceptual dominance [Holbrook, J. E. (1992). Bringing Piaget's preoperational thought to the minds of adults: A classroom demonstration. *Teaching of Psychology, 19,* 169-170].

Students might also work on the pendulum problem (described in the text). Within each pair or group of students, one or two might try working on the problem while another student keeps track of the problem solving approach (this is easiest if those working on the problem verbally describe what they are thinking as they work on through the problem).

Students may find traditional formal operational tasks such as the pendulum problem difficult. Kuhn and Brannock (1977) used a formal operational task that had more familiarity, or external validity, for our adolescents than traditional Piagetian tasks. In this task, participants are given a description of four plants that are treated differently and have different outcomes. Based on this, participants are asked what to do with a fifth plant (see Transparency Master 7.5 for this task). The problem is constructed so that one variable (plant food) influences plant outcome and the other variables are irrelevant to plant outcome. The Kuhn and Brannock article provides sample answers for four different levels of performance on this task.

3.   Provide an opportunity to observe children of various ages working on Piagetian tasks, such as conservation. Depending on access, students may be able to actually test some children on Piagetian tasks and report on their findings. This is an excellent option if you assign an observational or interviewing project in the course. If young children are not readily accessible to a large number of students, it may be possible to videotape children of friends or children at a local preschool (or bring the children into the classroom).

4.   After students have had a chance to compare concrete operations, formal operations, and possibilities for post-formal-operational thought, ask them to think about the implications for relationships between people of different age groups. Have students (alone or in small groups) generate hypothetical conversations that different-aged children might have with their parents and with each other. For example, students might construct a discussion of a current social problem between 40-year-old, educated parents and their 16-year-old child, or a discussion of lying between a 16-year-old and his or her 8-year-old sibling. The conversations should show appropriate language and cognitive skills for the two speakers. For example, the above discussions might highlight the 8-year-old's difficulty grasping abstract concepts, the 16-year-old's quest for perfectly logical answers, and the adult's more pragmatic and relativistic thought.

5.   Have students complete the Imaginary Audience Scale (Elkind & Bowen, 1979) and also administer it to younger adolescents. Compare the answers from the two groups and discuss factors contributing to imaginary audience concerns.

6.   Have students discuss whether earlier stages of cognitive development are always left behind. Do they ever, for example, engage in egocentric thought (e.g., giving someone a present they would have wanted) or experience an imaginary audience? Under what circumstances? How are these processes the same or different now as compared to earlier in life?

7.   Videotape or audiotape language samples at a local nursery or preschool. Ideally, try to capture children of different ages. Have students identify different stages of language acquisition. Ask students if they can identify any examples of over- or under-extensions, overregularizations, holophrases, etc. Discuss the importance of context for young children's holophrases and individual differences in language acquisition.

Adolescent Mental Development (Insight Media, VHS, 30 minutes): Focuses on Piaget's formal operations stage and adolescent egocentrism, including the imaginary audience and personal fable.

Baby Talk (1985, Insight Media or many video stores sell NOVA programs, VHS, 60 minutes): Good program on development of language, theories of language, and the meaning of preverbal communication.

Beginning Language (Insight Media, VHS, 30 minutes): Covers early stages of language development and theories of language acquisition. Also presents some research with other species.

Cognitive Development (1990, Insight Media, VHS, 30 minutes): Examines Piaget's theory and points out concepts that have not been supported by recent research.

Concrete Operations (1994, Davidson Films, VHS, 30 minutes): Dr. David Elkind illustrates concepts of concrete operational thought through structured interviews with four to nine year olds.

Developing Language Skills (Insight Media, VHS, 30 minutes): Focuses on language skills of preschool-age children. Also discusses the theories of Piaget and Vygotsky, and the impact of the environment.

Formal Reasoning Patterns (Davidson Films, VHS or film, 32 minutes): Illustrates proportional reasoning, separation of variables, combinatorial logic, and the balance beam problem.

The Growth of Intelligence in the Preschool Years (Davidson Films, VHS or film, 31 minutes): Infants and preschoolers are presented with various tasks to illustrate several Piagetian concepts.

The Infant Mind (1992, Insight Media, VHS, 30 minutes): Covers Piaget's stage of sensorimotor development and recent challenges to his observations.

Language and Thinking (1992, Insight Media, VHS, 30 minutes): Looks at research connecting brain function to language, and language to thought.

Out of the Mouths of Babes (Filmakers Library, VHS or film, 28 minutes): Shows the progression of language in the first six years. Highlights research of Peter and Jill de Villiers on language acquisition.

Piaget's Developmental Theory: An overview (1989, Davidson Films, VHS, 30 minutes): Shows old footage of Piaget and new footage of David Elkind conducting interviews with children.

Preschool Mental Development (Insight Media, VHS, 30 minutes): Covers characteristics of Piaget's preoperational stage of development, and contrasts this to a behavioral approach to cognitive development. Also discusses the Head Start program.

SUGGESTED READINGS

Beilin, H., & Pufall, P. B. (Eds.). (1992). *Piaget's theory: Prospects and possibilities.* NJ: Lawrence Erlbaum Associates.

Commons, M., Richards, F. A., & Armon, C. (Eds.) (1984). *Beyond formal operations: Late adolescent and adult cognitive development.* NY: Praeger.

Elkind, David (1967). Egocentrism in adolescence. *Child Development, 38,* 1025-1034.

Elkind, D., & Bowen, R. (1979). Imaginary-audience behavior in children and adolescents. *Developmental Psychology, 15,* 38-44.

Flavell, J. H., Miller, P. H., & Miller, S. A. (1993). *Cognitive development,* 3rd ed. NJ: Prentice-Hall.

Ginsburg, H. P., & Opper, S. (1988). *Piaget's theory of intellectual developmentt.* NJ: Prentice-Hall.

Kuhn, D., & Brannock, J. (1977). Development of the isolation of variables scheme in experimental and "natural experimental" contexts. *Developmental Psychology, 13,* 9-14.

Rice, M. L. (1989). Children's language acquisition. *American Psychologist, 44,* 149-156.

Richardson, K., & Sheldon, S. (Eds.) (1988). *Cognitive development in adolescence.* NJ: Lawrence Erlbaum Associates.

Small, M. Y. (1990). *Cognitive Development.* CA: Harcourt, Brace, Jovanovich, Inc.

Weiskrantz, L. (Ed) (1988). *Thought without language.* NY: Oxford University Press.

Wertsch, J. V. (Ed.). (1985). *Culture, communication, and cognition: Vygotskian perspectives.* NY: Cambridge University Press.

TRANSPARENCY MASTERS

7.1   Piaget: How does intelligence develop?

7.2   Characteristics of preoperational thought

7.3   Characteristics of concrete operational thought

7.4   Characteristics of formal operational thought

7.5   Example of problem requiring formal operational thought (Kuhn & Brannock's plant problem)

7.6   Criticisms of Piaget's theory

7.7   Components of language

7.8   Developmental course of language

<u>Piaget: How does intelligence occur?</u>

1. **Organization**

Process of combining existing schemes into new and more complex ones

2. **Adaptation**

Process of adjusting to the demands of the environment

    a. <u>Assimilation</u>

Process of interpreting new information in terms of existing schemes

    b. <u>Accommodation</u>

Process of modifying existing schemes to better fit new information

These innate mechanisms imply a third innate process that stimulates intellectual growth:

3. <u>Equilibration</u>

Process of searching for balance between cognitive schemes or structures and the environment

Characteristics of Preoperational Thought

Symbolic function: Ability to make one thing represent something else (allows child to refer to the past and present, use language, engage in pretend play)

Perceptual Salience: Understanding is dominated by single most perceptually salient feature

                    Child reasons based on how things appear rather than on logic

Egocentrism   View the world solely from one's own perspective

Whole/Part errors   Trouble understanding that parts are included in the whole on classification tasks

Difficulty with conservation tasks

    Irreversible thought: Can't mentally undo an action

    Centration: Center on a single aspect of a problem, rather than 2 or more dimensions at one time

    Static thought   Failure to understand transformations or processes of change from one state to another

<u>Characteristics of Concrete Operational Thought</u>

<u>Thought is operational</u>: Consists of internalized, reversible, organized systems of action

<u>Thought is logical</u>: Can reason logically about concrete objects, events, and situations

This allows understanding of:

<u>Class inclusion</u>   Understand that parts are included within the whole

<u>Seriation</u>   Can arrange items mentally along a quantifiable dimension

<u>Transitivity</u>   Understand the relationship among elements in a series

<u>Conservation</u>   Understand that certain properties of an object don't change when its appearance is somehow altered

                            Reversibility of thought

                            Transformational thought

                            Decentration

Characteristics of Formal Operational Thought

Acquire formal operations, which are mental actions on ideas

Can think logically and systematically about abstract and hypothetical objects, events, and situations

Can contemplate possibilities rather than realities

Use hypothetical-deductive reasoning: Generating all possible hypotheses and systematically testing their predictions

Implications of formal operational thought:
>Confusion because of new-found ability to question

>Rebellion because of ability to detect inconsistencies and flaws in the world

>Idealism because of the ability to imagine perfectly logical solutions to world problems that perhaps can't be implemented in our imperfect real world

Other changes:
>Adolescent egocentrism, or trouble distinguishing one's own thoughts and feelings from those of others

>Imaginary audience, or confusing one's own thoughts with those of a hypothesized audience for your behavior

Plant Problem

Imagine you have 5 plants, all of the same type.

Plant A gets a large glass of water each week and a light colored plant food. It is doing well.

Plant B gets a large glass of water, dark colored plant food, and leaf lotion. It appears to be dying.

Plant C gets a small glass of water, light-colored plant food, and leaf lotion. It is doing well.

Plant D gets a small glass of water and dark plant food. It seems to be dying.

Plant E is new. How should you treat it?

On what basis do you draw your conclusions?

(Based on "Development of the Isolation of Variables Scheme in Experimental and 'Natural Experiment' Contexts," by D. Kuhn & J. Brannock, 1977, *Developmental Psychology, 13*, 9-14.)

Criticisms of Piaget's Theory

1. Underestimated the cognitive abilities of infants and young children.

For example, he claimed that preoperational children were egocentric, yet more recent research shows that children as young as 2 or 3 can assume another's perspective.

2. Failed to distinguish competence (what an individual is capable of) from performance (what an individual actually does when given a task).

3. Claimed that broad stages of development exist, and each stage is characterized by a coherent mode of thinking that is applied to many problems.

Recent research shows that there is often little consistency in an individual's performance on tasks that supposedly rely on the same ability. Cognitive ability is thought to be domain specific by a number of researchers.

4. Failed to adequately explain development: How exactly does development occur?

5. Gave limited attention to social influences on cognitive development.

Components of Language

1. **Phonology**   Sound system of language

                        Basic unit--phoneme

2. **Semantics**   Meaning aspect of language

                        Basic unit--morpheme (words, grammatical markers)

3. **Syntax**   Rules specifying how words are combined to form sentences.

4. **Pragmatics**   Rules specifying how language is appropriately used in different social contexts.

Developmental Course of Language

Prelinguistic Vocalizations

Newborns	Three types of cries: Hunger, mad, pain
3 weeks	Fake cries
3-5 weeks	Cooing--repetitive vowel-like sounds
4-6 months	Babbling--repetitive consonant/vowel combinations

Linguistic Vocalizations

12 months	Holophrases--single words used to convey the meaning of an entire sentence
18-24 months	Telegraphic speech--Combinations of two or more words into simple sentences that contain the critical content words and omit the "extras"
24-36 months	Increase in vocabulary and length of sentences

8

LEARNING AND INFORMATION PROCESSING

LEARNING OBJECTIVES

After students have read and studied the material in this chapter, they should be able to answer the following questions:

1. How does classical conditioning work? What is a good example of classical conditioning?

2. How does operant conditioning work? What is a good example of operant conditioning? What factors influence the success of operant conditioning?

3. What is the distinction between negative reinforcement and punishment?

4. How does learning take place through observation?

5. Can young infants learn? In what ways? What is the evidence?

6. How do basic learning capacities change with age?

7. What is the general orientation of the information-processing model to cognition? What are the specific components of the model?

8. How do researchers assess infant memory? What information can infants typically remember? What are the limitations of infants' memory?

9. What are four major hypotheses about why memory improves with age? Which of these hypotheses is (are) supported by research?

10. How do problem solving capacities change during childhood?

11. What developments occur in the information processing abilities of adolescents?

12. In what ways do memory and cognition change during adulthood? What are the strengths and weaknesses of older adults' abilities? What factors help explain the declines in abilities during older adulthood?

13. How can memory be improved?

I. **Basic learning processes**
  A. Classical conditioning
       1. Unconditioned stimulus (UCS)
       2. Unconditioned response (UCR)
       3. Conditioned stimulus (CS)
       4. Conditioned response (CR)
       5. Counterconditioning
  B. Operant conditioning (Skinner)
       1. Positive and negative reinforcement-- Consequences that strengthen a response
       2. Positive and negative punishment-- Consequences that decrease the strength of a response
       3. Extinction
       4. Frequency of reinforcement
            a. Continuous reinforcement-- for developing a new behavior
            b. Partial reinforcement-- for maintaining behavior over time
  C. Observational learning (Bandura)
       1. Distinction between learning and performance
       2. Vicarious reinforcement
  D. Stability and change in learning
       1. Can young infants learn?
            a. Classical and operant conditioning at birth
       2. Developmental changes
            a. Early improvements in imitation-- Deferred imitation
            b. Aging and losses

II. **The information-processing approach**
  A. Computer model of information-processing
       1. Hardware and software
       2. Sensory register, short-term memory, long-term memory
       3. Encoding, storage, and retrieval of information
       4. Recognition, recall, and cued recall memory
       5. Problem-solving, executive control processes

III. **The infant**
  A. Early memory
       1. Assessment of infant memory--often with habituation tasks or operant conditioning techniques
       2. Evidence of recognition and recall memory
       3. Cue-dependent and context-specific before 8-12 months
  B. Infantile amnesia

IV. **The child**
  A. Dramatic improvements in learning and memory in childhood
       1. Do basic capacities change?
            a. Speed of processing increases, not total capacity
            b. Automatization of information processing
       2. Do memory strategies change?
            a. Increasing use of rehearsal, organization (e.g., chunking), elaboration (creating links between objects)
            b. Rehearsal, organization, elaboration
       3. Does knowledge about memory change?

                a. Metamemory and metacognition--Increases with age and some relation to
                    memory performance
            4. Does knowledge of the world change?
                a. Knowledge base affects learning and memory
            5. A summing up
                a. Older children have greater information-processing capacity-- faster and
                    juggle more information
                b. Older children use more effective memory strategies
                c. Older children have greater metamemory
                d. Older children have a larger knowledge base
    B. Problem solving in childhood
            1. Siegler's rule-assessment approach (balance-beam problem)
                a. Most children use multiple strategies-- natural selection

V. The adolescent
    A. New strategies emerge
    B. Use of strategies is more deliberate, selective, and spontaneous
    C. Basic capacities and knowledge base increase
    D. Metamemory and metacognition improve

VI. The adult
    A. Developing expertise
            1. Effect of knowledge base on memory and problem solving
                a. Experts have larger, more organized knowledge base, and information
                    used efficiently
                b. Knowledge and processing is domain-specific
    B. Learning, memory, and aging
            1. Declines in learning and memory
                a. Areas of strength and weakness
                    i. Research cross-sectional, declines not until 60s, not all show
                        declines and not all declines problematic
                    ii. Declines among old in same areas as deficits in young children
                b. Timed tasks
                c. Unfamiliar tasks
                d. Unexercised skills
                e. Recall versus recognition
                f. Deliberate, effortful memory tasks
            2. Explaining declines in learning and memory in old age
                a. Knowledge-base
                b. Metamemory
                c. Memory-strategy
                d. Basic processing capacities--working-memory capacity may decrease
                e. Contextual contributors
                    i. Cohort differences in education, health, and lifestyle
                    ii. Motivational factors
                    iii. Kinds of tasks
                    iv. External memory aids
                f. Summing up
    C. Problem solving and aging
            1. Older adults use fewer constraint-seeking questions
            2. Performance on meaningless tasks decreases, but performance on meaningful,
                everyday tasks is stable or improves

VII. Applications: Improving memory

1. Tauber provides six different techniques to reduce students' misunderstandings of negative reinforcement, such as confusing negative reinforcement with punishment [Tauber, R. T. (1988). Overcoming misunderstanding about the concept of negative reinforcement. _Teaching of Psychology, 15,_ 152-153].

2.   Have students consider and generate examples of how habits (in many cases, bad habits) become part of our behavioral repertoires through conditioning techniques. As an example, discuss how parents can inadvertently reinforce children's whining or demands when they "give in" to whining or requests for a product at the grocery store. Because this behavior is often reinforced on a partial schedule, it is more resistant to extinction. Ask students to discuss ways to extinguish such behaviors.

3.   Students often appreciate hearing how fears are acquired through classical conditioning. Ask students to analyze a relevant example, such as delivering a speech in front of a group of people (a fear that many students can relate to). They should be able to provide the unconditioned and conditioned stimuli, and the unconditioned and conditioned responses.

4.   Ask students to report their earliest memories, including their age at the time of the occurrence and the content of these memories. Do students really recall the experience, or do they recall the feelings associated with the experience? Do they remember because the events have been retold, captured in pictures, or otherwise been made memorable for them?
    For an excellent sampling of the first memories recalled by scores of people, try the following web site: http://www.exploratorium.edu/memory/earlymemory/index.html. What sorts of events does it seem we tend to remember? Which senses predominate? What sorts of emotions are involved?
    For students who want more information about early memories, an easy-to-read article called "Voices, glances, flashbacks: Our first memories" by Huyghe can be found in _Psychology Today_ (1985, Sept.). It is also interesting to read the early memories of writers, who may have more heightened powers of perception and recall. Two examples may be found in _Moments of Being,_ by Virginia Woolf (1985; Harcourt Brace), and _An American Childhood_ by Annie Dillard (1987; Harper Row).

5.   Have students explore the web site LDOnline: The Interactive Guide to Learning Disabilities for Parents, Teachers, and Children (www.ldonline.org). In general, the information-processing approach underlies our understanding of learning disabilities. Can students exploring this site find evidence for the importance of other learning approaches (i.e., conditioning and observational learning)?

6.   Although research reported in the text suggests that spanking and other forms of physical punishment are not effective in the long run, spanking children remains a widely debated issue. _ParadeMagazine_ (May 15, 1994) compiled responses of 10,000 readers who called to offer their opinion of spanking a child. Although a majority, 56%, said they favored spanking, this percentage is lower than a 1991 survey (67%) and a 1986 survey (84%). Have small groups of students discuss the advantages and disadvantages of spanking as a means of discipline. Some points to consider include: the consistency of discipline across settings and among the adults in charge of the child; the gray line between harsh discipline and child abuse; and the constitutional rights of children. What do students make of the finding that Black children are more likely to be paddled in school than White children, and that poor White children are more likely to be paddled in school than middle-class children?
    What are the short-term versus long-term effects of spanking? A Newsweek poll also conducted in 1994 (April 18) reported that 47% of Americans believed there would be less crime if more parents spanked their children, while 73% believed that there is already too much physical

abuse of children by parents. What do students think about the link between spanking and crime? What sort of study might be devised to assess this link?

7.   Ask students to learn the material presented in Figure 8-7 of the text or a similar task (a transparency master is also provided). Then ask them how they tried to learn the material. This is a good way to stimulate discussion of memory strategies such as rehearsal, organization, and elaboration.

You might then have students review some of the memory technique information available on PsychWeb's Mind Tools (http://www.psych-web.com/mtsite/memory.html). Have students try a few techniques and determine which one(s) work best for them. Using information in this chapter and on the web site, can students explain how the techniques work? You might also set up a memory-technique demonstration by dividing the class into several groups, each of which utilizes a different memory technique. Then give a new memory task (e.g., bring in some items to show them and have them remember). Which group does best?

8.   To demonstrate constraint-seeking strategies, have pairs or small groups of students try the Twenty Questions Game in class, using items in Figure 8-14 of the text (a transparency master is also provided). One student thinks of a target item, and others ask yes-no questions until they can identify the chosen item. Have them try this several times and note if strategies improve. What are the most efficient constraint-seeking approaches (e.g., Is it in the top two rows? Is it an animal?)? If possible, ask students to try the Twenty Questions game with younger subjects and report the outcome in class. If enough students do this with children of different ages, the class can pool their data to see if any developmental trends in constraint-seeking questions emerge.

SUGGESTED FILMS AND VIDEOS

Learning (1990, Insight Media, VHS, 30 minutes): Includes the basic principles and classical and operant conditioning and a segment on how operant conditioning can be used to change the behavior of hyperactive children.

The Learning Infant (Insight Media, VHS, 30 minutes): Focuses on classical and operant conditioning, learning through imitation, and building mental structures. Explains Piaget's concept of object permanence.

SUGGESTED READINGS

Collins, A. F., Gathercolse, S. E., Conway, M. A., and Morris, P. E. (Eds.) (1993). *Theories of memory.* NJ: Lawrence Erlbaum.

Kail, R. (1990). *The development of memory in children*, 3rd ed. NY: W. H. Freeman and Co.

Langer, E. J. (1998). *The Power of Mindful Learning.* New York: Addison-Wesley Publishing Co.

Light, L. L., & Burke, D. M. (1988). *Language, memory, and aging.* NY: Cambridge University Press.

Neisser, U. (1982) *Memory Observed.* NY: W. H. Freeman and Co.

Nelson, C. A. (Ed.). (1993). *Memory and affect in development.* NJ: Lawrence Erlbaum Associates.

Skinner, B. F. (1948). *Walden two.* London: Macmillan.

Skinner, B. F. (1982). Baby in a box. In J. K. Gardner (Ed.). *Readings in developmental psychology* (pp. 119-125). Boston: Little, Brown & Co. [Originally appeared in 1946 in *Ladies' Home Journal*]

Weinert, F., & Perlmutter, M. (Eds.) (1988). *Memory development: Universal changes and individual differences*. NJ: Lawrence Erlbaum Associates.

TRANSPARENCY MASTERS

8.1	Three phases of classical conditioning
8.2	Operant conditioning: Positive and negative consequences of behavior
8.3	Guidelines for effective use of punishment
8.4	Possible explanations for learning and memory improvements during childhood
8.5	Siegler's balance beam problem and rules
8.6	Declines in learning and memory among older adults
8.7	A memory task
8.8	A Twenty Questions Game

Three phases of classical conditioning

Before conditioning:

      Neutral Stimulus ----->   No particular response
      (bell)

      Unconditioned   Unconditioned
      Stimulus (UCS) ----->   Response (UCR)
      (food)   (salivation)

During conditioning:

      Neutral stimulus (bell)
           plus   ----->   Salivation
      Unconditioned
      stimulus (food)

After conditioning:

      Conditioned   Conditioned
      Stimulus (CS) ----->   Response (CR)
      (bell)   (salivation)

Operant conditioning: Positive and negative consequences of behavior

Positive
Reinforcement

Something <u>positive</u> is <u>added</u> to the situation or given to the person that <u>strengthens</u> the behavior it follows.

EX:

Giving a child a treat for a desired behavior.

Negative
Reinforcement

Something <u>negative</u> is <u>taken away</u> from the situation or person that <u>strengthens</u> the behavior it follows.

EX:

Taking away a disliked chore following a desired behavior.

Punishment
(positive)

Something <u>positive</u> is <u>taken away</u> from the situation or person that <u>weakens</u> the behavior it follows.

EX:

Taking away a child's favorite game after the child misbehaves.

Punishment
(negative)

Something <u>negative</u> is <u>added</u> to the situation or given to the person that <u>weakens</u> the behavior it follows.

EX:

Yelling at a child after the child misbehaves.

Guidelines for effective use of punishment

1. Punish as soon as possible after the misbehavior.

2. Punish with intensity (but not too much intensity).

3. Punish consistently, otherwise the behavior may persist because it occasionally gets reinforced.

4. Be otherwise warm and affectionate.

5. Explain why the behavior was wrong and why the child is being punished.

6. Reinforce alternative behavior so the child learns what to do, as well as what not to do.

7. Consider alternative responses to misbehavior, such as time out.

Possible explanations for learning and memory improvements during childhood

1. Do basic capacities change?

YES: Although total short-term memory capacity doesn't change, constructive use of it does increase with age. Older children are faster and more efficient at executing basic processes.

2. Do memory strategies change?

YES: Older children use more effective memory strategies (e.g., rehearsal, elaboration, organization).

3. Does knowledge about memory and other cognitive processes change?

YES: Metamemory and metacognition both increase with age and are somewhat related to memory performance.

4. Does increased knowledge of the world in general contributes to improvements in memory?

YES: Older children have a larger knowledge base.

Siegler's Balance Beam Problem and Rules

RULE 1: The child predicts that the arm with more weight will drop, totally ignoring information about the distance of weights from the center.

RULE 2: Weight is still the most important factor, but if the weights on each arm are equal, the child will consider the distance of the weights from the fulcrum to break the tie.

RULE 3: Both weight and distance are considered, but if one side has more weight while the other has its weights farther from the fulcrum, the child is confused and will simply guess.

RULE 4: The child knows that the pull on each arm is a function of weight times distance, and as a consequence, can answer any of the balance beam problems correctly.

Declines in learning and memory among older adults

Declines in learning and memory tend to occur when:

1. Tasks are timed.

2. Tasks are unfamiliar.

3. Tasks require unexercised skills.

4. Tasks call for recall rather than recognition of information.

5. Tasks involve deliberate, effortful learning rather than automatic, unconscious, or unintentional learning.

Explanations for the declines in learning and memory:

Working-memory capacity decreases, but this can't explain all declines in learning and memory.

Other contextual contributors:

Cohort differences in education, health, and lifestyle

Motivational factors

The tasks used are removed from everyday contexts of learning and remembering

A Memory Task

Take 120 seconds to learn the 12 objects pictured here.

What tricks or strategies did you devise to make this task easier?

A Twenty Questions Game

Think of an item in the group and ask your testee to find out which one it is by asking yes/no questions.

INTELLIGENCE AND CREATIVITY

LEARNING OBJECTIVES

After students have read and studied the material in this chapter, they should be able to answer the following questions:

1. How do psychometric theorists define intelligence?

2. What is the difference between fluid and crystallized intelligence?

3. How does Gardner define intelligence?

4. What is Sternberg's triarchic theory of intelligence?

5. How do the Stanford-Binet and Wechsler intelligence tests compare and contrast to one another?

6. What is the dynamic assessment approach to intelligence testing?

7. How is infant intelligence measured? To what extent is infant intelligence related to later intelligence?

8. Are IQ scores stable during childhood? What factors contribute to gains and losses in IQ scores?

9. How well do IQ scores predict school achievement? To what extent is IQ related to occupational success?

10. How do IQ and mental abilities change with age?

11. What factors predict declines in intellectual abilities in older adults?

12. To what extent does wisdom exist in older adults?

13. What evidence shows genetic influence on IQ scores? What other factors influence IQ scores?

14. How are mental retardation and giftedness defined? What are the outcomes for individuals who are mentally retarded or gifted?

15. What is creativity? How does it change across the life span?

16. How can intellectual performance be improved across the life span?

I. **What is intelligence?**
    A. The psychometric approach
        1. A single attribute or many attributes?
            a. Factor analysis
            b. Spearman's general ability (g) and special abilities (s)
            c. Thurstone's seven primary mental abilities
            d. Guilford's structure-of-intellect model
        2. Fluid versus crystallized intelligence
            a. Cattell and Horn's work
    B. Gardner's theory of multiple intelligences
        1. Seven intelligences-- linguistic, logical-mathematical, musical, spatial, bodily-
            kinesthetic, interpersonal, intrapersonal
    C. Sternberg's triarchic theory
        1. Contextual component-- real-world adaptation versus test-taking
        2. Experiential component-- novelty and automatization
        3. Information-processing component

II. **How is intelligence measured?**
    A. The Stanford-Binet test
        1. Description of child's mental age (MA) with age-graded items
        2. Intelligence quotient (IQ = MA/CA x 100)
        3. Test norms-- standards of typical performance
    B. The Wechsler scales-- verbal, performance, and full-scale scores
    C. The distribution of IQ scores
        1. Normal distribution-- bell-shaped spread around average score
    D. Intelligence testing today
        1. Dynamic assessment
            a. Feuerstein's Learning Potential Assessment Device-- assesses the ability to
                learn new things quickly with minimal guidance

III. **The infant**
    A. Developmental Quotients
        1. Bayley Scales of Infant Development (2-30 months)
            a. Motor scale, mental scale, infant behavioral record
            b. Developmental Quotient (DQ)-- performance compared to norms
    B. Infant intelligence and later intelligence
        1. Low correlations between DQ scores and later IQ scores
        2. Explanations for this lack of relationship
            a. Each assesses different domains
            b. Infant intelligence based on universal maturation
        3. Relationship between measures of infant attention and later IQ
            a. Speed of habituation, preference for novelty, reaction time

IV. **The child**
    A. How stable are IQ scores during childhood?
        1. IQ scores are fairly stable starting at about age 4
        2. Correlations reflect groups of children, not individuals
    B. Causes of gains and losses
        1. Gains among children with parents who foster achievement and are neither too lax
            nor too strict
        2. Cumulative-deficit hypothesis-- IQ scores of children from impoverished
            environments decrease as negative effects accumulate

V.   **The adolescent**
A. Continuity between childhood and adulthood
    1. Rapid intellectual growth in early adolescence, then levels off
    2. Increasing stability of individual differences
B. IQ and school achievement
    1. IQ is good predictor of academic achievement, especially high school
      (versus college)

VI.   **The adult**
A. Does IQ affect occupational success in adulthood?
    1. Some occupations require more intellectual ability than others
    2. Performance on the job also related to IQ
B. Change in IQ with age?
    1. Answer depends on type of research-- Cross-sectional or longitudinal,
      or sequential (Schaie's study)
    2. Cohort effects on performance
    3. Declines occur fairly late in life--60's or 70's
      a. Fluid intelligence declines earlier and more steeply than crystallized
      b. Performance on speeded tests declines more
      c. More declines in performance than in verbal intelligence
    4. Patterns of aging differ for different abilities
    5. Declines are not universal
C. Predictors of decline
    1. Poor health
      a. Terminal drop of IQ
    2. Unstimulating lifestyle
D. Potential for Wisdom
    1. Wisdom is rare and related more to expertise than age
    2. Research does not yet support common belief of wisdom in old age

VII. **Factors that influence IQ scores**
A. Genes
B. Home environment
    1. HOME inventory
      a. Parental involvement with child
      b. Provision of developmentally appropriate stimulation
C. Social-class differences in IQ
    1. Flynn effect-- 20th century increases in IQ
    2. Adoption from lower-class into middle-class homes associated with higher IQ
D. Racial and ethnic differences in IQ
    1. Culture bias in testing
    2. Motivational factors
    3. Genetic influences
    4. Environmental influences

VIII. **The extremes of intelligence**
A. Mental retardation
    1. IQ score below 70-75 and limitations in meeting age-appropriate expectations
    2. Mild to profound
    3. Causes: Organic retardation or cultural-familial retardation
B. Giftedness--high IQ or special abilities in areas valued by society
    1. Terman's research

IX. **Creativity and special talents**
    A. What is creativity?
        1. Divergent versus convergent thinking
        2. Ideational fluency-- number of different ideas one can generate
        3. Creativity and IQ not highly correlated
    B. Creativity in childhood and adolescence
        1. Influenced by different factors than IQ
        2. Developmental course of creativity less predictable
    C. Creative achievement in adulthood
        1. Relationship between age and creative achievement depends on field
        2. Creative behavior possible, but less frequent in later life

XI. **Applications: Boosting intellectual performance across the life span**
    A. Early intervention for preschool children
        1. Head Start and early education programs work best if start early, last long, and
            involve several components
    B. Enrichment for low-IQ adolescents
        1. Feuerstein's Instrumental Enrichment program
    C. IQ training for aging adults
        1. Declining skills can be revived with coaching and practice

SUGGESTIONS FOR CLASS DISCUSSIONS OR PROJECTS

1.   Ask your students to name behaviors and traits that they associate with intelligent people or with nonintelligent people. Sternberg and his colleagues did this and found that the named behaviors fell into three categories: Practical problem-solving skills, verbal skills, and social competence. Examples of practical problem-solving include making good decisions, keeping an open mind, and using original sources for information. Examples of verbal ability include conversing well, reading with high comprehension, and having a good vocabulary. Examples of social competence include being on time for appointments, admitting mistakes, and sensitivity to other people's needs. Sternberg (1986-- see Suggested Readings) presents a checklist of behaviors in each category that students can use to evaluate themselves on a 9-point scale. Sternberg notes that higher ratings on the checklist are associated with better performance.
     The class might also try to generate lists of behaviors and traits associated with creative and non-creative people. Are the concepts of creativity and intelligence in any way related?

2.   This chapter describes the relationship between home environment and intellectual performance and provides sample items from the HOME inventory. Ask students to expand on this by "designing" (on paper) environments that would be rated high, moderate, and low on intellectual stimulation. There are often examples of environments shockingly low on appropriate stimulation in the news.

3.   Some people have recently argued that providing stimulation has gone overboard when parents begin coaching infants and young children with flashcards and enrolling them in numerous programs designed to promote some aspect of development. The Better Baby Institute, founded by Glenn Doman (author of *How to teach your child to read*), provides a good illustration of a program which uses early structured stimulation with infants to accelerate mental growth. In this program, parents are trained to educate their infants by using flash cards presented to the infants three times a day. Discuss pros and cons of such efforts. What do students think would be the effects of such a program (on intellectual and also other types of functioning)?

4.   The controversies surrounding the 1995 book *The Bell Curve: Intelligence and Class Structure in American Life* by Murray and Herrnstein are not new. Students might discuss why

controversies about group differences in intelligences persist, and how progress in the debate might be made. The Amoeba Web site offers a great deal of information that might enhance class discussions at:

> http://www.sccu.edu/Programs/Academic/Psych/webintelligence.html.

In particular, an interview with Robert Sternberg on *The Bell Curve* (http://www.skeptic.com/03.3.fm-sternberg-interview.html) touches on much of the material presented in this chapter. An APA review of *The Bell Curve* (http://www.apa.org/journals/bell.html) provides some additional insights. Review of these and other articles would allow students to debate the issue of group differences in intelligence with more insight.

5.	Given the many criticisms of IQ tests reflected in the chapter, have students discuss in small groups whether it is a good or a bad idea to have some method of assessing individual intelligence. When are intelligence tests used? Should they be used for those purposes? What alternatives to these tests might exist? Ask students to try to design a "new and improved" test that taps typical aspects of intelligence as well as aspects not well represented in current tests. The test should relate to everyday intellectual functioning, be practically administered, predict what students design it to predict, and be fair to such groups as minority children and older adults. This exercise often makes students appreciate why none of the current intelligence tests is perfect; tests that are high in one desired feature are often low in another desired feature.

6.	Among the features offered at the Creativity Web: Resources for Creativity and Innovations (http://www.ozemail.com.au/~caveman/Creative/Genius/index.html) is a "Creative Genius Gallery" hall of fame. Who would students include in their list of 20th century creative geniuses and why? Students might have people of different ages suggest who they consider to be creative geniuses. Are there people who tend to appear on lists across age groups? What enables creative geniuses to stand the tests of time?

SUGGESTED FILMS AND VIDEOS

Aspects of Intelligence (Insight Media, VHS, 30 minutes). Discusses intelligence and its measurement. Presents different conceptions of intelligence, including those of Piaget and Terman.

Intelligence (1990, Insight Media, VHS, 30 minutes): Overview of intelligence test construction and meaning of IQ test scores.

SUGGESTED READINGS

Aiken, L. R. (1994). *Psychological testing and assessment*, 8th edition. Boston: Allyn and Bacon.

Birren, J. E., and Schaie, K. W. (1990). *Handbook of the psychology of aging*, 3rd edition. NY: Academic Press. [Three chapters in this Handbook are relevant to this chapter: "Intellectual development in adulthood," "Cognitive competence and expertise in aging," and "Creativity and wisdom in aging."]

Ceci, S. J. (1990). *On intelligence...more or less: A bio-ecological treatise on intellectual development*. NY: Prentice-Hall.

Gardner, H. (1983). *Frames of mind: the theory of multiple intelligences*. New York: Basic Books.

Howe, M. J. (1989). *Fragments of genius: The strange feats of idiot savants*. NY: Routledge Press.

Sternberg, R. (1985). *Beyond IQ: A triarchic theory of human intelligence*. NY: Cambridge University Press.

Sternberg, R. (1986). *Intelligence applied*. NY: Harcourt, Brace and Jovanovich.

Sternberg, R. (Ed.) (1990). *Wisdom: Its nature, origins and development*. NY: Cambridge University Press.

Sternberg, R., Conway, B., Ketron, J., and Berstein, M. (1981). People's conceptions of intelligence. *Journal of Personality and Social Psychology, 41*, 37-55.

Storfer, M. D. (1990). *Intelligence and giftedness: The contributions of heredity and early environment*. CA: Jossey-Bass Publishers.

Walsh, W. B., & Betz, N. E. (1990). *Tests and assessments*. NY: Prentice-Hall.

TRANSPARENCY MASTERS

9.1   Characteristics of intelligence tests (Stanford-Binet and Wechsler)

9.2   Measuring infant intelligence

9.3   Factors that influence IQ scores

9.4   Classifying mental retardation

<u>Characteristics of Intelligence Tests</u>

<u>Stanford-Binet Intelligence Scale</u>, 4th edition (1986)

Standardized on individuals between 2 and 24 years
Includes items in 4 areas: Verbal reasoning, abstract-
    visual reasoning, quantitative reasoning, and
    short-term memory
The 4 area scores are totaled for a composite score

<u>Wechsler Tests</u>:

<u>Adult Intelligence Scale-Revised</u> (WAIS-R, 1981)

Standardized on individuals between 16 and 74 years
6 verbal subtests (e.g., information, comprehension,
    vocabulary) and 5 performance subtests (e.g., block
    design, object assembly)

<u>Intelligence Scale for Children</u> (WISC-III, 1991)

Standardized on individuals between 6 and 17 years
6 verbal subtests and 7 performance subtests

<u>Preschool and Primary Scale of Intelligence</u>
(WPPSI-R, 1989)

Standardized on individuals between 3 and 7 years
6 verbal subtests and 6 performance subtests

The Wechsler scales yield separate Verbal, Performance, and
Full-Scale IQ scores.

Measuring Infant Intelligence

Developmentalists have tried to measure infant intelligence by the rate at which infants achieve important developmental milestones.

The most commonly used of these assessments is the <u>Bayley Scale of Infant Development</u> for 2-30 month olds.

A developmental quotient (DQ) is assigned on the basis of an infant's responses on:

    1.   <u>Motor Scale</u> (e.g., grasping a cube)
    2.   <u>Mental Scale</u> (e.g., searching for hidden toy)

The Bayley also includes an <u>Infant Behavioral Record</u> (a rating of the infant's behavior on dimensions such as goal-directedness, fearfulness, and social responsivity).

<u>Why are correlations between infant DQ scores and child IQ scores are low to nonexistent</u>?
   --The Bayley doesn't assess the kinds of things that are assessed by standard intelligence tests.
   --Growth of intelligence during infancy may be strongly under the influence of universal maturational processes, while later intelligence is less strongly influenced by maturational factors (McCall).

<u>What does correlate with later intelligence</u>?
Some measures of infant attention (speed of habituation and preference for novelty) are moderately correlated with measures of later intelligence.

Factors that Influence IQ Scores

GENES

Twin studies suggests genes account for about half of the variation in IQ scores within a group of people. Identical twins raised in separate environments score more similarly on IQ tests than other pairs of individuals who have been raised in the same environment.

HOME ENVIRONMENT

Growing up in a disadvantaged home where the adults do not provide much intellectual stimulation is associated with lower IQ. Scores on the HOME inventory, especially parental involvement with child, provision of appropriate play materials, and opportunities for a variety of stimulation, are correlated with intellectual functioning.

SOCIAL-CLASS DIFFERENCES

Economic status of the family is associated with IQ scores such that increases in socioeconomic condition improve IQ scores.

RACIAL AND ETHNIC DIFFERENCES
Asian American and Euro-American children score higher than African American, Native American, and Hispanic American children.

These differences may be due to:
--Culture bias in testing
--Motivational differences

Classifying Mental Retardation

Three-pronged definition:

Significantly below-average general intellectual functioning

Limitations in adaptive behavior

Origination during the developmental period

Levels:

Mild (Score in 55-69 range on the Wechsler test)
May be able to work and live independently, with
occasional help from others

Moderate (Score in 40-54 range)
Will probably need supervision and support in order to
work and live

Severe (Score in 25-39 range)
Can learn basic self-help skills, but will need a good deal
of training and support as adults

Profound (Score less than 25)
Will need constant basic care, perhaps in an
institutional setting

SELF-CONCEPTIONS, PERSONALITY, AND EMOTIONAL EXPRESSION

LEARNING OBJECTIVES

After students have read and studied the material in this chapter, they should be able to answer the following questions:

1. How do psychoanalytic, psychometric (trait), and social learning theories explain personality development?

2. How does self-concept emerge during infancy? How does self-concept change across the life span?

3. How has infant temperament been categorized? How do these temperament styles interact with caregiver characteristics? How does temperament relate to later personality?

4. What changes occur in the development of children's and adolescent's self-esteem? What factors influence self-esteem?

5. What is the focus of each of Erikson's psychosocial stages? What factors can influence how each crisis is resolved?

6. What factors influence the development of identity during adolescence?

7. How does personality change during adulthood? Why do people change or remain the same?

8. How can self-esteem be improved throughout the life span?

I. **Conceptualizing the self**
   A. Theories of personality development
      1. Psychoanalytic theory
         a. Freud
            i. Biological urges push children through universal stages of psychosexual development
            ii. Personality is formed in first five years
         b. Erikson
            i. Biological maturation <u>and</u> social demands push an individual into the next psychosocial stage
            ii. Personality continues to develop in adulthood
      2. Psychometric Theory
         a. Big Five dimension-- neuroticism, extraversion, openness to experience, agreeableness, consientiousness
         b. Dimensions are genetically influenced and cross-cultural
      3. Social learning theory
         a. People changes as environments change-- situation is key

II. **The infant**
   A. The emerging self
      1. 2-3 month olds show sense of agency
      2. Recognition of one's mirror image-- 18 to 24 months
      3. Categorical self-- classification by socially meaningful dimensions
      4. Looking-glass self-- our view of self reflects others' views of us
      5. Development of the self depends on cognitive development and social interaction
   B. Temperament
      1. Three dimensions of temperament: Emotionality, activity, sociability
      2. Behavioral inhibition: Tendency to be extremely shy and reserved in unfamiliar situations
      3. Easy versus difficult temperament
         a. Easy, difficult, and slow-to-warm-up temperaments
         b. Goodness of fit between child and environment affects continuity of temperament

III. **The child**
   A. Elaborating on a sense of self
      1. Use of personal pronouns
      2. Preschoolers-- concrete and physical descriptions of self
      3. School-age-- inner qualities or traits and social comparisons
   B. Self-esteem
      1. Harter's self-perception scale
         a. Self-esteem is multidimensional and hierarchical
         b. Self-evaluations first inflated, then more realistic by school-age
   C. Influences on self-esteem
      1. Actual competence
      2. Positive social feedback
         a. Parental behavior-- warm, democratic
         b. Peers and others
      3. Self-esteem stable over school years and correlated with adjustment measures
   C. The personality stabilizes
      1. Stabilization in childhood, but then some traits change while others remain about the same

2. Behaviors that are socially valued may persist

IV. **The adolescent**
   A. Self-conceptions
      1. Self-conceptions become more psychological and abstract
      2. Self-awareness increases and self-portrait is more integrated
   B. Self-esteem
      1. Young adolescents have lower self-esteem; older adolescents return to their preadolescent high levels
   C. Forming a sense of identity
      1. Erikson: Identity versus role confusion and moratorium
      2. Developmental trends
         a. Marcia's identity statuses
            i. Diffusion status--No crisis, no commitment
            ii. Foreclosure status--No crisis, commitment made
            iii. Moratorium status--Crisis experienced, no commitment
            iv. Identity achievement--Crisis experienced, commitment made
         b. Identity formation takes a long time and occurs at different rates for different domains
      3. Influences on identity formation
         a. Cognitive development
         b. Relationships with parents
         c. Experiences outside the home
         d. Broader social and historical context

V. **The adult**
   A. Self-perception
      1. No major differences in self-esteem and self-conceptions of young, middle-aged, and older adults
      2. How do elderly people maintain positive self-image despite losses?
         a. Gap between real and ideal self closes
         b. Goals and standards change
         c. The people we compare ourselves to changes
   B. Continuity and discontinuity in personality
      1. Do people retain their rankings on trait dimensions over the years?
         a. Personality traits relatively enduring but change does occur
      2. Do the personalities of adults change systematically?
         a. There is much cross-age consistency in rankings on Big Five
         b. Different generations have somewhat distinctive personality profiles as groups
         c. There is some personality growth from adolescence to middle adulthood
         d. There are few ways in which personality traits of adults systematically change in similar directions as they age
      3. Why do people change or remain the same?
         a. Stability may be accounted for by genetic inheritance, lasting effects of childhood experiences, or environments remaining stable
         b. Changes may be explained by biological factors, changes in social environments (including major life events), or a poor fit between person and the environment
   C. Psychosocial growth-- Erikson
      1. Before adulthood
         a. Trust versus mistrust
         b. Autonomy versus shame and doubt
         c. Initiative versus guilt

     d. industry versus inferiority
   2. Early adult intimacy
     a. Intimacy versus isolation
   3. Middle-age generativity
     a. Generativity versus stagnation
   4. Old age integrity
     a. Integrity versus despair
     b. Life review

VII. **Applications: Boosting self-esteem throughout the life span**

SUGGESTIONS FOR CLASS DISCUSSIONS OR PROJECTS
_____

1.   Thomas, Chess, and Birch (1968) introduced the labels "difficult," "easy," and "slow-to-warm-up" to characterize different temperament styles of infants and young children. The labels convey much value-laden information that might inspire t he following questions:
   • What are the messages implicit in these labels?
   • Would any parent want to have a difficult or slow-to-warm-up infant?
   • Would there be advantages to informing parents of their child's temperament style? How
     might the label affect parent-infant interactions?
   • Are there other, less value-laden labels that might describe the same temperament styles?
   • What would be a good fit for a child with one of these temperaments? In other words, in
     what kind of environment might a difficult or slow-to-warm-up child thrive?

2.   Adams, Shea, and Fitch (1979) provide a potentially useful measure of identity status that illustrates the meaning of the four statuses, and allows students to assess their own progress toward identity [Toward the development of an objective assessment of ego identity status. *Journal of Youth and Adolescence*, 8, 223-237). This instrument asks respondents to agree or disagree with statements that represent the achievement, moratorium, foreclosure, and diffusion statuses.
   Similarly, a 1986 article by Ochse and Plug (*Journal of Personality and Social Psychology*, 50, 1240-1252) presents a relatively short scale designed to assess progress through Erikson's stages (with the exception of integrity versus despair). There has been no research on the actual validity of the instrument, but the items do have face validity, and administering the scale in class (or asking students to listen to items and guess which stage they are supposed to assess) can help students grasp the relevance of such qualities as initiative versus guilt to adult personality.

3.   Have students right ten or so answers to the questions, "Who am I?," and then have them analyze their answers to determine how much they emphasize physical traits; social roles (e.g., student, mother); psychological traits; and membership in social groups (e.g., gender, ethnicity, religion). You might capitalize on diversity within the classroom to see if people in different groups (males versus females, students in early versus late adulthood, ethnic minority versus majority students) use different types of descriptors. Students might also pose the "Who Am I?" question to children and adults of different ages to see if they can identify the developmental trends in self-descriptions delineated in the text.

4.   For many people, ethnic identity is an important part of their sense of self. Jean Phinney (1992) has developed a measure of ethnic identity that is relevant to diverse ethnic groups. This questionnaire enables students to think about the importance of ethnic identity in their own life. Discussion questions might include:
   • Why do members of minority groups more often feel their ethnic identity is an important
     part of who they are, as compared to members of majority groups?
   • How does ethnic identity develop?
   • How is ethnic identity the same and different from other aspects of the self-concept?

5.   Given the emphasis on adolescence in this chapter, now might be a good time for an exercise described by McManus [McManus, J. L. (1986). Student composed case study in adolescent psychology. *Teaching of Psychology, 13*, 92-93]. In this variation of a case study method, students working in groups compose a hypothetical case study, a dilemma or problem, and possible solutions or outcomes to the problem.

6.   The headline of an article in a local newspaper proclaimed "Personality change after 30 unlikely." The article described a study showing that personality changes very little after about the age of 30. The article concluded by saying that if you have a personality trait that you are not happy about, work on changing it before you hit your late 20's. Ask students to discuss the extent to which personality can be modified. Is there a point when personality becomes more or less fixed? Does the research discussed in the text provide any support for the somewhat dire warnings in the newspaper? Can students think of cases where individuals have changed features of their personality? What factors influence personality change? Are some aspects of personality easier to modify than others?

7.   Some research shows that the course of development for self-concept and self-esteem differ for males and females. For example, Block and Robins (1993) found that self-esteem increased in males but decreased in females from early adolescence to early adulthood. Ask students to generate possible explanations for this gender difference, and any ideas for interventions that might seem warranted.

SUGGESTED FILMS AND VIDEOS

Adolescent Personality Development (Insight Media, VHS, 30 minutes): Discusses adolescents' search for identity, development of independence, and developing sexuality. Discusses several theoretical perspectives.

Childhood: The House of Tomorrow (WNET co-production, 1991by Ambrose Video, reissued 1995 by American Brain Tumor Association, VHS, 57 minutes): Part 7 of this 7-part series looks at the many emotional and physical transformations that characterize puberty and adolescence.

The Child's Personality (Insight Media, VHS, 30 minutes): Discusses peer groups and the growth of certain personality concepts including self concept, independence, and achievement.

The Emerging Personality (Insight Media, VHS, 30 minutes): Discusses four major theories of personality development: Freud, Erikson, social learning, and Mahler's separation-individuation theory.

Everybody Rides the Carousel (Insight Media, VHS, 72 minutes): Animated portrayal of Erikson's eight stages of psychosocial development.

Preschool Personality (Insight Media, VHS, 30 minutes): Discusses Freud's Oedipal and Electra complexes, illustrates Erikson's initiative vs. guilt conflict, presents replication of research on aggression with Bobo doll, and discusses relationship between television viewing and aggression.

SUGGESTED READINGS

Adams, G., Gullotta, T., & Montemayor, R. (Eds.). (1992). *Adolescent identity formation.* CA: Sage Publications.

Block, J., & Robins, R. (1993). A longitudinal study of consistency and change in self-esteem from early adolescence to early adulthood. *Child Development, 64*, 910-923.

Costa, P. T., & McCrae, R. R. (1989). Personality continuity and the changes of adult life. In M. Sorandt & G. R. VandenBos (Eds.), *The adult years: Continuity and change*. Washington, DC: American Psychological Association.

Lewis, M., & Haviland, J. (Eds.). (1993). *Handbook of emotions*. NY: Guilford Publications.

Malatesta, C. Z., Culver, C., Tesman, J. R., & Shepard, B. (1989). The development of emotion expression during the first two years of life. *Monographs of the Society for Research in Child Development, 54* (Nos. 1-2, Serial No. 219)

Marcia, J. E. (1966). Development and validation of ego-identity status. *Journal of Personality and Social Psychology, 3*, 551-558.

Markus, Hazel & Kitayama, Shinoba (1991). Cultural variation in the self-concept. In Jaine Strauss & George R. Goethals (Eds.), *The self: Interdisciplinary approaches*. New York: Springer-Verlag (pp. 18-48).

Pedlow, R., Sanson, A., Prior, M., & Oberklaid, F. (1993). Stability of maternally reported temperament from infancy to 8 years. *Developmental Psychology, 29*, 998-1007.

Phinney, J. S. (1992). The multigroup ethnic identity measure: A new scale for use with diverse groups. *Journal of Adolescent Research, 7 (2)*, 156-176.

Saarni, C., & Harris, P. L. (1989). *Children's understanding of emotion*. NY: Cambridge University Press.

Schiedel, D., & Marcia, J. (1985). Ego identify, intimacy, sex role orientation, and gender. *Developmental Psychology, 21*, 149-160.

TRANSPARENCY MASTERS

10.1   Theories of personality development

10.2   Erikson's eight psychosocial stages of development

10.3   Harter's research on self-perception

10.4   Influences on identity formation during adolescence

<u>Theories of Personality Development</u>

<u>Psychoanalytic Theory</u>

<u>Freud</u>: Personality develops during the first five years as the three personality structures (id, ego, superego) develop and clash with one another.

It is strongly influenced by biological forces that propel children through the psychosexual stages.

<u>Erikson</u>: Personality develops through systematic stages across the entire life span and is strongly influenced by both maturation and social and cultural forces.

<u>Social Learning Theory</u>

Personality is shaped by our interactions with other people in specific social situations, and it can change whenever the environment changes.

Erikson's Psychosocial Stages of Development

1.   Trust vs. Mistrust (birth to 1 year)

Infants must learn to trust their caregivers to meet their needs. Responsive parenting is critical.

2.   Autonomy vs. Shame and Doubt (1 to 3 years)

Children must learn to be autonomous-- to assert their wills and do things for themselves-- or they will doubt their abilities.

3.   Initiative vs. Guilt (3 to 6 years)

Preschoolers develop initiative by devising and carrying out bold plans, but they must learn not to impinge on the rights of others.

4.   Industry vs. Inferiority (6 to 12 years)

Children must master important social and academic skills and feel competent when they compare themselves to their peers, or they will suffer from feelings of inferiority.

5.   Identify vs. Role Confusion (12 to 20 years)

Adolescents must grapple with the question "Who am I?" They must establish social and vocational identities by exploring their possibilities or else remain confused about the roles they should play as adults.

6. Intimacy vs. Isolation (20 to 40 years)

    Young adults seek to form an intimate relationship (or a shared identity) with another person, but they may fear intimacy or may not want to give up their independence and may experience loneliness and isolation instead.

7. Generativity vs. Stagnation (40 to 65 years)

    Middle-aged adults must feel that they are producing something of value-- something that will outlive them-- either by successfully raising their children or by contributing to society through their work; otherwise, they will become stagnant and self-centered.

8. Integrity vs. Despair (65 and older)

    Older adults must come to view their lives as meaningful in order to face death without worries and regrets over unfulfilled goals and frustrations.

Harter's Research on Self-Perception

Children rated themselves on:

Scholastic competence (feeling smart, doing well in school)

Social competence (being popular, liked by others)

Behavioral competence (behaving appropriately, not getting in trouble)

Athletic competence (being good at sports)

Physical appearance (feeling good-looking)

Findings:

Third graders have distinctly negative or positive feelings about themselves

Children can distinguish between their competencies in different areas

Young children (4-7 years) tend to have inflated self-esteem scores (they don't always match their actual competencies)

Around age 8, ratings of self-esteem are consistent with actual competencies

<u>Influences on Identity Formation During Adolescence</u>

1. <u>Cognitive development</u>

   Formal operational thought allows adolescents to imagine and consider possible future identities.

2. <u>Relationships with parents</u>

   Whether relationship with parents is close, warm, and caring, or is distant, neglectful and rejecting affects whether adolescents experience a crisis of identity and make a commitment.

3. <u>Social experiences outside the home</u>

   Exposure to diverse ideas and people and encouragement to think independently influences process of identity formation.

4. <u>Broader social and historical context</u>

   The culture in which identity formation occurs affects its development, including whether or not developing a separate identity is even valued by the culture.

11

GENDER ROLES AND SEXUALITY

LEARNING OBJECTIVES

After students have read and studied the material in this chapter, they should be able to answer the following questions:

1. What are gender norms and stereotypes? How do they play out in the behaviors of men and women?

2. What actual psychological differences exist between males and females?

3. How does Eagly's social role hypothesis explain gender stereotypes?

4. How do gender role stereotypes influence infants' behavior and treatment?

5. How do children acquire gender role stereotypes? In what ways do children exhibit gender-typed behavior?

6. What theoretical explanations account for gender-typed behaviors? How well supported are these theories?

7. How do gender roles change throughout adulthood?

8. What is androgyny? To what extent is it useful?

9. How are infants are affected by their sex? What do we know about infant sexuality?

10. What do children know about sex and reproduction? How does sexual behavior change during childhood?

11. What factors contribute to the development of sexual orientation? What are adolescents' sexual attitudes and behavior today?

12. What changes occur in sexual activity during adulthood?

I. **Male and female**
  A. Gender norms and stereotypes
      1. Expressive role-- stereotypically female
      2. Instrumental role-- stereotypically male
  B. Actual gender differences
      1. Maccoby & Jacklin study
          a. Females have greater verbal abilities than males (but recent research indicates this difference may have disappeared)
          b. Males show greater visual/spatial ability than females
          c. Males outperform females on tests of mathematical ability starting in adolescence
          d. Males are more physically and verbally aggressive than females, starting as early as age 2
      2. Some research shows additional sex differences, but others argue that "actual" sex differences are trivial
      3. Most gender stereotypes are unsupported overgeneralizations
      4. Eagly's social-role hypothesis-- different roles males and females play in society create and maintain gender-role stereotypes
      5. Contextual factors also contribute to evidence of sex differences

II. **The infant**
  A. Differential treatment-- adults respond differently to infants on basis of gender
  B. Early learning-- by end of first year, infants distinguish different categories of people based on gender
  C. Development of gender identity by age 2 1/2 to 3, accompanied by differences in behavior

III. **The child**
  A. Acquiring gender stereotypes
      1. Child learns some stereotypes by 2 1/2, and continue to learn them
      2. Rigid adherence at 6 or 7 may be followed by more flexibility in thinking
  B. Gender-typed behavior
      1. Gender segregation strong during elementary school
      2. Boys under greater pressure than girls to adhere to gender-role expectations

IV. **The adolescent**
  A. Adhering to gender roles
      1. Gender intensification-- sex differences are magnified by increased pressure to conform around the time of puberty
  B. Theories of gender-role development
      1. Biosocial theory (Money and Ehrhardt)
          a. Chromosomes, hormones, and social labeling
              I. Presence of Y chromosome and testosterone stimulates growth of male internal and external organs, brain and nervous system
              ii. Society labels and reacts to child on basis of male or female genitals
          b. Evidence of biological influences
              i. Evolutionary view & twin studies
              ii. Prenatal exposure to "wrong" hormones-- androgenized females
          c. Evidence of social-labeling influences
      2. Psychoanalytic theory
          a. Phallic stage of psychosexual development
              i. Identification with same-sex parent to resolve conflicts that arise with Oedipus complex (boys) or Electra complex (girls)

ii. Support for some aspects of Freud's theory
3. Social learning theory
   a. Differential reinforcement for sex-appropriate behaviors
   b. Observational learning-- parents, peers, media
4. Cognitive theory
   a. Cognitive-developmental theory
      i. Gender-role development depends on stage-like changes in cognitive development
      ii. Children engage in self-socialization
      iii. Three stages-- gender identity, gender stability, gender consistency
   b. Gender schema theory
      i. Children form an in-group/out-group schema based on gender
      ii. Interpret new information so it is consistent with schemata
5. An attempt at integration

V. **The adult**
A. Gender roles in adulthood
   1. Changes in roles with marriage and children, and after children are grown
B. Masculinity, femininity, and androgyny
   1. Androgyny (Bem)--Blending of positive masculine and feminine traits
   2. Changes with age
      a. Parental imperative-- gender role distinctions required by parents
      b. Androgyny shift-- add other-sex qualities in mid-life
   3. Is androgyny advantageous?
      a. Greater flexibility in behavior
      b. Masculine traits associated with high self-esteem and good adjustment

VI. **Sexuality over the life span**
A. Are infants sexual beings?
   1. Infants are biologically equipped and derive pleasure from oral activities and genital stimulation
B. Childhood sexuality
   1. Knowledge of sex and reproduction
   2. Sexual behavior
      a. Curiosity about bodies, masturbation, and sexual play in preschoolers and school-age children
      b. Around 10, first sexual attraction
      c. Societal differences contribute to diversity in sexual attitudes and behaviors: restrictive, semirestrictive, and permissive societies
   3. Child sexual abuse
      a. Estimates of prevalence vary, but may be widespread
      b. May result in lack of self-worth and difficulty trusting, sexualized behavior, posttraumatic stress disorder
C. Adolescent sexuality
   1. Sexual orientation
      a. Continuum of sexual orientation, although our culture tends to recognize only three: heterosexual, homosexual, and bisexual
      b. Sexual experimentation with same sex may be common
      c. Influenced by genetic and environmental factors
   2. Sexual morality
      a. Sex with affection is acceptable
      b. Decline of the double standard
      c. Increased confusion about sexual norms

3. Sexual behavior
    a. Increasing sexual involvement at earlier ages, especially females
    b. Females more likely to link emotional and physical intimacy
    c. Lack of contraception
    d. Some change in behavior in response to threat of AIDS
D. Adult sexuality
    1. Sexual beings throughout the life span, though activity declines with age, especially for women
    2. Explanations for declining activity
        a. Physical changes, mental health, societal attitudes, lack of a partner, lack of experience

VI.   **Applications: Changing gender-role attitudes and behavior**

SUGGESTIONS FOR CLASS DISCUSSIONS OR PROJECTS

1. In a classic study, Broverman and colleagues asked trained clinicians about their definitions of healthy adults, healthy males, and healthy females. [Broverman, I. K., Broverman, D. M., Clarkson, E. E., Rosenkrantz, P. S., & Vogel, S. R. (1970). Sex-role stereotypes and clinical judgments of mental health, *Journal of Consulting and Clinical Psychology, 34,* 1-7]. They found that if women lived up to their gender-role prescriptions, they were also, by definition, maladjusted adults. What do students think has and has not changed since this study was conducted? What does this study have to say about the power of psychologists to define abnormality? What special responsibilities might psychologists have? How can psychologists (and others) guard against the biases about social groups (e.g., based on gender, age, sexual orientation, social class, disability status) with which we *all* grow up?

2.   Have students go to a mall or other public area and record the number of people who are wearing sex-stereotyped clothes and hairstyles, and the number who are wearing unisex clothes and hairstyles. Have students record color differences in clothes, or differences in toys or other objects the people are carrying/buying. Each student might pick one or two ages on which to focus: Infants, young children, older children, adolescents, adults, or older adults. The class may initially need to discuss what is stereotypical and what is unisex. Students might do their observations individually or in pairs, then tally everyone's results in class to obtain a larger sample. Discuss findings in terms of gender, age, and source of sample.

3.   Gender roles and stereotypes are easily apparent in the media. Bring in (and ask students to bring in) advertisements from magazines and/or clips from television shows and commercials. Questions to consider: How are males and females portrayed? Does age of the person affect this portrayal? Does the portrayal of males and females by the media accurately reflect societal views?
    Many current analyses of print advertisements use Goffman's (1976) framework for classifying ads in a variety of traditional poses (men are somehow shown in dominant or executive positions with women) or in reverse-sex poses (the opposite of traditional sex-role stereotypes is shown, often for humor value). A nice exercise and background material for conducting an analysis of gender in advertisements can be obtained by writing to: Media and Values, 1962 South Shenandoah Street, Los Angeles, CA 90034 (Phone 213-559-2944). Ask for "The lies that bind." They have a two-part series on gender and the media; one part is devoted to women's portrayals and the other to men's portrayals.

4.   Loki Games Ltd. markets a game called "Gender Bender," which can be used to improve awareness about attitudes and perceptions of the other sex. Participants are asked to respond to questions as if they were the other sex. Examples include "Suppose you were a man, what if someone at a bar called you a wimp or a sissy?" "Suppose you were a woman, what was your

biggest worry when you were 13 years old?" Loki Games LTD can be contacted at Fourth Line America Ltd. P. O. Box 78, Bolton, Ontario). It is, however, quite possible to use this idea without using the game itself. Simply make up some questions (or have students make up questions) and have students role-play the response of someone of the other sex.

5.   If possible, obtain a copy of the BEM Sex-Role Inventory . The BEM Inventory is available from Consulting Psychologists Press, Inc., 577 College Ave., Palo Alto, CA 94306. It contains 20 items that are feminine stereotyped (e.g., affectionate, sympathetic, warm), 20 items that are masculine stereotyped (independent, assertive, dominant), and 20 items that are gender-neutral. Respondents rate themselves on each item using a 7-point Likert-type scale ranging from "never or almost never true" to "always or almost always true" of me. Someone who is androgynous would have high scores on both the feminine and masculine scales. Have students complete the inventory and calculate their femininity and masculinity scores to determine if they are androgynous. Many students are surprised at their results. Ask them to comment on factors that they think have contributed to their sex-role profile.

6.   The Amoeba Web site on Gender and Sexuality. has a number of interesting articles, including several that focus on the role of gender in education (e.g., Gender differences in academic achievement and self-concept; Gender Differences: Learning Styles and Classroom Behavior; Teaching Mathematics Effectively to Females). Based on these articles and the text, how would students modify classroom and educational experiences at different levels (e.g., preschool, elementary school, high school, and college) to increase gender equity? The web site address is:
        http://www.sccu.edu/Programs/academic/psych/webgender.html

7.   Have students identify sex differences that people often believe are true, and then search for research evidence that does or does not support the existence of these differences (again, the information available in the text, on Amoeba Web, and from other references would be useful). The following question might be considered:
        • What ideas do students have about why differences exist? Do they serve any purposes?
        • What about differences we think exist but do not? What purposes do they serve?
        • Are there some differences that parents and others should try to help children resist or
            overcome? Why/why not?

SUGGESTED FILMS AND VIDEOS

Sex Hormones and Sexual Destiny (Films for the Humanities and Sciences, VHS, 26 minutes): Focuses on the effects of hormones on behavior and anatomical differences between male and female brains.

Sex Role Development (CRM Films, VHS and film, 23 minutes): Illustrates how parents often unconsciously socialize their sons and daughters differently.

Sex Roles: Charting the Complexity of Development (1991, Insight Media, VHS, 60 minutes): Includes an overview of Freudian, social learning, and cognitive-developmental explanations of sex-role stereotyping.

The Secret of the Sexes (Insight Media or many video stores sell NOVA programs, VHS, 60 minutes): This NOVA program looks at male and female stereotypes, socialization differences between males and females in our society.

The Sexes: What's the Difference (Filmakers Library, VHS and film, 25 minutes): Jerome Kagan and Eleanor Maccoby discuss biological and cultural factors that contribute to sex differences.

Understanding Sex Roles (Insight Media, VHS, 40 minutes): Discusses evolution of sex differences, romance, sex, relationships, marriage and career development.

SUGGESTED READINGS

Basow, A. (1992). *Gender stereotypes and roles*, 3rd ed. CA: Brooks/Cole.

Beal, C. R. (1994). *Boys and girls: The development of gender roles*. NY: McGraw-Hill, Inc.

Brooks-Gunn, J., & Furstenberg, F. (1989). Adolescent sexual behavior. *American Psychologist, 44*, 249-257.

Gilligan, C. (1993). *In a different voice*. MA: Harvard University Press. [New preface since the 1982 edition]

Jacklin, C. N. (1989). Female and male: Issues of gender. *American Psychologist, 44*, 127-133.

Jordan, J. V., Kaplan, A. G., Miller, J. B., Stiver, I. P., & Surrey, J. L. (1991). *Women's Growth in connection: Writings from the Stone Center*. New York: The Guilford Press.

Morgan, M. (1982). Television and adolescents' sex-role stereotypes: A longitudinal study. *Journal of Personality and Social Psychology, 43*, 947-955.

Serbin, L. A., Powlishta, K. K., & Gulko, J. (1993). The development of sex typing in middle childhood. *Monographs of the Society for Research in Child Development, 58*, Serial no. 232.

Silverstein, O., & Rashbaum, B. (1994). *The courage to raise good men*. New York: Viking.

Tavris, C. (1992). *The mismeasure of woman*. NY: Touchstone.

Tavris, C., & Offir, C. (1985). *The longest war: Sex differences in perspective*, 2nd edition. NY: Harcourt Brace Jovanovich, Inc.

TRANSPARENCY MASTERS

11.1   Actual psychological differences between males and females

11.2   Gender-role development

11.3   Theories of gender-role development

Actual Psychological Differences between Males and Females

Maccoby and Jacklin's 1974 review of over 1500 studies found four actual differences between males and females:

1. <u>Verbal Abilities</u>: Females outperformed males

2. <u>Visual/Spatial Abilities</u>: Males outperformed females

3. <u>Mathematical Abilities</u>: Males outperformed females

4. <u>Aggression</u>: Males were rated more aggressive than females, both physically and verbally

Since 1974, other research suggests sex differences in:

1. Activity level (boys higher)

2. Vulnerability to prenatal and perinatal problems, and to disorders such as speech and reading problems, mental retardation (boys higher)

3. Compliance to requests from adults (girls higher)

4. Methods of achieving compliance (girls are tactful and cooperative while boys are forceful and demanding)

5. Self-reports of nurturance and empathy (girls higher)

Gender-Role Development

Understanding Gender Identity

2 1/2 to 3 year olds can label themselves as either boys or girls

Around 5-7 years, children understand that their biological sex will remain the same

Acquiring Gender Stereotypes

By 2-3 years, children are learning what society thinks is appropriate male or female activity

4 year olds believe it is OK to engage in other-sex behaviors

6 year olds are intolerant of violations of traditional gender-role standards

By 9 years, children are more flexible once again in their thinking about gender stereotypes

Theories of Gender-Role Development

1. <u>Money and Ehrhardt's Biosocial Theory</u>

   Different chromosomes (XX or XY) and different levels of hormones (in particular, testosterone) lead to male or female genitals.

   These biological developments set the stage for the influence of social factors: People label and react to the child on the basis of male or female genitals.

2. <u>Freud's Psychoanalytic Theory</u>

   During phallic stage of psychosexual development, children experience the Oedipus complex (boys) or Electra complex (girls). To resolve the conflicts that arise as part of this, children identify with their same-sex parent and take on that parent's attitudes and behaviors.

3. <u>Social Learning Theory</u>

   Gender-Roles acquired through the same processes that all other behavior is acquired:

   <u>Differential reinforcement</u>--Rewarded for sex-appropriate behaviors and punished for behaviors not considered sex-appropriate.

   <u>Observational learning</u>--Imitate same-sex models

4.   Cognitive-Developmental Theory

Certain cognitive understandings about gender are needed before gender roles can be acquired. Need gender identity, gender stability, and gender consistency.

Then children actively socialize themselves to behave in sex appropriate ways.

5.   Gender Schema Theory

Children acquire gender schemata that influence the kinds of information they attend to and remember.

Children form an in-group/out-group schema for classifying things as appropriate for males or for females.

Children form an own-sex schema that has expanded information about the role of their own sex.

For example, if you know you are a girl, and you know that societal expectations sanction cooking for girls and lawn mowing for boys, then when you are exposed to cooking information, you tend to pay attention and remember it because you believe it is relevant to you. When you are exposed to lawn mowing information, you tend not to pay attention and so don't remember it because you don't believe it is relevant to you.

12

SOCIAL COGNITION AND MORAL DEVELOPMENT

LEARNING OBJECTIVES

After students have read and studied the material in this chapter, they should be able to answer the following questions:

1. What is social cognition?

2. What is a theory of mind? How is it assessed? What developmental changes occur in the understanding of a theory of mind?

3. How does person perception develop? How do role taking skills develop? Why are these skills important?

4. What is morality? What are the three basic components of morality?

5. What is Freud's explanation for the development of morality?

6. How did Kohlberg assess moral reasoning? What are the important characteristics of each level and stage of Kohlberg's theory? What are examples of responses at each stage of reasoning?

7. How do social learning theorists explain moral behavior?

8. What do infants understand about morality and prosocial behavior?

9. What changes in moral reasoning and behavior occur during childhood?

10. What is Piaget's view of moral reasoning during childhood?

11. What parenting characteristics contribute to the development of morality?

12. What changes in moral reasoning occur during adolescence? How is moral development related to antisocial behavior of adolescents? What other factors influence antisocial behavior?

13. What changes in moral reasoning and behavior occur during adulthood?

14. How does Kohlberg's theory of moral reasoning fare in light of research findings? In what ways might the theory be biased or incomplete?

I. **Social Cognition**
   A. Developing a theory of mind
      1. False belief task-- assesses understanding that people can have, and be influenced by, incorrect beliefs
      2. Research on normal development as well as autism
         a. Joint awareness and pretend play in infancy
         b. Around 3-4-- deception and belief-desire psychology
      3. Theory of mind requires cognitive development and social interaction
   B. Person perception
      1. Children younger than 7-8 describe people in physical terms
      2. By 11 or 12, children make social comparisons, see personality traits
   C. Role-taking skills
      1. Ability emerges with concrete operations
      2. Adolescents can juggle multiple perspectives
   D. Social-cognitive development in adulthood
      1. Involves both gains and losses
      2. Depends more on social experience than age

II. **Perspectives on moral development**
   A. Moral affect: Psychoanalytic theory
      1. Formation of superego during phallic stage
      2. Internalization of moral standards
   B. Moral reasoning: Cognitive-developmental theory
      1. Piaget's view
         a. Premoral period in preschool
         b. Children 6-10 believe in unalterable rules of authorities and attend to consequences
         c. At 10 or 11, children believe rules are changeable agreements and attend to intentions
      2. Kohlberg's theory-- universal, invariant sequences
         a. Level 1: Preconventional morality
            i. Punishment and obedience orientation (Stage 1)
            ii. Instrumental hedonism (Stage 2)
         b. Level 2: Conventional morality
            i. "Good boy" or "good girl" morality (Stage 3)
            ii. Authority and social-order-maintaining morality (Stage 4)
         c. Level 3: Postconventional morality
            i. Morality of contract, individual rights, and democratically accepted law (Stage 5)
            ii. Morality of individual principles of conscience (Stage 6)
   C. Moral behavior: Social learning theory
      1. Concern with moral habits and probable consequences of actions
      2. Morality is situation-specific

II. **The infant**
   A. Early moral training
      1. Initially viewed as amoral
      2. Must learn to experience negative emotions when they violate rules, and control impulses to engage in prohibited behaviors
      3. Parents and temperament important
   B. Prosocial behavior
      13-15 month olds capable of prosocial behavior

III. **The child**
   A. Research on Kohlberg's view
      1. Preconventional reasoning
   B. Research on Piaget's view
      1. Ignoring intentions-- Young children base moral judgments on intentions and consequences
      2. Viewing rules as sacred
         a. Turiel found children do distinguish moral rules from social-conventional rules
   C. Moral behavior
      1. Inconsistencies in moral behavior
      2. How does one raise moral children?
         a. Social learning-- reinforce moral behavior, punish immoral behavior, and model moral behavior
         b. Parental approaches
            i. Love withdrawal--sometimes found to have positive effects and other times negative effects
            ii. Power assertion--associated with moral immaturity
            iii. Induction--more often associated with moral maturity
            iv. Role of child's temperament

IV. **The adolescent**
   A. Changes in moral reasoning
      1. Conventional reasoning dominates
   B. Antisocial behavior
      1. Dodge's social information-processing model
         a. Encoding, interpretation, clarification of goals, response search, response decision, and behavioral enactment
         b. Faulty processing at any step can result in an interpretation of a social situation that leads to aggression
      2. Contributors to aggression
         a. Genetic influences
         b. Social influences
            i. Cultural contexts
            ii. Family influences-- coercive family environments

V. **The adult**
   A. Moral development
      1. Postconventional moral reasoning may emerge in adulthood
      2. No real differences in moral reasoning across adulthood
   B. Religion and adult life
      1. Moral and religious growth possible in early and middle adulthood, and these levels are likely maintained
      2. Particularly important to well being of older adults, especially African Americans

VI. **Kohlberg's theory in perspective**
   A. Support for Kohlberg
      1. Stage progression from 1 to 4 does appear to occur as outlined
      2. One individual's stage of reasoning may depend on context
   B. Factors that promote moral growth
      1. Cognitive growth
         a. Perspective-taking abilities and general cognitive abilities are necessary but not sufficient

2. Relevant social experience
    a. Exposure to different views creates cognitive disequilibrium
    b. Roles of parents and peers
    c. Societal context
C. Is the theory biased?
    1. Culture bias
    2. Liberal bias
    3. Gender bias
        a. Carol Gilligan: Morality of care versus morality of justice
D. Is the theory incomplete?
    1. Ignores moral affect and behavior

VII. **Applications: Combating youth violence**
    A. Improving moral reasoning
        1. Peer discussion groups
        2. Improvements in moral reasoning, but need link to delinquent behavior
    B. Building social information processing skills
        1. Training in looking for cues and controlling impulses
        2. Short-term versus long-term changes
    C. Breaking Coercive cycles
        1. Parent training and family therapy
        2. Partially successful

SUGGESTIONS FOR CLASS DISCUSSIONS OR PROJECTS

1.   Students might report on moral dilemmas they have experienced in their own lives. Do they remember any early moral dilemmas? Do they remember how they chose to act, and the reasons for their actions? Was there any difference between how they thought about the dilemma (e.g., what they knew they should do) versus how they acted (what they did do)? Is their thinking about the dilemma different now? Would their course of action be different now? If so, what accounts for these cognitive and behavioral changes? What about more recent moral dilemmas. How are they the same and different from earlier dilemmas? Do students think that if a recent dilemma occurred again later in life, they would behave the same way? Why/ Why not?

2.   An excellent film by Pierre Sauvage (VHS, 1997) allows students to think about moral dilemmas of the most serious kind. *Weapons of the Spirit* tells the story of a Christian mountain community in France that defied the Nazis and turned itself into a haven of refuge for 5,000 Jews, including the filmmaker and his parents. One of the intriguing aspects of this experience is that an entire town of people made the decision to help the Jews, largely without conferring with each other. This would be a good opportunity to revisit Bronfenbrenner and think about moral decision-making beyond the individual level. Other questions for discussion include: What in the development of these individuals might have prepared to make the choices they made? Why do these rescuers resist the label of "hero"?
There are a number of books available on the subjects, as well. Here are a few:
    Hallie, P. P (1994). *Village of Le Chambon and How Goodness Happened There.*
        Harperperennial.
    Block, G., & Drucker, M. (1992). *Rescuers : Portraits of Moral Courage in the Holocaust*t.
        Holmes & Meier.
    Fogelman, E. (1995). *Conscience & Courage : Rescuers of Jews During the Holocaust.*
        Anchor.

3.   Sison (1985) used the characters from the TV show M*A*S*H to illustrate each of Kohlberg's stages of moral reasoning. Reading the article prior to discussion of Kohlberg's theory

may enable students to take a more active role in the discussion. Students find the article engaging, easy to read, and informative. Even if students have never watched the show (or reruns), they still benefit from being able to associate the clear character descriptions with the stages. As an example, Sison used the character of Corporal "Radar" O'Reilly in order to illustrate the "good boy-good girl" stage of moral reasoning. Much of what Radar does is governed by his desire to be a good boy and please the people he looks up to (the Colonel of the M*A*S*H unit and Hawkeye Pierce, one of the surgeons). Radar regularly acts in ways that he thinks will be approved by these significant others and by society in general.

4.   Many students have trouble relating to the traditional Kohlberg moral dilemmas such as the "Heinz dilemma" because they find them out-of-date or unrealistic. (This and other moral dilemmas can be found in Colby, Kohlberg, Gibbs, & Lieberman, 1983-- see Suggested Readings.) Pick a more contemporary topic, such as obeying (or disobeying) traffic rules or cheating (or not cheating) on tests, and ask students to generate responses that fit into each stage of Kohlberg's theory.

5.   You may want to discuss Gilligan's theory of moral reasoning in more detail. See references in the Suggested Readings for more information. There is not a lot of empirical support for Gilligan's theory, but it has been influential in drawing to our attention a different way that people may approach moral dilemmas, and it has served in some ways to balance Kohlberg's emphasis on rights and rules as the way people approach moral dilemmas.

6.   Have students discuss whether moral education or values clarification should be included in the school curriculum. What are the pros and cons? At what age should children be exposed to values clarification? How can values be presented so that they are not offensive to students with different cultural and religious backgrounds?

SUGGESTED FILMS AND VIDEOS

Moral Development (Insight Media, VHS, 30 minutes): Discusses various theoretical models of moral development: Piaget's and Kohlberg's cognitive-developmental models, social learning theory, Freud's psychoanalytic explanation, and Hogan's framework for viewing moral thought and behavior.

Moral Development (CRM Films, VHS and film, 28 minutes): Dramatic recreation of Milgram's classic experiment on obedience which is framed in terms of Kohlberg's stages of moral reasoning.

Morality: The Process of Moral Development. (Davidson Films, VHS and film, 28 minutes): Illustrates unfolding of morality from preschool-age children to young adults and discusses Kohlberg's stages of moral reasoning. Examines children's concepts of sharing, fairness, theft, etc. Elliot Turiel narrates some sections.

Socialization: Moral Development (Harper & Row Media, film, 22 minutes): Covers different theoretical perspectives of moral development, including Piaget, Kohlberg, and Darley.

SUGGESTED READINGS

Colby, A., Kohlberg, L., Gibbs, J., & Lieberman, M. (1983). A longitudinal study of moral judgment. *Monographs of the Society for Research in Child Development, 48* (Nos. 1-2, Serial No. 200).

Gilligan, C. (1993). *In a different voice.* MA: Harvard University Press. [New preface since the 1982 edition]

Gilligan, C., & Attanucci, J. (1988). Two moral orientations: Gender differences and similarities. *Merrill-Palmer Quarterly, 34*, 223-237.

Gilligan, C., Ward, J. V., & Taylor, J. M. (Eds.). (1988). *Mapping the moral domain.* MA: Harvard University Press.

Ginsburg, G., & Bronstein, P. (1993). Family factors related to children's intrinsic/extrinsic motivational orientation. *Child Development, 64*, 1461-1474.

Kruger, A. (1992). The effect of peer and adult-child transactive discussions on moral reasoning. *Merrill-Palmer Quarterly, 38*, 191-211.

Richards, H., Baer, G., Stewart, A., & Norman, A. (1992). Moral reasoning and classroom conduct: Evidence of a curvilinear relationship. *Merrill-Palmer Quarterly, 38*, 176-190.

Schrader, D. E., & Damon, W. (Eds.) (1990). The legacy of Lawrence Kohlberg. *New Directions for Child Development*, vol 49.

Sison, G. (1985). M*A*S*H: An illustration of Kohlberg's stages of moral development. *Journal of Humanistic Psychology, 25*, 83-90.

TRANSPARENCY MASTERS

12.1   Perspectives on moral development

12.2   Piaget's view of moral reasoning

12.3   Kohlberg's theory of moral reasoning

12.4   Dodge's social-information processing model

12.5   Factors that promote growth in moral reasoning

Perspectives on Moral Development

Moral Affect: Psychoanalytic Theory

How a person feels about an action such
as cheating.

Negative emotions: Shame, guilt, anxiety
Positive emotions: Pride, self-satisfaction

Moral Reasoning: Cognitive-Developmental Theory

How a person makes a decision about whether an
action is right or wrong.

Moral Behavior: Social Learning Theory

How a person actually behaves in a situation
when faced with temptation.

Piaget's View of Moral Reasoning

Premoral Period during preschool period

Heteronomous Morality (6-10 years)

"Being under the rule of another"

Rules are moral absolutes; they are unalterable

Consequences are more important than intentions

Punishment is valued for its own sake, not as a teaching tool

Immanent justice: Rule violations <u>will</u> be punished

Autonomous Morality (from about 10-11 years)

"Being self ruled"

Rules are agreements among individuals and can be altered

Intentions are more important than consequences

Punishment should fit the crime and should have some teaching value

Justice is less than perfect; some rule violations go undetected and unpunished

KOHLBERG'S THEORY OF MORAL REASONING

Level I: Pre-Conventional Morality

Stage 1: Punishment-and-obedience orientation
Act is judged in terms of its consequences
If you can get away with it, it's not really bad
Obedience in order to avoid punishment

Stage 2: Instrumental hedonism
Rules are followed if it is in own best interest to do so

Level II: Conventional Morality

Stage 3: "Good boy" or "Good girl" morality
Acts that please or help others are considered good

Stage 4: Authority and social-order-maintaining morality
Acts are good if they conform to social rules and conventions

Level III: Post-Conventional Morality

Stage 5: Morality of contract, individual rights, and democratically accepted law
Concern for individual rights and the general welfare of society; laws are valid if they have been democratically agreed upon

Stage 6: Morality of individual principles of conscience
Concern for living up to self-chosen universally ethical moral princ

Dodge's Social Information Processing Model

1. Encoding
   Search for, attend to, and register cues in the situation

2. Interpretation
   Interpret the situation; infer the other's motive

3. Response Search
   Generate possible ways of responding to the situation

4. Response Evaluation
   Assess likely consequences of the responses generated, and choose the one that seems best

5. Enactment
   Act on the chosen response

Factors that Promote Growth in Moral Reasoning

Cognitive Growth

--Preconventional reasoning-- egocentric perspective
on moral issues

--Conventional reasoning--Need to be able to take
other people's perspectives

--Postconventional reasoning--Need formal operational
thought to reason about abstract   principles

Relevant Social Experience

Interactions with other people who hold different views

--Parents who can encourage children to think about
moral issues

--Parents who use inductive discipline styles

--Peers with whom children (and adults) can discuss
their respective positions on an equal footing

--Advanced schooling

--Living in a diverse, democratic society that successfully
integrates the opinions of many groups

ATTACHMENT AND SOCIAL RELATIONSHIPS

After students have read and studied the material in this chapter, they should be able to answer the following questions:

1.   How do relationships with others contribute to development?

2.   How does Bowlby's attachment theory explain attachment?

3.   In what ways are infants emotional beings? How are emotions socialized and regulated?

4.   What factors contribute to a caregiver's attachment to an infant?

5.   How do infants become attached to a caregiver? What are some observable signs of infant attachment?

6.   How is quality of attachment assessed? What are the types of attachment relationships between infants and caregivers? How do these relate to later development?

7.   What infant and caregiver factors determine the quality of early attachments between infant and caregiver?

8.   What features characterize peer relations and friendships at different points of the life span?

9.   What different types of play evolve during the first few years of life? What are the developmental benefits of play?

10.   What factors contribute to peer acceptance and popularity, or to peer rejection, during childhood?

11.   How do relationships with peers and parents change during adolescence? How do peers and parents influence adolescents' lives?

12.   How do social networks and friendships change during adulthood?

13.   What factors contribute to mate selection? How does type of early attachment style relate to type of romantic relationship?

14.   How can socially isolated and lonely people develop more rewarding relationships?

I.   **Perspectives on relationships**
    A. What do we gain from social relationships?
        1. Learning experiences
        2. Social support
            a. social networks and social convoys
    B. Which relationships are most critical?
        1. Attachment theory (Bowlby and Ainsworth)
            a. First attachment is to caregiver around 6 or 7 months of age
            b. Throughout the life span, attachments are to special, irreplaceable people
                with whom we seek proximity and from whom we derive security
            c. Nature, nurture, and attachment
                i. Biological predisposition to form attachments
                ii. Imprinting, critical periods, and sensitive periods
            d. Implications of attachment-- internal working models of relationships
        2. Peers and the two worlds of childhood
            a. Piaget-- child/child relationships important as well as adult/child
            b. Sullivan-- chumships

II.   **The infant**
    A. Early emotional development
        1. Development of specific emotions
            a. At birth-- interest, distress, disgust and contentment
            b. At 3-7 months, anger then sadness
        2. Socialization of emotions
            a. Mothers encourage positive emotions
            b. Social referencing-- infants seek emotional cues from mothers in
                ambiguous situations
        3. Emotion regulation
            a. Infants rely less and less on caretakers and more on their own emotion
                regulation strategies
    B. The first relationship
        1. Caregiver's attachment to the infant
            a. Infant characteristics affect attachment
            b. Synchronized routines between infants and caregivers
            c. Some adults may have trouble responding to infants
            d. Broader social context influences attachment
        2. Infant's attachment to the caregiver
            a. Undiscriminating social responsiveness
            b. Discriminating social responsiveness
            c. Active proximity seeking/True attachment
            d. Goal-corrected partnership
            e. Attachment-related fears-- Separation and stranger anxieties
        3. Exploratory behavior
            a. Attachment facilitates exploration-- Secure base
    C. Types of attachment
        1. Four types assessed in the Strange Situation
            a. Secure attachment
            b. Resistant attachment
            c. Avoidant attachment
            d. Disorganized/disoriented attachment
        2. Influences on the quality of early attachments
            a. The caregiver's contributions

        i. Freud-- oral pleasure

        ii. Harlow-- contact comfort

        iii. Erikson-- general responsiveness

        iv. Parenting styles

    b. The infant's contributions

        i. Cognitive development

        ii. Temperament

D. Early attachment and later development

    1. The effects of social deprivation in infancy

        a. Grief at early separation from attachment figure

            i. Protest, despair, and detachment

        b. Studies of institutionalized infants

    2. Later development of securely and insecurely attached infants

        a. Securely attached: leaders, curious, self-directed

        b. Insecurely attached: socially and emotionally withdrawn, hesitant, less curious, less goal-oriented

        c. Insecure attachment to mother may be mitigated

            i. Affectionate ties with father

            ii. Attachment status with mother may change

            iii. Social relationships after infancy may be important

E. First Peer Relations

    1. Development of infant sociability

        a. Stages

            i. Object-centered

            ii. Simple interactive

            iii. Complementary interactive

III.   **The child**

A. Parent/child attachments-- goal corrected partnerships

B. Peer networks

    1. From 2-12, increasing time spent with peers and less with adults

    2. Gender segregation increases with age

C. Play

    1. Play becomes more social

        a. Unoccupied play

        b. Solitary play

        c. Onlooker play

        d. Parallel play

        e. Associative play

        f. Cooperative play

    2. Play becomes more imaginative

        a. Pretend play, then social pretend play

    3. Play becomes more rule-governed

    4. What is good play?

        a. Play sharpens skills and contributes to development

D. Peer acceptance and popularity

    1. Social status

        a. Four categories-- popular, rejected, neglected, and controversial

        b. Popularity affected by attractiveness, academic skills, social competence

        c. Rejected status associated with negative outcomes

E. Friendships

    1. Importance of at least one reciprocated friendship

    2. Meaning of friendship depends on developmental level-- common activities, mutual loyalty, and psychological similarity

F. Contributions of peers to development
    1. Important for learning social skills
    2. Contribute to emotional well-being
    3. Foster cognitive growth
    4. Acceptance by peers may boost self-esteem

IV. **The adolescent**
    A. Attachment to parents
        1. Continue to need security and support
            a. Facilitates adjustment to autonomy, e.g., going to college
            b. Contributes to sense of identity
    B. Friendships
        1. Mutual intimacy and self-disclosure
        2. Psychological similarity
        3. Gender differences in same-sex friendships
        4. Comparison of same-sex to cross-sex friendships
    C. Changing social networks-- From same-sex peer groups to dating relationships
        1. Cliques and crowds
        2. Dating
    D. Parent and peer influence on adolescents
        1. Conformity
            a. Conformity to parents decreases and conformity to peers increases
            b. Parents and peers influence different aspects of behavior

V. **The adult**
    A. Social networks
        1. Selectivity hypothesis to explain shrinking social network
    C. Romantic relationships
        1. Partner selection (Udry)
            a. Similarity in backgrounds
            b. Complementarity of strengths and weaknesses
            c. Readiness for marriage
        2. Attachment styles
            a. Types of attachment-- Secure, preoccupied, dismissing, fearful
            b. Styles grow out of early experiences
    D. Adult friendships
        1. Importance of equity
    E. Adult relationships and adult development
        1. Quality, not quantity, of social relationships affects well-being
        2. Importance of confidants

VI. **Applications: Building good relationships**

SUGGESTIONS FOR CLASS DISCUSSIONS OR PROJECTS

1.   In 1993, a 2 1/2-year-old known as "Baby Jessica" was permanently separated from her adoptive parents after her biological parents succeeded in regaining custody of her. Many were haunted by the image of a screaming Jessica being driven off in a van from the only family she had known. Ask students to predict this little girl's short-term adjustment and long-term adjustment based on Bowlby's attachment theory. Then report that 8 months later, Jessica, now named Anna Jacqueline, was apparently thriving and had experienced none of the serious traumatic effects (e.g., eating problems, sleeping problems, weepiness) that had been predicted by all the experts (see _Newsweek_, March 21, 1994).

The course of Baby Jessica's transition into her new family appears to be quite different than the courses experienced by internationally-adopted children as described in the *New York Times Magazine* (May 24, 1998). What are some of the differences in these situations that might account for the poorer prognosis of the children described in the *New York Times*?

2.	Why do some children become attached to soft objects like blankets or stuffed animals? Passman and Weisberg (1975) suggest that these attachments may help children manage stress and anxiety and they designed an experiment to test this, which is reported in *Developmental Psychology* (*11*, pp. 170-177). Many students find this article interesting to read and discuss because they, or someone close to them, had an attachment to an inanimate object. There is more information on this subject in Passman and Halonen (*Journal of Genetic Psychology*, 1979, *134*, 165-178).

3.	Hazan and Shaver have done research on adult attachment styles [Hazan, C. & Shaver, P. R. (1990). Love and work: An attachment-theoretical perspective. Journal of Personality and *Social Psychology*, *59*, 270-280]. Students might enjoy seeing the short descriptors of avoidant, anxious/ambivalent, and secure adults. Do these adult styles seem to map well to the infant styles? How much continuity in styles would students expect to exist across the life span? What experiences *after* infancy might alter one's attachment style?

4.	Have students discuss what makes someone popular at different points of the life span. If possible, have students talk with middle-aged and older adults about what makes someone popular with these age groups.
	• What are the characteristics of popular peers at different ages?
	• Do these characteristics remain stable across the life span?
	• Do students expect the "in-crowd" from their high school to still be "in" when they return for their tenth or twenty-fifth class reunion?
Now consider the issue of rejection. How are the dynamics of rejected status consistent versus inconsistent across the life span?

5.	To help students think more about friendship development, have them reflect on their first friend. Before beginning the class discussion, you might ask for a show of hands in response to the following questions so that students can assess the diversity in the classroom:
	• How old were the students (preschool, middle childhood, preadolescent, other)?
	• Were their friends younger, older, or the same age?
	• Were the friends the same sex?
	• Were they biologically related?
	• How long did the friendship endure (less than a year, 2 to 5 years, more than 5 years)?
After gaining an appreciation for these parameters of friendships, students might then discuss the nature of their friendships.
	• What made that person a friend?
	• What factors are important at different ages?
	• What led to the end of the friendship (if it ended) and what contributed to its maintenance for as long as it lasted?
	• For friendships that lasted, how did the interpersonal dynamics change over time?

6.	How does the college environment affect development of friendships? How might college friendships differ from friendships developed in other settings? Ask students if they have friends who have not attended college. Do they see any differences between their friendships with these individuals and their friendships with individuals who have attended college? Do they believe that two people who have gone to college together have a different quality to their friendship than two people who have not gone to college together? Why or why not?

SUGGESTED FILMS AND VIDEOS

Childhood: Among Equals (WNET co-production, 1991by Ambrose Video, reissued 1995 by American Brain Tumor Association, VHS, 57 minutes): Part 5 of this 7-part series examines the importance of peer relationships as a crucial component of development. The film shows how boys interact with boys at an early age, and how girls interact with girls in distinctive and different ways.

Life's First Feelings (COR, VHS, 58 minutes): A NOVA program that discusses the emotional development of human infants.

Mother Love (IND, film, 26 minutes): An old film that shows Harlow's experiments on the mother-infant relationships in rhesus monkeys.

SUGGESTED READINGS

Ainsworth, M. D. (1964). Patterns of attachment behavior shown by the infant in interaction with his mother. *Merrill-Palmer Quarterly, 10(1),* 51-58.

Asher, S. R., & Coie, J. D. (1990). *Peer rejection in childhood.* Cambridge: Cambridge University Press.

Bowlby, J. (1980) *Attachment and Loss, Vols. I-III.* New York: Basic Books.

Bennett, M. (Ed.). (1993). *The development of social cognition.* NY: Guilford Publications.

Brazelton, T. B. (1982). *On becoming a family: The growth of attachment.* NY: Dell.

Brazelton, T. B., & Yorgman, M. E. (1986). *Affective development in infancy.* NY: Ablex.

Calkins, S., & Fox, F. (1992). The relations among infant temperament, security of attachment, and behavioral inhibition at twenty-four months. *Child Development, 63,* 1456-1472

Gottman, J. M., & Parker, J. G. (1987). *Conversations of friends.* NY: Cambridge University Press.

Hartup, W. W. (1996). The company they keep: Friendships and their developmental significance. *Child Development, 67,* 1-12.

Howes, C. (1988). Peer interaction of young children. *Monographs of the Society for Research in Child Development, 53* (1, Serial No. 217).

Isabella, R. (1993). Origins of attachment: Maternal interactive behavior across the first year. *Child Development, 64,* 605-621.

Lyons-Ruth, K., Alpern, L., & Repacholi, B. (1993). Disorganized infant attachment classification and maternal psychosocial problems as predictors of hostile-aggressive behavior in the classroom. *Child Development, 64,* 572-585.

Nugent, J. K., Lester, B. M., & Brazelton, T. B. (1989), *The cultural context of infancy.* Norwood, NJ: Ablex Publishing Co.

Sperling, M., & Berman, W. (Eds.). (1994). *Attachment in adults: Clinical and developmental perspectives.* NY: Guilford Publications.

Stern, D. N. (1973). *The interpersonal world of the infant*. New York: Basic Books.

TRANSPARENCY MASTERS

Phases of attachment development

1. <u>Undiscriminating social responsiveness</u>
    (birth to 2-3 months)

    Any person will do; no specific preference

2. <u>Discriminating social responsiveness</u>
    (2-3 months to 6-7 months)

    Preference for familiar people

3. <u>Active proximity seeking/True attachment</u>
    (6-7 months to 3 years)

    Clear attachments, often to mother

4. <u>Goal-corrected partnership</u>
    (3 years and older)

    Can adjust behavior in order to remain close to attachment figure

Theories of Attachment

1. Psychoanalytic

   I love you because you feed me.

   Freud: Oral pleasure

   Erikson: General responsiveness

2. Learning

   I love you because you are reinforcing.

   Caregiver becomes associated with pleasurable sensations.

3. Cognitive-Developmental

   I love you because I know you.

   Discrimination of social from nonsocial stimuli
   Person permanence

4. Ethological

   I love you because I was born to love.

   Infants and adults are biologically predisposed to respond to one another and form attachments.

Quality of Attachment (Ainsworth)

1. Secure Attachment

Protests mother's leaving; welcomes her back; uses her as a secure base for exploration; interacts with   strangers when mother is present.

(70% of 1-year-olds)

2. Resistant Attachment

Strongly protests mother's leaving; ambivalent about   her return; doesn't use her as a secure base; wary of strangers even when mother is present.

(10% of 1-year-olds)

3. Avoidant Attachment

Not distressed by mother's leaving; doesn't welcome   her back; ignores contact initiated by mother; indifferent   with strangers, as with caregiver.

(20% of 1-year-olds)

Developmental outcomes for securely and insecurely attached infants

Securely attached as infants

Initiate play activities

Sensitive to needs and feelings of other children

Popular among peers

Described as curious, self-directed, eager to learn

Insecurely attached as infants

Socially and emotionally withdrawn

Hesitant to engage other children in play activities

Described as less curious, less likely to pursue goals, and less eager to learn

Changes in family situation can change the quality of attachments later on, and so quality of infant attachment does not always predict later behaviors.

Are the theories of attachment supported by research?

1. Freud's theory about oral gratification as the basis of attachment lacks support

2. Erikson's notion of responsive parenting is supported

3. Learning theory's emphasis on reinforcing qualities of caregivers is supported

4. Cognitive-developmental theory's claim that certain cognitive milestones are necessary is supported

5. Bowlby-Ainsworth's ethological theory is well supported, possibly because it is a broad theory

   Internal working models of relationships can influence later relationships, but also can be altered by later relationships.

Categories of Social Status

Popular Children: Well liked by most; rarely disliked

Rejected Children: Rarely liked; often disliked

Neglected Children: Neither liked nor disliked; seem to be
                           invisible

Controversial: Liked by many and disliked by many

What factors influence popularity?

Personal characteristics: Names, attractiveness

Social competencies: Good role-taking skills, cooperative, responsive to others, good conflict resolution

Secure attachments as infants

Contextual factors (cultural definitions of popular)

14

THE FAMILY

After students have read and studied the material in this chapter, they should be able to answer the following questions:

1. How is the family viewed by the family systems theory?

2. How do individual family systems change? How have families in general changed during the 20th century?

3. How is the father/infant relationship similar to and different from the mother/infant relationship?

4. How do parents indirectly affect their children?

5. What are two basic dimensions of parenting? What patterns of child rearing emerge from these dimensions? How do these parenting styles affect children's development?

6. How do social class, culture, and ethnic variations affect parenting style?

7. What effects do children have on their parents?

8. What features characterize sibling relationships across the life span? How do siblings contribute to development?

9. What are relationships like between adolescents and their parents?

10. How does marriage and parenthood affect adults? What changes occur in the family as the children mature and leave home?

11. What sorts of roles do grandparents establish with their grandchildren?

12. How do various family relationships change during adulthood?

13. What sorts of diversity exist in today's families? What is the life satisfaction of people in these different types of families?

14. How does divorce affect family relationships?

15. How can spouse abuse and child abuse be reduced?

I. **Understanding the family**
   A. The family as a system
      1. Nuclear family
            a. reciprocal influence
      2. Extended family household
   B. The family as a system within other systems
      1. Ecological approach
   C. The family as a changing system
      1. Family development theories
            a. Family life cycle-- eight stages
   D. A changing family system in a changing world
      1. More single adults
      2. Postponed marriages
      3. Fewer children
      4. More women working
      5. More divorce
      6. More single-parent families
      7. More children living in poverty
      8. More remarriages (and reconstituted families)
      9. More- years without children
      10. More multigeneration families

II. **The infant**
   A. The mother/infant relationship
   B. The father/infant relationship
      1. Fathers are as capable of caring for infants as mothers
      2. Mothers and fathers differ in both quantity and quality of interactions with infants
   C. Mothers, fathers, and infants: The system at work
      1. Indirect effects of parents
      2. Children benefit when parents are mutually supportive

III. **The child**
   A. Dimensions of child rearing
      1. Dimensions of parenting
            a. Acceptance/responsiveness: Extent of parents' support, sensitivity to needs, warmth and praise
            b. Demandingness/control: How much control parents have over decisions
      2. Patterns of child rearing
            a. Four patterns (based on crossing two dimensions above)
                  i. Authoritarian parenting-- highly restrictive with expectations for strict obedience, low acceptance/responsiveness
                  ii. Authoritative parenting-- parents establish and explain rules, listen to their children, and are flexible
                  iii. Permissive parenting-- parents make few demands and exert little control over children
                  iv. Neglectful parenting-- parents uninvolved in upbringing
            b. Child outcomes associated with patterns
                  i. Best outcomes from warmth combined with moderate parental control (authoritative)
                  ii. Worst outcomes from uninvolved parents (neglectful)
      3. Social class, economic hardship, and parenting
            a. Class differences associated with differences in parenting styles

          i. Different goals and values
          ii. Different stressors
          iii. Different skills required for success
    4. Cultural and ethnic variation in parenting
        a. Authoritative style associated with positive outcomes in most groups
        b. Differences in beliefs and values still lead to some differences in parenting style and outcomes
    5. Child effects on parents
        a. Parenting style changes, for example, in response to child's age, competence, and temperament
  B. Sibling relationships
    1. A new baby arrives
        a. Sibling rivalry
    2. Ambivalence in sibling relationships
        a. Relationships characterized by both closeness and conflict
        b. Personalities and parenting behaviors affect sibling relationships
    3. Contributions to development
        a. Emotional support
        b. Caretaking services
        c. Teachers

IV.   **The adolescent**
  A. Parent/child closeness
    1. Adolescent-parent relationships similar to child-parent relationships
  B. Renegotiating the relationship
    1. Task of achieving autonomy
    2. Conflicts temporarily increase; parents turn over more power
    3. At the same time, adolescents try to maintain attachment with parents

V.   **The adult**
  A. Establishing the marriage
    1. Life transition with new roles
    2. Honeymoon is short-lived
  B. New parenthood
    1. Stressful transition with both positive and negative changes
        a. Marital satisfaction declines, especially for women
        b. Individual differences in adjustment to parenthood
           i.   Personal resources
           ii. Outside resources
  C. The child-rearing family
    1. Additional children
        a. Added strain on the family
        b. Slight decline in marital satisfaction continues
    2. Challenges when children reach adolescence
  D. The empty nest
    1. Parents generally respond positively to children leaving home
    2. Trend toward delayed empty nest and "refilling"
  E. Grandparenthood
    1. Styles of grandparenting
        a. Remote
        b. Companionate
        c. Involved
  F. Changing family relationships
    1. The marital relationship

a. Dips and recoveries in marital satisfaction, more so for women

b. Usually marital quality stable

2. Sibling relationships

a. Decreased contact, less conflict than during childhood

b. More closeness

3. Parent/child relationships

a. Forming more mutual relationships

b. Modified extended family

c. Myth of role reversal in parents' old age

d. Caring for aging parents

i. Middle generation squeeze-- middle aged adults experiencing heavy demands from young and older generation

ii. Caregiver burden-- psychological distress from caring for someone with impairments

VI. **Diversity in family life**

A. Singles

1. Cohabitation

B. Childless married couples

C. Gay and lesbian families

D. Families experiencing divorce

1. Before the divorce

a. Marital distress, trial separations

2. After the divorce

a. Emotional distress; higher risk for depression and health problems

b. Disturbance of parent-child relations

c. Most problems disappear a couple of years post-divorce

E. Remarriage and reconstituted families

1. Period of conflict and disruption

VII. **Applications: Confronting the problem of family violence**

A. Why does family violence occur?

1. The abuser

2. The abused

3. The context

B. What are the effects of abuse?

C. How do we solve the problem?

SUGGESTIONS FOR CLASS DISCUSSIONS OR PROJECTS

1.   Have the students locate a child, preferably one that they do not know very well. The child should be old enough to draw and explain a picture. Have the child to draw a picture of his/her family (colored pencils, crayons or markers would be good to have on hand). After the child draws the picture, ask him/her to explain the picture and record the explanation on the picture, or on a separate piece of paper (but not on the back of the picture-- the class needs to be able to see both the picture and the description at once). Also write the chlid's age. The students should separately record any of their observations. Display all the pictures on the classroom wall, perhaps grouped by age, and have the class reflect on developmental changes in children's conceptions of the family (observations about perception and creativity across the life span might also be collected).

2.   In order to gain a better understanding of the experience of being in different types of families, students might read the Message Boards at the Parent's Place web site. There are message boards where parents can converse with each other on a vast number of topics, including transracial

adoption, adopting an older child, stepfamilies, military parents, teenage parents, gay and lesbian parents, multiple births. Before students search through the message boards, they might want to do a brief research report on a particular family type, and then see if any of the topics that are of concern to researchers also emerge as parental concerns. Does it sound as if the researchers and the parents are talking about the same population? Do parents seem informed about the current research? The web address is: http://www.parentsplace.com/genobject.cgi/talking.html. In addition to web sites, students might also look for internet discussion groups on a family structure of interest to them.

3.   Many students in class have experienced divorce either directly or indirectly. If students feel comfortable, ask them to discuss the impact of divorce on themselves or people they know. A number of question might be discussed:
  • How is the experience of divorce related to the child's age at the time of the divorce?
  • What about the age of the parents?
  • How are the effects of divorce the same and different for male versus female children and parents?
  • How does culture come into play? What about historical factors (e.g., the effects of divorce now versus 10 years ago versus 30 years ago)?
  • Should there be any interventions for children or for parents undergoing divorce? What might these intervention look like?

4.   Have students determine how parents manifesting different styles (e.g., authoritarian, permissive, or authoritative) would respond to various family situations. For example, what if a child is watching television or playing with friends and the parent says it is time to go to bed and the child does not want to go? Or suppose parents have repeatedly told their child not to keep going through the fence into the neighbor's yard and the child continues to do so? Or a child who knows she is supposed to make her bed in the morning before going to school, but always waits until it's too late--if she makes the bed, she'll miss the school bus and will need a ride to school. How would parents using Baumrind's different styles of parental control respond in these situations?

5.   Have students consider competency testing for parents. This issue emerges in several contexts. For example, when a child who has been abused on numerous occasions and removed from the abusive home, is returned only to be killed by the abusive parents. As another example, the competency of parents has been questioned in cases of mildly retarded parents of children with normal intelligence. Should there be any requirements for parents? What would they be? How would they be monitored?

6.   Consider the "sandwich" generation--Middle-aged adults caring for their children and their aging parents. What impact do aging parents have on their children? What effects is this situation likely to have on grandchildren? Ask students if any of their parents are experiencing middle generation squeeze. What stresses does this place on the entire family? What benefits are realized from this experience?

7.   Discuss how changes in society such as geographic mobility, daycare, and divorce have contributed to changes in the quality of grandparent-grandchildren relationships. If possible, have students interview people of different ages about their experiences with their grandparents (and grandchildren, if any). Is it possible to identify the different styles of grandparenting noted in the text? Are there other styles of grandparenting that are evident from students' descriptions of their relationships with grandparents? How many factors can they identify that contribute to different patterns of grandparent-grandchildren relationships.

Childhood: In the Land of Giants (WNET co-production, 1991by Ambrose Video, reissued 1995 by American Brain Tumor Association, VHS, 57 minutes): Part 4 of this 7-part series features children from age 3-5 learning the psychological and social intricacies of family life. It demonstrates how the world affects the family, and in turn how the family teaches children to interact socially at day care and school.

Children of Divorce (Films for the Humanities, VHS, 28 minutes): This is a specially adapted Phil Donahue program that addresses the influence of parents' divorce on children into their adulthood.

Coping with Family Crisis: Violence, Abuse, Divorce (Insight Media, VHS, 52 minutes): People who have experienced family violence, abuse, or divorce talk about survival.

Do Children Also Divorce? (Filmakers Library, VHS, 30 minutes): Portrays typical behaviors expressed by children of different ages in response to divorce.

Fathers and Toddlers (Films for the Humanities, VHS, 28 minutes): Another specially adapted Phil Donahue program that looks at what fathers have learned and experienced during their child's first two years.

Life with Baby: How do the Parents Feel? (Filmakers Library, VHS and film, 27 minutes): This documentary shows how three families adjust to the demands of a new baby.

Parenting our Parents (Films for the Humanities and Sciences, VHS, 26 minutes): Looks at middle age adults who have children and parents to care for.

Violence in the Family (Insight Media, VHS, 55 minutes): Uses case histories to examine causes, characteristics, and possible solutions to family violence.

SUGGESTED READINGS

Boer, F., & Dunn, J. (Eds.). (1992). *Children's sibling relationships: Developmental and clinical issues.* NJ: Lawrence Erlbaum Associates.

Brooks, G. R., & Gilbert, L. A. (1995). Men in families: Old constraints, new possibilities. In R. F. Levant & W. S. Pollack (Eds), *A new psychology of men.* New York: Basic Books.

Coontz, S. (1992). *The way we never were : American families and the nostalgia trap.* New York: Basic Books

Coontz, S. (1998). *The Way We Really Are : Ending the War over America's Changing Families.* New York: Basic Books.

Cowan, P. A., & Hetherington, E. M. (Eds.) (1990). *Family transitions.* NJ: Lawrence Erlbaum Associates.

Elder, G. H., & Liker, J. K. (1984). Parent-child behavior in the Great Depression: Life course and intergenerational influences. *Life-span Development and Behavior, 6,* 109-158.

Emery, R. E. (1989). Family violence. *American Psychologist, 44,* 321-328.

Harrison, A. O., Wilson, M. N., Pine, C. J., Chan, S. Q., & Buriel, R. (1990). Family ecologies of ethnic minority children. *Child Development, 61*, 347-362.

Hetherington, E. M., & Clingempeel, W. G. (1992). Coping with marital transitions. *Monographs of the Society for Research in Child Development, 57* (Serial No. 227).

Hetherington, E. M., Stanley-Hagan, M., & Anderson, E. R. (1989). Marital transitions. *American Psychologist, 44*, 303-312.

Hinde, R. A., & Stevenson-Hinde, J. (Eds.) (1988). *Relationships within families.* NY: Oxford University Press.

Huston, A. C. (Ed.) (1991). *Children and poverty: Child development and public policy.* NY: Cambridge University Press.

Kotzlowitz, A. (1991). *There are no children here.* New York: Anchor Books.

Parke, R. D., & Ladd, G. W. (Eds.). (1992). *Family-peer relationships: Modes of linkage.* NJ: Lawrence Erlbaum Associates.

Patterson, C. J. (1995). Lesbian mothers, gay fathers, and their children. In A. R. D'Augelli & C. J. Patterson (Eds). *Lesbian, gay, and bisexual identities over the lifespan.* New York: Oxford University Press.

Smith, P. K. (Ed.) (1991). *The psychology of grandparenthood: An international perspective.* NY: Routledge.

Wallerstein, J., & Blakeslee, S. (1989). *Second chances: Men, women and children a decade after divorce.* Virginia Barber Literary Agency. [Excerpted in *The New York Times Magazine* (January 22, 1989; pp. 18-21 and 41-44).]

TRANSPARENCY MASTERS

14.1   Changes in the family system

14.2   Dimensions of parenting

14.3   Factors that influence adjustment to divorce

Changes in the Family System

1. Increased number of single adults.

2. Postponement of marriage.

3. Decreased childbearing (having fewer children).

4. Increased female participation in the labor force.

5. Increased divorce (up to 60% of newly married couples).

6. Increased numbers of single-parent families.

7. Increased numbers of children living in poverty.

8. Increased remarriage (formation of reconstituted families).

9. Increased years without children.

10. More multigenerational families.

Dimensions of Parenting

	Warmth	Hostility
Permissive	Loving, affectionate, autonomy granting, liberal or lax	Cold, distant, neglectful, ignoring
Restrictive	Loving, affectionate, strict, firm	Cold, distant, strict, harsh

The best child outcomes are associated with warmth and moderate parental control. Too much control can lead to lack of confidence and lack of self-reliance; too little control can lead to being selfish and unruly because children haven't learned self-control.

Children whose parents are hostile and restrictive tend to be withdrawn, inhibited, and low in self-esteem.

Children whose parents are hostile and permissive tend to be hostile and rebellious, and are likely to engage in delinquent acts and abuse drugs.

Factors Influencing Adjustment to Divorce

1. Adequate financial support following the divorce.

2. Adequate parenting by the custodial parent.
   Parenting that continues to be warm, authoritative, and consistent following the divorce.

3. Emotional support from the noncustodial parent.
   Regular contact with supportive fathers (if custodial parent is the mother) facilitates adjustment.

4. Additional social support.
   Supportive friends and family for the divorcing parents and the children aids adjustment.

5. A minimum of additional stressors.
   The more stressors there are (moving, finding a new   job, losing the children, etc.), the more difficult the adjustment to divorce.

15

ACHIEVEMENTS

After students have read and studied the material in this chapter, they should be able to answer the following questions:

1. What is the need for achievement? What factors influence achievement motivation? How do attributions affect achievement?

2. What factors influence mastery motivation of infants? How is this related to later achievement?

3. How does play promote mastery motivation?

4. What factors contribute to differences in levels of achievement motivation during childhood?

5. How does school affect children? What factors characterize effective schools?

6. What changes in achievement motivation occur during adolescence? What factors contribute to these changes?

7. How do adolescents make vocational choices? How does work affect adolescence?

8. How does achievement motivation change during adulthood?

9. How do career paths change during adulthood? How does Levinson's theory conceptualize family and work roles?

10. How does work affect women's lives?

11. How are older adults influenced by retirement?

12. How can the quality of education be improved?

I. **Achievement motivation**
    A. Need for achievement (McClelland)-- "learned motive to compete and strive for
        success whenever one's behavior can be evaluated against a standard of excellence"
    B. The value placed on achievement
    C. Expectancies of success
    D. Attributions for success and failure
        1. Locus of control-- internal or external
        2. Stability of causes of success

II. **The infant**
    A. Early origins of achievement motivation
        1. Effectance motivation-- desire to have an effect on or control objects and people
        2. Influences on effectance motivation
            a. Sensory stimulation
            b. Responsive environment
            c. Secure attachment
    B. Mastery through play
        1. Developmental sequence
            a. Before 1 year-- body play, acting on world, interest in toys,
            b. After 1 year
                i. Functional play
                ii. Pretend play (symbolic capacity)

III. **The child**
    A. Mastery-oriented and helpless achievement styles
        1. Age differences
            a. Before age 7
                i. Unrealistic optimism
                ii. Incremental view of ability and learning goals
            b. Older children
                i. Entity view of ability and performance goals
        2. Parent contributions
    B. Schooling and school achievement
        1. Benefits of preschool
            a. Overemphasis on academics may undermine achievement motivation
            b. May have greatest positive impact on disadvantaged children
        2. Benefits of school
            a. Transmit basic knowledge and academic skills
            b. Informal curriculum-- how to fit into the culture
        3. Effective schools
            a. Factors that often have little to do with a school's effectiveness
                i. Level of funding
                ii. Average class size
            b. Factors that matter more
                i. Student aptitude
                ii. Emphasis on academics
                iii. Task-oriented but comfortable environment
                iv. Effective discipline
                v. Supportive parents and communities
                vi. Aptitude-treatment interaction-- match between learner and
                    teaching method
        4. Making integration and inclusion work

a. Cooperative learning methods

IV. **The adolescent**
   A. Declining achievement motivation
      1. Cognitive growth
      2. Negative feedback
      3. Peer pressures
      4. Pubertal changes
      5. Poor person-environment fit
   B. Making vocational choices
      1. Fantasy stage (younger than 10)
      2. Tentative stage (11-18 years)
         a. Consider interests, capacities, and values
      3. Realistic stage (over 18)
         a. Also consider realities of job market
   C. Working after school
      1. More work hours associated with disengagement from school and distress
   D. Pathways to adulthood
      1. Choices constrained by traditional gender role norms

V. **The adult**
   A. Achievement motivation
      1. More affected by changing work and family contexts than by age
   B. Daniel Levinson's conception of adult development
      1. Life structure
      2. Stages of adult development
   C. Career paths during adulthood
      1. Exploration and establishment
         a. In early adulthood, explore options, before settling into a particular career
      2. Midlife crisis?
         a. Adults may experience intense inner struggles and disturbing realizations in early 40s
      3. Aging workers
         a. No decline in job performance
            i. Selective optimization with compensation
         b. Increase in job satisfaction
   C. Women, work, and the family
      1. Sex discrimination
         a. Traditional female jobs pay less
         b. Women may not rise as far in organizations or make as much
         c. Women receive less support for careers
      2. Role conflict and overload
         a. Conflicting demands of work and family
         b. Role overload--Too much to do in the time available
         c. Quality of a person's experience in work and family roles associated with well-being
      3. Implications for children
         a. No indication that maternal work is negative for children
         b. More positive for female children
   D. Work and adult development
      1. Substantive complexity
         a. Intellectually challenging work associated with greater intellectual flexibility and greater self-direction
   E. Retirement

1. Phases of adjusting to retirement: Preretirement, honeymoon, disenchantment, reorientation
2. Reduction in income
3. Change in activity patterns but no decline in health
F. Successful aging
  1. Activity theory-- Need to maintain existing levels of activity
  2. Disengagement theory-- Need a mutual withdrawal of individual and society
  3. Successful aging is not activity alone
    a. Relationship between level of activity and well-being is often weak
    b. Some features of disengagement theory have merit
    c. Individual differences in personality traits and preferences

VI.   **Applications: Improving the quality of education**

SUGGESTIONS FOR CLASS DISCUSSIONS OR PROJECTS

1.   Have students reflect on early career choices. What do they remember as their earliest answers to the question "What do you want to be when you grow up?" Can they identify some career choices that reflect the three stages discussed in the text (fantasy stage, tentative stage, realistic stage)? Do they have any memories of what led them to abandon some of their earlier career choices? Students might also ask children, preadolescents, and adolescents about their career choices and look for evidence of the different stages in these responses. Adults could also be interviewed about when and how they decided on the careers in which they currently work. What factors might be involved in someone always knowing what they wanted to be versus still not being sure, even as adults?

2.   Have students develop a set of "ideal" conditions for day care of infants and young children. You might present the class with the standards for day care licensing in your state, and have them discuss how the standards compare to the ideal conditions.
      The web site for the Children's Defense Fund is a very worthwhile site that is mentioned here because of its attention to day care issues. Students might go to this site to compare statistics for their state with other states. What factors at different levels of analysis (Bronfenbrenner's model) account for the variety of standards? The Children's Defense Fund web site can be found at: http://www.childrensdefense.org (see "Children in the States: 1998" data under News and Reports).

3.   Ask students to discuss factors that should or could be used to indicate readiness for school. Traditionally, age (6 years) has been used as the indicator, and this works fine for the average child. Besides age, what other factors should be considered?

4.   Discuss the topic of ageism (discrimination on the basis of age, usually referring to older adults). A good starting point might be Fried's five activities designed to increase students' awareness of attitudes, stereotypes, feelings toward aging [Fried, S. B. (1988). Learning activities for understanding aging. *Teaching of Psychology, 15*, 160-162]. See also the exercises developed by Pulos and by Palmore mentioned in the Chapter 5 course suggestions.
      The discussion of ageism might include the following questions:
      • What factors contribute to ageism?
      • What techniques could be used to reduce ageism?
      • How has ageism changed historically?
      • How does culture come into play?
      • Does ageism affect men and women differently? How and why?
      • Are the elderly the only age group that experience ageism?
      An episode of *Primetime Live* on ABC recently (June 9, 1994) reported on one aspect of ageism particularly relevant to this chapter--age discrimination in the workplace. Age discrimination was demonstrated by having the same person apply for a job, in one instance dressed as usual, and in

the other instance dressed and made-up as an older (but not elderly) person. In both cases, the person presented the same qualifications, but the "younger" person was treated more favorably during the interview and was offered the job.

5.   Have students discuss what psychologists know about the advantages and disadvantages of adolescents working while they are in high school. *U.S. News & World Report* has noted (May 17 1993, p. 68) that three out of every four high school juniors and seniors work part- or full-time jobs. Several recent studies (e.g., L. Steinberg, S. Fegley & S. Dornbusch, 1993, *Developmental Psychology*, *29*, 171-180) have found that teenagers who work more than 15-20 hours per week get lower grade point averages, are absent from school more often, and spend less time on homework than other teenagers. Other negative correlates of working include an increase in alcohol and other drug use, an increase in somatic complaints, a decrease in closeness to parents, and less involvement in extracurricular school activities. Steinberg and Dornbusch (in *Developmental Psychology*, 1991, *27*, 304-313) also found that working did not increase self-esteem, self-reliance, or work orientation of adolescents. Leaving the work force, or cutting back on long hours, has been associated with an increase in school performance. When discussing this in class, you might have students reflect on their own work experiences, and see if they can develop recommendations for teenagers who want to work during the school year.

In the context of young people and work, students might also look at Ellen Greenberger's 1983 article (see Suggested Readings). This article demonstrates the impact that developmental research can have on public policy. Would any of the policy recommendations you would make be different now than they were in 1983? Is there any developmental research in other areas that you have learned about that seems to have important implications for current social policy?

6.   Discuss whether Levinson's theory of adult development, which was based on male experiences, applies to women. Do women go through the same transitions? Where might there be differences between males and females? Levinson (1997) recently wrote a follow-up to his 1986 book on men's development entitled *The Seasons of a Woman's Life* (1997; written with Judy Levinson). Students might wish to compare these two texts.

7.   Have students discuss what would characterize "successful" aging in their own lives. Do students know any people who they believe model successful aging? Where would students like to be and what would they like to be doing in late adulthood? The recent article by Schulz and Heckhausen (see Suggested Readings) offers one view of successful aging that might be a starting point for alternative views. This might also be a good topic for which to organize a panel discussion of older adults, or perhaps plan a field trip to a Senior Center to conduct some interviews. (Seniors' contributions to discussions of life span development need not be limited to their experience of aging, however. The wisdom of seniors might be tapped for insights into more general issues, as well.)

SUGGESTED FILMS AND VIDEOS

Childhood: Life's Lessons (WNET co-production, 1991by Ambrose Video, reissued 1995 by American Brain Tumor Association, VHS, 57 minutes): Part 5 of this 7-part series observes the behavior of children of different cultures between the ages of 5-7. The film depicts the first day of school in several countries, observing what recent research says makes for effective education.

Child's Play (Insight Media, VHS, 30 minutes): Examines the role, function, and types of play, including how play facilitates problem solving and self expression.

I Never Planned on This (Filmakers Library, VHS, 46 minutes): Positive look at normal, health aging. Looks at factors that contribute to a positive outlook in older adults.

<u>Productivity and the self-fulfilling prophecy: The Pygmalion effect</u> (CRM Films, VHS and film, 31 minutes): Revised version of the classic film on how expectations can affect performance.

SUGGESTED READINGS

Arthur, H. B., Hall, D. T., & Lawrence, B. S. (1989). *Handbook of career theory.* NY: Cambridge University Press.

Booth, A. (Ed.) (1992). *Child care in the 1990's: Trends and consequences.* NJ: Lawrence Erlbaum.

Clarke-Stewart, K. A. (1989). Infant day care. *American Psychologist, 44,* 266-273.

Comstock, G., with Paik, H. (1991). *Television and the American child.* CA: Academic Press.

Greenberger, E. (1983). A researcher in the policy arena: The case of child labor. *American Psychologist, 38 (1)* , 104-111.

Lande, J. S., Scarr, S., & Gunzenhauser, B. (Eds.) (1989). *Caring for children: Challenge to America.* NJ: Lawrence Erlbaum Associates.

Lepper, M. R., & Gurtner, J. (1989). Children and computers. *American Psychologist, 44,* 170-178.

Liebert, R. M., & Sprafkin, J. (1988). *The early window: Effects of television on children and youth,* 3rd ed. NY: Pergamon Press.

Rutter, M. (1983). School effects on pupil progress: Research findings and policy implications. *Child Development, 54,* 1-29.

Schulz, R. & Heckhausen, J. (1996). A life span model of successful aging. *American Psychologist, 51,* 702-714.

Stambak, M., & Sinclair, H. (Eds.) (1993). *Pretend play among 3-year-olds.* NJ: Lawrence Erlbaum Associates.

Stern, D., & Eichorn, D. (Eds.) (1989). *Adolescence and work.* NJ: Lawrence Erlbaum Associates.

Zillmann, D., Bryant, J., & Huston, A. (Eds.) (1994). *Media, children, and the family.* NJ: Lawrence Erlbaum Associates.

TRANSPARENCY MASTERS

15.1   Factors that contribute to quality day care

15.2   Which infants fare best in alternative care settings?

15.3   Contributions of play to children's development

15.4   Effective schools

Factors that Contribute to Quality Day Care

1. A reasonable child-to-caregiver ratio (One adult for every 3 infants, or 4 toddlers, or 8 preschoolers)

2. Caregivers who are warm, emotionally expressive, and responsive to children

3. Low staff turnover

4. Planned activities that are age appropriate

Which Infants Fare Best in Alternative Care Settings?

1. Infants who are from disadvantaged homes and at risk of developmental delay

2. Girls, as compared to boys

3. Infants and toddlers with easy temperaments

4. Infants who have already formed attachments to their parents

5. Infants who have parents with positive attitudes about work and parenting, and who are warm and sensitive

Contributions of Play to Children's Development

Physical Development

Practice body movements
Get physical exercise
Improve manipulation skills and coordination
Receive skill training

Intellectual Development

Refine language and communication skills
Gain experience imagining fantasy situations, planning
strategies, and solving problems
In particular, engaging in symbolic play enhances
cognitive development and language skills

Social Development

Enhance perspective-taking skills
Help children learn about adult roles
Help children learn how to resolve conflicts and
cooperate with others

Emotional Development

Express their feelings and resolve emotional conflicts
Try out roles and tasks that they can't yet master in
real life

Effective Schools

According to Michael Rutter, effective schools "promote academic achievement, social skills, polite and attentive behavior, positive attitudes toward learning, low absenteeism, continuation of education beyond the age at which attendance is mandatory, and the acquisition of skills that will enable students to find and hold jobs."

What contributes to an effective school?

1.   Student body is in good shape coming into the school setting.

2.   Effective management of classroom activities.

3.   Effective management of discipline problems.

4.   Team work among the faculty.

5.   Aptitude-treatment interaction-- Need to consider the interaction of student characteristics and school environment:
No single "best" teaching method will work well for all students.

16

PSYCHOLOGICAL DISORDERS THROUGHOUT THE LIFE SPAN

LEARNING OBJECTIVES

After students have read and studied the material in this chapter, they should be able to answer the following questions:

1. What criteria are used to define and diagnose psychological disorders?

2. What is the perspective of the field of developmental psychopathology? What sorts of questions or issues are studied by developmental psychopathologists?

3. What are the characteristics, suspected causes, treatment, and prognosis for individuals with infantile autism?

4. In what ways to infants exhibit depression-like conditions? How is depression in infants similar to, or different from, depression in adults?

5. What is the difference between undercontrolled and overcontrolled disorders?

6. What are the symptoms, suspected causes, treatment, and long-term prognosis for children with attention-deficit hyperactivity disorder?

7. How is depression during childhood similar to, or different from, depression during adulthood?

8. How do interactions of nature and nurture contribute to psychological disorders? Do childhood problems persist into adolescence and adulthood? Explain.

9. Are psychological problems more prevalent during adolescence than other periods of the life span? Explain.

10. What are the characteristics, suspected causes, and treatment of eating disorders?

11. What factors are associated with adolescent alcohol and drug use?

12. What is the course of depression and suicidal behavior during adolescence?

13. What sorts of stress confront adults? How do adults cope with stress? What factors influence stress and coping strategies?

14. What factors influence depression during adulthood?

15. What are the characteristics and causes of dementia?

16. What are some of the treatments for psychological disorders across the life span?

I. **What makes development abnormal?**
  A. Criteria for diagnosing psychological disorders
    1. Three criteria for diagnosis
      a. Statistical deviance: Does the person's behavior fall outside the normal range of behavior?
      b. Maladaptiveness: Does the person's behavior interfere with personal and social adaptation or pose a danger to self or others?
      c. Personal distress: Does the behavior cause personal anguish or discomfort?
    2. Considering social norms
    3. Considering age norms
    4. Specific diagnostic criteria
      a. Diagnostic and Statistical Manual of Mental Disorders
  B. Developmental psychopathology
    1. Psychopathology as development, not disease
    2. Developmental issues
      a. Concerned with nature-nurture issue and continuity-discontinuity issue as they relate to maladaptive behaviors

II. **The infant**
  A. Infantile autism
    1. Deviant social development
    2. Deviant language and communication skills
      a. Echolalia--parrot back what someone else says
    3. Repetitive, stereotyped behavior
    4. Without a theory of mind
    5. Suspected causes
      a. Cognitive impairments
        i. Lack of theory of mind
        ii. Deficiency in symbolic thinking
        iii. Poor executive or integrative abilities
      b. Genes and environment
    6. Developmental outcomes
      a. Prognosis usually poor
      b. Intensive behavioral training beginning early in life
  B. Depression
    1. Behavioral and somatic symptoms
    2. Failure to thrive-- neglected, abused or otherwise stressed

III. **The child**
  A. Undercontrolled (externalizing) and overcontrolled (internalizing) disorders
  B. Attention-deficit hyperactivity disorder (undercontrolled)
    1. Criteria: Inattention, impulsivity, hyperactivity
    2. Developmental course
    3. Suspected causes
      a. Neurological abnormalities
      b. Nature and nurture
    4. Treatment
      a. Often treated with stimulant drugs
  C. Depression
    1. Masked depression-- depression expressed in atypical symptoms
    2. Suicide attempts

D. Nature, nurture, and childhood disorders
    1. Genetic factors and disturbances in family relations
E. Do childhood problems persist?
    1. Continuity more likely if problems are severe and little help received

IV. **The adolescent**
A. Is adolescence really a period of storm and stress?
    1. In general, no
    2. Heightened vulnerability to some disorders
B. Eating disorders
    1. Anorexia nervosa
    2. Bulimia nervosa
    3. Suspected causes
        a. Social pressures and values
        b. Genetic predisposition
        c. Disturbed family relationships
        d. Pileup of stressors
    4. Treatment
        a. Behavior therapy, family therapy, drug therapy
C. Drinking and drug use
    1. Factors distinguishing problem drinkers from others
        a. Personal qualities-- alienation from conventional values and little emphasis on academic achievement
        b. Social environment-- unsupportive parents and peers who model and reinforce problem behaviors
        c. Other behavior problems-- more likely to engage in other problem behaviors and less likely to engage in conventional behavior
D. Depression and suicidal behavior
    1. More vulnerable to depression than in childhood
    2. Express cognitive symptoms and may exhibit problem behaviors
    3. Suicide attempts fairly common, but less successful than adult suicide attempts

V. **The adult**
A. Stress and coping
    1. Types of stressors
        a. Major life events
            i. Normative transitions-- typical events
            ii. Nonnormative transitions-- unusual events
        b. Daily hassles
    2. Age and stressful experiences
        a. Young adults experience greatest number of life changes and stress
    3. Age and coping skills
        a. Different coping strategies across the life span; signs of growth and regression
            i. Middle-aged adults use problem-focused coping (change the problem)
            ii. Older adults use emotion-focused coping (change one's appraisal of the problem)
        b. Strategies may be determined by age differences in type of stressor
    4. When coping fails: Age and sex differences in psychopathology
        a. Psychopathology more prevalent among young adults
        b. Men and women display different sorts of problems
            i. Men-- substance abuse
            ii. Women-- affective disorders such as depression

B. Depression
   1. Age differences
      a. Elderly adults less vulnerable
      b. May be difficult to diagnose in older adults
   2. Sex differences
      a. Different stressors
      b. Difference in reporting symptoms
      c. Different coping mechanisms
         i. Men-- distraction strategies
         ii. Women-- rumination strategies
   3. Diathesis-stress
      a. Interaction of a predisposition or vulnerability to psychological disorder and experience of stressful events
C. Aging and dementia
   1. Alzheimer's disease-- difficulty learning and remembering progresses to inability to care for self, loss of verbal abilities, and death
   2. Other causes of cognitive impairment
      a. Vascular dementia
      b. Delirium

VI. **Applications: Treating psychological disorders**
A. Treating children and adolescents
   1. Differs from treatment for adults
   2. How well does psychotherapy work?
   3. A success story: Behavioral treatment of autism
B. Treating elderly adults
   1. Less likely to seek treatment than younger adults
   2. Ageism
   3. Those who do seek treatment are responsive and can change

SUGGESTIONS FOR CLASS DISCUSSIONS OR PROJECTS

1. Divide the chalk board into sections according to major life stages (e.g., infancy, childhood, adolescence, adulthood, late adulthood). Then have students think of normative life events that tend to occur at different ages and list them on the board under the appropriate heading. When students have finished generating events, ask them to characterize what types of normative events tend to occur at different ages. They will likely notice, for example, that infancy and childhood entail events that happen within the family context, adolescence entails many entry events (e.g., first drive, first kiss, first job), and that late adulthood entails many loss events. Do students think that respondents in each of these age groups would come up with the same list of events that they devised, or are the events generated dependent on the age groups represented in the classroom? They might check out their ideas by having people of different ages complete this task.

2. Much debate has centered on Hall's notion that adolescence is a period of storm and stress. Entertain the possibility that adolescence *is* a period of storm and stress, but for the *parents*, not the adolescent. How many reasons can students think of as to why this period might be stressful for parents? Examples include adolescent rebellion, financial stress of college, the parents' own mid-life crisis, and ambivalence about having an "empty nest."

3. Students generally have some personal experience with delinquent behavior or illicit drug use. Ask them to be the "experts" and analyze why adolescents become involved in such activities. Encourage them to consider theoretical concepts such as Erikson's conflict of identity versus role confusion and Elkind's concept of adolescent egocentrism. Students are also likely to know people

who have crossed the line between experimental drug use and abuse. Discuss where the line between normal and abnormal lies, and what factors explain why some of their fellow students become drug abusers and others do not.

Can students think of any interventions for juvenile delinquency based on their insights? They might visit the web site of the Office of Juvenile Justice and Delinquency Prevention [http://www.ncjrs.org/ojjhome.htm] and look at some of the new programs that are being developed in this area. They could report about one that they think would be likely to work well, or not work well, and explain the reasons behind their assessment. To what extent is the program sensitive to the developmental issues of adolescence? Are there ways of possibly strengthening such programs by attending more to developmental issues?

4.   Ask students how psychological disorders are portrayed by the media. Are the portrayals stereotypical or accurate? What television shows, commercials, or movies have the most and the least accurate portrayals? A recent analysis (Rider in *Studies in Popular Culture*, 1994, *16*, pp. 85-93) found that portrayals of people with handicaps in movies and television shows are still somewhat negative. Those portrayals that are not negative are often inaccurate or uninformative because they highlight a single case study that may not be representative of the group of people with a particular condition. To what extent do students find this to be the case in their analyses of the representation of disorders? Research shows that viewers believe these portrayals *are* representative of the larger group. This may have practical consequences because the belief structures people form from watching television and movies affect their future actions. Do students have any ideas on how to address this problem?

5.   The Diagnostic and Statistical Manual of Mental Disorders, published by the American Psychiatric Association, delineates that defining characteristics of psychological disorders, and is generally viewed as the standard for the field. Standards do, however, change. A brief history of Attention-Deficit/Hyperactivity Disorder (ADHD) as described in the DSM demonstrates how changes in the depiction of disorders reflect ongoing research discoveries, and philosophical changes in how we view the disorder.

Researchers, diagnosticians, and therapists have wrestled over whether inattention or hyperactivity is the primary problem in ADHD. In DSM-II (1968), the label was Hyperkinetic Reaction of Childhood and the main characteristic was hyperactivity. In DSM-III (1980), there were two different categories. One was Attention Deficit Disorder with Hyperactivity (ADDH) and the characteristics were inattention, impulsivity, and motor hyperactivity. The second category was Attention Deficit Disorder without Hyperactivity (ADD/noH) and the characteristics were inattention, disorganization, and difficulty completing tasks, but no hyperactivity. In the revision of DSM-III (1987), the category was changed to Attention-Deficit Hyperactivity Disorder (ADHD) because there seemed to be a lack of clinical cases of ADD/noH and a shift in thinking about the relative importance of hyperactivity and inattention. DSM-III-R did include a category of Undifferentiated Attention Deficit Disorder (U-ADD) that focused on developmentally inappropriate and marked inattention for children who didn't quite fit ADHD. In DSM-IV (1994), a child can show inattention or hyperactivity-impulsivity to be classified as ADHD. There are three subtypes of ADHD in DSM-IV: 1) ADHD, Combined Type for children who show roughly equal symptoms of both inattention and hyperactivity-impulsivity; 2) ADHD, Predominantly Inattentive Type for children who show numerous inattention symptoms and few hyperactivity-impulsivity symptoms; and 3) ADHD, Predominantly Hyperactive-Impulsive Type for children who show numerous symptoms of hyperactivity-impulsivity symptoms and few inattention symptoms.

After discussing ADHD, students might look up descriptions of disorders mentioned in the text in DSM-IV, and perhaps compare them to descriptions in earlier versions of the manual. Some questions to consider include:
   • What has changed in the descriptions over time?
   • What assumptions are embedded in current descriptions?
   • Is there any recent research that might affect how we think about disorders?
   • What sorts of research studies might be helpful?

6.	There are typically students in the class who have aging relatives with dementia (Alzheimer's or another form). You might ask them to describe their relatives' symptoms and how they progressed over time to help impress on students the nature of the disease. Having done that, it is worth emphasizing that only some cases of Alzheimer's (especially early onset cases) are genetic in origin and place descendants at higher risk.

SUGGESTED FILMS AND VIDEOS

Alzheimer's Disease: The Long Nightmare (Films for the Humanities and Sciences, VHS, 19 minutes): Shows both the medical aspects and the personal aspects of this disease.

An Alzheimer's Story (Filmakers Library, VHS, 28 minutes): A documentary that follows a family with an Alzheimer's patient for two years. Shows the typical declines associated with Alzheimer's and the struggles faced by the family. No narration.

An Anorexic's Tale: The Brief Life of Catherine (Films for the Humanities and Sciences, VHS, 80 minutes): A docudrama of Catherine Dunbar's fight against anorexia, from age 15 until her death at age 22.

Anorexia (Films for the Humanities and Sciences, VHS, 28 minutes): This is an adapted Phil Donahue program in which Donahue talks with recovered anorexics and physicians about this eating disorder.

Autism: Breaking Through (Films for the Humanities and Sciences, VHS, 26 minutes): Examines causes, symptoms, and treatments of autism. Treatments include fenfluramine, behavior modification, and a Japanese program using physical exercise and interaction with non-autistic children.

Bulimia (Films for the Humanities and Sciences, VHS, 28 minutes): Another adapted Phil Donahue program. Focuses on causes and treatments of bulimia.

Childhood's End: A Look at Adolescent Suicide (Filmakers Library, VHS and film, 28 minutes): Documentary format which profiles three suicidal teenagers, two survivors and one death.

Depression: Biology of the Blues (Films for the Humanities and Sciences, VHS, 26 minutes): Focuses on biological, rather than environmental, causes of depression. Differentiates between sadness and depression, discusses drug therapies, use of electro-convulsive therapy, and genetic links.

Out of Control: Hyperactive Children (Filmakers Library, VHS, 14 minutes): This is from an ABC "20/20" segment. It covers symptoms and treatments of hyperactivity.

SUGGESTED READINGS

Berkson, G. (1993). *Children with handicaps: A review of behavioral research.* NJ: Lawrence Erlbaum Associates.

Berman, A., & Jobes, D. (1991). *Adolescent suicide: Assessment and intervention.* Washington, D.C.: American Psychological Association.

Dugan, T. F., & Coles, R. (Eds.) (1989). *The child in our times: Studies in the development of resiliency.* Brunner Mazel.

Field, T. M., McCabe, P., & Schneiderman, N. (Eds.) (1988). *Stress and coping across development.* NJ: Lawrence Erlbaum Associates.

Henker, B., & Whalen, C. K. (1989). Hyperactivity and attention deficits. *American Psychologist, 44,* 216-223.

Kazdin, A. E. (1989). Developmental psychopathology. *American Psychologist, 44,* 180-187.

Luthar, S.S., Burack, J. A., Cicchetti, D., & Weisz, J. (1997). *Developmental psychopathology: Perspectives on adjustment, risk, and disorder.* Cambridge University Press.

Stark, K. (1990). *Childhood depression: School-based intervention.* NY: Guilford Press.

Werner, C. (1994). *Developmental psychopathology: From infancy to adolescence,* 3rd edition. NJ: McGraw-Hill.

TRANSPARENCY MASTERS

16.1   Criteria for major depressive episode

16.2   Key features of autism

16.3   Characteristics of depression during childhood

16.4   Attention deficit hyperactivity disorder

16.5   Characteristics of eating disorders

16.6   Characteristics of dementia

Diagnostic Criteria for Major Depressive Episode

At least five of the following symptoms during the same 2-week period, with one of the symptoms being either depressed mood (1) or decreased interest (2):

1. Depressed mood (or irritable mood in children and adolescents) most of the time.

2. Greatly decreased interest or pleasure in usual activities.

3. Significant weight loss (or weight gain)

4. Insomnia (or too much sleeping)

5. Psychomotor agitation (or sluggishness, slowing of behavior)

6. Fatigue and loss of energy

7. Feelings of worthlessness or extreme guilt

8. Decreased ability to concentrate or indecisiveness

9. Recurring thoughts of death, suicidal ideas, or a suicide attempt.

Key Features of Autism

1. <u>Early onset</u>
    Autistic at birth; diagnosed within first 3 years

2. <u>Deviant social development</u>
    Unable to form normal social relationships
    Don't respond appropriately to social cues
    Don't make eye contact or seek others for comfort

3. <u>Deviant language and communicative skills</u>
    Mute or limited language
    Flat monotone
    Pronoun reversals
    Echolalia
    General limitations in ability to use symbols

4. <u>Repetitive, stereotyped behavior</u>
    Need for sameness in their world

5. <u>Cognitive deficits</u>
    Lack a theory of mind
    Most are mentally retarded

Characteristics of Depression
During Childhood Infancy

Symptoms: Loss of interest in activities, psychomotor slowing, loss of appetite, disruption of normal sleep patterns

Lack of or disruption of a secure attachment relationship, unresponsive parents, neglect or abuse can increase the likelihood of depression

Childhood

Symptoms: Preschoolers often show the behavioral and somatic symptoms of depression. School-aged children begin to show cognitive symptoms of low self-esteem, hopelessness, and self-blame.

Adolescence

Symptoms: Show both the behavioral and cognitive symptoms; very similar to adults

Other indirect signs: Delinquency, drug or alcohol abuse, becoming sulky, grouchy, aggressive

More vulnerability to depression than in childhood

Attention-Deficit Hyperactivity Disorder

Symptoms:

Inattention	Doesn't listen, easily distracted, trouble finishing tasks
Impulsivity	Acts before thinking, can't wait for turn in a group
Hyperactivity	Perpetual fidgeting, finger tapping, chattering, restlessness

ADHD infants often characterized as very active, having difficult temperaments and irregular habits.

ADHD preschool-age children are noted for their constant motor activity.

ADHD school-age children show more fidgeting, restlessness, and inattention than motor excess.

ADHD adolescents and adults tend not to be overactive, but still have problems with inattention and impulsivity.

Characteristics of Eating Disorders

Anorexia Nervosa

Refusal to maintain weight that is at least 85% of expected weight

Strong fear of becoming overweight

Distorted body image

Absence of regular menstrual cycles in females

Bulimia Nervosa

Binge and purge syndrome: Repeated episodes of consuming large quantities of food and then purging (e.g., self-induced vomiting, laxatives, fasting)

Strong fear of becoming overweight

Negative feelings associated with their binging, which might be alleviated by their purging

Found among all weight ranges

Characteristics of Dementia

Family of diseases with similar symptoms:

Impaired memory

Impaired intellect

Impaired judgment

Impaired orientation

Exaggerated or shallow emotions

Causes:

Alzheimer's disease (irreversible, slow and steady progression)

Multi-infarct dementia from a series of minor strokes (irreversible, steplike progression with each stroke)

Medications, infections, metabolic disorders, alcoholism, malnutrition (reversible)

17

THE FINAL CHALLENGE: DEATH AND DYING

LEARNING OBJECTIVES

After students have read and studied the material in this chapter, they should be able to answer the following questions:

1.   How is death defined? Why is the definition of death controversial? How does the social meaning of death vary across groups?

2.   What factors influence life expectancy?

3.   What is the difference between programmed theories of aging and damage theories of aging? What are specific examples of each type of theory?

4.   What are Kübler-Ross's stages of dying? How valid and useful is this theory?

5.   What is the Parkes-Bowlby attachment explanation of grief?

6.   What is the infant's understanding of separation and death?

7.   How do children's conceptions of death compare to a "mature" understanding of death? What factors might influence a child's understanding of death?

8.   What is a dying child's understanding of death? How do dying children cope with the prospect of their own death?

9.   How do children grieve?

10.   What is the adolescent's understanding of death?

11.   How do family members react and cope with the loss of a spouse, a child, and a parent?

12.   What factors contribute to effective and ineffective coping with grief?

13.   What can be done for those who are dying and for those who are bereaved to better understand and face the reality of death?

I. **Life and death issues**
   A. What is death?
      1. Biological definitions of death
         a. Biological death is a process not a single event
         b. Total brain death
            i. Totally unresponsive to stimuli
            ii. Fail to move for one hour and fail to breathe for three minutes after removed from ventilator
            iii. Have no reflexes
            iv. Register a flat EEG
         c. Euthanasia
      2. Social meanings of death
         a. Cultural and historical differences in experiences of death
   B. What kills us and when?
      1. Life expectancy has increased this century-- in U.S., it's almost 76 years
      2. Infancy is most vulnerable period
      3. Leading causes of death change across the life span
   C. Theories of aging: But why do we age and die?
      1. Programmed theories
         a. Maximum life -- 110-120 years
         b. Genetic influence
         c. Hayflick limit-- human cells can divide a limited number of times
            i. Shortening of telomeres
         d. Genetically-guided systematic changes in neuroendocrine and immune systems.
      2. Damage theories of aging
         a. Error accumulation theory-- damage caused by free radicals
      3. Nature and nurture conspiring
      4. Theories of aging and life extension
         a. Dietary restriction

II. **The experience of dying**
   A. Kubler-Ross's stages of dying
      1. Five stages
         a. Denial and isolation
         b. Anger
         c. Bargaining
         d. Depression
         e. Acceptance
      2. Hope--runs throughout the other five responses
   B. Criticisms and alternate views
      1. Use of term "stage" is inappropriate
      2. Little attention on how responses are shaped by specific illnesses and events
      3. Does not account for how individual personality influences the experience of dying

III. **The experience of bereavement: An attachment model**
   A. Terminology
      1. Bereavement-- state of loss
      2. Grief-- emotional response to loss
      3. Mourning-- culturally defined ways of expressing grief
   B. Parkes-Bowlby model of grieving
      1. Numbness

      2. Yearning
          a. Separation anxiety--distress at being parted from object of attachment
      3. Disorganization and despair
      4. Reorganization

IV.   **The infant**
    A. Acquisition of object permanence
    B. Distress at being separated from caregivers
    C. Lack understanding that death is permanent separation

V.   **The child**
    A. Grasping the concept of death
      1. "Mature" understanding of death
          a. Finality
          b. Irreversibility
          c. Universality
          d. Biological causality
      2. Preschool children believe the dead retain some life functions, view death as reversible, do not believe it is universal, and believe that an external agent caused the death
      3. School-age children understand that death involves the cessation of life, it is irreversible and universal, but do not completely understand causality of death
      4. Understanding of death depends on both level of cognitive development and life experiences
    B. The dying child
      1. Typically more aware that they are dying than adults realize
      2. Experience a wide range of emotional responses
    C. The bereaved child
      1. Children do grieve
      2. Their grief is expressed differently than an adult's grief
      3. Particularly vulnerable to long-term negative effects of bereavement

VI.   **The adolescent**
    A. Achieves a mature understanding of death, but reactions to death reflect themes of the adolescent period
    B. Expresses grief more directly than younger children

VII.   **The adult**
    A. Death anxiety
      1. Factors influencing death anxiety
          a. Gender
          b. Religious involvement
          c. Personality
          d. Age
    B. Death and the family life cycle
      1. The loss of a spouse
          a. Precipitates other changes
          b. At-risk for illness and even death
          c. Changes in life-style
          d. First year most difficult, but recovery may take years
          e. Reactions are diverse
      2. The loss of a child
          a. Experienced as unexpected and untimely
          b. Can be devastating

          c. Effects on marriage-- strains
          d. Effects on siblings-- may feel neglected by parents, anxious about own
                    health, guilty, pressure to replace lost child for parents
          e. Effects on grandparents-- guilty, helpless
     3. The loss of a parent
          a. Not as disruptive as death of spouse or child
C. Who copes and who succumbs?
     1. Defining pathological grief
          a. Chronic grief--longer than normal
          b. Distorted grief--some symptoms are exaggerated and others are minimized
          c. Absence, inhibition, or delay of grief
     2. Personal resources
          a. Early experiences in attachment relationships
          b. Personality and coping style
     3. The nature of the loss
          a. Relationship to the deceased
          b. Suddenness or unexpectedness of the death
          c. Cause of the death
     4. The context of supports and stressors
          a. Social support helps
          b. Additional stressors hurt
     5. Bereavement and human development
          a. Potential to foster growth

VIII. **Applications: Lessening the sting of death**
     A. For the dying
     B. For the bereaved

SUGGESTIONS FOR CLASS DISCUSSIONS OR PROJECTS

1.   Have students discuss medical and moral concerns raised by euthanasia. They will need to distinguish among passive euthanasia, active euthanasia, and assisted suicide. Assisted suicide has gotten much media attention because of Dr. Jack Kevorkian's role in helping several terminally ill patients to commit suicide, and more recently around the legalization of assisted suicide in Oregon. If the right to die becomes more firmly established, what safeguards would student like to see to ensure that this option is used responsibly?

2.   Have students discuss the understanding of death at different points in the life span. Compare a young child's understanding of death to an adolescent's understanding to an adult's understanding, etc. One way to do this would be to use Piaget's stages of cognitive development as a framework. Another way to approach this issue would be to have students role-play explaining death (or a death) to people of different ages.

3.   Recently there have been many incidents of students killing other students across the country. Among these is the March 1998 tragedy in which two boys, aged 11 and 13 years, opened fire on their classmates in Jonesboro, Arkansas. More recently, in May 1998, a 15-year-old boy killed both his parents and then opened fire on his fellow students in the school cafeteria in Springfield, Oregon. As difficult as it is to explain these tragic events, do students think that preadolescent and adolescent views of death and dying contribute anything to our understanding of how children can kill?
        While the two boys in Arkansas are being prosecuted as juveniles and could be released at the age of 18, the boy in Oregon will be charged as an adult and faces a life sentence. There is currently a trend toward stiffer and stiffer penalties for younger and younger children. Should developmental considerations lead us to treat young people who commit murders (or other crimes) differently than

adults who commit these crimes? ? Why/why not? What are the relevant considerations?

4.   Have students generate factors that should be taken into account when "shopping" for a nursing home. Factors might include the physical facility (safety, cleanliness, attractiveness), staff, activities, cost, and connection with other organizations or community events. This might also be a good time to look at the chapter on "Mindful Aging" in Ellen Langer's 1990 book, *Mindfulness* (Addison-Wesley Publishing Co.).

5.   Jonathan Swift once commented that we all want to live long lives but none of us wants to become old. Ask students to respond to this. How old do they want to become? What factors or conditions are important to students when considering their longevity? If you knew that you were going to live to be 100, would you change any of your current behaviors?

6.   What would be a "perfect" death? Do students wish to have time to say good-bye, or would they rather die suddenly? Where would they like to be, both in their lives (in terms of accomplishments, etc.), and also and in terms of physical location (e.g., in own bedroom or in a field, perhaps a favorite song playing)? Would they want someone with them?

SUGGESTED FILMS AND VIDEOS

Bereaved Parents (Films for the Humanities and Sciences, VHS, 28 minutes): An adapted Phil Donahue program which explores issues of grief and guilt that parents experience when they lose a child.

Coping with Loss (Films for the Humanities and Sciences, VHS, 19 minutes): Uses the Challenger disaster to illustrate how children learn to cope with death. Also profiles the family of a person who is dying and shows the importance of the grieving process.

Crib Death (Films for the Humanities and Sciences, VHS, 59 minutes): The maker of this film lost his 7-month-old son to Sudden Infant Death Syndrome and relates his experiences and those of another family who experienced the death of a child.

Death and Dying: A Teenage Class (CRM Films, VHS and film, 10 minutes): This short clip shows a high school course covering funerals, cemeteries, embalming, cremation, and attitudes toward death. Although directed toward high school audiences, this film can initiate good discussion.

Dying Wish (Films for the Humanities and Sciences, VHS, 52 minutes): The is a CBS "48 Hours" program which explores the meaning of death in our technologically advanced world, and the issues involved in euthanasia.

Elderly Suicide (Films for the Humanities and Sciences, VHS, 28 minutes): An adapted Phil Donahue program covering the factors that sometimes lead elderly to the conclusion that suicide is the best alternative.

SUGGESTED READINGS

Kalish, R. A. (1984). *Death, grief, and caring relationships*, 2nd ed. CA: Brooks/Cole.

Kastenbaum, R. (1985). Death and dying: A life-span approach. In J. E. Birren & K. W. Schaie (Eds.), *Handbook of the psychology*, 2nd ed. (pp. 619-643). NY: Van Nostrand Reinhold.

Kubler-Ross, E. (1969). *On death and dying*. NY: Macmillan.

Kubler-Ross, E. (1983). *On children and death*. NY: Macmillan.

Papadatou, D., & Papadatos, C. (Eds.) (1991). *Children and death*. NY: Hemisphere.

TRANSPARENCY MASTERS

TM 17.1	Theories of aging
TM 17.2	Kubler-Ross's stages of dying
TM 17.3	Developmental changes in understanding of death

Theories of Aging

Programmed Theories

Emphasis on systematic genetic control of aging

Hayflick limit-- limited number of times that a human cell can divide

Endocrine theory-- genes program hormone changes that bring about death

Immune system theory-- immune system becomes less effective as we age and may produce antibodies to attack normal body cells (autoimmune reactions)

Damage Theories

Emphasis on less systematic processes that cause cells and organ systems to deteriorate

DNA repair theory-- DNA is damaged over the years and the body's capacity to repair this damage slows down

Cross-linkage theory-- molecules of collagen become interlinked resulting in signs we associate with aging

Free radical theory-- molecules with an extra electron react with other molecules to produce substances that damage normal cells

Kubler-Ross's Stages of Dying

1. Denial and isolation
   "This can't be happening."

2. Anger
   "Why me? It's not fair."

3. Bargaining
   "I just need a little bit more time."

4. Depression
   "I feel as if everything is hopeless; I feel as if I'm all alone--abandoned."

5. Acceptance
   "I feel calm and reasonably comfortable with the thought of dying"

Problems with this characterization of dying:

1. Dying process is not stage-like.

2. Ignores the course (dying trajectory) of an individual's illness.

3. Minimizes the large individual differences in emotional responses to dying.

Developmental Changes in Understanding of Death

Understanding influenced by level of cognitive development and specific life experiences.

Infants:
Need to have object permanence before they will show any distress at being separated from object of attachment
Lack understanding that death is a permanent separation

Preschool children:
Believe the dead retain some life functions, view death as reversible, do not believe it is universal, and believe that an external agent caused the death

School-age children:
Understand that death involves the cessation of life, it is irreversible and universal, but do not completely understand causality of death

Adolescents:
Achieve a mature understanding of death, but reactions to death reflect themes or concerns of the adolescent period

"Mature" understanding includes knowing that death is final, irreversible, universal, and caused by internal processes.

EPILOGUE: FITTING THE PIECES TOGETHER

LEARNING OBJECTIVES

1. What are the significant trends (physical, cognitive, personal, and social) of each major age or stage of the life span (infants, preschool children, school-aged children, adolescents, young adults, middle-aged adults, and older adults)?

2. What are the major developmental themes running throughout the text?

CHAPTER OUTLINE

I. **Major trends in human development**
    A. Infants (birth to age 2)
        1. Development is rapid
        2. Newborns are equipped with reflexes and sensory capabilities that allow them to learn from and respond to their environment
        3. Automatic reflexes are replaced by voluntary motor behaviors
        4. Improved perceptual and motor skills (e.g., walking) allow increasing activity in contributing to their own development
        5. Piaget's sensorimotor period of cognitive development
            a. Development of object permanence
            b. Acquisition of the symbolic capacity
        6. Linguistic breakthroughs through social interaction
        7. More aware of selves as individuals
        8. Resolution of Erikson's trust vs. mistrust conflict
            a. Affected by temperament and parents' style
            b. Affects formation of attachments
        9. Parent-child relationship as training ground for later social relationships
    B. Preschool children (ages 2 through 5)
        1. Improved gross motor control and fine motor skills
        2. Piaget's preoperational stage
            a. Symbolic capacity
                i. Basic language rules
                ii. Imaginative play
            b. Egocentrism
        3. Erikson's conflicts of autonomy vs. shame and initiative vs. guilt
            a. Self confidence and esteem if resolution successful
        4. Lack of self control but internalize rules
        5. Learn about themselves and others, including gender roles
        6. Caregivers still central, but form friendships with peers
    C. School-aged children (ages 6 through 11)
        1. More self-controlled, serious, skilled, logical
        2. Physical growth is slow; motor skills continue to improve
        3. Piaget's concrete operations stage
            a. Logical actions performed mentally
            b. Conservation
        4. Master the finer points of language and communication
        5. Better perspective-taking
        6. Improved memory and problem solving abilities

7. Better understanding of self and others based on inner traits
8. Erikson's conflict of industry vs. inferiority
9. Formation of a more stable personality
10. Kohlberg's preconventional level of moral reasoning
11. Expanded social world; socialization increasingly affected by agents other than parents (television, school)

D. Adolescents (ages 12 through 19)
1. Dramatic physical changes
   a. Growth spurt
   b. Puberty
2. Piaget's formal operations stage
   a. Can think systematically and abstractly about hypothetical situations or problems
3. Think about self and others in more sophisticated ways, though susceptible to adolescent egocentrism
4. Erikson's conflict of identity versus role confusion
5. Conventional moral reasoning for most adolescents
6. More serious about preparing for adult roles
7. Power relationships in family shift-- more decision making
8. Peer involvement and conformity peak

E. Young adults (ages 20 through 39)
1. Peak physical capacity with gradual declines beginning
2. Sophisticated cognitive skills, particularly in areas of expertise
3. Some will move from conventional to postconventional moral reasoning
4. Erikson's conflict of intimacy vs. isolation
5. Exploration of romantic relationships and career choices
6. Many become parents

F. Middle-aged adults (ages 40 through 64)
1. Gradual declines in physical and sensory capacities
2. Physical changes-- menopause, vulnerability to chronic illnesses
3. Generally stable intellectual functioning and personality
4. Expertise allows adults to effectively solve everyday problems
5. Creative achievement in careers often peaks
6. Erikson's conflict of generativity vs. stagnation
7. Emptying of the nest associated with satisfaction

G. Older adults (age 65 and up)
1. Continued physical and sensory declines
2. Likelihood of chronic disease increases
3. Take more time to learn things
4. Experience some memory lapses
5. No big change in cognitive and linguistic skills used everyday
6. Typically active and involved; self-esteem, and life satisfaction remain fairly stable
7. Erikson's conflict of integrity versus despair
8. Immense diversity among capabilities of older adults

II. **Major themes in human development**

A. <u>We are whole persons throughout the life span</u>.
1. Physical, cognitive, personal, and social developments are intertwined

B. <u>Development proceeds in multiple directions</u>.
1. Development becomes increasingly differentiated and integrated.
2. Development involves gains, losses, and changes

C. There is both continuity and discontinuity in development.
     1. Questions about whether change is stagelike (qualitative) or continuous
         (quantitative),
     2. Discontinuities mean early experiences may not predict later behaviors

D. There is much plasticity in human development.
     1. Human beings have the capacity to change in response to their experiences.

E. Nature and nurture truly interact in development.
     1. Biological and environmental factors together explain both universal trends in
         development and individual differences in development.
     2. The best developmental outcomes arise from the goodness of fit between a person
         and the person's unique environment.

F. We are individuals, becoming even more diverse with age.
     1. There is a great diversity among humans, which makes generalizations difficult.
     2. As we age, human development becomes less and less predictable.

G. We develop in a cultural and historical context.
     1. Development is affected by broad cultural and historical contexts, as well as the
         individual's immediate environment.

H. We are active in our own development.
     1. The person and environment reciprocally interact and influence one another.

I. Development is best viewed as a lifelong process.
     1. Development in any one phase of life is best understood as part of a lifelong
         process.

J. Development is best viewed from multiple perspectives.
     1. Importance of a multidisciplinary approach
     2. Many different theories make important contributions

SUGGESTIONS FOR CLASS DISCUSSIONS OR PROJECTS

The first two introductory exercises described as suggestions for Chapter One might also be nice closing exercises for the semester. These ideas were:

1) Have students break up the life span into meaningful eras, and describe each portion of the life span

2) Have students break into small group to discuss the tenets of life-span developmental psychology. With which do they agree and disagree?

See Chapter One of this Manual for more details.

If either of these exercises was done in the beginning of the semester, it might be interesting to revisit the results from that early class after doing this exercise again. Or, the earlier results could serve as a starting point for a final discussion on how people's ideas have changed or deepened.

Major Trends in Human Development

Infants (birth to age 2)

1. Development is rapid

2. Reflexes and sensory capabilities allow newborns to respond to their environment

3. Automatic reflexes disappear and are replaced by voluntary motor behaviors

4. Infants actively contribute to their cognitive development

5. Piaget's sensorimotor period of cognitive development
    Development of object permanence
    Acquisition of the symbolic capacity

6. Recognition of selves as individuals

7. Resolution of Erikson's trust vs. mistrust conflict

8. Development of attachment to caregivers

Preschool children (ages 2 through 5)

1. Improved gross motor control and fine motor skills

2. Piaget's preoperational stage of cognitive development
   Symbolic rather than logical reasoning
   Egocentric

3. Master basics of language

4. Short attention spans

5. Limitations in information processing skills

6. Erikson's conflicts of autonomy vs. shame and initiative vs. guilt

7. Increasing amount of time spent with peers

School-aged children (ages 6 through 11)

1. Physical growth is slow; motor skills continue to improve

2. Piaget's concrete operations stage
   Logical actions performed mentally
   Conservation

3. Master the finer points of language and communication

4. Improved memory and problem solving abilities

5. Better understanding of self and others based on inner traits

6. Erikson's conflict of industry vs. inferiority

7. Formation of a more stable personality

8. Kohlberg's preconventional level of moral reasoning for most children

9. Expanded social world; socialization increasingly affected by agents other than parents (television, school)

Adolescents (ages 12 through 19)

1.   Dramatic physical changes
Growth spurt
Puberty

2.   Piaget's formal operations stage
Can think systematically and abstractly about
hypothetical situations or problems

3.   Think about self and others in more sophisticated ways;
self-descriptions are more abstract

4.   Erikson's conflict of identity versus role confusion

5.   Conventional moral reasoning for most adolescents

6.   More serious about preparing for adult roles

7.   Increasingly participate in making decisions about their
lives

8.   Peer involvement and conformity peak

<u>Young adults</u> (ages 20 through 39)

1. Peak physical capacity with gradual declines beginning

2. Sophisticated cognitive skills, particularly in areas of expertise

3. Some will move from conventional to postconventional moral reasoning

4. Erikson's conflict of intimacy vs. isolation

5. Experimentation with romantic relationships and marriage

6. Many become parents

7. Face a number of family and career responsibilities

<u>Middle-aged adults</u> (ages 40 through 64)

1. Gradual physical and sensory declines

2. Menopause and male climacteric

3. Stable intellectual functioning

4. Expertise allows effective solutions to everyday problems

5. Creative achievement is often at its peak

6. Erikson's conflict of generativity vs. stagnation

7. Emptying of the nest as children leave home

Older adults (age 65 and up)

1. Continued physical and sensory declines

2. Likelihood of chronic disease increases

3. Take more time to learn things

4. Experience some memory lapses

5. No big change in cognitive and linguistic skills used everyday

6. Personality, self-esteem, and life satisfaction remain fairly stable

7. Erikson's conflict of integrity versus despair

8. Immense diversity among capabilities of older adults

Major Themes in Human Development

1. We are whole persons throughout the life span.

2. Development proceeds in multiple directions.

3. There is both continuity and discontinuity in development.

4. There is much plasticity in human development.

5. Nature and nurture truly interact in development.

6. We are individuals, becoming even more diverse with age.

7. We develop in a cultural and historical context.

8. We are active in our own development.

9. Development is best viewed as a lifelong process.

10. Development is best viewed from multiple perspectives.

1

UNDERSTANDING LIFE-SPAN HUMAN DEVELOPMENT

MULTIPLE CHOICE QUESTIONS

p. 2
F

1. Development is BEST defined as:
   a. individual differences in human behavior
   * b. systematic changes and continuities from conception to death
   c. the way people change in positive ways across time
   d. the systematic unfolding of genetic potential

p. 2
F

2. Developmentalists define development as the
   a. advances in physical functioning throughout the developmental period
   * b. changes and continuities across the life span
   c. biological unfolding of individuals based on a genetic plan
   d. growth in early life and declines in later life

p. 2
F

3. Developmentalists explore changes in three basic domains. These are:
   a. motor, interpersonal, cognitive
   * b. physical, cognitive, psychosocial
   c. personality, motor, learning
   d. interpersonal, maturational, learning

p. 2
C

4. Jane, a developmental psychologist, conducts research on children's emotional reactions to studying math in school. Jane is concerned with children's _____ development.
   a. cognitive
   b. maturational
   c. physical
   * d. psychosocial

p. 2
C

5. John is interested in the development of children's perceptual skills. Which developmental realm does his interest represent?
   * a. cognitive
   b. physical
   c. psychomotor
   d. psychosocial

p. 2
C

6. Vicki is impressed with how abstract and logical her teenage son's views have become regarding controversial issues such as AIDS, abortion, and assisted suicide. The changes Vicki observes in her son's thinking represent which kind of development?
   * a. cognitive
   b. psychosocial
   c. physical
   d. life-span

p. 2   7.   Zelda's research focuses on the acquisition of fine motor skills. In which developmental
C   domain does her interest fall?
             a. psychosocial
        *   b   physical
             c. cognitive
             d. perceptual

p. 3   8.   Growth is BEST defined as:
F   *   a. physical changes that occur from conception to maturity
             b. the biological unfolding of genetic potential
             c. positive changes across the life-span
             d. gains, changes, and losses at each stage of the life cycle

p. 3   9.   Maturation is BEST defined as:
F   a. physical changes that occur from conception to maturity
        *   b. the biological unfolding of genetic potential
             c. physical gains, changes, and losses across the life-span
             d. the effects of experience on thoughts, feelings and behavior

p. 3   10. Which of the following represents a maturational process?
C   a. a close relationship between parent and child
             b. learning to read
             c. learning to tie shoes
        *   d. ovulation in women

p. 3   11. Developmental change
C   a. occurs mainly during infancy and childhood
www   *   b. occurs through the processes of maturation and learning
             c. refers to increases that naturally unfold from a genetic plan
             d. involves the gains and losses that are associated with aging

p. 4   12. Developmentalists typically divide the life-span into a number of relatively distinct
F   age periods. Of these, the infancy period spans:
             a. the first six months of life
             b. the first one year of life
        *   c. the first two years of life
             d. the first three years of life

p. 4   13. Among the aging population, the "old-old" are
F   a. between 55 and 75 years and relatively healthy and involved
        *   b. between 75 and 85 years with some impairments in functioning
             c. over the age of 65 with varying degrees of impairment
             d. over the age of 85 and seriously impaired

14. The term "age grade" refers to:

    a. a group of individuals who are all the same chronological age

*   b. a socially defined age group, with culture-specific assigned roles privilege and responsibilities

    c. a universally defined age group, with universal roles, privileges and responsibilities

    d. the group of children assigned at a specific age to a specific in school

15. Many companies require employees to retire at the age of 65. This policy is an example of

*   a. age norms

    b. age stratification

    c. the young-old principle

    d. growth norms

16. In the United States, it is generally thought that an eight-year-old is too young to babysit and an eighty-year-old is too old to work. This BEST illustrates:

    a. age grades

    b. stereotyping

*   c. age norms

    d. young-old

17. Manuel, age 47, is romantically interested in 20-year-old Pam. Pam's parents voice strong disapproval of the relationship, claiming that Manuel is far too old for Pam. Their objection to the relationship BEST demonstrates which concept?

    a. age grades

*   b. age norms

    c. maturational differences

    d. standardization

18. Our society has shifted towards a concept of children in which they are viewed as:

    a. miniature adults

    b. economic possessions

    c. self-sufficient and knowledgeable

*   d. innocents who require guidance and protection

19. Which contributed MOST to the development of adolescence as a distinct period of the life-span in Western societies?

    a. the need for cheap factory labor

*   b. the need for an educated labor force

    c. the need for farm laborers

    d. the need for an immigrant labor force

20. Adolescence:

    a. is a recognized part of the life-cycle in all cultures

*   b. is a socially-constructed phenomenon

    c. emerged as a distinct period of the lifespan during the Middle Ages

    d. follows the "youth" period in the human life cycle

p. 6　21. Which of the following has had the MOST significant impact on lengthening the
C　　　　average life-span in the United States?
　　　　　a. improved health care for the elderly
　　　　　b. improved nutritional habits
　　* 　　c. major decreases in infant mortality
　　　　　d. disease prevention among school-age children

p. 6　22. The average life expectancy for a baby born in the United States today is highest for
F　　　　_____ and lowest for _____.
　　　　　a. a white male; a black male
　　　　　b. a black male; a white male
　　* 　　c. a white female; a black male
　　　　　d. a black female; a black male

p. 6　23. America is experiencing an ever-aging population: By the year 2030, 20% of the population
C　　　　is expected to be age 65 or older! This phenomenon has been termed "the graying of
　　　　　America." Which of the following has contributed MOST to this phenomenon?
　　* 　　a. major declines in the birth rate
　　　　　b. delayed marriage and childbearing
　　　　　c. growth of nursing homes
　　　　　d. improved nutritional habits

p. 7　24. Paul and Leah are in their mid-fifties. Their four children are all grown, employed, and
F　　　　living on their own. Paul and Leah are BEST described as experiencing:
　　* 　　a. middle age
　　　　　b. old age
　　　　　c. optimization of life goals
　　　　　d. the baby-boomer effect

p. 8　25. The meaning of development and aging:
C　　　　a. are basically the same across cultures
　　　　　b. are different for each cohort group
　　* 　　c. vary considerably based on cultural and historical context
　　　　　d. are positive in all cultures

p. 8　26. Su-Lee, a developmental psychologist, spends many hours observing children on
C　　　　playgrounds. She records the amount of time little boys spend playing on different pieces of
www　　playground equipment compared to little girls. Su-Lee's activity BEST fits which goal of
　　　　　developmentalists' investigation?
　　* 　　a. description
　　　　　b. optimization
　　　　　c. explanation
　　　　　d. control

p. 8

C

27. Dr. Benjamin Spock wrote a popular book for parents, providing information on what behaviors can be expected of a typical infant. This sort of publication PRIMARILY reflects which goal of developmental psychology?
   a. prediction
   b. optimization
   c. explanation
* d. description

p. 9

C

28. Galen is a developmental psychologist who is concerned with helping adolescents learn to deal constructively with divorce. His work focuses PRIMARILY on which goal of developmental psychology?
   a. description
   b. explanation
* c. optimization
   d. prediction

p. 9

C

29. Which of the following represents the goal of "optimization" of human development?
   a. Discovering why changes in cognitive capacity occur.
   b. Discovering how infants' senses function at birth.
* c. Discovering ways to help children with learning problems achieve more success in school.
   d. Discovering the effects of a particular parenting style on personality development.

p. 9

F

30. Early developmentalists recorded the growth and development of their children and published these reports as:
   a. journal articles
   b. case studies
* c. baby biographies
   d. life span reports

p. 9

F

31. Who is most often cited as the founder of developmental psychology?
   a. Charles Darwin
* b. G. Stanley Hall
   c. Sigmund Freud
   d. Jean Piaget

p. 9

C

32. Bryna is studying to become a developmental psychologist. When her son was born, Bryna began to keep a detailed account of his development. Her work might BEST be called:
   a. an autobiography
   b. a correlational study
   c. a sequential study
* d. a modern-day baby biography

p. 10

F   *

33. Who coined the phrase "storm and stress" to describe the adolescent period?
* a. G. Stanley Hall
   b. Charles Darwin
   c. Sigmund Freud
   d. Urie Bronfenbrenner

p. 10 34. G. Stanley Hall, often cited as the founder of developmental psychology, generally
F   viewed adolescence as:
       *   a. an emotional roller-coaster
           b. a time of withdrawal from family and friends
           c. a period of little significance in relation to overall development
           d. a time when logical thinking dominates activity

p. 10 35. Dr. Tesu studies how people adapt to economic, psychological, and physical changes
C   following retirement. Her field is known as:
           a. psychobiology
           b. anthropology
           c. sociology
       *   d. gerontology

p. 10 36. Which is NOT an assumption of the life-span perspective?
F   a. Development must be viewed in historical context.
           b. Development can take multiple directions.
       *   c. Development is due to environment rather than maturation.
           d. Development is multiply influenced.

p. 10 37. According to the life-span perspective
F   a. Development is determined largely by genetic factors
www   b. Development involves gains during infancy and childhood and declines during old age
           c. Developmental paths are not easily changed by experiences
       *   d. Development is influenced by multiple factors

p. 10 38. Which is NOT an assumption of the life-span perspective?
F   a. One is never too old to be a developing person.
           b. Human beings change in both negative and positive directions.
           c. Development is influenced by history and culture.
       *   d. Development is primarily determined by environmental influences.

p. 11 39. A theory is BEST defined as a:
F   a. set of concepts and propositions used to control developmental outcomes
       *   b. set of concepts and propositions intended to describe and explain some aspect of
               experience
           c. factual description of developmental phenomena
           d. series of systematic tests of hypotheses

p. 11 40. A specific prediction about what will hold true if we observe a phenomenon that
F   interests us is called a(n):
           a. fact
       *   b. hypothesis
           c. positive prediction
           d. theory

p. 11 41. Theories generate specific _____ which can be tested to determine the validity of the
F theory.
    a. methods
    b. variables
    c. case studies
  * d. hypotheses

p. 12 42. Dr. Hu is interested in children's affective responses to studying science. She spends many
C hours sitting quietly and observing in elementary school classrooms during science
instruction, and makes careful notes on all she observes. While observing, Dr. Hu is careful
not to interact with the children, or to interfere with their behavior in any way. This form of
data collection is known as:
    a. self-report investigation
  * b. naturalistic observation
    c. structured observation
    d. case study analysis

p. 12 43. The GREATEST advantage of the naturalistic observation method is that it:
C * a. can tell us what people do in everyday life
    b. is relatively inexpensive
    c. can lead to the discovery of cause-effect relationships
    d. untangles age effects from cohort effects

p. 12 44. Ruth is a developmental psychologist who is interested in preschool children's helping
C behavior. She spends hours observing at the campus preschool, taking great care not to
interfere with the children or to influence their behavior in any way. What data collection
technique is Ruth using?
    a. case study
  * b. naturalistic observation
    c. social survey
    d. structured observation

p. 12 45. Holly is interested in children's perceptions of what it means to be a good student in
C school. She constructs an interview in which all children are asked the same questions in the
same order. Holly is using a(n) _____ interview.
    a. guided
    b. nonstandard
  * c. standardized
    d. unstructured

p. 12 46. Max is doing an interview study to examine children's reactions to the death of a
C sibling. The interview he uses starts with some specific questions, but permits the use of
individualized follow-up questions. Max is using a(n)_____ interview.
    a. guided
    b. standardized
    c. unreliable
  * d. unstructured

p. 14   47.   If you watch and record the play behavior of 3-year-olds and compare it to that of
C   5-year-olds on playgrounds, you would be doing research that involves the:
              a.   cross-sectional method and experimental method
       *   b.   cross-sectional method and naturalistic observation
              c.   longitudinal method and experimental method
              d.   longitudinal method and naturalistic observation

p. 14   48.   Dr. Reese is interested in the development of children's beliefs about death and dying.
C   He decides to interview a group of children when they enter kindergarten, and to repeat these
www   interviews with the same children when they are in the second, fourth, and sixth grades.
              Which type of research design does Dr. Reese's study represent?
              a.   cross-sectional
              b.   experimental
       *   c.   longitudinal
              d.   sequential

p. 14   49.   In a(n) _____ research design, the performance of one group of individuals is
F   assessed repeatedly across a portion of the life-span.
              a.   cross-sectional
              b.   experimental
       *   c.   longitudinal
              d.   sequential

p. 14   50.   For her senior project, Shantae wants to study children's moral reasoning. During the
C   fall semester, she interviews twenty individuals in each of the following grades: first, fourth,
              seventh, tenth, and college sophomores. She asks each participant to solve a series of
              practical moral dilemmas. What sort of research design is Shantae using?
       *   a.   cross-sectional
              b.   experimental
              c.   longitudinal
              d.   sequential

p. 14   51.   Linda is interested in how people develop strategies for conflict resolution. She selects
C   group of preschoolers, and uses both interviews and naturalistic observation to explore their
              approaches to dealing with conflict. Every two years thereafter, Linda again interviews and
              observes this same group of youngsters, concluding her study when the children reach
              adolescence. Linda has been using a(n)_____ research design.
              a.   behavioral observation
              b.   cross-sectional
       *   c.   longitudinal
              d.   sequential

p. 14   52.   Dr. Farrell talks to preschoolers about what they want to be when they grow up, and
C   then compares their responses to those of fifth graders, high school students, and college
              students. This research design:
       *   a.   is cross-sectional
              b.   is longitudinal
              c.   is sequential
              d.   has three control groups

p. 14 53. Jim, a developmental psychologist, has a niece who was sexually abused by an intruder when
C   she was 8 years old. He carefully follows her behavior throughout adolescence and into early
           adulthood, to examine the impact of this early experience on later personality development
           and sexuality. This type of investigation is BEST classified as a:
    *   a. case study
           b. cross-sectional study
           c. sequential study
           d. quasi-experiment

p. 14 54. Lynn is interested in how women adjust to life as university professors. She invites a
C   young colleague who has just joined the psychology department to keep a journal detailing
           her experiences, and her thoughts about those experiences, across the first two years of
           employment. Lynn also arranges to interview her new colleague periodically across the same
           time span. Later, Lynn and her colleague will analyze the contents of the journal, as well as
           the interviews, and will see what conclusions they might draw. This type of study is BEST
           classified as _____ research:
           a. cross-sectional
           b. sequential
    *   c. case study
           d. correlational

p. 14 55. Shonda observes and records the free-play-activity choices of 2 1/2-year-olds and 4-
C   year-olds in a preschool setting. From the information given here, her research design is
           BEST classified as:
           a. naturalistic and longitudinal
    *   b. naturalistic and cross-sectional
           c. experimental and cross-sectional
           d. contrived and cross-sectional

p. 14 56. Dr. Forrest is interested in how students define "good" teaching. He conducts a
C   structured interview about teaching techniques with 20 youngsters from each of the following
           grade levels: Kindergarten, third, sixth, tenth, and college freshmen. Dr. Forrest's research
           design is BEST described as:
           a. experimental
    *   b. cross-sectional
           c. longitudinal
           d. sequential

p. 14 57. Dr. Bariella is interested in the development of children's attitudes toward school. She
C   interviews a group of children who are entering kindergarten, and then periodically
           re-interviews these same children as they progress through grade-school, middle-school and
           high-school. This type of research design is called:
           a. cross-sectional
    *   b. longitudinal
           c. sequential
           d. social-survey

p. 14   58.   In a cross-sectional study, groups of subjects should differ with respect to:
C   *   a.   age, only
           b.   gender, only
           c.   gender and age
           d.   social class

p. 14   59.   Which two research designs are MOST similar?
C   a.   cross-sectional and longitudinal
    *   b.   case-study and longitudinal
           c.   cross-sectional and cross-cultural
           d.   experimental and sequential

p. 14   60.   A _____ is a group of people born in a specified, limited span of years.
F   *   a.   cohort
           b.   cross-section
           c.   population
           d.   sample

p. 15   61.   What advantage does the cross-sectional design have over the longitudinal design?
C   a.   it can tell us more about the development of individuals over time
www   *   b.   it is less costly and less time-consuming
           c.   it can untangle the effects of age and the effects of cohort differences
           d.   it is not affected by the time of measurement

p. 15   62.   Which research design does NOT provide information about the development of
C   individuals over time?
           a.   case study
    *   b.   cross-sectional
           c.   longitudinal
           d.   sequential

p. 15   63.   Which is NOT an advantage of the cross-sectional design over the longitudinal
C   design?
           a.   it is less time-consuming
    *   b.   it yields more significant information about the development of individuals
           c.   it tells us more about how people of different cohorts differ
           d.   it generally costs less

p. 15   64.   The effects on research findings produced by historical events occurring at the time
F   when the data were collected are referred to as
           a.   content validity
    *   b.   time of measurement effects
           c.   age effects
           d.   placebo effects

p. 15   65.   In which research design are age differences and cohort differences hopelessly tangled?
F   a.   cross-cultural
www   *   b.   cross-sectional
           c.   longitudinal
           d.   sequential

p. 16   66.   A major disadvantage of the cross-sectional method is that:
C   *   a.   it cannot tell us about changes in individuals
        b.   it is time-consuming and expensive
        c.   the groups studied are too similar to each other
        d.   subjects of the study drop out over time

p. 16   67.   Measuring different age groups of subjects repeatedly over time is called a _____ design.
F   a.   longitudinal
        b.   cross-sectional
    *   c.   sequential
        d.   cross-cultural

p. 16   68.   The following are all disadvantages of the longitudinal research design EXCEPT:
C   a.   it is costly and time-consuming
        b.   different conclusions can emerge depending on which cohort is studied
        c.   the sample may not be representative of the population being studied
    *   d.   it can tell us nothing about the development of individuals over time

p. 16   69.   In which type of study are the effects of age and the effects of time of measurement
C   confounded with one another?
        a.   correlational
        b.   cross-sectional
    *   c.   longitudinal
        d.   sequential

p. 16   70.   Which is NOT an advantage of the longitudinal research design?
C   *   a.   it facilitates the untangling of age effects and time of measurement effects
www   b.   it can effectively explore the relationship between early life experiences and later
             personality traits
        c.   it can be used to examine the stability of character traits over time
        d.   it can be used to explore individual differences in development

p. 16   71.   An advantage of the longitudinal research design is that it:
C   a.   eliminates observer bias
    *   b.   can be used to explore individual differences in development
        c.   permits the disentanglement of age effects and time of measurement effects
        d.   can be used to determine cause-effect relationships

p. 16   72.   Sol is investigating the effects of divorce on children's self-esteem. His initial sample
C   consists of a group of ten 5-year-olds, whom he plans to follow over a period of at least
              fifteen years. When this group of children reaches age 15, Sol adds a second group of
              5-year-olds to his study, and plans to follow them for another fifteen years. Sol is setting up
              a research design BEST classified as _____ research:
        a.   correlational
        b.   cross-sectional
        c.   longitudinal
    *   d.   sequential

p. 16 73. The sequential design for studying development:
F
   a. combines the longitudinal and experimental methods
   b. has the advantage of not requiring any repeated testing of individuals
   c. simplifies the study of development by focusing on only one cohort
   * d. would allow a researcher to separate age effects from cohort effects

p. 16 74. Which research design helps us separate the effects of age, cohort, and time of
F   measurement?
   a. cross-sectional
   b. experimental
   c. longitudinal
   * d. sequential

p. 17 75. In an experimental design, the _____ is manipulated by the experimenter.
F
   a. control group
   b. dependent variable
   * c. independent variable
   d. sample

p. 17 76. George sets up an experimental study to examine the effects of method of reading instruction
C   on reading achievement. In this study, reading achievement is the _____ .
www a. control variable
   * b. dependent variable
   c. independent variable
   d. sampling variable

p. 17 77. The hallmarks of a true experiment include all of the following EXCEPT:
C * a. control over responses on the dependent measure
   b. manipulation of an independent variable
   c. control over extraneous variables
   d. random assignment of participants to experimental conditions

p. 17 78. Sam is interested in the effects of different types of advertisements on college
C   student's eating habits. In Sam's study, the different types of advertisements represent the:
www a. control variable
   b. dependent variable
   c. correlation variable
   * d. independent variable

p. 17 79. Holly conducts an experiment to examine the effects of various classroom discipline
C   programs on children's attitudes toward school. In this study, attitude toward school is the
     _____ variable:
   a. control
   b. experimental
   c. independent
   * d. dependent

p. 17 80. Dr. Hart sets up an experiment to see which method of science instruction has the greatest
C   impact on students' achievement as measured by a standardized, state-wide science test. In
       this study, instructional method is the _____ variable:
       a. standardized
       b. dependent
    * c. independent
       d. cohort

p. 17 81. A study is done examining whether rewarding children for good behavior reduces
C   their aggressive behavior. In this study, level of aggression would be the:
       a. control variable
    * b. dependent variable
       c. experimental variable
       d. independent variable

p. 18 82. The PRIMARY advantage of the experimental design is that it can be used to:
C   a. untangle age and cohort effects
       b. examine individual differences in development
    * c. uncover cause-effect relationships
       d. discover universals in human development

p. 18 83. Faith wants to know whether there is a cause-effect relationship between the amount
C   of time parents spend reading to their children and their children's attitudes toward reading.
       What type of research design should Faith use?
       a. cross-sectional
    * b. experimental
       c. longitudinal
       d. naturalistic observation

p. 18 84. Marci is designing an experimental study to explore the relationship between type of
C   reward and children's prosocial behavior. Which of the following would NOT be an essential
       part of a true experiment on this topic?
       a. randomly assigning children to treatment groups
       b. giving different kinds of rewards to different treatment groups
    * c. assessing prosocial behavior repeatedly as children get older
       d. keeping factors other than type of reward controlled

p. 18 85. Paul thinks he has developed a new way to teach math that will help children learn
C   fractions more easily. He trains teachers in three classrooms to use the new method of
       instruction. He then has them teach, using the new method, while in a fourth classroom there
       is no training or implementation of the new method of instruction. After the unit on fractions
       has been taught, Paul compares the results from the first three classrooms with those of the
       fourth. In this experiment, the fourth classroom represents the _____:
    * a. control group
       b. independent variable
       c. dependent variable
       d. experimental group

p. 18   86.   In an experiment, a researcher exposes different groups of infants to different types of
C   stimulation in a hospital nursery and then measures the neurological development of the
              infants. In this study, the independent variable is the:
              a.   family histories of the infants
              b.   neurological development of the infants
              c.   hospital nursery
       *   d.   type of stimulation provided in the nursery

p. 18   87.   If you wanted to show that a cause and effect relationship existed between teaching
C   style and academic performance, you would use
              a.   naturalistic observations of children in different classrooms
              b.   questionnaires given to large numbers of children from different teaching situations
       *   c.   an experimental study of children randomly assigned to different classes
              d.   teacher reports of how student's academic performance relates to the teacher's classroom
                   style

p. 19   88.   A correlation coefficient measuring the relationship (if any) between aggressive
C   behavior in children and the amount of violent TV that they watch produces a value of +1.5.
              This result indicates
              a.   as TV viewing increases, aggression increases
              b.   as TV viewing increases, aggression decreases
       *   c.   the math was done wrong
              d.   there is no relationship between TV and aggression

p. 19   89.   Mara finds that the correlation between variables A and B is +.43, while the
C   correlation between variables A and C is -.78. These results indicate that:
www   *   a.   the relationship between A and C is stronger than the relationship between A and B
              b.   the relationship between A and B is stronger than the relationship between A and C
              c.   variable A is responsible for whether another variable increases or decreases
              d.   variable A is greater than variable B, which in turn is greater than variable C

p. 19   90.   Tom finds a correlation of +.81 between number of years in school and salary of first
C   job. This shows that:
              a.   the more education one has, the lower their starting salary is likely to be
       *   b.   the more education one has, the higher their starting salary is likely to be
              c.   education level determines whether or not someone will get a job after graduation
              d.   increases in education level cause employers to offer higher salaries

p. 18   91.   Dr. Gerard wants to study the negotiation strategies of men and women who are
C   divorced and those who are still married. Dr. Gerard will need to use:
              a.   an experimental or a contrived study
       *   b.   a quasi-experimental or correlational study
              c.   a longitudinal and experimental study
              d.   an experimental and naturalistic study

p. 18   92.   What is the GREATEST strength of the experimental method?
F   a.   it is inexpensive
                b.   it can be used to examine individual differences
        *   c.   it can be used to determine cause-effect relationships
                d.   it less time consuming than the correlational method

p. 18   93.   Which of the following is a WEAKNESS of the experimental method?
C   *   a.   results from the laboratory do not always generalize to the real world
www   b.   results do not show which variable caused variations in the other variable
                c.   participants cannot be randomly assigned to experimental conditions
                d.   participants are not representative of the general population

p. 18   94.   Jack wishes to determine whether watching TV programs where males are depicted in
C   non-traditional sex-roles causes males to have more nonsexist attitudes than males who
                watch TV programs where males are depicted in traditional masculine sex-roles. Which
                research design would be MOST appropriate for this sort of study?
                a.   case study
        *   b.   experiment
                c.   correlational study
                d.   naturalistic observation

p. 18   95.   Mary is designing an experiment to look at the effects of a particular training program
C   on children's problem-solving skills. She knows she must have both a treatment group and a
                control group. Mary has a total of 20 children to work with. How should she decide which
                children go into which group?
                a.   she should ask the children which group they want to be in
                b.   she should put the first 10 children to volunteer in the treatment group, and the remaining
                     10 children in the control group
                c.   she should put the first 10 children to volunteer in the control group, and the remaining
                     10 children in the treatment group
        *   d.   she should randomly assign the children to the treatment and control groups

p. 18   96.   What is an advantage of using a quasi-experiment?
C   a.   Researchers can predict how experimental conditions will affect participants.
                b.   Researchers can maintain control over all possible extraneous variables
        *   c.   Researchers can study variables that do not permit random assignment of participants to
                     conditions.
                d.   Researchers can conclusively establish which factors caused differences among their
                     participants.

p. 18   97.   Dr. Peck wants to determine whether there are gender differences in reaction to
C   televised violence. He asks male and female participants to watch a 15-minute video clip of
www   a violent program and then complete a rating scale. This research is BEST classified as:
                a.   experimental
        *   b.   quasi-experimental
                c.   naturalistic
                d.   laboratory experimentation

p. 18   98.   Which of the following is a major drawback of the experimental method?

C
- a. experiments only occur in contrived, laboratory settings
- b. experiments can not be used to determine the relationship between two or more variables
- *   c. experiments can not be used to address many important questions about human development
- d. experiments do not yield results that are useful in explaining human behavior

p. 19   99.   Dr. Walker and Dr. Kotecki have completed an investigation of the relationship

C   between the use of harsh physical punishment and children's level of aggressive behavior. The results of their study yield a correlation coefficient of +.8. The MOST accurate interpretation of this finding is that:
- a. use of harsh punishment causes an increase in aggressive behavior
- *   b. children who are harshly punished tend to be more aggressive
- c. children who are aggressive should be harshly punished
- d. a decrease in use of harsh physical punishment will cause a reduction in aggressive behavior

p. 19   100.   Correlational methods can tell us:

F
- a. whether two variables are causally related

www   *   b. the strength and direction of a relationship between variables
- c. whether participants have been randomly assigned to treatments
- d. that a mismatch between two variables exists

p. 19   101.   The correlational method differs from the experimental method because only in an

C   experiment is:
- a. a representative group of children studied
- b. the relationship between two variables studied
- c. there little risk of violating ethical standards of research
- *   d   some variable manipulated by the researcher

p. 19   102.   Which is a primary advantage that correlational studies often have over experimental

C   studies?
- *   a. correlational studies often have a "real world" quality that experimental studies lack
- b. correlational studies are more useful in terms of determining cause-effect relationships
- c. correlational studies are less expensive than experimental studies
- d. correlational studies can be used to explain human behavior while experimental studies cannot

p. 20   103.   Sheri wants to examine the TV-viewing habits of 18 to 25-year-old males in the

C   United States. As it is quite impossible to include all males of this age group in her study, she randomly selects a smaller group of 18 to 25-year old males to survey. The group included in her study is called a(n):
- a. population
- *   b. sample
- c. target group
- d. experimental group

p. 20
C

104. Jack interviews a group of 50 teen mothers to determine what sort of knowledge they had regarding use of contraceptives prior to the time they became pregnant. He then writes an article where he speaks in broad terms about what teen mothers, in general, know about the use of contraceptives prior to becoming pregnant. In this study, the group of 50 teen mothers is called the _____ , while teen mothers in general are called the

_____ .

   a. control group; population
   b. population; sample
   c. sample; control group
* d. sample; population

p. 20
C
www

105. The MAJOR goal behind random sampling is to:
   a. ensure that the population is representative of the sample
* b. ensure that the sample is representative of the population
   c. cut down on the cost of the research project
   d. ensure that the control group is identical to the treatment group(s)

p. 20
C

106. Dr. Vandepolder is conducting a study on mid-west American college-students' radio-listening habits. He doesn't have the resources to survey all college students in the mid-west, so he uses census data to randomly select a group of several thousand students from Michigan, Wisconsin, Illinois and Minnesota to participate in the study. In this study, the group of all mid-west American college students is called the _____, while the group randomly selected from Michigan, Wisconsin, Illinois and Minnesota is called the _____:
   a. sample; control group
   b. sample; population
   c. control group; population
* d. population; sample

p. 20
C

107. What would be a drawback of using 2-year-olds who attend a private mother's-day-out program three mornings a week as a research sample?
   a. they don't represent a cross cultural group
   b. you cannot test participants this young and get valid responses
* c. the children are not a representative sample of the population
   d. they can only serve as the control group

p. 20
C

108. Ethical considerations are critical when conducting research with human beings. Guidelines for ethics are provided by various associations, such as the American Psychological Association and the Society for Research on Child Development. The guidelines stipulate all of the following EXCEPT:
   a. informed consent
   b. the avoidance of physical and psychological harm
   c. debriefing participants
* d. testing participants using multiple methods

p. 21 109. In terms of ethics in conducting research, why might research with young children be
C considered particularly problematic?
   a. young children are likely to be more fearful of the research situation
 * b. young children are less likely to fully understand the implications of their participation in
      the research process
   c. young children are more likely to be harmed psychologically by participating in the
      research process
   d. young children are likely to be less willing to participate in the research process

p. 3 110. Development results from biologically programmed changes called _____ and
F from specific environmental experiences called _____.
SG a. aging; learning
    b. learning; growth
 * c. maturation; learning
    d. age changes; age differences

p. 4 111. Neugarten uses the term "old-old" to refer to individuals who are
F   a. past retirement age
SG b. between 55 and 75 and still active
    c. over the age of 85 and frail
 * d. between 75 and 85 with some impairments in functioning

p. 5 112. a 65-year-old woman who feels as though it is time for her to become a grandmother is
C feeling the influence of
SG a. age grade
 * b. social clock
    c. age norms
    d. physiological needs

p. 6 113. What are the most striking historical <u>changes</u> in how the life span is perceived?
C   a. Infancy and childhood are regarded as important periods of time.
SG b. Adulthood is viewed as more important than childhood.
 * c. Periods of adolescence and middle adulthood have emerged.
    d. Increasing birth rates have focused greater attention on infancy.

p. 7 114. An increase in life expectancy during the past century has resulted in
C * a. an increased awareness of, and interest in, middle adulthood
SG b. more attention to adolescence as a distinct period of the life span
    c. changes in the way we treat our children
    d. more research on infant capabilities

p. 8 115. The goals of developmental psychology are BEST described by which of the following?
C   a. Developmental psychologists seek to modify behavior wherever possible.
SG b. Developmental psychologists seek to identify behaviors that should be changed.
    c. Developmental psychologists seek to construct a single unifying theory to explain
       development.
 * d. Developmental psychologists seek to describe and explain behavior, and where possible,
       optimize behavior.

p. 10   116. One of the assumptions of the life-span perspective is that development is multidirectional.
C   This means that
SG   a. development is caused by any number of factors and determining which cause is most
                 influential can't be done
             b. developmental changes are universal across most people
             c. developmental outcomes can never be predicted
       *   d. development at all ages consists of some gains and some losses as well as some abilities
                 that remain the same

p. 10   117. An assumption of the life-span perspective is that there is plasticity in development. This
C   means that
SG   a. most of our acquisition of new skills will occur during infancy when our brain is not fully
                 developed
       *   b. developmental changes can occur in response to our experiences across the life span
             c. development is never really complete
             d. all skills can be developed at any time of the life span

p. 12   118. Which of the following is an example of using naturalistic observation to collect data?
C   *   a. watching how children behave on their playground
SG   b. asking participants to orally answer questions rather than fill out questionnaires
             c. asking parents to keep track of their children's TV viewing habits
             d. seeing how children behave when they are asked to play a game with unfamiliar children

p. 14   119. Cross-sectional designs provide information about age _____; longitudinal designs
F   provide information about age _____.
SG   *   a. differences; changes
             b. changes; differences
             c. differences; differences
             d. changes; changes

p. 14   120. Cross-sectional designs confound age effects with _____; longitudinal designs confound
F   age effects with _____.
SG   a. cohort effects; cohort effects
             b. time of measurement effects; cohort effects
             c. cohort effects; type of measurement effects
       *   d. cohort effects; time of measurement effects

p. 14   121. If you wanted to assess individual changes over time in prosocial behavior, you would need
C   to use
SG   *   a. a longitudinal design
             b. a cross-sectional design
             c. a correlational design
             d. an experimental design

p. 17 122. Suppose you have one group of children role play (children assume the role of someone else)
C   while another group of children does not role play. You then observe the level of empathy in
SG   children from both groups as they interact with other children. The independent variable
            would be
    *   a. whether children role played or not
            b. children's level of empathy
            c. the relationship between role playing and level of empathy
            d. children's ability to role play

p. 19 123. a positive correlation between viewing televised violence and aggressive behavior would
C   indicate that
SG   a. children who watch less televised violence tend to be more aggressive
    *   b. children who watch more televised violence tend to be more aggressive
            c. increases in aggression are caused by watching more televised violence
            d. watching televised violence is not related to level of aggressive behavior

p. 18 124. Ensuring that all subjects have an equal chance of participating in any of the experimental
F   treatments is accomplished
SG   a. through experimental control
            b. by selecting a random sample from the population
    *   c. through random assignment
            d. by administering a questionnaire

TRUE-FALSE QUESTIONS

p. 3   125. Developmental psychologists use the term development to refer to both gains and
            losses across the life span.
    *   a. true
            b. false

p. 3   126. Maturation refers to the gains that occur across the life span from experiences and genetic
            influences.
            a. true
    *   b. false

p. 4   127. Lis thinks that age 22 is the perfect time to get married because all of her friends plan to
            marry at this age. This is an example of an age norm.
    *   a. true
            b. false

p. 5   128. Children in modern society tend to be treated worse than children in earlier times.
            a. true
    *   b. false

p. 7   129. The periods of adolescence and middle adulthood are relatively new constructions.
    *   a. true
            b. false

p. 7 130. Definitions of when it is appropriate for people to do certain things, such as marry or have children, are fairly consistent across cultures.
   a. true
 * b. false

p. 8 131. Developmentalists are interested in describing development in general as well as individual differences in development
 * a. true
   b. false

p. 8 132. Observing children in their classroom and recording how often they get out of their seats or talk out of turn illustrates the explanation goal of developmentalists.
   a. true
 * b. false

p. 8 133. According to the life-span perspective, development proceeds from individual accomplishments to global achievements.
   a. true
 * b. false

p. 10 134. According to the life-span perspective, both positive and negative change is possible across the entire life span.
 * a. true
   b. false

p. 12 135. Developmentalists believe that structured observations work best with young children and unstructured observations work best with older children and adults.
   a. true
 * b. false

p. 14 136. A 40-year-old New Yorker and a 40-year-old San Franciscan would be described as members of the same cohort.
 * a. true
   b. false

p. 15 137. Cross-sectional studies are better suited than longitudinal studies to the examination of individual differences.
   a. true
 * b. false

p. 16 138. Longitudinal designs can be used to separate the effects of cohort from effect of age.
 * a. true
   b. false

p. 16 139. In a sequential design, time of measurement is confounded with cohort effects
www
   a. true
 * b. false

p. 17   140. In an experimental research design, an independent variable represents the outcome of
         interest.
         a.   true
    *   b.   false

p. 17   141. In an experimental research design, the variable that is manipulated by the experimenter is
         called the independent variable.
    *   a.   true
         b.   false

p. 18   142. Quasi-experiments are used when researchers cannot randomly assign participants to
         experimental conditions.
    *   a.   true
         b.   false

p. 19   143. Correlational studies can demonstrate that one variable caused another, although they cannot
         show the probability of this occurring in the future.
         a.   true
    *   b.   false

p. 19   144. Correlational studies can indicate the strength and direction of relationships between
         variables.
    *   a.   true
         b.   false

ESSAY QUESTIONS

145.   How have conceptions of the life span changed over time? What factors have contributed to these
        changes?

146.   Suppose you are interested in how the college experience affects people's thought processes.
        Design a study to address this question. Be as complete as possible and justify your choice of
        design.

147.   A researcher is interested in what children of different ages understand about their parent's jobs.
www   Design a study to address this question. Be as complete as possible and justify your choice of
        design.

148.   Under what conditions would a researcher choose to conduct a correlational study? When would a
        researcher conduct a quasi-experimental design?

149.   Fred, Sheila, and Tamra disagree about the importance of early childhood education on children's
        later cognitive achievement. Design a study to determine whether Fred (who believes early
        childhood education is valuable), Sheila (who believes early childhood education has no effect), or
        Tamra (who believes early childhood education can actually be harmful) is correct.

150.   Many people in our society are interested in the possibility of "speeding up" some aspect of
SG   development, such as the ages when children can print or read. Similarly, parents are often
        concerned about providing appropriate learning experiences for their children to enhance their
        abilities. Design a study to test the possibility that some specific aspect of development can be
        accelerated. Indicate the type of design and the variables used to test this hypothesis.
        [Sample answer is provided in the Study Guide]

151.   Another current concern is the effect of divorce on children of all ages. Design a study to assess
SG   whether divorce has a negative impact on children at different ages. Specify the type of design
        needed for this question and how you would measure the impact of divorce.

152.   Suppose you would like to study how nutrition, both before birth and after birth, affects the three
SG   major areas of development: physical, cognitive, and psychosocial. How would you ethically
        conduct this study? Discuss factors that would need to be considered when designing an ethical
        study and specify how you would define and measure your variables.

153.   The age range for when it is considered appropriate to engage in various activities (e.g. sexual
SG   intercourse, marriage, settling down in career, having children, etc.) has changed over the years.
        How and why?

THEORIES OF HUMAN DEVELOPMENT

MULTIPLE CHOICE

_____

p. 26   1.   A theory is BEST defined as a:
F
             a.   proven set of facts about the way things are
      *   b.   set of ideas proposed to describe and explain certain phenomena
             c.   set of ideas proposed to predict and control certain phenomena
             d.   technique used to optimize developmental outcomes

p. 26   2.   A theory is all of the following EXCEPT:
F
             a.   a perspective on some issue
             b.   an organizational framework to guide interpretation of events
      *   c.   a proven set of facts about the way things are
             d.   a guide for generating hypotheses and predictions

p. 27   3.   A good theory
F
             a.   is a complex set of explanations for all possible phenomenon
www *   b.   should generate specific hypotheses that can be tested
             c.   must account for physical, cognitive, and psychosocial developments
             d.   must include a set of developmental stages covering the entire life span

p. 27   4.   A good theory should do all of the following EXCEPT:
F   *   a.   contain many propositions
             b.   be parsimonious
             c.   be falsifiable
             d.   have validity

p. 28   5.   The view that children were inherently selfish and bad was held by
F   *   a.   Thomas Hobbes
             b.   John Locke
             c.   B. F. Skinner
             d.   Jean Jacques Rousseau

p. 28   6.   Jean Jacques Rousseau believed which of the following?
F
             a.   an infant is a "tabula rasa," or blank slate
             b.   children are inherently bad in nature
      *   c.   children are innately good
             d.   children are like miniature adults, and should be treated as such

p. 28   7.   Melissa has just given birth to her first child. She feels an enormous sense of
C   responsibility, believing that it is up to her whether her child develops into an essentially
              good or essentially bad individual. Her views are MOST in line with those of:
              a. Thomas Hobbes
        *   b. John Locke
              c. Jean Jacques Rousseau
              d. Jean Piaget

p. 28   8.   John Locke believed that human nature was
F   a.   inherently selfish and aggressive
              b.   innately good
        *   c.   determined by a person's experiences
              d.   determined equally by both genetic and environmental factors

p. 28   9.   Sharon believes that all children are essentially good, and that they have a natural
C   understanding of right and wrong. Her perspective is most consistent with that of:
              a.   John Locke
              b.   Sigmund Freud
        *   c.   Jean Jacques Rousseau
              d.   Thomas Hobbes

p. 28   10.   Paul is very excited about the birth of his first child, although he is also a bit anxious. He
C   believes that the child is an empty book, and he and his wife will be the primary "authors"
              in terms of how the child's story unfolds. Paul's view is MOST similar to that of:
              a.   Thomas Hobbes
              b.   Jean Jacques Rousseau
        *   c.   John Locke
              d.   Jean Piaget

p. 28   11.   Lyn and Chris have just brought their infant daughter home from the hospital. They
C   imagine they will have tough times ahead, for they firmly believe that all children are born
              with selfish tendencies, and they take their job seriously as the ones who must keep their
              child in line. Lyn and Chris hold a view that is MOST like that of:
        *   a.   Thomas Hobbes
              b.   Albert Bandura
              c.   Jean Jacques Rousseau
              d.   John Locke

p. 28   12.   Dr. Johnson falls on the "nurture" side of the nature-nurture controversy. She is
C   MOST LIKELY to believe that:
              a.   if infants are given normal opportunities to move about, their motor skills will naturally
                   unfold in a universal sequence
              b.   teachers' expectations for their students' success will have little effect on how they
                   actually achieve
              c.   while a child's experiences in school will have an impact on his/her intellectual
                   development, what the child is "born with" matters more
        *   d.   it is a mother's responsibility to provide optimal care by staying home from work to
                   raise the child

p. 28　13. With regard to the nature-nurture debate, a strong believer in nurture would suggest that:

C

www
   a.　environmental influences are less important than genetic makeup in determining human behavior

   b.　maturation is more influential than environmental experiences in determining human behavior

*   c.　teaching and enrichment of the environment are often more influential than genetics in determining human behavior

   d.　heredity and environment interact

p. 28　14. A parent who falls on the "activity" side of the "activity-passivity issue" is MOST

C
   LIKELY to believe:

   a.　if a child is aggressive, the parents were not active enough in parenting

   b.　if new skills are not regularly used, they will disappear

   c.　we are naturally more active when young and become more passive with age

*   d.　children play an important role in shaping their own development

p. 29　15. The continuity-discontinuity issue concerns all of the following EXCEPT:

C
   a.　whether development is gradual or abrupt

   b.　whether development is quantitative or qualitative in nature

   c.　whether or not earlier development is connected to later development

*   d.　whether developmental stages naturally unfold or are determined by experiences

p. 29　16. Discontinuity theorists believe which of the following?

C

www
   a.　Early development is connected to later development.

   b.　Developmental changes are primarily quantitative in nature.

   c.　Developmental processes occur in small steps.

*   d.　Developmental changes are primarily qualitative in nature.

p. 29　17. Jerome believes that development proceeds through a series of stages, each of which

C
   represents distinct changes. He might BEST be called a(n):

   a.　continuity theorist

*   b.　discontinuity theorist

   c.　interactional theorist

   d.　context-specificity theorist

p. 29　18. Gail's daughter is approaching adolescence. Gail shudders at the thought, because

C
   she is convinced that adolescence is awful, and like no other time across the life-span. As she puts it, adolescents are like creatures from another planet! Her perspective on the matter fits BEST with that of _____ theorists:

   a.　quantitative

*   b.　discontinuity

   c.　particularity

   d.　continuity

p. 29   19.   The universality/context-specificity issue is concerned with:
*   a.   whether we all follow the same or different developmental paths
    b.   whether environmental or biological factors are more influential in development
    c.   whether we pass through abrupt developmental stages or develop in small, gradual steps
    d.   whether we all participate in our developmental outcomes or not

p. 29   20.   Lee sees development as proceeding much like the a video tape being played in slow
C   motion. She is BEST identified as a(n) _____ theorist:
    a.   environmental
    b.   activity
    c.   qualitative
*   d.   continuity

p. 29   21.   Dr. Hajak believes that development follows a highly similar path for most
C   individuals; in particular, she points to systematic and predictable changes in children's thinking skills to support her position. Dr. Hajak is BEST termed a(n):
*   a.   universalist
    b.   individualist
    c.   particularist
    d.   purist

p. 30   22.   Which theoretical perspective places the greatest emphasis on the unconscious
F   workings of the mind?
    a.   Piaget's cognitive developmental theory
    b.   Bronfenbrenner's ecological theory
    c.   Skinner's learning theory
*   d.   Freud's psychoanalytic theory

p. 30   23.   Dr. Chones believes that it is normal for a one-year-old to bite, pull hair, pinch, and
C   throw tantrums when she doesn't immediately get what she wants. Her views are MOST in line with those of:
    a.   Piaget
*   b.   Freud
    c.   Skinner
    d.   Bandura

p. 30   24.   Lola is a developmental psychologist who believes that the behavior of young
C   children is driven by a host of inborn instincts. Her views are MOST in line with which of the following theoretical perspectives?
    a.   cognitive-developmental
    b.   ecological
*   c.   psychoanalytic
    d.   psychosocial

p. 30　25.　According to Freud, the mission of the "id" is to:
F　　*　　a.　internalize the moral values and standards of the parents
　　　　　b.　satisfy the instincts
　　　　　c.　find acceptable ways to meet instinctual needs
　　　　　d.　mediate between the go and the superego

p. 30　26.　In Freud's theory of personality development, the "pleasure principle" refers to:
F　　*　　a.　the need for immediate gratification of needs
　　　　　b.　the good feeling one gets from doing the right thing
　　　　　c.　the personality structures of id, ego, and superego
　　　　　d.　the feelings experienced during the phallic stage of development

p. 30　27.　The PRIMARY function of the ego is to:
C　　　　a.　help the child learn right from wrong
www　　　b.　raise the child's self-esteem
　　　*　　c.　help the child find realistic ways to get his/her needs met
　　　　　d.　provide for immediate gratification

p. 30　28.　Lisa and Jimmy both want to stay up past their bedtimes to watch a show on TV.
C　　　　When their parents say "no," Lisa throws a fit, while Jimmy says, "Please? I'll brush my teeth and get into PJs and be all ready, so I can just pop into bed the minute the show is over!" From a Freudian perspective, Lisa is responding from her ___ while Jimmy is communicating through his ___ .
　　　*　　a.　id; ego
　　　　　b.　ego; superego
　　　　　c.　id; superego
　　　　　d.　ego; id

p. 30　29.　Leah, age two months, is hungry. She cries in order to signal her hunger. Sam, age
C　　　　2 years, is also hungry. He takes Dad's hand and leads him to the kitchen while repeating "cookie, cookie." According to Freudian theory, Sam is communicating his needs through the _____, while Leah is communicating her needs through the _____.
　　　*　　a.　ego; id
　　　　　b.　id; superego
　　　　　c.　id; ego
　　　　　d.　superego; ego

p. 31　30.　Which personality component emerges as children internalize, or take on as their
F　　　　own, the moral standards and values of their parents?
　　　　　a.　ego
　　　　　b.　id
　　　*　　c.　superego
　　　　　d.　the unconscious

p. 31　31.　Freud called the sex psychic energy the _____.
F　　　　a.　superego
　　　　　b.　ego
　　　*　　c.　libido
　　　　　d.　collective unconscious

p. 31   32.   After her mother says "no," Sandra takes some cookies from the cookie jar and eats
C   them when her mother isn't looking. Later, she feels bad because she knows this was not a
               good thing to do. The fact that she feels bad indicates that:
               a.   her id is in control
               b.   she has the ability to delay gratification
        *   c.   her superego is reasonably well developed
               d.   she is responding to her libido

p. 31   33.   Sam doesn't mind cheating on an exam, as long as he can get away with it. From a
C   Freudian perspective, one might say he has an:
        *   a.   under-developed superego
               b.   overly-developed ego
               c.   inadequate id
               d.   excess of libido

p. 31   34.   Which is the MOST accurate description of the relationship between the three
F   personality components proposed by Freud, the id, ego, and superego?
               a.   a well-oiled machine
*   b.   normal sibling rivalry
               c.   a broken-down car
               d.   a harmonious marriage

p. 31   35.   To control anxiety, the ego
F   a.   fulfills all of the id's desires
www   b.   turns over control to the superego
               c.   progresses through different psychosexual stages
        *   d.   adapts defense mechanisms

p. 31   36.   Maria, a university professor, smokes like a chimney and bites her nails. Freud
C   might say:
        *   a.   Maria has become fixated at the anal stage of development.
               b.   Maria did not strongly identify with her same sex parent.
               c.   Maria is suffering from an unresolved Electra complex.
               d.   Maria has an inadequate superego.

p. 31   37.   Brad, a high school teacher, is a tight-wad. He is also overly concerned with rules,
C   and with keeping everything in its place at all times. Freud might say:
               a.   Brad's id is too strong.
        *   b.   Brad has become fixated at the anal stage of development.
               c.   Brad was nursed for too long as an infant.
               d.   Brad is suffering from an Oedipal complex.

p. 31   38.   It is MOST accurate to say that Freud believed:
F   a.   nurture is more important than nature in determining the course of development
               b.   nurture and nature are equally important in determining the course of development
        *   c.   nature is more important than nurture in determining the course of development
               d.   the effects of nurture work against the effects of nature in determining the course of
                    development

p. 31   39.   Which of the following BEST characterizes Freud's position on the nature-nurture
F   issue?
              a.   He emphasized nurture more than nature.
        *   b.   He emphasized nature more than nurture.
              c.   He emphasized both nature and nurture equally.
              d.   He did not really take a stand on this issue.

p. 31   40.   Linda's son seems very aggressive with other children. She is concerned about this, and
C   consults with a psychologist who tells her it is normal for a child to go through an
              aggressive stage. Which of the following theorists is most likely to agree with this
              perspective?
              a.   Bandura
              b.   Erikson
        *   c.   Freud
              d.   Skinner

p. 32   41.   When Greg and Alice go out to dinner with friends, Greg brings a calculator so he
C   can figure out exactly how much his share of the bill is. Alice things Greg is a tight-wad
              and finds his behavior embarrassing. Freud would be MOST LIKELY to attribute Greg's
              stingy behavior to:
              a.   an unresolved Oedipus complex
        *   b.   stressful toilet-training
              c.   abusive parenting
              d.   a big ego

p. 32   42.   Brynn is three years old. She has been out of diapers for over a year. When her
C   mother comes home from the hospital with a new baby brother, Brynn begins to suck her
              thumb and wet the bed at night. Brynn is experiencing:
              a.   denial
        *   b.   regression
              c.   repression
              d.   sublimation

p. 33   43.   Freud proposed a 5-stage theory of personality development. In order, these stages
F   are:
              a.   anal, oral, genital, phallic, latency
              b.   oral, anal, genital, latency, phallic
        *   c.   oral, anal, phallic, latency, genital
              d.   anal, oral, genital, latency, phallic

p. 33   44.   Four-year-old Steven says, "Mommy, when I grow up will you marry me?" Steven
C   is most likely in which psychosexual stage of development:
              a.   anal
              b.   genital
              c.   oral
        *   d.   phallic

p. 33　45.　Ginny gives her daddy a valentine, on which she has written "Will you marry me?"
C　　　According to Freud's psychosexual theory, Ginny is MOST LIKELY in the _____ stage.
www　*　a.　phallic
　　　　b.　anal
　　　　c.　genital
　　　　d.　latency

p. 33　46.　Samantha adores her daddy and does not get along well with her mother. The
C　　　parents are concerned, and consult a therapist. The therapist, taking a Freudian
　　　　perspective, attributes Samantha's behavior to:
　　　　a.　an underdeveloped superego
　*　　b.　the Electra complex
　　　　c.　poor parenting
　　　　d.　repressed hostility

p. 33　47.　For a boy, the purpose of identification during the Oedipus complex is to
C　　　　a.　reduce anxiety
　　　　b.　learn his masculine sex role
　　　　c.　further develop his superego
　*　　d.　all of the above

p. 33　48.　Aaron frequently complains of stomach-aches and asks to stay home from school
C　　　with his mommy. Even though he has been home all day, Aaron always has to tell mommy
　　　　"something special" just when daddy gets home from work. Aaron's behavior suggests he
　　　　is in the _____ stage.
　　　　a.　genital
　　　　b.　latency
　　　　c.　anal
　*　　d.　phallic

p. 33　49.　Steven is working hard on perfecting his soccer and baseball skills, and is also
C　　　trying to improve his understanding of what he reads in school. After school, Steven likes
　　　　best to go roller-blading or shoot hoops with Nate and Jeff. Steven's behavior is MOST
　　　　typical of children in the _____ stage:
　　　　a.　Oedipus
　　　　b.　phallic
　*　　c.　latency
　　　　d.　genital

p. 33　50.　Freud described one developmental period when children suppress most of their
F　　　sexual feelings. He termed this period:
　　　　a.　fixation
　　　　b.　genital
　*　　c.　latency
　　　　d.　phallic

p. 33　51. According to Freud, the process of "identification" facilitates:

     F
        a. moral development in boys, but not girls
        b. gender-role development for girls, but not boys
        c. gender-role development for boys, only, and moral development for girls, only
     * d. moral and gender-role development for both boys and girls

p. 33　52. A reasonable criticism of Freudian psychoanalytic theory is that it puts TOO

     C   LITTLE emphasis on the:
        a. biological instincts or urges that underlie behavior
     * b. effects of later life experiences on development
        c. emotional side of development
        d. ways in which parents influence development

p. 33　53. Freud has been criticized for all of the following EXCEPT:

     F
        a. his theory is not falsifiable
        b. his propositions are difficult to test
     * c. he has ignored the matter of individual differences in development
        d. he is preoccupied with sexuality

p. 34　54. Which is generally NOT considered a strength of Freud's theory?

     C
     www
        a. a focus on unconscious motivation
        b. a focus on the role that early experiences play in shaping later personality development
        c. an emphasis on emotional development
     * d. a sound research methodology

p. 34　55. In comparison to Freud, Erikson placed:

     F
        a. greater emphasis on infantile sexuality
     * b. greater emphasis on social relationships
        c. less emphasis on parenting
        d. greater emphasis on biological determinants of behavior

p. 34　56. Erikson's theory is DIFFERENT from Freud's because it:

     C
        a. places greater emphasis on biological influences
        b. describes development in terms of stages
     * c. focuses on possibilities for growth beyond adolescence
        d. involves the resolution of crises

p. 34　57. Erikson's theory is different from Freud's because it:

     C
        a. describes development in terms of stages
        b. ignores development during adulthood
        c. puts more emphasis on biological drives
     * d. puts more emphasis on peers, school, and other social influences

p. 35 58. Erikson differs from Freud in his views of personality development in all of the
C   following EXCEPT:
            a. Erikson is more optimistic than Freud about the human organism's capacity for
                overcoming problems that originate in early childhood.
            b. Erikson believes that there are significant changes with regard to personality
                development that go beyond adolescence, whereas Freud does not.
            c. Erikson sees humans as basically rational and governed by the ego, whereas Freud sees
                humans as basically irrational and ruled by the id.
      *   d. Erikson pays less attention than does Freud to social influences on personality
                development.

p. 35 59. Which of the following is TRUE regarding the theories of Freud and Erikson?
C   a. Erikson leans more toward the "nature" side of the nature-nurture issue than does
www   Freud.
            b. Erikson and Freud both place a primary emphasis on infantile sexuality in their theories
                of personality development.
      *   c. Erikson places a greater emphasis on the influence of culture on personality
                development than does Freud.
            d. Freud places more emphasis on the "nurture" side of the nature-nurture issue than does
                Erikson.

p. 35 60. Which of Erikson's psychosocial stages corresponds to Freud's oral stage of
F   development?
            a. autonomy vs. shame and doubt
            b. industry vs. inferiority
            c. initiative vs. guilt
      *   d. trust vs. mistrust

p. 35 61. Freud's latency period corresponds to which of Erikson's psychosocial stages?
F   a. autonomy vs. shame and doubt
            b. initiative vs. guilt
      *   c. industry vs. inferiority
            d. trust vs. mistrust

p. 35 62. Maya has recently given birth to a healthy baby boy, Jason. Whenever Jason cries,
F   Maya goes to him, tries to figure out the reason for his crying, and then promptly does all
            she can to meet his needs. According to Erikson's theory, Jason is well on his way toward
            mastering which of the following developmental conflicts:
            a. autonomy vs. shame and doubt
            b. industry vs. inferiority
            c. initiative vs. guilt
      *   d. trust vs. mistrust

p. 35 63. Jimmy is two years old. His favorite word is "No!" According to Erikson, Jimmy is
C   working on developing:
      *   a. a sense of autonomy
            b. feelings of trust
            c. his own initiative
            d. a sense of industry

p. 35 64. The preschool-aged child is typically in which of Erikson's psychosocial stages?
F
www
          a. autonomy vs. shame and doubt
          b. industry vs. inferiority
    *   c. initiative vs. guilt
          d. trust vs. mistrust

p. 35 65. Rachel is 15 years old. She spends countless hours alone and in conversation with
C   her peers trying to figure out what it is she wants to do with her life. Rachel is in which of
          the following of Erikson's psychosocial stages?
    *   a. identity vs. role confusion
          b. industry vs. inferiority
          c. initiative vs. guilt
          d. intimacy vs. isolation

p. 35 66. Seven-year-old Rafi is MOST LIKELY in which of the following stages?
F
          a. trust vs. mistrust and latency
          b. initiative vs. guilt and phallic
          c. genital and industry vs. inferiority
    *   d. industry vs. inferiority and latency

p. 35 67. Molly is wants to do everything for herself, from eating to dressing to toileting, even
C   though she often makes "mistakes" (such as putting her pants on backward, or forgetting to
          wipe her bottom). Molly is MOST LIKELY in which of Erikson's stages?
          a. trust vs. mistrust
    *   b. autonomy vs. shame and doubt
          c. initiative vs. guilt
          d. industry vs. inferiority

p. 35 68. A child in the phallic stage is MOST LIKELY also in the _____ stage:
F
          a. autonomy vs. shame and doubt
    *   b. initiative vs. guilt
          c. industry vs. inferiority
          d. trust vs. mistrust

p. 35 69. Margie is in college and is having a very hard time deciding on a major. She just
C   doesn't know what she wants to be when she "grows up!" Erikson would say Margie is
          experiencing the conflict of:
          a. initiative vs. guilt
          b. autonomy vs. industry
    *   c. identity vs. role confusion
          d. industry vs. isolation

p. 35 70. What does Erikson see as the central developmental task facing those in the period
F   of young adulthood?
          a. establishing a sense of trust in others
    *   b. establishing intimate relationships with others
          c. the development of a social conscience
          d. deciding on a career path to follow

p. 36 71. Ruth is 80 years old and is terminally ill with cancer. As she reflects back on her life
C   she comes to the conclusion that she has lived a full and productive life, and that it could
           not have been better lived in any other way. Ruth has successfully mastered the
           developmental task of:
           a. generativity vs. isolation
           b. generativity vs. stagnation
           c. industry vs. inferiority
     *   d. integrity vs. despair

p. 36 72. Which of the following is a major criticism of Erikson's theory of personality
C   development?
           a. he is pessimistic regarding one's ability to overcome problems that have their roots in
               early childhood experiences
           b. he portrays adulthood as a period of little growth and change
     *   c. his theory is rather vague and difficult to test
           d. his theory focuses too strongly on unconscious drives and motives

p. 36 73. Erikson's theory has been praised for:
F   a. focusing attention on unconscious maturation
           b. its emphasis on cognitive development
     *   c. looking at personality development across the life span
           d. pointing out the importance of early childhood experiences

p. 37 74. Which theoretical camp suggests that we should study only what we can directly
C   observe and measure?
     *   a. behaviorists
           b. cognitive-developmentalists
           c. ecologists
           d. psychoanalysts

p. 37 75. Which of the theoretical camps discussed in your text would be LEAST interested in
C   unconscious drives and motives?
     *   a. behaviorists
           b. cognitive-developmentalists
           c. ecologists
           d. humanists

p. 37 76. Joy comes home from work exhausted and is surprised to find that her daughter,
C   Michelle, has set the table and started dinner. Joy is thrilled. She praises Michelle and
           spends an extra half-hour reading with her before bed. The same thing happens the next
           day, and soon this has become a daily event. This is an example of:
           a. classical conditioning
           b. observational learning
     *   c. operant conditioning
           d. respondent conditioning

p. 37
C

77. John is upset with his son for keeping his room so messy. His neighbor, Bill, suggests that John give his son a dollar for cleaning his room on Saturday mornings. Bill's approach is MOST in line with which of the following theorists?
   a. Urie Bronfenbrenner
   b. Erik Erikson
   c. Jean Piaget
*   d. B. F. Skinner

p. 37
F

78. Watson believed that:
   a. a person's behavior is primarily determined by his/her genetic makeup
   b. while the forces of nature are dominant, parents may also have a powerful influence on a child's development
   c. most human characteristics and behaviors are determined by multiple influences, including both genetic and environmental factors
*   d. a person's environment controls the course of his/her development

p. 37
F

79. Watson believed all of the following EXCEPT:
*   a. most children progress through a predictable series of stages that are programmed by biological maturation
   b. children have no inborn tendencies
   c. how a person turns out depends entirely on the environment s/he grows up in
   d. development is continuous and particularistic

p. 37
F
www

80. According to the behaviorists, development is:
*   a. continuous and particularistic
   b. universal and continuous
   c. universal and discontinuous
   d. discontinuous and particularistic

p. 37
F

81. A reinforcer:
   a. weakens an undesired response
   b. weakens a desired response
*   c. can strengthen whatever response that happened to produce it
   d. can weaken an undesired response or strengthen a desired response

p. 37
F

82. The purpose of a reinforcer is to:
*   a. strengthen a behavioral response
   b. weaken a behavioral response
   c. strengthen a desired response while weakening an undesired response
   d. weaken a desired response

p. 37
C

83. Steve taught his dog, Spot, to ring a bell hanging on the doorknob to signal when he had to go outside to "do his business." Each time Spot rang the bell, he received a treat, and soon he had learned just what to do. This approach to BEST exemplifies the perspective of:
   a. Albert Bandura
*   b. B.F. Skinner
   c. Jean Piaget
   d. Erik Erikson

p. 37   84. Mr. Jones is upset because his third-graders are too noisy during independent work time.
C   A colleague recommends that he give children stickers when they are being quiet, and
               withhold the stickers when they are noisy. This practice is consistent with the views of:
               a. Bandura
               b. Freud
         *   c. Skinner
               d. Pavlov

p. 38   85. Bandura would argue that Skinner
C   a. is totally correct in his approach
               b. didn't define reinforcement correctly
               c. agreed with Freud too much
         *   d. didn't stress cognitive factors enough

p. 38   86. Social learning theorists claim that:
C   a. all children progress through the same stages of social development
         *   b. behaviorists do not pay enough attention to the role of cognition in learning
               c. learners are passively shaped by the consequences of their behavior
               d. observational learning is not as important as other forms of learning

p. 38   87. Lisa learns to bake bread by watching her Grandpa bake bread. This is an example of:
F   *   a. observational learning
               b. respondent learning
               c. selective reinforcement
               d. social conditioning

p. 38   88. Traci goes along with her brother Joe to his gymnastics class and watches closely while he
C   works on the balance beam. One day Traci's Mom finds her out in the back yard, with a
               board spread across two big boxes, doing some of the same maneuvers that she has seen
               Joe do in class. This is an example of:
         *   a. observational learning
               b. operant conditioning
               c. respondent conditioning
               d. selective reinforcement

p. 38   89. Nick, age 3, has always been cooperative about going to bed at night. Then the family
C   takes a trip and stays with relatives where Nick's cousin, Becky (also age 3), has a royal fit
               at bed time. Nick watches while Becky's parents read her extra stories and bring her a
               glass of juice to calm her down. After Nick and his family return home, Nick begins to
               throw tantrums at bed time. This is an example of:
         *   a. observational learning
               b. operant conditioning
               c. respondent conditioning
               d. selective reinforcement

p. 38 90. Sara watches her big sister, Jenny, get ready for a big date. After Jenny leaves with her
C   boyfriend, Sara's mom finds her in the bathroom, putting on make-up just like Jenny did.
           This BEST demonstrates:
           a. mechanistic learning
           b. instrumental conditioning
    *   c. observational learning
           d. respondent conditioning

p. 39 91. Skinner and Bandura would AGREE that:
C   a. children progress through a predictable series of stages in normal development
           b. biological maturation plays a primary role in determining the course of development
           c. human beings are passively shaped by the environment
    *   d. development is continuous and particularistic

p. 39 92. Reciprocal determinism refers to a continuous, back and forth interaction between:
F   a. parent and child
           b. a person and the environment
    *   c. a person, his/her behavior, and the environment
           d. a reinforcer and a behavior

p. 39 93. Which of the following is NOT a strength of learning theory?
F   a. a focus on learning as a life-long process
    *   b. a focus on universal stages in cognitive development
           c. practical applications in psychotherapy
           d. it is precise and testable

p. 40 94. Skinner's and Bandura's explanations for the high rate of teen pregnancy include all
C   of the following except
    *   a. the influence of subconscious drives
           b. attention and reinforcement
           c. possible punishment for not engaging in sex
           d. bad role models

p. 41 95. Piaget was a "constructivist," which means he believed that in order for children to learn
C   they must be:
www   a. vicariously reinforced
    *   b. given opportunities to interact with their environment
           c. provided with models to imitate
           d. given lots of opportunities to build with blocks

p. 41 96. According to Piaget, cognitive development occurs as a result of:
F   a. differential reinforcement of behavioral responses
           b. the unfolding of one's genetic "blueprint"
    *   c. the interaction of a biologically maturing child with his/her environment
           d. observation and imitation

p. 41   97. Piaget would be MOST LIKELY to say that children:
C   *   a. learn by doing
          b. learn by watching
          c. learn through guidance from an adult
          d. learn through reinforcement

p. 42   98. Which of the following is NOT a characteristic of an invariant sequence of stages?
C   a. Progress through the stages is orderly
     *   b. People can become fixated at earlier stages
          c. Stages can't be skipped
          d. There is no regression to earlier stages

p. 42   99. At the end of what stage of cognitive development are children able to use symbols
F   to stand for objects and events?
          a. concrete operations
          b. formal operations
          c. preoperational
     *   d. sensorimotor

p. 42   100. As a child moves from the sensorimotor stage to the preoperational stage, s/he
F   becomes able to:
          a. conserve
     *   b. think symbolically
          c. engage in assimilation
          d. use abstract reasoning

p. 42   101. Which BEST describes the problem-solving approach of the concrete operational
F   child?
          a. systematic hypothesis testing
          b. scientific
     *   c. trial and error
          d. they cannot devise solutions to problems

p. 42   102. Ten-year-old Trixie is MOST LIKELY to:
C   *   a. use a trial and error approach to solving problems
          b. be able to think ahead to the long-term consequences of her actions
          c. be able to think about hypothetical situations
          d. be unable to think symbolically

p. 43   103. According to Piaget, what is likely to be MOST difficult for 8-year-old Fern, who is
C   in the concrete operations stage?
          a. solving conservation problems
     *   b. thinking through all the hypothetical consequences that might result from something
              she does
          c. overcoming her egocentric tendencies enough to understand that other people have
              different perspectives than she does
          d. adding or subtracting items in her head

p. 43 104. A major cognitive accomplishment made by children as they move from the pre-
F operational to the concrete-operational stage is a newly acquired capacity to:
www a. think symbolically
b. think hypothetically
* c. use a trial-and-error approach to solving problems
d. engage in systematic testing of hypotheses

p. 43 105. Molly has just entered the stage of formal operational thought. Something she can do now,
C that she could not do before, is:
a. engage in trial-and-error problem solving
* b. consider the long-range consequences of her actions
c. think symbolically
d. mentally classify objects in her head

p. 43 106. Piaget's explanation for today's high rate of teen pregnancy would
F a. suggest that teens were engaging in systematic hypothesis testing
* b. focus on their limited cognitive abilities
c. stress ethological factors
d. pinpoint the need for equilibrium

p. 43 107. Piaget has been criticized for all of the following EXCEPT:
C a. saying too little about the influences of motivation and emotion on thought processes
b. choosing formal operational thinking as the most mature form of thought
* c. portraying children as passive learners
d. providing an inadequate explanation of how children progress from one stage of
thought to the next

p. 43 108. A major criticism of Piaget's theory is that it:
C a. has had little influence on educational practice
b. focuses too heavily on the importance of social relationships in determining the course
of development
c. portrays children as passive learners
* d. says little about the influence of motivation on children's cognitive development

p. 43 109. Which theoretical perspective suggests that changes in an individual result in
F changes in his/her environment, and vice versa?
a. cognitive-developmental
b. behaviorism
* c. contextual
d. psychoanalytic

p. 44 110. Piaget and Bronfenbrenner would agree that
C a. development is stagelike
* b. nature and nurture interact to shape development
c. nurture is more influential in development than nature
d. development occurs through continuous change across the life span

p. 44   111. According to the ecological approach to development
F   a. ecological conditions have a significant impact on development
www   b. development naturally unfold according to a genetic blueprint
         *   c. environmental systems interact with one another and with the person to influence
                  development
              d. the environment determines a person's developmental path

p. 44   112. Which of the following characterizes Urie Bronfenbrenner's position on developmental
C   research?
              a. Research often does not take into account the affects of age.
              b. Research has too often used cross-sectional designs rather than longitudinal designs.
              c. Research places too much emphasis on how individuals shape their own development,
                  ignoring universal developmental changes.
         *   d. Research often separates the context of development from development itself.

p. 44   113. The effects of Lisa's family on her development are considered part of the:
C   a. exosystem
              b. macrosystem
              c. mesosystem
         *   d. microsystem

p. 45   114. According to the ecological approach to human development put forth by
C   Bronfenbrenner, a nation-wide economic recession would be considered a part of the:
              a. exosystem
         *   b. macrosystem
              c. mesosystem
              d. microsystem

p. 45   115. For German children, the tearing down of the Berlin Wall in 1989-1990 represents a
C   major change in the:
              a. exosystem
         *   b. macrosystem
              c. mesosystem
              d. microsystem

p. 45   116. Parent-teacher conferences best represent a part of the:
C   a. exosystem
              b. macrosystem
         *   c. mesosystem
              d. microsystem

p. 45   117. Mr. Jones writes a weekly newsletter which he sends home with his third grade
C   students in order to keep parents informed. For his students, this newsletter is part of what
www   Bronfenbrenner calls the:
         *   a. exosystem
              b. macrosystem
              c. mesosystem
              d. microsystem

p. 45   118. Thomas just lost his job with the Department of Social Services. As a result, money
C   is tight and the stress level at home has risen. With regard to Thomas's children, Steve and
               Angie, this represents an effect of the ___ on the ___:
               a. microsystem; macrosystem
               b. mesosystem; microsystem
        *   c. exosystem; microsystem
               d. macrosystem; exosystem

p. 45   119. In Jonesville, the proposal to increase the funding base for the public schools was
C   defeated. For the children of Jonesville, this BEST represents an aspect of the ___, which
               may have a significant impact on their development:
        *   a. exosystem
               b. macrosystem
               c. mesosystem
               d. microsystem

p. 45   120. Which is the BEST example of a change in the microsystem which could affect a
C   child's development?
        *   a. the birth of a sibling
               b. a school budget cut
               c. parent-teacher conferences
               d. a reconciliation between the child's father and his grandfather

p. 45   121. According to Bronfenbrenner, a dramatic decline in the national unemployment rate
C   would BEST be considered a change in the:
               a. exosystem
        *   b. macrosystem
               c. mesosystem
               d. microsystem

p. 45   122. Parent's work and friends can affect children indirectly through the:
F   a. microsystem
        *   b. mesosystem
               c. exosystem
               d. macrosystem

p. 47   123. Which of the following is NOT an organismic theorist?
F   a. Piaget
               b. Freud
        *   c. Skinner
               d. Gesell

p. 47   124. Proponents of the mechanistic view include all of the following except
C   a. B. F. Skinner
        *   b. Piaget
               c. Bandura
               d. Watson

p. 47   125. A mother who takes a mechanistic view of child development is MOST LIKELY to:
C   a. allow her child to watch whatever s/he wants on TV
             b. believe that what she does as a parent will have little influence on how her child
                 develops
             c. believe that children all develop in much the same way
        *   d. believe that children are relatively passive in the developmental process

p. 47   126. Which is NOT an assumption of the mechanistic model?
F   a. individual children develop in very different ways
             b. children develop in response to stimulation from the environment
        *   c. development occurs in a series of predictable stages
             d. development throughout the life-span is continuous and gradual

p. 49   127. MOST developmentalists today AGREE that:
C   a. nature is more important than nurture in determining the course of development
             b. nurture is more important than nature in determining the course of development
        *   c. nature and nurture are both critical in determining the course of development
             d. nature and nurture both play a role in determining the course of development, but they
                 tend to operate quite independently of one another.

p. 50   128. A developmentalist who is "eclectic" is one who:
C   *   a. draws from a number of different theoretical perspectives to help explain human
                 development
             b. uses organismic and contextual theories, but rejects mechanistic perspectives
             c. rejects all formal theories in favor of developing one's own personal theory of human
                 development
             d. believes that theory gets in the way of learning about the way things really are

p. 29   129 A theorist who believes that humans progress through developmental stages is likely
C   to believe in
SG   *   a. discontinuous changes
             b. continuous changes
             c. quantitative changes
             d. multiple paths of development

p. 29   130. The universality-particularity issue concerns
C   a. the degree to which developmental changes are quantitative or qualitative in nature
SG   *   b. the extent to which developmental changes are common to everyone or different from
                 person to person
             c. whether development is multiply caused
             d. whether or not development follows universal paths determined by genetic factors or
                 environmental factors

p. 30   131. According to Freud's theory, the _____ must find ways of realistically satisfying
C   the demands of the _____.
SG   a. superego, ego
             b. defense mechanisms, id
             c. id, ego
        *   d. ego, id

p. 33
C
SG

132. Boys resolve their Oedipus complexes by
    a. fearing their father
* b. identifying with their father
    c. distancing themselves from their parents
    d. redirecting their psychic energy to another part of their body

p. 32
F
SG

133. Regression occurs when
* a. a person reverts to an earlier stage of development
    b. a person pushes anxiety-provoking thoughts out of conscious awareness
    c. development becomes arrested because part of the libido remains tied to an earlier stage of development
    d. psychic energy is directed toward socially acceptable activities

p. 35
F
SG

134. Which of the following BEST characterizes Erikson's position on the nature-nurture issue?
    a. He emphasized nurture more than nature.
    b. He emphasized nature more than nurture.
* c. He emphasized nature and nurture equally
    d. He didn't really take a stand on this issue.

p. 35
F
SG

135. According to Erikson, the main task facing adolescents is
* a. developing a sense of identity
    b. achieving a sense of intimacy with another person
    c. mastering important academic tasks
    d. building a sense of self-confidence

p. 37
C
SG

136. A basic premise of John Watson's behaviorism is that development is
    a. a series of qualitative behavior changes
* b. a continuous process of change dependent on learning experiences
    c. a combination of inborn tendencies and environmental experiences
    d. best understood by studying mental activities

p. 38
C
SG

137. Which of the following explanations for developmental change would a social learning theorist be most likely to give?
    a. Children are unconsciously motivated by internal conflict.
* b. Children observe the world around them and actively process this information.
    c. Children are passively influenced by environmental rewards and punishments.
    d. Children actively construct an understanding of the world through interactions with their environment.

p. 47
C
SG

138. Which two theorists believe that development occurs through the interaction of an active person with the environment?
    a. Piaget and Freud
    b. Skinner and Bronfenbrenner
    c. Skinner and Bandura
* d. Piaget and Bandura

p. 42 139. A child in Piaget's preoperational stage is able to solve problems
C   a. that are concrete by using logical reasoning
SG   b. that are abstract by using logical reasoning
       *   c. using symbols
          d. through their sensory experiences and their actions

p. 43 140. Of the following, Piaget has been MOST criticized for his
C   a. emphasis on sexual instincts during childhood
SG   b. belief that children are actively involved in their development
          c. description of cognitive development
       *   d. belief that cognitive development occurs through an invariant sequence of coherent stages

p. 44 141. Urie Bronfenbrenner's ecological approach to development contends that
F   *   a. development is influenced by interacting environmental systems
SG   b. the home environment is the only really important influence on development
          c. children have a passive role in development and are unable to shape their futures
          d. the environment has a similar effect on all children

p. 44 142. According to the ecological approach to development, a person's most immediate
F   environment is the
SG   *   a. microsystem
          b. mesosystem
          c. exosystem
          d. macrosystem

p. 47 143. Which of the following theories is (are) based on an organismic world view?
F   a. Piaget's cognitive-developmental theory
SG   b. Freud's psychoanalytic theory
          c. Skinner's operant learning theory
       *   d. Both a and b
          e. Both b and c

TRUE-FALSE

p. 28 144. Most developmental theorists believe that children are relatively passive when it comes to their own development.
          a. true
       *   b. false

p. 29 145. Discontinuity theorists believe that development involves primarily quantitative changes in
www   human behavior.
          a. true
       *   b. false

p. 29   146. Theorists who believe that development occurs through qualitative changes usually do not
         propose stages to describe development.
         a.   true
    *   b.   false

p.29   147. The universality/particularity issue concerns whether we all follow similar or unique paths.
www *   a.   true
         b.   false

p. 30   148. Freud's theory was valuable in highlighting the importance of unconscious motivation.
    *   a.   true
         b.   false

p. 31   149. Freud believed that nurture was more important than nature.
         a.   true
    *   b.   false

p. 31   150. The superego's job is to realistically satisfy the demands of the id.
         a.   true
    *   b.   false

p. 31   151. Defense mechanisms are adopted to reduce or cope with anxiety created by conflict among
         the id, ego, and superego.
    *   a.   true
         b.   false

p. 35   152. Erikson believes that an infant should develop a certain amount of skepticism to balance a
         solid sense of trust.
    *   a.   true
         b.   false

p. 35   153. According to Erikson, middle-aged adults who are unproductive and wrapped up in their
         own concerns are experiencing isolation.
         a.   true
    *   b.   false

p. 35   154. The most important task facing adolescents is developing an identity.
    *   a.   true
         b.   false

p. 36   155. Erikson and Freud agree that personality changes very little after early childhood.
www   a.   true
    *   b.   false

p. 37   156. Behaviorists, in general, support the environmentalist position with regard to the nature-
         nurture debate.
    *   a.   true
         b.   false

p. 37   157. Skinner believed that learning occurred because learners associate actions with their
        consequences.
        *   a.   true
            b.   false

p. 38   158. Bandura believed that we actively process information that we observe in the environment.
        *   a.   true
            b.   false

p. 41   159. According to Piaget, children construct their own understanding of the world based on their
www   experiences.
        *   a.   true
            b.   false

p. 41   160. Piaget believes that changes in children's thinking are primarily quantitative in nature.
            a.   true
        *   b.   false

p. 44   161. Bronfenbrenner's ecological theory focuses on the way individuals develop in particular
        contexts.
        *   a.   true
            b.   false

p. 47   162. Learning theorists hold a contextual world view.
            a.   true
        *   b.   false

p. 48   163. Piaget's cognitive-developmental and Freud's psychoanalytic theories are examples of the
        organismic world view.
        *   a.   true
            b.   false

ESSAY QUESTIONS

164.   Susie, age four, climbed into her parent's bed one night because she was frightened by a scary
       dream. Because it was so late and Susie was obviously distressed, her parents comforted her and
       let her sleep with them for the remainder of the night. Now Susie does not want to sleep in her
       own bed and every night has been a battle of wills, usually ending with Susie sleeping in her
       parent's bed. How would psychoanalytic, learning, cognitive-developmental, and
       contextual/ecological theorists explain what is going on with Susie?

165.   What are the strengths and weaknesses of Freudian theory? How do neo-Freudians contribute to
       our understanding of development?

166.   Erikson and Freud both have psychoanalytic theories of development. How does Erikson's
       psychoanalytic theory compare to Freud's psychoanalytic theory?

167. How does Piaget's cognitive-developmental theory compare to each of the following theories: Erikson's psychoanalytic theory, Bandura's social-learning theory, and Bronfenbrenner's ecological theory? For each, note at least one point that is similar and one point that is different.

168. How would you create a new theory using the ideas of the theorists presented in this chapter? www   Which concepts would you keep and which would you eliminate? Explain your choices.

169. Consider the problem of shyness. Many children and adults in our society are socially SG   shy to a significant degree and express anxiety in many everyday, social situations. How would each of the theorists in this chapter interpret or explain the development of this condition? [Sample answer is provided in the Study Guide.]

170. In what ways do the learning theory explanations of development conflict with the SG   psychoanalytic explanations of development?

171. How do each of the theories address the goal of optimizing development in the example SG   of teenage pregnancy described in this chapter? Note that in this example, optimizing development would be somehow reducing the number of teenage pregnancies.

172. Freud and Piaget are often considered to be the "great stage theorists" of developmental SG   psychology. Discuss ways in which Freud and Piaget are similar in their views of development and ways in which they differ.

3

THE GENETICS OF LIFE-SPAN DEVELOPMENT

MULTIPLE CHOICE QUESTIONS

p. 55
F
1. The genetic endowment that members of a particular species have in common is called:
   a. dominant heredity
   b. Mendelian heredity
   c. natural selection
 * d. species heredity

p. 55
C
2. Most dogs bark but don't speak, and most humans speak but don't bark. This is due to:
   a. ethology
   b. environment
   c. individual heredity
 * d. species heredity

p. 55
C
3. All babies, regardless of which culture they live in or which language is spoken around them, begin to babble at about the same age. This is an example of
 * a. species heredity
   b. natural selection
   c. genetic adaptation
   d. ethology

p. 55
C
www
4. Ethologists argue that:
   a. genetic influences are much greater than environmental ones.
   b. behavior is best studied under controlled conditions.
 * c. behavior must be studied in the environment where it normally occurs.
   d. only behaviors that are adaptive to survival should be studied.

p. 56
F
5. The idea that some genes aid in adaption more than others is known as
   a. ethology
   b. dominant-recessive inheritance
 * c. natural selection
   d. species heredity

p. 56
F
6. Which of the following is NOT a major claim of Darwin's theory of evolution?
   a. There is genetic variation in a species.
   b. Some genes aid in adaptation to the environment more than other genes do.
 * c. Environmental changes can alter the individual's genetic material.
   d. Genes that aid in adaptation to the environment are more likely to be passed on to future generations than genes that do not aid in adaptation.

p. 56   7.   Kettlewell's research on the color of moths and their geographic location
C   demonstrates the principle of:
              a.   cultural evolution
              b.   Mendelian heredity
     *   c.   natural selection
              d.   species heredity

p. 56   8.   Evolutionary theory is concerned
C   a.   only with the influence of genes
              b.   only with the influence of environment
              c.   with DNA and gametes
     *   d.   with the interaction of genes and environment

p. 56   9.   Max is interested in the evolved behavior of various species in their natural environment.
C   Max is MOST likely a(n):
              a.   anthropologist
              b.   biologist
     *   c.   ethologist
              d.   sociologist

p. 56   10.   Which of the following would an ethologist be LEAST LIKELY to study?
C   *   a.   influence of training on level of preschooler's prosocial behavior
              b.   response of different species' young to separation from their mothers
              c.   the mating rituals of birds
              d.   preschooler's behavior on the playground

p. 56   11.   Researchers who test predictions drawn from Darwin's theory often referred to
F   themselves as
     *   a.   evolutionary psychologists
              b.   ecologists
              c.   ethologists
              d.   psychobiologists

p. 57   12.   Evolutionary theorists predict that:
C   a.   Learning and culture have no input on things such as mate selection.
     *   b.   Humans pick mates who will help pass along their genes to subsequent generations.
              c.   Women are likely to choose mates who are somewhat younger than themselves because
                  women live longer (on average), than men.
              d.   Humans have evolved about as far as they can go.

p. 58   13.   At conception, the genetic material of the mother's ovum and the genetic material of
F   the father's sperm unite, creating a new cell called a(n)
              a.   embryo
              b.   gamete
              c.   juvenile cell
     *   d.   zygote

p. 59　14. Normally, humans have _____ chromosomes in all cells, except the sex cells.
F
　　　　　a. 21
　　　　　b. 23
　　*　　c. 46
　　　　　d. 64

p. 58　15. The process by which a zygote becomes a multiple-celled organism is called:
F
　　　　　a. crossing over
　　　　　b. meiosis
　　*　　c. mitosis
　　　　　d. symbiosis

p. 58　16. Following mitosis, each daughter cell has
F
www　　　a. half the number of chromosomes as the mother cell had
　　　　　b. twice the number of chromosomes as the mother cell had
　　*　　c. the same number of chromosomes as the mother cell had
　　　　　d. an undetermined number of chromosomes

p. 58　17. A sperm cell and an ovum each contribute 23, rather than 46, chromosomes to a
F　　　　zygote because they:
　　*　　a. were produced through the process of meiosis
　　　　　b. were produced through the process of mitosis
　　　　　c. have undergone the process of crossing over
　　　　　d. have undergone the process of canalization

p. 58　18. Children of the same biological parents are typically quite different genetically from
C　　　　one another (assuming they are not identical twins). This can be explained by:
　　　　　a. a polygenic pattern of inheritance
　　　　　b. mutations
　　*　　c. the process of crossing-over
　　　　　d. species heredity

p. 58　19. We know that two people have precisely 50% of their genes in common if they are:
F
　　　　　a. fraternal twins
　　　　　b. identical twins
　　*　　c. parent and child
　　　　　d. siblings

p. 58　20. Siblings share:
F
　　　　　a. precisely 50% of their genes
　　*　　b. on average about 50% of their genes
　　　　　c. on average about 25% of their genes
　　　　　d. nearly 100% of their genes

p. 58　21. A normal male has _____ in each somatic cell:
F
　　　　　a. two X chromosomes
　　　　　b. two Y chromosomes
　　*　　c. one X and one Y chromosome
　　　　　d. an extra Y chromosome

p. 59   22.   Jack desperately wants to have a son. He and his wife already have three children, all girls.
C   Jack divorces his wife and remarries. He expects that his new wife will be more successful
                 in providing him with a son. Which of the following is TRUE?
                 a.   Jack's chances of having a son are better with his new wife.
                 b.   Jack's chances of having a son are worse with his new wife.
    *   c.   Jack's chances of having a son are not changed by a change in wife.
                 d.   Jack will be unable to have a son no matter how many children he fathers.

p. 59   23.   The sex of a zygote is determined by:
F   a.   the ovum
    *   b.   the sperm
                 c.   dominant genes
                 d.   both ovum and sperm

p. 59   24.   The sex of an individual human is determined by:
F   a.   the process of meiosis
www   b.   an X chromosome carried by the mother
                 c.   an X or Y chromosome carried by the mother
    *   d.   an X or Y chromosome carried by the father

p. 59   25.   Which of the following is MOST accurate?
C   a.   genes directly cause some behaviors
    *   b.   genes direct the production of proteins which are responsible for how different organs
                     function
                 c.   genetic blueprints cannot be altered by experiences
                 d.   genes contribute directly to physical traits but only indirectly influence personality and
                     intelligence traits.

p. 60   26.   The term _____ refers to the actual characteristics a person has.
F   a.   autotype
                 b.   dominant inheritance
                 c.   genotype
    *   d.   phenotype

p. 60   27.   Your phenotype is:
F   a.   a photograph of your chromosomes
www   b.   the effects on you of environmental factors as opposed to genes
                 c.   your genetic endowment
    *   d.   your various traits and characteristics

p. 60   28.   Phenotype is _____ ; genotype is _____ .
C   a.   a potential; actual reality
    *   b.   actual reality; a potential
                 c.   dominant traits; recessive traits
                 d.   recessive traits; dominant traits

p. 60　29.　Genotype is most accurately described as _____, while phenotype is _____.
F　　*　　a.　genetic potential; an observable characteristic
　　　　　b.　a genetic blueprint; a physical potential
　　　　　c.　a physical reality; the environment
　　　　　d.　a visual representation of chromosomes; environmental potential

p. 60　30.　A human trait is influenced by a single pair of genes with "D" representing the dominant
C　　　　gene and "d" representing the recessive gene. John has the genotype Dd and therefore:
　　　　　a.　carries a defective gene
　　　*　b.　exhibits the trait
　　　　　c.　does not exhibit the trait
　　　　　d.　is homozygous regarding the trait

p. 60　31.　A human trait is influenced by a single pair of genes with "M" representing the dominant
C　　　　gene and "m" representing the recessive gene. Richard (genotype Mm) and Dorothy
　　　　　(genotype mm) decide to have children. According to the principles of Mendelian
　　　　　heredity, what percentage f their children would exhibit the trait?
　　　　　a.　0
　　　　　b.　25
　　　*　c.　50
　　　　　d.　75

p. 60　32.　A human trait is influenced by a single pair of genes with "B" representing the dominant
C　　　　gene and "b" representing the recessive gene. George has the genotype Bb and therefore:
　　　　　a.　is a carrier of the trait but does not exhibit it
　　　*　b.　exhibits the trait
　　　　　c.　is not a carrier and does not exhibit the trait
　　　　　d.　is phenotypical for the trait

p. 60　33.　A human trait is influenced by a single pair of genes with "S" representing the dominant
C　　　　gene and "s" representing the recessive gene. Tim (genotype SS) and Leslie (genotype ss)
　　　　　decide to have children. According to the principles of Mendelian heredity, what
　　　　　percentage of their children would exhibit the trait?
　　　　　a.　0
　　　　　b.　50
　　　　　c.　75
　　　*　d.　100

p. 60　34.　A human trait is influenced by a single pair of genes with "T" representing the dominant
C　　　　gene and "t" representing the recessive gene. Joe (genotype Tt) and Meg (genotype Tt)
www　　　decide to have children. According to the principles of Mendelian heredity, what
　　　　　percentage of their children would exhibit the trait?
　　　　　a.　25
　　　　　b.　50
　　　*　c.　75
　　　　　d.　100

p. 61 35. An individual who is a carrier of a trait has:
C
  a. two dominant genes, both calling for the presence of the trait
  b. two recessive genes, both calling for the presence of the trait
* c. one dominant gene calling for the absence of the trait and one recessive gene calling for the presence of the trait
  d. one dominant gene calling for the presence of the trait and one recessive gene calling for the absence of the trait

p. 61 36. If a person needs a matching pair of genes in order to express a characteristic carried by
F this pair of genes, the characteristic is considered
* a. recessive
  b. dominant
  c. a mutation
  d. polygenic

p. 60 37. Two parents both have one dominant gene for Type A blood and one recessive gene for
C Type O blood. What are the chances that this couple's offspring will have Type O blood?
  a. 0%
* b. 25%
  c. 50%
  d. 75%

p. 60 38. A father has two genes that make for brown hair and a mother has red hair. What are the
C chances that this couple's offspring will have red hair?
* a. 0%
  b. 25%
  c. 50%
  d. 75%

p. 61 39. Tom and Mary are both carriers of the same defective gene. They know that each time
F they have a child there is a ___% risk that child will inherit the disorder.
* a. 25
  b. 50
  c. 75
  d. 100

p. 61 40. In sickle-cell disease, the dominant gene does not entirely mask the effects of the
F corresponding gene. This is called:
www * a. incomplete dominance
  b. codominance
  c. polygenic inheritance
  d. dual dominance

p. 62 41. Children of black/white interracial marriages usually have skin color that is somewhere
C between their mother's skin color and their father's skin color. This is an example of:
  a. incomplete dominance
  b. mutation
  c. polygenic inheritance
* d. codominance

p. 62 42. Michael is color blind. He inherited this characteristic from:
F
      *   a. his father
             b. his mother
             c. both of his parents
             d. neither parent, as this is most likely a fluke

p. 62 43. Jill and John have a son with color blindness. From this, we know that:
C   a. John must be at least a carrier of the color-blindness gene.
      *   b. Jill must be at least a carrier of the color-blindness gene.
             c. John must be color blind himself.
             d. Jill must be color blind herself

p. 62 44. Marcia has just given birth to a baby girl. She is concerned because she is a carrier
C   for hemophilia. Which of the following is TRUE?
             a. Marcia has good cause for concern because hemophilia is most often transmitted to
                 female offspring.
      *   b. Marcia has little cause for concern because hemophilia is most often transmitted to
                 male offspring.
             c. Marcia has little cause for concern because hemophilia can not be transmitted to
                 offspring unless both parents are carriers.
             d. Marcia should not worry because hemophilia almost always skips a generation.

p. 62 45. If a woman is a carrier of an X-linked disorder and a man is not a carrier and does
C   not have the X-linked disorder, what are the chances that this couple's daughter and their
            son will have the disorder?
      *   a. daughter--0%   son--50%
             b. daughter--50%   son--100%
             c. daughter--50%   son--0%
             d. daughter--100% son--50%

p. 62 46. Mr. and Mrs. Rainbow have a son with red-green color blindness. Therefore:
C   a. Mr. Rainbow must be at least a carrier of the color-blindness gene.
      *   b. Mrs. Rainbow must be at least a carrier of the color-blindness gene.
             c. Mr. Rainbow must be color-blind himself.
             d. Mrs. Rainbow must be color-blind herself.

p. 62 47. Color blindness, hemophilia, and Duchenne's muscular dystrophy are all examples of:
C   a. chromosomal abnormalities
             b. dominant inheritance
             c. polygenic inheritance
      *   d. sex-linked inheritance

p. 62 48. Most human characteristics, such as personality, are inherited through:
F   a. a single gene-pair
www   b. sex-linked inheritance
      *   c. polygenic inheritance
             d. mutation of one or more genes

p. 62   49.   Intelligence is an example of:
F   a.   dominant inheritance
        *   b.   polygenic inheritance
                c.   sex-linked inheritance
                d.   single gene-pair inheritance

p. 63   50.   A change in the structure or arrangement of one or more genes which produces a
F   new phenotype is called:
                a.   meiosis
                b.   mitosis
        *   c.   mutation
                d.   recessive inheritance

p. 63   51.   Trisomy 21 is another name for:
F   *   a.   Down syndrome
                b.   Duchenne's muscular dystrophy
                c.   Hemophilia
                d.   Tay-Sachs disease

p. 63   52.   Lisa gives birth to a Down syndrome child. Which of the following is TRUE?
C   a.   Lisa must have given her child an extra 21st chromosome.
                b.   The child's father must have given the child an extra 21st chromosome.
        *   c.   The child received an extra 21st chromosome from either its mother or its father.
                d.   Both parents contributed to the formation of the extra 21st chromosome.

p. 63   53.   Cheryl and Bob can tell at birth that something is wrong with their daughter. Genetic tests
C   indicate that the child has an extra chromosome in its cells. Which of the following does
              the child have?
                a.   Klinefelter syndrome
        *   b.   Down syndrome
                c.   Hemophilia
                d.   Turner syndrome

p. 63   54.   Larry and Kathleen can tell at birth that something is wrong with their son. The doctors
C   agree, and conduct a variety of genetic tests. The results of the tests indicate that the child
              has an extra chromosome in its cells. Which of the following does the child have?
                a.   Disomy 23
        *   b.   Down syndrome
                c.   Hemophilia
                d.   Turner syndrome

p. 64   55.   Which of the following is an accurate comparison of people with Down syndrome
C   and people with Klinefelter syndrome?
     *   a.   They both have cells with 47 chromosomes, but the extra chromosome in Klinefelter
                   syndrome is a sex chromosome and in Down syndrome it is one of the other
                   chromosomes.
              b.   They both have cells with 47 chromosomes, and in both cases it is an extra sex
                   chromosome.
              c.   There is an extra chromosome in Down syndrome, while there are fewer than the
                   normal number of chromosomes in Klinefelter syndrome.
              d.   There is an extra X chromosome in Klinefelter syndrome, and a missing X
                   chromosome in Down syndrome.

p. 64   56.   Margo and John are told that their infant daughter has been diagnosed with Turner
C   syndrome. Which of the following should they expect?
              a.   Their daughter will pass the disease on to her daughters.
              b.   Their daughter will be very tall and big-breasted.
              c.   Their daughter will most likely develop decidedly masculine tendencies.
     *   d.   Their daughter will score about average on tests of verbal intelligence.

p. 64   57.   Meg was born with only one X chromosome. She is short, of average verbal intelligence,
F   and lacking in spatial reasoning skills. Meg has:
              a.   Down syndrome
              b.   Fragile X syndrome
              c.   Klinefelter syndrome
     *   d.   Turner syndrome

p. 64   58.   Susan and Jeff are told that their child has Klinefelter syndrome. Which of the following is
C   TRUE of the child?
              a.   It is a female with unusually strong sexual urges.
              b.   It is a male who will most likely pass the disease on to his offspring.
     *   c.   It is a male who will develop some feminine sex characteristics at puberty.
              d.   It is a female who is sterile and masculine in appearance.

p. 64   59.   Matt has an extra X chromosome. He is tall, sterile, and has enlarged breasts. Matt
F   displays:
              a.   Down syndrome
              b.   Fragile X syndrome
     *   c.   Klinefelter syndrome
              d.   Turner syndrome

p. 64   60.   An individual who is clinically male but has an extra X chromosome has:
F   a.   Down syndrome
              b.   Fragile-X syndrome
     *   c.   Klinefelter syndrome
              d.   Turner syndrome

p. 64   61.   Glenda has several physical anomalies including short stature, stubby fingers and
C   under-developed breasts. She also has trouble with spatial tasks but does fine on verbal
             tasks. Glenda likely has:
             a.   Down syndrome
             b.   Fragile-X syndrome
             c.   Klinefelter syndrome
      *   d.   Turner syndrome

p. 64   62.   Heritability estimates refer to:
F   a.   how much of a trait is influenced by genetic factors
www   *   b.   the proportion of the differences in a trait among a group of people that is due to
                  genetic differences among these people
             c.   the percentage of pairs of people where, if one person in the pair has the trait in
                  question, the other person in the pair also has the trait in question
             d.   the degree to which one trait increases with increases in another trait

p. 65   63.   A trait that is highly heritable:
C   a.   is made-up almost entirely by genetic factors
             b.   has been inherited through the action of many genes
      *   c.   shows variation that can be attributed to variation in genetic endowments
             d.   cannot be influenced by the environment

p. 65   64.   Animal breeders often pick a highly desired trait (e.g. friendliness in golden retrievers) and
C   mate two animals with this trait. From their offspring, the one who displays the most
             friendliness is chosen and later bred with another animal who also shows the trait. This
             process is called
             a.   genetic engineering
             b.   evolutionary psychology
      *   c.   selective breeding
             d.   natural selection

p. 65   65.   When looking at Fluffy the cat's "family tree," Marilyn sees that over several generations a
C   particular trait has been deliberately cultivated by Fluffy's breeders through a process
             known as
      *   a.   selective breeding
             b.   natural selection
             c.   gene/environment correlation
             d.   heritability

p. 65   66.   Which of the following provides the BEST support for an hereditarian perspective
C   on development?
      *   a.   Identical twins reared apart are more alike than fraternal twins reared together.
             b.   Fraternal twins reared together are more alike than identical twins reared apart.
             c.   Fraternal twins reared together are more alike than fraternal twins reared apart.
             d.   Identical twins reared apart are more alike than identical twins reared together.

p. 65 67. Which one of the following sets of data would show a genetic influence on the trait?
C
    a. Identical twins raised together score more similarly to one another than identical twins raised apart.
    b. Fraternal twins raised apart score as similarly to one another as do biological siblings who are raised together.
*   c. Identical twins raised apart score more similarly to one another than fraternal twins raised together.
    d. Fraternal twins raised together score more similarly to one another than fraternal twins raised apart.

p. 65 68. Your text reveals that if one identical twin has schizophrenia, there is almost a 60% chance
C that the other identical twin will also be schizophrenic. On the other hand, if a fraternal twin is schizophrenic, there is only a 13% chance the other fraternal twin will be schizophrenic. The measure of likelihood that twins will share this mental illness in common is called a(n):
*   a. concordance rate
    b. correlation coefficient
    c. dominant trait
    d. heritability factor

p. 65 69. A researcher is looking at pairs of identical twins. One twin already has a particular
C disorder and the researcher wants to see if the other twin will get the disorder as well. The
www researcher is studying
    a. species heredity
    b. codominance
    c. karyotypes
*   d. concordance rates

p. 65 70. Concordance rates refer to the:
F
    a. percentage of pairs of people where, if one person in the pair has the trait in question, the other person in the pair does not have the trait in question
*   b. percentage of pairs of people where, if one person in the pair has the trait in question, the other person in the pair also has the trait in question
    c. degree to which you can determine one person's expression of a trait if another person's expression of the same trait is known
    d. degree to which one trait increases with increases in another trait

p. 66 71. Shared environmental influences tend to
C
    a. make individuals similar
    b. make individuals different
*   c. have no significant effects in terms of making siblings similar or different
    d. influence only identical twins

p. 66 72. If genes <u>alone</u> contributed to a trait, which of the following patterns of correlations
C   would be observed?
www   a. 1.00 for identical twins raised together but a lower correlation for those raised apart
          b. 1.00 for both identical and fraternal twin pairs raised together, but a lower correlation
              for those pairs raised apart
    *   c. 1.00 for identical twins and .50 for fraternal twins raised together and raised apart
          d. no significant correlation between identical twins or fraternal twins, regardless of
              whether they are raised together or apart

p. 66 73. If shared environmental influences <u>alone</u> contributed to a trait, which of the
C   following patterns of correlations would be observed?
          a. 1.00 for identical twins raised together but a somewhat lower correlation for those
              raised apart
    *   b. 1.00 for both identical and fraternal twin pairs raised together, but no correlation for
              those pairs raised apart
          c. 1.00 for identical twins and .50 for fraternal twins raised together and raised apart
          d. no significant correlation between identical twins or fraternal twins, regardless of
              whether they are raised together or apart

p. 66 74. If nonshared environmental influences <u>alone</u> contributed to a trait, which of the
C   following patterns of correlations would be observed?
          a. 1.00 for identical twins raised together but a lower correlation for those raised apart
          b. 1.00 for both identical and fraternal twin pairs raised together, but no correlation for
              those pairs raised apart
          c. 1.00 for identical twins and .50 for fraternal twins raised together and raised apart
    *   d. no significant correlation between identical twins or fraternal twins, regardless of
              whether they are raised together or apart

p. 66 75. Suppose identical twins raised apart have a correlation of .40 on a measure of some
C   aspect of personality, and identical twins raised together have a correlation of .60 on this
          same measure. From these data, what can we logically conclude about this trait?
    *   a. The nonshared environment has an impact because, even raised together, the identical
              twins do not show a perfect 1.00 correlation.
          b. The nonshared environment has no impact because the identical twins raised apart have
              a lower correlation than the identical twins raised together.
          c. The shared environment has no impact because identical twins raised apart have a
              correlation lower than 1.00.
          d. The shared environment has an impact because identical twins raised apart have a
              correlation of .40.

p. 67 76. As children get older:
C   a. shared environmental influences become more significant
    *   b. nonshared environmental influences become more significant
          c. genetic influences become insignificant as environmental influences take precedent
          d. genetic influences become more significant than environmental influences

p. 68   77.   As we get older, genetic influences are _____ in importance, while shared
C   environmental influences are _____ and nonshared environmental influences are
               _____ in importance.
               a.   decreasing; decreasing; increasing
               b.   decreasing; increasing; decreasing
               c.   increasing; increasing; decreasing
        *   d.   increasing; decreasing; increasing

p. 68   78.   The IQ scores of adoptive children show a positive correlation with:
C   a.   those of their biological parents, but not with those of their adoptive parents
               b.   those of their adoptive parents, but not with those of their biological parents
        *   c.   those of both their adoptive and biological parents
               d.   neither those of their adoptive nor biological parents

p. 68   79.   Consider the findings that identical twins score similarly to one another on intelligence
C   tests during early childhood, middle childhood, and adolescence, while fraternal twins
               score similarly to one another during early childhood but then become less similar during
               middle childhood and adolescence. What explanation can account for this finding?
        *   a.   The shared environmental influences become less influential over time and genetic
                    influences remain constant or increase over this same time.
               b.   The genetic influences become less influential over time and the shared environmental
                    influences remain constant over this same time.
               c.   The shared environmental influences become more influential over time and genetic
                    influences also increase over this time.
               d.   The nonshared environmental influences become less influential and the genetic
                    influences also decrease over this time.

p. 69   80.   Which best supports an hereditarian position?
C   *   a.   Adopted infants who are shy tend to have relatively unsociable biological parents
               b.   Adopted infants who are shy tend to have relatively unsociable adoptive parents.
               c.   Fraternal twins reared together are more similar in temperament than identical twins
                    reared apart.
               d.   Fraternal twins show more likeness in emotional tone than do identical twins.

p. 69   81.   Today, MOST developmentalists believe that:
C   a.   Genetic influences account for the majority of developmental characteristics.
               b.   Environmental influences are more important than genetics in determining
                    most developmental characteristics.
        *   c.   Genetic and environmental influences interact throughout the life-span.
               d.   We can determine quite precisely just how much of a given characteristic is due to
                    genetic versus environmental influences.

p. 69   82.   As we enter old age, the influence of genes on personality
C   a.   remains the same
               b.   gets a lot stronger
        *   c.   becomes somewhat weaker
               d.   none of the above

p. 69　83. Which of the following statements is TRUE regarding the effects of genes and
C　　　　environment on temperament?
www　　a. Genes contribute little to individual differences in temperament.
　　　　b. Genes account for nearly all of the individual differences in temperament.
　　　　c. Nonshared environmental influences contribute nothing to individual differences in
　　　　　 temperament.
　　*　　d. The shared environment of the home contributes little to individual differences in
　　　　　 temperament.

p. 69　84. The author of the text estimates that individual differences in personality reflect:
F　　　　a. genetic contributions of about 60%, and shared and nonshared environmental
　　　　　 contributions of about 20% each
　　*　　b. genetic contributions of about 40%, nonshared environmental contributions of about
　　　　　 55% and shared environmental contributions of about 5%
　　　　c. genetic contributions of about 55%, nonshared environmental contributions of about
　　　　　 5% and shared environmental contributions of about 40%
　　　　d. genetic contributions of about 5%, nonshared environmental contributions of about
　　　　　 40% and shared environmental contributions of about 55%

p. 69　85. Which of the following statements is TRUE regarding influences of genes and
C　　　　environments on personality?
　　　　a. Shared environmental influences impact the most on differences in personality.
　　*　　b. Nonshared environmental influences impact far more on personality than do shared
　　　　　 environmental influences.
　　　　c. Genetic influences impact far more on personality than do either shared or nonshared
　　　　　 environmental influences.
　　　　d. Genetic influences and the shared environment both contribute significantly to
　　　　　 personality, while nonshared environmental influences contribute little to personality
　　　　　 differences.

p. 69　86. If one or both parents is schizophrenic, we can conclude that their child will:
C　　　　a. not develop the disorder as long as he/she is raised in a separate environment
　　　　b. definitely develop the disorder regardless of the environment he/she is raised in
　　*　　c. have a greater than average risk of developing the disorder in response to an
　　　　　 environmental trigger
　　　　d. develop the disorder at a much younger age than another child who develops the
　　　　　 disorder but has no family history of schizophrenia

p. 70　87. Which of the following is probably LEAST influenced by heredity?
F　　　　a. height
　　　　b. blood pressure
　　*　　c. religiosity
　　　　d. IQ score

p. 70　88. Which of the following is probably MOST influenced by heredity?
F　　　　a. religiosity
　　*　　b. weight
　　　　c. occupational interests
　　　　d. personality traits

p. 70   89.   Which of the following is probably MOST influenced by heredity?
F   *   a. height
              b. IQ
              c. memory capacity
              d. sociability

p. 70   90.   Some traits are more influenced by genetic factors than other traits, as reflected in
C   the correlations between the traits of identical twins raised apart. Which one of the
              following series of traits is arranged from most to least heritable?
        *   a. height, alpha activity in the brain, IQ scores, personality
              b. alpha activity in the brain, height, personality, IQ scores
              c. alpha activity in the brain, IQ scores, height, personality
              d. height, personality, IQ scores, alpha activity in the brain

p. 72   91.   There are a number of ways in which genes and the environment interact. What sort
C   of gene/environment do we have when sociable parents provide a home environment
              abounding in social stimulation?
              a. active genotype/environment
              b. evocative genotype/environment
        *   c. passive genotype/environment
              d. negative genotype/environment

p. 72   92.   Lorri is a shy child who avoids social gatherings and who seeks out solitary
C   activities such as stamp collecting and reading a good book. Lorri's development will be
www   influenced by this pattern of behavior. In terms of genetic/environmental, this example
              BEST illustrates a(n):
        *   a. active genotype/environment
              b. evocative genotype/environment
              c. passive genotype/environment
              d. negative genotype/environment

p. 72   93.   Baby Mike smiles and coos so often and so delightfully that his parents feel
C   compelled to smile and chatter right back at him. This BEST illustrates which sort of
              genetic/ environmental?
              a. active genotype/environment
        *   b. evocative genotype/environment
              c. passive genotype/environment
              d. negative genotype/environment

p. 72   94.   The balance of various sorts of genotype/environment interactions shifts during
C   development. Which sort of genetic/environment interaction tends to predominate during
              infancy?
              a. active genotype/environment
              b. evocative genotype/environment
              c. negative genotype/environment
        *   d. passive genotype/environment

Test Bank--Chapter 3

p. 72   95.   Kendra is born into a family where both parents are physically very active and involved in sports. They take Kendra with them when they exercise and when they play in their weekly softball and volleyball games. From Kendra's perspective, this is an example of a(n):

C

a. active genotype/environment correlation
b. evocative genotype/environment correlation
* c. passive genotype/environment correlation
d. negative genotype/environment correlation

p. 72   96.   Sierra was born with such beautiful brown eyes that people stop to look at her, feel compelled to smile and talk to her, and comment on how alert and attractive she is. This is an example of a(n):

C

a. active genotype/environment correlation
* b. evocative genotype/environment correlation
c. passive genotype/environment correlation
d. positive genotype/environment correlation

p. 72   97.   Mary is born into a family where both parents are rather shy and quiet. Her parents don't invite many people over to their house or go out to socialize very often. From Mary's perspective, this is an example of a(n):

C

a. active genotype/environment correlation
b. evocative genotype/environment correlation
* c. passive genotype/environment correlation
d. negative genotype/environment correlation

p. 72   98.   Roger has discovered that he enjoys playing the piano and he is fairly talented in this area. He begins to take lessons and accepts several opportunities to play in public. This is an example of a(n):

C

* a. active genotype/environment correlation
b. evocative genotype/environment correlation
c. passive genotype/environment correlation
d. positive genotype/environment correlation

p. 74   99.   Diana and Phillip are in their late twenties. They are also Jewish, and of Eastern European ancestry. They seek genetic counseling before they attempt to become pregnant. They are MOST likely concerned about the possibility of their child having:

C

a. diabetes
b. hemophilia
c. sickle cell disease
* d. Tay-Sachs disease

p. 75   100.   Which of the following can be significantly affected by dietary modification?

F

a. cystic fibrosis
b. Tay-Sachs disease
c. Huntington's disease
* d. phenylketonuria

p. 74 101. All of the following are recessive disorders EXCEPT:
F
a. cystic fibrosis
b. Tay-Sachs disease
* c. Huntington's disease
d. phenylketonuria

p. 75 102. Phenylketonuria, or PKU, is a genetic disorder which, left untreated, will lead to
C
mental retardation and hyperactivity. Which is TRUE?
a. PKU can be detected before a child is born and treated prenatally through blood transfusions.
* b. PKU can be detected at birth and treated successfully with a special diet.
c. PKU cannot be detected until the child is about 8 years old.
d. PKU can be detected at birth and treated successfully with antibiotics.

p. 55 103. All children tend to walk and talk at about 12 months of age. This universal pattern of
C
development results from
SG
a. the crossing over phenomenon
b. societal expectations
* c. species heredity
d. single gene-pair inheritance

p. 58 104. A zygote
F
a. merges with a sperm cell at conception to form a fertilized cell
SG
b. is a cell that will split and develop into fraternal twins
c. contains only the sex chromosomes
* d. is a fertilized egg cell

p. 60 105. A person's phenotype is most accurately described as
C
a. a person's genetic inheritance
SG * b. the outcome of the interaction between a person's genotype and a particular environment
c. the result of the union between a sperm cell and egg cell
d. those characteristics that do not have a genetic basis

p. 61 106. Suppose two people are carriers for thin lips, which is a recessive trait. Each one of their
C
children would have a _____ chance of expressing this trait in their phenotype.
SG * a. 25%
b. 50%
c. 75%
d. 100%

p. 61 107. Incomplete dominance results when
F
a. two different genes in a pair are both expressed in a compromise of the two genes
SG * b. one gene in a pair cannot completely mask the effects of the other gene
c. several gene pairs contribute to the expression of a trait
d. both parents are carriers for a particular trait

p. 61   108. A person is a carrier for a genetic disorder if she/he
C   a. does not show the disorder and cannot pass on the disorder to offspring
SG   *   b. does not show the disorder but can pass on the disorder to offspring
                c. shows the disorder but cannot pass on the disorder to offspring
                d. shows the disorder and can pass on the disorder to offspring

p. 62   109. In X-linked traits
C   a. males and females are equally likely to express the trait
SG   b. males are carriers of the trait but do not always express the trait
        *   c. females can express the trait but do so much less often than males
                d. females and males typically carry but do not express the trait

p. 63   110. Down syndrome occurs when
F   a. a child receives too few chromosomes
SG   b. a male receives an extra X chromosome
                c. there is an abnormality associated with one of the sex chromosomes
        *   d. a child receives an extra 21st chromosome

p. 64   111. Heritability refers to
F   *   a. the amount of variability in a group's trait that is due to genetic differences between
SG   people in the group
                b. the degree to which an individual's characteristics are determined by genetics
                c. the degree of relationship between pairs of individuals
                d. a person's genetic makeup

p. 65   112. Some people have criticized the logic of twin studies because
C   a. identical twins are always the same biological sex while fraternal twins are not
SG   b. identical twins are more likely to participate in this type of study than fraternal twins
        *   c. identical twins are treated more similarly than fraternal twins, making it difficult to
                    separate environmental from genetic factors
                d. it is not always possible to accurately identify twins as fraternal or identical

p. 68   113. Which of the following statements is FALSE regarding genetics and intellectual ability?
C   a. Intellectual development in infancy is only weakly influenced by individual heredity
SG   and environment.
                b. Identical twins become more similar with age in their intellectual performance while
                    fraternal twins become less similar.
        *   c. Both identical and fraternal twins become more similar in intellectual performance
                    with increasing age.
                d. Genes influence the <u>course</u> of intellectual development.

p. 69   114. With regard to individual differences in intellectual ability, research suggests that
C   a. genes, shared environmental influences, and nonshared environmental influences
SG   contribute equally across the life span
                b. shared environmental influences have the greatest impact at all stages of the life span
        *   c. genetic influences become more influential and shared environmental influences
                    become less influential with age
                d. shared and nonshared environmental influences become more influential and genes
                    become less influential with age

p. 72　115. The concept of an evocative genotype/environment correlation suggests that
C
SG
　　　　　　　a. parents select environments for their children and their selection is determined by genetic factors
　　　*　　b. children's genotypes trigger certain reactions from other people
　　　　　　　c. children seek out environments that suit their particular genotypes
　　　　　　　d. genotypes limit the range of possible phenotypic outcomes

p. 72　116. Research shows that
C
SG　　*
　　　　　　　a. people directly inherit many psychological disorders
　　　*　　b. people inherit predispositions to develop psychological disorders
　　　　　　　c. psychological disorders have no genetic basis
　　　　　　　d. having a parent with a psychological disorder means that the child of that person will also have the disorder

p. 73　117. The goals of genetic counseling include all of the following EXCEPT
F
SG
　　　　　　　a. Identify traits that parents might be carrying
　　　　　　　b. Calculate probabilities that a particular trait might be transmitted to children
　　　*　　c. Make decisions for the couple about whether to terminate or continue a pregnancy
　　　　　　　d. Provide information about characteristics and treatment of genetic disorders

TRUE-FALSE ITEMS

p. 55　118. Species heredity is very important to our understanding of individual differences in human growth and development.
　　　　　　　a. true
　　　*　　b. false

p. 58　119. Genes are made up of chromosomes.
　　　　　　　a. true
　　　*　　b. false

p. 58　120. The process of mitosis results in daughter cells that have half the number of cells as the
www　　　original one.
　　　　　　　a. true
　　　*　　b. false

p. 58　121. Fraternal twins are no more alike genetically than brothers and sisters born at different times.
　　　*　　a. true
　　　　　　　b. false

p. 60　122. Phenotype represents a person's potential outcome.
　　　　　　　a. true
　　　*　　b. false

p. 61　123. If both parents are carriers of a particular genetic disorder, all their children will exhibit that disorder.
　　　　　　　a. true
　　　*　　b. false

p. 61 124. Incomplete dominance occurs when one gene in a pair cannot completely dominate the
other gene in the pair.
* a. true
b. false

p. 62 125. Most traits are inherited through a single dominant-recessive gene pair.
a. true
* b. false

p. 62 126. IQ is an example of polygenic inheritance.
* a. true
b. false

p. 62 127. Color blindness is inherited from the father.
a. true
* b. false

p. 63 128. Teenage mothers run an increased risk of bearing children with Down syndrome.
a. true
* b. false

p. 64 129. A male born with only one sex chromosome has Klinefelter's syndrome.
a. true
* b. false

p. 64 130. People born with Down's syndrome or Klinefelter's syndrome both have 47 chromosomes.
www * a. true
b. false

p. 65 131. Concordance rates show the likelihood that, if one member of a pair has a particular trait,
the other member of the pair also has it.
* a. true
b. false

p. 68 132. With regard to IQ, fraternal twins become LESS similar as they move from early childhood
www to adolescence.
* a. true
b. false

p. 68 133. Both twin studies and adoption studies have shown that environmental experiences
contribute to individual differences in infant mental development.
* a. true
b. false

p. 69 134. Sharing the same home environment does little to make children more similar in
www temperament or personality.
* a. true
b. false

p. 66   135. Sharing the same home environment is likely to make children more alike with regard to personality than with regard to tested intelligence.
         a. true
    *   b. false

p. 67   136. Individual differences among adolescents appear to be more closely linked to their genotypes than do the individual differences among infants.
    *   a. true
         b. false

p. 68   137. The association between the kind of home environment an individual experiences and his or her intellectual performance increases from childhood to adolescence.
         a. true
    *   b. false

p. 72   138. In an active gene/environment interaction, children provoke a certain kind of reaction from their environment.
         a. true
    *   b. false

p. 75   139. It is possible to determine the sex of the developing fetus by amniocentesis.
    *   a. true
         b. false

ESSAY QUESTIONS

140.   What is the evidence from the twin studies concerning the heritability of intelligence?

141.   What would be the strongest piece of evidence you could gather to show that genetic factors influenced personality?

142.   Why do children growing up in the same home often turn out to be quite different from one
www   another?

143.   How would you design a study to determine the contributions of genes, shared environment, and nonshared environment on alcoholism?

144.   Consider a characteristic such as humor. What evidence would you need to collect to convince
SG   someone that this trait is influenced by genetic factors? What evidence would you need to show the effects of shared and nonshared environmental influences on humor?
        [Sample answer is provided in the Study Guide.]

145.   How can you account for the findings that identical twins become more similar to one another in
SG   mental ability as they get older, and fraternal twins become less similar to one another in mental ability as they get older?

146.   How can you explain the intriguing finding that siblings, who share some common
SG   genetic material and who grow up in the same home, turn out to have such different personalities?

4

EARLY ENVIRONMENTAL INFLUENCES
ON LIFE-SPAN DEVELOPMENT

MULTIPLE CHOICE QUESTIONS

---

p. 81   1.   The story of Genie is described in the text. Because she was raised alone in a dark room
C   for most of her childhood,
   *   a.   Genie's IQ was borderline retarded
        b.   Genie had a great imagination
        c.   Genie preferred darkness to well lighted rooms
        d.   Genie had impaired sensory skills

p. 81   2.   What is the relationship between people and their environment?
C   a.   There is a one-to-one correspondence between them so that changes in one are
                  mirrored with the same changes in the other.
             b.   The environment affects the individual, but individuals cannot control their
                  environments.
   *   c.   They influences each other reciprocally.
             d.   Both are independent of each other.

p. 82   3.   Which of the following is FALSE regarding the environment?
F   * a.   The environment begins to influence development on the day a person is born.
             b.   Environments can be shaped by the people in them.
             c.   Environments can have substantial influences on development across the life span.
             d.   Environment includes both physical and social events.

p. 82   4.   The germinal period ends, on average, _____ days after conception.
F   a.   2-4
   *   b.   8-14
             c.   32-36
             d.   56-70

p. 82   5.   The germinal period ends when the:
F   a.   blastula burrows into the lining of the chorion
   *   b.   blastula is implanted in the wall of the uterus
             c.   zygote divides into two cells through mitosis
             d.   zygote travels through the fallopian tube into the uterus

p. 82   6.   Which happens during the germinal period of pregnancy?
F   a.   all the major body organs develop in primitive form
             b.   the placental relationship is established
   *   c.   the zygote divides to form the blastula
             d.   the chorion and amnion develop

p. 82   7.   From the moment Margo conceives, to the time she misses her period, is BEST
C   termed the _____ phase of pregnancy:
www   a.   chorionic
               b.   embryonic
       *   c.   germinal
               d.   fetal

p. 82   8.   What are the chances that a zygote will survive the initial phases of prenatal development?
F   *   a.   25%
               b.   50%
               c.   75%
               d.   100%

p. 82   9.   Natalie is six weeks pregnant. Her unborn child is MOST properly referred to as a(n):
F   a.   blastula
       *   b.   embryo
               c.   fetus
               d.   zygote

p. 82   10.   All major organs develop in some fashion:
F   a.   during the germinal period
       *   b.   during the process of organogenesis
               c.   from the amnion and chorion
               d.   during the fetal period

p. 82   11.   The function of the amnion is to:
F   a.   connect the placenta to the developing fetus
       *   b.   provide a cushion of protection for the developing embryo
               c.   provide nutrients and oxygen to the developing embryo
               d.   remove waste products from the developing fetus

p. 82   12.   The placenta, through the umbilical cord, provides the unborn child with:
F   a.   oxygen and blood cells
               b.   carbon dioxide and oxygen
               c.   nutrients and blood cells
       *   d.   oxygen and nutrients

p. 82   13.   The ___ provides nourishment to and removes waste from the fetus:
F   a.   amnion
www   b.   lanugo
       *   c.   placenta
               d.   uterus

p. 82   14.   The outer layer of the embryo forms the:
F   *   a.   amnion and chorion
               b.   placenta and umbilical cord
               c.   brain and spinal cord of the fetus
               d.   heart and internal organs

p. 82 15. In her human development class, Dr. Smith shows students several photographs of prenatal
C   development. She points out the placenta, explaining that its main purpose is to:
           a. provide the fetus with carbon dioxide and oxygen
           b. enable the maternal and fetal blood to mix so they will become compatible
      *   c. provide the fetus with oxygen and nutrients and remove carbon dioxide and wastes
               from the fetus
           d. protect and cushion the fetus from shock

p. 83 16. In vitro fertilization involves:
F   a. injecting sperm into a woman's uterus
      *   b. placing fertilized eggs directly into a woman's uterus
           c. artificially implanting a fertilized egg into the wall of a woman's uterus
           d. conceiving a child with a surrogate mother

p. 83 17. Children who were conceived through some type of reproductive technology:
C   a. are better off than children conceived the usual way
           b. are worse off emotionally than children conceived the usual way
      *   c. have parents who are somewhat more involved with them
           d. have parents who feel very guilty about how they were conceived

p. 84 18. The unborn child's heart begins to beat:
F   a. during the germinal period
      *   b. by about 4 weeks
           c. about 60 days after conception
           d. during the fourth month of pregnancy

p. 84 19. Sexual differentiation begins:
F   a. at the moment of conception
www   b. during the germinal period
      *   c. during the embryonic period
           d. during the fetal period

p. 84 20. Sensory organs:
F   a. are functioning by the end of the germinal period
      *   b. are functioning by the end of the second trimester
           c. do not function until the seventh month of pregnancy
           d. do not function until birth

p. 84 21. Maria, who just found out she is pregnant, wonders at what point her baby will be able to
C   hear. Her doctor is MOST LIKELY to tell her that her baby's sensory organs:
           a. begin to function during the embryonic phase
      *   b. will be functioning by the end of the second trimester
           c. do not function prior to the eighth or ninth month of pregnancy
           d. will not function prior to birth

p. 84   22.   The fetal period is BEST defined as:
F   a.   the last three months of pregnancy
              b.   all of the pregnancy that follows the implantation of the blastula in the uterine wall
              c.   the part of the pregnancy that extends from the age of viability to birth
       *   d.   the period from the ninth week of pregnancy to birth

p. 85   23.   The term "age of viability" refers to the point at which:
F   a.   a child will survive if born
       *   b.   survival outside the uterus might be possible
              c.   the embryo no longer requires oxygen from its mother
              d.   the heart starts beating

p. 85   24.   During the last trimester of pregnancy:
F   a.   sex differentiation begins
       *   b.   the brain develops rapidly
              c.   the senses begin to function
              d.   the heart begins to beat

p. 85   25.   Claire was 28 weeks pregnant when she went into labor and delivered a baby girl. Claire
C   and her doctor are concerned because:
www   a.   genitals are not completely formed until the 32nd week
              b.   the heart and other major organs are not yet functional
       *   c.   the nervous may not be completely organized
              d.   sensory organs are not ready to function in the world

p. 85   26.   Kate's grandson, Sol, was born 10 weeks premature and spent nearly a month in the
C   neonatal intensive care unit before coming home. Now two months old, Kate helps care
              for him and notices that:
              a.   Sol has already caught up to other babies in size and behavioral functioning.
       *   b.   Sol has rather irregular sleep and wake patterns.
              c.   Sol's heart rate does not vary in response to stimulation.
              d.   Sol does not seem to see objects that are directly in front of him

p. 85   27.   Research on infant states shows that:
F   a.   these develop soon after birth
              b.   there is a marked shift at birth from sleep states to waking states
       *   c.   fetuses who spend a lot of time in active states tend to be active as infants
              d.   infants who were born prematurely do not develop predictable states

p. 88   28.   Mariah, age 25, is wondering what the best age would be for her to begin a family. If the
C   only consideration is physical (in other words, factors such as emotional readiness are not
              an issue), her doctor is MOST LIKELY to respond by saying:
       *   a.   "Now would be a perfect time."
              b.   "You better get working on it, because you only have a few good years left."
              c.   "It would have been best to start your family sooner."
              d.   "You would do well to wait until you are in your thirties."

p. 88 29. What appears to be the optimal range of years for childbearing?

F   a. 15 to 25
      *   b. 18 to 35
           c. 20 to 25
           d. 25 to 30

p. 88 30. All of the following are considered to be major risk factors for pregnant teens EXCEPT:

F   a. an immature reproductive system
      *   b. an increased likelihood of chromosomal abnormalities
           c. complications during childbirth
           d. improper prenatal care

p. 88 31. Suzanne has been extremely stressed throughout her pregnancy. Her husband left her, she

C   was laid off from work, and her own mother died. Her doctor informs her that the extreme
           stress she has been under may have caused hormonal secretions which could affect her
           child. What effects might Suzanne expect her child to display?
           a. deafness
           b. impaired vision
           c. mild mental retardation
      *   d. sleep and feeding problems

p. 88 32. Barbara, 6 months pregnant, had a bad scare when her mother called to say her father was

C   in a car accident and had been taken to the hospital. Barbara flew home to visit her
           parents, and found that her father was going to be just fine, though he did have
           some bad breaks and lacerations. This stressful experience MOST LIKELY:
      *   a. had no lasting effect on Barbara's unborn child
           b. contributed to sleep and feeding problems that Barbara's baby exhibited following birth
           c. was the cause of Barbara delivering her baby three weeks early
           d. resulted in Barbara's baby being somewhat hyperactive during the preschool years

p. 88 33. While Cindy was pregnant, her husband was laid off work, her 2-year-old son was

C   diagnosed with severe allergies, and her own mother became critically ill with breast
           cancer. Cindy might reasonably conclude that these experiences while pregnant
           contributed to her baby's:
           a. visual impairment
      *   b. premature delivery
           c. extremely lethargic behavior
           d. heart murmur

p. 89 34. What would be an optimal weight gain during pregnancy?

F   a. 15 to 18 pounds
           b. 18 to 24 pounds
      *   c. 24 to 28 pounds
           d. 28 to 35 pounds

p. 89   35.   Malnutrition during pregnancy is likely to be MOST serious when it occurs during the:
F   a.   germinal period
www   b.   period of the embryo
                 c.   second trimester
      *   d.   last trimester

p. 89   36.   Shelly just found out she is pregnant. Regarding weight gain during pregnancy, her doctor
F   is MOST LIKELY to advise her to:
                 a.   gain no more than 15 pounds
                 b.   try not to gain weight, as she is already overweight
      *   c.   shoot for gaining about 25 pounds throughout the pregnancy
                 d.   not worry about how much weight she gains; she can always take it off later

p. 89   37.   Carrie, who used to be anorexic, is pregnant. She is still hung up about her body, and is
C   determined not to "get fat" while pregnant. Consequently, she puts herself on a
                 strict diet, and only gains 12 pounds during her pregnancy. Her physician is
                 MOST concerned that when the baby is born it will be:
      *   a.   mentally impaired
                 b.   physically deformed
                 c.   hyperactive
                 d.   blind or deaf

p. 89   38.   June is the mother of two young children and is pregnant with a third child. She is also a
C   single parent, out of work and living on welfare. June receives a letter telling her that her
                 benefits have been cut, once again, and that her food stamp allotment will be decreased by
                 a third. For the remainder of her pregnancy, June eats very little, trying to keep enough
                 food on the table for her two young children. What is the GREATEST concern with regard
                 to her unborn child?
                 a.   blindness
                 b.   deafness
      *   c.   mental impairment
                 d.   missing limbs

p. 89   39.   A teratogen is:
F   a.   a medication taken during labor and delivery
                 b.   anything that can cross the placental barrier
      *   c.   an environmental agent that causes birth defects
                 d.   a birth defect caused by genetic abnormalities

p. 89   40.   Which of the following is FALSE?
F   a.   A teratogen can result in a variety of birth defects.
                 b.   A teratogen may not affect all embryos or fetuses in the same way.
                 c.   The effects of a teratogen vary depending on the "dose" received.
      *   d.   An organ system is least vulnerable to the effects of a teratogen when it is developing
                       rapidly.

p. 89   41.   An organ is most vulnerable to teratogens during periods of rapid growth. This time is
F   called the:
        *   a.   critical period
                b.   mutation period
                c.   period of the fetus
                d.   viability period

p. 89   42.   Most teratogenic effects occur during the:
F   a.   germinal period
www   *   b.   embryonic period
                c.   fetal period
                d.   just prior to birth

p. 89. 43.   Which of the following is TRUE?
F   a.   The central nervous system is most vulnerable to teratogenic effects during the fetal
                     period.
                b.   Once a body part is formed, it is invulnerable to the effects of teratogens.
        *   c.   An organ is most vulnerable to teratogens during periods of rapid growth.
                d.   Most teratogenic effects to the vital organs occur during the fetal period.

p. 89   44.   Judy and Kathe are best friends. Judy contracts Rubella and Kathe catches it from her. At
C   the time they have the disease, Judy is 6-weeks pregnant and Kathe is 7 months
                pregnant. What is the MOST likely outcome?
                a.   Judy's child will be born unharmed, but Kathe's child will have some sort of birth
                     defect resulting from Rubella.
        *   b.   Kathe's child will be born unharmed, but Judy's child will have some sort of birth
                     defect resulting from Rubella.
                c.   Judy and Kathe will both give birth to children with birth defects resulting from
                     Rubella.
                d.   There is no need for Judy or Kathe to worry about birth defects as a result of having
                     Rubella.

p. 89   45.   Rubella, a form of measles, is most dangerous to the developing organism if contracted by
F   the mother:
        *   a.   during the first month of pregnancy
                b.   during the third month of pregnancy
                c.   during the fifth through seventh months of pregnancy
                d.   just prior to the birth of the child

p. 90   46.   Rubella and syphilis are both teratogens. They have all of the following in common
C   EXCEPT they:
                a.   can both cause brain damage
                b.   can both cause deafness and blindness
                c.   can both cause heart problems
        *   d.   are both most damaging if contracted during the period of the embryo

p. 90   47. Maggie, who just found out she is four weeks pregnant, has syphilis. Her doctor MOST
C   LIKELY:
                   a. advises her to have an abortion, as the child will be deformed from the disease
          *   b. treats her with antibiotics, and tells her that baby will probably not be harmed by the
                       disease
                   c. tells her that although he will treat her with antibiotics, her child will most likely be
                       born blind
                   d. tells her he will not treat the disease until the child is delivered as the medications he
                       would use would cross the placental barrier and cause more damage to the unborn child
                       than would the disease itself

p. 91   48. Lyla has genital herpes. When she goes into labor, she has active lesions in the genital
C   area. Lyla should expect that:
                   a. her baby will be born with genital herpes
          *   b. a cesarean delivery would prevent her baby from contracting genital herpes
                   c. her baby will not have to worry about contracting genital herpes unless someday he or
                       she has unprotected sex with someone who is infected with genital herpes
                   d. her baby will be mentally retarded

p. 91   49. Margaret has AIDS, and when her son, Peter, is born he also tests positive for HIV.
C   She wonders what this means for Peter's life expectancy. Margaret's doctor is MOST
              LIKELY to tell her that Peter will:
                   a. die within a few weeks
                   b. live one to two years
          *   c. might live to age six or beyond
                   d. probably live 10 to 15 years before dying of full-blown AIDS

p. 90   50. Ruth is pregnant and has AIDS. Her baby may catch the HIV virus:
C   a. during the prenatal period, as the HIV virus can cross the placental barrier
                   b. during the birth process, when maternal and fetal blood may mix
                   c. following birth, through breastfeeding
          *   d. all of the above

p. 90   51. Sandra, who is pregnant, tests HIV-positive. When her son is born, he does not have the
C   HIV virus. Sandra's doctor is MOST LIKELY to tell her:
                   a. she should breast feed her son so he can benefit from natural immunities to infection
                       that breast milk often provides
          *   b. she should not breast feed her son, as she might transmit the HIV virus through her
                       breast milk
                   c. she and her son are very fortunate, and she need no longer worry about transmitting the
                       virus to him
                   d. since she did not transmit the HIV virus to this child, it is unlikely that she would
                       transmit the virus to another child, should she become pregnant again

p. 91   52. Approximately ___% of babies born to HIV-infected mothers are themselves HIV infected:
F   *   a. 25
                   b. 40
                   c. 60
                   d. 80

p. 91 53. Myrna started taking the drug thalidomide in her sixth month of pregnancy.
F Chances are her baby will :
  a. be mentally retarded
  b. have heart problems
  c. have deformed or missing limbs
* d. suffer no harmful effects

p. 91 54. Thalidomide, a drug once taken during pregnancy to prevent morning sickness, has been
F shown to result in:
  a. mental retardation
* b. eye, ear, and nose malformations
  c. visual impairment
  d. all of the above

p. 92 55. Marcia smoked heavily throughout her pregnancy. Her husband was very worried about
C this, because of the possible effects on his unborn child. Which of the following did he
www have the GREATEST reason to be concerned about?
* a. the child's birth weight
  b. missing limbs
  c. visual impairment
  d. attention deficit disorder

p. 92 56. Hannah and Joe, both heavy smokers, are expecting a baby. Joe thinks Hannah should stop
C smoking. She says she will if he will. Which of the following is TRUE?
  a. Hannah's smoking is risky to the baby, but Joe's is not.
* b. Both Hannah and Joe's smoking is risky for their unborn child.
  c. Neither Hannah nor Joe should worry, because there are no long-term negative effects
     of smoking while pregnant on the development of the unborn child.
  d. If they continue to smoke, their child will be born prematurely, and will suffer from
     cognitive impairments.

p. 92 57. A child with fetal alcohol syndrome will MOST likely display the following:
F a blindness and deafness
* b. a small head, widely spaced eyes, and a flattened nose
  c. heart defects
  d. missing limbs

p. 92. 58. Ruth has just given birth to a baby girl. Right away it appears that something
C is wrong -- the child looks odd. She has a small head, widely spaced eyes, and a flattened
nose. What are the doctors MOST likely to suspect?
* a. Ruth consumed considerable quantities of alcohol during the pregnancy.
  b. Ruth had rubella during the second month of her pregnancy.
  c. Ruth had syphilis and did not seek treatment for it.
  d. Ruth did not eat properly throughout the pregnancy.

p. 92   59.   Louise did not know she was pregnant until she was about three months along. During
C   those first three months she drank alcoholic beverages quite frequently. Which of the
                  following could be the result for her unborn child?

                  a.   hyperactivity and attention disorder
                  b.   lowered intelligence
                  c.   irritability
      *   d.   all of the above

p. 92   60.   Lucy likes to drink a bit. When she finds she is pregnant, she asks her doctor what this
C   means in terms of her drinking. Her doctor is MOST LIKELY to tell her she:
      *   a.   should not drink at all while pregnant
                  b.   can have a drink now and then without worrying
                  c.   should hold off drinking during the first trimester, but after that it should be OK
                  d.   can only drink safely during the last two months of pregnancy

p. 93   61.   A baby is born to a woman who used cocaine throughout her pregnancy. The MOST
C   LIKELY effects on the baby will be
      *   a.   a low birth weight and a small head
                  b.   missing limbs
                  c.   widely spaced eyes and a flat nose
                  d.   serious heart problems

p. 93   62.   Diane frequently used cocaine while she was pregnant. The MOST LIKELY effect on her
C   baby is:
      *   a.   a premature birth
                  b.   extreme mental retardation
                  c.   blindness
                  d.   a hearing impairment

p. 94   63.   Sally is an X-ray technician. She takes special care to avoid exposure to radiation in her
C   work environment, because she is trying to get pregnant and she knows that there can be
                  negative effects of exposure to radiation such as:
                  a.   miscarriage
                  b.   still birth
                  c.   mental retardation
      *   d.   all of the above

p. 94   64.   Pollutants such as lead and PCBs:
F   a.   do not have a significant effect on development
                  b.   affect the mental functioning of children who are exposed during their first three years.
      *   c.   affect children who were exposed prenatally, with the effects proportional to the
                       amount of exposure
                  d.   are absorbed by pregnant women and may cause some ill effects in these women, but
                       do not pass to their unborn children

p. 94   65.   The MOST LIKELY effect of prenatal exposure to lead is:
F
www
                 a.   a weakened heart
                 b.   impaired kidney and liver functions
       *   c.   intellectual impairment
                 d.   physical deformities

p. 95   66.   Jim and Barbara are in the delivery room giving birth to their first child. The doctor tells
C
                them that the child's head has just passed through the cervix into the vagina. What stage of
                the birth process are they in?
                 a.   afterbirth
       *   b.   delivery
                 c.   labor
                 d.   transition

p. 95   67.   Paul and Kathy are having their first child. The nurse enters the birthing room, checks
C
                Kathy, announces that she is fully dilated, and tells her she can push with the next
                contraction. Kathy is entering the ___ stage of the birthing process:
                 a.   afterbirth
       *   b.   delivery
                 c.   labor
                 d.   transition

p. 95   68.   During the afterbirth phase of birthing:
F
                 a.   the child remains connected to the mother via the umbilical cord
       *   b.   the placenta is expelled
                 c.   the baby is under four-hour observation in the hospital nursery
                 d.   the child continues to receive oxygen through the placental system

p. 96   69.   Anoxia most clearly damages the infant's:
F   *   a.   brain and nervous system
www
                 b.   digestive system
                 c.   heart and circulatory system
                 d.   respiratory system

p. 96   70.   The following are all possible complications of anoxia except:
F
                 a.   cerebral palsy
                 b.   irritability
                 c.   mental retardation
       *   d.   a malformed heart

p. 96   71.   Most infants who suffered mild anoxia during the birthing process:
F
                 a.   are cognitively impaired for a lifetime
                 b.   have poor fine motor skills throughout childhood
                 c.   develop mild motor impairments which persist for a lifetime
       *   d.   overcome cognitive and motor delays by later childhood

p. 96.   72.   While Vicki is giving birth to her son, Chad, his heart rate drops suddenly. The doctors
C   perform an emergency Cesarean section, but Chad's oxygen supply is severely limited for
                 several minutes in the process. As a result, Vicki can expect that Chad may experience:

             a.   diminished intellectual functioning
             b.   muscular control problems
             c.   excessive irritability following birth
     *   d.   all of the above

p. 96.   73.   A child who is positioned for birth feet or buttocks first is:
F   *   a.   at risk for complications such as anoxia
             b.   called a Cesarean baby
             c.   undernourished in utero
             d.   sure to be mentally retarded

p. 96   74.   Doctors are likely to perform a Cesarean section in all of the following situations EXCEPT
C   when the:
             a.   child is positioned sideways in the uterus
             b.   mother has genital Herpes
             c.   child is experiencing respiratory distress
     *   d.   child is positioned head down in the birth canal

p. 96   75.   Babies that are positioned _____ are MOST DIFFICULT to deliver vaginally:
F   a.   head down
             b.   feet first
     *   c.   sideways
             d.   buttocks first

p. 96   76.   Compared to mothers who deliver their babies vaginally, women who have C-sections:
C   *   a.   are less satisfied with the birth process
www   b.   experience less distress
             c.   are more involved with the infants
             d.   are not as exhausted and take less time to recover

p. 97   77.   Regarding C-section deliveries:
C   a.   most mothers prefer this method because it is quicker than a vaginal delivery
             b.   doctors conduct C-sections only in clear cases of emergencies
             c.   the number of C-sections has steadily increased over the years to about one-third of all
                 deliveries
     *   d.   many people believe that C-sections are often performed unnecessarily

p. 97   78.   Obstetrical medications have been linked to all of the following EXCEPT:
F   a.   cognitive deficits during the first year of life
             b.   motor deficits during the first year of life
     *   c.   newborn blindness
             d.   sluggishness and irritability in the newborn

p. 97 79. Michelle's doctor advises her against using pain medications during labor and delivery
C   because they may:
          a. cause the baby to be sluggish and irritable
          b. result in motor impairments during the first year of life
          c. affect the baby's cognitive development
     *   d. all of the above

p. 97 80. The Apgar test is used to determine:
C   a. whether or not a C-section is required
www   b. whether or not the mother has ingested harmful drugs during pregnancy
     *   c. the newborn's condition immediately following birth
          d. the likelihood of congenital abnormalities

p. 97 81. A baby with an Apgar rating of 2
F   a. is normal
     *   b. will require intensive care to survive
          c. can score higher after a blood transfusion
          d. has above average reflexes

p. 97 82. The Apgar test yields information about all of the following EXCEPT:
F   a. heart rate
          b. muscle tone
          c. respiration
     *   d. vision

p. 97 83. Frieda receives an Apgar rating of 8. This means she:
C   a. is having difficulty breathing
     *   b. is doing just fine
          c. is probably going to die
          d. has visual and auditory deficits

p. 98 84. Research suggests that the mother's experience of giving birth:
C   *   a. is painful and anxiety-provoking, yet positive
          b. is overwhelmingly positive
          c. depends on whether they give birth to a boy or girl
          d. is forgotten very quickly because of medications used during delivery

p. 98 85. Cross-cultural research indicates that the child birth experience:
C   a. is interpreted very similarly in different cultural contexts
     *   b. is more medicalized in Western societies
          c. is less rewarding in most industrialized countries relative to nonindustrialized ones
          d. is generally viewed negatively

p. 98 86. According to Klaus and Kennell, the sensitive period for bonding between mother and
F   child is the first:
     *   a. 6 to twelve hours after birth
          b. 6 to twelve days after birth;
          c. six months of life
          d. year of life

p. 99   87. Due to complications during the birthing process, Nona and her son, Chris, were separated
C   for the first 24 hours following delivery. It is MOST LIKELY that:
         a. Chris and Nona will have a difficult time becoming attached
         b. Chris's temperament will be significantly affected by this separation
         c. Chris will, as a result, be closer to his father than his mother
      * d. Nona and Chris will have ample opportunities to bond with one another in the days and
             weeks to come

p. 99   88. Overall, the research evidence indicates that:
C   a. extended contact during the first few hours after birth is critical if bonding between
             parent and child is to occur
      * b. extended contact during the first few hours and days following birth is helpful but not
             necessary in establishing an affectional bond between mother and child
         c. affectional bonding is not influenced at all by the extent of early contact between
             mother and child
         d. as early contact between mother and child is essential for bonding, adoptive children
             and parents can not hope to achieve the same sort of bond that biological parents and
             children have

p. 99   89. A mother and her newborn do not have any contact in the period immediately after birth.
C   Research suggests that this will:
         a. strengthen their bond when they do meet because both will be more alert later on
      * b. slow up the bonding process, but will not really interfere with the formation of a close
             relationship in the long run
         c. mean that mother and child are likely to have a weaker relationship even years later
         d. not interfere with the parent-child relationship, but will seriously delay the baby's
             cognitive development

p. 99   90. Sheila gave birth to a healthy baby boy two days ago. Today she is sobbing uncontrollably,
C   feeling irritable, resentful, and depressed. Her husband has no idea what is going on. He
         consults with the family doctor who tells him Sheila is MOST likely suffering from:
         a. a psychotic neurosis
         b. denial
      * c. postpartum depression
         d. anoxia

p. 99   91. All of the following are considered to contribute to the postpartum depression EXCEPT:
C   a. drugs taken during childbirth
         b. hormonal changes
      * c. maternal psychosis
         d. visitors' attention to the newborn

p. 99   92. Mark can hardly bear to be separated from his tiny, newborn daughter. He loves to touch
C   and hold her and wiggle her little fingers and toes! When she's sleeping, he loves to sit and
         look at her. This BEST demonstrates what your text refers to as:
      * a. engrossment
         b. infatuation
         c. postnatal attraction
         d. neonatal neurosis

p. 100 93. The process by which an individual acquires the values, beliefs, and behaviors judged
F   important by a society is BEST termed:
                 a. cultural evolution
                 b. indoctrination
              * c. socialization
                 d. teaching

p. 100 94. Brad and Jill grew up in a blue-collar neighborhood and are themselves both blue-collar
C   workers. They are expecting their first child. Which socialization goal, as discussed in
www   your text, are Brad and Nona likely to be MOST concerned with?
              * a. the economic goal
                 b. the morality goal
                 c. the self-actualization goal
                 d. the prestige goal

p. 100 95. Socialization is BEST defined as:
F   a. teaching children social skills
                 b. teaching children to distinguish right from wrong
                 c. the transmission of universal beliefs and values
              * d. the process by which culturally-valued beliefs, values, and behaviors are acquired

p. 100 96. Marie and John tell their adolescent son, Jeremy, that he needs to study hard and get good
C   grades in high school so he can get into a good college, and one day get a good job where
                 he can support and take care of himself and a family. Marie and John are focused on the
                 _____ goal of socialization.
                 a. survival
              * b. economic
                 c. self-actualization
                 d. education

p. 100 97. Roma and Paul tell their daughter, Brooke, that she can be anything she chooses to be.
C   What matters most is that she, herself, be satisfied with what she is doing and who she has
                 become. Roma and Paul are emphasizing the _____ socialization goal.
                 a. survival
                 b. economic
              * c. self-actualization
                 d. prestige

p. 100 98. Scott and Jean are university professors. Terry and John are factory workers. In terms of
C   raising their children, it is MOST LIKELY that:
                 a. Scott and Jean place a higher emphasis than Terry and John on respect and obedience
                 b. Terry and John place a stronger emphasis than Scott and Jean on developing
                    independence skills and ambition
              * c. Scott and Jean are more permissive than Terry and John
                 d. Terry and John place less emphasis than Scott and Jean on conformity and respect for
                    authority

p. 101 99. Regarding the influence of culture on development, which is FALSE?
C
    a. Culture can affect both the rate and the direction of development.
    b. Culture can affect the behavior shown by children of a given age.
    c. Culture affects our understandings of influences on development.
*   d. Culture can affect the rate, but not the direction, of development.

p. 102 100. Research indicates that:
F
    a. children of mothers who smoked during pregnancy generally remain smaller and less cognitively skilled for a lifetime
    b. children who have intellectual and social problems that persist into adolescence will carry those same deficits into adulthood
    c. low-birth-weight babies never quite catch up to their more robust peers
*   d. the human organism is remarkably resilient, and many early deficits can be overcome given appropriate social support

p. 103 101. Infants who were at-risk for problems at birth:
C
    a. usually get progressively worse over time
www *   b. often show no serious long-term difficulties
    c. have long-lasting cognitive and intellectual problems
    d. recover completely during infancy

p. 103 102. Recovery from prenatal or perinatal trauma:
C *   a. depends on personal resources and a supportive environment
    b. depends on when the problem occurred
    c. must occur during a critical period if recovery is to occur at all
    d. is not possible in most cases

p. 103 104. Low-birth-weight babies are likely to have all of the following EXCEPT:
F
    a. immature immune systems
    b. respiratory problems
*   c. visual and auditory problems
    d. cognitive deficits

p. 103 104. What seems to be the MOST important factor for overcoming the problems of low-birth-
F   weight?
    a. good nutrition
*   b. attentive and responsive mothers
    c. establishing regular behavioral states
    d. being raised in a wealthy home

p. 104 105. The Lamaze method is a technique for:
F
    a. making birth more pleasant for babies
*   b. achieving childbirth without drugs
    c. measuring the difficulty a woman is having with the birth process
    d. stimulating premature infants

p. 104　106. Claire and her husband are taking classes to prepare them for the birth of their first child.
C　　　　They are learning to do exercises, to focus breathing, and to relax through the contractions
　　　　　of labor. Their instructor tells them that what they are learning will help them to have an
　　　　　easier delivery, With less pain and less need for obstetrical medications. This BEST
　　　　　demonstrates the _____ method of childbirth:
　　　　　　a.　Leboyer
　　　*　　b.　Lamaze
　　　　　　c.　Neugarten
　　　　　　d.　Brazelton

p. 105　107. Brazelton training is:
F　　　　　　a.　a method of prepared childbirth
　　　*　　b.　a process that helps parents understand their babies as individuals
　　　　　　c.　a technique for preparing midwives to assist in home births
　　　　　　d.　a method of preparing fathers to participate in the birthing process

p. 83　108. Research on reproductive technologies shows that children born with these procedures:
C　　　　　　a.　are more likely to be low birth weight or premature than other children
SG　　*　　b.　are more likely to be resentful about their atypical origins
　　　　　　c.　have parents who are more stressed and negative about their circumstances
　　　　　　d.　are equal to other groups of children in emotional adjustment and other developmental
　　　　　　　　outcomes

p. 82　109. The single cell that is formed by the union of a sperm cell and egg cell is called a(n)
F　　　　　　a.　blastula
SG　　　　　b.　embryo
　　　*　　c.　zygote
　　　　　　d.　germ cell

p. 82　110. All major organs begin to form between the second and the eighth week after conception.
F　　　　　This period of time is called the
SG　　*　　a.　period of the embryo
　　　　　　b.　germinal period
　　　　　　c.　period of the fetus
　　　　　　d.　age of viability

p. 82　111. The placental barrier
C　　　*　　a.　supports the developing embryo with oxygen and nutrients from the mother
SG　　　　　b.　blocks dangerous substances from reaching the developing embryo
　　　　　　c.　allows maternal blood to pass to the developing embryo
　　　　　　d.　is replaced by the umbilical cord at the end of the germinal period

p.84　112. Which of the following accurately represents the process of sex differentiation during the
C　　　　　prenatal period?
SG　　　a.　Sex differentiation is determined at conception by the inheritance of X and Y
　　　　　　　chromosomes.
　　　　　b.　Males and females begin with different tissue at conception that evolves into different
　　　　　　　reproductive systems
　　　　　c.　Sex differentiation begins around the 7th or 8th week with the development of male
　　　　　　　and female external genitalia.
　　　*　d.　Males and females begin with identical tissue that can evolve into male or female
　　　　　　　reproductive systems depending on genetic and hormonal factors.

p. 84　113. The presence or absence of testosterone affects the process of sexual differentiation in
F　　　　　a.　males only
SG　　　b.　females only
　　　*　c.　males and females
　　　　　d.　neither males or females

p. 85　114. The age of viability refers to
F　　　　　a.　the age at which a woman is still able to conceive
SG　　*　b.　the point at which a fetus has a reasonable chance of survival outside the womb
　　　　　c.　the point at which the brain and respiratory system are completely formed and
　　　　　　　functional
　　　　　d.　the point at which all the major organs can be identified

p. 88　115. Prolonged and severe emotional strain experienced by a mother during pregnancy can
C　　　　　result in
SG　　　a.　a miscarriage
　　　　　b.　prolonged and painful labor
　　　　　c.　a baby who is irritable and has irregular habits
　　　*　d.　all of the above

p.89　116. It is most important for mothers to consume ample amounts of protein, vitamins and
C　　　　　calories during
SG　　　a.　the first trimester
　　　　　b.　the second trimester
　　　*　c.　the third trimester
　　　　　d.　before becoming pregnant

p. 89　117. A critical period is a time when
C　　　　　a.　a fetus can survive outside the womb
SG　　　b.　conception occurs
　　　　　c.　the brain forms
　　　*　d.　a developing organ is particularly sensitive to environmental influences

p. 89   118. Mothers who contract rubella (German measles) during the first trimester of pregnancy
F   often have children who have problems such as
SG   *   a.   deafness, blindness, heart defects, and mental retardation
              b.   missing or malformed limbs
              c.   small head size and malformations of face, heart and limbs
              d.   slow growth and low birth weight

p. 98   119. Klaus and Kennell argue that emotional bonding between a mother and her newborn
C   a.   can occur at any time during the first three years of life
SG   b.   is unlike any other developing relationship
              c.   is necessary for later normal development to occur
         *   d.   develops during a sensitive period 6-12 hours after birth

p. 100   120. The process by which individuals acquire beliefs, values, and behavior important to
F   adaptation to the environment is called
SG   *   a.   socialization
              b.   survival goal
              c.   self actualization
              d.   culture

p. 103   121. Longitudinal studies of babies "at-risk"
C   a.   show that most at-risk babies continue to have problems throughout their lives
SG   b.   show that most of these children never develop any problems regardless of their
                   experiences
              c.   show that babies at greater risk have a better prognosis because they receive more
                   medical care than babies at less risk
         *   d.   suggest that children can "outgrow" their problems when placed in favorable
                   environments

p. 105   122. Parents who receive "Brazelton training"
C   *   a.   learn how to elicit various responses from their infant
SG   b.   typically have an easier time during delivery of their infant
              c.   can determine right after birth if their infant is healthy
              d.   can determine their infant's level of intelligence

TRUE-FALSE ITEMS

p. 82   123. Every major organ begins to take shape during the embryonic period.
              a.   true
         *   b.   false

p. 82   124. The fetus is protected from toxins by the placenta
              a.   true
         *   b.   false

p. 84   125. Every human organism that is conceived originally has the potential to develop either a
www   male or a female reproductive system.
         *   a.   true
              b.   false

p. 85   126. The fetus reaches the age of viability at around 32 weeks after conception.
www   a.   true
        *   b.   false

p. 85   127. The fetal heart rate is responsive to external stimulation.
        *   a.   true
               b.   false

p. 88   128. The best age to have a baby is somewhere between 16 and 35 years.
        *   a.   true
               b.   false

p. 89   129. The same teratogen can have different effects on different fetuses.
www   *   a.   true
               b.   false

p. 89   130. Most teratogens have their greatest (worst) effects during the last trimester when the fetus
             is putting on weight.
               a.   true
        *   b.   false

p. 98   131. Mothers must interact with their infants within hours of giving birth if they are going to
             develop a normal attachment relationship.
               a.   true
        *   b.   false

p. 101 132. Cross-cultural studies comparing parenting practices in Africa and the United States have
             shown that American mothers use a more verbal teaching style in their interactions with
             infants.
        *   a.   true
               b.   false

p. 101 133. Cross-cultural studies of socialization practices have shown that parents around the world
             are largely concerned with the same socialization goals for their young.
               a.   true
        *   b.   false

p. 101 134. Highly industrialized societies are more geared toward promoting cooperative behavior
             than are less industrialized societies.
               a.   true
        *   b.   false

p. 103 135. Maternal responsiveness is positively correlated with the resilience of at-risk infants.
        *   a.   true
               b.   false

136. What advice regarding prenatal care would you give to a woman who has just found out that she
www is pregnant?

137. What factors influence the effects of teratogens?

138. How does early socialization vary across cultures? How do these socialization practices affect infants?

139. To what extent are infants resilient? What factors increase or decrease resilience?

140. What advice concerning prenatal care would you give to a woman who has just learned that she
SG   is two months pregnant? Provide justification for your answer.
     [Sample answer is provided in the Study Guide.]

141. How do cultural variations affect infant care practices, and how do infant care practices relate to
SG   developmental outcomes?

142. How can we structure the environment to optimize development?
SG

5

THE PHYSICAL SELF

p. 110   1.   The endocrine glands:
F   *   a.   secrete hormones directly into the bloodstream
            b.   secrete neurotransmitters into the brain
            c.   are instrumental in producing myelin, which protects the neurons
            d.   transmits information from the sensory organs to the brain

p. 110   2.   Which body system is SLOWEST to develop across the life-span?
F   a.   circulatory system
            b.   digestive system
            c.   nervous system
      *   d.   reproductive system

p. 110   3.   The nervous system completes most of its important growth by
F   a.   birth
      *   b.   the end of infancy
            c.   puberty
            d.   the age of 21

p. 110   4.   The endocrine gland that is important to the development of muscles and bones is the:
F   a.   pituitary gland
            b.   thyroid gland
      *   c.   adrenal gland
            d.   testes gland

p. 110   5.   The endocrine gland that regulates growth and triggers the growth spurt during adolescence
F   is the:
www   *   a.   pituitary gland
            b.   thyroid gland
            c.   adrenal gland
            d.   testes and ovaries

p. 110   6.   Maya was born with a thyroid deficiency which was not diagnosed as such until she was
C   three years old. What is the LIKELY outcome for Maya?
      *   a.   Maya will be mentally handicapped to some extent.
            b.   There will be no long-lasting effects as long as Maya receives
               treatment once the problem is diagnosed.
            c.   Maya will grow to be over six feet tall.
            d.   Maya will become blind.

p. 110 7. Bill is 11 years old and has just recently developed a thyroid deficiency. What will be the
C LIKELY effects of his condition?
    a. Bill will become mentally retarded.
    b. Bill will grow to be extraordinarily tall.
  * c. Bill's growth will slow down dramatically.
    d. Bill will lose his vision and possibly his hearing.

p. 110 8. Which of the following is FALSE regarding the pituitary gland?
F   a. The pituitary is one of the most important endocrine glands.
    b. The pituitary is directly controlled by the hypothalamus.
    c. The pituitary secretes growth hormone.
  * d. The pituitary secretes sex hormones.

p. 110 9. Which of the following is FALSE regarding the thyroid gland?
F   a. Babies born with a thyroid deficiency will be mentally handicapped if not treated.
    b. The thyroid helps to regulate physical growth during childhood.
  * c. The thyroid triggers the release of hormones from all other endocrine glands.
    d. Children who develop a thyroid disorder will experience a significant decrease in their physical growth rate.

p. 111 10. Androgens do all of the following EXCEPT:
F   a. trigger the adolescent growth spurt
    b. contribute to sexual motivation in adulthood
  * c. cause ovulation in women
    d. trigger the development of male sex organs

p. 111 11. _____ is (are) to males as _____ is (are) to females.
F   a. adrenal glands; androgens
    b. estrogen; testosterone
    c. testosterone; androgens
  * d. testosterone; estrogen

p. 111 12. Which is responsible for the differentiation of the male reproductive system during the
F prenatal period?
    a. adrenal androgens
    b. estrogen
  * c. testosterone
    d. thyroxine

p. 111 13. Melissa is 15 years old. All of her friends have become notably "adolescent" in
C appearance: they have pubic hair and underarm hair and have experienced the "adolescent
www growth spurt." Melissa has no pubic or underarm hair, and still looks much more like a
young girl than an adolescent. The MOST likely culprit for Melissa's plight is
malfunctioning:
  * a. adrenal glands
    b. ovaries
    c. testes
    d. thyroid

p. 111 14. Which is responsible for controlling the menstrual cycle?
F
    a. adrenal androgens
  * b. estrogen
    c. testosterone
    d. thyroxine

p. 111 15. The growth spurt of males is triggered by the release of _____ and the growth spurt of
F   females is triggered by release of _____.
    a. estrogen; androgens
  * b. androgens; estrogen
    c. androgens; thyroxine
    d. adrenal androgens; thyroxine

p. 111 16. The basic unit of the nervous system is a(n)
F
    a. dendrite
    b. axon
    c. synapse
  * d. neuron

p. 111 17. Neurons "communicate" with one another
C   * a. by releasing neurotransmitters into the synaptic gap
    b. by releasing hormones from the hypothalamus
    c. through the pituitary, on "master" gland
    d. through the myelin sheath

p. 112 18. The function of myelin is to:
F
    a. trigger the adolescent growth spurt
  * b. speed the transmission of neural impulses
    c. inhibit the action of neurons
    d. trigger sexual maturation in females

p. 112 19. Myelin is important to the nervous system because it:
F
    a. transmits neural impulses from the brain to the body
www   b. directs the release of hormones from the endocrine glands
  * c. speeds transmission of neural impulses
    d. controls communication between the endocrine system and the nervous system

p. 112 20. Which of the following is NOT a key process of early brain development?
F
    a. a rapid multiplication of neurons
    b. migration of neurons to specific parts of the brain
  * c. production of myelin to facilitate communication among different brain areas
    d. formation of connections among neurons

p. 112 21. Synaptogenesis refers to
F
    a. the production of a waxy, protective coating on neurons
  * b. the formation of connections among neurons
    c. the specialized function that neurons assume
    d. the rapid development of neurons during the prenatal period

p. 112 22. All of the following are true regarding brain development during the prenatal period
F   EXCEPT
         a. neurons migrate to a particular location and assume specialized functions
         b. neurons have the potential to become any type of neuron
         c. neurons form connections with other neurons
    *   d. neurons begin to multiply and migrate, processes which continue during the first two
             years after birth

p. 112 23. Which of the following does NOT contribute to the brain growth spurt that occurs during
F   the last trimester of pregnancy and the first two years after birth?
         a. rapid proliferation of neurons
         b. myelinization of the neurons
         c. increase in levels of neurotransmitters
    *   d. hardening of the skull bones

p. 113 24. The following are all true of brain development EXCEPT:
F   a. a 2-year-old's brain has achieved 75% of its adult weight
         b. half of the neurons produced in early life die in early life
    *   c. the amount of myelin decreases from birth to age two
         d. the organization of synapses continues to change throughout life

p. 113 25. By age 2, a child's BRAIN has reached _____% of its adult weight.
F   a. 25
         b. 50
    *   c. 75
         d. 100

p. 114 26. The plasticity of the young infant's brain allows for all of the following EXCEPT:
F   *   a. The infant's brain is generally invulnerable to damage from drug and diseases.
         b. The brain can recover quite rapidly from many injuries.
         c. Brain cells are not fully specialized, so they can often take over for other damaged or
             dead brain cells.
         d. The brain is very responsive to environmental stimulation.

p. 114 27. Which of the following is FALSE regarding plasticity of an infant's brain?
C   *   a. Plasticity protects the brain from the negative effects of drugs and disease.
www   b. Plasticity allows the brain to benefit from positive influences.
         c. Plasticity allows the infant brain to recover more successfully from damage than an
             adult brain.
         d. Plasticity is greatest early in life and becomes less evident as we age.

p. 114 28. Jamie fell down the stairs and sustained a serious head injury. As a result, her language
C   skills have been seriously impaired. Which part of Jamie's brain was MOST LIKELY
         damaged?
    *   a. left hemisphere
         b. right hemisphere
         c. corpus callosum
         d. brain stem

p. 114 29. With regard to brain lateralization, or specialization of the two hemispheres of the cerebral
F   cortex, which is FALSE?
             a. The majority of individuals rely primarily on the left hemisphere of the brain to carry
                 out language activities.
             b. As children get older they come to rely increasingly on one brain hemisphere or the
                 other to carry out certain tasks.
        *   c. The majority of individuals rely primarily on the right hemisphere of the brain to carry
                 out language activities.
             d. The majority of individuals rely primarily on the right hemisphere of the brain for
                 spatial perception and listening to music.

p. 114 30. Lateralization refers to:
F   *   a. the specialization of the two hemispheres of the cerebral cortex
             b. the organizational structure of the nervous system
             c. the plasticity of the brain
             d. whether one is left handed or right handed

p. 115 31. Brain lateralization:
F   a. is complete at birth
             b. is not evident until the release of pubertal hormones
        *   c. is evident in at least rudimentary forms at birth
             d. develops across the entire lifespan and is never really complete

p. 115 32. The myelination of the brain continues:
F   a. through age 5
             b. through age 10
        *   c. through adolescence
             d. throughout the entire life span

p. 115 33. As we get older, we can expect all of the following changes in the brain to be part of the
C   NORMAL aging process EXCEPT:
        *   a. Alzheimer's disease and other forms of dementia
             b. decrease in the number of neurons
             c. longer and bushier neurons
             d. decreased levels of neurotransmitters

p. 116 34. Which of the following characterizes the aging brain?
F   a. degeneration, only
             b. plasticity, only
        *   c. degeneration and plasticity
             d. neither degeneration nor plasticity

p. 116 35. During the normal aging process, the nervous system:
F   a. slowly degenerates and is no longer able to grow or change in response to the
                 environment
             b. retains its capabilities, showing neither degeneration or regeneration
        *   c. undergoes both degeneration and growth of new capabilities
             d. continues to grow and shows no signs of degeneration

p. 116　36.　Which of the following is true regarding the aging of the brain?

F

　　　　　　a.　neuron loss is least severe in the portion of the brain which is responsible for sensory and motor activities
　　　　　　b.　brain weight and volume continue to increase into old age
　　　　　　c.　brain weight and volume remain stable after age 50
　　*　　d.　blood flow to the brain decreases in old age

p. 116　37.　From animal studies, as well as studies of the human brain, we have learned that:

F　　*　　a.　new synapses can develop during old age

www　　　b.　it is not possible to develop new synapses in old age
　　　　　　c.　there is no plasticity in an old brain
　　　　　　d.　plasticity increases significantly during old age

p. 116　38.　Greenough's (1986) research with adult rats demonstrated that:

F

　　　　　　a.　brain function is unaffected by exercise
　　　　　　b.　a complex, stimulating environment can be confusing and lead to neural degeneration
　　　　　　c.　learning a new task can change hemispheric specialization
　　*　　d.　learning a new task can increase synaptic connections in the brain

p. 117　39.　Which of the following is the best definition of a reflex?

F

　　　　　　a.　a behavior that has been repeated over and over
　　*　　b.　an unlearned and automatic response to stimulus
　　　　　　c.　a voluntary muscle movement
　　　　　　d.　a stimulus that provokes a response

p. 117　40.　A(n) _____ is an unlearned and automatic response to a stimulus.

F

　　　　　　a.　habit
　　　　　　b.　impulse
　　*　　c.　reflex
　　　　　　d.　synapse

p. 117　41.　Molly strokes the bottom of her baby Martin's foot and watches his toes fan out and then curl. Martin is exhibiting the _____ reflex.

F

　　*　　a.　Babinski
　　　　　　b.　Moro
　　　　　　c.　Palmer
　　　　　　d.　stepping

p. 117　42.　Which reflex disappears FIRST as the infant matures?

F　　*　　a.　grasping reflex
　　　　　　b.　rooting reflex
　　　　　　c.　Moro reflex
　　　　　　d.　breathing reflex

p. 117　43.　The following are all "survival" reflexes EXCEPT:

F

　　　　　　a.　breathing
　　　　　　b.　eye blink
　　*　　c.　Moro
　　　　　　d.　swallowing

p. 117 44. Dr. Troyer is examining newborn Danny's reflexes. He briefly removes support from
F behind Danny's head, and watches as Danny throws his arms outward, arches back, and
then brings his arms together. Dr. Troyer is checking for the presence of the
_____ reflex.
    a. Babinski
    b. grasping
*   c. Moro
    d. swimming

p. 118 45. Stewart and Timothy do not show a Moro reflex when tested for it. Stewart is one week
C old; Timothy is 12 months old. Which one shows an abnormal pattern of development?
www   a. Timothy only
*   b. Stewart only
    c. both Stewart and Timothy
    d. neither Stewart nor Timothy

p. 118 46. The disappearance of so-called "primitive" reflexes during the first few months of infancy
F signifies:
*   a. normal neurological development
    b. abnormal neurological development
    c. the emerging strength of the subcortical areas of the brain
    d. an inability of the infant to respond to stimulation in adaptive ways

p. 117 47. Becky thinks it is so neat that when she puts her finger in her baby Joe's hand, Joe hangs on
F to it tightly. Becky thinks this is because Joe loves her -- a nice thought! Actually, Joe is
simply exhibiting the _____ reflex.
    a. Babinski reflex
*   b . grasping reflex
    c. Moro reflex
    d. rooting reflex

p. 117 48. When Brenda sits down to nurse her baby, Alice, she strokes Alice's cheek on the side that
F is closest to her breast. Alice turns her head toward Brenda's breast and is ready to nurse.
Brenda is making good use of which reflex?
    a. Babinski
    b. grasping
*   c. rooting
    d. sucking

p. 118 49. If the primitive reflexes are not present in the neonate we are most concerned about:
F * a. neurological impairment
    b. psychological impairment
    c. survival
    d. there is no cause for concern

p. 118 50. Which of the following is TRUE of reflexes?
C
        a. Both primitive and survival reflexes should be present at birth and both disappear sometime during the first year.
        b. Both primitive and survival reflexes should be present at birth, but then the survival reflexes should disappear once the baby has survived.
*   c. Both primitive and survival reflexes should be present at birth, and then the primitive reflexes should disappear sometime during the first year.
        d. Both primitive and survival reflexes are present in rudimentary form at birth and both become stronger during the first year.

p. 117 51. Following an unexpected loud noise, a baby puts her arms out and then moves them together again. This is an example of the:
F
*   a. Moro reflex
        b. Turning reflex
        c. Babinski reflex
        d. rooting reflex

p. 117 52. When her baby brother came home from the hospital, Sarah was excited to see that he would suck on her finger when she put it in his mouth. The baby sucks her finger because he:
F
        a. wants to suck on something
        b. likes the slightly salty taste of it
        c. has a grasping reflex
*   d. has a sucking reflex

p. 117 53. Jimmy thinks his baby sister must be ticklish because she fans out her toes and then curls them up when he touches the bottom of her foot. The baby's behavior illustrates:
C
www
        a. Moro reflex
*   b. Babinski reflex
        c. rooting reflex
        d. stepping reflex

p. 119 54. Newborns, on average, sleep about _____ hours per day.
F
        a. 10 to 12
        b. 12 to 15
*   c. 16 to 18
        d. 19 to 21

p. 119 55. Which of the following is TRUE regarding infant states?
F
        a. Infants spend approximately the same amount of time everyday in each of the different states.
        b. Infant states are guided by a strong maturational program, which ensures that all infants spend similar amounts of time in each state.
        c. The amount of time infants spend in different states is determined by how parents interact with them.
*   d. Infants show individual differences in amount of time spent in different states and this can affect how parents interact with them.

p. 119 56. The purpose of REM sleep for infants may be to:

F

a. develop eye muscles
*   b. allow their nervous systems to mature
    c. keep their bodies moving about
    d. insure that the infant keeps breathing

p. 119 57. Cephalocaudal development means that:

F   *   a. physical development proceeds from the head downward
        b. physical development proceeds from the central axis out toward the extremities
        c. the torso develops more rapidly than the head
        d. the upper arms develop before the hands

p. 119 58. Which is the BEST example of cephalocaudal development?

C   a. The infant gains control over the arms before the hands.
www *   b. The infant can sit up before s/he can walk.
        c. The infant can roll over before s/he can grasp a small object.
        d. The infant can roll over before s/he can lift up his/her head.

p. 119 59. When laying flat, babies can hold their heads up before they can lift their hips or legs. This

C   illustrates the:
*   a. cephalocaudal direction of growth
    b. cephalodistal direction of growth
    c. proximodistal direction of growth
    d. proximocaudal direction of growth

p. 120 60. Sarah, like most babies, can swipe at objects in her crib long before she can pick up

C   Cheerios off her high-chair tray. This demonstrates the principle of:
    a. cephalocaudal development
    b. cephalodistal development
    c. proximocaudal development
*   d. proximodistal development

p. 120 61. Infants can flail their arms around before they can move their hands and fingers with any

C   precision. This illustrates the:
    a. cephalocaudal direction of growth
    b. cephalodistal direction of growth
*   c. proximodistal direction of growth
    d. proximocaudal direction of growth

p. 120 62. The ability to grasp an object develops later than the ability to move a hand back and forth

C   because development occurs in a:
    a. cephalocaudal direction
    b. cephalodistal direction
*   c. proximodistal direction
    d. proximocaudal direction

p. 120　63.　According to the orthogenetic principle:
F
www
         a.　growth occurs from the inside to the outside
         b.　growth occurs in a head-to-toe direction
  *   c.　growth is increasingly distinct and organized
         d.　growth consists of gains and losses

p. 120　64.　The average age when most infants have mastered a skill or milestone is referred to as the:
F   *   a.　developmental norm
         b.　normative curve
         c.　modal norm
         d.　growth period

p. 121　65.　What is the AVERAGE age at which infants begin to walk unaided?
F
         a.　9 months
         b.　10 months
  *   c.　12 months
         d.　14 months

p. 121　66.　By an infant's first birthday, we can expect him/her to _____, but not necessarily to _____.
F
         a.　sit up; walk
  *   b.　walk; go up stairs
         c.　roll over; sit up
         d.　lift their head; sit up

p. 121　67.　Most infants (90%) are able to sit without support by about _____ months, and can
F   walk without support by about _____ months.
         a.　4 ; 12
  *   b.　8 ; 14
         c.　6 ; 10
         d.　10 ; 12

p. 122　68.　Jimmy delights in his new-found ability to turn the TV on and off. How old do you think
C   Jimmy is, and which new motor skill is he experimenting with?
         a.　6 months; pincer grasp
         b.　7 months; palmer grasp
  *   c.　10 months; pincer grasp
         d.　12 months; palmer grasp

p. 122　69.　At around 9-12 months of age, there is marked improvement in what infants do with their
F   hands and fingers. This is due to the development of:
         a.　grasping reflex
  *   b.　pincer grasp
         c.　plasticity
         d.　visual perception

p. 122 70. Cross cultural studies suggest that infants will develop motor skills sooner if
C
    a. they are given opportunities to practice motor skills
    b. their limbs are rotated and stretched
    c. they are held by their ankles upside down
*   d. all of the above

p. 123 71. In order to develop normal motor skills, infants need:
F
    a. special training of motor skills
    b. to be swaddled and bound to cradle boards
*   c. opportunities to move around
    d. only a genetic blueprint for how motor skills should develop

p. 123 72. According to the dynamic systems approach of motor development:
C
    a. infants learn motor skills by watching others
    b. infants develop motor skills in a universal, invariant sequence
*   c. infants modify their movements in response to sensory feedback regarding their attempted movements
    d. infants must be taught how and when to perform various motor skills

p. 123 73. Ten-month-old Madra wants to get across the room to reach a favorite toy. She figures out
C that rolling over doesn't really get her where she wants to go, but pulling herself along on her belly does. Madra's behavior can be explained in terms of:
*   a. dynamic systems perspective
    b. orthogenetic principle
    c. proximodistal principle
    d. developmental norms

p. 124 74. How is a toddler likely to compare to a child in terms of physical behavior?
C   *   a. The toddler can control their movements as long as the world around them is
www   stationary, while the child can control movements even when the environment around them is changing.
    b. The toddler is not able to planfully direct future actions while the child is able to plan future actions.
    c. The toddler has developed gross motor skills that are as coordinated as the older child, but is just beginning to use fine motor skills.
    d. Toddlers are able to move more quickly than the older child, but are less coordinated in their movements.

p. 125 75. For girls, the beginning of puberty is marked by:
F
    a. turning twelve years of age
    b. the adolescent growth spurt
    c. the start of dating
*   d. menarche

p. 125 76. The mark of sexual maturation for a boy that is most comparable to menarche for a girl is
C
    a. deepening of the voice
*   b. first ejaculation of seminal fluid
    c. the appearance of pubic hair
    d. all of the above

p. 125 77. Sexual maturation in females is "officially" marked by _____ and the comparable event
F   in males is _____ .
              a. growth of pubic hair; growth of facial hair
              b. growth of pubic hair; growth of pubic hair
        *   c. first menstruation; first ejaculation
              d. breast development; penis growth

p. 125 78. On average, girls experience the adolescent growth spurt _____ sooner than boys.
F   a. 6 months
              b. 1 year
        *   c. 2 years
              d. 3 years

p. 125 79. Which is the correct sequence of development for MOST females?
F   a. menarche; breast buds; pubic hair
        *   b. breast buds; pubic hair; menarche
              c. underarm hair; pubic hair; breast buds;
              d. breast buds; underarm hair; menarche

p. 125 80. Which is the correct sequence of development for MOST males?
F   a. pubic hair; penis growth; enlarged testes
        *   b. enlarged testes; pubic hair; penis growth
              c. penis growth; pubic hair; enlarged testes
              d. penis growth; enlarged testes; pubic hair

p. 126 81. Over the past 100 years or so, people in industrialized societies have been maturing earlier,
F   as well as growing heavier and taller than in the past. This phenomenon is referred to as

              _____ .
              a. cultural determinism
              b. species enhancement
              c. the population growth spurt
        *   d. the secular trend

p. 126 82. The secular trend refers to:
F   a. the fact that people's rates of maturation are more variable than in the past
        *   b. the fact that people mature earlier and grow taller now than in the past
              c. a loosening of moral standards with regard to sexual preferences
              d. changes in the sequence of development over time

p. 126 83. Which of the following BEST explains the secular trend?
        *   a. better nutrition and medical advances
              b. genetic variation
              c. the political climate of the times
              d. genetic engineering

p. 126 84. Which of the following is evidence that physical and sexual maturation are influenced by
C   environmental factors?
www   a. Identical twins experience physical changes at about the same time.
             b. Timing of growth spurts is somewhat consistent within families.
    *   c. Overall, girls today experience menarche at an earlier age than girls of previous
                generations.
             d. Adopted children resemble their biological parents in timing of puberty.

p. 127 85. Overall, what can we conclude about boys' and girls' body images during adolescence?
C   a. Girls' body images are influenced by other people's reactions to them but not to actual
                physical changes, while boys show the opposite pattern.
             b. Both boys and girls experience puberty as a positive event.
             c. Girls show benefits from going through puberty but not from the changes associated
                with their growth spurt, while boys show the opposite pattern.
    *   d. Boys are more positive images than girls.

p. 127 86. Many cultures mark the transition from childhood to adulthood with:
F   *   a. rites of passage
             b. arranged marriages
             c. an end of formal schooling
             d. increased conflict with parents

p. 128 87. Which groups of adolescents might be expected to have the GREATEST difficulties
C   adjusting to the changes of puberty?
    *   a. late-maturing boys and early-maturing girls
             b. late-maturing boys and late-maturing girls
             c. early-maturing boys and late-maturing girls
             d. early-maturing boys and early-maturing girls

p. 130 88. Girls perform worse on some physical tasks in late adolescence than they did in early
C   adolescence. This is probably due to:
             a. a decrease in muscle strength of girls
    *   b. gender-role socialization of females in our culture
             c. hormone changes across the period of adolescence
             d. not understanding how to perform the tasks

p. 130 89. During adolescence, the physical performances of males continue to improve, while those
C   of females tend to level off, or even decline!   What is the most likely explanation for this?
             a. degeneration of muscle tissue in females
             b. decline in growth rate for females
    *   c. gender-role socialization
             d. the secular trend

p. 130 90. In old age, people tend to:
F   a. lose muscle and gain fat
             b. gain muscle and gain fat
    *   c. lose muscle and lose fat
             d. gain muscle and lose fat

p. 130 91. Sally is getting quite old. She should expect all of the following to occur EXCEPT a:
C   *   a. gain in body fat
             b. decrease in height
             c. loss in muscle mass
             d. loss in bone tissue

p. 130 92. Osteoporosis occurs when:
F   a. the cushioning between joints wears out and the joints become stiff
             b. maximal heart rates decrease so that any sort of work-out requires more effort
        *   c. lost minerals result in less bone mass
             d. vitamin deficiencies lower the efficiency of the major organs

p. 130 93. All of the following are known to help prevent or slow osteoporosis with the EXCEPTION
C   of:
             a. calcium supplements
             b. exercise
             c. estrogen therapy
        *   d. steroids

p. 130 94. Judith, age 68, suffers from osteoporosis. Which of the following is her doctor MOST
C   likely to recommend to slow the progression of her condition?
        *   a. regular exercise, such as walking one to two miles each day
             b. a diet low in calcium
             c. hormone therapy which involves taking massive doses of testosterone
             d. a low, daily dose of penicillin

p. 130 95. Stiff joints in older adults often occur as a result of:
F   a. osteoporosis
        *   b. osteoarthritis
             c. hypertension
             d. Alzheimer's disease

p. 131 96. Most older adults:
C   a. are unable to function independently
www   b. are unhappy and depressed about getting older
             c. believe that their health is poor
        *   d. report that they are in good, even great, health

p. 132 97. Which of the following is POSITIVELY associated with experiencing negative emotions
F   during the premenstrual and menstrual phases of the month?
             a. a high level of income
             b. a high level of education
             c. employment in a nontraditional occupation
        *   d. being a housewife

p. 132 98. The three most common premenstrual symptoms reported by women are:
F   *   a. mood swings, irritability, and weight gain
             b. weight gain, crying, and headaches
             c. cramps, painful breasts, and weight gain
             d. cramps, acne, and fatigue

p. 132 99. Which of the following would be LEAST likely to influence premenstrual and menstrual
C symptoms?
  * a. a woman's size and age
    b. societal expectations about what menstruation "should" be like
    c. genetic endowment
    d. levels of estrogen and progesterone

p. 132 100. Which of the following is TRUE regarding menopause?
C a. The earlier a woman experienced menarche as an adolescent, the earlier she will go
    through menopause.
  * b. There is no connection between age of menarche and age of menopause.
    c. Women are no longer ovulating but continue to menstruate each month.
    d. Levels of estrogen sharply increase leading to cessation of menstruation.

p. 132 101. Decreases in female hormones have been directly linked to:
F a. depression and breast tenderness
www b. hot flashes and irritability
  * c. hot flashes and vaginal dryness
    d. mood swings and irritability

p. 132 102. After going through menopause, a woman:
F * a. does not ovulate and is no longer fertile
    b. does ovulate but is no longer fertile
    c. does not ovulate but still menstruates
    d. menstruates, but is no longer fertile

p. 132 103. All of the following are quite commonly experienced by females who are going through
F menopause with the EXCEPTION of:
  * a. extreme depression
    b. a thinning of the vaginal wall
    c. hot flashes
    d. irritation during intercourse

p. 133 104. Men experience a loss of reproductive capacity in later life known as:
F a. menopause
    b. midlife crisis
    c. degeneration
  * d. the climacteric

p. 133 105. Which tends to be the MOST true with regard to sexual functioning during adulthood?
F a. sexual functioning declines quite rapidly for males after age 50
    b. sexual functioning declines quite rapidly for females after menopause
    c. sexual functioning improves with age
  * d. you either "use it or lose it"

p. 134　106. The main reason why older adults are slower on many tasks than younger adults is:
F
　　　　　　a.　they have fewer reasons to hurry or act quickly
　　　*　　b.　slowing of the nervous system
　　　　　　c.　a change from an impulsive style to a reflective style
　　　　　　d.　an increase in visual problems

p. 135　107. Research examining the physical and intellectual functioning of males indicates that, in
F　　　　　　general, old men in excellent health function:
　　　　　　a.　less well physically but better intellectually than do young men
　　　　　　b.　less well physically and intellectually than do young men
　　　*　　c.　just about as well as young men with regard to both physical and intellectual abilities
　　　　　　d.　just about as well as young men with regard to physical abilities, but are inferior with
　　　　　　　　regard to intellectual abilities

p. 135　108. Through a process called compensation for decline, older adults:
F
　　　　　　a.　gradually lose their ability to perform basic motor skills
　　　　　　b.　lose their reserve capacity
　　　*　　c.　find a way to get around losses that occur with age
　　　　　　d.　who exercise their skills, do not lose them

p. 136　109. The "use it or lose it" maxim applies to which of the following?
F
www　　　　a.　functioning of the brain but not the heart
　　　　　　b.　functioning of the heart but not sexuality
　　　　　　c.　functioning of the heart but not the brain
　　　*　　d.　sexuality, functioning of the heart, and functioning of the brain

p. 136　110. To maintain optimal functioning of an organ system across the lifespan, we should:
F　　　*　　a.　continue to use or exercise the system on a regular basis
　　　　　　b.　rest the system as much as possible to preserve it
　　　　　　c.　take medications to counteract any negative effects of aging
　　　　　　d.　increase use of the system to its maximum capacity for as long as possible

p. 136　111. Infants and young children who have experienced slow growth because they have been
F　　　　　　temporarily malnourished will:
　　　　　　a.　remain smaller than normal throughout their lifespan
　　　　　　b.　catch up in brain growth but not in physical growth
　　　　　　c.　require massive levels of calories to compensate for the earlier shortfall
　　　*　　d.　grow faster than normal when an adequate diet is restored

p. 137　112. Someone who is "obese" weighs at least ___% above the ideal body weight for someone of
F　　　　　　their age, height, and sex.
　　　　　　a.　10
　　　　　　b.　15
　　　*　　c.　20
　　　　　　d.　25

p. 138 113. Timmy, a second-grader, is obese. His parents want to know what to do to deal with the
F   problem. Which would be the best recommendation to give them?
              a. put Timmy on a strenuous diet
              b. leave Timmy alone; he'll grow out of it on his own
          *   c. plan family activities that include regular exercise
              d. ridicule Timmy so that he will feel he has to lose weight

p. 138 114. Moderate amounts of alcohol
F   a. have no effect on the body
          *   b. protects the heart from cardiovascular disease
              c. causes harm, regardless of the amount
              d. causes the same amount of harm as heavy drinking

p. 138 115. Of the following, who is likely to have the best physical functioning in old age?
C   a. A person who typically sleeps less than seven hours per night and rarely eats breakfast.
          *   b. A person who consumes a moderate amount of alcohol and regularly eats breakfast.
              c. A person who consumes no alcohol and sometimes snacks between meals.
              d. A person who rarely snacks between meals and smokes a moderate number of
                  cigarettes.

p. 110 116. Which structure is considered the "master gland" of the endocrine system?
F   a. thyroid gland
SG   b. hypothalamus
              c. adrenal gland
          *   d. pituitary gland

p. 112 117. Which of the following is NOT a key developmental process of early brain growth?
F   a. proliferation of neurons
SG   b. migration of neurons to select locations
          *   c. isolation of neurons into unique positions
              d. differentiation of neurons into specialized functions

p. 113 118. The brain growth spurt, a period of rapid brain development, occurs
F   *   a. during the prenatal period and the first two years after birth
SG   b. during the prenatal period only
              c. during infancy and childhood
              d. during puberty

p. 113 119. Which of the following is TRUE regarding early brain development?
F   a. Neurons continue to be produced until puberty.
SG   *   b. Neurons are rapidly forming connections with other neurons.
              c. The function of each neuron is determined at conception.
              d. The ultimate location of neurons is flexible throughout infancy and childhood.

p. 114 120. Plasticity ensures that the brain
C   a. can recover from any sort of damage
SG   b. receives the maximum benefits from stimulation throughout the life span
              c. is not influenced by adverse environments
          *   d. is responsive to individual experiences

p. 114 121. Lateralization is a process by which
F   a.   one hemisphere takes over for the other's functions after brain damage has occurred
SG   *   b.   specialization of the functions of the left and right hemisphere occurs
         c.   neurons in the brain develop rapidly
         d.   neurons are covered by a myelin sheath

p. 116 122. As the body ages from childhood to adulthood, the brain
C   a.   develops more neurons
SG   b.   begins to form a myelin sheath around many neurons
         c.   grows longer dendrites that may form new connections with other neurons
         d.   releases large quantities of neurotransmitters

p. 118 123. The primitive reflexes
F   a.   are essential to survival
SG   *   b.   disappear sometime during infancy
         c.   include rooting, sucking, and swallowing
         d.   protect the infant from various adverse conditions

p. 119 124. The cephalocaudal principle predicts that:
C   a.   growth of the brain and spinal cord will be the last to occur
SG   b.   growth will proceed from bones and cartilage to internal organs
     *   c.   growth will proceed from head to tail
         d.   growth will proceed from the midline to the extremities

p. 121 125. Based on the cephalocaudal principle of growth, infants typically can _____ before they
F   can _____.
SG   a.   stand; roll over
         b.   roll over; control their arms or hands
         c.   walk backward; walk up steps
     *   d.   sit; walk

p. 126 126. Which of the following hormone(s) trigger the adolescent growth spurt?
F   a.   progesterone
SG   *   b.   androgens
         c.   activating hormones
         d.   thyroxine

p. 128 127. Regarding the timing of maturation:
C   a.   Sheila, who matures early, is likely to be more popular than Mary, who matures late.
SG   b.   Bill, who matures late, is likely to be more academically skilled than Mark, who matures early
     *   c.   Tom, who matures early, is likely to be confident and poised relative to Steve, who matures late.
         d.   Mike, who matures "on time" is likely to be viewed most favorably by his parents and teachers, relative to other boys in his class who mature early or late.

p. 126 128. The secular trend refers to
F
SG
    a. earlier maturation and decreased body size
    b. later maturation and decreased body size
    c. historical changes in life expectancy
    * d. earlier maturation and increased body size from generation to generation

p. 130 129. The apparent decline of physical performance of females by the end of adolescence
C
SG
    a. is a myth not supported by any data
    * b. results largely from socialization differences between males and females
    c. results from an overall decline in the proportion of muscle mass relative to fat
    d. is similar to the decline that occurs in males

p. 132 130. Menopause is a time when
F
SG
    * a. women no longer ovulate or menstruate
    b. most women experience mood swings for extended periods of time
    c. women continue to ovulate but do not menstruate
    d. women experience an increase in hormone levels

TRUE-FALSE QUESTIONS

p. 111 131. Neurons "communicate" with one another by releasing hormones.
    a. true
    * b. false

p. 112 132. The cerebral cortex is responsible for voluntary body movements and perception.
    * a. true
    b. false

p. 112 133. Neurons migrate to specific locations during the prenatal period.
www * a. true
    b. false

p. 114 134. The plasticity of the brain means that it is impervious to harm.
    a. true
    * b. false

p. 114 135. The brain develops at its fastest rate during the school years.
    a. true
    * b. false

p. 115 136. Handedness (being a "lefty" or "righty") is already established at birth.
    a. true
    * b. false

p. 115 137. Lateralization of the brain is a process that continues throughout life.
    a. true
    * b. false

p. 115 138. In general, the left hemisphere of the brain governs language processing.
*   a. true
       b. false

p. 117 139. The Moro reflex occurs when infants curl their fingers around an object that touches their palm.
       a. true
*   b. false

p. 118 140. The endocrine glands secrete hormones directly into the bloodstream
*   a. true
       b. false

p. 118 141. Normal neurological development is signaled by the disappearance of the primitive reflexes sometime during the first year.
*   a. true
       b. false

p. 119 142. Infants will generally establish regular sleep cycles unless their nervous systems are in some way abnormal.
*   a. true
       b. false

p. 119 143. In general, an infant's bones will break less easily than those of an adult.
*   a. true
       b. false

p. 120 144. The proximodistal principle of growth refers to the fact that growth occurs in a head-to-tail
www   direction.
       a. true
*   b. false

p. 121 145. Motor skills follow the cephalocaudal principle but muscular development does not.
       a. true
*   b. false

p. 121 146. Locomotor development is largely a maturational process.
*   a. true
       b. false

p. 122 147. The emergence of motor skills follows a universal pattern, with infants all over the world
www   exhibiting the same skills at about the same time and in the same sequence.
*   a. true
       b. false

p. 125 148. Boys generally achieve sexual maturity earlier than do girls.
       a. true
*   b. false

p. 126   149. Sexual maturation occurs independent of environmental effects.
          a.   true
   *   b.   false

p. 128   150. Early sexual maturation is advantageous for both males and females.
          a.   true
   *   b.   false

p. 128   151. Boys who mature early are at a distinct social advantage as compared to those who mature early.
   *   a.   true
          b.   false

p. 131   152. Survey research indicates that old people are likely to view themselves as physically fit even though they typically have physical impairments.
   *   a.   true
          b.   false

p. 131   153. Males follow a hormonal cycle similar to that of females.
          a.   true
   *   b.   false

p. 132   154. Women who experience menarche at an early age will go through menopause earlier than those who experience menarche late in adolescence.
          a.   true
   *   b.   false

p. 132   155. Menopause is a major psychological crisis for most women.
          a.   true
   *   b.   false

p. 132   156. The female response to menopause is "universal," that is, women around the world tend to respond to menopause in much the same way.
          a.   true
   *   b.   false

p. 132   157. Senility is a part of the normal aging process.
          a.   true
   *   b.   false

p. 131   158. Most old people suffer from some sort of chronic disease or impairment.
   *   a.   true
          b.   false

ESSAY QUESTIONS

---

159.   What physical changes indicate the beginning of puberty for males and females? What are the psychological correlates of these changes?

160.   What physical changes accompany menopause? What variables influence how difficult or easy
www   this transition can be for women?

161.   What changes are brought about by an "an aging brain?"

162.   Suppose you are in charge of writing a newsletter for adults who are approaching
SG   retirement age. In one issue of the newsletter, you want to write an informative article on
        physical changes that these adults might experience as they age. What would this article
        say?
        [Sample answer is provided in the Study Guide.]

163.   Now write the same article but for a different readership: Parents with a newborn infant.
SG   What physical changes can they anticipate that their child will go through as she or he
        progresses through infancy, childhood, and adolescence?

164.   What evidence is there that lateralization takes place at an early age, yet still allows for
SG   plasticity in brain function across the life-span?

6

PERCEPTION

p. 143 1. Sensation refers to
F
          a. interpretation of incoming sensory messages
    * b. stimulation of nerve cells in the sense organs
          c. perceiving the surrounding environment
          d. innate processes of understanding the world

p. 143 2. Nerves are stimulated during the process of _____, and the brain interprets information
F   in the process of _____.
www * a. sensation, perception
          b. stimulation, selection
          c. perception, sensation
          d. selection, stimulation

p. 143 3. The brain does the _____, while the nerves do the _____.
F
          a. sensing, interpreting
          b. interpreting, sensing
          c. sensing, perceiving
    * d. perceiving, sensing

p. 143 4. Interpretation of the world around us is accomplished through the process of:
F
          a. sensation
    * b. perception
          c. distinction
          d. differentiation

p. 143 5. Which of the following is the best example of a perceptual process?
C
          a. hearing a sound in the room
          b. detecting that a light has been turned on in a dark room
          c. sensing that someone has touched your arm
    * d. realizing that the odor you smell is vanilla

p. 143 6. The idea that infants are born "tabulae rasae" means that they
C
          a. don't have depth perception so they see the world as flat images
    * b. are born without any perceptual knowledge
          c. prefer looking at tables compared to other stimuli
          d. instinctively know how to use their senses

p. 143 7. If an adult were created (cloned) from a single human cell, the empiricists would predict
C   that the clone would
*   a. have to learn to perceive the world as meaningful
      b. awaken with a meaningful understanding of the world
      c. not be able to function
      d. think and perceive like an adult

p. 143 8. If an adult were created (cloned) from a single human cell, the nativists would predict that
C   the clone would
      a. have to learn to perceive the world as meaningful
*   b. awaken with a meaningful understanding of the world
      c. be unable to learn because it has the brain of an adult rather than an infant
      d. think and perceive like an adult

p. 143 9. Empiricists are likely to say that infants:
C   a. are born with some understanding of the world around them
      b. have an innate tendency to seek out information
*   c. know nothing until they begin to take in information through their senses
      d. can sense information around them but do not understand this information

p. 143 10. Peter believes that his newborn already detects a difference between when he walks away
C   from her and when he walks towards her, and that she understands that these two actions
      will lead to different outcomes for her. Peter's beliefs are similar to those of:
      a. empiricists
*   b. nativists
      c. interactionists
      d. enrichment theorists

p. 144 11. If you turn on a floor fan, an infant will orient toward the sound. After awhile, he/she
C   appears to lose interest. This phenomenon is known as
www *   a. habituation
      b. discrimination
      c. generalization
      d. sound acuity

p. 144 12. Linda jingles her keys in front of baby Sam's face and he watches and smiles. Linda
C   continues to bring her keys up and jingle them in front of Sam because he appears to enjoy
      this "game." After a while, though, Sam seems to lose interest in the game and no longer
      focuses on the keys when Linda jingles them. This illustrates:
      a. cross-modal perception
      b. constancy
      c. visual accommodation
*   d. habituation

p. 144 13. All of the following methods are used to assess young infants' perceptual abilities
F   EXCEPT:
      *   a. classical conditioning to develop taste preferences
            b. preferential looking at an object
            c. habituation to a repeatedly presented stimulus
            d. operant conditioning to respond to one stimulus but not another

p. 145 14. What is the MOST accurate summary we can make regarding a newborn's visual sense?
C   *   a. The visual system works fairly well, but will improve during the first year.
            b. The visual system functions at its highest level shortly after birth.
            c. The visual system functions very poorly for the first 10 months of life.
            d. The visual system cannot be tested until infants understand verbal instructions, so we
                do not really know the full capabilities of an infant.

p. 145 15. If you want your two-week-old child to see you as clearly as possible, you should
C   a. have very bright light on your face
            b. move back and forth quickly so the child focuses on movement
      *   c. put your face within a few inches of their eyes
            d. all of the above

p. 145 16. One reason that infants see poorly is the fact that
F   a. the world is confusing to them
            b. they cannot distinguish between their senses
      *   c. they lack visual accommodation
            d. the cones of the retina do not function for the first six months

p. 145 17. Which of the following is TRUE regarding infants' vision?
F   a. Infants do not have color vision until around 6 months of age.
      *   b. Much of what young infants see is blurry.
            c. Pattern complexity has no impact on infants' visual preferences.
            d. Visual accommodation allows infants to focus clearly on far objects but not near
                objects.

p. 146 18. Which of the following would be LEAST LIKELY to attract an infant's attention?
C   *   a. a light yellow circle on a white page
            b. a picture that has a reasonably complex pattern
            c. a black and white geometric figure
            d. a moving object

p. 146 19. Research indicates that infants prefer to look at _____ more than other visual stimuli.
F   a. checkerboard patterns
            b. shiny discs
      *   c. faces
            d. rapidly moving objects

p. 146 20. Which of the following factors is the most important factor overall that determines what an
C   infant will stare at the longest?
www   a. the degree of contours that the object has
        b. whether the object is moving or not
        c. how complex the object is in terms of colors and patterns
    *   d. whether or not the infant can see it well

p. 146 21. What is the BEST explanation for why infants prefer to look at some objects more than
C   others?
        a. Some objects are circular and other objects have straight edges
        b. Some objects are colored and other objects are black and white
    *   c. Some objects can be seen more clearly by infants than other objects
        d. Some objects are more familiar to infants than other objects

p. 147 22. The tendency to perceive an object as not growing when it approaches our eyes or
F   shrinking as it moves away is _____ constancy.
        a. location
    *   b. size
        c. brightness
        d. form

p. 147 23. A woman is in a swimming pool. Her nine-month-old daughter is sitting on a blanket three
C   feet from the edge of the pool. The woman coaxes her child to crawl to her. The child is
        most likely to:
        a. crawl off the edge of the pool and fall into her mother's arms
    *   b. crawl to the edge of the pool and stop
        c. crawl away from her mother because her whole body isn't visible
        d. not do anything because of lack of location constancy

p. 147 24. The visual cliff experiment demonstrates that infants develop _____ before their first
F   birthday.
    *   a. depth perception
        b. size constancy
        c. location constancy
        d. shape constancy

p. 147 25. Which of the following does NOT illustrate perception of three-dimensional space?
C   a. reaching your hands out to catch a ball moving towards you
        b. showing habituation to the same stimulus regardless of the distance of the stimulus
           from your face
    *   c. crawling from an opaque platform onto a platform with an apparent drop-off
        d. blinking in response to an object moving towards your face

p. 147 26. As his mom walks towards him, the retinal image of her changes, but 6-month-old Marc
C   still recognizes her every step of the way. This suggests that Marc has:
www *   a. size constancy
        b. distance adaptation
        c. visual accommodation
        d. cross-modal perception

p. 147 27. The visual cliff has been used to assess whether infants:

C   a. can detect the distinct features of a visual display

         b. show visual preferences

         c. become habituated to an object that is repeatedly presented

     *   d. recognize and understand the implications of depth

p. 148 28. Testing infants of different ages with the visual cliff apparatus has found that:

C   a. 6-7 month old infants perceive drop-offs but do not fear them

     *   b. 2-month old infants perceive drop-offs but do not fear them

         c. 6-month old infants show no response to the deep side of the cliff

         d. both 2- and 6-month old infants will crawl across the shallow side of the cliff but will cry when enticed to crawl over the deep side of the cliff

p. 148 29. The bulk of the research with infants indicates that perception of space

F   a. develops gradually over several years

     *   b. develops rapidly in early infancy

         c. emerges at different rates for boys and girls

         d. is innate and present at birth

p. 148 30. All of the following contribute to infants' fear of drop-offs EXCEPT:

C   a. experience crawling

         b. moving around in a walker

     *   c. improved visual acuity

         d. maturation

p. 148 31. Infants can best organize the world into distinct objects when:

C   a. the environment they are trying to make sense of is stationary

     *   b. the environment they are trying to make sense of is moving

         c. the environment is made up of objects that are similar to one another

         d. the environment is made up of novel objects

p. 149 32. Which of the following is the best example of the infant as an intuitive theorist?

C   a. Infants look away when an object disappears from view

www   b. Infants get bored an look away when an object is repeatedly presented

     *   c. Infants show surprise when a ball that is dropped behind a screen is shown to be suspended in air

         d. Infants show surprise when a ball rolling down a hill is shown reaching the bottom of the hill

p. 149 33. According to the intuitive theories' perspective

F   *   a. Infants have innate knowledge of the world and can reason about the world like adults do

         b. Infants must construct their knowledge of the world from a blank slate

         c. Infants learn what they need to know about the world by observing people around them

         d. Infants may have some innate knowledge of the world, but do not yet have the capabilities to reason about the world.

p. 150 34. A 6-month-old infant watches as two dolls are placed behind a screen. When the screen is
C   removed, the infant sees either two dolls (possible) or one doll (impossible). Which of the
         following reactions is the infant likely to show?
         a. The infant will not notice any difference between the possible and impossible
             outcomes, as evidenced by no difference in looking times at the two outcomes.
    *   b. The infant will look longer at the impossible outcome than the possible outcome.
         c. The infant will look longer at the possible outcome because it is familiar to them.
         d. The infant will not look at either outcome because they will have habituated to the
             original stimulus.

p. 149 35. Concerning the ability of newborns to hear, research has shown that they can discriminate
F   a. loudness and frequency, but not direction and duration
         b. only frequency and loudness
    *   c. frequency, loudness, duration, and direction
         d. only between loud and soft sounds

p. 149 36. What advice would you give someone about how to speak to their newborn so that the baby
C   is most likely to listen?
         a. speak in a soft whisper
         b. speak extremely loud
         c. tickle the baby while whispering
    *   d. speak in a normal voice

p. 149 37. Three month old infants can discriminate between phonemes. This means that they can
F   *   a. tell the difference between various basic sounds
         b. discriminate between a doorbell and the bell on a telephone
         c. discriminate between various familiar odors
         d. discriminate between familiar and novel tastes

p. 149 38. The basic speech sounds that all humans are capable of making are referred to as
F   a. morphemes
         b. semaphores
    *   c. phonemes
         d. sensory thresholds

p. 149 39. Infants can detect the difference between the sound "pa" and the sound "ba." This shows
C   that they:
    *   a. can differentiate phonemes
         b. have cross-modal perception
         c. have phonological awareness
         d. can differentiate among languages

p. 149 40. Which of the following is FALSE regarding an infant's auditory sense?
F   a. They can localize sounds as newborns.
         b. They will turn away from loud noises.
         c. They can discriminate among different sounds
    *   d. They do not hear all sounds nearly as well as an adult.

p. 150 41. What can we conclude regarding developmental changes in speech perception?
C   *   a. With age, we become more sensitive to sound discriminations that are relevant in our own language and less sensitive to sound discriminations that are irrelevant.
          b. With age, we become more sensitive to all sound discriminations.
          c. There are no detectable differences in sound discriminations with age.
          d. With age, we become more sensitive to differences in consonant sounds and less sensitive to differences in vowel sounds.

p. 151 42. DeCasper and Fifer (1980) conducted research that demonstrated that infants can recognize
F   their mother's voices
          a. three months after conception
    *   b. within the first three days
          c. only after a month
          d. not until they are three months of age

p. 151 43. Three day old babies were given pacifiers to suck. Each baby learned to suck the pacifier
C   faster than usual in order to hear their mother's voice. The experiment demonstrated that
          a. each infant preferred his/her mother's voice to a pacifier
          b. each infant associated its mother's voice with nursing
          c. babies prefer pacifiers to their mothers
    *   d. babies learn to recognize their mothers by sound before they recognize them by sight

p. 151 44. Within days of their baby's birth, Carlotta and Jim are having an argument about him.
C   Carlotta claims that he recognizes her voice but Jim says that this is impossible. Knowing
www   the research in this area, you are able to tell them that:
          a. Jim is correct; voice recognition does not occur until around 6 months of age.
          b. Both could be correct; babies can recognize the first voice that they heard immediately following delivery. If this was Carlotta's voice, then she is correct. If this was not Carlotta's voice, then Jim is correct.
    *   c. Carlotta is correct; voice recognition is evident during the first few days after birth.
          d. We do not know who is correct because infants this young cannot be accurately tested.

p. 152 45. Experiments have demonstrated that infants learn to hear before they are born.
C   Consequently, potential parents
          a. should recite lists of vocabulary words to the unborn child
          b. should avoid loud arguments that might disturb the baby
          c. frequently play the type of music that they want their baby to appreciate after it is born
    *   d. should remember that the baby can hear but not understand the sounds

p. 152 46. Newborns will produce certain facial expressions depending on the taste of the liquid that
C   they are offered. They smile when offered sugar water and frown when offered quinine. This demonstrates that newborns
          a. prefer bitter tastes to sour ones
          b. inherit their mother's taste preferences
    *   c. can discriminate between various tastes
          d. prefer anything that tastes like milk

p. 152   47.   The senses of taste and smell are related in that
F   a.   both provide the same sensory experience
         *   b.   they are both triggered by chemical molecules
                  c.   they use the same nerves to send messages to the brain
                  d.   one will not work without the other

p. 152   48.   Which of the following senses is NOT working as well as the others at birth?
C   a.   hearing
         *   b.   vision
                  c.   taste
                  d.   smell

p. 153   49.   Which of the following does NOT demonstrate that infants have a well developed sense of
C   touch?
         *   a.   Newborns prefer their mother's milk over the milk of another nursing mother
                  b.   They reject milk that is too hot
                  c.   Infants habituate to strokes on the ear
                  d.   Infants prefer to touch novel objects rather than familiar ones

p. 153   50.   Analyses of the behavior of male infants as they undergo circumcisions indicate that they
F   a.   are unaware of the procedure
                  b.   sense something is going on but show little distress
         *   c.   feel a good deal of pain
                  d.   accept the procedure as a form of attention

p. 153   51.   Newborns look in the direction of a sound that they hear. They also try to grasp objects that
C   they can see. This suggests that newborns
                  a.   use the senses of sight, hearing, and touch, more than taste and smell
                  b.   use vision to coordinate all the senses
                  c.   cannot distinguish between their senses
         *   d.   can simultaneously use two or more senses

p. 153   52.   One month old infants were given either a smooth pacifier to suck on or one with hard
C   nubs. Although they had not seen the pacifier while sucking on it, when given the
                 opportunity to look, the infants stared longer at the type of pacifier that they had sucked on.
                 This shows that they have:
         *   a.   cross-modal perception
                  b.   inter-sensory sensation
                  c.   intra-modal integration
                  d.   none of the above

p. 153   53.   Cross-modal perception is the ability to:
F   a.   perceive three-dimensionality from a two-dimensional display
                  b.   perceive an object through two senses at the same time
                  c.   stop responding to a stimulus that is repeatedly presented
         *   d.   recognize with one sense an object that was learned through another sense

p. 153 54. Which of the following is NOT an example of cross-modal perception?
C * a. recognizing mom's face in photographs
       b. picking out by sight a toy that you had previously only touched
       c. identifying which cat has jumped onto the bed in the dark by running your hands over it
       d. a friend tells you to close your eyes and open your mouth for a treat, which you correctly identify as a tootsie roll pop because of the way it feels in your mouth

p. 153 55. Integration of sensory information:
C   a. begins to emerge sometime around the end of the first year
         b. is related to the acuity of senses but not to intellectual ability
    *   c. is present at birth or shortly thereafter
         d. is tested by using the visual cliff apparatus

p. 154 56. Riesen's research with chimpanzees raised in the dark showed that the optic nerve:
C   a. is not influenced by the amount of light exposure
    *   b. degenerates but can be rejuvenated if the exposure to the dark lasts no more than seven months
         c. degenerates and is permanently damaged regardless of the length of exposure to the dark
         d. degenerates but can be rejuvenated at any time regardless of the length of exposure to the dark

p. 154 57. In order to develop normally, the visual system needs:
C   a. any sort of stimulation to activate it
    *   b. patterned stimulation early in life
         c. constant stimulation throughout life
         d. no stimulation from the environment; maturation alone is sufficient

p. 154 58. The development of normal visual perception of features such as depth:
C   a. depends entirely on one's ability to move independently around the environment
         b. is present at birth and needs no particular environmental experience
         c. is guided by innate organizing principles
    *   d. requires regular exposure to moving objects in the environment that capture one's attention

p. 155 59. The activity that best helps the infant develop its perceptual skills is
C   a. sleeping, because that is when the brain areas develop the most
         b. sitting on a parent's knee listening to a conversation
         c. watching television
    *   d. exploratory crawling

p. 155 60. Research with kittens raised with restricted visual information suggests that infants
C   a. will develop normal vision regardless of what their early experiences consist of
www   b. need to be exposed to just one type of visual scene in order to develop normal vision
         c. have a fully developed nervous system that supports normal vision from the very beginning of life
    *   d. need to be exposed to a variety of visual experiences in order for normal vision to develop

p. 155 61. Research with infants suggests that:
C
    *   a. parents must find ways to bring the environment to their not-yet-crawling infants
         b. infants are active explorers who will find ways to get stimulation from the environment
         c. infants passively take in what is close by but do not seek stimulation
         d. parents need to take an active role in teaching their infants to explore their environment

p. 155 62. Perceptual development:
C
         a. is impervious to cultural differences
    *   b. varies across cultures because of socialization differences
         c. varies across cultures because of differences in sensory capabilities
         d. varies across cultures because of differences in levels of intellectual ability

p. 156 63. Much of the perceptual development that occurs during childhood is a matter of
F
         a. learning the names of things
         b. developing personal habits
    *   c. acquiring attention skills
         d. learning to control one's emotions

p. 156 64. During childhood, what factor has the greatest impact on perceptual development?
C   *   a. attention
         b. improved acuity of senses
         c. maturation
         d. metaperception

p. 156 65. Which of the following is NOT a typical change in attention during childhood?
F
         a. attention becomes more selective and controlled
         b. attention span becomes longer
    *   c. attention becomes linked to cognitive skills
         d. attention becomes systematic

p. 157 66. As children mature,
F
         a. their longer attention spans lead to boredom with simple tasks
    *   b. they can systematically search the most important features of a visual scene
         c. they can attend to visual information for seemingly endless amounts of time, but are limited in attention to auditory information
         d. their attention becomes fragmented

p. 157 67. Attention changes in all of the following ways over childhood EXCEPT:
C
www
         a. Children are more likely to plan what they will attend to.
         b. Children are better able to focus on relevant information and ignore irrelevant information.
         c. Children become more selective in what they attend to.
    *   d. Children are more likely to attend to all features of an object or display.

p. 157 68. According to Gibson and Levin, the first step in learning to read is:
F
        a. decoding letters
        b. sounding out words
    *   c. telling stories while looking at a storybook
        d. matching the spoken words of a story to what is thought to be the written symbols (letters or words) of the words

p. 158 69. According to Gibson, learning to read really involves learning to recognize:
C
        a. the proper order of words
    *   b. the distinctive features of letters
        c. that words are representations of objects
        d. relevant information and disregarding irrelevant information

p. 158 70. The knowledge of how printed words correspond to speech sounds is known as
F   *   a. phonological awareness
        b. phoneme recognition
        c. semantics
        d. morphology

p. 158 71. Acquisition of phonological awareness means that children realize that:
C
        a. consonants and vowels must be combined to create meaningful words
        b. words must be properly ordered to make sense
    *   c. spoken words can be broken into basic sound units
        d. meaningful sentences consist of at least a subject and a verb

p. 158 72. Children who are diagnosed with dyslexia:
F   *   a. have significant problems learning to read for a variety of reasons
        b. usually have lower overall intellectual ability
        c. have sensory impairments that impede their ability to read
        d. usually overcome the disability by the end of elementary school

p. 158 73. If a psychologist wanted to design a test that would reveal if a child has dyslexia, they
C   would design exercises that assessed
        a. nervousness
        b. how many phonemes the child knew
        c. morpheme recognition
    *   d. phonological awareness

p. 158 74. What is often found to distinguish good readers from poor readers?
C   a. understanding the meaning of printed words
www   b. ability to pronounce sounds
        c. attending to the letters and words on a page
    *   d. ability to decode letters and words

p. 158 75. In contrast to the "phonics" approach, the "whole language" approach teaches children how
F   to read by
         a. analyzing words into their component sounds
         b. teaching letter-sound correspondence rules
    *   c. recognizing specific words by sight
         d. stressing the idea that parts of words are more important than the whole word

p. 159 76. Research on teaching children how to read suggests that:
C   a. children become frustrated if instruction begins before kindergarten
         b. children must be able to fully control their attention before they can learn to read
    *   c. the phonics approach works best
         d. the whole-language approach works best

p. 159 77. Compared to nine year olds, adolescents can work better on tasks such as studying for
F   exams because their
    *   a. brain areas that regulate attention are more developed
         b. visual acuity is better
         c. hormones tend to make them more energetic
         d. visual accommodation skills are greater

p. 159 78. Perceptual skills of adolescents are advanced relative those of children because adolescents
C   a. have better sensory acuity
         b. have longer short-term memory space
    *   c. pay less attention to distracting information and more attention to relevant information
         d. pay more attention to each and every aspect of a task, even nonessential details

p. 160 79. The term sensory threshold refers to
F   *   a. the minimum amount of stimulation that can be detected
         b. the maximum amount of sensory stimulation that can be tolerated before
            pain is experienced
         c. the maximum number of senses that can be stimulated before the person
            gets confused
         d. all of the above are part of the definition

p. 160 80. Older people tend to raise the volume on their television sets and use more seasoning
C   because
    *   a. their sensory thresholds have increased with age
         b. they cannot concentrate on simple things
         c. their sensory thresholds decrease with age
         d. they forget that they already salted their food or raised the volume on the television

p. 160 81. As we get older:
C   a. sensory declines are normally quite sharp beginning in middle age
www *   b. sensory stimulation must often increase in order to be detected
         c. sensory capabilities decline but are compensated for with increases in perceptual
            capabilities
         d. the amount of sensory stimulation detected remains the same but the type of
            stimulation detected changes

p. 160 82. How do the sensory and perceptual abilities of adolescents compare to those of older
C   adults?
            a. There are no discernible differences between adolescents and older adults.
            b. Sensory capabilities are the same, but perceptual capabilities are poorer in older adults.
            c. Sensory capabilities decline with age but the loss is compensated for, so there are no
                differences in perceptual abilities.
        *   d. There are both sensory and perceptual declines with age.

p. 160 83. About half of all people over the age of 40, and 80% of people over 60 years old report
F   having trouble
            a. distinguishing similar colors
        *   b. with near vision
            c. reading large print
            d. all of the above

p. 160 84. When an optometrist is giving a sixty-year-old an eye exam, he or she would most likely
C   look for
            a. smaller changes in the pupil when light is shined on it
            b. yellowing of the lens of the eye
            c. clouding of the gelatinous liquid behind the lens
        *   d. all of the above

p. 160 85. All of the following are typical changes to the visual system EXCEPT:
F   a. difficulty focusing on objects at different distances
            b. the pupil changes less with changes in lighting conditions
        *   c. cells in the retina become entangled, impairing color vision
            d. the lens becomes less transparent

p. 160 86. What is one change in vision during adulthood that most of us can expect to experience?
C   *   a. loss of near vision
            b. development of an astigmatism
            c. weakening of the eye muscles leading to a "lazy" eye
            d. blindness

p. 161 87. The leading cause of blindness in old age is
F   a. detached retina
        *   b. cataracts
            c. degeneration of the optic nerve
            d. paralysis of the pupil

p. 161 88. Increased eye pressure that can eventually lead to blindness is called
F   *   a. glaucoma
            b. detached retina
            c. cataracts
            d. presbyopia

p. 161 89. When driving at night, an elderly person may have trouble seeing well when they exit a
C   lighted freeway onto an unlighted road because they have
          a. reduced sensory thresholds
          b. intermittent phonological awareness
       * c. slower dark adaption abilities
          d. trouble with near vision

p. 161 90. Older adults are similar to young children in that they both have trouble:
C   a. discriminating objects in low light levels
          b. perceiving moving objects
       * c. filtering out irrelevant information on some tasks
          d. focusing clearly on objects

p. 161 91. Older adults seem to have the greatest perceptual problems:
C   a. when tasks consist of color objects rather than black and white objects
www   * b. on tasks that are complex and novel
          c. when they must focus on tasks one at a time, in a sequential manner, rather than in a
             simultaneous manner
          d. when they are given oral instructions rather than written instructions

p. 162 92. Hearing loss in the elderly is most frequently caused by
F   a. hardening of the eardrum
          b. buildup of ear wax over the years
          c. decline of the brain areas associated with hearing
       * d. problems in the inner ear

p. 163 93. Decline in the ability to comprehend a conversation at a noisy party is most likely to be the
F   result of
          a. hardening of the eardrum
          b. buildup of ear wax over the years
       * c. decline of the brain areas associated with hearing
          d. problems in the inner ear

p. 163 94. With regard to speech perception, most older adults:
C   a. have no difficulties under ideal conditions
          b. have problems understanding speech only if they have an underlying hearing problem
       * c. show significant problems when there is a lot of background noise
          d. have an easier time understanding speech over a telephone because it is presented
             directly to their ear

p. 163 95. The ability to taste _____ does not seem to decline with age.
F   a. sour fruit
          b. bitter herbs
          c. lightly salted crackers
       * d. sweet candy

p. 163   96.   The ability to taste and smell in older adults changes in all of the following ways EXCEPT:
F   *   a.   they are less able to discriminate varying degrees of sweetness
              b.   they have some cognitive problems remembering and naming tastes
              c.   losses of smell contribute to changes in ability to identify tastes
              d.   they are less sensitive to faint odors

p. 164   97.   Old people may keep their homes too hot or too cold because
F   *   a.   they tend to be less sensitive to changes in temperature
              b.   aging makes them forget to change the thermostat
              c.   arthritis makes it necessary
              d.   all of the above

p. 164   98.   In terms of their ability to sense pain, old people
F   *   a.   are less sensitive to mild pain
              b.   show more sensitivity to mild pain
              c.   experience mild pain in the same way that they did in their youth
              d.   frequently forget that they are in pain

p. 164   99.   Older adults' sensitivity to pain:
C   a.   increases substantially for all types and levels of pain
              b.   increases for low levels of pain and stays the same for intense pain
              c.   decreases for all types and levels of pain
         *   d.   is fairly similar to that of younger adults

p. 165   100. Children who have been diagnosed with a hearing problem will benefit most from
F   a.   a hearing aid
              b.   auditory training
         *   c.   hearing aids combined with auditory training
              d.   being placed in a home for deaf children

p. 166   102. Most hearing problems:
F   a.   show up during infancy
              b.   can be corrected to normal hearing with hearing aids
              c.   are corrected with surgery
         *   d.   can be improved by altering the environment to compensate

p. 143   103. Sensation refers to _____ of stimuli while perception refers to _____ of this
F   information.
SG   *   a.   detection; interpretation
              b.   sense; the value
              c.   interpretation; detection
              d.   recognition; the use

p. 143   104. Nativists argue that a child is
C   a.   born knowing nothing and learns through interaction with the environment
SG   *   b.   born with knowledge and is very similar to an adult in terms of perceptual ability
              c.   influenced intellectually by genetics, maturation and the environment
              d.   learns mainly through cultural experiences

p. 144   105. Suppose you repeatedly present a stimulus until an infant loses interest in it. This
C   technique is known as
SG   a.   visual accommodation
              b.   color discrimination
              c.   visual acuity
         *   d.   habituation

p. 145   106. Which of the following is TRUE about young infants' visual capabilities?
F   a.   Infants are not able to perceive color until sometime during the second half of the first
SG   year.
              b.   Infants as young as two months can detect details of a patterned stimulus as well as
                   adults.
         *   c.   Infants are fairly good at detecting differences in brightness levels of stimuli.
              d.   Infants' visual systems are at their peak performance.

p. 146   107. Newborns appear to have a preference for viewing human faces. This probably reflects
C   a.   an innate ability to recognize faces
SG   *   b.   a preference for patterned stimuli with contour and some complexity
              c.   the fact that infants will learn to look at what they have been reinforced for in the past
              d.   the fact that infants can focus only on faces

p. 146   108. At around 2 or 3 months of age, infants prefer to look at "normal" faces as opposed to faces
C   that have been distorted in some way. This suggests that
SG   a.   infants cannot really detect a difference between them
              b.   infants have organized their perceptions according to Gestalt principles
              c.   infants prefer the simplest form or pattern
         *   d.   infants are developing mental representations of what a normal face looks like

p. 146   109. Very young infants are most visually attracted to
F   a.   a highly complex stimulus
SG   *   b.   a moderately complex stimulus
              c.   a colorful stimulus
              d.   a black and white stimulus

p. 147   110. The visual cliff is an apparatus used to determine
F   *   a.   depth perception
SG   b.   size constancy
              c.   visual acuity
              d.   visual accommodation

p. 148   111. Two-month-olds tested on the visual cliff typically show a slower heart rate on the deep
C   side than on the shallow side of the cliff. This suggests that two-month-olds
SG   a.   are afraid of falling off the apparent cliff
         *   b.   detect a difference between the two sides of the visual cliff
              c.   perceive size constancy
              d.   have learned to avoid potential drop-offs

p. 149   112. Normal hearing in young infants is different from normal hearing in adults in that infants
F   a.   are better able to hear soft sounds and whispers
SG   b.   have more difficulty discriminating between speech sounds
               c.   are unable to localize sound
        *   d.   can distinguish between all speech sounds, including those not used in the language of
                    adults around them

p. 160   113. The point at which a dim light can still be detected is termed
F   a.   dark adaptation
SG   *   b.   sensory threshold
               c.   visual accommodation
               d.   visual acuity

p. 153   114. An infant who sucks on an object and then recognizes this object visually is showing
C   evidence of
SG   a.   selective attention
               b.   habituation
        *   c.   cross-modal perception
               d.   recognition of the object's distinctive features

p. 154   115. Research findings with animals suggest that, in order for normal perceptual development to
C   occur, infants
SG   a.   must be able to actively move through their environment
               b.   must be able to watch movement in the environment
               c.   must be exposed to different colors
        *   d.   Both B and C

p.162   116. Most age related hearing problems originate in the
F   a.   hearing center of the brain
SG   *   b.   auditory nerves and receptors
               c.   structures of the middle ear
               d.   outer ear membrane

p. 166   117. When speaking to people who are hard of hearing, the speaker should
C   a.   elevate the voice--shout if necessary
SG   b.   talk directly into the person's ear so they can hear better
               c.   repeat what she has just said instead of rewording the misunderstood statement
        *   d.   make sure the hearing impaired person can see him/her

TRUE-FALSE QUESTIONS
_____

p. 143   118. Sensation refers only to stimulation of sensory receptors.
        *   a.   true
               b.   false

p. 143   119. The brain's interpretation of sensory information is known as sensation.
               a.   true
        *   b.   false

p. 143 120. Empiricists believe that we enter the world with knowledge that helps us understand the world.
　　　　　　a.　true
　　　* 　　b.　false

p. 144 121. Habituation refers to learning to be bored by repeatedly presented stimuli.
www 　* 　　a.　true
　　　　　　b.　false

p. 145 122. Young infants can only see about 8 inches in front of their face.
　　　* 　　a.　true
　　　　　　b.　false

p. 147 123. Three month old infants prefer to look at normal face forms.
　　　* 　　a.　true
　　　　　　b.　false

p. 148 124. When tested on the visual cliff, 7 month old infants will usually cross the cliff to reunite
www 　　　　with their mothers.
　　　　　　a.　true
　　　* 　　b.　false

p. 147 125. It is not necessary to perceive in three dimensions in order to experience size constancy.
　　　　　　a.　true
　　　* 　　b.　false

p. 148 126. To determine where one object ends and another one begins, babies often use common
　　　　　　motion cues.
　　　* 　　a.　true
　　　　　　b.　false

p.149 127. Infants construct intuitive theories about how the world works.
　　　* 　　a.　true
　　　　　　b.　false

p. 153 128. The newborn's sense of hearing is inferior to its ability to see.
　　　　　　a.　true
　　　* 　　b.　false

p. 154 129. Babies can hear before they are born.
　　　* 　　a.　true
　　　　　　b.　false

p. 154 130. The senses of taste and smell do not function at birth.
　　　　　　a.　true
　　　* 　　b.　false

p. 156   131. Infant males who undergo circumcision do not feel pain.
               a.   true
     *   b.   false

p. 157   132. Periods of sensory deprivation early in life can have long lasting effects.
     *   a.   true
               b.   false

p. 159   133. Cultural differences can produce perceptual differences in people.
www   *   a.   true
               b.   false

p. 162   134. One brain hemisphere dominates over the other only in individuals with dyslexia.
               a.   true
     *   b.   false

p. 164   135. Cataracts are the leading cause of blindness in old age.
     *   a.   true
               b.   false

p. 166   136. As they age, men tend to suffer greater hearing losses than women.
     *   a.   true
               b.   false

ESSAY QUESTIONS

137.   What do newborns know about the world around them? How are their sensory-perceptual abilities measured?

138.   What factors influence what an infant will look at?
www

139.   What sorts of experiences are necessary for the development of normal perception?

140.   How do cultural differences produce perceptual differences among people?

141.   Given a choice among the various sensory problems that develop with aging, which one do you believe would be the most difficult to deal with? Why?

142.   What sensory and perceptual abilities decline with age?

143.   In light of their sensory and perceptual abilities, what do young infants know about the people
SG   and world around them?
      [Sample answer is provided in the Study Guide.]

144.   Discuss the likely outcomes for an infant born with congenital cataracts that preclude any sort of
SG   visual stimulation.

145.   What sensory and perceptual changes can an older adult expect? What implications do these
SG   changes have with respect to an older adult's lifestyle?

146.   Based on what you know from this chapter about perceptual capabilities and preferences, what
SG   recommendations would you make for designing an infant's nursery? What recommendations
       would you make for an older adult's living quarters?

COGNITION AND LANGUAGE

MULTIPLE-CHOICE QUESTIONS

p. 171　1.　Piaget was interested in how children come to know reality, a field that he called:
F　　*　a.　genetic epistemology
　　　　b.　clinical methodology
　　　　c.　hypothetical-deductive reasoning
　　　　d.　cognitive psychology

p. 171　2.　With regard to his work on the development of standardized intelligence tests, Piaget was
F　　　　MOST intrigued by:
　　　*　a.　age-related errors in children's responses
　　　　b.　determining the age at which children could correctly answer certain questions
　　　　c.　sex differences in the ability to problem-solve
　　　　d.　similarities in problem-solving skills across age groups

p. 171　3.　Which of the following illustrates Piaget's clinical methods?
C　　　　a.　asking children standardized questions and recording their answers
　　　　b.　giving children paper and pencil questionnaires to learn the ages when children can
　　　　　　solve certain problems
　　　　c.　questioning children as a group to learn about general problem solving strategies
　　　*　d.　asking children questions that are individually tailored to their previous responses

p. 171　4.　The clinical method involves:
F　　　　a.　uncovering unconscious motives for behavior
　　　　b.　presenting standardized questions to all children tested
　　　　c.　observing children in their natural environment
　　　*　d.　tailoring questions to individual children's responses on previous questions

p. 171　5.　According to Piaget, intelligence is the ability to:
C　　*　a.　adapt to one's environment
www　　b.　respond to reinforcement
　　　　c.　process information
　　　　d.　solve problems effectively

p. 171　6.　Which of the following is the BEST description of a scheme?
F　　*　a.　an organized way of thinking or acting that allows us to interpret our experiences
　　　　b.　a standard way of solving a problem in the fewest possible steps
　　　　c.　changing our experiences in order to adapt to our environment
　　　　d.　interpreting new experiences by using previously stored information

p. 171 7. Which of the following is an example of a behavioral scheme?
C   a. using a block to represent a car
     b. asking about grandma even when she's not present
   *   c. grasping a block or a lock of hair
     d. calling the dog by the cat's name

p. 171 8. Which of the following is an example of a symbolic scheme?
C   a. counting the number of holes on a belt
   *   b. pointing a finger and saying "Bang!"
     c. sucking on an object
     d. grasping an adult's finger

p. 172 9. Piaget refers to the process of combining existing schemes into new and more complex
F   ones as:
     a. accommodation
     b. adaptation
     c. assimilation
   *   d. organization

p. 172 10. Adaptation is BEST defined as:
F   *   a. adjusting to the demands of the environment
     b. combining schemas
     c. interpreting new experiences through existing schemas
     d. organizing one's thoughts

p. 172 11. Adaptation involves two major processes. These are:
F   a. accommodation and symbolic thinking
   *   b. assimilation and accommodation
     c. assimilation and organization
     d. organization and equilibration

p. 172 12. Micky, age 18 months, is visiting a zoo for the first time. As soon as he sees the zebras,
C   he yells "look at the horseys." This BEST demonstrates the concept of:
     a. accommodation
     b. adaptation
   *   c. assimilation
     d. organization

p. 172 13. Leisl was so excited when her son Henry began to call her "Mommy." But then she
C   noticed that he also called other women Mommy. Piaget would say that this illustrates:
www   a. accommodation
     b. adaptation
   *   c. assimilation
     d. organization

p. 172 14. Cody likes to play with his stuffed animals, dragging them around the house by their arms
C or ears or tails. He tries to do this with Fluffy the cat one day, but she hisses at him and
runs off, leaving Cody perplexed and crying. Cody's attempts to play with the cat illustrate
the concept of:
a. accommodation
* b. assimilation
c. disequilibrium
d. fixation

p. 172 15. Linda always thought of herself as being incapable when it came to fixing things. She
C easily developed the habit of asking her husband, Jake, to do even the simplest "fix-it"
tasks, like changing a light bulb. Then one day Linda got a flat tire on a country road. She
managed to struggle through the process of changing the tire all on her own. From then on,
she felt much more capable, and stopped asking Jake to fix everything. This best
illustrates:
* a. accommodation
b. assimilation
c. disequilibrium
d. fixation

p. 172 16. Assimilation is
F * a. interpreting the world around us in terms of our current cognitive structures
b. the modification of existing schemas to account for new experiences
c. the innate tendency to meaningfully organize information
d. combining existing schemes into more complex ones

p. 172 17. Which of the following is an example of assimilation?
C a. naming your dog Barney after the famous purple Barney on TV
b. changing the name of your dog after finding out that a classmate has a dog with the
same name
c. pretending that your dog is a horse
* d. calling all dogs by the name of your dog, Spot

p. 172 18. Young Will tries to fit the square peg into the round hole several times, thinking that pegs
C can go into holes of any shape. After a number of unsuccessful attempts, Will figures out
www that square pegs must go into square holes. This is an example of:
a. assimilation
* b. accommodation
c. organization
d. object permanence

p. 172 19. Richie knows that the dog has to be walked outside on a leash several times a day so the
C dog does not have an accident in the house. Richie always wants to take the cat along on
these trips even though the cat uses an indoor litter box. This is an example of:
* a. assimilation
b. accommodation
c. organization
d. object permanence

p. 172 20. Peggy is puzzled about why her dad tells her not to yell at her brother when she is mad at
C   him, but her dad seems to yell whenever <u>he</u> is mad at someone. Piaget would say that
             Peggy's confusion reflects:
             a. conservation
             b. adaptation
             c. equilibrium
        *   d. disequilibrium

p. 172 21. According to Piaget, which of the following is FALSE?
C   a. adaptation = assimilation + accommodation
             b. intelligence develops as a result of interactions between the individual and the
                 environment
        *   c. intelligence is determined by biological maturation
             d. assimilation involves interpreting new experiences through existing schemas

p. 172 22. To say that we construct reality means that we:
C   a. are genetically predisposed to understand the world
             b. construct more complex schemes by combining simple schemes
        *   c. create our own understanding of the world from our experiences
             d. progress through stages as we develop

p. 172 23. According to Piaget, which is MOST apt to stimulate cognitive growth?
C   a. focusing intently on only one aspect of a problem at a time
        *   b. an imbalance between one's schemes and the environment
             c. a balance between one's schemes and the environment
             d. persisting with a method of problem-solving that has always worked in the past

p. 173 24. An infant's first schemas for interacting with the environment are:
C   a. cross-modal reactions
             b. primary circular reactions
        *   c. reflexes
             d. trial-and-error accommodations

p. 173 25. Baby Timmy seems to love to suck his thumb and has learned to do it over and over again.
C   This is an example of:
www   a. coordination of secondary schemes
        *   b. a primary circular reaction
             c. a secondary circular reaction
             d. a tertiary circular reaction

p. 173 26. Baby Carolyn likes to suck on her blanket when she's going to sleep. This is an example
C   of:
             a. coordination of secondary schemes
             b. a primary circular reaction
        *   c. a secondary circular reaction
             d. a tertiary circular reaction

p. 173 27. At what substage of the sensorimotor period do infants first exhibit truly intentional
C behavior?
  a. primary circular reactions (1-4 months)
  b. secondary circular reactions (4-8 months)
  * c. coordination of secondary schemes (8-12 months)
  d. beginnings of thought (18-24 months)

p. 173 28. Jacob is playing in his playpen. He pushes all the toys out of the way until he can reach his
C Jack-in-the-box, which is on the far side of the playpen. What is the EARLIEST substage
  of the sensorimotor period that Jake could be in?
  a. secondary circular reactions (4-8 months)
  * b. coordination of secondary schemes (8-12 months)
  c. tertiary circular reactions (12-18 months)
  d. beginnings of thought (18-24 months)

p. 173 29. Jackie is enjoying a fine lunch in her high chair. She picks up a handful of spaghetti and
C stuffs it in her mouth. Next, she picks up two handsful and shoves them in her ears. The
  next handful goes in her hair, and the next is casually thrown on the floor. Jackie's
  behavior is MOST typical of infants in which sensorimotor substage?
  a. secondary circular reactions (4-8 months)
  b. coordination of secondary schemes (8-12 months)
  * c. tertiary circular reactions (12-18 months)
  d. beginnings of thought (18-24 months)

p. 173 30. Rachel is playing with pots and pans in the kitchen. First she bangs two lids together.
C Then she beats on a pot with a wooden spoon. Next she throws a pot across the room.
  Finally she stands on top of the asparagus steamer. Rachel's antics typify those of infants
  in which sensorimotor substage ?
  a. secondary circular reactions (4-8 months)
  b. coordination of secondary schemes (8-12 months)
  * c. tertiary circular reactions (12-18 months)
  d. beginning of thought (18-24 months)

p. 173 31. A primary circular reaction is:
F * a. the repetition of a pleasurable action involving the body
  b. the repetition of a pleasurable action involving objects in the environment
  c. the exercise of inborn reflexes
  d. experimentation to find new ways of solving problems

p. 173 32. A secondary circular reaction is:
F a. the repetition of a pleasurable action involving the body
  * b. the repetition of a pleasurable action involving objects in the environment
  c. the exercise of inborn reflexes
  d. experimentation to find new ways of solving problems

p. 173 33. Infants often enjoy blowing bubbles with the milk in their mouth. This is an example of:
C
a. reflexive activity
b. primary circular reaction
* c. secondary circular reaction
d. coordination of secondary schemes

p. 173 34. Piaget's first stage is called sensorimotor because:
C   * a. infants use sensory information and motor responses to learn about the world
www
b. understanding of the world is based on symbolic reasoning about sensory and motor input
c. thought is not yet operating; infants are developing sensory capabilities
d. sensory operations allow children to solve problems

p. 173 35. A father is playing a peek-a-boo game with his son by holding a towel in front of his face
C   and saying"peek-a-boo" when his son pulls the towel away and sees his father's face.
          What is the EARLIEST sensorimotor substage that this infant could be in?
a. reflex activity
b. primary circular reaction
* c. secondary circular reaction
d. coordination of secondary schemes

p. 173 36. Which of the following plays the MOST significant role in the capacity of infants to
C   engage in pretend play?
a. The ability to conserve.
b. The emergence of the object permanence concept.
* c. The ability to use symbols.
d. The capacity for coordination of secondary schemes.

p. 173 37. Several years ago, a television commercial for floor products showed an infant who was
C   pretending that his plate of food was an airplane and sent it soaring out over the floor.
          During which sensorimotor substage could this first occur?
a. secondary circular reactions
b. coordination of secondary schemes
c. tertiary circular reactions
* d. beginning of thought

p. 173 38. Danny has discovered that even though his mom won't let him play with her set of car keys,
C   he can use a ring of metal tabs and pretend that these are his car keys. What is the
          EARLIEST sensorimotor substage that Danny could be in?
a. secondary circular reactions
b. coordination of secondary schemes
c. tertiary circular reactions
* d. beginning of thought

p. 174 39. To a young infant, out-of-sight is literally out-of-mind. This relates to what Piaget has
C   termed:
             a. assimilation
             b. insight
        *   c. object permanence
             d. selective attention

p. 174 40. We know that Suzie's object concept is fully mature when she searches for:
C   a. partially concealed objects
             b. fully covered objects
        *   c. an object that has been displaced from where she last saw it
             d. an object at the place where it disappeared

p. 174 41. Which BEST demonstrates the object permanence concept?
C   *   a. crying when Mommy leaves the room
             b. repeatedly swiping at a mobile hanging over the crib
             c. crying when someone grabs a toy out of your hand
             d. trying to grab a toy that is out of reach

p. 174 42. Sarah loved to play with the family dog, Maggie, and even though the pet has died, Sarah
C   keeps asking about her. This demonstrates that Sarah has:
www   *   a. object permanence
             b. secondary circular reaction
             c. conservation
             d. class inclusion

p. 174 43. Recent research on the early understanding of object permanence shows that:
F   a. infants will not search for an object at its correct location until they are 18-24 months
                 of age
             b. 4 month old infants can search for a hidden object as well as 24 month old infants
        *   c. 8 month old infants may remember the correct location of an object but not be able to
                 initiate a search for the object at this location
             d. infants younger than 4 months show no signs of understanding that an object exists
                 when it is hidden from view

p. 174 44. Five-year-old Bill is playing with his baby sister, Lucy. He takes Lucy's teddy bear and
C   hides it behind a pillow while Lucy watches. Lucy quickly finds the bear. Then Bill puts
             teddy in a bag, puts the bag behind a chair (where he dumps teddy), and then brings out the
             empty bag. Lucy looks inside the bag, but doesn't look for teddy behind the chair. What
             sensorimotor substage is Lucy in?
             a. secondary circular reactions
             b. coordination of secondary schemes
        *   c. tertiary circular reactions
             d. beginning of thought

p. 174   45.   We know that infants are ready to progress from sensorimotor intelligence to the next
C   highest stage when they:
               a.   display secondary circular reactions
               b.   coordinate secondary schemes
               c.   display trial-and-error experimentation
     *   d.   demonstrate insight in problem-solving

p. 175   46.   The MOST remarkable distinguishing feature between the thought of preschoolers and
C   infants is the ability to:
www   a.   assimilate
               b.   accommodate
     *   c.   use symbols
               d.   equilibrate

p. 175   47.   Piaget's second stage is called preoperational because:
F   a.   children are no longer using symbols to solve problems
               b.   precursors of primary and secondary circular reactions allow children to solve
                   problems
     *   c.   logical thought is not yet operating
               d.   mental operations allow children to solve problems

p. 175   48.   Jimmy watches as his Mommy pours all of his juice out of a tall, skinny glass, into a short,
C   wide cup. He puts up a fuss, because he now thinks he doesn't have as much juice as he
              started with! Jimmy is unable to:
               a.   center
     *   b.   conserve
               c.   seriate
               d.   transform

p. 175   49.   Asked to choose between two cookies of equal size, Jenny takes the broken cookie, saying
C   that three cookies are better than one. Piaget would say that Jenny lacks:
               a.   centration
               b.   object permanence
               c.   seriation
     *   d.   conservation

p. 175   50.   The Piagetian concept of "decentration" refers to:
C   *   a.   the ability to focus on more than one dimension of a problem at one time
               b.   the ability to mentally reverse simple operations
               c.   an understanding that the amount of something remains the same regardless of a
                   change in shape or position
               d.   the ability to attend to a transformational process

p. 175   51.   Molly's Mommy is mad, and Molly doesn't believe it when Mommy says "I'm angry, but I
C   still love you!" Molly thinks that Mommy can't be mad and still love her at the same time.
               Molly's thinking demonstrates:
        *   a.   centration
               b.   conservation
               c.   irreversibility
               d.   overextension

p. 175   52.   The tendency to focus on only one aspect of a situation or problem at a time is known as:
F   a.   assimilation
        *   b.   centration
               c.   conservation
               d.   identification

p. 175   53.   All of the following characterize the thinking of preoperational children EXCEPT:
F   a.   centration
               b.   irreversible thought
               c.   static thought
        *   d.   transformational thought

p. 175   54.   Billy always walks to Kindergarten, and Mommy always picks him up at school after
C   Kindergarten on her way home from work. One day, Mommy asks Billy to walk home
               from Kindergarten, because she is not going to work and will already be at home. Billy
               insists he does not know how to walk home from Kindergarten -- he only knows how to
               walk to Kindergarten. Which cognitive operation does Billy apparently lack?
               a.   centration
               b.   equilibration
        *   c.   reversibility
               d.   transformation

p. 175   55.   Marcia, a college student, is checking 7-year-old Jeffrey out to see what cognitive skills he
C   has. She asks him to do some basic conservation tasks. Jeffrey has correctly responded
               that there is still the same amount of clay, whether it is in a round ball or rolled out into a
               hotdog-type shape. When Marcia asks why, Jeffrey demonstrates how the hotdog-type
               shaped piece of clay can be rolled back into a ball. This shows that Jeffrey has a good
               grasp of:
               a.   assimilation
               b.   centration
               c.   equilibrium
        *   d.   reversibility

p. 175   56.   Piaget suggested that preoperational children have difficulty understanding conversation
C   because they
www   a.   tend to concentrate on all the dimensions of the problem at the same time
        *   b.   tend to focus on only one aspect of a problem when more aspects are relevant
               c.   persist in mentally reversing actions performed in the transformation
               d.   have not yet achieved abstract reasoning

p. 177　57.　Four-year-old Steven is shopping for a birthday present for Mommy. Finally he finds just
C　　　　　the right thing: a Batman action figure! This demonstrates:
　　　　　　a.　animism
　　　　　　b.　centration
　　*　　　c.　egocentrism
　　　　　　d.　static thought

p. 177　58.　The inability to take a point of view other than one's own is referred to as:
F　　　　　a.　animism
　　*　　　b.　egocentrism
　　　　　　c.　nontransformational thought
　　　　　　d.　static thought

p. 177　59.　Daddy is upset and crying. Five-year-old Micky brings his favorite old Teddy out for Dad
C　　　　　to hold, thinking this will comfort him. This demonstrates:
　　　　　　a.　animism
　　　　　　b.　centration
　　*　　　c.　egocentrism
　　　　　　d.　transformational thought

p. 177　60.　When her mommy is sick in bed, Jenna brings her a pacifier and a rattle, thinking these
C　　　　　will help mommy feel better since they always make Jenna feel better. This demonstrates:
　　　　　　a.　centration
　　*　　　b.　egocentrism
　　　　　　c.　animism
　　　　　　d.　static thought

p. 177　61.　Jack is taking a class on Piaget, and as part of an assignment he is "testing" some
C　　　　　youngsters on various Piagetian tasks. He gives 4-year-old Meg a bag of red and blue
　　　　　　marbles. They discuss the fact that marbles are made of glass. Meg counts the marbles --
　　　　　　7 reds and 18 blues. Jack asks: "Are there more blues marbles or more glass marbles?"
　　　　　　Meg says: "There are more blue marbles." This demonstrates difficulty with:
　　*　　　a.　class inclusion
　　　　　　b.　conservation
　　　　　　c.　identity
　　　　　　d.　transformations

p. 177　62.　What can be concluded from recent research showing that children as young as three years
C　　　　　can act in ways that indicate they know what another person is thinking or feeling?
www　*　a.　Children in the preoperational stage are not as egocentric as Piaget claimed.
　　　　　　b.　Children this age are not in the preoperational stage.
　　　　　　c.　Children in the preoperational stage are able to reason logically.
　　　　　　d.　Children this age can solve conservation tasks.

p. 179　63.　Piagetian conservation tasks are:
C　　　　　a.　all mastered at age 7 or 8
　　*　　　b.　mastered gradually in a fairly predictable sequence
　　　　　　c.　mastered gradually in very different orders by different children
　　　　　　d.　all mastered at age 11 or 12

p. 178 64. A hallmark of concrete operational thought is being able to:
F
          a.   solve object permanence tasks
    *   b.   solve conservation tasks
          c.   solve hypothetical problems
          d.   use relativistic thinking

p. 179 65. Molly is asked to arrange a group of jars from shortest to tallest. This is a test for:
C
          a.   classification
          b.   conservation
    *   c.   seriation
          d.   transductive reasoning

p. 179 66. Seriation involves
F
          a.   the realization that properties of objects do not change even though appearance might be altered
          b.   understanding that subclasses are included in the whole class
          c.   understanding the relationships among elements in a series
    *   d.   mentally arranging elements along a quantifiable scale

p. 179 67. Becky can quickly and accurately arrange sticks from shortest to longest, and crayons from
C   lightest to darkest. This demonstrates a capacity for:
          a.   animism
          b.   centration
    *   c.   seriation
          d.   transitional thinking

p. 179 68. "Pete is older than Jill, and Jill is older than Pat. Who is older, Pete or Pat?" The ability to
C   solve problems such as this demonstrates the concept of:
          a.   decentration
          b.   identity
          c.   transductive reasoning
    *   d.   transitivity

p. 179 69. One difference between formal operational thought and concrete operational thought is that
C   formal operational thinkers:
www
          a.   are less egocentric
          b.   can reason logically about objects
          c.   can solve conservation tasks
    *   d.   can think about possibilities

p. 179 70. The MOST remarkable feature of adolescent thought is the ability to:
F
          a.   conduct mental actions on objects
          b.   attend to transformations
    *   c.   think about hypothetical situations
          d.   conserve

p. 179 71. A researcher asked students of different ages "What would the world be like if humans had
C   tails?" According to Piaget's theory, which one of the following answers would we be
likely to hear from an adolescent in the formal operational stage?
     a. "People don't have tails, so this is a useless exercise."
     b. "I guess they could swing from trees just like the monkeys I saw at the zoo."
*   c. "People would be able to hold tails and pass notes under the table while still keeping
        both hands on the table."
     d. "I wouldn't like having a tail all the time."

p. 181 72. In what sort of reasoning does one move from general ideas to their specific implications?
F   a. empirical-inductive
     b. empirical-deductive
     c. hypothetical-inductive
*   d. hypothetical-deductive

p. 181 73. Which of the following illustrates hypothetical-deductive reasoning?
C   a. Uncovering and resolving possible contradictions between ideas.
     b. Using observations to formulate a conclusion about a particular problem.
*   c. Developing a hypothesis and then testing the specific implications of this hypothesis.
     d. Logically reasoning about an event based on the appearances of the event.

p. 182 74. One implication of formal operational thought is that adolescents are more likely than
C   children to:
     a. have idealized notions about their parents
*   b. rebel against the inconsistencies they are able to detect in the world
     c. accept the realities of the world
     d. solve problems by using a trial and error approach

p. 182 75. Phillip is moping around because his "steady" girlfriend, Janet, is going on a date with
C   another boy she's interested in. His dad comes up to him and says, "I know just how you
feel, son...." Phillip cuts him off, saying "You don't know how I feel. No one knows how I
feel! Just leave me alone!" This demonstrates a phenomenon known as:
*   a. adolescent egocentrism
     b. adolescent neurosis
     c. concrete operational thinking
     d. the imaginary audience

p. 182 76. Rhonda spends the last week of summer vacation at the mall, looking for just the right
C   outfit for the first day of tenth grade. Finally she finds something she likes, and feels sure
that everyone will notice her smashing outfit! This is an example of:
*   a. adolescent egocentrism
     b. the personal fable
     c. school phobia
     d. transductive reasoning

p. 182   77.   Which of the following is an example of a personal fable?
C   a.   believing that life is a tragedy, thus every precaution needs to be taken to ensure
                      everyone's safety
                b.   feeling self-conscious in front of an audience
                c.   believing that everyone is aware of your feelings
          *   d.   believing that no one has ever felt grief more strongly than you

p. 182   78.   If an adolescent believes that they cannot die regardless of reckless behavior, they are
C   exhibiting
                a.   adolescent neurosis
                b.   transformational thinking
                c.   transductive reasoning
          *   d.   personal fable

p. 182   79.   Sally has just gotten her hair trimmed, and even though it doesn't look very different than
C   before, she is sure everyone in homeroom will notice a big change. This is an example of:
          *   a.   imaginary audience
                b.   personal fable
                c.   hypothetical-deductive reasoning
                d.   relativistic thinking

p. 182   80.   Jamie doesn't worry very much about contracting the HIV-virus from unprotected sex,
C   saying "I'm a good guy. It can't happen to me." This is an example of:
www   a.   imaginary audience
          *   b.   personal fable
                c.   transductive reasoning
                d.   hypothetical-deductive reasoning

p. 182   81.   Jerry drives his motorcycle very fast and rarely follows laws about protective helmets. He
C   tells his friends and parents that nothing bad will happen to him. This is an example of:
                a.   imaginary audience
          *   b.   personal fable
                c.   transductive reasoning
                d.   hypothetical-deductive reasoning

p. 184   82.   Which seems to be the most important factor in facilitating formal operational thought
C   among college students?
www   a.   basic intelligence
                b.   amount of schooling
                c.   the presence of appropriate models in the environment
          *   d.   expertise in a domain of knowledge

p. 184   83.   People are most likely to regularly use formal operational thinking:
F   a.   in all areas of their work and living
          *   b.   in areas where they have some expertise
                c.   in high school and college courses but not on nonacademic tasks
                d.   on new and complex tasks

p. 184 84. College students are most likely to use formal operational thought

C   *   a. in their major area

            b. in the areas of social science

            c. when they are presented with a new and challenging task

            d. when they are enrolled in general education classes

p. 185 85. Mary understands that the "right" thing to do in one set of circumstances may well not be

C   the "right" thing to do in a different situation. Mary's thinking is best characterized as:

            a. absolute

            b. dialectical

            c. formal

     *   d. relativistic

p. 185 86. Some research comparing adults and adolescents suggests that the adults are:

F   a. less likely to recognize and resolve inconsistencies between opposing views

www   b. less likely to develop mental shortcuts to get around using formal operational thought

            c. more likely to view knowledge as having an absolute existence in the world

     *   d. more likely to view knowledge as being relative to the person with the knowledge

p. 185 87. Darion doesn't understand why her psychology instructor doesn't just tell the class the

C   right answer. When asked, her instructor says that there is no single answer, it depends on

            each individual's interpretation. Darion has not yet developed:

            a. dialectical thinking

            b. systematic thinking

     *   c. relativistic thinking

            d. concrete thinking

p. 186 88. In general, which is true for older adults?

C   a. Older adults are likely to do better than adolescents on tasks requiring formal operational thought.

            b. Older adults are likely to outperform younger adults on concrete-operational tasks.

     *   c. Older adults are likely to perform less well than younger adults on concrete- and formal-operational tasks.

            d. As compared to younger adults, older adults are likely to perform less well on concrete-operational tasks, but better on formal-operational tasks.

p. 186 89. Which of the following statements is TRUE regarding cognitive capacities during later

C   adulthood?

     *   a. Older adults do not perform as well as younger adults on concrete-operational and formal operational tasks.

            b. Older adults perform better than younger adults on novel tasks.

            c. Older adults don't perform as well as younger adults on concrete-operational tasks, but do better than younger adults on formal operational tasks.

            d. Older adults perform just as well as younger adults on concrete-operational and formal operational tasks.

p. 187 90. Piaget has been criticized on all of the following grounds EXCEPT that he:

C
    a. portrays the young child as more limited than s/he really is
    b. portrays changes in cognitive skills as being more abrupt and absolute than they really are
  * c. places too great an emphasis on the ways in which language shapes thought
    d. pays too little attention to the influence of social interactions on the shaping of children's minds

p. 187 91. Which of the following is NOT a criticism of Piaget's theory?

F
    a. He did not give enough attention to social influences on cognitive development.
    b. He did not clearly distinguish competence from performance.
  * c. He did not clearly describe developmental changes in cognitive performance.
    d. He underestimated young children's abilities.

p. 188 92. The main theme of Vygotsky's theory is:

F   * a. cognitive growth is a product of the child's social interactions within a cultural and historical context
    b. cognitive growth results from independent interactions with objects in the environment
    c. cognitive development is a necessary building block for social and language development
    d. culture passively shapes a child's cognitive abilities

p. 188 93. Compared to Piaget, Vygotsky:

C
    a. believed that greater emphasis should be placed on creating disequilibrium
    b. believed that we learn best through reinforcement and punishment
    c. placed greater emphasis on developing independent cognitive skills
  * d. placed greater emphasis on culture and social interactions

p. 189 94. Which of the following is an example of Vygotsky's zone of proximal development?

C   * a. Figuring out the answer to your math homework after your sister gives you a hint.
    b. Getting a better grade on the math test than you usually get.
    c. Using trial and error to eliminate incorrect answers to a problem.
    d. Having your dad tell you the answer to your homework problems.

p. 189 95. Rana never had any formal training in breeding animals, but had always participated with his father in the family's business of breeding sheep. Consequently, Rana is now quite skilled at this practice. Vygotsky called this process:

C
    a. zone of proximal development
    b. genetic epistemology
  * c. guided participation
    d. transformational thought

p. 189 96. A major difference between Vygotsky and Piaget is:

C
    a. Vygotsky believed that private speech interfered with normal cognitive development.
www * b. Vygotsky believed social interactions were important to cognitive development.
    c. Vygotsky believed social development was driven by cognitive development.
    d. Vygotsky believed children's understanding of the world was arrived at through independent exploration.

p. 189 97. Four-year-old Jackie often mutters to herself as she builds things with her blocks. Her
C utterances (e.g., "the blue one goes first") seem to be a running dialogue of her actions.
Vygotsky called this:
* a. private speech
b. social speech
c. inner speech
d. telegraphic speech

p. 190 98. Which of the following is an accurate comparison of Piaget and Vygotsky?
C a. Piaget believed that children create knowledge through interactions with others while
Vygotsky believed that children construct knowledge independently.
b. Piaget believed that adults are most important to a child's cognitive development while
Vygotsky believed that peers are most important.
c. Piaget thought that language influences how children are able to think while Vygotsky
thought that cognition determines language.
* d. Piaget believed that people in different cultures went through universal stages of
cognitive development while Vygotsky believed that cognitive development varied
across cultures.

p. 190 99. With respect to children's use of private speech, research suggests that private speech:
C a. is unrelated to children's cognitive capabilities
* b. is a sign of cognitive maturity
c. is a sign of immature egocentrism
d. reflects what the child does not know

p. 191 100. The sound system of a language is referred to as:
F * a. phonology
b. pragmatics
c. semantics
d. syntax

p. 191 101. Jimmy has difficulty sounding out words such as "enough," "sophisticated," and "gnome."
C Jimmy's difficulties lie in which of the following aspects of language?
* a. phonology
b. pragmatics
c. semantics
d. syntax

p. 191 102. The rules for how to combine sounds into words are the rules of:
F * a. morphology
b. phonology
c. syntax
d. semantics

p. 191   103. Every language system has a set of rules that governs the ways in which words are strung
F   together to make meaningful utterances. This aspect of language is known as:
               a. phonology
               b. pragmatics
               c. semantics
        *   d. syntax

p. 191   104 Jake turned in a paper in his English composition class. The teacher returns it with a note
C   that he needs to work on sentence structure. Which aspect of language is this comment
              referring to?
               a. phonology
               b. pragmatics
               c. semantics
        *   d. syntax

p. 191   105. Tammy knows that she needs to put the subject first, followed by the verb, in order to make
C   the simple sentence, "the dog ran." This demonstrates that Tammy has an understanding
              of:
               a. phonology
               b. semantics
        *   c. syntax
               d. pragmatics

p. 191   106. Frances brings home a math assignment from kindergarten and shows it to her Mom. Her
C   mom says, "Wow, Frances, that looks really rough!" Frances runs her hand over the paper
              and says "No, Mommy, it's not rough; it's smooth!" Which aspect of language is causing
              Frances and her Mommy to have some communication difficulties?
               a. phonology
               b. pragmatics
        *   c. semantics
               d. syntax

p. 191   107. Which aspect of language deals with the meanings assigned to words?
F   a. phonology
               b. pragmatics
        *   c. semantics
               d. syntax

p. 191   108. Which of the following terms refers to the set of rules that govern the appropriate use of
F   language in different social contexts?
www   a. phonology
        *   b. pragmatics
               c. semantics
               d. syntax

p. 191   109.   Understanding that you need to use language differently with your professors than with
C   your friends shows mastery of:
                  a.   phonology
                  b.   semantics
                  c.   syntax
       *   d.   pragmatics

p. 192   110.   All of the following cries are present at birth except:
F
                  a.   anger
                  b.   hunger
                  c.   pain
       *   d.   sadness

p. 192   111.   At about one month of age, babies begin to combine vowel-like sounds into what we call
F   _____, and by six months of age, babies have added consonant sounds to produce

             _____.
                  a.   babbling, cooing
       *   b.   cooing, babbling
                  c.   morphemes, phonemes
                  d.   holophrases, telegraphic speech

p. 192   112.   At what age would you expect an infant to first demonstrate an understanding of the rule of
F.   "turn-taking" in conversation?
                  a.   2 months
                  b.   4 months
       *   c.   8 months
                  d.   12 months

p. 192   113.   Joel reaches up to Daddy with outstretched arms and says "Up!", meaning "Daddy, pick me
C   up!" This is an example of:
                  a.   caretaker speech
                  b.   echolalia
       *   c.   a holophrase
                  d.   telegraphic speech

p. 193   114.   Children substantially increase their vocabulary when they:
F   a.   have older siblings to listen to
                  b.   turn one year of age
                  c.   attend preschool
       *   d.   realize that everything has a name

p. 193   115.   Two-year-old Jill calls all the women she knows "Mommy." This is an example of:
C   *   a.   overextension
www   b.   overregularization
                  c.   telegraphic speech
                  d.   social speech

p. 193   116. Reserving the use of the word "kitty" to refer only to the cat at home and not other cats is
C   an example of:
               a.   babbling
               b.   functional grammar
        *   c.   underextension
               d.   overextension

p. 194   117. Karla speaks with very simple two- and three-word sentences, such as "Daddy gone." This
C   shows that Karla has developed:
               a.   holophrastic speech
        *   b.   telegraphic speech
               c.   overregularized speech
               d.   overextended speech

p. 194   118. Young children's early sentences are based on:
F   a.   correct grammar
        *   b.   functional grammar
               c.   transformational grammar
               d.   organizational grammar

p. 194   119. Rachel says "Ouch! I hurted myself!" This is an example of:
C   a.   animism
               b.   metacognition
        *   c.   overregularization
               d.   overextension

p. 194   120. Nelson and his Dad are at the zoo. "Look at those huge foots!" exclaims Nelson, as they
C   watch the elephant in its cage. Nelson's speech demonstrates:
               a.   overextension
        *   b.   overregularization
               c.   telegraphic speech
               d.   transitivity

p. 195   121. Changes in language use during elementary school include all of the following EXCEPT:
C   a.   increased command of grammatical rules
               b.   increased vocabulary size
               c.   decreased egocentrism
        *   d.   decreased use of transformational rules

p. 195   122. Which of the following is NOT a typical change in children's language use during the
C   elementary school years?
               a.   They communicate more effectively because they are not as egocentric.
               b.   Their pronunciation of words improves.
               c.   Their vocabulary increases.
        *   d.   They are able to produce shorter sentences that more effectively convey what they want
                    to say.

p. 196 123. Older adults experience all of the following changes in language EXCEPT:

F   a. they use less complex sentences than younger adults do

          b. they may not be able to distinguish all speech sounds if their hearing is impaired

          c. their knowledge of semantics increases

*   d. their knowledge of grammar decreases

p. 196 124. According to the learning theory explanation of language:

C   a. We learn language by listening to speech around us and generating rules from this speech.

          b. We must acquire certain cognitive milestones before language acquisition can begin.

*   c. We learn language the same way we learn everything else -- through observation and imitation.

          d. The way we learn language is unique from the way we learn other major skills.

p. 196 125. Learning theory is LEAST informative with regard which aspect of language development?

C   a. morphology

          b. phonology

          c. semantics

*   d. syntax

p. 197 126. With regard to language learning, nativists believe that:

C   a. language is learned as a result of differential parental reinforcement

          b. children learn language by listening, observing, and imitation

*   c. children are biologically programmed for language learning

          d. the social environment plays the most critical role in language learning

p. 197 127. Noam Chomsky asserts that humans have an inborn mechanism for mastering language.

F   He calls this the:

          a. executive grammar governor

          b. inborn language processor

*   c. language acquisition device

          d. programmed language center

p. 197 128. All of the following are arguments in support of the nativist perspective on language

C   learning EXCEPT:

          a. Children learn language at an amazingly rapid rate.

          b. Children progress through the same sequence in acquiring language skills, and at roughly the same ages.

*   c. Children exhibit remarkable cultural differences in early language learning.

          d. Overregularization, and other characteristics of early language, appear to be universal phenomena.

p. 197 129. The learning theory of language seems to best explain the acquisition of _____,

C   while the nativist theory seems to best explain the acquisition of _____.

www *   a. semantics; syntax

          b. syntax; semantics

          c. semantics; phonology

          d. semantics; pragmatics

p. 197　130. Which of the following is NOT a valid criticism of nativist theory of language
C　　　　development?
　　　　　a.　It doesn't really explain how built-in language devices operate.
　　　　　b.　It underestimates the role of the environment in language development.
　　　　　c.　It assumes that mere exposure to language is sufficient for acquisition of language.
　　*　　d.　It assumes that there are some universal aspects of language development.

p. 197　131. Which of the following claims does Chomsky make regarding language acquisition?
C　　　　　a.　Humans have an inborn knowledge of all components of language.
　　*　　b.　Humans have an inborn mechanism for sifting through the language they hear and
　　　　　　　generating rules for that language.
　　　　　c.　Humans are able to listen to the language around them and imitate the sounds they
　　　　　　　hear.
　　　　　d.　Humans must be exposed to language at a developmentally appropriate time in order
　　　　　　　for language to develop.

p. 197　132. Which of the following arguments is NOT support for Chomsky's nativist theory of
C　　　　language acquisition?
　　　　　a.　Children of all cultures babble at about the same age and with the same vowel-
　　　　　　　consonant combinations.
　　*　　b.　Children tend to develop the accents and speech mannerisms of the people around
　　　　　　　them.
　　　　　c.　Most children make the mistake of overregularizing the language rules of their culture.
　　　　　d.　Children learn language quickly and without formal instruction.

p. 198　133. Which is TRUE with regard to the acquisition of language?
C　　　　　a.　The nativist perspective is primarily concerned with the branch of language known as
　　　　　　　semantics.
　　*　　b.　The interactionist perspective is most helpful in coming to an understanding of how
　　　　　　　children acquire language.
　　　　　c.　The learning perspective is extremely useful in understanding the acquisition of syntax.
　　　　　d.　The nativist perspective is concerned primarily with the influence of the social
　　　　　　　environment on early language learning.

p. 198　134. Which of the following is FALSE regarding the interactionist view of language
C　　　　acquisition?
　　*　　a.　Biological predispositions outweigh the effects of the environment.
　　　　　b.　Biological factors and the environment are both critical components of language
　　　　　　　acquisition.
　　　　　c.　Acquisition of language depends on accomplishments in other areas, including
　　　　　　　cognitive, perceptual, and social developments.
　　　　　d.　Language develops in the context of social interactions.

p. 198　135. When talking to their 2-year-old, Sue and Jim typically use short, simple sentences, lots of
C　　　　repetition, and high pitched voices. This sort of speech is known as:
　　　　　a.　abbreviated speech
　　　　　b.　caretaker speech
　　*　　c.　child-directed speech
　　　　　d.　telegraphic speech

p. 198　136. When her toddler holds her cup up and says "Milk," her mother says "You're ready for
C　　　　　more milk." The mother's response is an example of:
　　　* 　a. expansion
　　　　　b. holophrastic speech
　　　　　c. child-directed speech
　　　　　d. recast speech

p. 199　137. Which of the following is evidence of a critical period for language acquisition?
C　　　* 　a. Children have an easier time learning a second language than adults do.
　　　　　b. Deaf children are never able to develop language.
　　　　　c. Adults are more likely to study multiple languages than children are.
　　　　　d. Children do not acquire large vocabularies until after they learn to read.

p. 172　138. An example of accommodation is
C　　　　　a. believing that all four-legged animals with fur are dogs
SG　　* 　b. realizing that a cat fits into a different category than a dog
　　　　　c. the confusion that a child experiences when new events challenge old schemas
　　　　　d. a child who sees a cat and refers to it as a dog

p. 172　139. Which of the following statements best characterizes Piaget's position on the nature-nurture
C　　　　　issue?
SG　　　　a. The environment is primarily responsible for providing children with cognitive skills.
　　　　　b. Innate mechanisms are primarily responsible for determining intelligence.
　　　* 　c. Ideas are not innate or imposed by others, but are constructed from experiences.
　　　　　d. Some cognitive skills result from innate characteristics while others are influenced only
　　　　　　 by environmental experiences.

p. 173　140. Throughout the sensorimotor stage, infants change from
C　　　　　a. focusing on symbols to using simple mental operations
SG　　　　b. an egocentric perspective to one that considers other viewpoints
　　　* 　c. relying on reflexes for understanding their world to mentally planning how to solve
　　　　　　 simple problems
　　　　　d. focusing on sensory information to focusing on motoric information for gaining
　　　　　　 knowledge about their world

p. 173　141. Which of the following is an example of object permanence?
C　　　　　a. visually tracking a moving object
SG　　　　b. searching for a shoe under the bed because this seems like a likely hiding place
　　　* 　c. searching for a toy where the child just watched it being hidden
　　　　　d. using goal directed behavior to systematically check all possible hiding locations for a
　　　　　　 toy

p. 175 142. Which of the following responses to a conservation problem indicates that the child has
C   reversibility of thought?
SG
           a. The amount of water in the two cups is the same because even though one is taller, the
              other one is wider.
           b. The amount of water in the two cups looks about the same, so I'd say they were equal.
           c. I didn't see you spill any water, so the amounts are the same.
       *   d. If you'd pour the water back into the original container, you'd see it has the same
              amount of water as the other container.

p. 177 143. Research on Piaget's description of preoperational thought has found that
C   *   a. when task demands are reduced, young children can successfully solve some problems
SG   at a more sophisticated level.
           b. when task demands are reduced, it has little impact on performance because children
              do not yet have the cognitive capabilities to solve the problem.
           c. Piaget was correct in his description of when certain abilities emerged, but was not
              always accurate in his description of what underlying thought was required for these
              abilities.
           d. Piaget overestimated what most preschool-age children can do.

p. 179 144. Formal operational children are different from concrete operational children in that
C   *   a. formal operational children can deal with possibilities
SG   b. formal operational children focus on realities
           c. concrete operational children systematically test all possible solutions to a problem
           d. concrete operational children are more likely to be egocentric.

p. 187 145. Piaget has been criticized by modern developmentalists who suggest that
C   a. Piaget was somewhat pessimistic concerning the timing of cognitive abilities in
SG   adolescents
           b. Piaget was overly optimistic concerning the abilities of infants and young children
       *   c. development is a gradual process rather than a stagelike process
           d. development is stagelike but stages follow a different pattern than what Piaget
              suggested

p. 185 146. Research by Perry with college students suggests that their thinking progresses from:
F   *   a. assuming that truth is absolute to understanding that truth is relative
SG   b. uncertainty about the "correctness" of answers to absolute certainty about the
              correctness
           c. considering all possible options to selecting a single answer
           d. being able to think logically about ideas to thinking logically about multiple sets of
              ideas

p. 186 147. Research with older adults solving Piagetian tasks shows that
F   a. nearly all are reasoning at the formal operational level
SG   *   b. older adults perform worse than younger adults on many concrete operational tasks
           c. older adults perform similarly to younger adults on all Piagetian tasks
           d. older adults are more egocentric than younger adults and tend to use transductive
              reasoning

p. 190 148. In comparing Piaget's perspective to Vygotsky's perspective, which of the following is
C   TRUE?
SG   *   a. Piaget believed that knowledge was constructed through independent exploration of the
                world while Vygotsky believed that social interactions were needed for development of
                more advanced thinking.
            b. Both believed that language development was independent of cognitive development.
            c. Vygotsky believed that private speech was not a developmentally important
                phenomenon, while Piaget used it as evidence of egocentrism.
            d. Piaget and Vygotsky both proposed that children progress through major stages in
                reaching mature cognitive understanding of the world.

p. 189 149. Vygotsky used the term <u>zone of proximal development</u> to refer to:
F   a. the influence that thought and language have on one another
SG   b. the child's approximate level of cognitive skill on a particular task
      *   c. the difference between what someone can do independently and what they can do
                with another person's help
            d. the point at which the child progresses from one level of understanding to another

p. 191 150. Phonology refers to the _____ of language, while semantics refers to the _____
F   of language.
SG   *   a. sound system; meaning
            b. rules for forming sentences; meaning
            c. meaning; rules for how to use language
            d. rules for combining sounds; rules for forming sentences

p. 193 151. Calling all four-legged animals "doggie" is an example of
C   a. overregularization
SG   b. underextension
      *   c. overextension
            d. telegraphic speech

p. 196 152. Learning theorists argue that language is acquired through
F   a. biologically programmed learning capacities
SG   *   b. imitation of others' language and reinforcement for recognizable speech
            c. cognitive understanding of speech sounds and their relationship to real objects and
                actions
            d. a device that allows children to sift through language and generate rules that govern the
                language

TRUE-FALSE QUESTIONS

p. 172 153. With regard to intelligence, Piaget takes a "nativist" position on the nature/nurture issue.
            a. true
      *   b. false

p. 172 154. It is possible for a child to move directly from the sensorimotor period to concrete
            operations.
            a. true
      *   b. false

p. 173 155. According to Piaget, infants are first able to search for a hidden toy during the sixth sensorimotor substage.
   a. true
 * b. false

p. 175 156. Preoperational children have a good grasp of cause-effect relationships.
   a. true
 * b. false

p. 178 157. Recent research has supported Piaget's conclusions that young children (age 3) have no ability to take another person's point of view.
   a. true
 * b. false

p. 178 158. Concrete-operational thinkers can conserve, but they are still unable to use
www   transformational thought.
   a. true
 * b. false

p. 180 159. In general, concrete operational thinkers are more impulsive in their attempts to solve problems than are formal operational thinkers.
 * a. true
   b. false

p. 184 160. High-school teachers can safely assume that the vast majority of their students are formal operational thinkers.
   a. true
 * b. false

p. 184 161. Research indicates that formal operations is the most advanced form of adult thought.
   a. true
 * b. false

p. 184 162. Once an individual has attained formal operational thought, s/he can easily generalize www problem-solving skills across all content areas.
   a. true
 * b. false

p. 188 163. With regard to Piaget's stages of cognitive development, cultural factors have been shown to influence both the rate and sequence of development.
   a. true
 * b. false

p. 189 164. Piaget was highly concerned with developing ways to accelerate children's progression through the stages of concrete and formal-operational thought.
   a. true
 * b. false

p. 189 165. Training studies have indicated that it is possible to accelerate children's progression through the preoperational and concrete-operational stages of cognitive development.
* a. true
   b. false

p. 192 166. Babies "coo" before they "babble."
* a. true
   b. false

p. 192 167. Deaf infants never learn to coo or babble.
   a. true
* b. false

p. 192 168. Infants only understand the meanings of words they, themselves, can produce.
   a. true
* b. false

p. 196 169. Learning theorists tend to stress the role of the social environment in language learning.
* a. true
   b. false

p. 197 170. Nativists assume that all children need in order to acquire language is exposure to language.
* a. true
   b. false

ESSAY QUESTIONS

171. Why did Piaget call his first stage "sensorimotor" development?

172. How are children in the concrete operational stage advanced relative to those in the preoperational stage and deficient relative to those in the formal operational stage?

173. How is an adult's thinking different from that of an adolescent?

174. In light of current research, what are some of the main concerns about Piaget's theory?
www

175. What educational recommendations can you make based on Piaget's theory? What educational recommendations can you make based on Vygotsky's theory?

176. How does Vygotsky's perspective on cognition and language compare to Piaget's perspective?

177. How do the learning, nativist, and interactionist theories explain language acquisition?

178.	Apply Piaget's description of cognitive development to a social issue such as divorce, birth of a
SG	new sibling, or adoption. What would a child's understanding of one these events be in each of
	Piaget's four stages of cognitive development?
	[Sample answer is provided in the Study Guide.]

179.	Piaget's theory has stimulated a tremendous amount of research on cognitive development over
SG	the past 30 years. Considering what we have learned from this research, how would Piaget's
	theory need to be updated to account for the findings that have emerged since the theory was
	developed?

180.	Suppose you need to design a program to teach 6-year-old children a new academic skill.
SG	How would you approach this from Piaget's perspective? How would you approach this
	from Vygotsky's perspective? How would the two programs be similar or different?

181.	Consider how deafness affects the language development of children. Questions to think about
SG	include: Do you need to hear speech to develop speech? More generally, do you need to be
	exposed to a language (spoken or unspoken) in order to develop a language? What is the
	relationship between thought and language? Is language an important basis for thought (Is it a
	necessary basis for thought)?

8

LEARNING AND INFORMATION PROCESSING

MULTIPLE-CHOICE QUESTIONS

p. 206 1.   Learning is typically defined as a relatively permanent _____ that results from _____ :
F
- a. change in belief; maturation
- * b. change in behavior; one's experiences
- c. knowledge base; one's formal education
- d. change in behavior; maturation

p. 206 2.   In Watson and Raynor's experiment with "little Albert," Watson hit a steel rod with a
C   hammer when Albert reached for a white rat. Eventually, Albert came to fear the rat.
www   Which set of terms is synonymous to and in the same order as: <u>present the rat</u>, <u>loud noise</u>, and <u>fear of rat</u>?
- a. unconditioned stimulus (UCS), conditioned response (CR), conditioned stimulus (CS)
- b. UCS, CS, CR
- * c. CS, UCS, CR
- d. CR, UCS, CS

p. 206 3.   In Pavlov's experiments with classical conditioning, he rang a bell just before feeding dogs.
C   Eventually the dogs salivated whenever the bell rang. Which set of terms is synonymous to and in the same order as: <u>sound of bell</u>, <u>food</u>, and <u>salivation in response to bell ringing</u>?
- a. unconditioned stimulus (UCS), conditioned response (CS), conditioned stimulus (CS)
- b. UCS, CS, CR
- * c. CS, UCS, CR
- d. CR, UCS, CS

p. 206 4.   During her first physical education class a 6th grade student is severely criticized for her
C   performance. Now she gets a sick feeling in her stomach before each physical education class. This BEST illustrates:
- * a. classical conditioning
- b. negative reinforcement
- c. observational learning
- d. counter-conditioning

p. 206 5.   When newborn Baby Joe cried for food, his mother promptly nursed him, each and every
C   time. At first, Joe would cry and cry until he got the breast milk. Soon, however, Joe stopped crying as soon as his mother picked him up and sat down in the rocker where they typically nursed. Eventually, he stopped crying and made sucking motions as soon as his mother appeared. At this point, Joe's mother is BEST referred to as a(n):
- a. unconditioned stimulus
- * b. conditioned stimulus
- c. positive reinforcer
- d. negative reinforcer

p. 206 6. The last time Kurt went to the dentist, he had two cavities filled and experienced a lot of
C   pain and anxiety. When the dental office calls to remind Kurt it is time for his next
            appointment, he gets tense. On his way to the dentist's office, he starts to feel queasy! This
            BEST illustrates:
    *   a. classical conditioning
            b. counterconditioning
            c. instrumental conditioning
            d. habituation

p. 206 7. Which of the following is an example of using classical conditioning in the classroom?
C   *   a. Associate pleasant events with learning.
            b. Model the behaviors you want the students to learn.
            c. Give students an extra ten minutes of recess as a reward for doing well.
            d. Use test scores as a means of determining semester grades.

p. 206 8. While her fifth-grade students work on their math sheets in class, Mrs. Abrams lets them
C   listen to their favorite CDs on a portable CD player she provides. She doesn't know if this
            affects their performance, but she hopes it will help them to enjoy mathematics more. Mrs.
            Abrams is using:
            a. operant conditioning
    *   b. classical conditioning
            c. bribery
            d. habitual stimuli

p. 206 9. Jake is afraid of a new puppy. His parents gradually get him used to the puppy by only
C   bringing the puppy into the room when Jake is eating ice cream (his favorite!). Soon, Jake
            comes to associate the puppy with eating the good feelings he has while he is eating ice
            cream, and he loses his fear of the puppy. This BEST illustrates the concept of _____
            conditioning:
            a. operant
    *   b. counter
            c. negative
            d. instrumental

p. 207 10. The fact that people tend to repeat behaviors that have pleasant consequences and cut down
C   on behaviors that have negative consequences is the basis for:
            a. classical conditioning
            b. habituation
            c. observational learning
    *   d. operant conditioning

p. 207 11. Positive reinforcement and negative reinforcement are used to:
C   *   a. strengthen a behavior
            b. weaken a behavior
            c. strengthen and weaken a behavior, respectively
            d. weaken and strengthen a behavior, respectively

p. 207 12. Positive reinforcement is to _____ as negative reinforcement is to _____ :
C
    a. reward; punishment
    b. giving something positive; giving something negative
    c. giving something positive; taking away something positive
  * d. reward; taking away something negative

p. 207 13. Regina and her friends started car pooling to work after the city instituted a new policy:
C   Cars with more than two passengers do not have to pay the hefty toll fees to cross the main
       bridge into the city. The increased car pooling resulted from using:
    a. positive reinforcement
  * b. negative reinforcement
    c. classical conditioning
    d. observational learning

p. 207 14. Marsha works very hard and raises her grade in Biology from a C to an A. When she
C   shows her dad her report card, he lets her go out with her friends on a school night, which
       thrills Marsha! This BEST illustrates the concept of:
  * a. positive reinforcement
    b. bribery
    c. a conditioned response
    d. continuous reinforcement

p. 207 15. A teacher constantly nags at a student to settle down and get to work. When the student
C   does so, the teacher stops nagging. Now the student works just to avoid the nagging. This
www example BEST demonstrates:
    a. elaboration
  * b. negative reinforcement
    c. positive reinforcement
    d. punishment

p. 207 16. Negative reinforcement is the:
F
    a. same as punishment
    b. removal of a pleasant stimulus
  * c. removal or avoidance of an unpleasant stimulus
    d. best way to decrease an inappropriate behavior

p. 207 17. The primary difference between negative reinforcement and punishment is:
C   * a. punishment is intended to decrease behavior
    b. punishment occurs after a behavior
    c. punishment has fewer harmful side effects
    d. there is no difference

p. 207 18. In _____ conditioning, a learner must first emit a response, while in _____
F   conditioning, a stimulus elicits a response from the learner.
    a. classical; operant
  * b. operant; classical
    c. operant; observational
    d. observational; classical

p. 208 19. Which of the following is an example of negative punishment?
C * a. Taking away TV privileges after misbehaving.
      b. Yelling at a child for fighting on the playground.
      c. Taking away a disliked chore.
      d. Ignoring a child in hopes that the undesirable behavior will disappear.

p. 208 20. When Polly breaks her mother's favorite vase, her allowance is taken away for a month.
C   This BEST illustrates:
      a. negative reinforcement
  *   b. negative punishment
      c. counterconditioning
      d. positive punishment

p. 208 21. Studying ONLY to avoid failing a course is an example of:
C   a. continuous reinforcement of desired behavior
      b. partial reinforcement of desired behavior
  *   c. negative reinforcement
      d. punishing undesirable behaviors

p. 208 22. Ginny ignores her daughter's whining at bedtime, and soon the whining stops. Ginny is
C   using:
      a. classical conditioning
  *   b. extinction
      c. negative reinforcement
      d. love withdrawal

p. 208 23. The BEST way for a teacher to maintain students' desirable behavior over long time
C   periods is to:
www * a. reinforce the behavior on an unpredictable schedule
      b. reinforce the behavior the first twenty times it occurs and then stop the reinforcement
      c. harshly punish the entire class of students whenever one misbehaves
      d. have an initial talk with the students about your expectations and then say no more

p. 208 24. Mark and Shiela want their children to learn to clear their places after every meal. They
C   should:
      a. praise them every time, until it becomes a habit, and then abruptly stop
      b. pay them $5 a month "up front" so they will want to do the job
      c. punish them if they don't clear the table
  *   d. praise them every time, until it becomes a habit, and then occasionally thereafter

p. 208 25. Mr. Levin's students have learned to work quietly, without talking, while he meets with
C   individual reading groups. To BEST MAINTAIN his students' quiet working behavior
      across the school year, Mr. Levin should:
      a. punish the students when they misbehave
  *   b. periodically reinforce the students on an unpredictable schedule
      c. ignore students who misbehave
      d. reward the students only on Fridays

p. 209 26. Which of the following is the LEAST desirable guideline for effective punishment?

F

        a. Explain to the child why s/he is being punished.

*   b. Delay the punishment as long as possible after the child misbehaves.

        c. If you are going to punish a particular act, always punish it.

        d. Be warm (affectionate) toward the child when you are not punishing him/her.

p. 209 27. Mr. Peters opens the front door and steps inside, right on a pile of poop! He finds the dog

C   (the guilty one!) sleeping on his dog bed and whacks him hard with a newspaper. The dog

          will MOST LIKELY:

        a. learn to sleep by the front door

*   b. not want to sleep on the dog bed any more

        c. poop on the dog bed next time

        d. poop outside from now on

p. 209 28. Harsh physical punishment is MOST LIKELY to:

F

        a. eliminate negative behaviors effectively

*   b. result in increased levels of aggressive behavior

        c. cause the child to respect his/her parents

        d. teach children their parents care about them

p. 209 29. If Mr. and Mrs. Snooks want to use punishment effectively in disciplining their children,

C   they should do all of the following EXCEPT:

        a. punish their children with moderate intensity

        b. explain why the behavior being punished is unacceptable

*   c. always have the same parent do the punishing

        d. punish their children during the act

p. 210 30. Observational learning is MOST likely to account for the appearance of:

C

        a. metamemory

        b. simple habits

        c. emotional likes and dislikes

*   d. brand-new, complex behaviors

p. 210 31. A teenager who smokes after seeing his/her friends do so MOST likely learned this

C   through:

        a. classical conditioning

        b. habituation

*   c. observational learning

        d. operant conditioning

p. 210 32. Day after day Donna admires her Kindergarten teacher. One day, while at home, Donna

C   lines up her stuffed animals and begins to pretend to teach them. Her actions BEST

          illustrate:

        a. behavior modification

        b. positive reinforcement

*   c. observational learning

        d. rehearsal and verbal mediation

p. 210 33. Molly watches as her friend, Jill, throws a temper tantrum because she wants a cookie
C   and her mother said "No!" She then watches as Jill gets spanked! Molly MOST LIKELY:
         a. will try the temper-tantrum technique with her mom to see if she has better luck
         b. will not learn how to throw a tantrum, because she saw Frieda get punished
     *   c. will learn how to throw a tantrum, but won't try it because she doesn't want to get
            spanked
         d. will not want to play with Frieda any more because she was bad

p. 211 34. Which of the following is TRUE regarding classical conditioning?
F   a. Newborns can be easily classically conditioned.
         b. Classical conditioning is not possible until at least 8-12 months of age.
     *   c. Newborns can be classically conditioned but not always reliably or easily.
         d. Infants can be classically conditioned if they understand what it is the experimenter is
            trying to condition.

p. 211 35. With regard to newborns' learning, which is FALSE?
F   a. newborns can learn through classical conditioning
www   b. newborns take longer to be conditioned than older infants do
     *   c. newborns can learn entirely novel behaviors through observation and imitation
         d. newborns can learn through operant conditioning

p. 211 36. While visiting friends, 9-month-old Bobby watches Lucy play with a busy box in her
C   playpen. Lucy pushes a button that squeaks and rolls a bar that rattles. The next day,
         Bobby's mother buys Bobby the same busy box and sets it up in his crib. Right away,
         Bobby pushes the button that squeaks and rolls the bar that rattles. This BEST illustrates:
         a. operant conditioning
         b. classical conditioning
     *   c. deferred imitation
         d. habituation

p. 211 37. Research has conclusively shown that newborns (1 day old) can learn in all of the
F   following ways except:
         a. classical conditioning
         b. habituation
     *   c. observational learning
         d. operant conditioning

p. 213 38. The information-processing approach to learning:
F   a. ignores the inner workings of the mind
         b. relies heavily on modeling and imitation
     *   c. likens the human mind to a computer
         d. is concerned primarily with affective responses to the environment

p. 213 39. In the information-processing approach, hardware is to ____ as software is to _____:
C   *   a. the central nervous system; the retrieval of information
         b. memory; the brain
         c. the brain; the central nervous system
         d. the brain; sensory receptors

p. 213 40. The information-processing approach stresses all of the following except:
F
* b. reinforcers
   a. encoding
   c. retrieval
   d. storage

p. 213 41. In the information-processing model, the purpose of the sensory register is to:
F * a. briefly hold a piece of information for possible processing
   b. control the activities of long-term memory
   c. retrieve data from short-term memory
   d. develop strategies for storing encoded data

p. 213 42. Shirley is introduced to her friend's mother, but has no idea what the woman's name is
C   immediately after it was spoken! It is MOST ACCURATE to say that the woman's name:
* a. never made it past Shirley's sensory register
   b. is trapped in Shirley's short-term memory
   c. is lost in Shirley's long-term memory
   d. could be cued to recall later on if Shirley would relax a bit

p. 213 43. In the information-processing model, long-term memory and short-term memory differ in
C   that:
   a. the sensory register is located in long-term memory
   b. short-term memory has a much larger storage capacity
* c. short-term memory provides a working space for processing information
   d. long-term memory does not become functional until someone is at least 6 years old

p. 213 44. Gayle looks up a phone number and remembers it just long enough to walk over to the
C   telephone and dial. The number was held in her:
   a. sensory register
* b. short-term memory
   c. long-term memory
   d. perceptual register

p. 213 45. Short-term memory:
F   a. can hold about 20 bits of information at a time
   b. is where we retain information for a day or two before we forget about it
* c. is what is on one's mind at a given moment
   d. controls the storage of information for later retrieval

p. 213 46. Encoding involves information that is
F * a. moved from a sensory register to short-term memory to long-term memory
   b. maintained in long-term memory
   c. pulled out from long-term memory when needed
   d. simple to process

p. 214 47. Professor Jacobs gives her students a multiple-choice test. This method of assessment
C requires students to use ___ memory:
www   a.   recall
      *   b.   recognition
           c.   cued-recall
           d.   meta-memory

p. 214 48. Mr. Jones gives his students the following test item: "The capitol of the United States is
C ___." To answer this question, students must use:
           a.   recognition memory
           b.   metamemory
      *   c.   recall memory
           d.   selective memory

p. 214 49. In general, MOST people find that test questions requiring _____ memory are easier to
F answer than those requiring _____ memory:
           a.   recall; recognition
           b.   cued recall; recognition
      *   c.   recognition; recall
           d.   recall; cued recall

p. 214 50. Jill has good recognition memory, but lousy recall memory, of the story she just read. This
C suggests that her main problem is a deficiency in:
           a.   storage
           b.   encoding
      *   c.   retrieval
           d.   metamemory

p. 214 51. Ten-month-old Vicki pulls away a couch cushion to find a toy bear she watched her mother
C hide there. This BEST demonstrates the use of:
           a.   recognition memory
      *   b.   recall memory
           c.   cued-recall memory
           d.   observational learning

p. 215 52. Which statement is TRUE regarding "recall" memory and "recognition" memory in
F newborns?
      *   a.   only recognition memory is present
           b.   only recall memory is present
           c.   both recall and recognition memory are present
           d.   neither recall memory nor recognition memory is present

p. 216 53. By age ___, MOST infants can deliberately recall and remember an event that happened
F quite some time ago.
           a.   6 months
           b.   12 months
           c.   18 months
      *   d.   2 years

p. 216 54. "Infantile amnesia" refers to the lack of human ability to remember:
F
        a. extremely traumatic events
    *   b. anything that happened during the first three years of life
        c. insignificant events in our lives
        d. things we don't want to remember

p. 217 55. Greg has difficulty remembering anything that happened in his life prior to the time he was
C   about 3 years old. This means that Greg:
    *   a. is like most normal people
        b. suffered some traumatic event early on that has caused him to block off memory of his
            early years
        c. has a mental impairment
        d. has an unusually small amount of space in his working memory

p. 217 56. Older children can learn faster and remember more than younger children because older
F   children have a:
        a. significantly larger sensory register
        b. greater storage capacity in short-term memory
        c. greater storage capacity in long-term memory
    *   d. larger working memory space available for constructive use

p. 217 57. Research shows that basic capacities
F
        a. are unrelated to actual performance
        b. are very consistent across the life span
    *   c. become faster with age as some functions are automatized
        d. become larger in size with age

p. 217 58. Which component of the information-processing model is thought to improve most as
F   students get older and thus become more proficient learners?
www   a. sensory register
    *   b. working space in short-term memory
        c. storage capacity of short-term memory
        d. storage capacity of long-term memory

p. 218 59. Estelle, age 6, can learn faster and remember more than her 3-year-old brother, Harry. This
C   is MOST LIKELY so because:
        a. Estelle is smarter than Harry
        b. Estelle has a larger sensory register than Harry
        c. Harry has significantly less storage space in his short-term memory than does Estelle
    *   d. Estelle has more working memory space available for constructive use than Harry does

p. 218 60. Which memory strategy is being used when a long number is easily memorized by
C   breaking it into subunits?
    *   a. chunking
        b. elaboration
        c. metamemory
        d. rehearsal

p. 218 61. An example of elaboration is
C
    a. repeating "red, chair, dog" several times
    b. consolidating "red" and "green" into a color group and "chair" and "table" into a furniture group
  * c. noting that the red chair and the green piano remind you of Christmas when you sit on the chair and play the piano
    d. saying the words to be remembered out loud

p. 218 62. The purpose of "chunking" is to:
C
    a. make rote learning meaningful
    b. increase the capacity of long-term memory
    c. increase the capacity of the sensory register
  * d. improve the efficiency of short-term memory

p. 218 63. Sam and Sue are shopping for groceries. Sam looks at the list and tells Sue: "I'll get the cat food, soap, toilet paper, and flour, and I'll meet you by the lettuce." He takes off, muttering to himself over and over: "cat food, soap, t.p., flour." This BEST illustrates the use of which memory strategy?
C
    a. chunking
    b. elaboration
    c. organization
  * d. rehearsal

p. 218 64. Peter is playing a party game where a tray of objects is displayed for one minute and then covered with a cloth while the players write down as many objects on the tray as they can remember. Peter notices there is a plum, a pear, and a peach. Also, there is a knife, a fork, and a spoon. He notes, too, there is a crayon, a pencil, and a magic marker. This BEST demonstrates the use of which memory strategy?
C
    a. elaboration
  * b. organization
    c. rehearsal
    d. mediation

p. 218 65. Wayne has trouble remembering the last 4 digits of his phone number until he makes the connection that the last 2 digits are exactly half of the first 2 digits. Once he makes this connection, he has no trouble remembering the number! This BEST demonstrates the memory concept of:
C
    a. chunking
    b. organization
  * c. elaboration
    d. mediation

p. 219 66. Jack knows that he can more easily memorize and recall a list of ten familiar words than he can ten unfamiliar words. His knowledge of this is an example of:
C
    a. short-term memory
    b. chunking
    c. recall memory
  * d. metamemory

p. 219 67. Which is NOT an example of metamemory?
C   * a. knowing the difference between metaphysics and metaphysical
       b. knowing which memory strategies are most effective for you
       c. knowing which memorization tasks are most difficult for you
       d. being able to plan and control your memory processes as you learn

p. 219 68. The BEST example of metacognition is a:
C   * a. student thinking about how to improve his/her study techniques
       b. group of researchers trying to solve a problem
       c. chemistry teacher preparing a lecture
       d. student taking lecture notes

p. 219 69. Matilda knows that she remembers the material better when she takes notes from a chapter
C   she is reading, than when she simply highlights passages in the text. Her knowledge of this
www   BEST illustrates:
       a. chunking
       b. elaboration
    * c. metamemory
       d. organization

p. 219 70. In comparing memory capabilities in children who were experts at chess with the memories
C   of adults who weren't, Chi (1978) tested both groups on memory of location of chess pieces
        and on ability to remember sequences of digits. She found that the:
       a. children did better on both tests
       b. adults did better on both tests
    * c. children did better on memory of chess, but not sequences of digits
       d. children did better on memory of digits, but not on memory of chess

p. 220 71. In their area of expertise, expert children perform
F   * a. better than novice adults
       b. the same as novice adults
       c. worse than novice adults
       d. the same as children with good overall problem solving skills

p. 220 72. Which statement is TRUE regarding the development of learning in children?
C   a. Younger children have a greater information-processing capacity and a larger
          knowledge base than older children do.
       b. Younger children have a greater information-processing capacity, but older children
          have a larger knowledge base.
       c. Younger children have a larger knowledge base, but older children have a greater
          information-processing capacity.
    * d. Older children have a greater information-processing capacity and a greater knowledge
          base.

p. 220 73. Which statement is TRUE regarding the development of memory in children?

C   *   a. Older children know more about their memory and have more effective memory strategies than younger children do.
           b. Older children know more about their memory, but younger children have more effective memory strategies.
           c. Older children have more effective memory strategies, but younger children know more about their memory.
           d. Younger children know more about their memory and have more effective memory strategies than older children do.

p. 220 74. Which is TRUE regarding the development of learning and memory in children?

C   *   a. Older children have a greater information-processing capacity and know more about their memorization strategies than younger children do.
           b. Older children have a greater information-processing capacity, but younger children know more about their memorization strategies than older children do.
           c. Older children know more about their memorization strategies but younger children have a greater information-processing capacity.
           d. Older children have a lesser information-processing capacity and know less about their memorization strategies than younger children do.

p. 222 75. According to Siegler, children are LIKELY to begin using rule-governed problem-solving

F   strategies:
           a. as early as age 2
       *   b. by the time they are in Kindergarten
           c. during the later elementary-school years
           d. when they reach the stage of formal-operational thought

p. 221 76. Research on problem solving shows that children

C   a. pick a single strategy and stick with it
www   *   b. use multiple strategies to solve problems
           c. progress through distinct stages of using different strategies
           d. prefer to guess rather than use a strategy

p. 222 77. During the adolescent years, what generally happens to an individual's learning, memory,

F   and problem-solving abilities?
           a. learning improves, but memory and problem-solving abilities do not
           b. learning and problem-solving improve, but memory does not
           c. problem-solving improves, but learning and memory do not
       *   d. they all improve

p. 222 78. Throughout his high school years, it is MOST LIKELY that Gregory will:

C   a. improve his use of memory strategies such as organization and elaboration
           b. develop problem-solving skills which are increasingly rule-governed
           c. develop new learning strategies
       *   d. all of the above

p. 223 79. If one compares people who are new to a chosen field of study (novices) to those who are
F experienced in this field (experts), what can be expected in terms of ability to solve
problems in that field of study?

    a. Experts solve problems more quickly, but novices develop solutions that are especially
       effective.

    b. Novices solve problems more quickly, but their solutions are not nearly as effective as
       those of experts.

    c. There are no appreciable differences in the problem-solving capabilities of the two
       groups.

*   d. Experts solve problems more quickly and their solutions are more effective.

p. 224 80. With which of the following tasks would older adults have the LEAST problem?
F

    a. a memory task where the material is unfamiliar

    b. a task where they are asked to recall rather than recognize names

*   c. a memory task where they can use well-practiced memory strategies

    d. a timed memory task

p. 224 81. Which statement is TRUE regarding "recall" memory and "recognition" memory in elderly
C adults?

*   a. they are likely to be more deficient in recall than in recognition memory

    b. they are likely to be more deficient in recognition than in recall memory

    c. they are likely to be equally deficient in both types of memory

    d. neither type of memory diminishes with age (except in extreme cases)

p. 225 82. Research shows that older adults
F   *   a. have trouble with explicit memory tasks

    b. have trouble with implicit memory tasks

    c. show no differences in their explicit and implicit memories

    d. show declines in implicit memory earlier than declines in explicit memory

p. 225 83. Which is the LEAST probable cause of memory problems in older adults?
F

    a. ill health

    b. deficiencies in information-processing capacity

*   c. deficiencies in knowledge base

    d. failure to use effective memory strategies

p. 226 84. Which statement is generally true regarding adult memory?
C

    a. Older adults use effective memorization strategies more often and can recall
       information better than young adults.

    b. Older adults use effective memorization strategies more often, but cannot recall
       information as well as young adults can.

    c. Older adults can recall information better, but are less likely to use effective
       memorization strategies.

*   d. Older adults are less likely to use effective memorization strategies and are less able to
       recall information.

p. 227 85. Which statement is TRUE regarding adult learning?
C   *   a. Older adults are slower at learning and retrieving information from long-term memory than younger adults are.
            b. Older adults are slower at learning but better at retrieving information.
            c. Older adults are faster at learning but slower at retrieving information.
            d. Older adults are faster at learning and retrieving information.

p. 228 86. Jeff, age 65, is finding that he has more difficulty remembering things than he did when he was a younger man. The MOST LIKELY cause of his memory difficulties is:
C
            a. a diminished knowledge base
        *   b. a decline in working memory capacity
            c. deterioration in metamemory skills
            d. degenerative disease

p. 227 87. Older adults often perform worse than younger adults on learning and memory tasks for all of the following reasons EXCEPT:
F
www   a. They are not as motivated.
            b. They are less educated.
        *   c. They have less knowledge about the world.
            d. They have slower processing of material.

p. 228 88. Problem-solving skills:
F   a. tend to improve steadily across the life-span
            b. decline rapidly during middle age
        *   c. frequently depend on the meaningfulness of the problem at hand
            d. decline more rapidly in women than in men

p. 231 89. One of the problems encountered while coaching subjects in the effective use of memory strategies was the lack of transfer; that is, subjects seldom used the strategies in "new" situations. What appears to be the BEST solution to this lack of transfer?
C
            a. teach a wider variety of strategies
        *   b. teach subjects how to plan and control their use of strategies
            c. give the subjects more training in each of the major strategies
            d. no solution has been found to correct this problem

p. 230 90. The method of loci involves:
F   a. learning to focus on one thing
            b. making lists to help memory
            c. teaching local memory control
        *   d. devising a mental map of a route through a familiar place

p. 206 91. You turn on the can opener to open the dog's food and the dog comes running into the
C   room. In this example, food is the _____; the sound of the can opener is the
SG   _____; and running into the room in response to the sound is the _____.
            a. unconditioned stimulus; conditioned stimulus; unconditioned response
            b. conditioned stimulus; unconditioned stimulus; conditioned response
        *   c. unconditioned stimulus; conditioned stimulus; conditioned response
            d. conditioned stimulus; conditioned response; unconditioned response

p. 207 92. A stimulus can serve as reinforcement or as punishment depending on whether it
C
        a. is pleasurable or not (negative) for the subject receiving it
SG   *   b. increases or decreases the frequency of the behavior it follows
        c. occurs before or after the behavior in question
        d. is administered or taken away from the person

p. 207 93. Which of the following is an example of negative reinforcement?
C
        a. Giving a child dessert as a reward for eating his/her vegetables at dinner
SG
        b. Paying a child for each "A" received on his or her report card
    *   c. A parent stops nagging a child when the child finally cleans his or her room
        d. Cutting a child's television viewing by 30 minutes each time the child misbehaves

p. 210 94. Which of the following is <u>necessary</u> in order to learn through observation?
C
        a. Observing the model get a reward or punishment for his/her actions
SG
        b. Being provided with an opportunity to imitate the model's actions immediately after the observation
        c. Hearing the model describe the consequences of his/her actions
    *   d. Observing and remembering the model's actions

p. 208 95. Partial reinforcement
F
        a. is the best way to initially tech a child an unfamiliar behavior
SG   *   b. is a good way to maintain behaviors over a long period of time
        c. allows a child to accurately predict when a behavior will be reinforced
        d. leads to extinction of most responses

p. 208 96. In order to effectively use punishment as a deterrent to bad behavior a parent should
C
        a. delay punishment until both parents can address the behavior together with the child
SG
        b. speak quietly so the child does not feel intimidated
    *   c. explain the inappropriateness of the behavior and the reasons for punishment
        d. punish the behavior when it is extreme but not necessarily punish when the behavior is mild or moderate

p. 211 97. Which of the following is NOT true regarding infants' abilities to learn?
F
        a. Infants need many trials in order to learn simple behaviors.
SG
        b. Infants can be conditioned as long as the responses are already familiar to them.
        c. Even newborns can be conditioned.
    *   d. The easiest way for young infants to learn is through observation.

p. 211 98. Research on imitation suggests that
C   *   a. young infants can show imitation but this may be a reflex-like action
SG
        b. infants of all ages reliably show imitation
        c. young infants reliably imitate novel acts but older infants have lost this ability
        d. imitation is not evident at all until about 8-12 months of age

p. 214 99. Taking an essay exam is an example of _____, while taking a multiple choice
C   exam uses _____ memory.
SG   a. long term memory; short term
             b. recall; reconstruction
       *   c. recall; recognition
             d. recognition; long term memory

p. 215 100. Habituation occurs when an infant
F   *   a. stops responding to a repeatedly presented stimulus
SG   b. is conditioned to respond to a familiar stimulus
              c. learns to respond to a desired stimulus
              d. turns in the direction of a novel stimulus

p. 218 101. Strategies tend to develop in order, with _____ appearing first, followed by
F   _____, and then _____.
SG   a. organization; elaboration; rehearsal
              b. organization; rehearsal; elaboration
              c. rehearsal; elaboration; organization
       *   d. rehearsal; organization; elaboration

p. 221 102. Siegler's research on children's use of rules on the balance beam problem shows that
C   a. most children master the correct rule by age 8
SG   b. even the youngest children, age 3, use logical rules to solve the problem
              c. children master a single rule, applying it to all tasks, before moving on to another rule
       *   d. children progress from guessing to trying several rules to selection of correct rules

p. 222 103. One difference between the memory strategy use by preadolescents and use by adolescents
C   is that adolescents
SG   a. randomly select a strategy
              b. use fewer strategies to remember important information
              c. remember more irrelevant information than younger children
       *   d. are better able to distinguish the more relevant points from the irrelevant points

p. 225 104. Which of the following statements accurately describes memory performance of adults?
C   a. Memory systematically declines throughout adulthood.
SG   *   b. Memory declines may occur after age 60 and are typically slight.
              c. Memory does not change from adolescence through middle adulthood, but after this,
                  memory declines quite rapidly.
              d. Older adults experience no memory declines because they use more memory strategies
                  than younger adults.

p. 223 105. Research on expertise shows that
C   a. experts do not know any more than nonexperts but are able to organize their knowledge
SG   more effectively
       *   b. it depends on domain-specific knowledge and strategies
              c. experts spend more time thinking through all possible options on a problem before
                  selecting the correct one
              d. expertise generalizes from one area to another, so experts tend to be good on all tasks

p. 206 106. The classic study with "little Albert" demonstrated that emotional responses could be conditioned.
     * a. true
        b. false

p. 206 107. A neutral stimulus comes to elicit a conditioned response after being paired with an unconditioned stimulus.
     * a. true
        b. false

p. 207 108. While classical conditioning involves automatic responses, operant conditioning focuses more on emotional responses.
        a. true
     * b. false

p. 207 109. Negative reinforcement refers to applying something unpleasant after an unwanted
www   behavior occurs.
        a. true
     * b. false

p. 208 110. The best way to sustain a learned response is to reinforce it every single time it occurs.
        a. true
     * b. false

p. 209 111. In order to be effective, punishment should be swift and consistent.
     * a. true
        b. false

p. 210 112. Bandura's classic research with the "Bobo" doll demonstrated that children could learn a behavior without receiving reinforcement.
     * a. true
        b. false

p. 211 113. Research shows that newborns can be operantly conditioned.
www * a. true
        b. false

p. 213 114. Short-term memory can hold an unlimited amount of information.
        a. true
     * b. false

p. 214 115. Executive control processes are responsible for moving information around the memory stores.
     * a. true
        b. false

p. 215 116. Infants demonstrate memory when they habituate to a stimulus that is repeatedly presented.
*   a. true
       b. false

p. 217 117. Older children have better learning and memory abilities because they have larger storage capacity to hold information.
       a. true
*   b. false

p. 218 118. The memory strategy of rehearsal usually develops first, followed by organization and elaboration.
*   a. true
       b. false

p. 221 119. Children are unable to formulate logical plans for solving problems until about ten years of age.
       a. true
*   b. false

p. 224 120. Older adults perform worse than younger adults on all types of learning and memory tasks.
       a. true
*   b. false

p. 225 121. Older adults perform better on implicit memory tasks than explicit ones.
*   a. true
       b. false

p. 227 122. A contextual explanation of learning and memory suggests that older adults perform worse because of a combination of personal and task factors.
*   a. true
       b. false

ESSAY QUESTIONS

123.   What is the difference between positive reinforcement, negative reinforcement, positive punishment, and negative punishment? Provide an example of each.

124.   Why are the problem solving abilities and memories of a 10-12 year old better than the abilities of a 4-5 year old?

125.   What are three reasons why old people tend to have poorer memory skills?
www

126.   What is the role of executive control processes in the information processing model?

127.   To what extent are infants able to learn from their experiences? Provide evidence of different types of learning in infants.

128.   Use several different learning principles to describe ways you might reduce a child's
SG   temper tantrums.
       [Sample answer is provided in the Study Guide.]

129.   How could you use learning principles to change a child's television viewing habits?
SG

130.   What practical suggestions regarding the memory and problem solving skills of older
SG   adults would be helpful to someone who works with older adults?

131.   In what ways are the memory, learning, and problem solving skills of young children and
SG   older adults similar?

132.   As children's eyewitness testimony in court proceedings has increased, we have seen
SG   more research on children's reliability as witnesses. Based on what you know about memory
       development from this chapter, what conclusions and suggestions can you make regarding use of
       children as witnesses?

INTELLIGENCE AND CREATIVITY

MULTIPLE-CHOICE QUESTIONS

p. 236   1.   According to the psychometric approach to intelligence, intelligence:
F
- a. aids in adaptation to the environment
- *   b. is made up of traits that vary and can be measured
- c. is fixed at conception by genetic factors
- d. is organized by stages or levels

p. 236   2.   The statistical procedure of factor analysis is used to:
C
- a. determine the extent to which intelligence is genetically influenced
- b. establish a person's range of potential intelligence scores
- *   c. determine whether intelligence is made up of one or many abilities
- d. eliminate questions from intelligence tests that do not assess abstract reasoning

p. 237   3.   Guilford's structure-of-intellect model of intelligence suggests that intelligence is
F   composed of ___ distinct mental abilities.
- a. 2
- b. 7
- *   c. 180
- d. an unlimited number

p. 238   4.   The ability to solve a variety of tasks using untaught skills is:
F   *
- a. fluid intelligence
- b. crystallized intelligence
- c. primary intelligence
- d. triarchic intelligence

p. 238   5.   Using previously learned information to act intelligently is:
F
- a. fluid intelligence
- *   b. crystallized intelligence
- c. primary intelligence
- d. triarchic intelligence

p. 238   6.   Fluid intelligence refers to one's ability to:
F
- a. recognize words (verbal fluency)
www   *
- *   b. solve novel problems
- c. engage in inductive reasoning
- d. see spatial relationships

p. 238   7.   Cattell and Horn's view of crystallized intelligence was that this dimension of intelligence
C   includes all of the following abilities EXCEPT:
              a. numerical abilities (arithmetic skills)
              b. word comprehension
        *   c. solving novel problems
              d. ability to recall general information

p. 238   8.   According to Howard Gardner, intelligence consists of at least seven distinct abilities.
F   Which of the following is NOT among Gardner's forms of intelligence?
              a. musical
              b. spatial
              c. linguistic
        *   d. creative

p. 239   9.   People with savant syndrome illustrate that intelligence
C   a. is a single unified ability
              b. is consistent with Spearman's notion of a general mental ability
              c. fluctuates across time in individuals
        *   d. consists of multiple and distinct abilities

p. 239   10. Which of the following is NOT a component of Sternberg's triarchic theory of
F   intelligence?
              a. Intelligence depends on the context in which it occurs.
              b. What is considered an intelligent response will vary with task familiarity.
        *   c. Intelligent responses depend on cognitive style.
              d. There are variations in the information processing components used to solve a task,
                  which can lead to more or less intelligent responses.

p. 239   11. With regard to experience, Sternberg believes that:
C   a. intelligent responses to tasks can be accurately assessed only after extensive experience
www   with the tasks
              b. experience with a tasks has no impact on ability to intelligently respond to the task
              c. there is no way to assess familiarity with a task
        *   d. intelligence can be measured by a person's responses on novel tasks

p. 239   12. Sternberg's triarchic theory of intelligence emphasizes all of the following factors
F   EXCEPT:
        *   a. heredity
              b. information-processing components
              c. role of experience
              d. sociocultural context

p. 240   13. _____ refers to an efficiency of information processing that appears with practice.
F   a. experience
        *   b. automatization
              c. factor analysis
              d. giftedness

p. 240 14. The first intelligence tests (circa 1900) were designed to:
C
    a. measure the intelligence quotient (IQ) of adults
    b. identify gifted children
    c. predict which high school students would be successful in college
*   d. determine which school children were likely to be slow learners

p. 240 15. The IQ test developed by Binet and Simon (1904) was composed of tasks that were:
F
    a. believed necessary for success in adapting to one's environment
    b. found to be too difficult, even for educated adults
    c. primarily analytical
*   d. believed necessary for success in the classroom

p. 240 16. The concept of mental age (MA):
C
    a. was originally used by itself to indicate a person's level of intelligence
*   b. has been replaced by test norms reflecting how an individual performs relative to others the same age
    c. is still used today to calculate a person's intelligence quotient (IQ)
    d. is used to calculate IQ for as long as MA keeps increasing with chronological age (CA)

p. 241 17. The original IQ formula (MA/CA x 100) would be LEAST appropriate to use with:
C
    a. kindergarten children
    b. elementary school children
    c. high school students
*   d. college students

p. 241 18. Suppose an 8-year-old child is found to have a mental age of ten. According to the Stanford-Binet Scale, this child has an IQ (intelligence quotient) of about:
F
    a. 80
    b. 100
    c. 110
*   d. 125

p. 241 19. What is meant by the term "test norms?"
C
    a. a set of procedures for properly administering a test
    b. information specifying the number and types of items found on a test
    c. a statement indicating the purpose of the test along with information on appropriate and inappropriate use of test results
*   d. a table of test scores which indicates the average score and how to interpret the range of scores around that average score

p. 241 20. The Wechsler verbal IQ score is based on performance on all of the following EXCEPT:
F
    a. arithmetic reasoning
    b. general knowledge
*   c. solving mazes
    d. vocabulary

p. 241   21.   A person's IQ as measured on one of the Wechsler tests:
C   *   a.   is a combination of a verbal IQ score and a performance IQ score
               b.   is primarily a measure of one's mathematical ability
               c.   is a good measure of ability to adapt to one's environment
               d.   would not change as the person grows older

p. 241   22.   The Wechsler intelligence tests differ from the Stanford-Binet tests because they (the
C   Wechsler tests):
               a.   are administered in groups rather than individually
               b.   emphasize verbal abilities
       *   c.   have separate scores for verbal and performance abilities
               d.   are administered only to children

p. 241   23.   To say that test scores are normally distributed around the average score means that:
C   *   a.   most people score in the average range and few people score very high or very low
www   b.   there are equal numbers of low, average, and high scores
               c.   scores obtained on repeated testings are fairly consistent
               d.   the test is a good measure of the trait that it is supposed to be measuring

p. 241   24.   The dynamic assessment approach:
C   a.   is intended to assess infant intelligence
www   b.   is used to assess children who fall outside the normal range of intelligence
       *   c.   is used to assess a person's ability to learn new material
               d.   has been found to be the best measure of school performance

p. 241   25.   Concerning intelligence and its measurement, many psychologists
C   *   a.   criticize both the definition, and the tests used to measure it
               b.   accept the definition of intelligence but criticize the IQ tests
               c.   criticize the definition but accept the tests used to measure it
               d.   accept both the definition of intelligence and the tests used to measure it

p. 243   26.   Which statement about the Bayley Scales of Infant Development is FALSE?
C   a.   They are useful in diagnosing mental retardation.
               b.   They are designed for infants ages 2 to 30 months.
       *   c.   They are useful in predicting success in school.
               d.   They are useful in charting infants' developmental progress.

p. 243   27.   The Bayley Scales of Infant Development measure:
C   a.   an infant's ability to solve problems
               b.   likelihood of success in school
               c.   mental retardation, learning problems, and giftedness
       *   d.   the rate at which infants achieve developmental milestones

p. 243   28.   Bayley DQ scores:
C   a.   include non-verbal, performance items in addition to the verbal items
       *   b.   are useful for monitoring developmental progress
               c.   can accurately predict intelligence during childhood, but not during adulthood
               d.   can accurately predict later intelligence at any point of the lifespan

p. 243 29. Which statement regarding infants' development is TRUE?

C
               a. Infant development scales do an excellent job of predicting children's later IQ.
*   b. Infants who score very low on developmental tests often turn out to be mentally retarded.
               c. Infants who score very high on developmental tests often turn out to be mathematically gifted.
               d. Infants who get bored easily tend to have low IQs.

p. 243 30. If you want to predict later intelligence using some infant measure, which of the following
C   measures would be best to use with the infants?
www
               a. Bayley DQ scores
               b. Stanford-Binet IQ scores
               c. Wechsler performance scores
*   d. speed of habituation scores

p. 243 31. An intelligent infant can be characterized as one who:
C
               a. prefers familiar information over novel information
               b. achieves developmental milestones more quickly than other infants
*   c. gets bored quickly with familiar information and seeks out novel information
               d. slowly habituates to stimuli

p. 243 32. Which measure during infancy would be most useful in predicting a child's later IQ?
C
               a. scores on the Wechsler performance scale
               b. Bayley DQ scores
*   c. measures of attention such as speed of habituation
               d. measures of motor skills such as rate of achieving motor milestones

p. 244 33. Stability of IQ scores is:
C
www *   a. high during early childhood and then declines
               b. fairly high starting at around age four
               c. higher with longer times between testings
               d. high for individual children but low for large groups of children

p. 244 34. Between the ages of 6 and 18, individual IQ scores:
F
               a. remain constant after age six
               b. remain constant after age twelve
               c. always increase steadily
*   d. show sizable ups and downs

p. 244 35. Some children show gains in IQ during their school years. Which factor appears to be the
F   PRIMARY cause of such gains?
               a. strict child rearing practices
               b. relaxed child rearing practices
*   c. parents who foster achievement
               d. effective schools

p. 244 36. Some children show a lowering of their IQs during their school years. Which factor seems
F to be the MOST common cause of this decline?
    a. accidental injury to the brain
  * b. living in poverty (impoverished environment)
    c. chronic illness
    d. ineffective schools

p. 244 37. The cumulative-deficit hypothesis is often used to explain:
C   a. how deficits in school funding create ineffective schools
    b. how people with lower IQs have more children, thus lowering the average IQ in a
       society
    c. how the cumulative effects of a superior education create a feeling of never being
       satisfied
  * d. how the negative effects of an impoverished environment "snowball" over time to
       create lowered IQs

p. 244 38. Children from impoverished environments may show progressively lower IQ scores over
F time, a phenomenon called:
    a. terminal drop
    b. culture bias
  * c. cumulative-deficit hypothesis
    d. cultural-familial hypothesis

p. 245 39. IQ scores are BEST at predicting:
C   a. whether a person will graduate from college
  * b. a person's high school grades
    c. a person's choice of occupation
    d. how well a person performs in his/her chosen occupation

p. 245 40. IQ scores do NOT do a very good job at predicting:
C   a. high school grades
    b. college grades
  * c. choice of occupation
    d. scores on subsequent IQ tests

p. 245 41. To what extent does a person's IQ predict his/her degree of occupational success
F (productivity)?
    a. not at all (r = .00)
    b. only very weakly (r = .15)
  * c. fairly well (r = .50)
    d. extremely well (r = .90)

p. 246 42. Schaie's sequential study of stability of intellectual abilities showed that:
F * a. both cohort and age affect intellectual performance
    b. cohort, but not age, affects intellectual performance
    c. age, but not cohort, affects intellectual performance
    d. neither cohort or age affects intellectual performance

p. 248 43. Which of the following accurately describes how intellectual abilities change with age?
C
www   a. Longitudinal studies show that intellectual abilities decline gradually across the lifespan.
     b. Intellectual abilities peak while one is still in school.
     c. Intellectual abilities increase across the entire lifespan.
  *   d. There are modest gains in intellectual abilities until about age 60 when they level off before starting to decline at about age 70.

p. 247 44. Research on changes in intellectual abilities during adulthood indicates that:
C
     a. fluid and crystallized intelligence decline at the same rate
  *   b. fluid intelligence declines earlier and more quickly than crystallized intelligence
     c. crystallized intelligence declines earlier and more quickly than fluid intelligence
     d. crystallized and fluid intelligence fluctuate up and down throughout the entire lifespan

p. 247 45. Which type of test is MOST apt to put an older adult at a disadvantage?
C
     a. test of general knowledge
  *   b. "speeded" (timed) test
     c. vocabulary test
     d. test on arithmetic operations

p. 247 46. Which of these mental abilities tends to decline FIRST (and most) in older adults?
F
     a. numerical ability (arithmetic problems)
     b. verbal meaning (vocabulary)
  *   c. reasoning (applied to novel problems)
     d. spatial ability (imagining how an object would look if rotated in space)

p. 247 47. Which of the following can we conclude about intellectual functioning across the lifespan?
C
     a. Preference for familiar items and tasks is associated with higher levels of intellectual performance.
     b. Intellectual functioning is not affected by practice or familiarity.
  *   c. The speed with which someone processes information is related to intellectual performance.
     d. The speed with which someone processes information is important only in later adulthood.

p. 248 48. What is most likely to lead to declines in intellectual performance of older adults?
F   *   a. poor health
     b. being female
     c. being wealthy
     d. participation in too many activities

p. 248 49. "Terminal drop" is the name given to:
F
     a. a low score on an IQ test brought about by the child not feeling well on the day of the test
  *   b. a rapid decline in the mental abilities of elderly people a few years prior to dying
     c. placing an underachieving child in a special education class
     d. a gifted student dropping out of high school and remaining underemployed during his/her adult life

p. 249 50. Research on wisdom suggests that:
C
        a. most older adults achieve a degree of wisdom
   *   b. only adults with expertise or experience display wisdom
        c. wisdom is closely related to measures of creativity
        d. wisdom is strongly correlated with age

p. 249 51. Research on wisdom shows that:
C
        a. it is fairly common among older adults
www *   b. expertise is more predictive of wisdom than age
        c. there is a strong positive correlation between IQ and wisdom
        d. it is more strongly associated with creativity than IQ

p. 250 52. Which of the following is the STRONGEST piece of evidence showing that genetic factors
C   influence intelligence (as measured by IQ tests)?
   *   a. Identical twins reared apart are more alike than fraternal twins reared together.
        b. Fraternal twins reared together are more alike than identical twins reared apart.
        c. Fraternal twins reared together are more alike than fraternal twins reared apart.
        d. Identical twins reared apart are more alike than identical twins reared together.

p. 250 53. Which is a better predictor of the IQ of a 4-year-old: His/her performance on an infant
F   intelligence test or the quality of his/her home environment?
        a. performance on the IQ test
   *   b. quality of home environment
        c. they predict equally well
        d. neither can be used as a predictor

p. 251 54. Which "home" factor seems to be most important for the intellectual development of a
F   child?
        a. having several older siblings
        b. having several younger siblings
        c. a permissive parenting style
   *   d. parental involvement with the child

p. 252 55. The BEST predictor of a child's IQ at age 2 is the:
F
        a. socioeconomic status of the family
www   b. income of the parents
        c. racial background of the family
   *   d. mother's IQ

p. 252 56. Which of the following is TRUE regarding early IQ?
F
        a. The effects of home environment on IQ can be explained by the mother's IQ.
        b. Early IQ is determined mainly be environmental factors.
        c. Quality of home environment is the best predictor of a 2-year-old's IQ.
   *   d. The best predictor of a 2-year-old's IQ is his/her mother's IQ.

p. 252 57. Which statement regarding child IQ scores and family socioeconomic class is FALSE?

C

    a. IQ scores of children from lower-class homes average 10 to 20 points below the IQ scores of children from middle-class homes.

    b. Babies of lower-class biological parents who are adopted by well-educated middle-class parents end up with above-average IQ scores in elementary school.

*   c. Improving the economic conditions of children's homes usually will not improve their IQs.

    d. Poor nutrition and disruptive family experiences are factors associated with lowered IQ scores.

P. 252 58. Scarr and Weinberg's research on social class and IQ showed that:

C   * a. children from disadvantaged homes could raise their IQs if adopted into middle-class homes with intelligent adoptive parents

    b. children from disadvantaged homes continue to show significant deficits in IQ even after being adopted into middle-class homes with intelligent adoptive parents

    c. children from poor economic conditions do not differ significantly in IQ from children from average or above average economic conditions

    d. improving the economic conditions of the home has no significant impact on children's IQs because IQ is so strongly affected by genes

p. 253 59. Which of the following statements is FALSE?

C   * a. Genetic differences between whites and blacks account for the group differences in IQ scores.

    b. IQ tests seem to predict future school achievement as well for blacks and other minorities as they do for whites.

    c. Black children in more advantaged homes score higher on IQ tests that black children in disadvantaged homes.

    d. Disadvantaged children tend to do better on IQ tests when given a chance to become familiar with the examiner.

p. 253 60. On average, black students score 12-15 points lower than white students on IQ tests due to all of the following EXCEPT:

C

    a. the tests are more representative of white culture

*   b. genetic differences between blacks and whites

    c. black children more often grow up in unstimulating environments

    d. children from minority backgrounds are less comfortable with the testing situation

p. 253 61. Which statement is FALSE?

C

    a. IQ tests seem to predict future school achievement as well for blacks and other minorities as they do for whites.

*   b. Translating existing IQ tests into the Black English dialect results in a large increase in the average IQ score for black students.

    c. When a friendly examiner "warms" children up prior to an IQ test, they tend to have significantly higher IQ scores.

    d. Black children adopted into middle-class homes subsequently score higher on IQ tests than black children in disadvantaged homes.

p. 253 62. A culture fair test is BEST defined as one that:
F
    a. completely eliminates cultural bias from testing
    b. can be administered to children from more than one culture
   * c. includes questions that are equally familiar or unfamiliar to children from all cultures
    d. includes questions about all cultures

p. 255 63. Mental retardation is defined as
F * a. significantly below average IQ and deficits in adaptive behavior
    b. significantly below average IQ alone
    c. problems in everyday functioning beginning during childhood
    d. significant impairments in basic academic skills

p. 255 64. Individuals diagnosed with mild mental retardation:
F
    a. are likely to show significant delays in all areas of development
www
    b. are likely to need constant supervision in order to work
    c. are unable to live or work independently
   * d. are often able to live and work independently

p. 255 65. Mildly retarded individuals tend to adjust to:
C
    a. school demands better than they do to the demands of adult life
   * b. demands of adult life better than they do to the demands of school
    c. school demands and demands of adult live, equally well
    d. only the demands of institutional settings

p. 255 66. Individuals diagnosed with severe mental retardation:
F
    a. can learn most academic and social skills in school
    b. are usually able to work and live independently
    c show delays in all areas of development and typically have trouble with even the most basic self-help skills
   * d. can usually learn self-care and communication skills but not academic skills

p. 255 67. Organic retardation is the term given to retardation caused by:
F * a. heredity, disease, or injury
    b. lack of schooling
    c. lack of intellectual stimulation
    d. poor nutrition

p. 255 68. Which is the MOST common form of mental retardation?
F * a. cultural/familial retardation
    b. organic retardation
    c. retardation caused by disease or injury
    d. Down syndrome

p. 255 69. Examples of causes of organic mental retardation include all of the following EXCEPT:
F
    a. Down syndrome
    b. Fetal alcohol syndrome
   * c. impoverished environment
    d. prenatal exposure to rubella

p. 256 70. Follow-up studies of individuals who are mentally retarded show that they:

C
    a. usually fare no worse in the long run than nonretarded people
    b. usually end up being unemployed and dependent on others
    c. are more successful than high school dropouts with normal IQs
*   d. are usually employed in semi-skilled or unskilled jobs

p. 256 71. Today's MOST common standard for identifying a gifted child is that she must have an:

F
    a. IQ of at least 140
    b. IQ of at least 160
*   c. IQ of at least 140 or special abilities
    d. IQ of at least 140 and special abilities

p. 256 72. Gifted children can be identified at an early age by their

C   *
*   a. advanced language skills
    b. good social interaction skills
    c. high level of motor activity
    d. personality traits

p. 257 73. Which set of characteristics BEST describes a typical high-IQ child?

F
www
    a. physically frail; emotionally immature
    b. physically frail; emotionally mature
    c. better-than-average health; emotionally immature
*   d. better-than-average health; emotionally mature

p. 258 74. As compared to the general population, when gifted children become adults they tend to:

F
    a. have more health problems
*   b. be more satisfied with their marriages
    c. have more emotional problems
    d. enter careers and achieve at the same rate as those who were not labeled as gifted

p. 258 75. As adults, gifted women in Terman's longitudinal study:

F
    a. achieved more in science than gifted men
*   b. tended to focus on family and community service
    c. worked in professional careers to the same extent as gifted men
    d. showed more mental illness

p. 258 76. Which of the following accurately summarizes Terman's findings regarding gifted

F   children?
    a. Gifted children are often emotionally immature and experience more frequent physical problems.
    b. Gifted children are not as well adjusted as their age mates.
*   c. Gifted children are well adjusted and emotionally mature.
    d. Gifted children are well adjusted but physically frail.

p. 258 77. Creativity is usually defined as:

F
    a. high intelligence
    b. the ability to come up with the most bizarre answer to a problem
*   c. the ability to produce novel responses that are valued by others
    d. the ability to adapt to a variety of situations

p. 258 78. Standard intelligence tests measure:
F   *   a. convergent thinking
           b. divergent thinking
           c. everyday problem-solving skills
           d. wisdom

p. 258 79. Ideational fluency refers to one's ability to:
C   a. pick the most appropriate idea to solve a problem
           b. quickly recall synonyms when given a word
           c. solve a problem quickly and accurately
      *   d. generate many interesting, novel ideas

p. 258 80. Which of the following accurately characterizes the relationship between intelligence and
C   creativity?
           a. Differences in both intelligence and creativity are related to differences in genetic factors.
           b. Scores on the two tests show a moderate positive correlation.
           c. Increases in IQ typically lead to increases in creativity.
      *   d. For the most part, creativity scores are independent from IQ scores.

p. 258 81. Which of the following statements is TRUE?
C   a. Creativity is relatively easy to define.
      *   b. Highly creative people rarely have below average IQs.
           c. Among people of high IQs, a person's level of creativity can be predicted by knowing the person's IQ score.
           d. Convergent thinkers tend to be creative.

p. 259 82. Which of the following is TRUE of creative children?
F   *   a. They engage in more fantasy or pretend play than other children.
www   b. They engage in less fantasy or pretend play than other children.
           c. They are less popular with peers because of their unconventional ideas.
           d. They are more successful and receive more approval from teachers.

p. 259 83. Characteristics of the home environment that seem to foster creativity in children include
C   all of the following EXCEPT:
           a. parents who encourage curiosity in their children
           b. parents who give their children opportunities to independently explore new possibilities
      *   c. parents who are particularly warm and close their children
           d. parents who value nonconformity

p. 259 84. Which of the following statements regarding creativity is false?
C   *   a. Overall, creativity seems to decrease over the childhood and adolescent years.
           b. There are no consistent differences between children of different races and social classes in their scores on creativity tests.
           c. Parents of creative children give their children a good deal of freedom.
           d. Parents of creative children tend to accept their children as they are.

p. 259 85. Research on age-related changes in creativity suggests that:

C
         a. creativity tends to steadily increase across the lifespan

   *   b. creativity dips during periods of the life span when pressure to conform is high

         c. creativity peaks in elementary school and then slowly declines

         d   creativity increases throughout childhood and adolescence and remains steady throughout adulthood

p. 260 86. Creativity during adulthood:

F
         a. is independent of field of study or work

         b. is highest during early adulthood

   *   c. increases until around 40 years of age and then gradually declines

         d. increases until around 60 years of age and then gradually declines

p. 262 87. Which is TRUE of children who participate in early intervention programs such as Project

F
      Head Start?

         a. These children are just as likely to drop out of high school as are children in the control group.

         b. These children show no immediate gain in scores on IQ tests.

   *   c. These children tend to score higher on tests of reading, language, and mathematics achievement.

         d. At age 20 these children appear to be no different than non-participants.

p. 262 88. Which of the following is TRUE of early intervention programs for preschool children?

C
         a. The programs affect grades but have no impact on attitudes about achievement and

www
            education.

         b. The programs lead to long-term improvements on IQ tests but no significant short-term improvements.

   *   c. The programs lead to short-term improvements on IQ tests but no significant long-term improvements.

         d. The programs lead to short-term and long-term improvements on IQ and achievement tests but have no effect on social-emotional measures.

p. 264 89. Training studies with older adults show that:

C
         a. IQ can be improved for some adults but only with extensive training that would be impractical to provide in most cases.

   *   b. IQ can be improved with training for older adults who have already experienced some declines in abilities.

         c. IQ can be slightly improved with training, but the effects disappear as soon as the training ends.

         d. IQ cannot be improved once it begins to decline.

p. 238 90. Which of the following is an example of crystallized intelligence?

C
         a. remembering unrelated word pairs (e.g., dog-couch)

SG
         b. solving verbal analogies

         c. realizing the relationship between geometric figures

   *   d. solving word comprehension problems (e.g, what does "participate" mean?)

p. 239 91. The _____ emphasizes the importance of context, experience and information-
C   processing components in defining intelligent behavior.
SG   * a. triarchic theory of intelligence
          b. psychometric approach to intelligence
          c. factor analysis approach
          d. structure-of-intellect model

p. 239 92. Sternberg's contextual component of intelligence suggests that intelligence
C   * a. depends on expectations of particular cultures
SG   b. is consistent across different contexts
          c. varies with the amount of experience a person has
          d. consists of general and specific mental abilities

p. 241 93. If someone achieves a score of 100 on the Stanford-Binet intelligence test, it means that
C   this person
SG   a. scored higher than approximately 68% of the population
          b. is somewhat below average in intelligence
       * c. has the same chronological (CA) and mental age (MA) levels
          d. could answer all the questions appropriate for 10-year-olds

p. 243 94. The Bayley Scale of Infant Development is a useful indicator of
C   a. childhood intelligence
SG   b. whether or not the child is gifted
       * c. a child's developmental progress through major milestones
          d. problem solving abilities that the child possesses

p. 241 95. Feuerstein's Learning Potential Assessment Device measures
F   a. what children have learned
SG   b. infant intelligence
          c. children's abilities to learn by observing an adult solve the task
       * d. children's potential to learn new things with minimal guidance

p. 244 96. Correlations between scores on infant intelligence tests and scores on later intelligence
C   tests show
SG   a. that infants who score high typically score high as children and adolescents
          b. that infant intelligence scores can predict later intelligence for those who score around
              the mean of 100
       * c. little relationship between infant intelligence and later intelligence
          d. that infant intelligence scores can predict childhood intelligence but not adult
              intelligence

p. 244 97. Correlations of IQ measured during early and middle childhood with IQ measured during
C   adolescence and young adulthood indicate that for individuals, IQ scores
SG   a. are quite stable
       * b. can fluctuate quite a bit
          c. generally increase with age
          d. generally decrease with age

p. 244 98. The cumulative-deficit hypothesis suggests that
C
SG   a. lack of intellectual stimulation produces an overall deficit in intelligence that is stable over time
   * b. lack of intellectual stimulation depresses intellectual growth more and more over time
    c. lack of intellectual stimulation early in life is less damaging than lack of intellectual stimulation later in life
    d. parents with low IQ scores will have children with low IQ scores

p. 245 99. The relationship between IQ and occupational status indicates that
C   a. IQ scores are more likely to predict job preference than job performance
SG   b. people with high IQ scores do not work in low status occupations
   * c. people with high IQ scores are more likely to work in high status occupations than people with low IQ scores
    d. there is no relationship between these two factors

p. 247 100. Which of the following describes how intellectual abilities change with age?
C   a. Overall, intellectual abilities decline significantly with age.
SG   b. Crystallized intelligence declines with age more than fluid intelligence.
   * c. Fluid intelligence declines with age more than crystallized intelligence.
    d. No decline in intelligence occurs with age.

p. 248 101. Declines in intellectual performance among older adults may occur because of all of the
C   following EXCEPT:
SG   a. unstimulating life styles
    b. slower response times
    c. poor health
   * d. lack of sufficient knowledge base

p. 253 102. Research on ethnic and racial differences in IQ scores shows that differences
C   a. do not really exist
SG   b. result from genetic differences between racial groups
   * c. can be reduced with the appropriate environmental intervention
    d. do exist but cannot be reduced or eliminated

p. 255 103. Mental retardation is defined by:
F   * a. deficits in intelligence and difficulties with adaptive behavior, both evidenced during
SG   the developmental period
    b. abnormal brain development
    c. inability to function at grade-level in school
    d. low scores on standardized intelligence tests that become increasingly poor over time

p. 261 104. With respect to creativity in adulthood,
C   a. creative endeavors decrease throughout adulthood
SG * b. creative endeavors increase in young adulthood and then usually peak and remain steady in middle adulthood
    c. creative endeavors are at their peak during college years and early adulthood
    d. creative endeavors decline significantly for older adults in all fields

p. 238   105. Crystallized intelligence is the ability to use one's mind actively to solve novel problems.
                   a.   true
         *   b.   false

p. 239   106. According to Sternberg, intelligent people are able to adapt to their environment.
         *   a.   true
                   b.   false

p. 240   107. According to Sternberg, in order to know how intelligently someone performs a task, you
www   must know how familiar the person is with the task.
         *   a.   true
                   b.   false

p. 240   108. The Stanford-Binet intelligence test yields both a performance and a verbal IQ score.
                   a.   true
         *   b.   false

p. 241   109. The dynamic assessment approach is interested primarily in what a person has learned.
                   a.   true
         *   b.   false

p. 243   110. The Bayley DQ score does a good job of predicting later school grades.
                   a.   true
         *   b.   false

p. 243   111. A good infant measure of later IQ is a test that assesses attention.
         *   a.   true
                   b.   false

p. 244   112. Children whose IQ scores fluctuate tend to come from unstable home environments.
         *   a.   true
                   b.   false

p. 245   113. Most people with high IQs work in high-prestige occupations.
                   a.   true
         *   b.   false

p. 246   114. For many adults, declines in mental abilities occur sometime during their 60s or 70s.
         *   a.   true
                   b.   false

p. 246   115. Older adults usually experience a decline in their crystallized intelligence before a decline
                   in their fluid intelligence.
                   a. true
         *   b. false

p. 248 116. Elderly people who retain their physical and mental health throughout old age usually maintain their intellectual skills as well.
  *   a. true
       b. false

p. 249 117. Very few older adults develop wisdom.
www *   a. true
       b. false

p. 250 118. Children who live in stimulating homes are likely to have higher IQs than children in unstimulating homes.
  *   a. true
       b. false

p. 253 119. Research indicates that there are genetic differences that account for the differences between racial groups on intelligence tests.
       a. true
  *   b. false

p. 255 120. Cultural-familial mental retardation typically leads to mild mental retardation.
  *   a. true
       b. false

p. 257 121. Gifted children tend not to be as well adjusted as "average" children.
  *   a. true
       b. false

ESSAY QUESTIONS

122. What do scores on IQ tests seem to predict (during childhood as well as adulthood)?

123. To what extent are IQ scores stable over time? What factors influence whether IQ scores stay
www the same or change?

124. How would you go about optimizing intelligence across the life span?

125. What evidence demonstrates that intelligence is influenced by genetic factors? What evidence demonstrates that intelligence is influenced by environmental factors? Which source seems to have greater influence? Justify your response.

126. In order to make the most accurate prediction about later IQ based on infant measures,
SG   what information or test would you want to have access to? Justify your answer.
     [Sample answer is provided in the Study Guide.]

127. Discuss evidence that supports the conclusion that IQ scores are influenced by genetic
SG   factors. Discuss evidence that supports the conclusion that IQ scores are influenced by environmental factors.

128. It has been noted that there may be culture bias in intelligence testing, resulting in certain
SG groups of people scoring lower or higher than other groups of people. Another finding regarding
intelligence tests is that they are relatively accurate at predicting academic success and job
performance. What conclusions can be logically drawn from these two seemingly disparate
findings?

SELF-CONCEPTIONS AND PERSONALITY

MULTIPLE-CHOICE QUESTIONS

p. 268   1.   What is the primary distinction between "self-concept" and "self-esteem?"
C
           a.   One's self-concept is realistic, while self-esteem is idealistic.
www   b.   Self-concept is an accurate reflection of reality, while self-esteem is not.
      *   c.   Self-concept is cognitive in nature, while self-esteem is affective (or emotional) in nature.
           d.   One's self-concept is objective in nature, while self-esteem is subjective.

p. 268   2.   Self-concept is mostly _____ in nature while self-esteem is mostly _____ in
C   nature:
      *   a.   cognitive; emotional
           b.   objective; subjective
           c.   subjective; objective
           d.   cognitive; objective

p. 269   3.   Freud believed that personality:
C   a.   continues to develop across the life-span
           b.   is essentially formed during the infancy period
           c.   is largely unaffected by parenting practices
      *   d.   changes very little after the first five years of life

p. 269   4.   According to Erikson, individual differences in personality are:
C   a.   innate
           b.   determined by age 6
           c.   largely attributable to the id
      *   d.   a reflection of one's experiences in coping with life crises

p. 269   5.   In comparing the views of Freud and Erikson with regard to personality development, it is
F   MOST ACCURATE to say that Erikson placed MORE emphasis than Freud on _____
           and LESS emphasis than Freud on _____:
           a.   the impact of early experiences; the selfish side of human nature
      *   b.   the rational ego; the impact of early experiences
           c.   potential for growth and change; the rational ego
           d.   the impact of early experiences; sexual urges

p. 269   6.   Erikson believed that:
F   a.   a person's personality is primarily genetically determined
           b.   there are four stages in the development of personality
           c   while personality develops gradually over the first 15 to 20 years of life, people change very little throughout the years of adulthood
      *   d.   social and cultural factors have a strong influence on the development of personality

p. 269 7. The psychometric approach to personality has led researchers to believe that

F   * a. there are five basic dimensions of personality

          b. personality develops through a series of stages

          c. personality is formed from experiences during the first few years

          d. a series of life crises shape personality over the life span

p. 269 8. The psychometric approach to personality development assumes:

C   * a. personality traits remain stable across situations and times

          b. personality traits vary across situations and times

          c. the concept of traits is not useful in the study of personality

          d. paper and pencil tests are not a productive way to examine personality

p. 270 9. The big five personality dimensions include:

F   * a. neuroticism, extraversion, openness to experience, agreeableness, and conscientiousness

          b. curiosity, sociability, stability, discipline, and conscientiousness

          c. introversion, compliance, seriousness, aggressiveness, and conscientiousness

          d. integrity, extraversion, aggressiveness, trustworthiness, and competence

p. 270 10. The key characteristics of someone with the personality dimension of openness to experience would be:

F   * a. openness to fantasy, esthetics, and interest in variety

          b. anxiety, hostility, and emotional instability

          c. trust, altruism, and compliance

          d. competence, achievement striving, and self-discipline

p. 270 11. The key characteristics of someone with the personality dimension of agreeableness would be:

F   a. openness to fantasy, esthetics, and interest in variety

          b. anxiety, hostility, and emotional instability

      * c. trust, altruism, and compliance

          d. competence, achievement striving, and self-discipline

p. 270 12. The key characteristics of someone with the personality dimension of conscientiousness would be:

F

www   a. openness to fantasy, esthetics, and interest in variety

          b. anxiety, hostility, and emotional instability

          c. trust, altruism, and compliance

      * d. competence, achievement striving, and self-discipline

p. 270 13. The key characteristics of someone with the personality dimension of extraversion would be:

F   a. openness to fantasy, esthetics, and interest in variety

      * b. warm, excitement seeking, and sociable

          c. trust, altruism, and compliance

          d. competence, achievement striving, and self-discipline

p. 270 14. The key characteristics of someone with the personality dimension of neuroticism would
F   be:
             a. openness to fantasy, esthetics, and interest in variety
        *   b. anxiety, hostility, and emotional instability
             c. trust, altruism, and compliance
             d. competence, achievement striving, and self-discipline

p. 270 15. The social learning perspective assumes that:
C   a. there are universal stages in the development of personality
             b. one's personality is "set in stone" during infancy and early childhood
             c. personality traits emerge consistently in a wide variety of situations and across long
                 periods of time
        *   d. personality development depends on each person's social experiences

p. 270 16. Frieda believes that each individual follows a unique path toward the development of
C   personality, and that one's personality is constantly changing across the life-span. Her
             views are most similar to those of:
        *   a. Bandura
             b. Erikson
             c. Freud
             d. Costa and McCrae

p. 270 17. With regard to personality development, a contextual theorist is MOST LIKELY to believe
C   that:
             a. one's personality is "set in stone" during the first six years of life
             b. people have enduring tendencies called personality traits
             c. one's basic personality is determined by early social relationships
        *   d. the development of each individual's personality is unique, and dependent upon social
                 experiences

p. 270 18. Vicki was reserved as a baby, shy as a child, and shy as an adult. Social learning theorists
C   would say that Vicki
www   a. was genetically predisposed to be shy
        *   b. is a product of environments that consistently fostered the same personality trait
             c. was unable to resolve psychosocial crises in positive ways
             d. identified with her shy mother and adopted her traits

p. 270 19. Social learning theorists believe that
C   *   a. personality is situation specific
             b. there are universal stages of development
             c. there are five basic dimensions of personality
             d. personality is fairly consistent over time and situations

p. 270 20. Bill and Gloria wonder what their baby will be like when he grows up. He seems very
C   difficult to them as an infant, and they are concerned about the future. They ask their
       family doctor what she thinks. Their doctor takes a social learning perspective and
       answers:
       a. Since he's a difficult baby, he will be a difficult adult.
       b. By the time he's 5 or 6, you'll be able to predict what he'll be like as a grown-up.
       c. He probably inherited his temperament from you and it's not likely to change.
   *   d. He may very well change if you alter his environment and social experiences.

p. 270 21. With regard to personality development, what belief do Albert Bandura and Erik Erikson
C   share in common?
       a. There are universal, age-related changes in personality development.
       b. One's basic personality is determined by experiences during infancy
          and early childhood.
       c. People have enduring tendencies called personality traits.
   *   d. Personality continues to change and develop during adulthood.

p. 271 22. Which is one of the FIRST signs of the infant's emerging sense of self?
C   a. Crying when hungry.
       b. Enjoying games such as peek-a-boo and hide-and-seek.
       c. Expressing recognition of one's self-image in the mirror.
   *   d. The infant's incorporation of objects external to his/her own body into his/her actions.

p. 271 23. An infant's sense of self:
F   a. is established right from birth
       b. is well-established by 6 months (the stage of secondary circular reactions)
       c. is fully formed by age 1
   *   d. develops gradually over the first two years of life

p. 271 24. Which of the following suggests the infant's emerging awareness of self as separate from
C   the world around them?
       a. repeatedly kicking one's legs
   *   b. repeatedly throwing a spoon off the high-chair tray
       c. crying when hungry
       d. sucking on one's thumb

p. 271 25. Jimmy's mother paints his face like a clown for Halloween and holds him up to look at
C   himself in the mirror. Jimmy laughs, and rubs his hands all over his own cheeks making a
       mess of the paint job! Given his behavior, the YOUNGEST you should expect Jimmy to
       be is:
       a. 6 months
       b. 12 months
   *   c. 18 months
       d. 2 years

p. 271 26. Naomi looks into the mirror, sees her reflection, begins to vocalize, and reaches out to
C touch the baby in the mirror. From her behavior, we can infer that Naomi is MOST
www LIKELY:
    a. about 3 months old
  * b. less than 18 months old
    c. about 20 months old
    d. at least 2 years old

p. 271 27. Put in front of a mirror, infants will wipe at a spot of rouge on their nose by about age
C _____; it is fitting that they are also in Erikson's stage of:
    a. 8-12 months; autonomy vs. shame and doubt
  * b. 18-24 months; autonomy vs. shame and doubt
    c. 8-12 months; trust vs. mistrust
    d. 18-24 months; trust vs. mistrust

p. 271 28. Which of the following utterances clearly demonstrates the development of a categorical
C sense of self?
    a. "My car!"
  * b. "I big girl!"
    c. "Me pick up."
    d. "Daddy book."

p. 272 29. The "looking-glass self" refers to:
F   a. the sense of self we get from observing our own behavior
    b. a baby looking in the mirror and reaching out to touch the image s/he sees
  * c. perceptions of self based on social interactions
    d. looking into a mirror and realizing it is one's own image reflected there

p. 272 30. Which of the following accomplishments is NOT generally in place by the beginning of
F toddlerhood?
    a. recognition of self-image in the mirror
    b. knowledge of one's own names
    c. recognition of self as physically distinct from others
  * d. comparison of self to others

p. 272 31. Which of the following is NOT one of the three main components of temperament?
F   * a. identity
    b. emotionality
    c. activity
    d. sociability

p. 272 32. With regard to temperament, research indicates that:
F   a. most babies are alike during the first few months of life
  * b. babies can differ significantly from early on
    c. genetics is the sole determinant of temperament
    d. one's temperament in infancy bears no relation to one's temperament
       later on in life

p. 273　33.　Children who are behaviorally inhibited:
F
www
　　　　　　a.　have high levels of activity and regularity
　　　　　　b.　are low in emotionality and reactivity
　　　*　　c.　are high in emotionality and low in sociability
　　　　　　d.　are low in sociability and neuroticism

p. 273　34.　Baby Jake is moody, inactive, and hesitant about new situations. With regard to
F　　　　　temperament, he is best classified as:
　　　　　　a.　avoidant
　　　　　　b.　easy
　　　　　　c.　difficult
　　　*　　d.　slow-to-warm-up

p. 273　35.　Marissa cries and throws tantrums when she doesn't get her way. Moreover, she has
C　　　　　frequent digestive difficulties, and rarely sleeps through the night, even though she is two
　　　　　　years old. With regard to temperament, Marissa is BEST classified as:
　　　　　　a.　sensitive
　　　*　　b.　difficult
　　　　　　c.　slow-to-warm up
　　　　　　d.　avoidant

p. 273　36.　With regard to temperament, which statement is MOST ACCURATE?
C
www
　　　　　　a.　Easy babies usually always grow up to be easy-going adults.
　　　　　　b.　Difficult infants grow up to be maladjusted adults.
　　　　　　c.　Parents can have little effect on a child's temperament.
　　　*　　d.　A good person-environment fit can change a child's temperament.

p. 274　37.　Research on early temperament and later development suggests that:
C
　　　　　　a.　early temperament directly predicts adult temperament
　　　　　　b.　there is no systematic relationship between early temperament and adult personality
　　　*　　c.　the relationship between early temperament and later development is strongly
　　　　　　　　influenced by the nature and course of the parent-child relationship
　　　　　　d.　"easy" children MAY turn out to be maladjusted adults, but "difficult" children are
　　　　　　　　certain to do so

p. 275　38.　A significant change in self-descriptions that appears at about age 8 is a shift from:
F　　　*　　a.　physical characteristics to inner qualities.
　　　　　　b.　inner qualities to action statements.
　　　　　　c.　subjective to objective self-evaluations.
　　　　　　d.　action statements to physical characteristics.

p.273　39.　Goodness of fit refers to:
F　　　*　　a.　the extent to which the child's temperament is compatible with the social world to
　　　　　　　　which the child must adapt
　　　　　　b.　the compatibility of the child and his/her siblings
　　　　　　c.　whether or not the home provides all of the child's physical needs
　　　　　　d.　the extent to which a child develops an attachment to a caregiver

p. 275 40. As compared to preschoolers, grade-school children are:
C * a. more likely to notice how they differ from one another
      b. less likely to view themselves as part of a social unit
      c. less likely to understand how they are like others
      d. more likely to judge themselves unrealistically

p. 275 41. Research has indicated that children's self-perceptions of competence
F   a. are quite accurate even in the preschool years
    * b. become more accurate over the elementary school years
      c. are generally overinflated throughout the elementary school years
      d. are most often at odds with the perceptions of teachers and peers

p. 275 42. What change in cognitive development permits children to engage in social comparison,
C   where judgment of self is made in relation to others?
      a. development of the object permanence concept
    * b. a shift from preoperational to concrete-operational thought
      c. moving from concrete operations to formal operations
      d. the emergence of stranger anxiety

p. 275 43. Rachel and Ed invite some friends, the Bartleys, over for dinner. When they introduce the
C   Bartleys to their daughter, Louise, Mr. Bartley says "So tell me about yourself, Louise."
      Louise says: "I have a new doll, see?" Louise is MOST LIKELY:
      a. 2 years old
    * b. 4 to 6 years old
      c. at least 8 years old
      d. 10 years or older

p. 275 44. Joshua is 9 years old. When asked to describe his best friend, Lou, Joshua is MOST
C   LIKELY to say:
      a. "Lou is a boy and he's in third grade, and he's tall and has dark hair."
      b. "Lou has neat toys and that's why I like him."
    * c. "Lou is really neat and funny and he's a good friend, and we both play soccer, but I
         play better than him."
      d. "Lou lives around the corner, and I ride my bike over to play with him."

p. 275 45. According to the research on self-perceptions, which is FALSE?
C   a. Preschoolers generally think they are the greatest, regardless of evidence to the
         contrary.
      b. Children make important distinctions between their competency in one area as
         compared to another area.
      c. The accuracy of children's self-perceptions increases throughout the elementary school
         years.
    * d. As early as kindergarten, most children become very concerned with how they "stack
         up" in comparison to their peers.

p. 276　46.　School-age children tend to:
F
　　　　　　a.　see how they are like others, but not how they are different
www　*　　b.　understand ways in which they are both similar and different from others
　　　　　　c.　avoid comparing themselves to others
　　　　　　d.　assess others primarily in terms of physical characteristics and personal possessions

p. 276　47.　Which is FALSE?
F
　　　　　　a.　The accuracy of children's self-evaluations increases across the grade-school years.
　　*　　　b.　Preschool children tend to underestimate their skills and abilities.
　　　　　　c　Upper-elementary school children generally hold self-perceptions that match the evaluations of their teachers and peers.
　　　　　　d　Children tend to make distinctions between their ability in one domain as compared to another.

p. 277　48.　Children who are high in self-esteem have parents who:
F
　　　　　　a.　have few rules, and generally let children decide for themselves what is best
　　　　　　b.　make decisions for their children so they are not burdened with making choices
　　*　　　c.　allow children to participate in decision-making
　　　　　　d.　do not discipline their children

p. 276　49.　Harter's research with children show that self-esteem
C
　　　　　　a.　emerges as a single entity and remains unchanged after this
　　　　　　b.　is unidimensional, consisting of a global sense of self
　　　　　　c.　becomes less realistic as children enter adolescence
　　*　　　d.　is multidimensional, consisting of several distinct components

p. 276　50.　Research on the stability of personality shows that _____ are relatively stable across
F　　　　　time for BOTH males and females.
　　　　　　a.　dependency and aggression
　　*　　　b.　achievement orientation and sex-typed behavior
　　　　　　c.　passivity and anger
　　　　　　d.　sexual behavior and hostility

p. 277　51.　Regarding the stability of behavior, which of the following statements is FALSE?
F
　　　　　　a.　Achievement orientation is relatively stable across time for both males and females.
　　　　　　b.　Gender-stereotyped behaviors tend to remain stable for males and for females.
　　　　　　c.　Behaviors that conflict with cultural norms tend not to be very stable for males or females.
　　*　　　d.　Tendencies toward anger and aggression are remarkably stable across time for both males and females.

p. 277　52.　Which is true regarding the relationship between child behavior and adult behavior?
F　　*　　a.　Behaviors that are socially valued tend to persist.
　　　　　　b.　There is no systematic relationship between child and adult behaviors.
　　　　　　c.　Those traits that do persist from childhood to adulthood are the same for both males and females.
　　　　　　d.　Only those traits that are innate persist from childhood to adulthood.

p. 277 53. Five-year-old Missy really wants to do well in school. Sometimes, however, she ends up in
C   trouble because when she gets angry, she gets really aggressive with the other children.
         She also has a tendency to be rather dependent on her teacher. As Missy gets older,
         research on the stability of personality suggests it is MOST LIKELY that Missy will:
         a   continue to be motivated to achieve, remain dependent, and remain aggressive in her
              interactions with peers
         b   lose her motivation to achieve, remain dependent, and continue to act out aggressively
              toward her peers
    *   c   continue to be motivated to achieve, remain dependent, and lose her aggressive
              tendencies
         d   lose her motivation to achieve, remain dependent, and become quite passive in her
              interactions with peers

p. 279 54. The integration of conflicting self-perceptions, such as "I am popular" and "I am lonely" is
F   achieved during:
         a.   the early elementary school years
         b.   the later elementary school years
         c.   the beginning of adolescence
    *   d.   late adolescence

p. 279 55. The developmental shift from more concrete to more abstract self-conceptions corresponds
C   BEST with a shift from:
    *   a.   concrete-operational to formal-operational thought
         b.   preoperational- to concrete-operational thought
         c.   the phallic stage to the latency period
         d.   the initiative vs. guilt stage to the stage of industry vs. inferiority

p. 279 56. Regarding self-esteem in adolescence, which is true?
F   *   a.   Most individuals leave adolescence with the same general level of self-esteem they had
              at the outset.
         b.   Most individuals suffer from very low levels of self-esteem during adolescence.
         c.   Early adolescents generally have a higher level of self-esteem than do later adolescents.
         d.   Self-perceptions during the adolescent period are remarkably stable.

p. 279 57. Mara is very popular in school: She has lots of friends, gets along well with her teachers,
         and is generally quite happy. At home, however, Mara often feels depressed and lonely.
         Mara understands that this difference is partly related to her family situation: her parents
         are rarely at home, and when they are, they are usually fighting. Mara is MOST LIKELY:
         a.   in elementary school
         b.   in middle school
         c.   just beginning high school
    *   d.   in her senior year of high school

p. 279 58. Lisa has just entered middle school. Compared with when she was in grade school, Lisa is
C   MOST LIKELY to experience:
    *   a.   a decrease in self-esteem
         b.   an increase in self-esteem
         c.   no change in self-esteem
         d.   severe swings in level of self-esteem

p. 279 59. Who is MOST LIKELY to experience the greatest decline in self-esteem?
C   a. Molly, who just entered middle school
    *   b. Jane, who just moved to town and is beginning middle school.
     c. Sheri, who just started menstruating.
     d. Linda, who is in eighth grade.

p. 279 60. Which is TRUE?
F   a. Most boys and girls experience an increase in self-esteem as they enter puberty.
www   b. Most boys and girls experience a steady, gradual decline in self-esteem as they move through adolescence.
     c. Most boys and girls experience a steady increase and then a decrease in self-esteem during adolescence.
    *   d For most boys and girls, level of self-esteem at the end of adolescence is about the same as it was when they entered the adolescent period.

p. 280 61. According to Erikson, the major task one faces during adolescence is:
C   a. the establishment of meaningful love relationships
     b. gaining acceptance into the peer group
    *   c. the establishment of an integrated sense of self
     d. breaking away from dependence on parents

p. 281 62. Donna's mother and father are both medical doctors, as are her two older brothers. Donna
C is in college, enrolled in a pre-med curriculum. When asked about her career goals, Judy states "I'll be a doctor, of course. Everyone in my family is a doctor. I've never thought of being anything else." Donna's identity status is BEST described as:
     a. diffusion status
     b. moratorium status
    *   c. foreclosure status
     d. identity achievement status

p. 281 63. Which BEST represents "identity diffusion?"
C   a. Fred plans to be a teacher because his parents and siblings are all teachers.
    *   b. Erica doesn't really know what she wants to be when she "grows up" and couldn't care less about even exploring the possibilities.
     c. Margo has taken a battery of interest inventories and is exploring different majors at the university, thinking about possibilities for her future career.
     d. Lee has talked with career counselors, his parents, peers and instructors, and has determined that he is best suited for a career in teaching. He is now doing his student teaching.

p. 281 64. The period of trying on roles that is so common during adolescence is referred to as:
C   a. foreclosure period
     b. identity diffusion
    *   c. moratorium period
     d. identity period

p. 281   65.   Which is FALSE regarding the achievement of identity status?
F   a.   Males and females generally achieve a clear sense of identity at about the same age.
        *   b.   By age 20, most individuals have reached identity achievement status.
               c.   Generally speaking, the process of achieving identity is quite uneven.
               d.   Most individuals move into the moratorium status during the college years.

p. 281   66.   In which identity status group do adolescents appear to have the closest and most
F   dependent relationship with parents?
               a.   diffusion status
        *   b.   foreclosure status
               c.   moratorium status
               d.   identity achievement status

p. 282   67.   David and Peggy believe that their children should have the freedom to be who and what
C   they want to be. They are loving and warm parents, who respect their children's opinions
               and encourage their participation in decision-making. What effect is David and Peggy's
               parenting likely to have on their child's identity status?
        *   a.   Their child is likely to be classified in either the moratorium or identity
                    achievement status group.
               b.   Their child is likely to be classified in the diffusion status group.
               c.   Their child is likely to be classified in the foreclosure status group.
               d.   Their parenting will have little effect on their child's identity status

p. 282   68.   George is planning to enter the family business as soon as he graduates from high school.
C   His parents have a job for him in their frame shop, and they all expect that George will
www   eventually run the business. George has never questioned this. According to Erikson,
               George's identity status is BEST described as:
               a.   identity diffusion
               b.   identity achievement
               c.   moratorium status
        *   d.   identity foreclosure

p. 281   69.   Sue's mother is Jewish and her father is a non-practicing Lutheran. For the past two years
C   Sue has been exploring various religions--she has attended a Lutheran church, a local
               synagogue, and the Unitarian church. Finally, Sue joined the Presbyterian church, which
               she believes it a good fit for her. Sue's identity status is BEST described as:
               a.   moratorium status
               b.   identity diffusion
        *   c.   identity achievement
               d.   identity foreclosure

p. 281   70.   Joni doesn't read the newspaper or watch the news. She claims she doesn't care for politics
C   and cannot even recall the name of the vice president of the United States. She does not
               take a stand on political issues, and doesn't see the point in worrying about all that stuff.
               Joni's position BEST fits with Erikson's _____ status:
               a.   moratorium
               b.   foreclosure
        *   c.   diffusion
               d.   achievement

p. 281 71. Joe is a college sophomore who has changed his major three times. Currently he thinks he
C   might like to go into business, so he's taking some basic management and accounting
        classes to see how he likes them. Joe's identity status is BEST described as:
        a. foreclosure
        b. achievement
        c. diffusion
    *   d. moratorium

p. 282 72. Which is FALSE?
F   a. Males and females generally move toward identity achievement at about the same rate.
        b. Most adolescents do not complete the identity formation process by the time they finish
           high school.
        c. It is normal to struggle with identity issues well into adulthood.
    *   d. For most adolescents, identity issues relating to career choice, religion, and politics are
           resolved at about the same time.

p. 283 73. The process of developing an ethnic identity
C   *   a. is very similar to developing other forms of identity
        b. is quite distinct from forming other identities since ethnicity is not chosen
        c. is easier than the process of forming other types of identities
        d. is completed earlier than the formation of other identities

p. 284 74. In which identity status group are adolescents MOST LIKELY to be neglected or rejected
F   by their parents?
    *   a. identity diffusion
        b. identity foreclosure
        c. moratorium
        d. identity achievement

p. 285 75. Which is FALSE regarding self-conceptions in adulthood?
C   a. Self-conceptions change relatively little during adulthood.
    *   b. Old people generally suffer from a poor self-image.
        c. Adults most often describe themselves in terms of unique personal qualities and social
           roles.
        d. Younger and older adults often have different reasons for feeling good about
           themselves.

p. 285 76. Which is TRUE regarding self-perceptions during adulthood?
F   a. Self-esteem generally declines with age.
        b. The gap between one's real self and one's ideal self tends to widen with age.
    *   c. With age, people generally tend to take a more positive view of what they have done in
           the past.
        d. Most old people generally suffer from a poor self-image.

p. 286 77. Which is TRUE regarding personality during adulthood?
F   a. Older adults are more rigid than younger adults with regard to personality traits.
www *   b. Broad personality dimensions, such as extroversion and neuroticism, are quite stable across adulthood.
           c. Personality is more rigid during the early adulthood years than it is later on.
           d. There is little support for the notion that enduring personality traits exist.

p. 286 78. Which of the following correctly ordered from MOST stable over the life span to LEAST
F   stable?
           a. attitudes, intelligence, extraversion
           b. extraversion, attitudes, intelligence
           c. extraversion, intelligence, attitudes
     *   d. intelligence, extraversion, attitudes

p. 286 79. Research on personality has confirmed that:
F   a. personalities tend to become firmly established by late adolescence
           b. there is little continuity in personality across the life-span
     *   c. most personality traits show considerable stability from middle- to old age
           d. personality is more rigid during early adulthood than during middle- or old age

p. 286 80. With regard to personality development during adulthood, which is TRUE?
F   *   a. There is generally more change in personality between adolescence and middle age than there is between middle age and old age.
           b. There are virtually no changes in personality beyond adolescence.
           c. The historical context in which people grow up appears to have little influence on personality development.
           d. Most people undergo highly significant personality changes as they progress from middle age to old age.

p. 287 81. Rhonda wants to know whether or not people's personalities undergo significant change as
C   they age. To determine this, Rhonda will need to use a(n) _____ design:
           a. cross-sectional
     *   b. longitudinal
           c. naturalistic observation
           d. experimental

p. 287 82. Research on stability of personality across the life span shows
C   a. very little stability throughout adulthood because of life changes
           b. change is most likely as people move from middle age to old age
     *   c. substantial stability throughout adulthood, but also some change
           d. stability is greater among women than men

p. 287 83. People's personalities tend to stay the same for all of the following reasons EXCEPT:
F   a. long lasting childhood experiences
     *   b. changes in cognitive growth
           c. genetic influences
           d. consistent environments

p.287 84. Which is likely to contribute MOST to change in personality across the life-span?
F
   a. biological maturation
   b. genetic inheritance
   c. childhood experiences
* d. changes in the social environment

p. 288 85. Which is FALSE regarding personality change?
F
   a. Some people are more likely than others to change during adulthood.
* b. Personality changes are most dramatic during old age.
   c. People are most likely to change when there is a clash between personality and the environment.
   d. Early childhood experiences can have lasting effects on personality development.

p. 288 86. Which is likely to contribute MOST to personality change?
F
   a. disease
   b. early childhood experiences
* c. a poor fit between a person's lifestyle and their personality
   d. genetic inheritance

p. 288 87. Quite often, a person who experiences a "poor fit" between his/her lifestyle and personality
C   will experience a personality change. This is MOST similar to the Piagetian concept of:
   a. assimilation
   b. animism
   c. egocentrism
* d. accommodation

p. 288 88. Children's recognition of themselves as physically separate from others and the
C   environment corresponds with which of Erikson's psychosocial stages?
* a. trust vs. mistrust
   b. autonomy vs. shame and doubt
   c. initiative vs. guilt
   d. industry vs. inferiority

p. 289 89. Timmy is concerned with how he compares to his peers. For example, he always wants to
C   know if he can kick the ball farther or read better than his friends. Timmy is in which of
www   Erikson's psychosocial stages?
   a. autonomy vs. shame and doubt
   b. initiative vs. guilt
* c. industry vs. inferiority
   d. identity vs. role confusion

p. 289 90. At which stage of Erikson's psychosocial theory of development does a child develop a
F   sense of purpose by making bold plans and taking great pride in their accomplishments?
   a. autonomy vs. shame and doubt
* b. initiative vs. guilt
   c. industry vs. inferiority
   d. identity vs. role confusion

p. 289 91. Sammy wants to pour the milk on his cereal all by himself. When Mommy starts to pour
C the milk he puts his hands over the bowl and shouts "No, ME do it!" Sammy is MOST
LIKELY in Erikson's _____ stage, and is approximately ___ years old:
    a. trust vs. mistrust; 2
    b. initiative vs. guilt; 3
   * c. autonomy vs. shame and doubt; 2
    d. industry vs. inferiority; 5

p. 289 92. Kristi's mother finds 4-year-old Kristi in the kitchen, mixing up a muffin mix and making a
C marvelous mess! Kristi announces: "Surprise! I'm making dinner!" Kristi's mother
squelches her desire to yell at Kristi and with great control says "Oh, how nice! Can I
help?" She responds in this way because she has been studying Erik Erikson's theory in her
psychology class and she knows that Kristi's behavior is typical of a child in the stage of:
    a. autonomy vs. shame and doubt
    b. industry vs. inferiority
   * c. initiative vs. guilt
    d. trust vs. mistrust

p. 289 93. Seven-year-old Sven is signing up to play Little League baseball for the first time. He
C worries that the other kids will play better than he does, and asks his Mom to help him
practice his fielding skills by hitting him some pop-ups to catch. Sven's concerns are
typical of children in Erikson's stage of:
    a. initiative vs. guilt
   * b. industry vs. inferiority
    c. identity vs. role confusion
    d. autonomy vs. shame and doubt

p. 289 94. According to Erikson, successful resolution of the _____ stage leads to the development of
F an individual's ability to engage in setting goals.
    a. generativity vs. stagnation
    b. autonomy vs. despair
    c. industry vs. inferiority
   * d. initiative vs. guilt

p. 289 95. Research investigating Erikson's claim that identity paves the way for the establishment
C of intimate relationships has revealed that:
    a. there is no relationship between identity and intimacy
   * b. the acquisition of a well-formed identity does indeed facilitate
      intimacy in relationships
    c. the psychologically healthy individual has completed the identity-formation
      process by the time s/he graduates from college
    d. we can truly love another even though we do not "know ourselves"

p. 289 96. According to Erikson, successful resolution of the "identity vs. role confusion" conflict
C faced in adolescence leads to which of the following basic personality strengths:
    a. a sense of purpose
    b. feelings of competence
   * c. the ability to commit oneself
    d. investment in future generations

p. 290 97. Zelda is proud of the tutoring she is doing at school with kids who have learning problems
C   and feels that she is doing something positive for future generations. Chances are Zelda is
www   in Erikson's stage of:
           a. integrity vs. despair
           b. identity vs. role confusion
           c. intimacy vs. isolation
      *   d. generativity vs. stagnation

p. 290 98. Margaret's children are all in college. Margaret works as a legal secretary, and most of
C   what she earns goes toward paying her children's college tuition. Her own children lead
           busy lives, with friends and school activities occupying most of their time, so Margaret
           volunteers one evening each week at the Boys' Home, reading bedtime stories to the young
           delinquents there. Margaret is BEST classified as fitting into Erikson's stage:
           a. intimacy vs. isolation
      *   b. generativity vs. stagnation
           c. integrity vs. despair
           d. identity vs. role confusion

p. 291 99. Psychologically healthy middle-aged adults are MOST likely to:
F   a. engage in reflection on their lives in order to come to terms with unresolved conflicts
           b. be concerned with personal advancement relating to careers
      *   c. develop a deep concern with making a contribution to society and passing on
               something of value to younger generations
           d. focus on the establishment of intimate relationships with others

p. 291 100. Most old people:
F   a. would make significant changes if they had their lives to live over again
           b. feel a keen sense of despair
           c. spend little time dwelling on the past
      *   d. think about the past in an effort to integrate the pieces of their lives

p. 293 101. Parents who wish to enhance their children's self-esteem should:
C   a. not express their disapproval of their children's misbehavior
           b. provide unconditional acceptance of their children's behavior
           c. allow the children to determine consequences for misbehavior
      *   d. set clear guidelines for behavior

p. 294 102. Which of the following teaching practices is MOST likely to have a positive impact on
C   children's self-esteem?
           a. placing a child in the appropriate ability groups in reading and mathematics
           b. encouraging children to strive to be the best in the class
      *   c. helping children to focus on their own unique strengths
           d. providing public feedback so that children can learn from each others' mistakes

p. 295 103. Researchers have found that a good way to boost self-esteem among nursing home
C residents is to encourage them to:
  a. simply blame the process of aging for their difficulties in functioning
 * b. view the nursing home environment as contributing to their problems
  c. see that they are not in control of what happens to them so they should stop worrying
     about it
  d. expect less of themselves, and therefore be less disappointed in their lack of ability to
     function well

p. 268 104. Self-esteem refers to a person's
F a. cognitive understanding of self
SG b. perception of his or her abilities and traits
 * c. overall evaluation of his or her worth as a person
  d. knowledge of who they are

p. 269 105. According to Erik Erikson, personality
F a. develops in the first five or six years after birth and changes little after this
SG * b. develops and changes throughout the life span
  c. development is complete in adolescence once a sense of identity has been achieved
  d. is formed in childhood and only changes later in life under extreme environmental
     conditions

p. 270 106. Someone who adheres to social learning theory would believe that
C a. personality develops through a series of systematic stages that are similar for all people
SG b. personality is shaped by the environment during childhood, but once it is formed,
     changes very little in response to environmental changes
  c. some aspects of personality are determined only by genetic factors while other are
     determined only by environmental factors
 * d. personality traits are only consistent across the life span if the person's environment
     remains the same

p. 271 107. Infants with a spot of rouge on their noses who recognize themselves in a mirror will
F a. reach for the nose of their mirror image
SG * b. reach for their own nose
  c. look behind the mirror
  d. begin to cry indicating that they are confused

p. 273 108. An infant who is classified as "slow-to-warm-up"
F * a. follows a somewhat regular schedule, is inactive, and somewhat moody
SG b. follows a somewhat regular schedule, is active, and tolerates frustrations fairly well
  c. follows a regular schedule, appears content, and is adaptable to new experiences
  d. does not follow a regular schedule, is inactive, and reacts very negatively to new
     experiences

p. 272 109. Research on behavioral inhibition suggests that
C a. whether one is inhibited as a toddler determines whether one will be shy as an adult
SG * b. inhibited toddlers are more likely to turn out to be shy than uninhibited toddlers
  c. inhibited toddlers were securely attached as infants
  d. inhibited children show the same patterns of physiological arousal to events as
     uninhibited children

p. 275 110. A child who can compare her abilities to those of her companions is likely to be in Piaget's
C   _____ stage of cognitive development.
SG   a. sensorimotor
           b. preoperational
     *   c. concrete operational
           d. formal operational

p. 276 111. When Harter's self-perception scale was administered to children in third through ninth
C   grades, it was found that
SG   a. only the oldest children had well-defined self-concepts
           b. children typically did not distinguish between their competencies in different areas
           c. children showed a "halo effect" by evaluating themselves high in all areas
     *   d. children's ratings of themselves were consistent with how others rated them

p. 289 112. According to Erikson, a third grader who has problems with reading and math may develop
F   a sense of
SG   a. doubt
           b. guilt
     *   c. inferiority
           d. role confusion

p. 281 113. Adolescents who have experienced a crisis involving identity but have not resolved the
F   crisis or made a commitment are classified in Marcia's _____ status.
SG   a. diffusion
     *   b. moratorium
           c. foreclosure
           d. identity achievement

p. 281 114. An adolescent who says "My parents taught me that abortion is wrong and so I just would
C   not consider having an abortion or voting for someone who supports abortion." This
SG   statement reflects which identity status?
           a. diffusion
           b. moratorium
     *   c. foreclosure
           d. identity achievement

p. 287 115. Longitudinal research on the major dimensions of personality suggests that
C   *   a. they are relatively consistent over time in adults
SG   b. they change considerably over time in adults
           c. they are strongly correlated with infant temperament
           d. they cannot be reliably measured in adults

p. 286 116. Findings from cross-sectional research that, as a group, adult personalities change
C   systematically over time, may reflect
SG   *   a. the fact that personality is affected by the historical context in which it develops
           b. changes in the way personality has been measured over the years
           c. the fact that personality begins to disintegrate as we age
           d. the fact that people grow more similar as they get older

p. 291 117. Older adults face Erikson's psychosocial conflict of
F
SG   a. integrity versus stagnation
                b. generativity versus stagnation
                c. intimacy versus despair
        *   d. integrity versus despair

p. 289 118. Compared to adults who do not achieve a firm sense of identity, those adults who <u>do</u>
C   achieve a sense of identity are
SG   a. equally likely to form genuine intimacy with another person
        *   b. more likely to form genuine intimacy with another person
                c. are less likely to form intimate relationships because they feel very good about
                    themselves as individuals
                d. more likely to form many pseudo intimate relationships but no intimate relationships

TRUE-FALSE QUESTIONS
_____

p. 268 119. Self-concept refers to how people perceive themselves while self-esteem is how they
               evaluate themselves.
        *   a. true
                b. false

p. 269 120. Erikson and Freud both view adult personality as being primarily determined by
www   experiences during infancy and early childhood.
                a. true
        *   b. false

p. 269 121. According to the psychometric approach, personality can be characterized as a set of
               distinct traits on which people differ.
        *   a. true
                b. false

p. 270 122. Social learning theorists believe that personality is unchanging after childhood.
                a. true
        *   b. false

p. 272 123. Self-awareness depends on both cognitive development and social experiences.
        *   a. true
                b. false

p. 272 124. A person's temperament is partially determined by genetics.
www   *   a. true
                b. false

p. 273 125. Babies with DIFFICULT temperaments tend to be very passive.
                a. true
        *   b. false

p. 273 126. Infants who are behaviorally inhibited usually outgrow this temperament by the time they start elementary school.
a. true
*   b. false

p. 275 127. School-age children spend a lot of time comparing themselves to others.
*   a. true
b. false

p. 276 128. Self-esteem is a general, undifferentiated attribute.
a. true
*   b. false

p. 276 129. Level of self-esteem tends to remain quite stable across the grade-school years.
*   a. true
b. false

p. 279 130. Going through adolescence results in a drop in self-esteem for most individuals.
www
a. true
*   b. false

p. 280 131. Adolescents who engage in false self behavior often feel that their "true selves" are unsupported.
*   a. true
b. false

p. 282 132. Most individuals achieve an "adult"sense of identity by the time they graduate from high school.
a. true
*   b. false

p. 284 133. The same sort of parenting practices that promote self-esteem lead children to forge a separate identity.
*   a. true
b. false

p. 285 134. Most older adults suffer from a poor self-image.
a. true
*   b. false

p. 287 135. Observed age differences in adult personality may be due more to generational effects than to maturational processes.
*   a. true
b. false

ESSAY QUESTIONS

136.   In what ways does Erikson's view of personality development differ from Freud's view?

137. What factors influence identity formation?
www

138. Why do personalities change or stay the same over the life span?

139. How does "goodness of fit" influence temperament, self esteem, and personality?

140. Taking into consideration everything you have read about personality, how would you
SG   summarize the findings on stability of personality characteristics across the life span?
     [Sample answer is provided in the Study Guide.]

141. Based on research, what could you tell parents who are concerned about their infant's or
SG   toddler's temperament (perhaps it is a difficult temperament, or the infant is inhibited)?

142. How does self-esteem change across the life span, and what factors influence self-esteem
SG   in positive or negative directions?

GENDER ROLES AND SEXUALITY

MULTIPLE-CHOICE QUESTIONS

---

p. 298   1.   Each society generally has a set of expectations regarding the behaviors and traits that are
F   considered appropriate for males as compared to females. These sets of expectations are:
   * a.   gender role norms
      b.   gender-role stereotypes
      c.   gender types
      d.   gender identities

p. 298   2.   While Nicki is growing up she gets the message that a woman should stay home and take
C   care of the children while men go off to work and "bring home the bacon." This message
               BEST reflects what your text refers to as a:
      a.   gender-role stereotype
      b.   gender type
      c.   gender identity
   * d.   gender-role norm

p. 298   3.   Mr. and Mrs. Hill have two children, Jack and Jill. They make no bones about telling Jack
C   that he should be an engineer, since men are good at math, and that Jill should be a nurse,
www   since women are good at taking care of other people. The Hill's message BEST reflects
               what your text calls:
      a.   gender-role norms
   * b.   gender-role stereotypes
      c.   instrumental roles
      d.   expressive roles

p. 298   4.   Mary tries to be everything a good wife and mother should be, whereas Tim tries to be a
C   good provider for his family. This BEST illustrates:
      a.   gender types
      b.   gender roles
   * c.   gender-role norms
      d.   gender-role stereotypes

p. 298   5.   John says he's not going to cry at the funeral because men are not as emotional as women.
C   This illustrates:
      a.   gender types
      b.   gender roles
      c.   gender-role norms
   * d.   gender-role stereotypes

p. 298   6.   Which is the BEST example of an expressive role?

C

           a.   Women are expected to be good at reading, but not at math.

           b.   Males are not supposed to cry, or otherwise express emotions.

*   c.   Women are expected to be cooperative and sensitive to others.

           d.   Males are supposed to have a greater need to express their sexuality than are females.

p. 298   7.   Which is the BEST example of an instrumental role?

C

           a.   Women are expected to be good at reading, but not at math.

           b.   Women are expected to be cooperative and sensitive to others.

*   c.   Males are expected to provide for the family.

           d.   Males are supposed to be taller and have greater upper body strength than females.

p. 299   8.   Which is TRUE regarding common gender stereotypes?

C

           a.   There is solid research evidence that females generally have better visual/spatial skills than males.

*   b.   There is consistent research support for the fact that males are more aggressive than females.

           c.   Females are more vulnerable to diseases and disorders than males.

           d.   There are no gender stereotypes that are consistently supported by research.

p. 299   9.   With regard to actual psychological differences between males and females, research has

F

www

consistently found that, on average:

           a.   females perform better than males on both verbal and spatial tasks

           b.   females are more verbally aggressive while males are more physically aggressive

           c.   males perform better than females on mathematical and verbal tasks

*   d.   males perform better than females on mathematical and spatial tasks

p. 299   10.   According to the research on sex differences, which of the following is TRUE?

F

           a.   Girls have lower self-esteem than boys.

           b.   Boys excel at tasks that require higher-level cognitive processing.

           c.   Girls are more social than boys.

*   d.   Boys are more verbally aggressive than females.

p. 299   11.   Males out perform females on tests of visual spatial ability:

F

           a.   only until about ten years of age.

           b.   only during adolescence

           c.   only during adulthood.

*   d.   throughout the lifespan

p. 300   12.   Recent research on sex differences suggests that:

F

           a.   girls are more compliant than boys in all situations

*   b.   girls are more compliant than boys with authority figures but not with peers

           c.   girls are much more persuasive than boys

           d.   girls are more likely than boys to have developmental problems

p. 300　13.　The sex differences between males and females indicate that:

C
      a.　nearly all males score higher than nearly all females on mathematical skills
      b.　gender accounts for 95% of the observed differences in aggressiveness
*　c.　even though there are group sex differences on some traits, gender accounts for very little of the variability on the traits
      d.　there are lots of individual differences, but no significant group differences due to gender

p. 300　14.　What can we conclude about psychological differences between the sexes?

C　*　a.　Males and females are far more similar than different.
      b.　Gender stereotypes that are not supported by research can have no effect on actual behavioral or psychological differences between males and females.
      c.　Most gender-role stereotypes have been eliminated in our society.
      d.　When differences <u>are</u> found between males and females, it means that nearly all members of one gender perform better or worse than nearly all members of the other gender.

p. 300　15.　Which of the following conclusions can be made regarding sex differences?

C
      a.　Gender differences are larger when boys and girls are in same-sex situations than when they are in mixed-sex groups.
      b.　Males and females differ on more traits than they share in common.
*　c.　Most gender stereotypes have no empirical support.
      d.　Whether we are male or female has little impact on how others in society view us.

p. 300　16.　Alice Eagly argues that gender differences:

F
      a.　result from biological differences between males and females
*　b.　can only be understood in light of the social context in which they occur
      c.　result from early childhood experiences
      d.　are virtually nonexistent

p. 300　17.　The social-role hypothesis predicts that:

C
      a.　once formed, gender differences cannot be changed
www
      b.　men and women adopt different roles in society because they differ in basic traits and abilities
*　c.　gender differences vary from culture to culture depending on the roles men and women hold in each society
      d.　gender differences are fairly universal because they originate in biological differences

p. 301　18.　Adults are asked to interact with an unknown infant. Half of the adults are told that the infant is "Stevie" and the other half of the adults are told that the infant is "Stacy." What are you likely to observe of these interactions?

C
      a.　At such a young age, there are not likely to be any differences in how adults treat the infant in the two conditions.
      b.　Adults will treat the infant similarly until the infant begins to act in stereotypical ways, and then there will be differences in the adults' reactions to the infant.
      c.　Adults will be able to detect the real biological sex of the infant, regardless of whether they are told the infant is "Stevie" or "Stacy."
*　d.　Adults are likely to rate "Stevie" as strong and brave and "Stacy" as soft and cuddly.

p. 301 19. Most children clearly demonstrate basic gender identity by:
F
           a. 1 to 1 1/2 years of age
     *   b. 2 1/2 to 3 years of age
           c. 3 1/2 to 4 years of age
           d. 5 to 6 years of age

p. 302 20. Children become quite rigid in their thinking about gender-role standards:
F   *   a. at about the time they understand that they can not change their sex
           b. as soon as they can accurately label themselves as male or female
           c. at the point that they can accurately determine whether a person (self included) is male or female
           d. around the end of the elementary school years

p. 302 21. With regard to children's views of what is "for boys" and what is "for girls," research
F   indicates that:
           a. 9-year-olds are more bothered than 6-year-olds when kids engage in activities that violate gender-role stereotypes
     *   b. 6-year-olds are more upset by violations of gender-role stereotypes than are 9-year-olds
           c. 4-year-olds are quite rigid in their thinking about what boys and girls can and should do
           d. it isn't until the onset of puberty that youngsters become concerned with what is sex-appropriate behavior and what is not

p. 303 22. When asked if it is OK for a boy to play with dolls, Tim replies, "Yes, if he feels like it."
C   Based on Damon's research on gender-roles and stereotypes, what age is Tim likely to be?
           a. 2 or 6 years
           b. 4 or 6 years
           c. 6 or 9 years
     *   d. 4 or 9 years

p. 303 23. One likely theory proposed by Maccoby about why boys and girls segregate themselves
C   into same-sex peer groups is that:
     *   a. their play styles are different from one another making it difficult for the two groups to play together
           b. the physical differences between boys and girls make it unlikely that they could find common interests and activities
           c. biological predispositions lead children to interact with others who are most like them
           d. children are reinforced by adults for playing with same-sex children

p. 303 24. Gender segregation:
F   *   a. tends to escalate as children move into elementary school
           b. is highest among preschoolers and then slowly declines
           c. is uncommon in today's equality-minded society
           d. is low until adolescence, at which time it sharply increases

p. 303 25. Children with strong gender-typed preferences (i.e., they strictly avoid playing with
C   members of the other sex):
www   a. are more likely to be rejected by their peers than children with weak gender-typed
                 preferences
             b. are less well adjusted than children with weak gender-typed preferences
        *   c. are more popular than children with weak gender-typed preferences
             d. are less popular than children with weak gender-typed preferences

p. 303 26. With regard to gender typing, which is FALSE?
C   a. Boys are more pressured to "be boys" than girls are to "be girls."
        *   b. Children do not evidence a clear preference for same-sex playmates until age 5.
             c. Boys show earlier preferences than do girls for gender-appropriate toys.
             d. The masculine role is more clearly defined than the feminine role in American society.

p. 304 27. In terms of gender role expectations:
C   a. females are expected to adhere more to gender role expectations
        *   b. males are expected to adhere more to gender role expectations
             c. males and females are equally expected to adhere to gender role expectations
             d. males and females are no longer expected to adhere to gender role expectations

p. 304 28. Which of the following requests for toys are you LEAST likely to find?
C   a. Patty asking for a doll.
        *   b. Billy asking for a stuffed rabbit.
             c. Sherry asking for a bicycle.
             d. John asking for a building set.

p. 304 29. An example of gender intensification would be:
C   a. boys noticing that some girls like romance
        *   b. a boy asserting his masculinity among his peers
             c. a girl acting like a "tomboy"
             d. a boy acting like a "sissy"

p. 304 30. Heightened concern with conformity to gender roles during adolescence:
F   a. is an unusual occurrence in the United States
             b. is a sign of poor psychological adjustment
        *   c. may serve an adaptive purpose with regard to preparation for dating, family, and career
                 roles
             d. occurs for females, but not for males

p. 304 31. In general, adolescents:
F   *   a. view gender-role violations as a sign of psychological abnormality
             b. are more accepting of peers' cross-sex interests than they are likely to be as adults
             c. make less negative judgments of peers who violate traditional gender roles than do
                 those in middle childhood
             d. are more like 5th graders than kindergartners with regard to judgments of those
                 exhibiting cross-sex behaviors

p. 304 32. Most adolescents:

C

    a. are very tolerant of girls acting and dressing like boys

    b. are very tolerant of both boys and girls acting in ways inconsistent with traditional gender roles

    c. minimize any sex differences between males and females

*   d. view violations of gender-role expectations as a sign that there is something psychologically wrong with the person

p. 304 33. Gender differences tend to _____ as children enter adolescence.

F

    a. decrease

    b. stay the same

*   c. increase

    d. show no consistent pattern of change

p. 304 34. Which two groups view cross-sex behaviors most negatively?

F   *   a. kindergartners and adolescents

www   b. preschoolers and elementary school-age children

    c. elementary school-age children and adolescents

    d. elementary school-age children and adults

p. 305 35. According to Money and Ehrhardt's biosocial theory of gender-role development:

C

    a. Freud was correct when he said that "biology is destiny."

    b. children begin acting like boys or girls once they acquire gender identity and constancy

*   c. several critical biological events set the stage for different social reactions to males and females

    d. pubertal hormones create differences in how males and females react to social events

p. 305 36. With regard to biological differentiation of the sexes, which is FALSE?

C

    a. It is possible for a male (XY) fetus to develop female external genitalia.

    b. The male hormone testosterone affects the development of the brain and nervous system.

*   c. External genitalia are fully differentiated by the 8th week after conception.

    d. The sex chromosomes influence the development of the testes and ovaries.

p. 305 37. Which biological event leads to the growth of a penis in a male fetus?

F

    a. receiving a Y chromosome at conception

*   b. secretion of testosterone by the testes

    c. absence of the release of female hormones

    d. secretion of growth hormone from the pituitary gland

p. 305 38. Money and Ehrhardt's biosocial theory of gender typing suggests all of the following EXCEPT:

C

    a. Gender-role development is strongly influenced by socialization.

    b. There is a critical period for the establishment of gender identity.

    c. Early biological developments influence how parents label and treat a child at birth.

*   d. Biology is more important than experience in determining gender identity.

p. 306   39.   Some individuals inherit two X chromosomes but are exposed prenatally to drugs that are
C   converted to male hormones once in the body. These individuals are likely to:
                   a.   physically resemble females but behaviorally act like males
                   b.   look and act no differently as a result of this prenatal exposure
                   c.   have masculinized genitalia at birth but lose this appearance at puberty and become
                       indistinguishable from others
      *   d.   have masculinized genitalia and behave in more "masculine" ways

p. 306   40.   Androgenized females are:
F   *   a.   girls who have been exposed prenatally to male hormones
                   b.   boys who have been exposed prenatally to female hormones
                   c.   girls who fail to develop any external genitalia
                   d.   girls who inherit two X chromosomes and one Y chromosome

p. 307   41.   What evidence did John Money use as the basis for concluding that there is a critical period
C   for the establishment of gender identity?
                   a.   Hormones must be released prenatally to have any impact on behavior
                   b.   Sex reassignment can be successfully done when a child has achieved gender identity,
                       but not once a child has achieved gender stability.
      *   c.   Sex reassignment before 18 months of age causes few adjustment problems while
                       reassignment after 3 years of age is very difficult.
                   d.   Sex reassignment while still in the preoperational stage of development causes few
                       adjustment problems while reassignment once concrete operational thought has begun
                       is very difficult.

p. 307   42.   According to Freud, 3- to 6-year-old little boys love their mothers, are jealous of their
F   fathers, secretly wish that they could take Dad's place with Mom, and fear that Dad will
           retaliate by castrating them. This is known as:
                   a.   the Electra complex
      *   b.   the Oedipus complex
                   c.   identification
                   d.   projection

p. 307   43.   Boys go through a phase where they adore their mothers and resent, even fear, their fathers.
F   Freud referred to this phase as:
      *   a.   Oedipus complex
                   b.   Electra complex
                   c.   androgyny complex
                   d.   parental complex

p. 307   44.   According to psychoanalytic theory, gender-role development occurs primarily as a result
F   of:
www   *   a.   children patterning themselves after their same-sex parents
                   b.   differential reinforcement for sex-appropriate behavior
                   c.   observational learning
                   d.   hormonal influences

p. 308 45. Regarding the Freudian perspective on sex-role development, which of the following has
C   NOT been supported by research?
      a. The preschool period is a critical time for gender-role development.
      b. Boys are more powerfully motivated than girls to learn their gender roles.
      c. Fathers play an important role in the gender typing of both daughters
          and sons.
   * d. Boys identify with fathers primarily out of fear.

p. 309 46. With respect to social learning theory, which of the following is FALSE?
C   * a. Children begin the process of gender-typing by classifying objects and events as either
          male or female appropriate.
      b. Children observe and imitate same-sex models
      c. Gender-role development depends on how we are treated by society.
      d. Gender-roles can be "created" by reinforcing behaviors thought to be sex-appropriate.

p. 309 47. Research on reinforcement of sex-appropriate behavior indicates that:
C   * a. Fathers are more likely than mothers to punish youngsters for playing with gender-
          inappropriate toys.
      b. Peers are more critical of cross-sex behavior in the preschool years than in later
          childhood.
      c. Mothers are more likely than fathers to praise youngsters for playing with
          gender-appropriate toys.
      d. Teachers generally do not engage in the differential reinforcement of sex-appropriate
          behavior that parents engage in at home.

p. 311 48. With regard to gender-role development, social learning theorists have been criticized for:
C   * a. portraying children as passive participants in the developmental process
      b. overemphasizing the role of biological factors
      c. placing too little emphasis on the role of differential reinforcement
      d. denying the role that peers play in promoting gender typing

p. 309 49. The Freudian concept that is closely related to observational learning is:
C   * a. identification
      b. The Oedipus complex
      c. The Electra complex
      d. partial reinforcement

p. 311 50. "I am a boy. Therefore I want to do the things boys do." This statement is reflective of
C   which theoretical perspective regarding gender-role development?
www   a. biosocial theory
   * b. cognitive-developmental theory
      c. psychoanalytic theory
      d. social-learning theory

p. 312 51. According to the cognitive-developmental perspective on gender typing, which is the most
C   mature understanding?
             a. The understanding that some things are "boy things" and some things are "girl things"
                 to do.
             b. The ability to correctly label one's self as male or female.
        *   c. The understanding that gender identity is stable across situations.
             d. The understanding that gender identity is stable across time.

p. 312 52. According to cognitive-developmental theory, the notion that gender doesn't change despite
C   change in appearances is closely linked to the:
        *   a. ability to conserve
             b. object permanence concept
             c. notion of class inclusion
             d. the emergence of formal operational thought

p. 312 53. A mature gender identity is achieved when a child:
C   a. begins to act in gender-appropriate ways
             b. can accurately label him/herself as male or female
             c. can accurately distinguish between male and female strangers
        *   d. understands that a his/her biological sex will always remain the same
                 despite a change in clothing, hairstyle, etc.

p. 312 54. Phillip knows he is a boy, but sometimes he says things that worry his father. For example,
C   when his mom and aunt are talking about a friend who is expecting a baby, young Philip
             says that when he's expecting a baby, he's going to exercise a lot so he doesn't get such a
             big stomach. Statements like this suggest that Phillip has not yet acquired:
             a. gender roles
             b. gender identity
        *   c. gender stability
             d. gender schemata

p. 312 55. According to cognitive-developmental theory, children do not achieve a full understanding
C   of what it means to be a female or a male until they:
             a. achieve symbolic thought
             b. attain the object permanence concept
        *   c. acquire conservation skills
             d. can engage in systematic problem-solving

p. 312 56. Gender consistency is really a form of:
C   a. object permanence
www   b. identification
        *   c. conservation
             d. androgyny

p. 312 57. Which of the following is NOT part of the cognitive-developmental explanation of gender
C typing?
  a. Certain cognitive understandings must be achieved before gender typing will occur.
  b. Children actively socialize themselves to act in ways appropriate with their gender.
* c. Children begin to identify with their same-sex parent after they realize their parent's
     gender is not going to change.
  d. After realizing their gender, children try to act in ways consistent with their
     understanding of who they are.

p. 312 58. One problem with Kohlberg's cognitive-developmental explanation of gender-typing is
C that:
* a. Children often acquire gender-typed behaviors and preferences before they acquire
     gender stability and consistency.
  b. Some children do not engage in gender-typed behaviors until elementary school age.
  c. Cognitive developments seem to be unrelated to the development of gender typing
  d. It places too much emphasis on hormonal factors.

p. 312 59. Martin and Halverson's schematic-processing model suggests that:
C
www a. children learn gender roles as a result of parental reinforcement of sex-appropriate
        behaviors
* b. children are particularly interested in learning about objects or activities that fit their
     own-sex schemas
  c. inaccurate gender-stereotypes are easily changed
  d. children are passive participants in gender-role development

p. 312 60. A major difference between Kohlberg's cognitive-developmental theory and Martin and
C Halverson's gender-schema theory is that gender-typing in the gender-schema theory:
  a. does not begin to develop until after children have developed gender stability and
     gender consistency
* b. begins as soon as children acquire gender identity at around 2-3 years of age
  c. develops through passive exposure to external models of appropriate gender-typed
     behaviors
  d. is unrelated to cognitive developments

p. 312 61. Gender schemata:
C a. must develop before gender identity can develop
  b. help children realize whether they are male or female
  c. are objective, accurate representations of what males and females are like
* d. influence what people pay attention to and remember regarding gender

p. 313 62. On which of the following points do ALL the theories of gender-role development agree?
C a. Gender roles develop from reinforcement of gender appropriate behaviors.
www b. Children identify with their same-sex parent in order to resolve painful feelings of
        family conflict.
* c. The gender roles that children develop depend on what their society offers in terms of
     gender models.
  d. Gender roles depend on acquiring a certain level of cognitive development.

p. 314 63. In general, gender roles:
C
    a. are more differentiated during adolescence than they are among newlyweds
*   b. become more differentiated with the birth of a child
    c. tend to remain constant across the adult years
    d. are more pronounced for couples when both partners are working

p. 315 64. Androgyny refers to individuals who are:
F
    a. high in masculine traits and low in feminine traits
*   b. high in masculine traits and high in feminine traits
    c. low in masculine traits and low in feminine traits
    d. low in masculine traits and high in feminine traits

p. 316 65. Which is true with regard to androgyny?
C
    a. Androgynous males are more nurturant than most females.
    b. Androgynous females are more aggressive than most males
*   c. Androgynous individuals possess both "masculine" and "feminine" personality traits.
    d. Androgynous individuals score very low on virtually all traditionally "masculine" and traditionally "feminine" personality traits.

p. 315 66. The theory of psychological androgyny suggests that:
C
www
    a. if one scores very high on masculine traits one must be low in feminine traits
    b. psychologically healthy individuals score very low on all sex-typed personality traits
*   c. it is desirable for an individual to simultaneously possess a number of traditionally masculine- and feminine-stereotyped traits
    d. inborn biological differences account for virtually all gender differences in personality traits

p. 315 67. People with androgynous personalities tend to:
C
    a. have sexual problems
    b. be social misfits
*   c. have a higher level of self-esteem
    d. to have difficulty making close friends

p. 315 68. What can we conclude about androgyny?
C
    a. There are no truly androgynous people.
    b. Young adults with children tend to be the most androgynous.
*   c. Androgynous people are better adjusted and have higher self-esteem, but only because they have stereotypical masculine traits.
    d. Androgynous people tend to be rated as less well adjusted because they do not fit into a single neat package of the stereotypical male or female that our society is comfortable with.

p. 315 69. Gutmann's hypothesis regarding the "parental imperative" suggests that:
C
    a. most women in our society feel they must have children
    b. most males and females in our society feel they must have children
*   c. becoming parents pressures males to be more "masculine" and females to be more "feminine"
    d. becoming parents pressures young men and women to take on non-traditional gender roles

p. 315 70. According to Gutmann's hypothesis of the parental imperative:

C

          a. women must become more masculine and men must become more feminine when they begin to have children

    *   b. mothers and fathers must establish distinct roles in order to successfully raise their children

          c. it is necessary for both parents to adopt a masculine gender role so they can effectively raise their children

          d. it is essential that parents adopt flexible gender roles to be able to meet the variety of demands placed on them by children

p. 315 71. Research on Guttmann's hypothesis about sex differences in adulthood has found that:

C

          a. after having children, men become more feminine and women become more masculine

          b. having children fosters a more androgynous gender-role orientation

    *   c. once adults have finished parenting, both males and females become more androgynous

          d. adults who are not parents typically have an undifferentiated gender-role orientation

p. 317 72. Regarding infantile sexuality, which is TRUE?

F

          a. Infants are not sexual beings.

    *   b. Both male and female babies have been observed to experience what appear to be orgasms.

          c. Infants experience masturbation in much the same way as do adults.

          d. Male infants are incapable of having an erection.

p. 317 73. Observations of infants suggest all of the following EXCEPT:

F

          a. they are curious about all their body parts

          b. their genitals are sensitive to stimulation

    *   c. they can experience adult-like sexual pleasure

          d. they can experience physical arousal

p. 317 74. Which of the following is TRUE regarding children's knowledge of sex and reproduction?

F   *   a. Children's level of understanding is linked to their cognitive development.

          b. Most children know by age 3 that sexual anatomy is what distinguishes males from females.

          c. By age 6 most youngsters understand that sexual intercourse plays a role in making a baby.

          d. By age 11 or 12, all children have a complete understanding of how a child is created.

p. 318 75. Which is TRUE regarding sexual experimentation such as masturbation and same- and cross-sex sexual play?

F

          a. Boys engage in less such sexual experimentation overall than do girls.

          b. Sexual experimentation decreases during the grade school years.

          c. Children do not engage in masturbation prior to puberty.

    *   d. Girls engage in less same-sex sexual play than do boys.

p. 318 76. Research supports all of the following EXCEPT:
F
    a. Parental attitudes toward sexuality have an effect on children's sexual behavior.
    b. Sexual socialization varies from one cultural context to the next.
    c. Sexual experimentation appears to increase with age during the grade-school years.
   * d. Children are more interested in sexuality during the phallic period than they are during the latency period.

p. 318 77. Regarding childhood sexuality, Freud was:
C
    a. correct in his claim that sexual play activities are infrequent among school-age children
   * b. correct when he claimed that children are not only interested in their bodies, but also seek bodily pleasure through manipulation of their genitals
    c. correct when he said that sexual experimentation declines after children enter elementary school
    d. wrong when he claimed that preschoolers are interested in their bodies

p. 318 78. In cultures where sexual attitudes and behaviors are semirestrictive:
F
    a. there are rules prohibiting sexual behaviors and strict sanctions for violating these rules
www * b. there are rules prohibiting sexual behaviors but they are often violated without negative consequences
    c. there are very few rules prohibiting sexual behaviors, and indeed, expression of sexuality is encouraged
    d. strict rules govern adult behavior, but children are free to do as they please

p. 319 79. Which of the following is NOT generally true regarding children who are victims of sexual
F   abuse?
    a. They may become aggressive or depressed as a result of the abuse.
    b. They can experience flashbacks to the abuse long after it has ended.
   * c. They are usually abused by strangers.
    d. They engage in sexualized behavior.

p. 320 80. Research on sexual orientation shows that:
C
    a. a strong, domineering mother and a weak, ineffectual father lead to male homosexuality
    b. same-sex sexual activity during adolescence is a good predictor of adult sexual orientation
   * c. certain patterns of prenatal hormones may predispose some individuals to adopt a homosexual orientation
    d. sexual orientation is determined by how one is treated by important individuals that one interacts with on a regular basis

p. 320 81. Twin studies on sexual orientation show that:
C
    a. genes are much more influential than environmental factors in determining sexual
www   orientation
    b. sexual orientation is determined almost completely by environmental factors
    c. a genetic link cannot be established because not enough twins will participate in this kind of research
   * d. genetic and environmental influences are about equally responsible for sexual orientation

p. 321 82. Research indicates that MOST teenagers today believe premarital sex is:
F
        a. always morally wrong
    *   b. acceptable as long as the partners are emotionally involved
        c. acceptable for males but not for females
        d. perfectly acceptable under almost all circumstances

p. 321 83. In regards to adolescent attitudes about premarital sex, which of the following is FALSE?
F
        a. There has been a decline in the double standard.
        b. Sex with affection is acceptable to most adolescents.
        c. There is increased confusion about sexual norms.
    *   d. There is an increased gap between males' and females' sexual attitudes.

p. 321 84. Which of the following is NOT one of the components of the new sexual morality of
F   teenagers?
    *   a. There is a high degree of consistency in the decisions that teenagers make regarding
            sexual behaviors.
        b. Sex with affection is all right.
        c. There is greater confusion about sexual norms than in the past.
        d. The double standard--what's OK for males is not as OK for females--is decreasing.

p. 321 85. Which of the following is FALSE regarding the sexual behaviors of teenagers?
C
        a. The rate of sexual intercourse has increased over the years.
        b. More adolescents report that they masturbate and believe that it is a normal aspect of
            sexuality.
    *   c. There are still large differences in sexual behaviors of males and females.
        d. Petting and intercourse occur at earlier ages than in previous decades.

p. 321 86. Regarding changes in sexual attitudes and behaviors during adolescence, it is accurate to
C   say that over the past 30 years:
        a. attitudes have changed, but behaviors have not
        b. there have been virtually no changes in attitudes or behaviors
        c. attitudes and behaviors have changed for males, but not for females
    *   d. there have been significant changes in attitudes and behavior for both males and
            females

p. 321 87. In comparing the sexual behaviors of males and females, we find that:
C
        a. females are more likely to describe their sexual encounters as satisfying
www   b. males are more likely to insist on using contraception
        c. males are more likely to think about the long-term consequences of their behavior
    *   d. females are more likely to insist that emotional intimacy go along with physical
            intimacy

p. 322 88. With regard to adolescent sexuality, which is FALSE?
F
        a. More adolescents are having sexual intercourse today than in the past.
        b. More adolescents masturbate today than in the past
    *   c. More adolescents are engaging in homosexual behavior than ever before.
        d. The "double standard" regarding premarital intercourse still has an impact on teenage
            sexuality.

p. 323　89.　Regarding sexuality during old age:

F
　　　　　　a.　there is a greater decrease in sexual activity among men than among women
　　　　　　b.　the majority of old women lose interest in sex entirely
　　　*　　c.　the majority of old men and women maintain an interest in sexual activity
　　　　　　d.　only a very small minority of people over age 65 continue to engage in sexual intercourse

p. 323　90.　Which is NOT a likely explanation for the decline in sexual activity reported among older
C　　　　adults?
www　　　a.　Health problems are more common among older adults
　　　　　　b.　Older adults are discouraged by society from being sexually active.
　　　　　　c.　There are fewer available partners for older adults.
　　　*　　d.　There is little interest in sexual activities among older adults.

p. 324　91.　Which appears to contribute MOST to the lack of sexual activity among old women?
F
　　　　　　a.　a physiological incapacity to engage in intercourse
　　　*　　b.　lack of a partner
　　　　　　c.　negative social attitudes toward sex during old age
　　　　　　d.　lack of interest in having sex

p. 325　92.　Projects intended to change (reduce) gender-role behavior have found that:
C　　　*　a.　short-term reduction of stereotypical gender behavior, but no long-term effects
　　　　　　b.　overall reduction of stereotypical gender behaviors among males but not females
　　　　　　c.　a change in attitudes regarding stereotypical gender behaviors, but no corresponding change in behavior
　　　　　　d.　gender roles are so firmly ingrained that not even short-term changes are possible

p. 298　93.　The process by which children learn their biological sex and acquire the motives, values,
F　　　　and behaviors considered appropriate for the members of that sex is called
SG　　*　a.　gender typing
　　　　　　b.　gender-role norms
　　　　　　c.　gender differences
　　　　　　d.　gender consistency

p. 298　94.　Females in our society have historically been encouraged to assume a(n)
F　　　　　a.　gender role
SG　　　　b.　instrumental role
　　　*　　c.　expressive role
　　　　　　d.　androgynous role

p. 299　95.　Which one the following is <u>true</u> regarding psychological differences between males and
C　　　　females?
SG　　　　a.　Males and females do not actually differ on any psychological traits or abilities.
　　　　　　b.　Wherever there is a difference between males and females, males outperform females.
　　　　　　c.　There are no differences between males and females throughout childhood, but beginning in adolescence, males outperform females in most areas.
　　　*　　d.　Females typically outperform males on verbal tasks and males typically outperform females on tests of mathematical reasoning.

p. 302 96. Most children can correctly label themselves as males or females by age _____ and
F   begin to understand that one's sex does not change around age _____.
SG   a. 5 years; 11 years
       *   b. 3 years; 6 years
           c. 18 months; 3 years
           d. 2 years; 3 years

p. 305 97. Money and Ehrhardt's biosocial theory of gender-role development suggests that
C   *   a. there are real biological differences between boys and girls and these differences
SG   influence how people react to the children
           b. biological differences between males and females cause them to behave differently and
               to have different levels of expertise in areas such as math and verbal skills
           c. biological differences males and females may exist, but these differences have no
               impact on psychological differences between males and females
           d. biological factors affect males' behavior but not females' behavior

p. 306 98. A woman who receives male hormones while she is pregnant may deliver a child who is
C   a. genetically XY and has external genitals that appear feminine
SG   *   b. genetically XX and has external genitals that appear masculine
           c. genetically XX and becomes very masculine appearing following puberty
           d. mentally retarded

p. 307 99. According to Freud's psychoanalytic explanation, boys resolve their Oedipus complexes
F   and girls resolve their Electra complexes
SG   a. when they move into the phallic stage of development
           b. out of love for their parents
           c. by identifying with the parent of the other sex
       *   d. by identifying with the same-sex parent

p. 309 100. Social learning theorists explain sex-typing as the result of
C   a. the child's understanding of gender identity and gender constancy
SG   b. the child's desire to be like his or her parents
       *   c. the parents differentially reinforcing behaviors and the child's observation of same-sex
               models
           d. chromosomal and hormonal differences between males and females

p. 311 101. According to cognitive-developmental theorists, gender-role development
C   *   a. begins with children's understanding that they are girls or boys
SG   b. begins with children imitating same-sex models
           c. begins when parents differentially reinforce boys and girls
           d. depends on observational learning

p. 312 102. When children realize that their gender is stable over time, they have achieved
C   _____, and when they realize that their gender is stable over situations, they have
SG   achieved _____.
           a. gender stability; gender identity
           b. gender identity; gender consistency
           c. gender consistency; gender stability
       *   d. gender stability; gender consistency

p. 312 103. Gender schemas
F
SG   *   a. determine a child's behavior in ambiguous situations
             b. influence the kinds of information that children attend to
             c. refer to the child's understanding that their gender is stable over time
             d. reflect the fact that children have difficulty understanding their appropriate gender roles

p. 312 104. Which of the following accurately characterizes developmental changes in thinking about
C   gender roles?
SG   a. Preschoolers are the most rigid in their thinking about gender roles.
             b. The period of young adulthood is when people hold the most rigid beliefs about gender roles.
      *   c. Children in early elementary school and adolescence hold the most rigid beliefs about gender roles.
             d. Children in middle childhood hold the most rigid beliefs about gender roles.

p. 321 105. Which of the following is <u>true</u> regarding changes in sexual attitudes?
F   a. Regardless of how they may act, most adolescents believe that premarital sex is wrong.
SG   b. Most adolescents are quite knowledgeable about sex and clearly understand today's sexual norms.
             c. The "double standard" for males and females sexual behavior no longer exists.
      *   d. Most adolescents believe that sex with affection is OK.

p. 315 106. In Sandra Bem's model, an androgynous individual is a person who is
F   *   a. high in both masculine and feminine traits
SG   b. high in masculine traits and low in feminine traits
             c. low in masculine traits and high in feminine traits
             d. low in both masculine and feminine traits

p. 317 107. With respect to androgyny, research indicates that
F   a. androgynous people are less flexible in their behavior than sex-typed people
SG   b. children of androgynous parents are more socially responsible and assertive than children of sex-typed people
      *   c. the possession of masculine traits leads to higher self-esteem and good adjustment
             d. the possession of feminine traits by men leads to better adjustment

TRUE-FALSE QUESTIONS

p. 298 108. In general, traditional sex-role stereotypes such as "women are nurturant" and "men are strong" have disappeared, primarily as a result of the women's-liberation movement and the increased number of women entering the work force.
             a. true
      *   b. false

p. 298 109. An instrumental role is illustrated by expectations for females to take care of children.
www   a. true
      *   b. false

p. 299   110. Young adults today no longer embrace traditional stereotypes regarding masculinity and femininity.
    a. true
*   b. false

p. 299   111. There are no gender stereotypes that are consistently supported by research.
    a. true
*   b. false

p. 300   112. According to the social-role hypothesis, roles in society are determined by biological sex.
    a. true
*   b. false

p. 301   113. Adults treat male and female infants differently.
*   a. true
    b. false

p. 302   114. Gender stereotypes are generally not acquired by youngsters until they begin formal www schooling at age 4 or 5.
    a. true
*   b. false

p. 302   115. Third graders are likely to be more concerned and troubled by violations of traditional gender-role standards than are first grade youngsters.
    a. true
*   b. false

p. 302   116. Infants begin to behave in what are considered to be "gender-appropriate" ways even before they are aware that they are a boy or a girl.
*   a. true
    b. false

p. 303   117. Children often become very rigid about what males and females "should" do at about the time they acquire gender stability.
*   a. true
    b. false

p. 305   118. A fertilized egg has to potential to develop the anatomical genitalia of either sex regardless
www   of whether it carries XX or XY chromosomes.
*   a. true
    b. false

p. 307   119. Freud's claims regarding infantile sexuality have been totally discredited.
    a. true
*   b. false

p. 307   120. According to Freud, gender identity is achieved during the genital stage.
    a. true
*   b. false

p. 307　121. In order to resolve the internal conflict that arises during the phallic stage, children identify with their opposite parent.
　　　　　　a.　true
　　　*　　b.　false

p. 308　122. Boys identify more strongly with fathers who are warm and nurturant than with those who are threatening and punitive.
　　　*　　a.　true
　　　　　　b.　false

p. 309　123. Children develop distinct preferences for "boy toys" or "girl toys" even before they are clear about their own gender identity.
　　　*　　a.　true
　　　　　　b.　false

p. 309　124. In general, little boys learn gender stereotypes and gender-typed behaviors more rapidly than do little girls.
　　　*　　a.　true
　　　　　　b.　false

p. 309　125. Fathers are more likely than mothers to differentially reinforce children's play with gender-typed toys.
　　*　　　a.　true
　　　　　　b.　false

p. 313　126. Most observed differences between males and females are due to biological causes.
　　　　　　a.　true
　　　*　　b.　false

p. 313　127. Gender identity and gender-role development are influenced by both biological and social factors.
　　　*　　a.　true
　　　　　　b.　false

p. 314　128. During middle childhood, relationships between the sexes are relatively ambivalent.
　　　*　　a.　true
　　　　　　b.　false

p. 314　129. Gender-role socialization is relatively independent of cultural influence.
　　　　　　a.　true
　　　*　　b.　false

p. 314　130. Research suggests that becoming parents tends to decrease psychological differences between men and women.
　　　　　　a.　true
　　　*　　b.　false

p. 321　131. In the United States, the double standard is on the decline.
　　　*　　a.　true
　　　　　　b.　false

p. 322 132. Most adolescent couples today regularly use some form of contraceptive.
  a. true
* b. false

p. 323 133. In general, sexual activity tends to increase over the course of the child-bearing years.
  a. true
* b. false

p. 323 134. Older adults are usually no longer interested in sex.
  a. true
* b. false

p. 323 135. Level of sexual activity during young adulthood predicts level of sexual activity later in life.
* a. true
  b. false

ESSAY QUESTIONS

136. Why does gender segregation occur? When is gender segregation most pronounced? Why?

137. What evidence suggests that observed gender differences are due to differences in socialization?
www

138. How do the psychoanalytic, social learning, and cognitive explanations of gender typing compare to one another? Are there points on which they agree?

139. In what ways have sexual attitudes and behaviors changed over the last few decades? What is responsible for these changes?

140. How do sexual behaviors change over the life span?

141. One issue debated by scholars in the field of gender roles is the existence of actual differences
SG between males and females. Are there "real" gender differences? Discuss all sides of this issue and provide evidence to support each position.
  [Sample answer is provided in the Study Guide.]

142. Which theory of gender-role development seems to have the most empirical support? Justify
SG your answer.

143. Which ideas of Freud seem to be accurate regarding early sexuality and gender-role
SG development, and which ideas of Freud have not been supported?

144. What happens to gender roles and gender differences during adulthood?
SG

SOCIAL COGNITION AND MORAL DEVELOPMENT

MULTIPLE CHOICE QUESTIONS

p. 329 1. Social cognition is BEST defined as:
F
   a. knowledge of how to behave in social situations to make the best impression
   b. knowing who gets along with whom
 * c. thinking about the thoughts, feelings, motives, and behaviors of self and others
   d. being aware of current "codes" for dressing and dating

p. 329 2. Having a theory of mind indicates that an individual:
F
   a. understands how the mind works
   b. can draw inferences
 * c. understands that mental states exist and guide behavior
   d. can reason about abstract concepts

p. 329 3. Wendy puts her toys away in the toy chest and goes to eat dinner. Her brother,
C   unbeknownst to her, decides to "relocate" all her toys. A child who has a theory of mind
www would predict that, when Wendy returns after dinner, she will:
 * a. look for her toys in the toy chest
   b. look for her toys where her brother has relocated them
   c. not remember anything about her toys
   d. try to think of where her brother likes to hide things

p. 329 4. The "false belief" task is used to assess
F
   a. how a person would reason about a moral dilemma
 * b. the understanding that people have personal theories that influence their behaviors
   c. a person's stage of social cognition
   d. a person's cognitive understanding of the world

p. 330 5. Children are normally able to solve false beliefs tasks around age:
F
   a. 2
 * b. 4
   c. 6
   d. 8

p. 330 6. Infants show precursors of a theory of mind when they
C * a. engage in joint attention with their caregiver
   b. reach for their reflection in a mirror
   c. get upset when their caregiver leaves the room
   d. ask for more of something

p. 331 7. Sarah tries to wipe up the juice that she spilled all over the living room floor so that her dad
C doesn't see that she disobeyed him by taking juice out of the kitchen. This suggests that
Sarah:
   a. has an understanding based on desire psychology
   b. has developed a morality based on rules and authority
   * c. can engage in deceitful behavior, a sign of a theory of mind
   d. cannot be trusted to make appropriate moral decisions

p. 331 8. Someone with a belief-desire psychology understands that
C * a. people do not always hold accurate beliefs, but these beliefs still influence behavior
   b. beliefs accurately reflect what we desire
   c. desires shape our behavior
   d. people develop accurate beliefs based on interactions with others

p. 332 9. In describing other people, an 8-year-old child is MOST likely to:
F a. speak in terms of physical appearance and actions
www * b. refer to enduring psychological traits such as being friendly or bossy
   c. make social comparisons of psychological traits such as "Jenny is smarter than Joe."
   d. provide explanations regarding the underlying reasons why their friends behave as they
   really do

p. 332 10. Which description of a friend is MOST LIKELY to be offered by an 8-year-old child?
C a. She's pretty and she has dark hair and I like her toys.
   * b. She's nice and funny and friendly, and she's smart.
   c. She's smarter than anyone else and she's friendly and funny, but sometimes she's not as
   fun to be with as my other friends.
   d. Sometimes she's nice but sometimes she's mean. And she's smart in math, but not in
   reading.

p. 332 11. Jill tells Vicki about her mom, and then asks Vicky what her mom is like. Vicki says "My
C mom is pretty and tall and she makes great chocolate chip cookies." Vicki's description of
her mom is MOST typical of a ___ -year-old child.
   a. 2
   * b. 5
   c. 8
   d. 12

p. 332 12. What important advance in social cognition generally occurs at age 11 or 12?
F a. children begin to describe others in terms of the activities they engage in
   b. children begin to describe others in terms of inner, psychological traits and
   characteristics
   * c. children begin to compare people to one another on psychological dimensions
   d. children begin to focus heavily on others' physical appearance in their descriptions of
   them

p. 332 13. Hank is 12 years old. In describing a friend, Hank is MOST LIKELY to say:
C
        a. He's good at sports and he has a really cool bike.
        b. He's fun to be with, and I trust him.
*   c. He's about the smartest kid I know, and he's the best soccer player on our team. He's really fair, too, and he tries to help all the other kids score.
        d. He's pretty nice, but sometimes he's not. He's really strong, and he plays soccer.

p. 332 14. Which shows the greatest degree of sophistication in children's understanding of what other people are like?
F
        a. describing others in terms of personality traits
        b. describing others in terms of physical capabilities
        c. making social comparisons between classmates
*   d. explaining why other people behave as they do

p. 333 15. Studies on perspective taking indicate that:
C
        a. even preschool children usually understand that other people may not see things in the same way that they do
*   b. changes in cognition relate to changes in role-taking skills
        c. it is not until a child attains formal operational thinking that s/he is able to understand another person's point of view
        d. the shift from preoperational to concrete-operational thinking permits one to consider simultaneously a number of different perspectives

p. 333 16. At what point is a child first able to simultaneously consider the viewpoint of another person along with his/her own?
C
        a. with the attainment of the person-permanence concept
        b. when s/he makes the transition from preoperational to concrete-operational thought
*   c. when s/he begins to shift to formal operational thinking
        d. only when they can consider the perspective of a "generalized other"

p. 333 17. The social cognition of adolescents is best distinguished from that of younger children by the adolescent's ability to:
C
www
        a. understand that not all people see things in the same way
*   b. simultaneously consider all possible perspectives
        c. understand a parent's perspective
        d. recognize distinct personality traits in others

p. 334 18. A child who is able to see things from a number of different points of view is MORE LIKELY than an egocentric agemate to:
F
        a. be sociable
        b. be skilled at resolving social conflicts
        c. have close friends
*   d. all of the above

p. 334   19.   Which of the following is TRUE regarding the development of role-taking skills?
F   a.   Conflicts with peers get in the way of the development of perspective-taking skills.
           b.   Children as young as 4 understand that parents may not think the way they do.
           c.   Concrete-operational thinkers are capable of simultaneously considering several different points of view.
     *   d.   The ability to consider a situation from a number of different points of view increases the quality of one's social relationships.

p. 334   20.   The social-cognitive abilities of adults:
F   a.   decline steadily in old age
           b.   increase steadily between middle- and old age
     *   c.   depend more on social experiences than on chronological age
           d.   decline more rapidly than nonsocial cognitive skills

p. 335   21.   Which of the following is an example of the affective component of morality?
C   a.   knowing that you made the right decision in a difficult situation
           b.   feeling good about giving money to charity
           c.   taking some food from the cafeteria without paying for it
           d.   jumping up and down in joy after you win the lottery

p. 335   22.   Which perspective is MOST concerned with the affective (emotional) component of moral
F   development?
           a.   cognitive-developmental theory
     *   b.   psychoanalytic theory
           c.   social-learning theory
           d.   traditional learning theory

p. 335   23.   Empathy refers to:
F   *   a.   vicariously experiencing another's feelings
           b.   reading minds
           c.   being able to resist temptation
           d.   knowing that someone holds a false belief

p. 335   24.   Who is experiencing an empathic response?
C   a.   Margaret, who is depressed because she lost her job.
           b.   Ann, who feels sorry for her neighbors because their dog got run over by a car.
     *   c.   James, who cries as he watches a news documentary about a mother who lost her son to AIDS.
           d.   Gloria, who is excited about going on her first date.

p. 335   25.   An example of empathy would be:
C   a.   escaping pain
www   b.   sensing that you are about to get a phone call
     *   c.   being afraid for the hero in a movie
           d.   looking forward to watching the villain in a movie die

p. 335 26. Michelle wanted a "beanie baby" but didn't have the money to buy one. One day she was
C   in a store at the mall, and when she thought no one was looking, she slipped a beanie baby
             into her bag and left without paying for it. Later, when she was playing with it, she found
             she wasn't enjoying herself very much, and she felt bad that she had stolen the beanie baby.
             Taking the beanie baby from the store represents the _____ component of morality
             while the fact that she felt bad represents the _____ component of morality:
             a. affective; cognitive
       *   b. behavioral; affective
             c. cognitive; affective
             d. behavioral; cognitive

p. 335 27. After paying for her groceries, Linda went to her car and loaded the bags into her trunk.
C   On the bottom of the grocery cart, Linda found a case of beer and realized that she hadn't
             been charged for it. Linda popped it into her trunk and when she got home she told her
             roommate what had happened. She said: "Oh, well, it's a big store and they can do without
             the money. It's really not my fault. The cashier should have spotted it and rung it up."
             This response to the situation BEST illustrates the _____ component of morality:
             a. psychomotor
       *   b. cognitive
             c. behavioral
             d. affective

p. 335 28. According to Freud, a moral conscience is formed during the _____ stage with the
C   emergence of the _____.
www   *   a. phallic; superego
             b. phallic; ego
             c. genital; superego
             d. latency; Oedipus complex

p. 335 29. Jessica feels guilty after taking pocket change from her father's dresser drawer. According
C   to Freud, this emotional response BEST indicates:
             a. Jessica is in the genital stage.
             b. Jessica is responding from the id.
       *   c. Jessica has successfully resolved the Electra complex.
             d. Jessica's superego has not yet developed.

p. 336 30. According to Freud:
C   *   a. Females are generally less moral than males.
             b. Young infants are born with an innate understanding of right and wrong.
             c. Moral development begins with the emergence of the ego, prior to the phallic stage of
                development.
             d. A sense of morality develops during adolescence, as a result of engaging in dialogue
                and debate with peers.

p. 336   31.   A child's internalization of the same-sex parent's moral standards leads to the:
C
     *   a.   development of the id
     *   b.   development of the superego
         c.   development of the ego
         d.   reduction of the id

p. 336   32.   Which of Freud's assertions has been upheld by research?
F
         a.   females have weaker superegos than males
         b.   moral maturity is achieved by age 6 or 7
     *   c.   emotions play a critical role in moral development
         d.   threatening, punitive parents produce children who are more morally strong than
             parents who are warm and loving

p. 336   33.   Which theoretical perspective views a child's moral reasoning as more significant than
F   their actual behavior in a moral situation?
         a.   psychoanalytic theory
         b.   social-learning theory
         c.   traditional learning theory
     *   d.   cognitive-developmental theory

p. 336   34.   According to Piaget,
C   *   a.   children of elementary-school age believe that rules are "written in stone"
www   b.   children are premoral until they enter adolescence
         c.   starting in elementary school, children are able to take intentions as well as
             consequences into account in a moral situation
         d.   up until adolescence, children believe that rules are quite flexible

p. 336   35.   According to Piaget, children in second or third grade are MOST LIKELY to believe that:
C
         a.   if they are careful, they can do things they know they shouldn't do and get away with it
         b.   if somebody didn't mean any harm, they shouldn't be punished for what they did
     *   c.   rules are to be obeyed at all times
         d.   a punishment should fit the crime

p. 337   36.   The cognitive-developmental perspective assumes all of the following EXCEPT:
C
         a.   moral reasoning progresses through a series of invariant stages
         b.   moral development is dependent on cognitive development
         c.   what we actually do is less significant than how we decide what to do
     *   d.   the sequence of stages in moral development is determined by one's culture

p. 337   37.   Kohlberg's cognitive-developmental theory of moral development claims that:
C
         a.   regression from a higher to a lower stage of moral reasoning is quite common
         b.   through an exploration of moral dilemmas, it is possible to teach someone to skip over
             the lower stages of moral development
         c.   the sequence of stages one goes through may vary from one culture to another
     *   d.   a person's stage of moral development is determined by the person's thoughts, rather
             than his/her actions

p. 337 38. Which statement reflects Kohlberg's conventional morality?
C
www   a. "Do your own thing."
    b. "Scratch my back and I'll scratch your's."
    c. "Rules are made to be broken."
*   d. "Buckle up. It's the law!"

p. 337 39. At what level of moral development are the rules and standards of society internalized and
C   held as one's own?
    a. preconventional
*   b. conventional
    c. postconventional
    d. autonomous

p. 337 40. An individual who is at Kohlberg's conventional level of moral development is MOST
F   LIKELY to:
    a. follow the rules so they won't get punished
    b. do something nice for someone so that they will be rewarded in return
    c. believe that rules are made to be broken
*   d. behave in ways that earn the approval and avoid the disapproval of others

p. 338 41. Max refuses to pay his income tax because he believes that the government uses taxes for
C   poor purposes. Most notably, he is opposed to the use of tax funds to support war efforts,
    because he doesn't believe that violence is an acceptable way to solve problems. He is
    willing to go to jail for his belief. Max is BEST classified as being in Kohlberg's _____
    level of moral development:
    a. premoral
    b. preconventional
    c. conventional
*   d. postconventional

p. 338 42. According to Kohlberg, the most mature level of moral development is characterized by:
C   a. internalization of the rules and standards of one's own society
*   b. the creation of universal ethical principles
    c. behavior that is in accordance with the law
    d. an understanding that justice is immanent

p. 339 43. Regarding Kohlberg's theory of moral development, which cognitive skill is particularly
C   instrumental in promoting movement from one level of moral development to the next?
*   a. the development of perspective-taking abilities
    b. emergence of the object permanence concept
    c. the development of a theory of mind
    d. the development of conservation skills

p. 339 44. The social-learning perspective on moral development holds that morality is:
C   a. a generalized personality trait
*   b. situation-specific behavior
    c. driven by physiological motives
    d. determined more by level of reasoning than by actual behavior

p. 339 45. What do the psychoanalytic and cognitive-developmental perspectives on moral
C   development share in common?
             a. They both view moral reasoning as being more significant than actual behavior or
                 emotions.
             b. They both suggest that moral development proceeds through an invariant sequence of
                 three stages.
       *   c. They both view morality as a kind of personality trait.
             d. They both view experiences during early childhood as the critical determinant of one's
                 ultimate level of moral development.

p. 339 46. Dr. Barnes believes that we all have times when we do things we know we shouldn't do.
C   For example, we may roll through a stop sign if there is no police car around, or cheat on a
             test if we feel a great deal of pressure to do well and think we can get away with it.
             However, if we think we might get caught, by the police or a professor, we tend to behave
             differently. This perspective is MOST consistent with that of:
             a. Piaget
             b. Skinner
       *   c. Bandura
             d. Freud

p. 339 47. Pete sees his brother steal a pack of gum from the drug store and get away with it. The
C   next time Pete goes to the drug store, he pockets a pack of gum. According to the _____
             perspective on moral development, Pete's behavior is the result of _____ :
             a. psychoanalytic; observational learning
             b. cognitive-developmental; an underdeveloped superego
       *   c. social learning; observational learning
             d. psychoanalytic; a weak ego

p. 340 48. Regarding moral development in infancy, which is TRUE?
F   a. Infants are incapable of empathy.
             b. Infants are not motivated to help others in distress.
       *   c. Infants under age one cannot evaluate their own behavior in terms of right and wrong.
             d. Infants are incapable of learning moral lessons regarding such things as stealing and
                 sharing.

p. 340 49. Children as young as ___ tend to anticipate the disapproval of others:
F   *   a. 2
             b. 4
             c. 6
             d. 8

p. 341 50. Which of the following BEST exemplifies prosocial behavior?
C   a. doing chores to earn allowance
             b. driving no faster than the speed limit
             c. getting homework done on time
       *   d. stopping to help a stranger change a flat tire

p. 342   51.   Kohlberg believed that:
F   *   a.   most preschoolers are not really moral beings
           b.   children as young as 4 have generally adopted society's standards for behavior as their own
           c.   infants have an innate sense of right and wrong
           d.   environmental factors have very little impact on moral reasoning

p. 342   52.   What does the research on young children's moral development tell us?
F   a.   Nearly all young children place greater emphasis on intentions than on consequences in judging moral behavior.
     *   b.   Piaget underestimated the child's ability to consider intentions.
           c.   Piaget overestimated the moral development of young children.
           d.   Young children do indeed view all rules as rigid, absolute, and unchangeable.

p. 343   53.   Turiel made a distinction between "moral" rules and "social-conventional" rules.
C   Which BEST exemplifies the concept of a moral rule?
           a.   Don't run in the halls.
     *   b.   Don't take things that don't belong to you.
           c.   Don't chew gum in school.
           d.   Don't sneak snacks into the movie theater.

p. 343   54.   Which is the BEST example of a social-conventional rule?
C   a.   Don't take things that don't belong to you.
www   b.   Don't hit other people.
     *   c.   Don't eat or drink in the lecture hall.
           d.   Be kind to animals.

p. 343   55.   Carlos believes that rules such as "don't lie or steal" are more important than a rule such as
C   "don't eat food in the living room." The YOUNGEST Carlos is likely to be is:
     *   a.   3
           b.   6
           c.   8
           d.   10

p. 343   56.   Both Piaget and Kohlberg believed that:
C   *   a.   the moral skills of young children are quite limited
           b.   with regard to level of moral development, actions speak louder than words
           c.   an individual's moral character is determined by social interactions during the early childhood years
           d.   by age 3, children can distinguish between moral and social-conventional rules

p. 343   57.   Hartshorne and May, in their classic study of moral behavior in young children, found that:
F   a.   the behavior of most children is consistent with their values
           b.   children's behavior is highly consistent from one situation to another
           c.   children who cheat do not think cheating is wrong
     *   d.   morality is situation specific, rather than a stable personality trait

p. 343 58. Which BEST describes the relationship between moral thought and behavior in young
C children?
    a. Children's moral behavior is highly consistent with their level of moral reasoning.
  * b. Children often espouse a more rigid moral standard than they themselves adhere to.
    c. Children don't violate their own moral rules.
    d. Children are very nonjudgmental in their evaluations of others' moral transgressions.

p. 343 59. Which is TRUE?
F
    a. Young children tend to adhere to rigid standards of moral behavior.
    b. Young children (under age 8) do not understand that cheating is wrong.
    c. Young children tend to practice more rigid moral standards than they preach.
  * d. Young children's moral behavior is fairly inconsistent from situation to situation.

p. 344 60. Which is TRUE regarding the role of punishment in moral development?
F
    a. Punishment is a highly effective means of promoting moral development.
  * b. Punishment only temporarily suppresses unwanted behavior.
    c. To be effective in eliminating unwanted behavior, punishment must be very severe.
    d. Children generally believe that if their parents punish them it means they care.

p. 344 61. With regard to fostering moral development, punishment tends to:
F
    a. be more effective if it is harsh
    b. work better than an inductive approach
    c. be highly effective for boys only
  * d. have undesirable side effects

p. 344 62. With regard to moral development, the MOST influential models are those who:
F
    a. provide elaborate rationales regarding the need to modify behavior
  * b. provide developmentally appropriate rationales for what they are doing
    c. are themselves the same age as the misbehaver
    d. are perceived as threatening

p. 344 63. The BEST way to "teach a moral lesson" is to:
C
    a. punish a child
    b. threaten a child
    c. be highly disapproving of behavioral transgressions
  * d. explain why behavior should change

p. 344 64. Which sort of rationale would likely make the MOST sense to a preconventional child?
C
    a. Don't hit Jimmy because you should never hurt anyone.
    b. Don't hit Jimmy because it's against the rules.
  * c. Don't hit Jimmy because you'll get in trouble with the teacher.
    d. Don't hit Jimmy because there are better ways to get what you want.

p. 344 65. Tommy's fifth grade teacher reports that he frequently bullies other children on the
C playground. Tommy's parents are MOST likely to change his behavior if they:
    a. spank him
    b. tell him they won't love him if he acts that way
    c. ground him for a month
  * d. explain why his behavior should change

p. 344 66. Freddie practically killed his pet hamster when he popped him in the tub for a bubblebath.
C   His parents take an inductive approach in responding to this situation by:
              a. giving the hamster away so Freddy can't do any more damage
              b. spanking Freddie for doing the wrong thing
      *   c. explaining to Freddie that hamsters don't like baths, and can get sick or die from getting
                  too wet
              d. telling Freddie he's a very mean little boy and they are very disappointed in him

p. 344 67. Which approach to dealing with wrongdoing BEST promotes moral development?
F   a. showing children who's the boss
www   b. withholding affection or other forms of reinforcement when a child misbehaves
      *   c. explaining the effect of the wrongdoing on others
              d. taking away privileges

p. 345 68. Throughout adolescence, there is a decrease in _____ moral reasoning and an
F   increase in _____ moral reasoning.
              a. conventional; postconventional
      *   b. preconventional; conventional
              c. conventional; preconventional
              d. rule-based; social-conventional

p. 346 69. Studies have suggested that antisocial adolescents engage in:
F   *   a. preconventional moral reasoning
              b. conventional moral reasoning
              c. postconventional moral reasoning
              d. social-conventional reasoning

p. 346 70. According to Kenneth Dodge, the main thing wrong with teenagers who commit violent,
F   antisocial acts is:
www   a. their genetic makeup
              b. the coercive family environments in which they were raised
      *   c. the way they process social cues
              d. the culture in which they live

p. 347 71. Highly aggressive youth:
C   a. understand that what they are doing is wrong, but do not care
              b. consider all aspects of a task before acting aggressively
              c. normally have tried other, nonviolent options before acting aggressively
      *   d. believe that their aggressive acts will produce positive consequences

p. 348 72. Severe antisocial behavior:
F   a. is primarily determined by genetics
              b. is primarily due to environmental influences
      *   c. most likely results from a combination of genetic and environmental influences
              d. is equally prevalent in different societies

p. 348 73. Tim deliberately sneaks up on Paul and hits him over the head in retaliation for something
C   that Paul did earlier in the day. This is an example of
www   a. reactive aggression
      * b. proactive aggression
         c. coercive aggression
         d. power assertion

p. 348 74. Sammy gets frustrated at school because things are not going the way he wants them to.
C   When William bumps into Sammy's desk and knocks his work to the floor, Sammy
            quickly responds by shoving William into the wall. This is an example of:
      * a. reactive aggression
         b. proactive aggression
         c. coercive aggression
         d. power assertion

p. 348 75. Which of the following is TRUE regarding contributors to aggression?
C   a. Aggression is determined by genetic factors and does not vary cross-culturally.
            b. Aggression is solely a product of neglectful parenting.
      *   c. Some cultures tolerate and encourage more aggression than others.
            d. The social environment contributes very little to cases of severe aggressive behavior.

p. 349 76. According to Patterson's model of the development of antisocial behavior:
C   a. children fall in with a bad crowd when they are young, which leads to distancing from
                their parents and rejection by normal peers
      *   b. children with conduct problems and poor parental monitoring/discipline end up being
                rejected by their peers and doing poorly in school, which in turn leads to antisocial
                behavior
            c. children are genetically predisposed to act aggressively and this causes peer rejection,
                which in turn leads to antisocial behavior
            d. children have parents who engage in antisocial behavior and they begin to imitate this
                behavior and find that it is reinforcing

p. 349 77. Coercive family environments refer to situations where:
C   a. parents gain more and more power over their children
      *   b. family members are locked in power struggles
            c. family members use discussion to try to persuade others to adopt their position
            d. family members establish a power hierarchy that allows them to solve problems swiftly
                and smoothly

p. 349 78. Regarding moral development, which is TRUE?
F   a. By age 30, most individuals are postconventional moral reasoners.
            b. Moral reasoning deteriorates in old age.
      *   c. There is little change in moral reasoning from early adulthood to old age.
            d. Religion starts to play a significant role in moral choices during old age.

p. 349 79. Research on Kohlberg's model of moral development indicates that:

F
        a. it is possible to skip one or more stages

        b. the sequence of stages within a level (preconventional, conventional, postconventional) can be reversed, but the sequence of progression through levels is always the same

        c. regression to a lower stage or level is very common

*   d. most adults do not progress beyond stage 3 or 4

p. 350 80. Fowler's ideas regarding stages of faith:

F
        a. ignore the role of social experience in determining level of faith

        b. contradict those of Erikson and Piaget

*   c. are highly compatible with Kohlberg's stages of moral reasoning

        d. suggest that few people are truly motivated to find purpose and direction in life

p. 350 81. Which is TRUE with regard to involvement in religion during old age?

C
        a. Old people generally become disillusioned with religion as a result of their significant health problems.

*   b. The importance of religion does not change significantly with age.

        c. Old people generally become highly religious in preparation for death.

        d. Participation in organized religious activities increases from middle to old age.

p. 350 82. The primary developmental trend in moral reasoning during adolescence is a shift from:

F   *   a. preconventional to conventional moral reasoning

www   b. conventional to postconventional moral reasoning

        c. premoral to autonomous morality

        d. conventional to heteronomous morality

p. 350 83. One weakness of Kohlberg's theory of moral reasoning is that:

C
        a. people tend not to reason cognitively about moral dilemmas

        b. he overestimated what adolescents were able to do

        c. he did not include enough stages in his model

*   d. people use reasoning from several stages rather than a single stage

p. 351 84. What type of interaction BEST promotes the development of moral reasoning?

F   *   a. debating moral matters with peers

        b. lectures from parents on moral matters

        c. listening to religious sermons

        d. discussing moral issues with parents

p. 351 85. Research on the discussion of moral issues indicates that

C
        a. it is not possible to accelerate children's progression through Kohlberg's stages of moral reasoning

        b. cognitive disequilibrium is confusing to children and impedes their moral growth

*   c. groups designed to enhance moral reasoning should be made up of children who are at different levels of moral reasoning

        d. we can achieve equal gains by lecturing to children about morality as by having them discuss the issues

p. 352　86.　Which of the following is a common criticism of Kohlberg's theory of moral development?
F　　　　　a.　Kohlberg ignores the role cognition plays in moral development.
www　　　b.　Too much emphasis is placed on sex-differences in moral development.
　　　*　c.　The theory reflects a cultural bias in favor of Western, liberal values.
　　　　　d.　The approach is too behaviorally oriented.

p. 354　87.　Gilligan claims that:
F　　*　a.　women often think more in terms of responsibility to others than about issues of justice in resolving moral dilemmas
　　　　　b.　women are less sophisticated than men in their moral reasoning
　　　　　c.　there are no significant sex differences in moral reasoning
　　　　　d.　women have more definitive ideas of "right" and "wrong" than do men

p. 354　88.　Research on gender differences in moral reasoning has revealed that:
F　　　　　a.　women are generally morally inferior to men
　　　　　b.　men are generally morally inferior to women
　　　　　c.　there are systematic differences in the ways women and men approach moral matters, and these differences persist regardless of cultural context
　　　*　d.　both women and men often think about moral issues in terms of their responsibilities to others

p. 354　89.　Kohlberg's theory of moral development:
C　　*　a.　largely ignores the role of affect in moral development
　　　　　b.　ignores the role of social experience in promoting moral growth
　　　　　c.　is biased against those who hold individualistic and democratic values
　　　　　d.　contradicts the major principles of Piagetian theory

p. 355　90.　Kohlberg's theory of moral development has been criticized for all of the following
F　　　　　EXCEPT:
　　　　　a.　it ignores the role of culture in shaping moral reasoning
　　　*　b.　it emphasizes gender differences in moral development
　　　　　c.　it is biased against those from non-Western cultures
　　　　　d.　it largely ignores both the emotional and behavioral aspects of moral development

p. 356　91.　Research on the effectiveness of programs aimed at reducing youth violence shows that:
F　　　　　a.　they are highly effective
　　　*　b.　they bring short-term improvements but few long-term advantages
　　　　　c.　they are not able to alter patterns of antisocial behavior and violence
　　　　　d.　the ones that focus on cognitive change are effective while those that focus on behavioral change are not

p. 329　92.　Having a theory of mind shows an understanding that
C　　　　　a.　people's behavior is guided by a set of internalized set of rules about right and wrong
SG　　　　b.　more than one person is looking at an object at a particular time
　　　*　c.　people have mental states that influence their behavior
　　　　　d.　other people experience different emotions

p. 334 93. Children who are popular and have close friends
C
SG
    a. reason at the "good boy" "good girl" stage of moral reasoning
    b. tend to use more reactive aggression than proactive aggression
    c. are more likely to have an intuitive theory of emotions
    * d. tend to have more advanced role-taking skills than other children

p. 334 94. Social cognitive skills
C
SG   *
    a. reach a peak as adolescents finish their formal schooling and then slowly decline
    b. remain high in socially active older adults
    c. relate specifically to a person's educational level
    d. decline from young to older adulthood for most adults

p. 335 95. According to Freud's psychoanalytic theory
C   *
SG
    a. children reach moral maturity around age 6 or 7 when they resolve their Oedipal (or Electra) conflicts
    b. girls are more morally mature than boys since they have less to fear during the phallic stage of development
    c. children reach moral maturity in adolescence when they enter the genital stage of development
    d. the reasons behind an act are more important than how one feels about a moral action

p. 336 96. Research on Freud's explanation of morality shows that all of the following are PROBLEMS with the explanation EXCEPT:
C
SG
    a. males do not have stronger superegos than females
    b. children do not achieve moral maturity by resolving the conflicts of the phallic stage
    c. children do not develop greater moral maturity by interacting with cold, punitive parents
    * d. children do not experience feelings in conjunction with moral transgressions

p. 337 97. A child says that it is wrong to cheat because he or she might get caught would be in Kohlberg's _____ stage.
C
SG
    a. punishment-and-obedience orientation (stage 1)
    b. instrumental hedonism (stage 2)
    c. "good boy" or "good girl" morality (stage 3)
    d. authority and social-order-maintaining morality (stage 4)

p. 337 98. A teenager who begins smoking because all his friends are doing it, is probably in Kohlberg's _____ stage.
C
SG
    a. instrumental hedonism (stage 2)
    * b. "good boy" or "good girl" morality (stage 3)
    c. authority and social-order-maintaining morality (stage 4)
    d. morality of contract, individual rights, and democratically accepted law (stage 5)

p. 339 99. Social learning theorists argue that morality is
C
SG
    a. a generalized trait inherent to the person and subject to little change
    b. a situation-specific trait that is subject to change
    c. an emotional reaction and cannot be directly observed
    d. established in early childhood and changes little after this

p. 342   100. Piaget argued that elementary school children
C   a. are largely unaware of moral rules and so do not always act appropriately
SG   b. base decisions on both consequences of an action and intentions of the actor
               c. believe that rules can be changed at any time
               d. believe that the consequences of an action are more important than intentions of the
                   actor

p. 343   101. Standards of what behaviors are right or wrong based on rights and privileges of
F   individuals are termed
SG   a. postconventional rules
               b. social-conventional rules
         *   c. moral rules
               d. altruistic rules

p. 343   102. Recent studies of Kohlberg's and Piaget's theories of moral reasoning suggest that
C   a. there is no relationship between level of cognitive development and moral reasoning
SG   *   b. they underestimated children's moral reasoning capabilities
               c. they overestimated children's moral reasoning capabilities
               d. they focused too much attention on children's actions in a moral situation

p. 344   103. Parents who discipline their children by making them anxious about whether they will
F   receive affection or approval are using
SG   *   a. love withdrawal
               b. power assertion
               c. emotional assertion
               d. induction

p. 344   104. Parents who use an inductive style of discipline
F   a. indoctrinate their child with their own values and beliefs
SG   b. withhold attention until their child complies with rules
               c. use their power to get their child to comply with rules
         *   d. explain to their child why the behavior is wrong and emphasize how it affects other
                   people

p. 345   105. Moral maturity can be fostered by
C   *   a. using an inductive style of discipline
SG   b. using love-withdrawal as the major disciplinary method
               c. using power assertion as the major disciplinary method
               d. harsh discipline that leaves the child in no doubt about whether a behavior is acceptable
                   or not

p. 354   106. Carol Gilligan claims that men and women score at different levels on Kohlberg's moral
C   dilemmas because
SG   *   a. males operate on the basis of a morality of justice and women do not
               b. Freud was right--females are less morally mature
               c. males are more concerned about the needs of others
               d. males reason about real life dilemmas while women reason about hypothetical moral
                   issues

p. 329   107. A theory of mind allows children to understand that other people's behavior is governed by their belief systems.
*   a. true
         b. false

p. 331   108. Children begin to understand wants and desires before they understand beliefs.
*   a. true
         b. false

p. 331   109. Research with autistic children shows that acquiring a theory of mind depends solely on neurological maturation.
         a. true
*   b. false

p. 332   110. Preschool-age children are likely to describe other people in terms of their personality characteristics.
         a. true
*   b. false

p. 333   111. Children who have achieved formal operational thought can integrate multiple perspectives to resolve a problem.
*   a. true
         b. false

p. 334   112. Children with more advanced role-taking skills are usually more popular than children who
www   have weak role-taking skills.
*   a. true
         b. false

p. 336   113. Freud's claim that women have weaker superegos than do men has been substantiated by research.
         a. true
*   b. false

p. 336   114. According to the cognitive-developmental perspective, it is more important to understand how we decide what to do than how we actually behave when we face moral issues.
*   a. true
         b. false

p. 337   115. According to Kohlberg, individuals in the same stage of moral development may make totally opposite decisions regarding how to behave in a given situation.
*   a. true
         b. false

p. 342   116. Research on Piaget's theory of moral development confirms that children do not usually take a person's intentions into account when making a decision about the person's actions.
       a.   true
*   b.   false

p. 343   117. Research indicates that both Kohlberg and Piaget underestimated the young child's capacity for moral reasoning.
*   a.   true
       b.   false

p. 344   118. The most effective way to promote moral development is to temporarily withhold love and affection when a child does something wrong.
       a.   true
*   b.   false

p. 344   119. Parents who explain to their children why their misbehavior is wrong foster higher levels of moral reasoning than parents who use other approaches to misbehavior.
*   a.   true
       b.   false

p. 345   120. The majority of adolescents have achieved Kohlberg's postconventional level of moral
www   reasoning.
       a.   true
*   b.   false

p. 346   121. According to Dodge's social-information model, antisocial adolescents process information differently than other adolescents.
*   a.   true
       b.   false

p. 347   122. Aggressive adolescents usually believe that there will be negative consequences for their aggressive behavior.
       a.   true
*   b.   false

p. 349   123. By middle-age, a majority of adults have progressed to Kohlberg's post-conventional level of moral reasoning.
       a.   true
*   b.   false

p. 350   124. Adults who remain active in their religious faith tend to be better adjusted and happier than other adults.
*   a.   true
       b.   false

p. 354   125. Gilligan's claim that Kohlberg's theory of moral development is sex-biased has been heavily substantiated by research.
       a.   true
*   b.   false

126. Dr. Cairns must decide whether or not to give a lethal dose of narcotics to a dying patient who is in a great deal of pain. What sorts of things would Dr. Cairns consider in making his decision at each of Kohlberg's six stages of moral development?.

127. To what extent has research supported Kohlberg's theory of moral reasoning? How would the theory need to be strengthened to address concerns raised by recent research?

128. What makes some adolescents aggressive and antisocial? What factors might reduce antisocial www behaviors?

129. What is it about an induction approach to discipline that leads to greater moral maturity in SG comparison to children raised with power assertion or love withdrawal? [Sample answer is provided in the Study Guide.]

130. On Halloween night, several of your friends try to talk you into going out with them to SG pull some pranks in the neighborhood (e.g., soaping the neighbor's windows, scaring young children, and knocking over gravestones). You are considering it. What preconventional, conventional, and postconventional answers might you give (either to join in or to abstain)?

131. What can parents do to increase a child's social cognitive skills and foster moral SG maturity?

13

ATTACHMENT AND SOCIAL RELATIONSHIPS

MULTIPLE CHOICE QUESTIONS

p.361   1.   Social support
F
           a.   serves no significant function in life
   *   b.   can insulate people from stress
           c.   increases significantly across the life span
           d.   is more important for children than adults

p. 361   2.   A social convoy:
F
           a.   remains consistent over the life span
           b.   consists only of immediate family members
   *   c.   changes in size and makeup across the life span
           d.   is larger for males than for females

p. 362   3.   An attachment relationship is characterized by:
F
           a.   an extreme dependence on one another
   *   b.   a desire to maintain contact with one another
           c.   an inability to separate from one another without great distress
           d.   total responsiveness to one another

p. 362   4.   What do Freud, Erikson, and Bowlby share in common?
F
           a.   They are all continuity theorists.
           b.   They all believe that nurture is more influential than nature in determining infant-caregiver attachment.
   *   c.   They all agree about the importance of the parent/child relationship.
           d.   They all believe one's basic personality is determined during the first 5 or 6 years of life.

p. 362   5.   Which best reflects the ethological perspective regarding parent/child attachments?
C
           a.   attachments form automatically as a result of biological programming
www   *   b.   human infants and caregivers have a genetic predisposition to form close attachments
           c.   the key to forming close attachments lies in principles of conditioning and reinforcement
           d.   learning plays no significant role in the process of developing parent/child attachments

p. 362   6.   Imprinting refers to:
F   *   a.   an innate tendency to follow moving objects
           b.   the ability of parents to instill their values into their children
           c.   learning by observation
           d.   becoming attached to whomever provides oral gratification

p. 362 7. Evidence of human imprinting includes all of the following EXCEPT
C   a. crying and getting attention from a caregiver
            b. smiling and getting a smile and attention in return
      *   c. falling asleep after a caregiver has put you in your crib
            d. visually "following" a caregiver around the room

p. 363 8. The ethological perspective asserts that attachment relationships form:
F   a. automatically
            b. through the processes of conditioning and reinforcement
            c. as a result of the mother gratifying the child's oral needs
      *   d. through the responsive interactions that take place between parent and child

p. 363 9. According to Bowlby's attachment theory, through their interactions with caregivers,
C   infants:
            a. learn that they need to rely on themselves
            b. are reinforced for some kinds of behaviors and punished for others.
            c. develop a sense of trust or mistrust before moving on the next stage
      *   d. construct cognitive representations of self and others that influence their expectations
                about social relationships

p. 363 10. Internal working models:
F   a. are formed during a critical period when an infant first sees a moving object
www   *   b. are constructed through early interactions with caregivers and influence future social
                 relationships
             c. depend largely on the broad cultural context in which they are formed
             d. develop during the first few hours and days following birth

p. 363 11. The concept of internal working models that influence expectations of social interactions is
C   MOST similar to the concept of:
      *   a. gender schemas
             b. assimilation
             c. conservation
             d. conditioned response

p. 363 12. A peer is someone who is:
F   *   a. your social equal
             b. the same chronological age
             c. the same with regard to outlook on life
             d. of the same sex, race, creed, and religion

p. 364 13. According to Piaget, peer relationships have a unique influence on children's development
C   because:
www   a. ego strength develops as a result of resolving power struggles
             b. peers tend to see things in the same way, so conflicts are minimized
             c. values are more similar between peers than between parent and child
      *   d. peers foster the development of perspective-taking skills

p. 364 14. Which is the primary factor distinguishing between peer relationships and parent/child
F   relationships?
           a. Parent/child relationships are much more intimate than peer relationships.
      *   b. Peers have equal power in the relationship, while in parent/child relationships power is
               unevenly distributed.
           c. Peers see things the same way, while parents and children do not.
           d. Values are more similar in peer relationships than in relationships between parents and
               children.

p. 364 15. According to Sullivan, chumships tend to emerge:
F   a. with the onset of concrete-operational thinking
           b. during the preschool years
      *   c. during the late elementary-school years
           d. no earlier than the onset of puberty

p. 364 16. According to Sullivan, chumships:
F   a. can never compensate for the lack of a close parent/child relationship
      *   b. teach children about trust, loyalty, and honesty in relationships
           c. emerge as early as kindergarten or first grade
           d. have no significant effect on later relationships

p. 364 17. According to Sullivan, a child who never had a "chum:"
F   a. will be just as well adjusted as those who do have chums
           b. will find it easier to develop intimate relationships during adolescence
      *   c. will be poorly adjusted later in life
           d. will be incapable of forming an attachment relationship

p. 364 18. Which emotion is a newborn MOST likely to exhibit?
F   a. anger
           b. anxiety
      *   c. interest
           d. sadness

p. 364 19. In what order do the following emotions appear?
F   a. fear, interest, sadness, guilt
           b. interest, fear, guilt, sadness
      *   c. interest, sadness, fear, guilt
           d. interest, sadness, guilt, fear

p. 365 20. Early socialization of emotions in Western culture
C   *   a. usually results in less expression of negative emotions and more expression of positive
               ones
           b. is necessary to show infants how to express different emotions
           c. results in more intense displays of anger and fear, and less intense displays of joy and
               sadness
           d. teaches infants to verbally express emotions, rather than through their facial
               expressions

p. 366 21. It is most accurate to say that a parent's attachment relationship with his/her child:
F
    a. becomes firmly established before the child is born
    b. is formed during the few hours immediately following the child's birth
    c. will be seriously impaired if there are not opportunities for prolonged and immediate contact following the child's birth
*   d. builds gradually over a period of many months

p. 366 22. Kristi and Brad are adopting a baby boy named Troy. They are worried about how their
C   relationship with Troy will turn out, because Troy will be 3 months old when they get him. Kristi and Brad:
    a. have good reason to be concerned because they missed out on being with Troy during those first critical hours following birth
*   b. should relax, as they will have many opportunities to bond with Troy over many weeks and months
    c. will never have as close a relationship with Troy as they could with their own biological child
    d. shouldn't worry, because they will bond with Troy the minute they set eyes on him

p. 366 23. True social smiling:
F
    a. is present at birth
*   b. emerges as early as three weeks
    c. begins at about 4 months
    d. does not emerge until object permanence is achieved

p. 366 24. Shirley and John are so excited because when they peeked into their daughter's crib, she
F   smiled up at them for the first time as if she recognized their faces! Their baby girl is MOST LIKELY about ___ old:
    a. 1 week
*   b. 6 weeks
    c. 3 months
    d. 6 months

p. 366 25. Synchronized routines refer to:
F   a. the parent arranging a daily schedule
www   b. the baby adjusting to the parent's lifestyle
*   c. the parent and child taking turns determining their social interactions
    d. being able to consider another person's perspective

p. 367 26. Which of the following has NOT been shown to interfere with the development of
C   attachment relationships between parents and children?
    a. the child has a difficult temperament
    b. the parent was abused as a child
    c. an unhappy marriage
*   d. the child's intelligence

p. 367 27. Regarding the attachment process, which is FALSE?
F
     a. A child's temperament can affect the attachment process.
     b. Depressed mothers may experience difficulties in establishing attachment relationships with their infants.
     c. An unhappy marriage can upset the attachment process.
*   d. Attachments between parent and child develop independent of cultural context.

p. 367 28. Children who engage in active proximity-seeking behaviors with one particular caregiver
F   are likely to be:
     a. 2 - 6 weeks old
     b. 2 - 4 months old
     c. 5 - 6 months old
*   d. 7 months or older

p. 367 29. Lola shows a preference for familiar people but is still quite friendly to strangers as well.
F   Lola is MOST likely _____ old.
     a. 2
*   b. 5
     c. 8
     d. 14

p. 367 30. Kenny seems equally content to be held by his mother, father, or a stranger. He just doesn't
C   like it when no one is holding him. Kenny is MOST likely ___ months old:
*   a. 3
     b. 6
     c. 9
     d. 12

p. 367 31. Nicole shows a distinct preference for being with her mom. When mom leaves the room,
C   Nicole usually whimpers or cries. When mom returns, Nicole settles down, as long as
    mom holds her or is close by. Nicole is MOST likely about ___ months old:
     a. 2
     b. 5
*   c. 10
     d. 18

p. 367 32. Separation anxiety:
C   a. only occurs as a result of unresponsive parenting
*   b. is an important sign of attachment
     c. occurs mainly in children who attend preschool
     d. is a sign of an unhealthy attachment

p. 367 33. Who is MOST LIKELY to show signs of separation anxiety?
C   a. 6-month-old Larissa
*   b. one-year-old Timmy
     c. Mikey, who attends preschool
     d. four-year-old Randy, who does not attend preschool

p. 367 34.   Separation anxiety generally appears:
C
            a. at the time when infants begin to prefer human to nonhuman stimuli
            b. at the time when infants begin to express a preference for familiar people
    *   c. when the child forms his/her first genuine attachment
            d. toward the end of the sensorimotor period

p. 368 35.   _____ anxiety peaks first, followed by _____ anxiety.
F   *   a. stranger; separation
            b. separation; stranger
            c. goal; separation
            d. relationship; social

p. 368 36.   Regarding stranger anxiety, which is FALSE?
C
            a. Stranger anxiety is less likely to occur when Mommy is close by.
www *   b. Children are most wary of strangers when they are encountered in familiar surroundings where they don't belong.
            c. Stranger anxiety is lessened when the caregiver responds positively to the stranger.
            d. Stranger anxiety is affected by the appearance of the stranger.

p. 369 37.   When Clare takes her son, Joel, to the park one day, he demands to be held, and does not
C   want to get down to play on the equipment. When another young mother comes over and strikes up a conversation with Clare, Joel hides his head in his mother's skirt, and refuses to play with the other woman's child. Eventually, Clare leaves Joel with the other woman briefly so she can buy drinks for all of them at the concession stand. Joel screams and cries, and is inconsolable even after Clare returns. Joel's attachment relationship with his mother is BEST characterized as:
            a. secure
    *   b. resistant
            c. avoidant
            d. disorganized/disoriented

p. 369 38.   Pam loves to play with other children. As she plays in the sandbox at the park, she
C   frequently climbs out to run over to her mommy, gives her a hug, and then runs back to the sandbox. When her mother walks a short distance away to get a drink at a fountain, Pam begins to cry and runs after her. After they both get a drink, they head back toward the sandbox, with Pam running ahead to join the other children in play. Pam's attachment relationship with her mother is BEST described as:
    *   a. secure
            b. resistant
            c. avoidant
            d. disorganized/disoriented

p. 369 39.   The majority of infants develop a _____ attachment relationship with their caregiver(s):
F   *   a. secure
            b. insecure
            c. resistant
            d. avoidant

p. 369   40.   Gail takes her 1-year-old son Mike to visit an infant-toddler program that he will soon
C   join. Mike appears very anxious, and is unwilling to explore and play with toys, even
               though Gail is close by. When Gail leaves the room, Mike becomes extremely upset and
               remains that way all the time his mother is gone. When Gail returns, Mike stays close to
               his mother, but makes it clear he does not want her to touch him or pick him up. He
               appears angry at Gail. This BEST demonstrates which sort of attachment relationship?
               a.   disorganized
          *   b.   resistant
               c.   avoidant
               d.   secure

p. 369   41.   Frieda (18 months) and her mother are visiting at a friend's house. Although there are lots
C   of toys to play with, Frieda seems disinterested. When Frieda's mother and her friend go
www   into the kitchen for tea, Frieda appears undisturbed. Twenty minutes later her mother
               emerges from the kitchen and tries to pick Frieda up. Frieda is unresponsive, and wants to
               get down. When put down, Frieda ignores her mother and wanders around. This BEST
               demonstrates which sort of attachment relationship?
               a.   disorganized
               b.   resistant
          *   c.   avoidant
               d.   secure

p. 370   42.   When disorganized/disoriented infants are reunited with their parent, they tend to:
C   a.   not remember prior experiences
          *   b.   act dazed or seek attention
               c.   always scream in terror
               d.   sleep to escape the situation

p. 370   43.   Freud believed that the attachment relationship between parent and child occurs as a result
F   of:
               a.   conditioning and reinforcement
               b.   an innate tendency to engage in proximity-seeking behaviors
               c.   advances in the infant's cognition that enable the child to discriminate between familiar
                    and unfamiliar companions
          *   d.   early feeding experiences

p. 370   44.   Diana believes that her nursing relationship with her baby is critical to her child's well-
C   being, and that it will have a powerful impact on her overall relationship with her child.
               Based on this outlook, Diana's views with regard to the attachment process are MOST
               SIMILAR to those of:
               a.   Bowlby
               b.   Erikson
          *   c.   Freud
               d.   Ainsworth

p. 370   45.   Harlow's classic research regarding Freud's views of feeding practices and the attachment
C   process indicate that:
                 a. Freud was correct in assuming that the feeding process plays the central role in
                     establishing parent/child attachments
                 b. breast feeding is far superior to bottle feeding with regard to promoting parent/child
                     attachments
         *   c. contact with a soft, cuddly caregiver is more important than specific feeding practices
                     with regard to the establishment of parent/child attachments
                 d. attachments are biologically programmed, therefore feeding becomes irrelevant in the
                     attachment process

p. 370   46.   Research on the relationship between feeding practices and attachment suggests that:
F   a. breast-fed babies tend to be more securely attached to their mothers than are bottle-fed
                     babies
                 b. bottle-fed babies tend to be more securely attached to their mothers than are breast-fed
                     babies
                 c. a baby who nurses for 9 months is more likely to develop a secure attachment than one
                     who is weaned at 6 months
         *   d. feeding practices do not accurately predict the strength of a child's attachment to
                     his/her caregiver

p. 371   47.   Which appears to contribute MOST significantly to the formation of secure parent/child
C   attachments?
                 a. generosity in feeding practices
                 b. infant temperament
                 c. genetics
         *   d. responsive parenting

p. 371   48.   When a parent and child fail to develop a secure attachment relationship, it is MOST likely
C   that
                 a. there is something pathologically wrong with the parent
                 b. the child is incapable of establishing emotional bonds
                 c. the parent was unloved, neglected, or abused as a child
         *   d. there is a lack of responsiveness somewhere in the relationship

p. 371   49.   Lisa is a very high-strung, active mom. Her baby, Marie, is very laid-back and calm.
C   When Lisa bounces Marie on her knee, and tickles her, and talks to her in a loud and
www   excited voice, Marie turns away. Lisa turns Marie toward her, bounces her more
                 rigorously, and continues to talk and sing more loudly than before. Based on this pattern of
                 behavior, it is MOST LIKELY that:
         *   a. Marie will develop an avoidant response to her mother
                 b. Marie will develop a secure attachment to her mother
                 c. Marie will develop a resistant attachment to her mother
                 d. Marie's disposition will change rapidly to match that of her outgoing mother

p. 371   50.   The disorganized/disoriented style of attachment is associated with:
F   a.   disorganized parents
                b.   a noisy confusing home
                c.   being adopted
         *   d.   being physically abused

p. 371   51.   Who is MOST LIKELY to develop a disorganized/disoriented attachment?
C   a.   Linda, who was weaned at 3 months.
                b.   Mark, whose mother works outside the home.
         *   c.   Shonda, who was abused by her parents.
                d.   Su Lin, whose parents placed her in full-time child care at 6 months.

p. 371   52.   The cognitive-developmental perspective suggests that infants will not form attachments
C   until they:
                a.   have acquired conservation skills
         *   b.   have acquired an understanding of person permanence
                c.   are consistently reinforced for proximity-seeking behaviors
                d.   can decenter

p. 372   53.   With regard to the development of an attachment relationship, which is TRUE?
F   a.   An infant's temperament matters more than a caregiver's actions.
         *   b.   The caregiver's behavior is more significant than the infant's temperament.
                c.   Children with difficult temperaments are incapable of forming secure attachments.
                d.   Feeding practices appear to be the most critical factor.

p. 372   54.   David was raised in an orphanage until he was 4-years-old. The orphanage was under
C   staffed, and there were no adults who paid much attention to David other than to provide
               care for his physical needs. It is most likely that the effects of David's social deprivation:
                a.   were minimal overall
                b.   had a significant impact on his cognitive, but not social, development
                c.   had a significant impact on his social, but not cognitive, development
         *   d.   had an impact on both his cognitive and social development

p. 372   55.   The effects of social deprivation in infancy:
C   *   a.   are best recovered from when infants are placed with well-educated, financially
                     advantaged parents
                b.   are permanent if the deprivation lasts for more than six months
                c.   are likely to be minimal as long as the child is placed with a responsive caregiver by
                     age 5
                d.   are negligible overall

p. 372   56.   Studies of institutionalized children indicate that:
C   a.   a lack of a central "mother figure" during the first year of life leads to significant and
                     lasting developmental delays
         *   b.   normal development is dependent on sustained interactions with responsive caregivers
                c.   children who are deprived of responsive caregiving during the first six months of life
                     cannot achieve a full recovery, even when placed with responsive caregivers thereafter
                d.   as long as sensory stimulation is adequate, the absence of a responsive caregiver during
                     the first three years of life will cause no permanent damage

p. 373 57. Infants who are securely attached to their mothers are likely to be preschoolers who are:
C
 a. intellectually superior
 b. overly dependent
* c. social leaders
 d. hesitant to separate from their mothers

p. 373 58. Infants who are insecurely attached to their mothers are likely to be preschoolers who are:
C
 a. no different from those who were securely attached as infants
www
 b. extremely sensitive to the needs of other children
* c. less interested in learning than those who were securely attached
 d. physically immature

p. 373 59. Molly is securely attached to her mother and her father. When she enters preschool, she
C is MOST LIKELY to:
 a. strenuously resist separating from her parents
 b. cling to her teacher in her parents' absence
* c. be very popular with her peers
 d. be socially immature

p. 373 60. Kim has an avoidant relationship with her mother. When she enters preschool, Kim is
C MOST LIKELY to:
 a. be no different from children who were securely attached to their parents
 b. be hesitant to separate from her mother
* c. lack persistence in completing activities
 d. be very sensitive to the needs of other children

p. 374 61. Research shows that, compared to infants with secure attachments, infants with insecure
F attachments:
* a. process information differently
 b. are indistinguishable from other infants
 c. are likely to become high achievers to compensate for their lack of a secure attachment
 d. pay much less attention to positive events in their life

p. 375 62. Regarding attachment, which is TRUE?
F * a. A secure attachment to one's father can compensate for a poor attachment relationship
   with one's mother.
 b. Infants with insecure attachments suffer permanent damage in terms of social skills.
 c. Infants with avoidant attachments suffer permanent cognitive deficits.
 d. A child who develops a secure attachment with at least one caregiver is invulnerable to
   later social problems.

p. 376 63. Which is true regarding the effects of parent-child attachments on later development?
C
 a. An insecurely attached infant will have life-long emotional problems.
 b. A secure relationship with one's father cannot compensate for an insecure mother-child
   attachment relationship.
* c. A secure attachment may become insecure as a result of major stresses in the family,
   such as divorce or a mother returning to work.
 d. An infant who is securely attached to mother at age 1 automatically has a life-long
   advantage over the infant who is insecurely attached at age 1.

p. 377 64. With regard to the social interactions of infants, which of the following is TRUE?
F
  a. Infants engage in turn-taking behaviors with peers earlier than they do so with parents.
  b. Children younger than age two do not form specific attachments to other infants.
  c. Infants as young as 6 months of age engage in responsive, reciprocal interactions with other infants.
 * d. Infants are more proficient at social interactions with adults than with other infants because adults help structure the interaction.

p. 377 65. Tom and John are playing together. Tom hands John a ball. In return, John offers Tom a stuffed frog to play with. Tom and John are MOST LIKELY no younger than ___ old.
C
 * a. 18 months
  b. 2 years
  c. 3 years
  d. 4 years

p. 377 66. Lindy chases Matt around the living room, catches him, and they tumble down together. Then Matt chases Lindy. When he catches her, they fall down and laugh together. Lindy and Matt are AT LEAST ___ year(s) old:
C
  a. 1 year
 * b. 2 years
  c. 4 years
  d. 6 years

p. 378 67. Jimmy is watching a group of children who are playing with Lego blocks. Occasionally he says things like "that's a neat car" or "want some blocks?" However, he does not sit down and play with the Legos himself. This BEST demonstrates which form of play?
C
  a. associative
  b. cooperative
 * c. onlooker
  d. solitary

p. 378 68. Rachel and Donna are both playing with dolls in the doll corner. They are dressing and undressing the dolls, and pretending to feed them dinner. Rachel and Donna do not, however, talk to one another or involve each other in their play. This BEST demonstrates which type of play?
C
  a. associative
  b. cooperative
 * c. parallel
  d. solitary

p. 378 69. Jennifer and Ashante are playing school. Jennifer is the teacher and Ashante is the student. After a while, they decide they need a principal and some more students, so they ask Lee, Josh, and Steven to join them. This activity BEST demonstrates the concept of ___ play:
C
www
  a. associative
 * b. cooperative
  c. functional
  d. parallel

p. 378 70. Which is the PRIMARY distinction between associative and cooperative play?

C   *   a. Cooperative play involves activities directed toward a common goal and associative play does not.

       b. Cooperative play involves sharing the same materials while associative play does not.

       c. Cooperative play involves interaction between playmates while associative play does not.

       d. Cooperative play emerges during the concrete-operational period while associative play emerges during preoperational thought.

p. 379 71. With regard to Mildred Parten's classification system for types of childhood play, which forms of play become MORE frequent with age?

F

   *   a. associative and cooperative play

       b. solitary and parallel play

       c. solitary and cooperative play

       d. parallel and associative play

p. 379 72. In general, concrete-operational thinkers:

C   *   a. see game-rules as rigid and unalterable

       b. understand that game-rules can be changed, if a majority of players agree

       c. believe that game-rules can be changed only if all people playing the game agree

       d. really don't understand the concept of game-rules, and consequently tend to play games in a rather haphazard fashion

p. 379 73. At what point do children generally begin to see that game-rules are flexible and alterable?

C   a. when they enter grade school

       b. during the 5-to-7 shift

       c. with the attainment of concrete-operational thought

   *   d. when they enter the stage of formal-operational thought

p. 380 74. Angie has two imaginary friends named Ellie and Uppitz. They go everywhere with her, and she sets places for them at the lunch table. Angie is MOST LIKELY:

C   a. socially unskilled

       b. escaping from reality

       c. emotionally disturbed

   *   d. quite well adjusted

p. 380 75. Which is TRUE with regard to the effects of play on development?

C   *   a. Preschoolers who engage in considerable amounts of social pretend play tend to be more popular and more socially mature than those who do not.

       b. Play contributes significantly to physical and social development, but has little impact on the development of cognitive skills.

       c. While engagement in pretend play tends to stimulate creative thought processes, it tends to interfere with the development of logical thought.

       d. Play contributes to the emotional development of preschoolers by helping children work through unresolved conflicts, but it detracts from children's intellectual development by keeping them from engaging in more productive academic tasks.

p. 380 76. Sociometric techniques refer to:
F
  a. measuring maturity in children
  b. assessing level of play
  * c. determining who is liked or disliked in a group
  d. measuring social skills

p. 380 77. Molly is rarely chosen as a workmate or playmate by her classmates. She tends to be shy
C and quiet, and on those rare occasions that someone does ask her to play, Molly often says
no, and walks away. According to categories of sociometric status, Molly is BEST
classified as:
  * a. neglected
  b. rejected
  c. antisocial
  d. controversial

p. 380 78. "Controversial" children are:
F
  a. uniformly disliked by their peers
  * b. liked and disliked by about as many of their peers
  c. usually not very smart, but have good social skills
  d. socially isolated and seldom recognized by their classmates

p. 381 79. Which of the following is FALSE with regard to rejected children?
C a. A child who is rejected by peers one year will probably again be rejected the next.
www b. Rejected children are at risk for becoming juvenile delinquents.
  * c. Rejection by peers during the childhood years is unlikely to have long-term effects on
overall emotional adjustment.
  d. Rejected children tend to enter new situations expecting to be disliked.

p. 381 80. An elementary-school-aged child who is classified as "rejected" is most likely:
F a. nonassertive
  * b. aggressive
  c. unlikely to experience any long-term negative effects
  d. to hold back and watch, rather than attempt to join in on a group activity

p. 381 81. The MOST important factor with regard to determining popularity during the grade school
C years appears to be:
  * a. social competence
  b. physical attractiveness
  c. intellectual ability
  d. athletic ability

p. 381 82. Who is likely to be MOST popular?
C a. Pretty Polly
  b. Smart Alec
  * c. Cooperative Rachel
  d. Hold-back Harry

p. 382　83. Ross was "neglected" by his elementary-school classmates. Randy was "rejected" by his
C　　　peers. Which is TRUE?
　　　　　a. Ross is more likely than Randy to drop out of school.
　　　　　b. Randy is more likely than Ross to gain acceptance by his peers later on.
　　　　　c. Ross and Randy are equally likely to become antisocial, aggressive adolescents.
　　*　　d. Randy is more likely than Ross to have behavior problems during adolescence.

p. 382　84. Friendships based on mutual loyalty tend to FIRST emerge:
F　*　　a. during the later elementary school years
　　　　　b. during the early childhood years
　　　　　c. during adolescence
　　　　　d. along with intimate relationships during young adulthood

p. 382　85. Rachel's grandma asks her why Naomi is her best friend. Rachel explains she's best
C　　　friends with Naomi because they always help each other with their school work and they
　　　　can tell each other everything and know their secrets are safe! Rachel's answer is MOST
　　　　typical of a(n):
　　　　　a. preschooler
　　　　　b. 5- or 6-year-old
　　*　　c. 8- to 10-year-old
　　　　　d. adolescent

p. 382　86. Fourth and fifth graders are most likely to base their friendship choices on:
F　　　　a. similar physical characteristics
www　　b. shared interests
　　　　　c. prized possessions
　　*　　d. loyalty and respect

p. 382　87. Which best describes the nature of 10-year-olds' friendships?
C　　　　a. fickle and changeable
　　　　　b. self-serving
　　*　　c. reciprocal
　　　　　d. intimate and full of self-disclosure

p. 383　88. Twelve-year-olds Judy and Jenny are best friends. Fifteen-year-olds Mary and Marcia are
C　　　best friends. As compared to Mary and Marcia, Jenny and Judy are:
　　*　　a. less likely to confide in one another
　　　　　b. more likely to share similar values and interests
　　　　　c. more likely to talk about their feelings
　　　　　d. more likely to have respect for each other's points of view

p. 383　89. Which is MOST important with regard to friendship choices during adolescence?
C　　　　a. physical attractiveness
　　*　　b. shared thoughts and feelings
　　　　　c. involvement in the same extracurricular activities
　　　　　d. loyalty

p. 384 90. Linda and Jean are best friends. Frank and Thomas are best friends. All four attend
C high school. As compared to Linda and Jean, Frank and Thomas are:
    a. more likely to confide in one another
*   b. less likely to talk about their feelings with one another
    c. less likely to understand each other's point of view
    d. more likely to share an intense relationship

p. 384 91. Compared to girls, boys:
F   a. are more intense in their friendships
    b. develop intimate cross-gender relationships at an earlier age
    c. are less likely to base friendships on common interests
*   d. are less likely to talk about their feelings with each other

p. 384 92. Which is TRUE with regard to cross-sex friendships in adolescence?
C   a. Boys achieve intimacy in cross-sex friendships earlier than do girls.
*   b. Girls achieve intimacy in cross-sex friendships earlier than do boys.
    c. Boys and girls achieve intimacy in cross-sex friendships at about the same time.
    d. Cross-sex friendships are frequently more intimate for male adolescents than are same-sex friendships.

p. 384 93. According to Dunphy, the typical developmental sequence of events in the adolescent peer
F group is:
*   a. isolated unisex groups; interaction between unisex groups; heterosexual groups; groups of couples; the couple
    b. heterosexual groups; isolated unisex groups; interaction between unisex groups; the couple; groups of couples
    c. isolated heterosexual groups; interaction between heterosexual groups; unisex groups; the couple; groups of couples
    d. isolated unisex groups; heterosexual groups; interaction between heterosexual groups; the couple; groups of couples

p. 385 94. Research on conformity to parent- and peer-pressure indicates that conformity to:
F   a. peer pressure to engage in prosocial acts increases with age
    b. peer pressure to engage in prosocial acts decreases with age
*   c. peer pressure with regard to antisocial behavior increases from grade school to high school
    d. parental pressure to engage in prosocial acts increases with age

p. 385 95. Children are MOST susceptible to negative peer pressure during:
F   a. the grade-school years
www   b. very early adolescence
*   c. mid adolescence
    d. late adolescence

p. 386 96. During adolescence parents should:
F   a. expect to experience conflict with their children on most matters
    b. tighten their restrictions on their adolescent children to keep them out of trouble
    c. take a hands-off approach, as adolescents need freedom to develop their independence
*   d. understand that a certain amount of conformity to peers is in their child's best interest

p. 386 97. Adolescents must make decisions both with regard to their current lifestyle and their future
C   educational/vocational goals. For help in making these decisions they can turn to parents
             or peers. Research indicates that adolescents most often turn to:
             a. peers, for both current and future concerns
             b. parents, for both current and future concerns
        *   c. peers for current concerns and parents for future concerns
             d. parents for current concerns and peers for future concerns

p. 387 98. In what ways do the social networks of younger and older adults differ?
F   a. Middle-aged adults have more close friends than younger adults do.
             b. Old people feel more socially isolated and lonely than younger adults do.
        *   c. Younger adults have broader social networks than middle-aged adults have.
             d. Older adults are more likely than young adults to wish for more close relationships.

p. 387 99. With regard to partner selection, adults tend to favor partners who are:
F   *   a. similar to themselves
             b. an exciting contrast to one's self
             c. stronger morally and religiously then one's self
             d. highly independent

p. 388 100. A person's style of loving or romantic attachment is:
C   a. strongly determined by the quality of his/her parent/child attachment relationship
        *   b. somewhat related to the quality of his/her parent-child attachment
             c. unrelated to the quality of his/her parent/child attachment relationship
             d. largely due to innate tendencies to behave in one way or another

p. 388 101. Sandy (age 25) finds it difficult to get close to others. As soon as she feels herself getting
C   involved, she pulls out of a relationship. Her adult attachment type is BEST classified as:
www   a. secure
        *   b. dismissing
             c. preoccupied
             d. fearful

p. 389 102. Which is FALSE?
F   a. Younger adults generally have more friends than older adults do.
             b. Elderly males are less likely than elderly females to have close relationships outside the
                 family.
        *   c. Older people are relatively unconcerned with equity issues in friendships.
             d. For most married people, spouses are the most important confidant.

p. 389 103. An elderly adult is likely to be most uncomfortable and distressed if he or she is:
F   *   a. the overbenefitted person in a relationship
             b. the underbenefitted person in a relationship
             c. in a highly equitable relationship
             d. in a confidant relationship

p. 390 104. Which is TRUE of adult relationships?
C   a. Old people with restricted social networks are generally dissatisfied.
        b. Old people who have large social networks remain content in life.
    *   c. It is the quality of relationships, rather than the number of relationships, that
           determines one's level of satisfaction.
        d. Having a particular "confidant" appears to be less important in old age than it was
           during adolescence.

p. 362 105. Infants show attachment through which of the following behaviors?
F   a. showing a preference for one person over another
SG   b. trying to maintain proximity to a person
        c. showing distress when a person leaves
    *   d. all of the above

p. 362 106. According to Bowlby's attachment theory:
C   a. infants must develop an attachment during a critical period early in life or they will not
SG   form later attachments
        b. infants become attached to the caregiver who feeds them
    *   c. infants are biologically predisposed to form attachments
        d. through reinforcement, infants learn to form attachments

p. 367 107. In the discriminating social responsiveness phase of developing attachment, infants
F   a. respond to many different social stimuli such as voices and faces
SG   b. respond differently depending on the social situation
    *   c. show preferences for familiar companions
        d. show clear attachment by following the object of their attachment and protesting when
           this person leaves

p. 367 108. Stranger anxiety would be greatest in which of the following situations?
C   a. Seated on mother's lap at the doctor's office while mom warmly greets the doctor.
SG   b. Seated on mother's lap at home while mom warmly greets the next door neighbor.
        c. Seated on mother's lap at home while mom neutrally greets a salesperson.
    *   d. Seated across from mother at the doctor's office while mom neutrally greets the doctor.

p. 370 109. According to Freud, infants become attached to their mothers because
F   a. mothers become associated with pleasurable sensations
SG   b. mothers are generally responsive to their needs
        c. they are innately predisposed to form attachments
    *   d. mothers provide oral pleasure

p. 369 110. Which of the following describes infants who have resistant attachment?
F   a. Infants use their mother as a secure base, they are upset when she leaves them, and
SG   welcome her when she returns.
    *   b. Infants are upset when their mother leaves them and are ambivalent when she returns.
        c. Infants are not really distressed when their mother leaves them and do not welcome her
           back when she returns.
        d. Infants are not really distressed when their mother leaves them and express joy when
           reunited with mother.

p. 382　111. With respect to the relationship between security of attachment during infancy and social
C　　　　　competence during adulthood, research suggests that
SG　　*　a. quality of infant attachment does not predict adult social competence as well as peer
　　　　　　　relations during adolescence do
　　　　　b. quality of infant attachment has no relation to social competence during adulthood
　　　　　c. quality of infant attachment to parents is the most important predictor of adult social
　　　　　　　competence
　　　　　d. individuals who were securely attached as infants always have positive social
　　　　　　　relationships

p. 370　112. The finding that infant monkeys in Harlow's research preferred the cloth surrogate over the
C　　　　　wire surrogate regardless of which one provided food
SG　　　　a. supports Erikson's claim that general responsiveness is important to development of
　　　　　　　attachment
　　　　　b. shows that there is an innate predisposition to form attachments
　　*　c. shows that Freud's emphasis on feeding behavior cannot fully explain development of
　　　　　　　attachment
　　　　　d. supports learning theory explanations of attachment since infants become attached to
　　　　　　　the mother who reinforced them with food

p. 365　113. Social referencing refers to an infant's ability to
F　　　　　a. recognize familiar companion
SG　　　　b. compare self to others
　　*　c. use other people's reactions to guide their own behavior
　　　　　d. imitate other people's behavior

p. 372　114. Effects of early social deprivation in human infants
F　　　　　a. cannot be overcome
SG　　*　b. can be overcome if the infants are placed with affectionate and responsive caregivers
　　　　　c. can be overcome if the infants are exposed to multiple caregivers
　　　　　d. are usually not significant

p. 379　115. The capacity for pretend play emerges
F　　　　　a. at birth
SG　　　　b. around 6-7 months of age
　　*　c. around 1 year
　　　　　d. around 3 years

p. 378　116. Children who do not actually participate in play with others but watch others play are
F　　　　　engaged in _____ play.
SG　　　　a. solitary
　　　　　b. unoccupied
　　　　　c. parallel
　　*　d. onlooker

p. 379 117. Pretend play
C
SG *   a. can be used to assess children's level of intellectual functioning
     b. can provide children the opportunity to work through problems
     c. shows the same pattern in all children
     d. increases when children enter elementary school

p. 385 118. With respect to conformity to pressure during adolescence
C
SG
     a. there is no difference between conformity to pressure from adults and pressure from peers
  * b. conformity to peer pressure for antisocial acts increases, peaks around ninth grade, and then decreases
     c. adolescents are more likely to conform to peer pressure for prosocial acts than antisocial acts
     d. adolescents are more likely to conform to parental pressure than peer pressure

p. 385 119. Which of the follow accurately represents the order of filters used for mate selection
F   according to Udry's model?
SG *   a. proximity, attractiveness, social background, consensus, complementarity, readiness
     b. proximity, complementarity, attractiveness, consensus, social background, readiness
     c. social background, proximity, complementarity, attractiveness, consensus, readiness
     d. attractiveness, readiness, social background, proximity, complementarity, consensus

TRUE-FALSE QUESTIONS

p. 362 120. Most attachment theorists believe that the relationship between an infant and caregiver is essential to development
  * a. true
     b. false

p. 363 121. Physical contact shortly after birth is critical for the formation of parent/child attachments.
www   a. true
  * b. false

p. 363 122. According to Bowlby's attachment theory, infants form internal working models through their interactions with caregivers and these guide expectations about future interactions.
  * a. true
     b. false

p. 364 123. Children develop chumships at the beginning of preschool.
     a. true
  * b. false

p. 364 124. Emotions such as anger, sadness, and fear seem to be biologically programmed.
www * a. true
     b. false

p. 365   125. Infants learn how to react emotionally by monitoring their caregiver's responses in various situations.
*   a. true
     b. false

p. 366   126. Infant-caregiver interactions are largely unidirectional, with the caregiver directing the course of the interaction.
     a. true
*   b. false

p. 367   127. Separation anxiety generally appears toward the end of the sensorimotor period.
     a. true
*   b. false

p. 368   128. Stranger anxiety is greatest when meetings take place in the infant's home.
     a. true
*   b. false

p. 369   129. In today's troubled and stressful world, only a minority of infants in our society are securely attached to their mothers.
     a. true
*   b. false

p. 371   130. Children develop secure attachments to people who are generally responsive to their needs and signals.
*   a. true
     b. false

p. 372   131. Infants who are socially deprived can easily recover from any negative effects of this deprivation once they are given attention.
     a. true
*   b. false

p. 374   132. Some children do better in day care settings than similar infants do raised at home.
*   a. true
     b. false

p. 374   133. Children who form secure attachments tend to remember positive events while those with insecure attachments tend to remember negative events.
*   a. true
     b. false

p. 378   134. Children's play becomes more cooperative as they get older.
*   a. true
     b. false

p. 379   135. Children who engage in lots of pretend play tend to have cognitive deficits.
     a. true
*   b. false

p. 380   136.   Children who are rejected by their grade-school peers are at risk for psychological disturbance later in life.
*   a.   true
     b.   false

p. 383   137.   Adolescents typically select friends on the basis of shared, common activities.
*   a.   true
     b.   false

p. 383   138.   Most adolescents have close relationships with their parents
*   a.   true
     b.   false

p. 384   139.   Girls generally form intimate friendships earlier than do boys.
*   a.   true
     b.   false

p. 385   140.   It is typical for an adolescent to get highly conflicting messages from parents and peers regarding important future decisions.
     a.   true
*   b.   false

p. 387   141.   Adults tend to pick partners who are similar to them.
*   a.   true
     b.   false

p. 388   142.   A person's style of loving in adult relationships is largely determined b the quality of his/her early parent/child attachment relationship.
     a.   true
*   b.   false

ESSAY QUESTIONS

143.   What factors of the infant and the caregiver influence the quality of attachment that develops between them?

144.   How do Bowlby and Ainsworth integrate psychoanalytic, cognitive, and ethological concepts into their theory of attachment?

145.
www   What are the likely long-term effects of a secure or insecure attachment? What factors can "derail" a secure attachment or get an insecure attachment back on track?

146.   How do friendships change across the life span?

147.   How does a child's social status influence their social interactions with peers?

148.
SG   What are the likely outcomes for children who, as infants, were insecurely attached to their caregiver? What factors influence the outcome for these children?
[Sample answer is provided in the Study Guide.]

149. What aspects of children's development are fostered by engaging in pretend play?
SG

150. What factors influence whether a child is popular or rejected in peer relationships?
SG

THE FAMILY

MULTIPLE-CHOICE QUESTIONS

---

p. 396   1.   The systems approach to understanding families suggests that:
F
www
       a.   the larger the family network, the lower the quality of interaction between parent and child
       b.   the mother is the central influence on a child's development
  *   c.   every relationship within the system has an impact on every other individual in the system
       d.   families function in a similar manner from one culture to the next

p. 396   2.   Family systems theory includes all of the following points EXCEPT:
C
       a.   changes in family membership have an effect on the entire family system
       b.   there are distinct stages in the family life cycle
       c.   all relationships in the family system have reciprocal influence
  *   d.   the mother/child relationship is more significant than all other relationships in the family system

p. 396   3.   The nuclear family consists of:
F
       a.   the siblings in a family
  *   b.   mother, father, and one or more children
       c.   grandparents, parents, and offspring
       d.   one's family "tree"

p. 396   4.   Charlotte lives with her biological mother and father and her two younger brothers. Charlotte's family is BEST termed a(n) ___ family:
C
       a.   extended
       b.   multigenerational
  *   c.   nuclear
       d.   blended

p. 397   5.   The extended family is BEST defined as:
F   *
  *   a.   a mother and father, their children, and all their kin
       b.   mother, father, and one or more children
       c.   at least four generations
       d.   people who have divorced and remarried

p. 397   6.   Paul lives with his mother, his grandmother, his aunt, and his older brother. Paul's family is BEST termed a(n) ___ family:
C
www   *
  *   a.   extended
       b.   nuclear
       c.   reconstituted
       d.   beanpole

p. 397　7.　The concept of a family life cycle:

C

　　a.　shows how the broad cultural context affects the nuclear family

　　b.　applies to white middle-class families, but not to minority or lower-class families

　　c.　suggests that the nuclear family is the ideal family system

*　d.　highlights the role changes that occur within family relationships from marriage to death

p. 398　8.　Which of the following is TRUE regarding the changing nature of the American family?

F

　　a.　Family size (number of offspring) is once more on the rise.

　　b.　With more and more women in the work force, a majority of young couples today share equally in child-rearing and housework responsibilities.

*　c.　Close to half of all children born in the next decade will spend some time living in a single-parent family.

　　d.　Marriage in our society is fast going out of style.

p. 398　9.　The most likely cause of the increase in the number of adults is:

F　　　*　a.　career and educational goals come first

　　b.　they don't believe in marriage

　　c.　they can't afford to marry

　　d.　they can't find a suitable partner

p. 398　10.　Regarding the nature of today's families, which is TRUE?

F

　　a.　A majority of women who remain childless do so by choice.

*　b.　Over 90% of today's young adults will marry at least once.

　　c.　Today, most people who divorce choose to remain single, rather than remarry.

　　d.　Increased rates of teen-age pregnancy in recent years have led to a lower average age for first marriages

p. 398　11.　Karla and Ken are getting married. It is a first marriage for both of them. Which is

C　　　FALSE?

www　　a.　Karla and Ken are most likely older than their parents were when they got married.

　　b.　Chances are about 50-50 that Karla and Ken will get divorced.

　　c.　Karla is more likely than her mother was to work outside of the home.

*　d.　Karla and Ken are likely to have more children than their parents did.

p. 399　12.　Tommy is 5 years old. His mom and dad are getting a divorce. Chances are:

C

　　a.　neither of his parents will remarry

*　b.　at least one of his parents will remarry

　　c.　he will spend some time in a foster home

　　d.　he will not want to get married when he gets older

p. 399　13.　Which of the following is FALSE?

F

　　a.　Adults today are having fewer children than was true 20 years ago.

　　b.　The number of adults living as singles is on the rise.

　　c.　Most adult women now work outside the home.

*　d.　A majority of those who get divorced do not remarry.

p. 399 14. A "reconstituted" family is one where:
F
         a. the parents have divorced and then remarried each other once again
 *   b. a parent, stepparent, and child (or children) live together
         c. at least three generations reside in the same household
         d. children who have grown up and "left the nest" return to "roost" after a failed marriage

p. 399 15. Jayme and Joshua live with their mom and her new husband, and their new baby. Every
C   other weekend, Jayme and Joshua go to stay with their dad and his girlfriend. Jayme and
       Joshua's family is BEST termed a(n) ___ family:
         a. beanpole
 *   b. reconstituted
         c. extended
         d. nuclear

p. 399 16. The mother/child relationship receives far more attention than the father/child relationship
F   because:
         a. having a competent mother is crucial to the psychological well-being of the child
 *   b. mothers are typically the caregivers for infants
         c. fathers have little impact overall on the psychological and intellectual development of
            their children
         d. fathers are not well suited for nurturant roles with children

p. 399 17. The nature of the mother/child relationship is PRIMARILY determined by the:
C
         a. child's gender
         b. innate temperament of the child
         c. temperament of the mother
 *   d. reciprocal contributions of both mother and child

p. 400 18. Regarding the amount of time parents spend with their children, which is TRUE?
F   a. With more women currently working outside of the home, the amount of time that
www   mothers and fathers spend with their children is now equal.
         b. Men whose wives hold nontraditional views of the male role spend no more time caring
            for their children than those whose wives hold traditional views of the male role.
 *   c. Today, as in the past, mothers spend a good deal more time in parenting than fathers
            do.
         d. The amount of time fathers spend interacting with their infants has increased
            dramatically in the past 25 years.

p. 400 19. Which is FALSE with regard to the nature of parent/child interactions?
F   a. Mothers spend more time in custodial care (e.g., feeding, diapering) than they do
            engaging in play with their young children.
         b. Of the time spent with their children, fathers spend proportionately more of this time
            playing with their children than mothers do.
         c. Mothers are typically more reserved than fathers in their play with young children.
 *   d. Fathers and mothers typically play with their children in much the same sort of way.

p. 400 20. Which is TRUE with regard to nature of early parent/child interactions?
F
* a. Fathers tend to play a more powerful role than mothers in the early gender-typing of young children.
b. Fathers are more accepting than mothers of their daughters' play with masculine-stereotyped toys.
c. Mothers are more upset than fathers when their little boys choose to play with feminine-stereotyped toys.
d. Mothers and fathers differ little in the ways in which they socialize young children into their gender roles.

p. 400 21. Which is TRUE according to research on parent/child attachments?
C
a. An infant generally develops a close attachment with only one parent or the other.
b. It is not possible for an infant to attach securely to its father unless it first establishes a secure attachment with its mother.
* c. Infants who are securely attached to both parents are more socially competent than those who are securely attached only to mother.
d. Attachment to mother predicts later social competence, while attachment to father does not.

p. 400 22. Which is FALSE regarding the effects of fathers on their children's later development?
C
a. Warm and nurturant fathers are more likely than cold, uninvolved fathers to produce "masculine" sons.
* b. Fathers have little impact on the feminine gender-typing of their daughters.
c. There is a positive relationship between having a nurturant father and achievement in school.
d. Fathers have a greater impact on their sons' gender development than on their daughters'.

p. 400 23. Sue and Mike have two children, Trent (age 3) and Lisa (age 5). It is MOST LIKELY that:
C *
a. Mike will be more concerned than Sue if Trent plays with Barbie dolls and Lisa plays with G.I. Joe.
b. Sue will be more upset than Mike if Trent wants to play dress-up and wear make-up.
c. Sue and Mike will be about equally concerned if Lisa refuses to wear dresses and wants to play Power Ranger and Superman all day long.
d. Of the time Mike spends with Trent and Lisa, he will spend proportionately less of this time playing with them than Sue does.

p. 401 24. "Do as I say, because I said so! And don't ask why!" This sort of statement is reflective of which pattern of child rearing?
C
a. authoritative
* b. authoritarian
c. neglectful
d. permissive

p. 401 25. Jimmy's parents have very clear rules about what is "OK" to do and what is not. They are
C   very careful to enforce the rules. However, they are willing to listen to Jimmy's side of the
            story, and are careful to explain why the rules are important. They even consider changing
            rules that don't seem to be working well. Jimmy's parents are BEST described as having
            which sort of child rearing pattern?
            a. neglectful
            b. authoritarian
        *   c. authoritative
            d. permissive

p. 401 26. Authoritative parents:
F   a. are highly restrictive
            b. often use physical punishment to discipline their children
            c. make relatively few demands on their youngsters
        *   d. respect their children's opinions

p. 401 27. Sixteen-year-old Becky wants to go on a weekend camping trip with a group of her friends
C   --some of whom are male. She brings up the idea with her parents. As they tend to be
            authoritative parents, their MOST likely response is to say:
            a. "Absolutely not. Case closed."
            b. "Do as you please. It's your life!"
        *   c. "Let's sit down and discuss this. We're not sure this is a good idea, but we'd like to hear
                your views. Then we'll come to some sort of agreement."
            d. "We don't approve, but if you insist....."

p. 401 28. Dan and Betsy set clear rules for their son, Sam, and they consistently enforce these rules.
C   They also are willing to listen to what Sam has to say, and they may decide to modify their
www   rules if Sam gives them with a good reason for doing so. Dan and Betsy's child-rearing
            style is BEST categorized as:
            a. authoritarian
        *   b. authoritative
            c. permissive
            d. harmonious

p. 401 29. "I'm willing to listen to what you have to say. If it makes sense, we will consider changing
C   your bedtime." This statement is reflective of a(n) ___ parenting style:
            a. authoritarian
        *   b. authoritative
            c. permissive
            d. neglectful

p. 401 30. Julie wants special permission to stay out on a date past her normal curfew. Her parents,
C   who tend to be authoritarian, are MOST LIKELY to respond:
            a. "Why should we let you do this?"
        *   b. "No."
            c. "I guess you'll have to make that choice, and suffer the consequences."
            d. "It doesn't matter to us what you do."

p. 402 31. Sam is bright, but doesn't do well in high school. He is aggressive with his peers, and
C   really has no particular interests in terms of career goals. MOST LIKELY his parents took
           a(n) ___ approach to child rearing:
           a. authoritarian
           b. authoritative
           c. moderate
        * d. permissive

p. 402 32. Marissa works two different jobs to make ends meet. She is so wrapped up in her own
C   problems that she has little time to devote to her children. They basically do whatever they
           want and Marissa seems not to care. Which style of child rearing does this reflect?
           a. authoritative
           b. authoritarian
           c. permissive
        * d. neglectful

p. 402 33. Kitty and David want their children to grow up to be self-reliant, cooperative, and
C   achievement-oriented. To achieve this, they should:
           a. Punish their children every time they break the rules.
        * b. Set firm limits and enforce them consistently.
           c. Place few restrictions on their children's behavior.
           d. Pay their children to get good grades in school.

p. 402 34. Linda, a senior in high school, is bossy and self-centered. She doesn't do very well
C   in school and doesn't have any plans for her future after graduation. It is MOST LIKELY
www   that her parents use a child rearing style that is:
           a. high in acceptance and high in control
        * b. high in acceptance and low in control
           c. low in acceptance and low in control
           d. low in acceptance and high in control

p. 402 35. Mark is a member of a teen-age gang. He's doing drugs, and is into petty crime. On the
C   rare days he shows up at school, he invariably ends up in a fight and leaves early. Mark's
           behavior is MOST typical of children raised by parents who are:
           a. authoritative
           b. authoritarian
           c. permissive
        * d. neglectful

p. 402 36. Children raised by authoritative parents tend to be:
C   * a. self-reliant and achievement oriented
           b. self-centered and lacking in self-control
           c. hostile and rebellious
           d. quiet and withdrawn

p. 402 37. Hostile, rebellious youngsters tend to have parents who are:
C
        a. low in acceptance and high in control
        b. from lower class backgrounds
     * c. low in both acceptance and control
        d. young and involved in their careers

p. 402 38. The LEAST successful parenting styles are those that are:
C
        a. high in acceptance and high in control
        b. high in acceptance and low in control
     * c. low in acceptance and low in control
        d. low in acceptance and high in control

p. 402 39. Which parenting style is MOST likely to be associated with positive child outcomes?
F
        a. authoritarian
     * b. authoritative
        c. permissive
        d. harmonious

p. 403 40. Children who look after themselves until their parents return from work:
C
        a. do just as well as other children regardless of their age
        b. do fine if they hang out with their friends during this time
        c. are OK as long as their parents have consistently used a strict, controlling child rearing style to ensure that their children know the rules
     * d. tend to do fine if they are older, remain home alone, and have parents who check in with them regularly

p. 403 41. Compared to middle- and upper-class parents, lower-class parents tend to do all of the following EXCEPT:
F
        a. place a greater value on obedience
        b. show less warmth and affection to their children
        c. spend less time reasoning with their children
     * d. be more permissive

p. 404 42. David and Viv are both business executives, while Ron and Sheila are factory workers. With regard to parenting, David and Viv are MORE LIKELY than Ron and Sheila to:
C
        a. demand that their children show respect for authority figures
     * b. be warm and affectionate with their children
        c. insist that their children obey them
        d. use physical punishment

p. 404 43. Social-class differences in parenting style are LEAST LIKELY to be related to:
F   * a. lack of love and attachment
        b. economic stress
        c. anticipated job skills
        d. marital conflict

p. 404 44. Compared to Euro-American families, African-American families:

C
    a. place greater emphasis on explaining their rationale for discipline

   *   b. are more likely to use physical forms of discipline

    c. are more permissive and indulgent with their children

    d. are very controlling with their children

p. 405 45. Compared to Euro-American families, Native-American families:

C
    a. are very controlling with their children

www
    b. tend to use physical punishment to discipline their children

    c. do not openly express warmth and acceptance

   *   d. are very indulgent with their children

p. 405 46. The effects of different child rearing practices:

F
    a. are the same in all cultures

    b. tend to balance out so that no single technique is particularly effective

   *   c. vary depending on the cultural context in which they are used

    d. cannot be measured because of all the other variables that influence development

p. 405 47. Which is MOST accurate with regard to interactions within the family system?

C
    a. The influence is unidirectional, from parent to child.

    b. Children have more influence on their parents than their parents have on them.

   *   c. The influence is reciprocal between parent and child.

    d. Children have no influence on their parents, as parent's personalities are already firmly cemented.

p. 405 48. According to a child effects model:

F   *   a. children influence their parents through variables such as their age and personality

    b. parents are most influential in the parent-child relationship

    c. parents are responsible for how children turn out

    d. parents and children find one style of interaction that works best for them

p. 405 49. Research indicates that:

F
    a. parents of conduct-disordered sons are worse disciplinarians than other parents

    b. children have little influence on their parents' parenting styles

    c. parents should increase their level of restrictiveness as children enter adolescence

   *   d. children's behavior can significantly impact parenting style

p. 406 50. The arrival of a new baby in the family is MOST likely to:

F
    a. be a joyous occasion for all

   *   b. promote feelings of resentment and dependency behaviors in first-born children

    c. result in parents overcompensating by paying more attention to older siblings than before

    d. enhance an older sibling's feelings of competence and self-reliance

p. 406 51. Mary and Barry have a toddler, Jack, and are expecting a new baby. Mary and Barry can
C   help Jack adjust by:
            a. making sure Jack knows he is their favorite
            b. letting Jack have special privileges such as staying up late and eating whatever he
                wants
      *   c. encouraging Jack to help take care of the new baby
            d. sending Jack to stay with his grandparents for a few weeks while they get settled with
                the new baby

p. 407 52. Regarding sibling relationships, which is FALSE?
C   a. If parents get along, brothers and sisters are likely to get along.
www   b. Conflict is normal in all sibling relationships.
            c. Children who responded early with affection to siblings are likely to remain
                affectionate later on.
      *   d. It is normal for the adjustment of siblings to one another to be a long and difficult
                process, taking a few years.

p. 408 53. Older siblings often serve as caretakers and teachers for their younger brothers and sisters.
C   Examination of the effects of assuming these roles on later development suggests all of the
            following EXCEPT:
            a. As a result of playing school, younger siblings often have an easier time learning to
                read.
            b. Engaging in the role of "teacher" may have important intellectual benefits for the older
                sibling.
      *   c. Placement of the older sibling in such roles tends to lead to life-long feelings of
                resentment over having to grow up too fast.
            d. Both older and younger siblings may experience significant social benefits from
                participating in such roles.

p. 408 54. Which is TRUE regarding parent-adolescent relationships?
F   a. The generation gap is rapidly expanding.
            b. The generation gap has shrunk dramatically during the past decade.
      *   c. Parents and adolescents generally get along better than is commonly assumed.
            d. Most adolescents go through a couple of years of hating their parents but eventually get
                over it.

p. 408 55. Conflicts between parents and adolescents:
F   *   a. play an important role in the development of adolescents' autonomy
www   b. are generally quite severe
            c. lead to the destruction of parent/child attachments
            d. tend to stifle psychological growth

p. 409 56. Adolescents' psychological growth toward emotional and behavioral autonomy is BEST
C   fostered in a home environment:
            a. which is devoid of conflict
      *   b. which permits disagreement in a climate of mutual support
            c. where children are permitted to make all their own decisions
            d. where parents protect their children so they can't get into trouble with drugs, sex, and
                the law

p. 409 57. Which parenting style is MOST likely to promote psychological maturity in adolescents?
C   *   a. authoritative
             b. authoritarian
             c. permissive
             d. harmonious

p. 409 58. Parents who wish to promote autonomy in their adolescent children should strive to:
C   a. let their children do as they please and learn from their mistakes
             b. maintain a tight rein on their children's activities
        *   c. keep rules to a minimum and be warm and supportive
             d. avoid conflict so as not to alienate their youngsters

p. 409 59. If Diana and Phillip want their adolescent to "make it" as an independent adult, they
C   should:
             a. exert strong control over their child's behavior during the adolescent years
             b. distance themselves from their adolescent, to weaken their attachment relationship
             c. let their adolescent make his/her own choices and withhold their own opinions, because
                 they won't be around to help their child forever
        *   d. gradually relinquish power and control so that their adolescent gains experience in
                 making wise choices

p. 409 60. In general, marital satisfaction tends to:
F   a. increase steadily over the first two to three years of marriage
        *   b. decrease somewhat over the first year of marriage
             c. remain stable for most couples until the "7 year itch"
             d. decrease drastically within 6 months of the wedding

p. 409 61. Lauren and Hal are nearing their first wedding anniversary. It is MOST LIKELY that:
C   *   a. they are less satisfied with their sex life than when they first married
             b. they share their feelings more openly now with each other than when they were first
                 married
             c. they would rather not be married
             d. they spend more time with each other now than ever before

p. 410 62. Becoming a parent tends to lead toward:
C   a. an increase in marital satisfaction for women, but not for men
             b. an increase in marital satisfaction for men, but not for women
             c. an increase in marital satisfaction for both partners
        *   d. a more traditional division of household responsibilities

p. 410 63. As children are added to the family, marital satisfaction tends to:
F   a. increase for both mothers and fathers
www   b. increase for mothers but decrease for fathers
             c. decrease for mothers but increase for fathers
        *   d. decrease for both mothers and fathers

p. 411   64.   Adjustment to parenthood is likely to be MOST difficult for those who:
C
            a.   have children in their early twenties
            b.   wait for several years after the marriage to have children
            c.   postpone childbearing until their thirties
      *   d.   do not have good spousal support

p. 411   65.   Liz and John are expecting their second child. Once the baby arrives, it is MOST LIKELY
C   that:
            a.   Liz and John will become more satisfied with their marriage
      *   b.   John will become more involved in caring for the children
            c.   The stress level in the family will lessen, as the two children will keep each other
                 company
            d.   Liz and John will experience a sharp decline in their overall level of marital satisfaction

p. 412   66.   Susan and Jeff's children are all grown up -- the youngest just graduated from college! It is
C   MOST LIKELY that Susan and Jeff:
            a.   are less satisfied with their marriage than when the children were at home
            b.   spend less time together now than when they had children at home
            c.   find it more stressful to be alone together than when their children were at home
      *   d.   will experience an increase in marital satisfaction

p. 412   67.   Tom and Phyllis have just "emptied their nest" by dropping their youngest son off at
C   college! It is MOST LIKELY that:
            a.   Phyllis will become very depressed
            b.   Tom will spend less time with Phyllis now that there are no children to keep him at
                 home
      *   c.   Phyllis will feel better about herself than when the children were living at home
            d.   Phyllis and Tom will become distant from one another without the children to bring
                 them together

p. 413   68.   The MOST common form of grandparenting appears to be one where there is:
C
            a.   little contact between grandparent and grandchild, largely due to geographical distance
            b.   frequent contact between grandparent and grandchild, with the grandparent often
                 assuming a parental role
      *   c.   frequent contact between grandparent and grandchild, with the primary goal being
                 enjoyment of one another
            d.   infrequent contact between grandparent and grandchild, but when together the
                 grandparents tend to meddle in the way the child is being reared

p. 413   69.   MOST grandparents:
F
www   a.   wish they could have greater caretaking responsibility of their grandchildren than they
                 currently do
            b.   are emotionally distant from their grandchildren
      *   c.   hesitate to interfere in the way their adult children are parenting their children
            d.   assume a parent-like role with their grandchildren

p. 413   70.   Which is TRUE with regard to grandparenting?
C
      a.   Grandfathers tend to be more satisfied with their roles than are grandmothers.
   *   b.   Relationships tend to be closest between grandchildren and their maternal grandmothers.
      c.   The closest relationships tend to be those between grandchildren and their grandfathers.
      d.   Most grandparents spend more time with their grandchildren than they really want to because the grandchildren tire them out.

p. 413   71.   The LEAST satisfied grandparents tend to be those who:
F
      a.   are often called on to help with child care
   *   b.   live far away from their grandchildren, and are relatively uninvolved in their lives
      c.   serve as companions, rather than parent substitutes
      d.   become grandparents during middle-age

p. 414   72.   All else being equal, who is likely to feel MOST satisfied with their marriage?
C   *   a.   Julie and Jim, who just got married.
      b.   Jane and Jake, who just had their first child.
      c.   Jessica and John, who have two young children.
      d.   Janet and Jack, whose children are in high school.

p. 414   73.   Marital satisfaction:
F   *   a.   varies somewhat, but tends to remain relatively stable over the years
      b.   is greatest among couples with contrasting personalities
      c.   tends to change dramatically with significant life events such as the birth of a child, and children's departure from the "nest"
      d.   is not influenced by characteristics of children in the family

p. 415   74.   Happily married couples tend to stay together because they:
F
      a.   believe marriage should be a lifelong commitment
      b.   believe it is best for the children
      c.   find it convenient to do so
   *   d.   enjoy each other's company

p. 415   75.   Which BEST describes sibling relationships over the adulthood years?
C
      a.   Sibling rivalry disappears once the children are out and on their own.
      b.   Most siblings share intimate problems frequently across the years.
   *   c.   Siblings often grow emotionally closer from middle age to old age.
      d.   Marriage generally brings siblings closer together.

p. 415   76.   Adult children and their parents:
C
      a.   usually find that their parent-child roles become exaggerated as they get older
      b.   tend to become emotionally distant and remote from one another
      c.   usually reverse their roles with one another
   *   d.   usually form more mutual friend-like relationships

p. 415 77. MOST families in the United States today:

F   a.   live as isolated nuclear units (mother, father, children)

        b.   have abandoned their elderly relatives

    *   c.   live in separate nuclear households but maintain close ties to other relatives

        d.   consist of three generations living in the same household

p. 416 78. MOST elderly people:

F   a.   want to live with their adult children when their health fails

        b.   become needy and dependent on their adult children

    *   c.   prefer to live in their own homes, with frequent contact with their adult children

        d.   prefer to live on their own, and interact infrequently with their adult children

p. 416 79. Len and Martha have children in high school and college. Their parents live in different

C   towns, all within an hour's drive. Len and Martha talk on the phone to their parents once or twice a week, and drive to visit them at least once each month. They all get together on holidays, or for other significant events such as a school play or high-school graduation. Len and Martha's family is BEST classified as a(n) ___ family:

        a.   nuclear

        b.   extended

        c.   reconstituted

    *   d.   modified extended

p. 416 80. The "middle generation squeeze" refers to:

F   a.   young grandparents who must simultaneously care for their own and their children's children

    *   b.   middle-aged adults who find themselves simultaneously caring for both younger and older generations

        c.   children of divorce who must split their time between living with both mother and father

        d.   children who are middle-borns in large families

p. 416 81. Who is MOST LIKELY to experience caregiver burden?

C   a.   Rita, who is married and cares for her 90-year-old mother who is mentally alert but

www   can't get around very well.

        b.   Jill, who cares for both of her 80-year-old parents living next door.

    *   c.   Sue, who is single and cares for her 85-year-old mother who is suffering from Alzheimer's and recently broke her hip.

        d.   Mary, who is single and has put her 70-year-old father in a nursing home following a stroke.

p. 418 82. Couples who live together before marriage tend to:

C   a.   experience greater satisfaction in the marriage relationship than those who do not live together before marriage

        b.   do so as a substitute for marriage

        c.   be less likely to divorce once they are married

    *   d.   be less similar in race, religion, and occupation than those who do not live together before marriage

p. 418 83. Couples who live together before getting married, compared to those who do not live
F   together, tend to be all of the following EXCEPT:
         a. less satisfied when they do get married
    *   b. more satisfied with their relationship
         c. more likely to divorce
         d. less committed to the idea of marriage

p. 418 84. In general, adults who never marry:
F   a. are more outgoing than married adults and don't want to be tied down to a partner
    *   b. have a lower sense of well-being than married adults do
         c. tend to be socially maladjusted
         d. are very lonely and maladjusted

p. 418 85. Adults who never marry tend to be:
F   a. very lonely
www   b. happier than those who do get married
         c. higher in self-esteem than those who marry
    *   d. happier than singles who have been divorced

p. 418 86. Married couples who voluntarily remain "childfree":
F   *   a. generally experience greater marital satisfaction than couples with children during the
                 child-rearing years
         b. tend to be less satisfied in middle-age and old age than couples whose children have
                 grown and gone
         c. are generally more lonely than couples with children
         d. are usually quite self-centered

p. 418 87. In general, MOST gay and lesbian couples:
F   a. have less satisfying relationships than married heterosexuals
www   b. assign the role of "wife" to one partner and the role of "husband" to the other
    *   c. tend to have more egalitarian relationships than married heterosexuals
         d. are less loyal and more promiscuous than married heterosexuals

p. 418 88. Compared to children of heterosexual couples, children raised in gay or lesbian families:
F   a. are much more likely to develop a homosexual orientation
    *   b. are just as well-adjusted
         c. perform worse at school
         d. are not as securely attached to their parents

p. 419 89. The couple at HIGHEST risk for divorce is one where partners:
F   a. postponed having children for 5 or more years following marriage
    *   b. are young and have been married for about 7 years
         c. married in their mid-thirties
         d. never had children

p. 419 90.   Who is MOST at-risk for divorce?

C

          a. Tim and Leslie, who were married at age 25 and waited for three years before having children.

          b. David and Rose, who are in their 50's and have an adult child still living them.

*   c. Margaret and Steve, who are in their 20's and have 3 children, the first of whom was conceived before they were married.

          d. Jess and Luke, who married in their thirties, and have one child.

p. 419 91.   Young children of divorce are MOST likely to be:

C

          a. extra cooperative and helpful to the custodial parent

          b. independent and obedient

*   c. fearful that they are somehow responsible for the divorce

          d. particularly motivated to achieve well in school

p. 419 92.   The negative effects of divorce on the parent-child relationship are likely to be MOST

C   intense:

          a. before the actual separation between spouses takes place

          b. immediately following the divorce

*   c. about one year after the divorce

          d. when the child reaches adolescence, whenever that may be

p. 419 93.   In the case of divorce, custodial mothers tend to be:

C

          a. extremely warm and loving with their children to make up for their loss of a father

          b. very permissive and overindulgent

*   c. less accepting and responsive to their children

          d. extra sensitive to their children's needs

p. 420 94.   Shari and Bill just got divorced. It is MOST LIKELY that, early on, Shari will be ___ and

C   Bill will be ___ with the children:

www   a. warm and loving; cold and distant

          b. permissive; highly controlling

*   c. inconsistent; indulgent

          d. cold and distant; inconsistent

p. 421 95.   Which of the following is FALSE with regard to the effects of divorce on children?

C

          a. Many emotional disturbances fade away within approximately two years.

          b. Children tend to fare better in the long run when they live with the same-sex parent.

*   c. Children of both sexes tend to fare best when they reside with the mother.

          d. Boys tend to recover more slowly than girls from the negative effects of divorce.

p. 421 96.   Which is FALSE with regard to the effects of divorce?

C

          a. Children may actually benefit from the ending of a dysfunctional marriage.

*   b. Staying together "for the children" is virtually always easier on the children than getting a divorce.

          c. Behavior problems exhibited by children of divorce are often present even before the divorce, and are due more to family conflict than to the divorce itself.

          d. Children whose parents divorce are themselves at increased risk for divorce.

p. 421   97.   When a stepfather comes on the scene, boys tend to:

C
        a.   suffer a loss in self-esteem
        b.   develop even more severe adjustment problems
        c.   become withdrawn and depressed
    *   d.   benefit more than girls

p. 421   98.   Which is FALSE?

F
        a.   A majority of those who get divorced will eventually remarry.
        b.   Second marriages are more at-risk for divorce than first marriages.
    *   c.   Girls tend to benefit more than boys when they gain a stepfather.
        d.   Boys tend to suffer more than girls when they live with a single-parent mother.

p. 424   99.   All of the following appears to be associated with the incidence of child abuse with the

C   EXCEPTION of:
    *   a.   maternal employment outside of the home
        b.   social isolation
        c.   infant temperament
        d.   family history of abuse

p. 424   100.   Parents who abuse their children:

C
        a.   were almost always abused themselves as children
        b.   cannot be helped, and should have their children taken away immediately
    *   c.   often tend to interpret their children's cries as criticism or rejection
        d.   suffer from severe mental illness

p. 424   101.   MOST child abusers:

F
        a.   abuse all of their children from a very young age
        b.   cannot be rehabilitated
        c.   feel their behavior is justified
    *   d.   have poor coping skills and little social support

p. 425   102.   Children who are abused are MOST LIKELY to:

F
        a.   become passive and withdrawn
    *   b.   act aggressively toward their peers
        c.   put their energy into succeeding in school
        d.   be particularly sensitive to the needs of their peers

p. 426   103.   Programs designed to help parents who are abusive or are at-risk to be abusive:

C
        a.   have proven to be largely useless for both groups of parents
        b.   have proven to work equally well for both groups of parents
    *   c.   seem to be most effective when they provide emotional support and teach improved coping techniques
        d.   work best for those who are actively abusive, because these are the parents who realize they have a problem

p. 397　104. The family life cycle
F
SG　　*　a.　refers to the sequence of changes in family membership and roles between marriage and death
　　　　　b.　refers to family units that consist of a parent, a stepparent and at least one child
　　　　　c.　refers to the changes that have occurred in the family system during the 20th century
　　　　　d.　undergoes dramatic changes every 10 years

p. 396　105. A family unit consisting of a mother, father, and at least one child is called a _____
F　　　　family.
SG　　　　a.　reconstituted
　　　　　b.　extended
　　　*　c.　nuclear
　　　　　d.　generational

p. 400　106. Compared to mothers, fathers in general
F　　　　　a.　spend as much time with their children
SG　　*　b.　spend less time with their children
　　　　　c.　treat boys and girls more similarly
　　　　　d.　serve as disciplinarian in the family

p. 402　107. Which type of parenting style places few demands on children and allows them to express
F　　　　their desires freely?
SG　　*　a.　permissive
　　　　　b.　authoritative
　　　　　c.　authoritarian
　　　　　d.　neglectful

p. 401　108. In which style of parenting do parents value obedience for its own sake and impose many
F　　　　rules that are typically not fully explained to children?
SG　　　　a.　permissive
　　　　　b.　authoritative
　　　*　c.　authoritarian
　　　　　d.　neglectful

p. 402　109. Children of parents who use a(n) _____ style of parenting are typically more self-
C　　　　reliant and achievement oriented than children raised with other styles of parenting
SG　　　　a.　permissive
　　　*　b.　authoritative
　　　　　c.　authoritarian
　　　　　d.　neglectful

p. 406　110. Feelings of rivalry or jealousy following the birth of a new sibling
C　　　　　a.　are strongest if parents maintain the same regular schedule they had for the first-born
SG　　　　　before the arrival of the new baby
　　　*　b.　can be minimized if the first-born had already established a good relationship with parents
　　　　　c.　can be minimized if the parents lavish the first child with attention
　　　　　d.　are always worse if the first-born is a boy

p. 409 111. With respect to adolescent-parent relationships, research indicates:
C
SG
        a. there is a huge gap between generations in their values and attitudes
        b. adolescents generally report being unhappy with the relationship
        c. boys are much more dissatisfied with the relationship than girls
  * d. adolescents are strongly influenced by their parents on important issues

p. 415 112. The relationship between adult siblings
F
SG   *
        a. disintegrates once the siblings leave school
  * b. remains close although less intense than during childhood
        c. involves a great deal of sharing and discussing feelings
        d. continues to be as intense as during childhood

p. 410 113. Which of the following is <u>true</u> regarding marital satisfaction?
F
SG
        a. Marital satisfaction is highest following the birth of a child.
        b. Because of the adjustments that must be made, marital satisfaction is lowest right after marriage
  * c. Marital satisfaction declines following the birth of a child
        d. Marital satisfaction declines across middle and older adulthood

p. 418 114. Cohabiting couples who later marry
F   *
SG
  * a. are more dissatisfied with their marriages than couples who had not lived together before marrying
        b. are more satisfied with their marriages than couples who had not lived together before marrying
        c. are less likely to divorce than couples who had not lived together before marrying
        d. are basically no different from couples who had not lived together before marrying

p. 418 115. Adults who never marry
F
SG
        a. typically have some psychological problem
        b. are lonely and maladjusted
        c. are much happier and better adjusted than married adults
  * d. are somewhat less happy than married adults

p. 420 116. Evidence indicates that following a divorce
C
SG   *
        a. both boys and girls settle quickly into a new lifestyle with few adjustment problems
  * b. boys take longer to adjust than girls and exhibit more behavior problems
        c. girls take longer to adjust than boys and exhibit more depression
        d. neither boys or girls adjust to the new lifestyle within several years of the divorce

p. 421 117. Reconstituted families where children in a mother-headed family acquire a stepfather
F   *
SG
  * a. seem to benefit boys more than girls
        b. seem to benefit girls more than boys
        c. seem to benefit boys and girls equally
        d. do not benefit any of the children, just the adults

p. 422   118. Child abuse is <u>less</u> likely in families where
C   a. the parents had been abused themselves and so they know the negative impact that
SG   abuse can have
                b. there are multiple sources of stress
    *   c. there is a strong support network available to parents
                d. parents have difficulty "reading" their child's signals

TRUE-FALSE QUESTIONS

p. 397   119. Extended families are more common among African-Americans than among Euro-
                Americans.
    *   a. true
                b. false

p. 398   120. Most women in American society today work outside the home.
    *   a. true
                b. false

p. 400   121. Fathers and mothers today spend about equal amounts of time in caring for their children.
                a. true
    *   b. false

p. 400   122. Mothers are more likely than fathers to treat young children differently on the basis of
                gender.
                a. true
    *   b. false

p. 400   123. The way parents interact with one another can influence how each parent individually acts
                with each child in the family.
    *   a. true
                b. false

p. 404   124. "Good parenting" is much the same in all cultures around the world.
                a. true
    *   b. false

p. 406   125. Conflict is normal, even in the best of sibling relationships.
    *   a. true
                b. false

p. 407   126. Older siblings who "teach" their younger siblings in games such as "playing school" make
                significant gains in their own academic achievement.
    *   a. true
                b. false

p. 409   127. The advantages children gain from authoritative parenting tend to wash out by adolescence.
                a. true
    *   b. false

p. 409 128. As a child matures, it is best to move from a more permissive to a more restrictive
parenting style.
a. true
* b. false

p. 409 129. The nature of the sibling relationship during childhood tends to predict the nature of the
adult sibling relationship.
* a. true
b. false

p. 409 130. To attain psychological maturity, adolescents must sever their emotional attachments to
parents.
a. true
* b. false

p. 409 131. Parents who wish to promote their adolescents' autonomy must learn to let their children do
www   as they please.
a. true
* b. false

p. 409 132. In many cultures, marriages are not formed on the basis of love.
* a. true
b. false

p. 410 133. The birth of a child generally leads to increased satisfaction in the marital relationship.
a. true
* b. false

p. 410 134. Children typically have a negative effect on the marital relationship.
* a. true
b. false

p. 412 135. Most parents experience a further decrease in marital satisfaction when the children leave
home.
a. true
* b. false

p. 413 136. Most old people would welcome the chance to move in with their adult children.
a. true
* b. false

p. 415 137. Contact generally increases between siblings from middle adulthood to old age.
a. true
* b. false

p. 418 138. Never-married adults tend to be happier, overall, than divorced single adults.
* a. true
b. false

p. 418 139. Most homosexual couples assume heterosexual roles, where one is the submissive "wife" and the other is the dominant "husband."
   a. true
 * b. false

p. 418 140. Homosexual couples are likely to have more egalitarian relationships than heterosexual couples do.
 * a. true
   b. false

p. 418 141. People who live together before getting married tend to have more satisfying marital
www   relationships than those who do not.
   a. true
 * b. false

p. 419 142. Following a divorce, custodial mothers tend to become extra-sensitive to the needs of their children, in order to compensate for their "loss" of a father.
   a. true
 * b. false

p. 420 143. In the case of divorce, noncustodial fathers tend to be highly punitive and controlling with their children.
   a. true
 * b. false

p. 420 144. Following a divorce, problems between mother and child are most severe when the child is female.
   a. true
 * b. false

p. 420 145. Girls tend to suffer more than boys from persistent negative effects of divorce.
   a. true
 * b. false

p. 421 146. Girls tend to fare better than boys in reconstituted families.
   a. true
 * b. false

ESSAY QUESTIONS

147. How do child-rearing styles influence children's development? In general, which style seems to work best? Why?

148. How does marital satisfaction change over the course of a marriage? What factors influence marital satisfaction?

149. In what ways do children influence their parents?

150. How does life satisfaction compare for individuals who marry, those who never marry, those who marry but later divorce, and those who marry but do not have children?

151. What factors contribute to child abuse?

152. How does divorce influence parents and their children?
www

153. What type of parenting dimensions and parent control have the best outcome for children? What
SG   makes these parenting styles effective?
     [Sample answer is provided in the Study Guide.]

154. What are potential advantages and disadvantages for children whose parents divorce?
SG

155. What affects can children have on their parents across the life span?
SG

156. What are potential advantages and disadvantages for individuals who marry, individuals who
SG   remain single, couples who have children, and those who do not have children?

ACHIEVEMENTS

MULTIPLE-CHOICE QUESTIONS

---

p. 431 1. Achievement motivation (n Ach) is best defined as a motive to:
F   a. gain approval
     * b. meet high standards of performance
     c. avoid failure and embarrassment
     d. master the environment

p. 431 2. Children with a high need for achievement:
F   * a. get better grades in school than children with a low need for achievement
     b. perform no differently than children with a low need for achievement
     c. do better than other children on easy tasks, but not on difficult tasks
     d. are also high in intelligence

p. 431 3. People work harder on a task when:
F   a. the outcome of the task is unknown to them
www   * b. they believe they might succeed
     c. they are faced with a very difficult task
     d. they are not worried about failure

p. 432 4. Maria has done poorly on an important math exam. She attributes this to a lack of ability
C   on her part. This attribution is:
     a. internal and unstable
     * b. internal and stable
     c. external and unstable
     d. external and stable

p. 432 5. Mark competes in a swim meet and doesn't do nearly as well as he had hoped. He
C   attributes his failure to the fact that the judges made a mistake. This attribution is BEST
     classified as:
     a. internal and stable
     * b. external and unstable
     c. internal and unstable
     d. external and stable

p. 432 6. Fred has just flunked an important geography test. To what might he attribute his failure
C   and have the BEST chance of feeling like he will do well next time around?
www   a. he isn't bright enough
     * b. he didn't study enough
     c. the test was unfair
     d. it was just bad luck

p. 432　7.　Which of the following represents an internal, unstable attribution?

C
　　　　　a.　"If I wasn't so dumb I would do better."
　　　　　b.　"If the teacher would give a fair test, I could do better."
　*　　c.　"If I had studied more I would have done better."
　　　　　d.　"If the teacher liked me more I could do better."

p. 433　8.　Effectance motivation:

C　*　a.　is present in very young infants
　　　　　b.　does not emerge until the end of the sensorimotor period
　　　　　c.　is a learned phenomenon
　　　　　d.　emerges only in a competitive environment

p. 433　9.　Which of the following has NOT been shown to influence effectance motivation?

C
　　　　　a.　type of attachment to a caregiver
　　　　　b.　sensory stimulation
　　　　　c.　parental responsiveness
　*　　d.　socioeconomic status of the family

p. 433　10.　Parents who wish to enhance their infants' effectance or mastery motivation should:

C
　　　　　a.　push their children to achieve
　*　　b.　be responsive to their children's needs
　　　　　c.　avoid stimulating their infants so that they learn to entertain themselves
　　　　　d.　place their infants in academic preschool programs

p. 434　11.　Jean Piaget viewed play as:

F
　　　　　a.　useless and a waste of time
　　　　　b.　getting in the way of cognitive development
　　　　　c.　an extrinsically motivated activity
　*　　d.　an opportunity to practice cognitive skills

p. 434.　12.　During the first three months of life, infants are most interested in playing with:

F
　　　　　a.　motorized toys
　　　　　b.　objects that make a nice sound
　　　　　c.　their mothers
　*　　d.　their own bodies

p. 434　13.　At about one year of age, infants engage in functional play. Which of the following is

F
　　　　　the BEST example of this?
　　　　　a.　kicking his/her legs repeatedly
　*　　b.　dialing a toy telephone
　　　　　c.　sucking on a rattle
　　　　　d.　shaking toy animals

p. 434　14.　Which of the following is ESSENTIAL for a child to be able to engage in symbolic play?

C
　　　　　a.　achievement of preoperational thought
　*　　b.　achievement of symbolic capacity
　　　　　c.　the development of conservation skills
　　　　　d.　an understanding of past and future, as well as present events

p. 434　15.　Symbolic play is BEST demonstrated by each of the following EXCEPT:

C　　　*　a.　sucking on toes
　　　　　b.　holding a plastic cup to a doll's lips
　　　　　c.　holding a block up to one's own lips and pretending to drink
　　　　　d.　pretending to be a mommy, putting a baby-doll to sleep

p. 434　16.　Which is NOT an example of symbolic play?

C　　　　　a.　flapping one's arms and chirping like a bird
　　　　　b.　pointing a finger at someone and shouting "Bang, you're dead!"
　　　　　c.　holding a block to one's ear and "talking on the phone"
　　　*　d.　splashing around in the bathtub

p. 434　17.　What is the BEST thing parents can do to foster the development of play activity?

F　　　　　a.　push their children to develop their language skills
　　　*　b.　play along with their children
　　　　　c.　encourage their children to play on their own, and to not be dependent on them as playmates
　　　　　d.　buy their children the latest, "trendy" toys

p. 435　18.　Mastery oriented students tend NOT to blame their failures on factors that are:

F　　　*　a.　internal and stable
　　　　　b.　internal and unstable
　　　　　c.　external and stable
　　　　　d.　external and unstable

p. 435　19.　High achievers generally make attributions regarding their academic performance that:

F　　　　　a.　give others the credit
　　　*　b.　enhance or preserve their self-esteem
　　　　　c.　threaten their self-esteem
　　　　　d.　always place the blame on others

p. 435　20.　Low-achieving students most often tend to make attributions regarding their academic performance that:

F　　　　　a.　enhance or preserve their self-esteem
　　　　　b.　give them renewed strength to try again
　　　*　c.　cause them to feel like giving up
　　　　　d.　place responsibility for their performance on others

p. 435　21.　Which statement is a high achiever MOST LIKELY to make?

C　　　　　a.　"I sure lucked out on that test!" (after doing well)
www　　　b.　"I tried as hard as I could." (after doing poorly)
　　　　　c.　"I must not be smart enough." (after doing poorly)
　　　*　d.　"I need to try harder." (after doing poorly)

p. 435　22.　Jeff is a low achiever. After doing well on an exam, he is LEAST LIKELY to say:

C　　　　　a.　"Boy, did I get lucky!"
　　　　　b.　"That was an easy test."
　　　　　c.　"I really studied hard for that."
　　　*　d.　"I knew I was smart enough!"

p. 435 23. As children get older, they tend to
C
a. place greater emphasis on luck and fate rather than ability and effort
b. try to improve their abilities as much as possible
* c. view ability as a fixed trait that cannot be changed
d. view ability as a changeable quality

p. 435 24. Children who adopt performance goals in school:
C   * a. strive to demonstrate their ability to others rather than really try to strengthen their ability
b. work hard to improve their ability
c. have an incremental view of ability
d. believe that all goals can be achieved by performing one's best

p. 435 25. Jill views every assignment that her teacher assigns as an interesting challenge. She works
C   hard to do a good job. When she doesn't understand something, she asks her teacher or she
reads up on the topic in the encyclopedia. This way, if the issue comes up again in the
future, she really understands what it means. This suggest that Jill has adopted a(n):
a. entity view of ability
* b. incremental view of ability
c. learned helplessness orientation
d. performance goals

p. 436 26. Parents can foster healthy attribution styles by helping children to:
C   * a. view themselves as competent
b. be eternally optimistic
c. blame others for their failures
d. expect less of themselves

p. 436 27. Rachel wants to help her children develop a mastery achievement orientation. She should:
C   a. push them to do things at a very early age
* b. encourage them to do things well
c. give her children rewards when they do the things she asks them to do
d. praise them lavishly for their accomplishments

p. 437 28. Angela doesn't seem to even want to try to do well in her high school math class. If her
C   teacher wants to help her change her self-defeating pattern of behavior, she should:
* a. encourage Angela to attribute her failures to a lack of effort
b. tell Angela her failures thus far have just been due to bad luck
c. tell Angela she should consider transferring to a less rigorous math class
d. encourage Angela to consider a profession that doesn't require a lot of math skills

p. 437 29. Research indicates that we can help youngsters overcome a "helpless" attribution style by
C   teaching them to attribute their failures to:
www * a. a lack of effort, rather than a lack of ability
b. bad luck, rather than a lack of effort
c. impossible task demands, rather than a lack of ability
d. unfair demands, rather than a lack of effort

p. 437 30. Teachers can help students who are prone to learned helplessness by:
F
    a. ignoring them so they are less self conscious
*   b. coaching them in more adaptive styles
    c. giving them easy tests and high grades to build self esteem
    d. teaching them that learning situations are tests of competence

p. 437 31. Which of the following teacher comments is LEAST LIKELY to have a positive effect
C   on a student's achievement motivation?
*   a. "It's not your fault you aren't doing well."
    b. "You can do this if you try!"
    c. "You can learn a lot from this experience."
    d. "You're really very smart, you know."

p. 437 32. Teachers who wish to develop their students' achievement motivation should:
C   a. encourage their students to compete with one another to see who can do the best
*   b. encourage students to strive for their own personal best
    c. use operant conditioning techniques (e.g., give rewards for good grades) to motivate students to achieve
    d. give students easy tasks so they will always succeed

p. 437 33. Which is FALSE with regard to the effects of attending preschool on later development?
C   a. Economically disadvantaged preschoolers who attend preschool programs designed to prepare them for school generally experience more success in school than similar youngsters who stay home.
    b. Children who attend preschool sometimes develop social skills sooner than those who stay at home.
*   c. Middle-class youngsters are far better off in their mothers' care than they are in day-care centers.
    d. Most children who go to preschool are no more intellectually advanced when they enter public school than those who remain at home.

p. 437. 34. Shelly attended a neighborhood play group three half-days per week during the year before
C   she went to kindergarten. Marie went to a prestigious preschool where children were drilled in basic skills in reading, writing, and mathematics. All else being equal, which of the following is MOST LIKELY?
    a. Marie will be academically advanced and will have a better attitude than Shelly toward school.
    b. Marie will be more creative, less anxious, and more cognitively advanced than Shelly when she begins kindergarten.
*   c. Marie will be more anxious and will have a more negative attitude toward school than Shelly will.
    d. There will be no differences in the development of Shelly and Marie.

p. 437 35. Becky's parents are looking for a high-quality day-care center to place her in. The center
C   they choose should have all of the following EXCEPT:
www   a. a low child-to-caregiver ratio
    b. an age-appropriate curriculum
    c. a stable staff the child can become attached to
*   d. an academically-oriented program of activities

p. 437 36. Edith and Leroy are trying to decide whether their son, Sam, should go to preschool before
C   kindergarten. Their neighbor is a developmental psychologist, so they decide to ask her
          advice. MOST LIKELY they are told:
          a. Keep your son at home. He'll do much better if you do.
          b. Send Sam to the Tots Academy, where they'll teach him to read and do math, and he'll
             always be at the head of his class.
      *   c. Put Sam in the Discovery Center, where they have a play-centered curriculum. This
             will benefit him most.
          d. It really doesn't matter what you do -- kids usually adapt just fine.

p. 438 37. Which does NOT appear to have an impact on school effectiveness?
F   *   a. class size
www   b. approach to discipline
          c. teacher expectations
          d. the characteristics of the students

p. 439 38. Effective schools:
F   a. have small classes
          b. do not use ability tracking
      *   c. emphasize academics
          d. have plenty of money

p. 439 39. What appears to matter MOST with regard to school effectiveness is:
C   a. the amount of support (e.g., amount of money spent per pupil; books in the library;
             quality of supplies and equipment)
          b. the use of ability tracking versus. mixed-ability grouping
      *   c. a good fit between the student and the classroom environment
          d. the nature of the student population (e.g., whether they are from economically
             advantaged or disadvantaged homes)

p. 439 40. Which of the following have been shown to relate to the effectiveness of schools?
F   a. small classes, an academic focus, and grouping by ability level
          b. high expectations for success, rewarding good work, and a high funding base
      *   c. a task-oriented environment, faculty involvement in curriculum development, and
             effective discipline
          d. mixed-ability grouping, high expectations for success, and small classes

p. 439 41. The "effective school environment" is best described as:
F   a. warm and loving, with few expectations
      *   b. comfortable and businesslike
          c. strictly academically oriented
          d. homey and laid-back

p. 440 42. In Brown vs. the Board of Education (1954), the courts mandated the:
F   a. integration of physically-disabled youngsters into regular classrooms
      *   b. racial desegregation of the public schools
          c. integration of emotionally-disturbed children into regular classrooms
          d. provision of public education services for the mentally handicapped from birth through
             adulthood

p. 440 43. Following the enactment of legislation to racially desegregate the public schools:
F
    a. there has been a remarkable improvement in the self-esteem of minority children in integrated classrooms
    b. there has been a notable decline in prejudicial attitudes among school children
    c. there has been a general decline in the achievement of both minority and non-minority youngsters in integrated classrooms
    * d. there is no evidence that the practice has had a positive impact overall on the reduction of prejudice or on the self-esteem of minority youngsters

p. 440 44. "Inclusion" refers to:
F
    a. the inclusion of physically-handicapped youngsters in special classrooms housed within the public schools
    b. the provision of public education services to mentally-handicapped youngsters from birth to age 26
    * c. the integration of handicapped children into regular education classes for at least portion of their educational programming
    d. the inclusion of handicapped youngsters in regular classrooms for 100% of their educational programming

p. 440 45. Research indicates that, overall, the practice of inclusion has resulted in:
F
www
    a. greatly enhanced academic performance for handicapped youngsters
    b. a great increase in the social acceptance of handicapped youngsters
    c. an overall decrease in academic performance for nonhandicapped children who have handicapped students in their classes, because the teacher has less time to give them
    * d. no particular systematic academic and social effects

p. 441 46. Handicapped children who are included in the regular classroom:
F
    a. do consistently better socially and academically than those who are not
    b. do better socially, but not academically, than those who are not
    c. do better academically, but not socially, than those who are not
    * d. show no generalized pattern of benefits in the areas of academics, social skills, and self-esteem

p. 441 47. Cooperative learning techniques have resulted in all of the following EXCEPT:
C
    a. more positive attitudes toward mathematics than when traditional instruction is used
    b. greater acceptance of minority students by nonminority peers
    c. enhanced self-esteem for members of the cooperative learning team
    * d. a slight decline in actual level of achievement in mathematics

p. 441 48. Children who participate in cooperative learning strategies at school tend to exhibit:
F
    a. improved attitudes toward school, but slightly lower levels of achievement
    * b. improved self-esteem, better attitudes toward school, and gains in academic achievement
    c. slight gains in academic achievement, but poorer attitudes toward school overall
    d. improved self-esteem and better attitudes toward school, but no improvement in academic achievement

p. 441 49. Which is TRUE with regard to achievement motivation during adolescence?
F
      a. Children value academic achievement less in high school than they did during grade school.
      b. Self-perceptions of competence tend to become more inflated as children progress through school.
      c. Attitudes toward school generally improve with age.
   * d. High school students are generally more concerned with extrinsic rewards than with intrinsic satisfaction in learning.

p. 441 50. Tina is graduating from elementary school, and will attend middle school in the Fall. She
C   is MOST LIKELY to exhibit an increase in:
      a. self-esteem
      b. motivation to do well
      c. grades
   * d. trouble-making behavior

p. 441 51. Reasons for decreased achievement motivation during adolescence include all of the
F   following EXCEPT:
   * a. increased belief that ability is a changeable quality
      b. advances in cognitive development
      c increasingly negative feedback from teachers regarding ability
      d. increased importance of peer acceptance

p. 441 52. Compared to those who are intrinsically motivated, children and adolescents with an
C   extrinsic motivation to achieve:
      a. see themselves as more competent at academic tasks
      b. prefer more challenging academic tasks
   * c. work to earn an incentive or grade
      d. adopt an incremental view of ability

p. 441 53. Children under age ten are MORE LIKELY than adolescents to:
F
      a. view ability as a highly stable characteristic
www
      b. experience learned helplessness
      c. be concerned with their peers' opinions
   * d. feel good about school

p. 441 54. One reason that achievement motivation changes as children get older is:
C
      a. their cognitive abilities do not keep pace with their need to achieve
   * b. they get increasingly negative feedback about their work from teachers
      c. they don't value any of the work that they are asked to do
      d. they are asked to participate in cooperative learning situations when they would prefer to work independently

p. 442 55. Which of the following is TRUE regarding peer pressure and academic achievement?
C
      a. Peer pressure normally increases academic achievement among both minority and majority students.
      b. Peer pressure normally decreases academic achievement among all groups of adolescents.
*   c. Among African-Americans, peer pressure is likely to decrease academic achievement.
      d. African-American and Hispanic adolescents use peer pressure to improve academic achievement so that they can improve their life options.

p. 443 56. Based on recent research of academic achievement, which of the following recommendations should be made to improve the transition from childhood to adolescence?
C
      a. Create a school that is intermediate between elementary school and high school.
      b. Emphasize getting good grades and competing with other students.
      c. Create an environment where students do not have to make any choices, assignments are easy, and teachers distance themselves so that students don't feel as if they have an adult watching over them.
*   d. Create an environment where teachers are supportive, academic tasks are interesting and challenging, and there is some opportunity for self-direction.

p. 443 57. With regard to career aspirations, which of the following is TRUE?
C
      a. As early as kindergarten or first grade, children are influenced by their awareness that some jobs are valued more highly by society than others.
      b. Concern with the gender-typing of occupations is not apparent until the later elementary school years.
      c. Girls show an earlier tendency toward gender-stereotyping in occupational choices than do boys.
*   d. As early as kindergarten, children of both sexes choose traditionally gender-typed occupations.

p. 443 58. Ginzberg's theory of vocational choice suggests that MOST adolescents:
F
      a. are largely still in a "fantasy" stage with regard to career goals
www * b. become increasingly realistic about what they can be
      c. become increasingly optimistic about the possibility that they can be anything they choose to be, as long as they work hard for it
      d. tend to feel that they have little control over who and what they can be in this troubled world

p. 443 59. Steve wants to be a firefighter or maybe a star football player. He is MOST LIKELY in Ginzberg's _____ stage of vocational choice:
C
*   a. fantasy
      b. tentative
      c. realistic
      d. gender-identity

p. 443　60.　Danielle is in tenth grade. She likes to solve problems, is good at science, and thinks she'll
C　　　　　　be a chemist one day. Danielle is MOST LIKELY in the ___ stage of vocational choice:
　　　　　　　a. fantasy
　　　*　　　b. tentative
　　　　　　　c. decision
　　　　　　　d. realistic

p. 443　61.　As adolescents become young adults, they tend to:
F　　　*　　a. become more realistic in their career choices
　　　　　　　b. place more emphasis on interests than on abilities in making career choices
　　　　　　　c. move toward living out their dreams, rather than being bound by reality
　　　　　　　d. pay increasing attention to their parents' aspirations for their vocational choice

p. 444　62.　Today, most women
C　　　*　　a. aspire to traditionally feminine-stereotyped jobs
　　　　　　　b. aspire to traditionally masculine-stereotyped jobs
　　　　　　　c. don't really care what kind of job they hold as long as they have one
　　　　　　　d. expect that their jobs will be more central in their lives than their family

p. 444　63.　In general, adolescents who work tend to:
F　　　　　　a. develop a more positive attitude toward the world of work
　　　　　　　b. stay out of trouble with drugs
　　　　　　　c. have better attendance in school
　　　*　　　d. get lower grades in school

p. 444　64.　Jeffrey is in high school and works part-time in a bakery, cleaning up and stacking shelves.
C　　　　　　MOST LIKELY Jeffrey will:
　　　　　　　a. do better in school because he has to organize his time wisely now that he is working
　　　　　　　b. be less anxious and depressed now that he is working and earning money
　　　*　　　c. be less interested in school than before he was working
　　　　　　　d. gain valuable practice at work in using what he is learning in school

p. 445　65.　All of the following have been associated with working while in high-school students
F　　　　　　EXCEPT:
www　　　　a. a decline in school performance
　　　*　　　b. an increase in self-direction and self-esteem
　　　　　　　c. an increase in depression and anxiety
　　　　　　　d. an increase in drug and alcohol use

p. 445　66.　Research on the effects of working during high school have found that challenging jobs can
F　　　　　　lead to positive outcomes. These include all of the following EXCEPT:
　　　　　　　a. a stronger sense of self-reliance
　　　*　　　b. greater organizational skills leading to enhanced school performance
　　　　　　　c. greater knowledge about the world of work
　　　　　　　d. stronger work orientation (e.g., pride in doing a good job)

p. 446 67. Overall, research suggests that changes in achievement motivation during adulthood are:
F
           a. influenced more by maturation than by the environment
      *   b. more likely the result of various life events than chronological age
           c. universal for both males and females
           d. orderly and predictable for men but not women

p. 446 68. Achievement motivation in females:
C
           a. usually increases from young adulthood to middle adulthood
           b. declines in highly successful career women across the adult years as they get frustrated with the work world
      *   c. often rebounds after a drop in educated and highly career-oriented women
           d. is particularly high in women in traditionally feminine-stereotyped jobs

p. 446 69. Regarding achievement motivation during adulthood, which is TRUE?
F
           a. Achievement motivation declines steadily from middle to old age for females, but not for males.
           b. Achievement motivation declines steadily from middle to old age for males, but not for females.
           c. For both females and males, achievement motivation increases steadily from young adulthood to middle age.
      *   d. Achievement motivation is more affected by social context than by the process of aging.

p. 447 70. Daniel Levinson's stage theory of adult development:
C
           a. posits different stages for males as compared to females
      *   b. revolves around the building, questioning, and re-building of life structures
           c. suggests that stages in adult development are largely culture-bound
           d. claims that environmental factors are more influential than maturational factors in determining the course of adult development

p. 447 71. According to Levinson, males in their mid-twenties are MOST likely to be concerned with:
F
           a. establishing independence from their parents
           b. questioning their career choices
           c. realizing their dreams
      *   d. working hard to get a good start in their careers

p. 447 72. David is 37 years old. According to Levinson, he is MOST LIKELY:
C
www   a. wondering what to do with his life
           b. working hard on establishing a career and beginning a family
      *   c. feeling settled in his career and family life
           d. serving as a mentor to other executives at the company he works for

p. 447 73. Levinson's theory of adult development suggests that a man in his early forties is MOST
C   likely to be concerned with:
      *   a. questioning the worthiness of his dreams
           b. becoming one's own man
           c. changing his marriage and career choices
           d. finding a mentor to support his career development

p. 448 74. Several studies suggest that:

  a. most males are likely to make very early, stable career choices, though females remain open to change throughout young adulthood

  b. most females are likely to make very early, stable career choices, though males remain open to change throughout young adulthood

  * c. both males and females tend to remain very open to changes in careers as young adults

  d. the vast majority of males and females have stabilized their career choices by age 25

F

p. 448 75. The term midlife crisis refers to:

  a. the time when a parent dies

  b. the loneliness caused when the last child leaves home

  c. getting a divorce

  * d. questioning your career and lifestyle

F

p. 448 76. Levinson's work on stages of adult development suggests that men between the ages of 40 and 45 that:

  a. most either seek a divorce or change their job

  * b. a vast majority experience some sort of life crisis

  c. only a small minority experience any sort of significant life crisis

  d. most are primarily concerned with becoming good at their current jobs

F

p. 448 77. Jay is experiencing what Levinson termed a "midlife crisis." This MOST LIKELY means he is:

  a. searching for someone to serve as a role model for his future career development

  * b. wondering if he's chosen the career that's best for him

  c. getting divorced and marrying a younger woman

  d. experiencing a mental breakdown

C

p. 449 78. Research on adult development indicates that:

  a. Levinson's claim that the early forties are a time of major upheaval for most people is correct

  b. the early forties are generally accompanied by significant changes in personality, often accompanied by emotional disturbance

  * c. many people engage in midlife questioning, but relatively few experience a full-blown midlife crisis

  d. middle-aged males and females are less satisfied with their work, in general, than are younger adults

F

p. 449 79. Applications of Levinson's theory to women suggest that:

  a. women go through the same stages as men

  b. women's life structures are even more predictable than men's

  * c. women follow more erratic and complex paths, dividing attention among career, family, and personal goals

  d. women's life structures follow a more qualitative pattern compared to men's quantitative paths

C

p. 449 80. The job performances of people in their 50's and 60's:
F
    a. is poorer than when they were in their 20's
    b. is poorer than when they were in their 30's
    c. shows a steady decline after age 40
  * d. is not much different than when they were younger

p. 449 81. Adults maintain a consistent level of job performance as they get older by:
C * a. compensating for some lost skills and practicing other skills to keep them in good working order
    b. changing jobs to easier ones
    c. watching how younger workers perform their job and working to keep up with them
    d. becoming less strict about the quality of their work

p. 450 82. In terms of sexual discrimination, which of the following is FALSE?
F
    a. men are still seen as the major breadwinners in the family
    b. women are still perceived as poor workers
  * c. discrimination today is rare
    d. women are paid less than men

p. 450 83. Which is TRUE regarding women assuming multiple roles such as wife, mother, and
C career person?
    a. Women who are wives, mothers, AND workers have lower self-esteem due to "role overload" than those who are trying to do less.
    b. Women who are wives, mothers, AND workers have higher self-esteem than those who are trying to do less due to feelings of great accomplishment.
    c. Women who work outside of the home have higher self-esteem than those who are career homemakers.
  * d. Women who feel the rewards of multiple roles outweigh the hassles have the greatest level of self-esteem.

p. 450 84. Role conflict and role overload have decreased for women in recent years because:
C   a. women are learning not to try to do so much
www b. sex discrimination in the workplace is a thing of the past
  * c. women are spending less time on family tasks
    d. men today tend to share equally in household tasks and child care

p. 450 85. Which is TRUE regarding women and work?
F * a. The majority of women today work in traditionally female-dominated jobs.
    b. The gap between men's and women's wages has been reduced dramatically in the past ten years.
    c. In today's society, a woman's career tends to be viewed as being equally important as her husband's.
    d. Women today are just as likely as men to have a "mentor" of the sort that Daniel Levinson describes as being essential to vocational success.

p. 451　86.　Which is TRUE regarding women in today's world and career achievement?

F

　　　　　a.　Women who climb to the top of the corporate ladder are no more likely than those who don't to be divorced, separated, or childless.

　　　　　b.　Few career women today interrupt their careers to bear and care for their children.

　　　　　c.　Modern society has dropped the old-time view of women as the homekeepers and men as the breadwinners.

　　*　　d.　Women who take time out from their careers to raise a family are hurting their chances to rise to a highly-paid, leadership position.

p. 451　87.　MOST women who are wives, mothers, and workers:

F

　　　　　a.　have lower self-esteem than those who do less

　　　　　b.　are less depressed and anxious than those who do less

　　　　　c.　have children who suffer because of their too-busy lives

　　*　　d.　tend to spend about as much time as non-working mothers in child-centered interactions with their children

p. 452　88.　Regarding the children of mothers who work, which is TRUE?

F

　　　　　a.　Sons of mothers who work have lower levels of self-esteem than sons of stay-at-home moms.

　　　　　b.　Daughters of mothers who work have poorer cognitive skills than daughters of stay-at-home moms.

　　*　　c.　Children of mothers who work fare just as well as children of stay-at-home moms as long as their mothers continue to make time for meaningful, child-centered activities such as reading, playing, and talking.

　　　　　d.　Sons of mothers who work tend to experience confusion with regard to gender-role development.

p. 452　89.　Work that is substantively complex, or intellectually challenging, is associated with all of

C　　　　the following except:

　　　　　a.　increased tolerance of others

　　　　　b.　enhanced self-confidence

　　　　　c.　independent thinking

　　*　　d.　acute anxiety

p. 453　90.　People tend to go through a series of stages in their adjustment to retirement. The usual

F　　　　sequence for progressing through these stages is:

　　　　　a.　preretirement; disenchantment; reorientation; honeymoon

　　　　　b.　preretirement; reorientation; honeymoon; disenchantment

　　*　　c.　preretirement; honeymoon; disenchantment; reorientation

　　　　　d.　disenchantment; preretirement; honeymoon; reorientation

p. 453　91.　Roger is considering retirement. He is concerned about how he will adjust. He talks with a

C　　　　responsible counselor who tells him it is MOST LIKELY that the greatest change will be in the area of:

　　*　　a.　finances

　　　　　b.　social networking

　　　　　c.　physical fitness

　　　　　d.　mental alertness

p. 453 92. Dr. Hart will soon retire from a long, successful career. If he is like MOST retirees, he
C will:
  a. quickly develop a more negative outlook on life
  b. begin to feel quite socially isolated within a short period of time
  c. begin to suffer health problems as a result of inactivity and depression
 * d. be just as satisfied with life after work as he was with life during work

p. 454 93. With regard to aging, activity theory suggests that:
C   a. psychological needs change as people enter old age
  b. successful aging involves accepting a significant decrease in activity level as one gets
   older
 * c. as a person ages, s/he will be most content if s/he maintains preexisting activity levels
  d. those who are happiest in old age are those who significantly increase their physical
   activity level

p. 454 94. Disengagement theory of aging suggests that:
C * a. successful aging involves the ability to leave old roles behind and to reduce one's
   activity level
  b. psychological needs remain the same throughout adulthood
  c. society suffers from the withdrawal of elderly citizens from positions of power
  d. it is important to emotionally sever ties from loved ones in preparation for death

p. 455 95. A person is MOST LIKELY to adjust well to retirement if s/he:
F   a. remains very active, both physically and in terms of maintaining some connections
www   with the world of work
  b. gradually disengages from the world of work and relinquishes former social roles
  c. makes a clean break from the world of work, and doesn't look back
 * d. does whatever feels "right" with regard to activity level and engagement with his/her
   former "work world"

p. 455 96. Which provides for the healthiest adaptation to aging?
F   a. maintaining an active lifestyle
  b. disengaging from roles and relationships
 * c. doing whatever suits one's own personality and lifestyle preferences
  d. substantially increasing the amount of time spent in the pursuit of leisure activities

p. 455 97. Comparative studies of American and Asian students and schooling practices indicate that:
F   a. Asian parents are less likely than American parents to be satisfied with their children's
   academic progress
  b. compared to American parents, Asian parents place a greater emphasis on effort, rather
   than ability, in determining success
  c. Asian children generally spend more time in school AND more time on homework than
   American children do
 * d. all of the above

p. 456 98. Noriko (Japanese) and Molly (American) are best friends. If their parents are like most
C   parents in their respective cultures:
           a. Noriko's parents will focus more on ability, and Molly's on effort, in explaining their
              children's school success.
           b. Noriko's parents will feel more satisfied with her school performance than Molly's will
              with hers.
       *   c. Noriko will be pressured by her parents to spend more time and effort on her
              homework than Molly will receive from her parents.
           d. Molly's parents will hold higher expectations for her academic performance than
              Noriko's will for hers

p. 432 99. A child with an internal locus of control might say which of the following?
C   a. I did well on that test because it was easy.
SG   b. I did well on that test because the teacher likes me.
       *   c. I did well on that test because I knew the material.
          d. I did well on that test because I wanted to earn the money Dad promised me for getting
             an "A."

p. 432 100. Children who score high in need for achievement
C   a. have parents who use an authoritarian style of parenting
SG   b. have parents who praise success with external rewards and punish failures
          c. get the same grades as other children but feel happier about them
       *   d. tend to get better grades than children who score low on need for achievement

p. 432 101. Research on attributions indicates that
F   *   a. high achievers tend to attribute their successes to internal and stable causes
SG   b. high achievers tend to attribute their failures to internal and stable causes
          c. low achievers tend to attribute everything to external causes
          d. high achievers tend to give up once they fail a task

p. 433 102. Research indicates that
F   a. infants do not have sense of motivation
SG   *   b. from a very early age, infants are motivated to control their environments
          c. infants can develop effectance motivation if they are externally rewarded for all their
             efforts
          d. infants who are insecurely attached to their parents will not develop any mastery
             motivation

p. 435 103. Children with a learned helplessness attributional style
C   a. have high expectations for success and get upset when they cannot achieve these high
SG   standards
          b. work hard to achieve only small gains in performance
       *   c. have low expectations for success and give up easily
          d. believe that external factors are responsible for their failures

p. 435   104. Young children are often more confident than older children about their chances for
C   success because younger children:
SG   *   a.   adopt an incremental view of ability
               b.   adopt an entity view of ability
               c.   are given easier tasks than older children
               d.   attribute outcomes to external factors while older children attribute outcomes to
                    internal factors

p. 435   105. Which of the following strategies would likely lead to the greatest success?
C   a.   Viewing failures as evidence that ability is lacking.
SG   b.   Viewing success as a result of luck or fate.
          *   c.   Viewing ability as something that can change.
               d.   Viewing ability as a fixed characteristic that cannot change.

p. 439   106. One factor that contributes significantly to school effectiveness is
F   *   a.   a comfortable setting where the emphasis is on academics
SG   b.   average class size
               c.   level of monetary support that the school receives
               d.   strict guidelines and adherence to rules

p. 441   107. Achievement motivation declines during adolescence for all of the following reasons
F   EXCEPT:
SG   a.   cognitive advances that allow adolescents to understand their strengths and weaknesses
               b.   pressure from peers to be popular or athletic
               c.   increasingly receiving positive feedback based on quality of their accomplishments
                    rather than effort
          *   d.   having teachers who use cooperative learning styles

p. 443   108. Vocational choices
F   a.   are stable across an individual's life span
SG   *   b.   become increasingly realistic across adolescence
               c.   are usually not related to one's ability
               d.   are influenced very little by environmental opportunities

p. 444   109. Research on adolescents and work indicates that
C   a.   working while in high school is beneficial for most adolescents
SG   *   b.   there are more potential disadvantages than advantages to working while in high school
               c.   work contributes to improvements in social-emotional development, but does not
                    influence cognitive development
               d.   work is associated with higher levels of achievement and self-esteem

p. 447   110. Levinson's theory of adult development focuses on
C   *   a.   the interaction of one's self with other people and society
SG   b.   the role of stress in adult development
               c.   how adult males differ from females in values and career choices
               d.   how career choices are made

p. 448   111. According to Levinson's theory of adult development, men
F   a. typically settle into their final career choice in early adulthood
SG   b. follow career paths that are similar to women's paths
                 c. question their career and family choices very little
        *   d. experience a midlife crisis and question their life structure

p. 450   112. Role conflict refers to
F   a. the belief that hard work pays off and relaxation promotes moral decay
SG   b. the feeling that one has too much to do and too little time to accomplish it
        *   c. the competing demands of various roles such as family and work
                 d. the feelings that women experience when they are in careers traditionally held by men

p. 454   113. The theory that successful aging requires a gradual withdrawal from society is
F   a. Levinson's theory
SG   *   b. disengagement theory
                 c. withdrawal theory
                 d. activity adjustment theory

TRUE-FALSE QUESTIONS

p. 431   114. People have stable needs for achievement that are determined by genetic personality traits.
                 a. true
        *   b. false

p. 432   115. Children who believe that their achievement outcomes are due to luck are making a stable
               and external attribution.
                 a. true
        *   b. false

p. 432   116. Children who consistently adopt an internal locus of control assume that they are
               responsible for their success and failures.
        *   a. true
                 b. false

p. 432   117. Someone who attributes outcomes to internal and unstable factors is likely to think that
               he/she can change the course of future outcomes.
        *   a. true
                 b. false

p. 433   118. Infants who are securely attached to their parents are more likely to have a strong sense of
www   effectance motivation than infants who are insecurely attached.
        *   a. true
                 b. false

p. 434   119. As children move from infancy to preschool-age, they progress from symbolic play to
               functional play.
                 a. true
        *   b. false

p. 435　120. Children with a mastery orientation take credit for their successes and blame their failures on things that can be changed.
*　　a. true
　　b. false

p. 435　121. Children who attribute their successes to internal and stable causes and their failures to internal and unstable causes tend to be high achievers.
*　　a. true
　　b. false

p. 435　122. Children with a learned helplessness orientation attribute successes to stable factors and failures to things that can be changed.
　　a. true
*　　b. false

p. 435　123. As children get older, they move from an entity view of ability to an incremental view of ability.
　　a. true
*　　b. false

p. 435　124. Adolescents tend to work hard so that they can improve their abilities.
www
　　a. true
*　　b. false

p. 436　125. Parents who use an authoritarian style of parenting tend to raise children who are high in achievement.
　　a. true
*　　b. false

p. 437　126. Children who attend an academically challenging preschool are likely to fare much better in terms of achievement later on than children who attend a play-oriented preschool.
　　a. true
*　　b. false

p. 438　127. Research indicates that a school that has large classes and spends relatively little per pupil is likely to be significantly less effective than one that has smaller classes and is well-off financially.
　　a. true
*　　b. false

p. 439　128. Academic achievement tends to be lower in schools with a high proportion of economically disadvantaged students.
*　　a. true
　　b. false

p. 440　129. The practice of inclusion has been successful both academically and socially for children with developmental disabilities.
　　a. true
*　　b. false

p. 441　130. As children enter adolescence, their achievement motivation often drops.
　　　　*　　a.　true
　　　　　　　b.　false

p. 444　131. Adolescents who work part time while going to high school tend to get better grades, have better attendance records, and stay out of trouble with drugs, more so than those who do not work at least part time.
　　　　　　　a.　true
　　　　*　　b.　false

p. 447　132. In general, research on adult development supports Levinson's claim that the early forties are for the vast majority of individuals a time of upheaval and crisis.
　　　　　　　a.　true
　　　　*　　b.　false

p. 448　133. Middle-aged men and women are generally less satisfied with their work than are younger adults.
　　　　　　　a.　true
　　　　*　　b.　false

p. 449　134. Older workers in their fifties and sixties tend to perform their jobs less capably than they did earlier on in their careers.
　　　　　　　a.　true
　　　　*　　b.　false

p. 450　135. Most women today feel very comfortable with their blend of work, family, and personal roles.
　　　　　　　a.　true
　　　　*　　b.　false

p. 452　136. Most retired people are less satisfied with their lives after retirement than they were while working.
　　　　　　　a.　true
　　　　*　　b.　false

p. 454　137. With regard to aging, there is more support for disengagement theory than for activity theory.
　　　　　　　a.　true
　　　　*　　b.　false

ESSAY QUESTIONS

138. Would you put your infant or preschooler in a "daycare" or preschool program? Why or why not? Based on what you have read in this chapter and others (such as Chapter 13 on Attachment and Social Relationships and Chapter 14 on The Family), what recommendations would you make regarding infants, preschoolers, and care by non-family members?

139. What factors influence a person's adjustment to retirement? What recommendations would you
www　have for a parent, spouse, or friend who is close to retirement?

140. Why does achievement motivation drop as children move into adolescence? What can be done to maintain a high level of achievement motivation during adolescence?

141. Based on research described in the text, what recommendations would you make regarding
SG   adolescents and work?
      [Sample answer is provided in the Study Guide.]

142. What factors are likely to increase or decrease our achievement motivation as we move through
SG   childhood and adolescence?

143. What attributions do you typically use to explain your successes and failures? How would you
SG   modify these attributions to create healthier ones? (And what is a healthy attribution?)

PSYCHOLOGICAL DISORDERS THROUGHOUT THE LIFE SPAN

MULTIPLE-CHOICE QUESTIONS

p. 462 1. All of the following are criteria that have been used for identifying abnormal behavior
F   EXCEPT:
            a. behavior that is statistically outside of the normal range
        *   b. behavior that cannot be used as a model for other's behavior
            c. behavior that interferes with personal and social adaptation
            d. behavior that causes personal distress

p. 462 2. Social norms are best defined as:
F   a. the tendency to go along with what others are doing
            b. cross-cultural expectations for behavior
            c. expectations of how to behave at different times of the life span
        *   d. expectations of how to behave in a given social context

p. 462 3. Whether or not children are thought to have a psychological problem:
C   a. is determined by performance on standardized tests
        *   b. depends on cultural expectations of normal behavior and socialization practices
            c. is normally determined by the children's physician
            d. can be determined by examining how successfully children interact with others

p. 463 4. An age norm is BEST defined as:
F   a. societal expectations for behavior in a particular social context
        *   b. expectations regarding behavior that is appropriate or inappropriate at a given age
            c. expectations for how to behave at a party
            d. cross-cultural expectations for behavior

p. 463 5. We normally think that it is OK for a 2-year-old to suck his thumb, but not for a 22-year-
F   old. This is most likely because of:
www   a. lack of tolerance
            b. contextual norms
            c. cultural norms
        *   d. age norms

p. 463 6. The Diagnostic and Statistical Manual of Mental Disorders (DSM-IV):
F   a. uses social norms to diagnose disorders
        *   b. is based on observable symptoms of disorders
            c. is based on underlying causes of disorders
            d. uses theoretical models to explain psychological disorders

p. 464   7.   With regard to depressive disorders, the Diagnostic and Statistical Manual of Mental
C   Disorders:
         *   a.   defines major depression by the presence of a group of symptoms consistently evident
                    for a 2-week period
               b.   makes no distinction between major depression and depressed moods that occur as
                    responses to specific events
               c.   includes affective symptoms like sad moods in the definition of depression but
                    excludes behavioral symptoms like sleep disturbance
               d.   recognizes that some people may suffer from major depression with as few as one or
                    two symptoms

p. 464   8.   According to the DSM-IV, which of the following is FALSE regarding major depression?
C   a.   The definition can be applied to people of all ages.
               b.   A depressive episode must be at least two weeks in duration to be diagnosed as major
                    depression.
               c.   Children and adults may not express their depression in the same way.
         *   d.   Cultural and developmental variations are irrelevant to diagnosis.

p. 464   9.   Symptoms of major depression include all of the following EXCEPT:
F   a.   irritable mood
               b.   weight loss
         *   c.   lack of guilt
               d.   loss of energy

p. 464   10. Developmental psychopathologists focus on:
C   a.   developing therapies for treatment of psychological disorders
               b.   disorders of infancy and early childhood
         *   c.   studying the origins and the path of abnormal behaviors
               d.   trying to establish genetic contributions to maladaptive behavior

p. 464   11. Developmental psychopathologists view psychopathologies as:
C   a.   diseases that can be treated with medicine
www   b.   qualitative disorders that people either have or no not have
         *   c.   a series of intertwined developmental pathways that people can pass into and out of
               d.   biological conditions residing in the person

p. 465   12. Autistic children are:
F   a.   extremely attached to their parents
               b.   most likely to communicate through the use of elaborate symbols
               c.   oblivious to changes in the world around them
         *   d.   unable to form normal social relationships

p. 466   13. Autistic children exhibit deviant development in all of the following areas EXCEPT:
F   *   a.   physical development
               b.   social development
               c.   language development
               d.   intellectual development

p. 466   14.   The development of an autistic child is:

C
        a.   determined by early experiences
    *   b.   qualitatively different from that of other children
        c.   delayed but not different in comparison to that of other children
        d.   erratic throughout infancy and early childhood but evens out during adolescence and adulthood

p. 466   15.   Most autistic children exhibit:

F
        a.   normal intelligence
        b.   exceptionally high intelligence in some areas
    *   c.   mental retardation
        d.   substantial fluctuations in intelligence throughout childhood

p. 466   16.   Autistic children are believed to lack a theory of mind, which means they:

C
        a.   have trouble with the storage and retrieval of information in long term memory
        b.   are unable to convey their thoughts to another person
        c.   experience intellectual deficits that prevent them from developing and testing theories
    *   d.   do not understand mental states, such as emotions and intentions, and how these affect behavior

p. 467   17.   All of the following are currently suspected causes of autism EXCEPT:

F
        a.   inability to plan and organize functions of the brain
www   *   b.   cold, rigid parenting
        c.   inability to engage in representational though
        d.   lack of a theory of mind

p. 467   18.   Autism is likely caused by:

F
        a.   strict and disinterested parenting
    *   b.   genetic factors combined with early environmental influences
        c.   living in an impoverished environment
        d.   brain injury that occurs during the prenatal or perinatal period

p. 467   19.   The long-term prognosis for autistic children:

C
    *   a.   depends on their level of intelligence and communication skills
        b.   is generally quite good once they reach adulthood
        c.   can be improved significantly through drug treatment
        d.   is determined by how well they get along with other children

p. 467   20.   The MOST effective way to treat autistic children is to use:

F
        a.   a special diet to eliminate allergies
    *   b.   behavioral training to teach them better social and language skills
        c.   drug therapy
        d.   counseling with the entire family

p. 468   21.   Which is TRUE regarding depression in infancy?
F
        a.   Infants do not exhibit depression-like symptoms.
        b.   Infants experience the same cognitions that are common among adults (e.g., feelings of low self-esteem, worthlessness, hopelessness).
        c.   Infants who display depression-like symptoms are those who are most securely attached to their caregivers.
    *   d.   Infants can and do sometimes display depression-like symptoms and states.

p. 468   22.   Somatic symptoms in infants are best described as:
F
        a.   numbing of the body
    *   b.   physical symptoms without physical base
        c.   motor problems
        d.   anxiety problems

p. 468   23.   Infants who exhibit depression-like states:
C
        a.   are cognitively very similar to depressed children and adults
        b.   have experienced various prenatal and perinatal complications
        c.   were unable to form any meaningful attachment relationships
    *   d.   have often experienced the loss of an important attachment figure

p. 468   24.   Failure to thrive in otherwise healthy infants:
C
        a.   can be attributed to prenatal and perinatal complications
        b.   can lead to delays in physical development that cannot be undone
    *   c.   usually results from having unresponsive or rejecting caregivers
        d.   have caregivers who do not adequately provide for their nutritional needs

p. 468   25.   The young children of parents who are depressed:
C
        a.   are clinically depressed as well
        b.   tend to be hyperactive and difficult children
    *   c.   vocalize very little and often appear sad
        d.   are usually unaffected by their parents' depression

p. 469   26.   Which of the following is NOT an example of an externalizing disorder?
C
        a.   a child who constantly interrupts the activities of others
    *   b.   a child who constantly worries about whether he/she is performing adequately
        c.   a child who refuses to follow the rules established for the classroom
        d.   a child who regularly gets in trouble for hitting other children

p. 469   27.   Internalizing problems are:
C
        a.   problems that are undercontrolled
        b.   particularly disruptive to people who come in contact with the child
        c.   easier to observe than externalizing disorders
    *   d.   more prevalent among girls than boys

p. 469 28. Which of the following is TRUE regarding the pattern of developmental disorders?
C   *   a. Externalizing problems tend to decrease throughout childhood and adolescence while
www   internalizing problems tend to increase.
.   b. Externalizing and internalizing problems both increase throughout childhood and
                adolescence.
             c. Internalizing problems tend to increase throughout childhood and adolescence while
                internalizing problems tend to decrease.
             d. Externalizing and internalizing problems both decrease throughout childhood and
                adolescence.

p. 469 29. David is easily distracted, very inattentive and impulsive. He is also extremely active and
F   unable to sit still. The most likely diagnosis for David's behavior is:
        *   a. attention deficit disorder
            b. depression
            c. dyslexia
            d. autistic disorder

p. 469 30. Children with Attention-Deficit Hyperactivity Disorder:
F   a. typically become calmer if they stop eating sweets
            b. outgrow all the behaviors associated with the disorder as they get into adolescence and
                adulthood
            c. are indistinguishable from other children except in the classroom
        *   d. display behaviors similar to those seen in normal children at younger ages

p. 469 31. Hyperactivity has gone from being viewed as primarily a problem of _____, to being
C   viewed as primarily a problem of _____.
www   a. cognitive deficit; learning disorder
            b. excess motor activity; cognitive deficit
            c. attention; excess motor activity
        *   d. excess motor activity; attention

p. 469 32. DSM-IV includes all of the following symptoms as criteria for Attention-Deficit
F   Hyperactivity Disorder EXCEPT:
            a. impulsivity
            b. inattention
        *   c. cognitive delays
            d. excess motor activity

p. 470 33. Hyperactive children tend to:
F   a. outgrow their problems before reaching adolescence
            b. outgrow their problems by the time they are young adults
            c. continue to be extremely overactive throughout their lives
        *   d. experience continued effects on cognitive, social, and emotional development
                into the young adult years

p. 471   34.   All of the following have been linked to Attention-Deficit Hyperactivity Disorder as
F   possible causes EXCEPT:
               a.   prenatal exposure to alcohol or drugs
       *   b.   a need to gain attention from teachers and parents
               c.   an inherited predisposition
               d.   brain chemistry of the frontal cortex

p. 472   35.   Which of the following is a valid criticism of using stimulant drugs to treat Attention-
C   Deficit Hyperactivity Disorder?
               a.   The drugs reduce the hyperactive behaviors but do not have any effect on academic
                    performance.
               b.   The drugs only work for a limited number of individuals and only when they are
                    young.
       *   c.   The drugs temporarily improve behavior but do not have any lasting effects on
                    adjustment.
               d.   The drugs help the individual child to feel better but do not influence the way that
                    others view the child.

p. 472   36.   Research on diet and Attention-Deficit Hyperactivity Disorder has found that:
C   a.   food intolerance and allergic reactions to foods are more common among children with
                    ADHD
       *   b.   food additives and sugar do not seem to have an impact on the behavior of most ADHD
                    children
               c.   food additives such as coloring and preservatives decrease the level of some
                    neurotransmitters in the brain, the same ones that are then increased with stimulant
                    drugs
               d.   food additives and sugar in the diet both play a role in most cases of ADHD

p. 473   37.   Depressed young children:
C   a.   display the same behavioral and cognitive symptoms as do depressed adults
               b.   are most often extremely aggressive
               c.   usually mask their depression such that it is nearly impossible to detect
       *   d.   are unlikely to display cognitive symptoms of depression such as guilt and
                    hopelessness

p. 473   38.   Children with depression:
C   *   a.   are judged by the same criteria that are used to diagnose depression in adults
www   b.   show the same behavioral and cognitive symptoms as adults with depression
               c.   show symptoms of masked depression but not direct symptoms of depression
               d.   are cognitively unable to think about their circumstances at a deep enough level to
                    develop depression

p. 473   39.   Which of the following is an example of masked depression?
C   a.   A child talking about a doll that is sad.
       *   b.   A child acting aggressively.
               c.   A child who is silent for hours.
               d.   A child who pretends that his/her doll is dead

p. 474   40.   Which is TRUE regarding the causes of childhood disorders?
C   a.   Most childhood psychological disturbances are the result of poor parenting.
                 b.   Depressed and hyperactive children are no more likely than normal children to have
                       come from homes where parents are hostile and rejecting.
                 c.   Children with psychological disorders are no more likely to have parents who are
                       themselves psychologically disturbed than normal children are.
        *   d.   Many childhood psychological disorders are partially genetic, and may be the
                       cause, as well as the effect, of problems in the parent/child relationship.

p. 474   41.   Children who have a depressive disorder:
C   a.   differ from adolescents and adults with depression because children never attempt
                       suicide while the older age groups often do
                 b.   are easy to identify because they frequently talk about their negative feelings
                 c.   usually overcome the disorder and suffer no problems as adolescents or adults
        *   d.   often have problems with depression as adolescents and adults

p. 474   42.   From a family systems perspective, research on the causes of childhood disorders shows
C   that:
                 a.   parents who are inexperienced and lack good parenting skills often socialize their
                       children to behave in disordered ways
                 b.   parents have no influence on the course of developmental disorders because of the
                       strong genetic component to these disorders
                 c.   children with developmental disorders do not act any differently with their parents than
                       other children until after their parents exhibit disordered behavior
        *   d.   children with developmental disorders often act in ways that evoke a negative response
                       from parents, which worsens the child's problem

p. 476   43.   What can we conclude regarding the persistence of childhood problems?
C   *   a.   Problems of early childhood are more likely to disappear than to persist.
www   b.   Problems related to personality such as shyness persist, while behavior problems such
                       as aggression disappear.
                 c.   Most problems of childhood persist to adulthood
                 d.   Overcontrolled problems are more likely to persist into adulthood than undercontrolled
                       problems.

p. 476   44.   What determines whether a childhood disorder will persist into adulthood?
C   a.   whether the disorder early or late in childhood
        *   b.   its severity and whether or not the child's environment stays the same or changes
                 c.   whether or not it is treatable with drug therapy
                 d.   the extent to which it interferes with the child's daily functioning

p. 476   45.   Which of the following is TRUE?
C   a.   Most children who have problems grow up to have problems as adults.
        *   b.   Many adults who have problems also experienced problems as children.
                 c.   Children are most likely to overcome undercontrolled problems.
                 d.   There is very little change over time in the course of any psychological disorder.

p. 476 46. Adolescents:
C
        a. are particularly resilient to different environmental stressors
        b. reveal greater genetic vulnerabilities than younger children
  *   c. are more vulnerable than other age groups to some psychological disorders
        d. recover more quickly from problems than other age groups

p. 476 47. Which is TRUE with regard to psychological "health" during adolescence?
C
        a. Most adolescents suffer at some point from some sort of significant psychological disturbance.
  *   b. Most adolescents who are psychologically disturbed were maladjusted before they reached puberty.
        c. Individuals at adolescence are no more vulnerable to psychological disturbance than they are at any other point in the life span.
        d. Adolescents are far more likely than younger children or adults to experience some sort of psychological disturbance.

p. 477 48. At age 18, Marie is 5'6" and weighs about 90 pounds. She thinks of herself as being fat,
F   and she is desperately afraid she will become overweight. Marie MOST likely suffers from:
  *   a. anorexia
        b. bulimia
        c. drug addiction
        d. a metabolic disorder

p. 477 49. Denise is about average in height and weight, and is often dieting. From time to time,
F   however, she sits down and eats huge quantities of food all at once, after which, she makes herself vomit. Denise suffers from:
        a. anorexia
  *   b. bulimia
        c. anorexia and bulimia
        d. a thyroid deficiency

p. 477 50. How do anorexia nervosa and bulimia nervosa compare to one another?
C *   a. In both cases, individuals have a distorted image of their bodies.
        b. Anorexia affects far more women than bulimia.
        c. Anorexia, but not bulimia, can be life threatening.
        d. Individuals with either disorder can be found in all weight ranges.

p. 478 51. Girls who develop eating disorders:
C
        a. over-react to media images about food products
  *   b. have a genetic vulnerability that is triggered by some disturbance in family relationships
        c. have parents who are distant and unresponsive
        d. have trouble controlling their weight because of hormone imbalances

p. 478 52.   Many adolescent girls with eating disorders:

C
www
        a. have parents who typically use a permissive style of child rearing
        b. are personally satisfied with their appearance but diet because they believe others expect them to
  *   c. view themselves negatively and expect others to do so as well.
        d. have achieved autonomy or a sense of independence from their parents

p. 479 53.   The prognosis for girls with eating disorders is:

C
        a. better if girls are older when they first develop the disorder
        b. the same whether or not they receive treatment
  *   c. better for those who start treatment early in the course of the illness
        d. better for those with anorexia than those with bulimia

p. 479 54.   As early as 7th grade, most adolescents have tried:

F
  *   a. alcohol
        b. cigarettes
        c. marijuana
        d. inhalants

p. 479 55.   Regarding drinking and drug use:

C
        a. adolescents who drink or use drugs are otherwise no different from teens who do not
  *   b. the earlier a person starts, the more likely s/he is to develop a problem
        c. most adolescents will wait until they are 18 years old to experiment with drugs and alcohol
        d. adolescents believe that drug use will enhance their academic performance

p. 480 56.   Which of the following is FALSE with regard to adolescent problem drinkers?

C
        a. Adolescent problem drinkers tend to place little value on academic achievement.
        b. Adolescent problem drinkers feel there are huge differences between their parents' and their peers' values.
  *   c. Adolescent problem drinkers are no more likely than other adolescents to use other drugs as well.
        d. Adolescent problem drinkers tend to be tolerant of other forms of deviant behavior.

p. 480 57.   What seems to account for the fact that some adolescents end up abusing alcohol, while others merely engage in typical experimentation without developing a problem?

C
        a. Problem drinkers conform to what they believe are conventional adult behaviors.
        b. Problem drinkers use alcohol to escape from what they perceive as over involved and controlling parents.
  *   c. Problem drinkers do not value academic achievement or religious ideals the way other teens do.
        d. Problem drinkers saw that their older siblings received reinforcement for their excessive drinking.

p. 480 58. All of the following have been identified as characteristics that distinguish problem
F drinkers from other teens who may experiment with alcohol but do not develop a problem
EXCEPT:
    a. a pattern of violating rules
    b. alienation from conventional values
*   c. alienation from other teens
    d. a belief that their parents are nonsupportive and unimportant in their lives

p. 481 59. Which is true with regard to depression in adolescence?
C   a. Major depression abounds in adolescence at a rate that far exceeds that found in the
        adult population.
    b. Depression in adolescence is less common than during the early childhood years.
    c. Most depressed adolescents mask their depression through aggressive acting-out
        behaviors.
*   d. Depressed adolescents often display feelings of hopelessness and worthlessness, as
        well as suicidal tendencies.

p. 481 60. Which of the following is TRUE with regard to suicide?
F   a. More males than females attempt and are successful at committing suicide.
    b. More females than males attempt and are successful at committing suicide.
    c. More males attempt suicide, but more females are successful at committing suicide.
*   d. More females attempt suicide, but more males are successful at committing suicide.

p. 481 61. According to statistics, who is MOST likely to commit suicide?
F   a. an 18-year-old black male
*   b. an 80-year-old white male
    c. a 45-year-old white male
    d. a 25-year-old black male

p. 481 62. In comparison to depressed children, depressed adolescents are:
C   *   a. more likely to express hopelessness and thoughts of suicide
www   b. more likely to benefit from therapy
    c. easier to accurately diagnose
    d. more likely to show other problems along with the depression

p. 481 63. Adolescents attempt suicide:
F   *   a. relatively frequently, but are far less likely than adults to succeed in killing themselves
    b. relatively frequently, and are more likely than adults to actually succeed in killing
        themselves
    c. with relative infrequency, and are rarely successful in completing their attempts
    d. infrequently, but when they do, they get the job done

p. 482 64. Events that are likely to be MOST stressful and take the greatest toll on mental health are:
F   a. normative major life events
    b. nonnormative major life events
    c. major life events
*   d. ongoing, daily hassles

p. 482　65.　What seems to be MOST important in defining whether or not an event is stressful to
C　　　　　someone?
　　＊　　a.　how individuals appraise the event and their abilities to cope with it
　　　　　b.　whether or not the event has been experienced previously
　　　　　c.　whether or not other people respond to the event as stressful
　　　　　d.　the age of the person experiencing the event

p. 482　66.　A person is MOST likely to experience negative effects of stress with which event?
F　　　　　a.　major events that are predictable
　　　　　b.　major events that are not predictable in advance
　　＊　　c.　small events that occur regularly and repeatedly
　　　　　d.　small events that are unusual and infrequent

p. 482　67.　Which of the following is likely to be MOST stressful?
C　　　　　a.　getting married
　　　　　b.　becoming a parent
　　　　　c.　retiring from work
　　＊　　d.　getting fired

p. 483　68.　Who typically experiences the MOST stress?
F　　　　　a.　an adolescent
　　＊　　b.　a young adult
　　　　　c.　a middle-aged adult
　　　　　d.　an older adult

p. 69　69.　Which is TRUE with regard to coping capacities?
C　　　　　a.　Ability to cope with life strains increases steadily with age.
　　　　　b.　Ability to cope with life strains decreases gradually across the life span.
　　　　　c.　Ability to cope increases steadily between young adulthood and middle age, and then
　　　　　　　drops off as one moves toward old age.
　　＊　　d.　When facing similar sorts of life events, younger and older adults generally cope in
　　　　　　　similar ways.

p. 483　70.　Barbara is going through a divorce and spends her time trying to convince herself that
C　　　　　everything will be OK. Her coping strategy is best described as:
www　　　a.　diathesis/stress
　　　　　b.　learned helplessness
　　　　　c.　problem-focused
　　＊　　d.　emotion-focused

p. 483　71.　Which of the following is the BEST example of a problem-focused coping style?
C　　　　　a.　becoming busy in order to avoid thinking about the problem
　　　　　b.　telling yourself that the problem really isn't so bad after all
　　＊　　c.　vowing to get up early and attack the problem head on
　　　　　d.　deciding that the problem is not going to go away and developing ways to live with it

p. 483 72. Elderly adults are likely to:
C   a. try to fix all their problems
             b. approach their problem directly and aggressively
             c. not perceive anything as being a problem
        *   d. try to make the best of their problems

p. 484 73. Which is TRUE with regard to the incidence of psychopathology?
F   a. Affective disorders (e.g., depression) are most common among elderly females.
        *   b. Alcohol abuse is more common among young adults than middle-aged or elderly
                  adults.
             c. Men are more likely than women to experience major depression.
             d. Most affective disorders occur among elderly males.

p. 484 74. Which of the following are we MOST LIKELY to find?
F   a. a middle-aged female with alcohol dependence
        *   b. a female in early adulthood who has an affective disorder
             c. an elderly male with alcohol dependence
             d. a male in early adulthood who has an affective disorder

p. 485 75. Depression during older adulthood:
C   a. is more typical than during younger or middle adulthood
             b. is most likely to be expressed in direct, rather than indirect, ways
        *   c. may be confused with signs of "normal" aging
             d. is easier to diagnose than at younger ages

p. 485 76. Which of the following is true with regard to gender and psychopathology?
C   a. Males and females are equally likely to engage in alcohol abuse.
www   b. Across the life span, males have a higher incidence of psychological disturbance than
                  do females.
             c. Across the life span, females have a higher incidence of psychological disturbance than
                  do males.
        *   d. Though the types of disorders may vary, males and females have a similar rate of
                  diagnosable psychological disorders across the life span.

p. 485 77. The gender gap in rates of depression:
F   a. is readily apparent, even in early childhood
             b. is most extreme during the adolescent period
        *   c. peaks during the 30-to-60 age range
             d. is greatest in old age

p. 485 78. According to the diathesis/stress model, psychopathology results:
C   *   a. when a stressful event triggers an already existing vulnerability or predisposition
             b. when stress in the environment reaches a critical level and overwhelms a person's
                  ability to cope
             c. from a gene that is programmed to activate at a certain point during the life span
             d. when environmental toxins alter the nuclei of cells, opening the way for stress to
                  further erode the normal operations of the cells

p. 485 79. Which of the following is TRUE?
C
  a. Men are more likely than women to report their symptoms of depression and face the problem directly.
 * b. Men often try to divert their attention from feelings of depression while women often focus their attention on the depression.
  c. Men are more and more likely to mask their feelings of depression as they get older, while women become less able to hide feelings of depression as they get older, which leads to a large gender gap in depression during old age.
  d. Women's hormones make them more vulnerable to depression at all ages of the life span.

p. 485 80. Suppose two people experience the same stressful events and as a result of the experience, one person develops an affective disorder while the second person shows no ill effects.
C
  The diathesis/stress model would MOST LIKELY explain this by saying that:
  a. the person who developed the disorder was older than the other person and thus, had a larger accumulation of stressful events that finally resulted in the disorder
  b. the one person must be female and the other person male
 * c. the personal resources of the two individuals were different
  d. the person who developed the disorder had a gene that guaranteed the disorder would develop at some point, while the other person had a gene that protected him/her from the effects of stress

p. 486 81. Dementia is BEST defined as:
F
  a. forgetfulness
  b. an inevitable change in the brain with age
 * c. a gradual loss of cognitive skills
  d. loss of control over motor responses

p. 487 82. The first sign of Alzheimer's disease is typically:
F * a. trouble learning and remembering verbal material
  b. a loss of language skills
  c. personality changes
  d. difficulty on recognition tasks

p. 487 83. Which of the following is TRUE of Alzheimer's disease?
F * a. Alzheimer's patients eventually experience personality changes as well as cognitive losses.
  b. Female hormones make women more vulnerable to Alzheimer's disease.
  c. Alzheimer's is an inevitable part of aging and will eventually happen to everyone.
  d. Alzheimer's is curable if caught and treated early enough.

p. 487 84. Which of the following has NOT been generated as a possible cause of Alzheimer's disease?
F
  a. an inherited predisposition, possibly located on the 21st pair of chromosomes
  b. lower levels of, or insensitivity to, the neurotransmitter acetylcholine
 * c. a life-long accumulation of stress that finally overwhelms the person
  d. a slow working virus activated later in life in some people

p. 488 85. Vascular dementia:

F   a. is a slowly progressive deterioration of memory and thinking skills

www   *   b. results from a series of small strokes, each adding rather quickly to the observed deterioration

     c. is marked by periods of disorientation and confusion interspersed with periods of lucidity

     d. results from taking medications or having a poor diet and can be reversed when these problems are corrected

p. 488 86. Delirium is:

F   a. the same as dementia

     b. incurable

   *   c. a reversible state of confusion and disorientation

     d. a normal part of the aging process

p. 489 87. Treatment of children with psychological disorders:

C   a. is much the same as that which is used with adolescents and adults

     b. is generally unsuccessful

   *   c. must include consideration of the entire family system

     d. works best when the child is seen alone

p. 489 88. Which is TRUE with regard to the treatment of childhood psychological disorders?

C   a. Psychotherapy generally does not work as well with children and adolescents as it does with adults.

     b. Internalizing disorders are generally treatable, while externalizing disorders are not.

   *   c. Behavioral therapies tend to be more successful than nonbehavioral techniques.

     d. Children who do not receive treatment generally outgrow their difficulties and are just as competent later on as those who received treatment.

p. 489 89. Treatment for children and adolescents with psychological disorders is likely to differ from

F   treatment for adults in all of the following ways EXCEPT:

     a. children's cognitive levels of understanding are less sophisticated than an adult's

     b. children typically do not initiate treatment

     c. children are usually treated as part of a family, rather than individually

   *   d. children can distract themselves from their problems more readily than adults

p. 489 90. Research on the effectiveness of psychotherapy suggests that:

F   *   a. children benefit about as much from therapy as adults do

www   b. children, because they are younger and more malleable, benefit much more than adults

     c. responsiveness to psychotherapy increases as children get older

     d. the success of psychotherapy with children depends largely on the type of disorder the child has

p. 490 91. Which is FALSE regarding the treatment of elderly adults with psychological disorders?

F   a. Treatment is made difficult by the fact that relatively few elderly adults seek treatment.

     b. Treatment is hampered by the fact that many of their problems are misdiagnosed.

   *   c. Elderly adults are generally less responsive than younger adults to psychotherapy.

     d. Treatment is hampered by a common misperception of mental health workers that elderly individuals are untreatable.

p. 463   92.   Age norms are defined as
F
               a.   the ages when it is appropriate to act in a deviant manner
SG   * b.   societal expectations about what behavior is appropriate at different ages
               c.   societal expectations about how to behave in different contexts
               d.   the average ages when people are most susceptible to various disorders

p. 463   93.   Which of the following persons is most likely to be diagnosed as having a psychological
C   disorder?
SG   a.   a child who cannot fall asleep at night because he is worried about goblins under the
               bed
     * b.   a woman who can no longer to work because she is so upset about her appearance
               c.   a man who quits his job because it is no longer challenging
               d.   a woman who is sobbing because her husband has recently died

p. 464   94.   According to developmental psychopathologists, psychopathology is
C   * a.   a pattern of behavior that develops over time
SG   b.   a medical condition that you either have or do not have
               c.   a disease that can be treated with medicine
               d.   a developmental disorder that lies solely within the person

p. 466   95.   A disorder that begins in infancy and is characterized by deviant social development and
F   communication skills is
SG   a.   an externalizing disorder
               b.   infantile dementia
     * c.   infantile autism
               d.   attention-deficit disorder

p. 466   96.   Which of the following is an example of echolalia?
C   * a.   using "you" to refer to one's self
SG   b.   hearing the echo of a phrase after someone has said something
               c.   substituting one phrase for another
               d.   repeating something that has just been said

p. 467   97.   Autistic children
F   a.   typically outgrow the disorder as they get older
SG   b.   have a number of physical problems in addition to their deficits in social and
               communication skills
     * c.   are often mentally retarded
               d.   show marked improvement after they enter elementary school

p. 467   98.   Which of the following seems to be a promising explanation of the cause of autism?
C   a.   Autistic children have cold, distant parents.
SG   b.   Autistic children have inherited a recessive set of genes for the disorder.
               c.   Autistic children are unable to verbalize their thoughts.
     * d.   Autistic children lack symbolic thought and/or the ability to organize information into
               meaningful chunks.

p. 469 99. Children who act in ways that conflict with rules and other people are said to have

F   a. an internalizing problem

SG   *   b. an externalizing problem

            c. masked depression

            d. autism

p. 469 100. Attention-deficit hyperactivity disorder is:

F   a. a disorder that is diagnosed on the basis of too much motor activity

SG   *   b. primarily an attention problem

            c. an overcontrolled disorder

            d. associated with mental retardation

p. 473 101. Depression

F   a. is displayed in similar ways across the life span

SG   b. is not present until children are old enough to verbally express their feelings

            c. is an undercontrolled disorder

        *   d. can be present throughout the life span but is expressed in different behaviors

p. 475 102. Problems that exist in early childhood

C   a. disappear when children enter elementary school

SG   b. are nonexistent by the time children leave school

        *   c. are more likely to disappear than persist, although some do persist

            d. typically are still present later in life

p. 477 103. Eating disorders such as anorexia and bulimia

F   a. are caused by the body's inability to properly metabolize food

SG   *   b. develop, in part, as a result of a genetic predisposition interacting with stress and social
                pressure

            c. are easily controlled with a properly managed diet

            d. are present during adolescence and then disappear

p. 480 104. Adolescent problem drinkers

F   a. are indistinguishable from other adolescents

SG   *   b. place less value on academic achievement and more value on independence than other
                adolescents

            c. typically have just this one area where they have a problem

            d. are generally intolerant of deviant behavior in others

p. 481 105. With respect to suicide,

F   *   a. adolescents are more likely to attempt suicide than adults but less likely to succeed

SG   b. adolescents successfully commit suicide at a higher rate than any other age group

            c. males and females are equally likely to end up killing themselves

            d. elderly adults commit suicide at a rate somewhat higher than adolescents and younger
                adults

p. 488 106. One difference between Alzheimer's disease and delirium is that

F
a. Alzheimer's disease affects mental functioning and delirium does not.

SG
b. Patients with Alzheimer's disease have periods of lucidity, while those with delirium do not.

c. Alzheimer's disease occurs only in old age, while delirium occurs only at younger ages.

* d. Alzheimer's disease is irreversible, while delirium is reversible.

TRUE-FALSE QUESTIONS

p. 462 107. To be classified as a psychological disorder, a person's behavior must be statistically deviant from the norm, maladaptive, AND the cause of personal distress.

a. true

* b. false

p. 464 108. Individuals who suffer from major depression, as diagnosed using the DSM-IV, must be suicidal.

a. true

* b. false

p. 466 109. In general, autistic children are very intelligent; they simply cannot interact socially in

www   a normal fashion.

a. true

* b. false

p. 468 110. Failure to thrive infants tend to improve immediately once they are removed from their dysfunctional home environment.

* a. true

b. false

p. 469 111. Externalizing disorders are more common among boys, and internalizing disorders are more common among girls.

* a. true

b. false

p. 469 112. Externalizing and internalizing disorders are relatively immune to cultural influence.

a. true

* b. false

p. 469 113. Hyperactivity is an example of an overcontrolled disorder.

a. true

* b. false

p. 474 114. Most clinically depressed children outgrow their depression before adolescence.

a. true

* b. false

p. 474 115. Poor parenting is the single most important cause of most childhood psychological disturbances.
        a. true
*   b. false

p. 475 116. Externalizing problems are more likely than internalizing problems to persist into
www   adolescence and adulthood.
        a. true
*   b. false

p. 477 117. Anorexia is more common than bulimia.
        a. true
*   b. false

p. 481 118. More male than female adolescents both attempt and commit suicide.
        a. true
*   b. false

p. 483 119. Coping skills tend to decline steadily, though gradually, from young adulthood to old age.
        a. true
*   b. false

p. 484 120. Across the life span, females generally have a higher rate of psychological disturbance than do males.
        a. true
*   b. false

p. 485 121. Elderly adults are generally more depressed than the rest of the population.
        a. true
*   b. false

p. 485 122. Depression is generally the result of the ongoing interaction between a person and his/her environment.
*   a. true
        b. false

p. 486 123. Becoming senile is a normal part of the aging process.
        a. true
*   b. false

p. 490 124. Behavioral therapies tend to work better than nonbehavioral approaches in the treatment of psychological disorders of young children.
*   a. true
        b. false

125. How does the diathesis/stress model account for psychopathology?

126. How does the expression of depression vary across the life span? How does age influence the treatment of depression?

127. Your neighbor has just learned that her little boy has a psychological problem. What can you tell
www   her about the persistence of childhood problems?

128. How do genetic or biological factors interact with environmental factors to create psychological disorders? Which factors seem most important?

129. Why are adolescents more vulnerable to some disorders than children or adults?

130. What gender differences are found across the life span in the diagnosis or course of
SG   mental disorders? What factors might account for these differences?
      [Sample answer is provided in the Study Guide.]

131. How would you explain the development of psychological disorders from the perspective
SG   of each of the major developmental theories (Freud and Erikson's psychoanalytic theories,
      Piaget's cognitive-developmental theory, Skinner and Bandura's learning theories, and
      Bronfenbrenner's ecological theory)?

17

THE FINAL CHALLENGE: DEATH AND DYING

MULTIPLE-CHOICE QUESTIONS

p. 495   1.   It is MOST accurate to say that biological death:
C   a.   is a single event with a clear-cut end point
              b.   occurs when a person stops breathing
        *   c.   is a process consisting of multiple events and the line between life and death is blurry
              d.   officially occurs when the heart stops beating.

p. 495   2.   Experts at Harvard Medical School developed a definition of biological death that includes
F   all of the following components EXCEPT:
              a.   the person is totally unresponsive to stimuli
              b.   there is a lack of reflexes
        *   c.   there is a lack of eye movements
              d.   there is no electrical activity in the cortex of the brain

p. 496   3.   In many modern societies, people approach death as:
F   a.   inevitable
        *   b.   a medical failure
              c.   a natural part of life
              d.   an opportunity to celebrate life

p. 496   4.   Compared to today, people in the middle ages:
F   a.   were more likely to fear death
              b.   usually went off to die alone
        *   c.   cared for their dying relatives at home
              d.   had no opportunity to think about death as we do today

p.497   5.   Nancy's elderly father had been in a nursing home for many years suffering with
C   Alzheimer's disease. He could no longer care for himself and did not recognize family
              members or friends. Nancy told her sister that she wished there was some way they could
              bring about his death so they could all stop suffering. Nancy's wish illustrates:
        *   a.   active euthanasia
              b.   passive euthanasia
              c.   manslaughter
              d.   assisted suicide

p.497   6.   Which of the following is an example of passive euthanasia?
C   a.   giving a terminally ill patient a lethal dose of drugs
www   b.   permitting a terminally ill patient to give him/herself a lethal dose of drugs
        *   c.   removing a respirator from a patient who is brain dead and in an irreversible coma
              d.   permitting a patient to refuse to eat

p. 497　7.　Which of the following is an example of active euthanasia?

C

　　　　　a.　withholding pain-killing drugs
　　　　　b.　removing a feed-tube from a patient who cannot feed him/herself
　　　*　c.　injecting a terminally ill patient with a lethal dose of drugs
　　　　　d.　removing a respirator from a patient who is totally brain dead

p. 497　8.　Which of the following is TRUE with regard to attitudes toward euthanasia?

F

　　　　　a.　The medical profession is generally opposed to all forms of euthanasia.
　　　　　b.　The medical profession is very supportive of both passive and active euthanasia.
　　　　　c.　The public generally supports active euthanasia for relatives but not for others.
　　　*　d.　The medical profession and the public are both very supportive of passive euthanasia, and somewhat supportive of active euthanasia.

p. 497　9.　Which of the following is an example of assisted suicide?

C　　*　a.　instructing someone on how to kill their self
　　　　　b.　injecting someone with a lethal dose of a drug that they are already taking
　　　　　c.　withholding medical treatment for a chronic disorder
　　　　　d.　removing someone from a respirator when their brain activity is nonexistent

p. 497　10.　The purpose of a living will is to:

F

　　　　　a.　make provisions for the division of property between loved ones after one's own death
　　　*　b.　specify how much medical care one wishes to receive if terminally ill
　　　　　c.　appoint guardians to care for all living minor offspring upon one's death
　　　　　d.　make active euthanasia legal for one's self

p. 497　11.　Some doctors will prescribe painkillers or sleeping pills for terminally ill patients, knowing that the patient may very well deliberately take a lethal overdose. This is an example of:

C

　　　　　a.　active euthanasia
　　　　　b.　passive euthanasia
　　　　　c.　manslaughter
　　　*　d.　assisted suicide

p. 498　12.　Cross-cultural observations of the social meanings of death show that:

F

　　　　　a.　the view of death in the United States is quite similar to other cultural views
　　　　　b.　Americans are socialized to express their grief more openly and more intensely than other cultural groups
　　　*　c.　there are many different interpretations of death
　　　　　d.　the experience of death is much the same across cultures

p. 498　13.　Which is TRUE with regard to life expectancies in the United States today?

F

　　　　　a.　The life expectancy for all people, regardless of race and gender, is 75 years.
　　　　　b.　Males are generally expected to outlive females, by about 5 years.
　　　*　c.　Females are generally expected to outlive males, regardless of race.
　　　　　d.　Black females have the greatest life expectancy of all.

p. 499   14.   Statistics on life expectancy show all of the following EXCEPT:

F   *   a.   individuals in the United States have the highest life expectancies compared to
                    individuals in other countries
               b.   white females can expect to live longer, on average, than white males
               c.   white Americans can expect to live longer, on average, than African Americans
               d.   individuals living in underdeveloped countries have lower life expectancies than those
                    living in developed countries

p. 499   15.   Life expectancy in the United States has increased dramatically during the past century.
F   This is PRIMARILY due to:
www   a.   advances in the treatment of cancer
               b.   new technologies in heart surgery
          *   c.   a decline in infant mortality
               d.   people exercising and eating a healthier diet

p. 499   16.   An 8-year-old child is MOST likely to die from:
F   a.   a terminal illness
               b.   congenital abnormalities
          *   c.   a car accident
               d.   child abuse

p. 499   17.   You see an obituary in the local newspaper for an adolescent. What is the most likely
F   cause of the adolescent's death?
               a.   congenital abnormality
               b.   cancer
          *   c.   accident
               d.   heart disease

p. 499   18.   When her 70 year old uncle died, Jen knew that, statistically, the most likely cause of his
C   death was:
               a.   congenital abnormality
               b.   stroke
               c.   an accident
          *   d.   heart disease

p. 499   19.   According to the programmed theories of aging:
C   a.   DNA becomes increasingly faulty with age and can no longer be repaired
               b.   exposure to environmental toxins damages genetic material over time
          *   c.   aging and death are under genetic control
               d.   aging and death result from a gradual build-up of damage to cells and organs

p. 500   20.   Over the last century, people's _____ has increased and their _____ has remained
F   about the same.
www   a.   total life span; longevity
          *   b.   average life expectancy; maximum life span
               c.   maximum life span; average life expectancy
               d.   longevity; total life span

p. 500   21.   Research with twins suggests that:
C   a.   there is no appreciable genetic contribution to aging and death
                b.   the shared environment has a significant affect on aging and death of family members
                c.   aging and death are determined almost entirely by a genetic program
        *   d.   about one-third of the differences in longevity are due to genetic factors

p. 500   22.   The Hayflick limit refers to:
F   a.   how much infection that the immune system can handle
                b.   a person's maximum life span
        *   c.   the number of times that a cell can reproduce itself
                d.   the amount of time that the hypothalamus can function before it malfunctions

p. 501   23.   Research on chromosomal contributions to aging suggests that:
C   *   a.   cells may be limited in how often they can divide because the tips of chromosomes do
www   not actually replicate
                b.   cells cannot make connections with other cells after the developmental period and the
                     lack of "communication" among cells leads to death
                c.   cells can only divide once; after this they slowly degenerate over the years
                d.   there are no limits on cell life; without environmental wear and tear, we could live
                     indefinitely

p. 501   24.   Some research suggests that telomeres:
C   a.   are responsible for the functioning of the immune system
                b.   begin to deteriorate after years of exposure to environmental toxins
                c.   slow the release of hormones and brain chemicals over time to eventually bring about
                     death
        *   d.   do not replicate during cell division, limiting the life of the cell

p. 501   25.   Damage theories of aging suggest that:
C   a.   aging and dying are simply a part of nature's plan
www   *   b.   death results from an accumulation of defects in cells and organs over time
                c.   the primary cause of death is damage to the organism caused by external forces
                d.   autoimmune reactions damage normal body cells, leading to aging and death

p. 501   26.   Some proponents of damage theories of aging suggest that:
C   a.   a highly restrictive diet and much exercise will extend the life span
                b.   strengthening the immune system is the only way to extend the life span
        *   c.   antioxidants may extend life by keeping free radicals under control
                d.   we may be able to increase longevity by cutting back on activities that tax the body's
                     major organs and muscles

p. 502   27.   Research with animals suggests that the BEST way to prolong life overall is to:
F   a.   exercise rigorously
                b.   take antioxidants to neutralize destructive free radicals
        *   c.   restrict your diet
                d.   strengthen your immune system through early exposure to contagious diseases

p. 502 28. When the doctor tells him that he is dying of cancer, Harley refuses to believe the doctor
F and insists that the laboratory results must be inaccurate. Harley is likely in Kubler-Ross's
www _____ stage.
* a. denial
b. anger
c. bargaining
d. depression

p. 502 29. Frieda has been told she is going to die, for she has an inoperable brain tumor. Her
C children are young, and she cannot stand the thought of leaving them behind. All day long
she thinks over and over again, "Why me?" Frieda is in which of Kubler-Ross's stages?
* a. anger
b. bargaining
c. denial
d. depression

p. 503 30. Jake has terminal cancer. After years of very irregular church attendance, Jake begins to
C go to church every Sunday, and often in between. He asks of God "Please let me live to
see my son graduate from college. I'll be a good Christian. I'll mend my ways. Just let me
live...." Jake is in which of Kübler-Ross's stages of death and dying?
a. anger
* b. bargaining
c. denial
d. depression

p. 503 31. The last stage of dying, according to Kübler-Ross, involves:
F a. anguish over unfinished business that must be left behind
b. depression and feelings of hopelessness
c. anger and resentment directed toward those who will go on living
* d. peaceful acceptance of the inevitable

p. 503 32. Kübler-Ross's stage-theory of death and dying has been criticized because:
F a. the stages appear to be incorrectly ordered
* b. the dying process is simply not stagelike
c. there appear to be several stages in the process she has missed
d. the emotional responses she describes largely don't occur

p. 503 33. Which of the following is NOT a criticism of Kübler-Ross's theory?
C a. The course of dying is not really stage-like.
* b. It does not describe any of the emotions experienced by people facing death.
c. It does not really take the course of the illness into account.
d. It does not account for how individual differences in personality affect reactions to
death.

p. 503 34. With regard to Kübler-Ross's theory, other researchers on death and dying have:
F a. substantiated her theory
www b. found that anger is not a typical reaction to death
* c. determined that the dying process is simply not stagelike
d. found that her theory holds in the United States, but not in other cultures

p. 503 35. Shneidman's work in the area of death and dying suggests that:
C
        a. it is more normal to remain depressed than to reach acceptance toward the end of the dying process
        b. there is a distinct sequence of stages that people pass through with regard to the acceptance of death
*   c. dying people experience a myriad of emotional responses, with many unpredictable ups and downs
        d. one's reaction to the dying process is much the same, regardless of the cause of death

p. 503 36. Which of the following appears to be TRUE with regard to death and dying?
C * a. A person's personality influences how s/he deals with dying.
        b. Most people do go through stages of dying as Kübler-Ross claimed.
        c. The nature and course of the illness seems to have little impact on an individual's reactions to dying.
        d. There are no common emotional reactions to dying

p. 504 37. The term bereavement refers to:
F
        a. a person's emotional response to loss
*   b. a state of loss
        c. death by terminal illness
        d. socially accepted ways of displaying grief

p. 504 38. Grief is BEST defined as:
F * a. the emotional response to loss
        b. culturally accepted ways of displaying one's reactions to loss
        c. the reaction a person has to learning that s/he is about to die
        d. a state of loss

p. 504 39. Nine-year-old Sarah died from cancer. Her teacher and her classmates made black
C arm bands to wear for a month following her death. This best demonstrates:
        a. bereavement
        b. depression
        c. grief
*   d. mourning

p. 504 40. Feelings of sadness and anger are typical of:
F
        a. bereavement
*   b. grief
        c. mourning
        d. denial

p. 504 41. The Parkes-Bowlby model of the grieving process suggests that:
C * a. a grieving adult is much like an infant experiencing separation anxiety
www
        b. there is a series of clear-cut stages one passes through in mourning one's loss
        c. grief that lasts much longer than six months is maladaptive
        d. longing to have the loved one return becomes most intense about one year following death

p. 504 42. According to Parkes and Bowlby, one of the first reactions to the death of a loved one is:
F
a. disorientation
* b. numbness
c. yearning
d. despair

p. 505 43. After her husband dies, Hannah gives away most of his belongings, but keeps a few
C treasured items. Among these is a sweater of her husband which Hannah begins to wear
and she finds that this brings her some comfort. Hannah is most likely experiencing:
* a. yearning
b. denial and isolation
c. bargaining
d. disorganization and despair

p. 506 44. According to the Parkes-Bowlby model of grieving:
C
a. despair and depression are at their highest peak during the first month after a loss
b. yearning increases in the months following a loss until it reaches a peak around 6-8
months after the loss
c. numbness and disbelief remain high throughout the first year following a loss
* d. despair and depression increase in the months following a loss until they reach a peak
around 4-6 months after the loss

p. 506 45. What can we conclude regarding an infant's experience of death?
C *
a. Infants who have developed an understanding of person permanence may show many
of the same reactions that adults do in response to loss of an attachment figure.
b. Most infants understand that death means that life processes stop, but they believe that
it can be undone or reversed.
c. Infants are biologically programmed to show grief responses to the loss of a caretaker,
regardless of the age of the infant.
d. Infants who show separation protest and depression-like symptoms have clearly
demonstrated that they have an accurate cognitive understanding of death.

p. 507 46. The MOST mature conception of death in Western culture involves understanding that
F death:
a. is the cessation of life
b. is final
c. happens to everyone
* d. results from internal or biological causes

p. 507 47. Steven now understands that death is final, and cannot be undone, but he thinks his
C Mommy and Daddy will never die. Steven is MOST likely:
a. age 3 or 4
* b. between the ages of 5 and 7
c. at least 8 years old
d. 10 or older

p. 507 48. Amber is upset at her grandfather's funeral because she is worried that he will be lonely a
C   and have no one to take care of him after he is buried. These specific concerns expressed
               by Amber suggest that she does not understand that:
               a. dead people cannot come back to life
    *   b. dead people do not retain any life processes such as feelings
               c. death has resulted from internal changes in the body
               d. death eventually happens to everyone

p. 507 49. When the family dog dies at home, Cory does not understand how this could be. He
C   doesn't see any marks on the dog and without any physical signs, Cory doesn't believe the
www   dog could actually be dead. This suggests that Cory does not understand that:
               a. dead things cannot come back to life
               b. dead things do not retain any life processes
    *   c. death has resulted from internal changes in the body
               d. death eventually happens to all animals

p. 507 50. Children's conceptions of death are influenced by all of the following except:
F   a. level of cognitive development
               b. religious beliefs
               c. social learning experiences
    *   d. their gender

p. 508 51. Why are children in the 5-to-7 age range particularly likely to make a major breakthrough
C   in their understanding of death?
               a. Because most of them are likely to have experienced a major death in their own family
                    by then.
    *   b. Because of important changes in cognition that occur as children move from
                    preoperational to concrete-operational thought.
               c. Because of their religious training.
               d. Because parents are generally very straightforward in their explanations of death once
                    children reach this age.

p. 508 52. Young children who encounter death firsthand will MOST likely:
F   a. be severely traumatized
                b. have night terrors
    *   c. develop a more mature understanding of death
               d. become overly dependent on their parents

p. 508 53. Telling a young child that death is like "going to sleep" is:
C   a. a good way to protect him/her from the brutality of death
               b. a good way to help him/her understand that death happens to everyone
    *   c. likely to contribute to his/her misconception that death is a temporary state
               d. likely to lead to a more mature conception of why people die

p. 508 54. As children move from Piaget's preoperational stage to the concrete operational stage of
C cognitive development, they are likely to:
   a. gain a fully mature understanding of death
 * b. understand that death is final, inevitable, and irreversible, but not that it is biologically
      caused
   c. continue to have trouble understanding that death is final and irreversible
   d. give accurate explanations about the causes of death

p. 508 55. Which two factors are MOST likely to contribute to a child's understanding of death?
C * a. level of cognitive development and specific life experiences
   b. gender and parent's explanations of death
   c. what they watch on television and where they live
   d. age and gender

p. 508 56. Research on young children with terminal illnesses shows that they:
F * a. usually know that they are going to die
   b. should not be told the details about their illness or that they are going to die
   c. do not have any idea that their illness will result in death
   d. understand and accept their impending death

p. 509 57. Preschool-aged children who are dying are likely to:
F   a. reason with their parents and doctors to find a way to save them
 * b. behaviorally act out their frustrations regarding the illness
   c. talk about their feelings regarding death
   d. cope as well as anyone else with their impending death

p. 510 58. With regard to the grief process, a young child who loses a parent is:
C   a. unlikely to feel grief
   b. likely to grieve for only a short while
 * c. particularly vulnerable to long-term negative effects of bereavement
   d. likely to proceed through the grieving process in much the same way
      as does an adult

p. 510 59. Which of the following is FALSE regarding children who have experienced the death of a
C loved one?
   a. They often experience problems with sleeping and eating.
   b. They can develop academic or behavioral problems.
 * c. They express grief in ways very similar to an adult.
   d. They are at-risk for long-term negative consequences as a result of the loss.

p. 510 60. Which of the following is FALSE regarding adolescent's understanding of death?
C * a. Adolescents are less likely than younger children to believe that death happens to
      everyone.
   b. Adolescents are more likely than younger children to think about the abstract meaning
      of death.
   c. Adolescents are more likely than younger children to say that death may be reversible.
   d. Adolescents are less likely than younger children to view death as just a biological
      ending of life.

p. 510 61. Adolescents who are dying are likely to be concerned with their appearance. This is
C   MOST LIKELY because:
            a. They are in denial about their illness and are trying to focus on other things.
            b. They want to look good so that other people will notice them.
     *   c. This is a typical concern of the adolescent period.
            d. They are probably unaware that they are dying.

p. 511 62. Which is TRUE with regard to "death anxiety?"
C   a. Males express more death anxiety than do females.
            b. Death anxiety is higher among elderly adults than among young adults.
            c. Death anxiety is greatest among highly religious individuals.
     *   d. Death anxiety is a normal part of the human condition throughout the life span.

p. 511 63. What can we conclude regarding death anxiety?
C   *   a. Personality, including self-esteem, is related to the extent to which individuals are
                anxious about their death.
            b. Death anxiety increases sharply in old age.
            c. There are no gender differences in expression of death anxiety.
            d. Death anxiety tends to be higher among people who are deeply religious.

p. 512 64. A middle-aged adult who is dying is MOST likely to be:
F   a. concerned about making sense of his/her life before death
     *   b. concerned about the welfare of family members
            c. feeling angry and cheated
            d. anxious to seek out new experiences and try new things

p. 512 65. A middle-aged adult who has a terminal illness is MOST LIKELY to focus on:
F   a. spending time in individual, private pursuits such as reading
www   b. finishing up projects that have been started
     *   c. spending time with family and other loved ones
            d. changing their lifestyle to make the most of the time left

p. 512 66. All of the following are true with regard to the loss of a spouse EXCEPT:
C   *   a. Widows are more at risk for death than are widowers.
            b. The year after death is the most difficult period of adjustment.
            c. Cognitive functioning of the survivor may be impaired.
            d. The surviving spouse is at risk for suicide.

p. 512 67. Other things being equal, which one of the following deaths is likely to be most disruptive
C   to an adult?
            a. parent
     *   b. spouse
            c. friend
            d. grandparent

p. 513 68. All of the following are true regarding widows and widowers EXCEPT:

F
    a. They are likely to have trouble sleeping and experience changes in appetite.
    b. They are likely to have impairments in memory and cognitive functioning.
    c. They are at higher risk of physical illness and death.
*   d. They are likely to remain debilitated physically, cognitively, and emotionally for the rest of their lives.

p. 514 69. Which of the following is TRUE regarding the loss of a child?

F * a. Parents are likely to feel more guilt and anger when they lose a child than when they experience another type of loss.
    b. The loss of a child is experienced by parents much the same way as other types of losses.
    c. The older the child is at the time of death, the more difficult it is for parents to cope with the loss.
    d. Fathers typically have more trouble coping with the loss than mothers.

p. 515 70. Research suggests that for an adult, the loss of a parent is:

C
    a. more difficult to deal with for women than for men
*   b. upsetting, but in some ways expected and therefore easier to deal with than some other types of losses
    c. typically the most difficult type of loss to cope with
    d. experienced as a complex combination of positive and negative emotions

p. 515 71. Joe's wife died five years ago. Joe still daily sets a place at the table for his wife, and

C   breaks into tears when he must sit down, once again, without his wife beside him at the table. Joe's grief reaction is BEST termed:
    a. normal
*   b. chronic grief
    c. distorted grief
    d. inhibited grief

p. 515 72. Bill's son, Mark, was killed suddenly in a car accident. A year following Mark's death, Bill

C   has still not cried or experienced pangs of grief over his death. Bill's behavior is:
    a. quite normal for a man
    b. a sign of his strong coping skills
*   c. a sign that he may be unable to express his grief
    d. a sign that he didn't love Mark

p. 515 73. Which of the following is NOT an example of pathological grief?

C
    a. A family that continues to set a dinner place for their deceased father and refuses to get rid of any of his belongings, preferring to continue as if he was still alive.
    b. A child who shows no reaction after her father is killed in an accident.
    c. A parent who shows anger and guilt but never any sadness or depression in response to the death of a child.
*   d. A person who experiences depression and sleeping problems during the year following the death of a spouse.

p. 517   74.   All of the following factors affect whether a person successfully copes with the death of a
C   loved one EXCEPT:
               a.   development of internal working models of love and trust
               b.   greater emotional independence from the person before the loss occurs
        *   c.   changes in life style following the death of a loved one
               d.   strong social supports including people who allow them to express their true feelings

p. 517   75.   All of the following contribute significantly to the ability of individuals to cope with the
C   death of a loved one EXCEPT:
        *   a.   whether the death was sudden and unexpected or somewhat anticipated
               b.   their personality and coping style
               c.   a sense of control over the outcome of events
               d.   how close they were to the deceased

p. 517   76.   Who is likely to have the MOST difficulty coping with the death of a loved one?
C   a.   A 60-year-old female who loses her mother.
www   b.   A 30-year-old male who loses his brother.
               c.   A 60-year-old female who loses her husband after a lengthy illness.
        *   d.   A 60-year-old male who suddenly loses his wife of 30 years.

p. 518   77.   The purpose of a hospice is to:
F   *   a.   make the dying person as comfortable as possible
               b.   prolong life for as long as possible
               c.   try new experimental methods for prolonging life
               d.   provide euthanasia

p. 519   78.   Which is NOT a feature of hospice care?
F   a.   a deemphasis on medical attempts to prolong life
               b.   the patient and his/her family determine what medical treatment is to be given
        *   c.   the regular practice of active euthanasia
               d.   liberal use of powerful "pain cocktails"

p. 519   79.   Hospice care compares to hospital care in that:
C   a.   pain control is emphasized more in the hospital setting
        *   b.   care in the hospice is less institutionalized than in the hospital
               c.   prolonging life is a main goal of hospice care
               d.   more choices and patient control are possible in the hospital setting

p. 495   80.   The Harvard definition of biological death is
F   a.   the point at which the heart stops beating
SG   b.   irreversible loss of functioning in the cerebral cortex
        *   c.   irreversible loss of functioning in the entire brain
               d.   failure to breathe without life support systems

p. 496   81.   Cross-cultural research on death and dying indicates that
F   *   a.   cultures have evolved different social meanings of death
SG   b.   all cultures have similar ways of coping with death
               c.   people of some cultures do not experience grief
               d.   there is universal agreement on the definition of death

p. 498 82. The average length of time that a person can expect to live is termed
F   a. life span
SG   *   b. life expectancy
                   c. age norm
                   d. maximum life span

p. 499 83. The leading cause of death in childhood is _____ and in middle age, the leading
F   cause of death is _____.
SG   a. congenital abnormalities; chronic diseases
                   b. accidents; suicides
                   c. hereditary defects; violent acts such as homicides
            *   d. accidents; chronic diseases

p. 500 84. The Hayflick limit is
F   a. the number of times that a gene can "turn on" or "turn off" to bring about maturational
SG   changes
                   b. the ceiling on the number of years that anyone lives
                   c. the speed with which the body can repair damaged cells
            *   d. the limited number times that a human cell can divide

p. 499 85. Theories that focus on the genetic control of aging are called _____ theories and
F   those that focus on gradual deterioration of cells are called _____ theories
SG   a. genetic; environmental
            *   b. programmed; damage
                   c. damage; programmed
                   d. biological; psychological

p. 502 86. According to Kübler-Ross's stages of dying, a person who expresses resentment and
F   criticizes everyone is in the stage of
SG   a. denial and isolation
            *   b. anger
                   c. bargaining
                   d. depression

p. 503 87. According to Kübler-Ross's stages of dying, a dying person who agrees to stop smoking
F   and drinking in return for a little more time is in the stage of
SG   a. denial and isolation
                   b. anger
            *   c. bargaining
                   d. depression

p. 503. 88. One of the biggest problems with Kübler-Ross's stages of dying is that
C   *   a. dying is not really stage-like
SG   b. patients go through the stages in order but at different rates
                   c. they are focused on a person's cognitive understanding of death rather than the person's
                       affective response
                   d. they describe a person's response to death of a spouse or parent but not the response to
                       one's own impending death

p. 504 89. The emotional response to death is referred to as
F   a. bereavement
SG   *   b. grief
            c. mourning
            d. depression

p. 504 90. In the first few days following the death of a loved one, the bereaved person
F   a. is usually unable to function
SG   b. experiences anticipatory grief
            c. experiences the worst despair of the mourning process
        *   d. is typically in a state of shock and numbness

p. 507 91. Preschool-aged children are likely to believe that
C   a. death is inevitable and will happen to everyone eventually
SG   *   b. dead people still experience sensations and perceptions, just not as intensely as live
                people
            c. people die because of changes in internal bodily functioning
            d. death is irreversible

p. 509 92. Terminally ill children typically
F   a. accept their impending death with equanimity
SG   b. have no idea that they are dying or what it means to die
            c. go through Kübler-Ross's stages of dying in sequential order
        *   d. experience a range of negative emotions and express a number of negative behaviors

p. 514 93. Grief over the loss of a child
C   a. is greatest if the child is young
SG   *   b. does not differ in intensity as a function of the age of the child
            c. is less intense if the child dies from an accident beyond the parent's control
            d. is more intense for fathers than mothers since mothers in our culture are encouraged to
                express grief more openly than fathers

p. 510 94. Children's grief
F   a. can be reduced by not talking about death and the deceased
SG   b. can be reduced if they have a number of other stressors to deal with at the same time
        *   c. can be reduced if appropriate social support systems are in place
            d. is always expressed openly through behavior such as crying

TRUE-FALSE QUESTIONS

p. 495 95. Experts today are in agreement that a person should be proclaimed dead when there is total
             brain death.
            a. true
        *   b. false

p. 496 96. Euthanasia refers to speeding up the death of a terminally ill person.
        *   a. true
            b. false

p. 498   97.   Different cultures have remarkably different ways of mourning their dead.
www   *   a.   true
                b.   false

p. 499   98.   Life expectancies in the United States have increased during the past century primarily due
                to advances in medical technologies used to prolong life.
                a.   true
          *   b.   false

p. 499   99.   The leading cause of death among young children is accidents.
          *   a.   true
                b.   false

p. 501   100. Damage theories of aging suggest that aging and dying are simply a part of nature's plan.
                a.   true
          *   b.   false

p. 501   101. Telomeres, the tips of chromosomes, do not replicate as do the chromosomes, which may
                limit how often a cell can divide.
          *   a.   true
                b.   false

p. 502   102. A severely restricted diet is the only technique proven to extend life span, at least among
                animals.
          *   a.   true
                b.   false

p. 503   103. Kübler-Ross's stages of death and dying have been shown to apply across most ages and
                cultures.
                a.   true
          *   b.   false

p. 505   104. Parkes and Bowlby claimed that grief is different from other emotional responses because
www   it contains the component of separation anxiety
          *   a.   true
                b.   false

p. 506   105. An infant age 6 months or more who is genuinely attached to his/her parents may well
                experience intense grief and display depression-like symptoms upon the death of a parent.
          *   a.   true
                b.   false

p. 507   106. A 7-year-old child is likely to view death as temporary and unlikely to happen to
                him/herself.
                a.   true
          *   b.   false

p. 507 107. Children's understanding of death is linked to important changes in cognitive development.
* a. true
b. false

p. 510 108. A young child is likely to "bounce back" from the death of a parent much more quickly than if s/he was an adult at the time of loss.
a. true
* b. false

p. 510 109. Adolescents generally grieve in much the same way as do adults.
* a. true
b. false

p. 511 110. Highly religious people experience more death anxiety than those who are less religious.
a. true
* b. false

p. 513 111. Widow(er)s of a conflict-ridden marriage are most likely to feel relief upon the spouse's death.
a. true
* b. false

p. 514 112. The death of a young child is more difficult for parents to bear than is the death of an adult child.
a. true
* b. false

p. 515 113. The death of a parent tends to be less disruptive than the loss of a spouse or child.
* a. true
b. false

ESSAY QUESTIONS

114. How do children of different ages (from infants through adolescents) understand death?

115. In general, which is harder to deal with, the death of a parent, spouse, or child? What determines how difficult a particular death will be for someone to cope with?

116. What personal and cultural factors influence a person's ability to cope with death?
www

117. In your job as a counselor, you must meet with a family in the hospital as they are confronted with the news that their son has been in a terrible car accident. He is on life support and not expected to regain consciousness. What do you tell them regarding the meaning of biological life and death? How do you counsel them regarding their response to death and dying?

118. In general, what factors contribute to the process of aging and death?
SG [Sample answer is provided in the Study Guide.]

119. Integrate the understanding of death with Piaget's stages of cognitive development and
SG apply this to the practical situation of coping with the death of a pet or the death of a parent. For example, how would you help a child in the preoperational stage understand and cope with death of a parent? How would you explain that the pet dog has died? How would your conversations with children in the concrete operational stage and adolescents or adults in the formal operational stage differ from the conversation that you have with the preoperational child?

FITTING THE PIECES TOGETHER

MULTIPLE-CHOICE QUESTIONS

p. 523   1.   Which of the following is FALSE regarding development during infancy?
C
        a.   Infants continue the brain growth spurt that began prenatally.
        b.   Infants can learn and remember from their experiences.
  * c.   Infants quickly acquire language and the ability to reason logically.
        d.   Many reflexes disappear and are replaced by voluntary behaviors as the brain matures.

p. 523   2.   As infants move through the second year of life, they acquire the "symbolic capacity,"
C   or the ability to engage in representational thought. This permits all of the following
       EXCEPT:
        a.   imitation
        b.   pretend play
        c.   location of hidden objects
  * d.   conservation

p. 523   3.   The "symbolic capacity" is:
F   * a.   acquired toward the end of the sensorimotor period
www   b.   acquired during the period of concrete-operational thought
        c.   acquired as children move from concrete-operational to formal-operational thought
        d.   present at birth

p. 523   4.   During which period of the life span do we see the most rapid physical changes?
F   * a.   infancy
        b.   early childhood
        c.   middle childhood
        d.   adolescence

p. 523   5.   Which of the following would we NOT expect to see during the first year of life?
C
        a.   disappearance of most reflexes
        b.   manipulation of objects with one's hands
        c.   the first spoken words
  * d.   emergence of social pretend play

p. 523   6.   Which of the following would 2-year-old Susie have trouble with?
C   * a.   understanding that objects remain the same despite changes in appearance
www   b.   understanding that objects still exist when they cannot be seen
        c.   knowing that she is a girl
        d.   recognizing herself in a mirror

p. 524   7.   Infants can be expected to be in which stages?
F   a. preoperational, oral, trust versus mistrust
         *   b. sensorimotor, oral, trust versus mistrust
                 c. sensorimotor, anal, autonomy versus shame
                 d. preoperational, oral, preconventional

p. 524   8.   Which of the following is within the capacity of a preoperational thinker?
C   a. classification of objects
                 b. conservation of number
                 c. ordering objects from biggest to smallest
         *   d. figuring out the rules of language

p. 524   9.   What cognitive event marks the move from the sensorimotor stage to the preoperational
C   stage?
                 a. development of trust
                 b. development of conservation
         *   c. development of the symbolic capacity
                 d. development of attachment

p. 524   10.   Which of the following tasks would a preschooler MOST LIKELY have trouble with?
F   a. object permanence
                 b. pretend play
         *   c. conservation
                 d. hide and seek games

p. 524   11.   Which of the following characterizes the preschool-age child?
C   a. They can reason logically about real-world objects and events.
                 b. They consider internal qualities of people such as personality and intentions.
         *   c. They can use symbolic information to guide their understanding of the world.
                 d. They understand that changes in the appearance of an object do not change the object.

p. 524   12.   Which BEST distinguishes the concrete-operational from the pre-operational child?
C   a. the capacity for symbolic thought
www   b. the capacity to engage in systematic testing of hypotheses
                 c. acquisition of the object permanence concept
         *   d. the ability to perform actions in one's own head

p. 524   13.   Concrete operational thinkers are different from preoperational thinkers because concrete
C   operations allow children to:
                 a. mentally allow a symbol to represent an object or event
                 b. solve hypothetical problems
                 c. learn more efficiently by comparing new information to information already stored in
                     memory
         *   d. mentally work through actions rather than having to physically work through actions

p. 524 14. Which of the following characterizes the school-age child?
C   *   a. They can reason logically about real-world objects and events.
            b. They can consider hypothetical situations.
            c. They understand that knowledge is relative and depends on the perspective of the knower.
            d. They can systematically form and test hypotheses.

p. 524 15. Compared to a preschooler, a school-age child is likely to do all of the following EXCEPT:
C   a. spend more time with peers
            b. compare themselves to others
            c. use more memory strategies
    *   d. show an increase in self-esteem

p. 526 16. School-aged children are GENERALLY in which of the following stages?
F   a. initiative vs. guilt; conventional morality; concrete operations
www   b. industry vs. inferiority; conventional morality; preoperations
            c. initiative vs. guilt; latency; conventional morality
    *   d. industry vs. inferiority; preconventional morality; concrete operations

p. 526 17. Which is characteristic of entering the stage of formal-operational thought?
C   *   a. obsession with what others are thinking
            b. a new-found respect for adult logic
            c. a decrease in confusion regarding religious and political beliefs
            d. a trial-and-error approach to problem solving

p. 526 18. MOST adolescents are in which of the following stages?
F   a. formal operational thought; postconventional morality
            b. intimacy vs. isolation; genital
            c. identity vs. role confusion; phallic
    *   d. formal operational thought; identity vs. role confusion

p. 526 19. A major preoccupation of adolescents is:
F   a. figuring out what to do with the rest of their lives
            b. what they look like physically
            c. achieving intimacy in relationships
    *   d. both a and b
            e. both a and c

p. 526 20. Adolescents who achieve formal operational thought are advanced compared to other
C   adolescents because they:
    *   a. can generate and systematically test hypotheses
            b. can efficiently process information in their short-term memory
            c. are no longer troubled by egocentrism
            d. have achieved a sense of identity

p. 526 21. When presented with a moral dilemma, an adolescent is likely to:
C   a. think that an action was OK because no one got caught doing it
     *   b. believe that something was immoral if laws or rules were broken
        c. argue that broad principles of justice be applied to determine who in the situation was correct
        d. not notice if there has been a violation of rules

p. 526 22. What can we conclude about social interactions or relationships during adolescence?
C   a. Increased maturity makes adolescents more compliant to their parent's requests.
www   b. Adolescents begin to form gender segregated cliques.
     *   c. Trying to conform to expectations of peers can lead to both positive and negative behaviors.
        d. Adolescents see this period of time as a last opportunity to engage in childish pursuits before the responsibilities of adulthood take over.

p. 526 23. When can most people expect to be at their peak physically and cognitively?
F   a. adolescence
     *   b. young adulthood
        c. middle adulthood
        d. late adulthood

p. 526 24. Cognitive advances during young adulthood:
C   *   a. may be made in a person's area of expertise
        b. are unlikely because intellectual capabilities reach their peak in late adolescence
        c. are likely to occur once a person has reached postconventional reasoning
        d. occur in a step-like fashion with age

p. 528 25. Young adulthood is a period that is characterized by:
C   *   a. higher divorce rates than later adulthood years
        b. fewer mental health problems (e.g., depression; alcoholism) than later adult years
        c. lower levels of sexual responsiveness as compared to adolescence and middle-age
        d. lower levels of stress compared to adolescence and middle-age

p. 528 26. MOST young adults are in the stages of:
F   a. postconventional morality and intimacy versus isolation
     *   b. conventional morality and intimacy versus isolation
        c. postconventional morality and generativity versus stagnation
        d. conventional morality and generativity versus stagnation

p. 528 27. Physical declines usually first become noticeable starting in one's:
F   a. 20's - 30's
     *   b. 40's - 50's
        c. 60's - 70's
        d. 80's - 90's

p. 528 28. In comparison to young adults, middle-age adults:
C   a. have developed more memory capacity
             b. have increased their scores on general intelligence tests
             c. perform better on measures of fluid intelligence
        *   d. perform better on measures of crystallized intelligence

p. 528 29. According to Erikson, middle-aged adults struggle with the crisis of:
F   a. identity versus role confusion
             b. intimacy versus isolation
        *   c. generativity versus stagnation
             d. integrity versus despair

p. 528 30. Most older adults:
F   *   a. can expect some physical and cognitive declines
www   b. develop dementia of some sort
             c. are unable to live independently
             d. experience a drop in social skills and self-esteem

p. 528 31. Older adulthood is characterized by:
C   a. sharp declines in physical and cognitive skills for most adults
        *   b. large variability across individuals in physical and cognitive abilities
             c. increases in cognition and decreases in physical health
             d. increasing similarity among adults as they lose physical and cognitive abilities

p. 529 32. The theme that we are whole persons throughout the life span suggests that:
C   a. development is stable across the life span
        *   b. developmental psychologists must study all aspects of development to fully understand
                 the person
             c. development occurs across the entire life span
             d. we are products of both heredity and environmental factors acting together

p. 529 33. According to the orthogenetic principle, development:
C   *   a. proceeds from being general to being specific and organized
www   b. moves from being differentiated to being global and diffuse
             c. becomes more malleable with age
             d. proceeds in a head-to-foot and an inward to outward direction

p. 529 34. Another way of stating the orthogenetic principle is to say that:
C   a. new developments become enriched by adding to them from previous knowledge of the
                 world
             b. we learn to sift through information and disregard the irrelevant while holding onto the
                 relevant information
             c. development is complete interaction of physical, cognitive, and social changes
        *   d. behaviors become more distinct from one another, which allows for greater integration
                 of responses

p. 529 35. How can we MOST accurately characterize development across the life span?
C
  a. Development increases through childhood and adolescence, then levels off during young and middle adulthood before declining in old age.
  b. Development increases until adulthood when it levels off and remains at this plateau through old age.
 * c. Some aspects of development improve, others decline, and still others change in neither positive or negative ways across the entire life span.
  d. Skills that are adaptive improve across the entire life span while skills that have no useful function disappear across the life span.

p. 529 36. Claire believes that the way her teenage son thinks is totally different from how he thought
C as a child. This suggests:
  a. a goodness of fit between the person and his environment
  b. the operation of the orthogenetic principle
  c. continuity in his development
 * d. discontinuity in his development

p. 529 37. Even though John has not seen his nephew for over 10 years, he is sure that the two of
C them will be able to pick up where they left off--doing the same things, sharing the same interests, laughing at similar antics. John's view suggests:
 * a. continuity across the life span
  b. discontinuity across the life span
  c. the strong impact of environmental factors
  d. the plasticity of human development

p. 530 38. Plasticity in development means that:
C
  a. We can recover from any insult to the brain.
 * b. We can change in response to experiences.
  c. We change in response to the unfolding of a genetic blueprint.
  d. Changes that occur are usually only temporary.

p. 532 39. It is MOST accurate to say that most human traits are:
C
  a. influenced more strongly by genetic factors than environmental factors
www b. influenced more strongly by environmental factors than genetic factors
 * c. influenced to some extent by genetic and environmental factors
  d. triggered by genetic factors and then enhanced by environmental factors

p. 532 40. Which of the following BEST characterizes the nature-nurture interaction?
C
  a. Nature determines the sorts of experiences that we are exposed to.
 * b. Nature influences how we react to environments and environments influence our genetic potential.
  c. Shared environmental influences determine whether family members are similar to one another.
  d. Nature determines physical traits and nurture determines psychological traits.

p. 532 41. We tend to function MOST like our peers during:
F   *   a. infancy
             b. adolescence
             c. young adulthood
             d. old age

p. 532 42. Which of the following is TRUE?
C   a. Humans become more similar to one another as they age.
        *   b. Species wide genetic factors make infants similar to one another while individual
                 genetic factors contribute to differences after infancy.
             c. A Species wide genetic blueprint ensures that we all express similar developmental
                 characteristics during adulthood and old age.
             d. Diversity among humans increases during childhood, then plateaus during adolescence
                 and early adulthood, and then begins to decline in old age.

p. 532 43. Which of the following themes helps us to better appreciate why Freud came up with many
C   of the ideas that he did?
www   a. We are active in our own development.
             b. There is much plasticity in human development
        *   c. We develop in a cultural and historical context.
             d. We are whole persons throughout the life span

p. 532 44. Most of the developmental norms and findings described in your text book are:
F   a. applicable across cultural contexts
        *   b. primarily applicable to 20th century Western societies
             c. likely to be as applicable in the future as they are today
             d. representative of subcultural differences in the United States

p. 533 45. Which of the following is MOST LIKELY to agree that we are active in our own
F   development?
        *   a. Piaget
             b. Freud
             c. Skinner
             d. Watson

p. 533 46. According to Piaget, children:
C   a. are strongly influenced by genetic influences
             b. are passively shaped by their experiences
        *   c. actively contribute to their development
             d. learn most of what they need to know through their interactions with adults

p. 533 47. Most current developmental theorists:
F   a. follow the psychoanalytic perspectives of Freud and Erikson
             b. are behaviorists or learning theorists
        *   c. integrate features from multiple theorists
             d. adhere to Piaget's stages of development

p. 523 48. Which advance in cognition is instrumental in helping the child to move from trial-and-
C   error problem-solving to a point where s/he can mentally devise a solution to a problem
SG   and then try it out?
           a. transformational logic
      *   b. acquisition of symbolic capacity
           c. movement from concrete-operational to formal-operational thought
           d. the ability to conserve

p. 524 49. Preschoolers are MOST likely to be in which of the following stages?
F   a. autonomy vs. shame and doubt; latency
SG   b. initiative vs. guilt; conventional morality
      *   c. autonomy vs. shame and doubt; preconventional morality
           d. industry vs. inferiority; preconventional morality

p. 524 50. A marked weakness of the preoperational stage is the inability to:
C   *   a. think logically
SG   b. use language effectively
           c. allow one thing to represent something else
           d. socially interact with their peers

p. 524 51. One drawback of concrete operational thinking is difficulty with:
C   a. any sort of problem solving task
SG   b. tasks that require mental consideration of tangible objects
      *   c. abstract or hypothetical tasks
           d. tasks that require understanding the perspective of another person

p. 526 52. Erikson believed that young adults were struggling with the issue of:
F   a. industry versus inferiority
SG   b. identity versus role confusion
      *   c. intimacy versus isolation
           d. generativity versus stagnation

p. 528 53. Older adults (age 65 and over) are typically:
F   a. lower in self-esteem and life satisfaction than younger adults
SG   b. in Erikson's stage of generativity vs. stagnation
           c. superior to younger adults with regard to fluid intelligence, though their crystallized
               intelligence has deteriorated significantly
      *   d. suffering from some sort of physical limitations

p. 530 54. With the evidence in, it is MOST accurate to say that cognitive development is:
C   a. discontinuous and stage-like, as Piaget asserted
SG   b. continuous, reflected in measures of quantitative change such as accumulation and loss
               of knowledge over time
           c. largely maturational and independent of environmental influence
      *   d. both stage-like and gradual, depending on the aspect being studied

p. 530 55. To say that there is discontinuity in development means that:
F   a. changes smoothly and gradually occur across the life span
SG   *   b. changes occur in distinct steps
              c. early traits carry over and form the basis of later traits
              d. change is a matter of quantitatively adding to what is already present

p. 532 56. We are MOST LIKELY to be similar to someone else our same age during:
C   *   a. infancy
SG   b. childhood
              c. adolescence
              d. old age

p. 529 57. Which is TRUE with regard to the course of development across the life span?
F   a. In general, there is growth throughout childhood and young adulthood, stability during
SG   middle-age, and a decline in functioning during old age.
              b. In general, there is growth throughout childhood and young adulthood, followed by
                  steady declines in functioning beginning with middle-age.
              c. In general, growth proceeds in an incremental fashion throughout childhood and
                  adolescence, levels off during young adulthood, and begins to decline by age 40.
        *   d. There is evidence of growth, loss, and change at every stage of the life span.

TRUE-FALSE QUESTIONS

p. 523 58. As infants mature, they lose many of the reflexes they were born with.
        *   a. true
              b. false

p. 523 59. By the end of the sensorimotor stage, infants have acquired symbolic capacity.
www   *   a. true
              b. false

p. 523 60. The ability to allow one thing represent something else is first acquired during the stage of
             concrete-operational thought.
              a. true
        *   b. false

p. 524 61. A child in the preoperational stage understands that changes in the appearance of an object
             do not change the nature of the object.
              a. true
        *   b. false

p. 524 62. A school-age child's IQ score is a fairly good predictor of adult intellectual standing.
        *   a. true
              b. false

p. 524 63. School-age children have trouble assuming another person's perspective.
www   a. true
        *   b. false

p. 526 64. Most adolescents have good relationships with their parents.
   *   a.   true
        b.   false

p. 526 65. Adolescents who achieve formal operational thought can form hypotheses and
             systematically test them.
   *   a.   true
        b.   false

p. 526 66. A fifteen-year-old adolescent is likely to be in Kohlberg's stage of postconventional
             morality.
        a.   true
   *   b.   false

p. 528 67. Early adulthood is characterized by lower divorce rates and fewer mental health problems
             than later adult years.
        a.   true
   *   b.   false

p. 528 68. There are noticeable declines in intellectual functioning over the course of middle
www   adulthood.
        a.   true
   *   b.   false

p. 528 69. Adults age 65 and beyond are generally lower in self-esteem, and are less satisfied with life
             in general, than are younger adults.
        a.   true
   *   b.   false

p. 529 70. Development is largely the result of reciprocal influences between the individual and
             his/her environment.
   *   a.   true
        b.   false

p. 530 71. Research indicates that early experiences generally determine later personality
             development, much as Freud surmised.
        a.   true
   *   b.   false

p. 532 72. We tend to become more distinct from one another as we get older.
   *   a.   true
        b.   false

ESSAY QUESTIONS

73.   What does it mean to say that development consists of continuity and discontinuity? What is an
       example?

74. What does it mean to say that "nature and nurture truly interact"? What is an example?

75. Consider the major theories that have been covered in the text: Freud and Erikson's psychoanalytic theories, social-learning theory, cognitive-developmental, and ecological theory. What are the main, distinctive features of each theory? Are there points on which all the theorists agree?

76. Considering the theories that have been covered in the text, which two do you believe are the most valuable theories for our understanding of development? Provide a rationale for your selection.

77. The notion "goodness of fit" came up in many chapters throughout the text. What does this mean? Provide an example of how a "good fit" and a "bad fit" can influence development.

78. The concept of "internal working models" came up in many chapters of the text. What does this mean? What factors contribute to the development of internal working models? Provide an example.

79. One theme that runs throughout the text is "There is both continuity and discontinuity in
SG development." Explain what this means and give a concrete example from any area of developmental psychology.
[Sample answer is provided in the Study Guide.]

80. Another theme that runs throughout the text is "Nature and nurture both contribute to
SG development." Explain what this means and indicate how research is typically conducted to study the effects of nature and nurture.